Birds and Climate Change
Impacts and Conservation Responses

From the red grouse to the Ethiopian bush-crow, bird populations around the world can provide us with vital insights into the effects of climate change on species and ecosystems. They are among the best studied and monitored of organisms, yet many are already under threat of extinction as a result of habitat loss, overexploitation and pollution.

Providing a single source of information for students, scientists, practitioners and policy-makers, this book begins with a critical review of the existing impacts of climate change on birds, including changes in the timing of migration and breeding and effects on bird populations around the world. The second part considers how conservationists can assess potential future impacts, quantifying how extinction risk is linked to the magnitude of global change and synthesising the evidence in support of likely conservation responses. The final chapters assess the threats posed by efforts to reduce the magnitude of climate change.

Supplementary material is available for download at www.cambridge.org/9780521114288.

JAMES W. PEARCE-HIGGINS is a Principal Ecologist at the British Trust for Ornithology, where he leads on climate change research across the organisation and manages the Population Ecology and Modelling team. He is responsible for a range of research projects to examine the evidence for climate change impacts on biodiversity, undertaking projections of future responses and conducting research to inform how conservation should adapt to climate change.

RHYS E. GREEN is Principal Research Biologist at the Royal Society for the Protection of Birds, and Honorary Professor of Conservation Science at the University of Cambridge. His research focuses on measuring the effects of human land use, disturbance, illegal killing, climatic change and conservation management on the demography of bird populations, using the insights this provides to devise conservation programmes.

ECOLOGY, BIODIVERSITY AND CONSERVATION

Series Editors
Michael Usher   *University of Stirling, and formerly Scottish Natural Heritage*
Denis Saunders   *Formerly CSIRO Division of Sustainable Ecosystems, Canberra*
Robert Peet   *University of North Carolina, Chapel Hill*
Andrew Dobson   *Princeton University*

Editorial Board
Paul Adam   *University of New South Wales, Australia*
H. J. B. Birks   *University of Bergen, Norway*
Lena Gustafsson   *Swedish University of Agricultural Science*
Jeff McNeely   *International Union for the Conservation of Nature*
R. T. Paine   *University of Washington*
David Richardson   *University of Stellenbosch*
Jeremy Wilson   *Royal Society for the Protection of Birds*

The world's biological diversity faces unprecedented threats. The urgent challenge facing the concerned biologist is to understand ecological processes well enough to maintain their functioning in the face of the pressures resulting from human population growth. Those concerned with the conservation of biodiversity and with restoration also need to be acquainted with the political, social, historical, economic and legal frameworks within which ecological and conservation practice must be developed. The new Ecology, Biodiversity and Conservation series will present balanced, comprehensive, up-to-date and critical reviews of selected topics within the sciences of ecology and conservation biology, both botanical and zoological, and both 'pure' and 'applied'. It is aimed at advanced final-year undergraduates, graduate students, researchers and university teachers, as well as ecologists and conservationists in industry, government and the voluntary sectors. The series encompasses a wide range of approaches and scales (spatial, temporal and taxonomic), including quantitative, theoretical, population, community, ecosystem, landscape, historical, experimental, behavioural and evolutionary studies. The emphasis is on science related to the real world of plants and animals rather than on purely theoretical abstractions and mathematical models. Books in this series will, wherever possible, consider issues from a broad perspective. Some books will challenge existing paradigms and present new ecological concepts, empirical or theoretical models and testable hypotheses. Other books will explore new approaches and present syntheses on topics of ecological importance.

Ecology and Control of Introduced Plants
Judith H. Myers and Dawn Bazely

Invertebrate Conservation and Agricultural Ecosystems
T. R. New

Risks and Decisions for Conservation and Environmental Management
Mark Burgman

Ecology of Populations
Esa Ranta, Per Lundberg and Veijo Kaitala

Nonequilibrium Ecology
Klaus Rohde

The Ecology of Phytoplankton
C. S. Reynolds

Systematic Conservation Planning
Chris Margules and Sahotra Sarkar

Large-Scale Landscape Experiments: Lessons from Tumut
David B. Lindenmayer

Assessing the Conservation Value of Freshwaters: An international perspective
Philip J. Boon and Catherine M. Pringle

Insect Species Conservation
T. R. New

Bird Conservation and Agriculture
Jeremy D. Wilson, Andrew D. Evans and Philip V. Grice

Cave Biology: Life in darkness
Aldemaro Romero

Biodiversity in Environmental Assessment: Enhancing ecosystem services for human well-being
Roel Slootweg, Asha Rajvanshi, Vinod B. Mathur and Arend Kolhoff

Mapping Species Distributions: Spatial inference and prediction
Janet Franklin

Decline and Recovery of the Island Fox: A case study for population recovery
Timothy J. Coonan, Catherin A. Schwemm and David K. Garcelon

Ecosystem Functioning
Kurt Jax

Spatio-Temporal Heterogeneity: Concepts and analyses
Pierre R. L. Dutilleul

Parasites in Ecological Communities: From interactions to ecosystems
Melanie J. Hatcher and Alison M. Dunn

Zoo Conservation Biology
John E. Fa, Stephan M. Funk and Donnamarie O'Connell

Marine Protected Areas: A multidisciplinary approach
Joachim Claudet

Biodiversity in Dead Wood
Jogeir N. Stokland, Juha Siitonen and Bengt Gunnar Jonsson

Landslide Ecology
Lawrence R. Walker and Aaron B. Shiels

Nature's Wealth: The economics of ecosystem services and poverty
Pieter J. H. van Beukering, Elissaios Papyrakis, Jetske Bouma and Roy Brouwer

Birds and Climate Change

Impacts and Conservation Responses

JAMES W. PEARCE-HIGGINS
British Trust for Ornithology, UK

RHYS E. GREEN
The Royal Society for the Protection of Birds (RSPB); and University of Cambridge, UK

CAMBRIDGE
UNIVERSITY PRESS

University Printing House, Cambridge CB2 8BS, United Kingdom

Cambridge University Press is part of the University of Cambridge.

It furthers the University's mission by disseminating knowledge in the pursuit of education, learning and research at the highest international levels of excellence.

www.cambridge.org
Information on this title: www.cambridge.org/9780521114288

© J. W. Pearce-Higgins and R. E. Green 2014

This publication is in copyright. Subject to statutory exception and to the provisions of relevant collective licensing agreements, no reproduction of any part may take place without the written permission of Cambridge University Press.

First published 2014

Printed in the United Kingdom by Clays, St Ives plc

A catalogue record for this publication is available from the British Library

Library of Congress Cataloguing in Publication data
Pearce-Higgins, James W.
Birds and climate change : impacts and conservation responses / James W. Pearce-Higgins, British Trust for Ornithology, UK, Rhys E. Green, The Royal Society for the Protection of Birds (RSPB); and University of Cambridge, UK.
    pages cm. – (Ecology, biodiversiy, and conservation)
Includes bibliographical references and index.
ISBN 978-0-521-11428-8 (Hardback) – ISBN 978-0-521-13219-0 (pbk.)
1. Birds–Climatic factors. 2. Birds–Conservation. I. Green, Rhys. II. Title.
QL698.95.P43 2014
598.15–dc23   2014006999

ISBN 978-0-521-11428-8 Hardback
ISBN 978-0-521-13219-0 Paperback

Additional resources for this publication at www.cambridge.org/9780521114288

Cambridge University Press has no responsibility for the persistence or accuracy of URLs for external or third-party internet websites referred to in this publication, and does not guarantee that any content on such websites is, or will remain, accurate or appropriate.

To my dear family (JWPH)

Contents

	Foreword Michael B. Usher	*page* x
	Acknowledgements	xii
1.	Birds and climate change	1

Part I. Impacts

2.	Altered timings	25
3.	The impact of altered timings	63
4.	Further mechanisms of population impacts	102
5.	Effects of climate change on distributions and communities	171

Part II. Conservation responses

6.	Using models to predict the effects of climate change on birds	201
7.	Conservation in a changing climate	250
8.	Effects of climate change mitigation on birds	308
9.	Overall conclusions	359
	References	383
	Index	451

Foreword

If you ask anyone what he or she considers to be the greatest environmental problem of our times, it is likely that *Climate Change*, or something similar to this, will be the reply. The unusual weather patterns – droughts in some parts of the planet, floods in other parts, temperature records (both maxima and minima) being broken, the frequency of cyclones and gales – are associated phenomena. A couple of decades ago, as well as predictions of rising average temperature, another prediction was that there would be more frequent extreme events. So it is not just the trends in warmth or rainfall, or those of the melting of Arctic sea ice or of glaciers, that affect birds, but also the extremes of all aspects of our climate.

Try asking people about their favourite wildlife and almost certainly *Birds* will feature strongly in the replies. Birds have a charisma which appeals to so many people. Small birds inhabit our gardens and parks, larger birds are a feature of our coasts, estuaries and seas, and the raptors – owls, hawks and eagles – have a particular appeal. Although there are other charismatic and iconic species of wildlife, birds have a particular appeal because they fly by day, occur everywhere and often interact with people because of their endearing habits.

Put these two replies – *Climate Change* and *Birds* – together, and what a tremendous appeal this book must inevitably have. The authors are extremely well known for their research and writing about ornithology in general and the potential effects of climate change on birds in particular. This breadth of knowledge is manifest in the chapters, reviewing the increasingly extensive literature. Entering the two words *climate change* into a popular internet search engine you get 495 million results. Add the third word *bird* and the search engine still indicates 75 million results. This is in October 2012, but by the time the book reaches anyone's bookshelf I suspect that these numbers will be much larger. However, they indicate the huge interest in the subject matter of this book.

I have no doubt that the chapter topics, and the wealth of examples, will fascinate many readers. It is important that the impact of climate change, not just on birds, but on wildlife in general, is understood if the planet's loss of biodiversity is ever to be halted. But equally, people involved in policy issues need to understand why mitigation to limit the magnitude of climate change may also have detrimental effects on birds and wildlife. These are important and difficult issues which the authors wrestle with. Whereas policy shifts are essential, so equally are the practical responses of the practitioners on the ground, and a key section of the book summarises how conservationists can help wildlife populations adapt to the changing environment in which they live. Given this wide-ranging subject matter, and the global focus of the book, I believe that *Birds and Climate Change: Impacts and Conservation Responses* has something for everyone, be they bird watchers, wildlife researchers, policy advisers or practical conservationists.

Michael B. Usher
University of Stirling

Acknowledgements

It was Michael Usher at the British Ecological Society annual meeting in Glasgow, 2007, who invited JWPH to submit a proposal for this book to Cambridge University Press. We are extremely grateful to Michael for this invitation, and for his continued encouragement, enthusiasm and patience during this project. Dominic Lewis and Megan Waddington at Cambridge University Press also provided much additional encouragement at various academic conferences, and continued advice and support whilst the book was being written and produced. Without them, and Cambridge University Press's initial agreement to publish this volume, this book would not have been written.

Many colleagues and friends have provided much support, encouragement and advice during the last few years. In particular, Jeremy Wilson offered much enthusiastic support whilst the proposal was drafted and the first chapters written. We are extremely grateful to Andrew Balmford, Derek Yalden, Paul Donald, Tim Sparks, Ken Smith, Will Peach, Stephen Baillie, Albert Phillimore, Robert Robinson, Rob Fuller, Stuart Butchart, Malcolm Ausden and Richard Bradbury for taking the time to read and comment on parts or all of individual chapters. Without their assistance and comments the final manuscript would have been much poorer. Any residual errors are ours alone.

The Intergovernmental Panel on Climate Change, Met Office, American Association for the Advancement of Science, Dartmouth Flood Observatory, National Academy of Sciences USA, John Wiley and Sons, the Royal Society for the Protection of Birds (RSPB), the British Trust for Ornithology (BTO) and BirdLife International all kindly gave permission for reproduction of technical diagrams from journals, publications or websites to which they hold copyright. We are particularly grateful to Jenny Bright and Paul Britten for producing the combined wind farm sensitivity map for Scotland and England (Box 8.7), Graeme Buchanan for the production of the forest habitat loss around the Harrapan Reserve (Figure 7.2), David Baker for producing the map of global bird diversity (Figure 5.1) and the species data for Figure 9.3, and to Dario Massimino for converting his excellent density and abundance change maps into Figures 5.1 and 7.12. Photographs were kindly supplied by Ben Darvill (Boxes 2.5, 2.6, 8.3), Neil Calbrade (Box 2.7), Andy Musgrove (Box 3.4), Paul Donald (Box 6.2) and Malcolm Ausden (Figure 7.5b). Figure 7.5a was taken by JWPH. We also wish to acknowledge BirdLife International's checklist of birds of the world (BirdLife International 2012b), which we have used as the taxonomy for this book.

Finally, the authors thank the RSPB, BTO and the University of Cambridge for their support during the course of writing the book. The views expressed are entirely our own.

1 · *Birds and climate change*

1.1 Introduction

This book is about the impact of global climate change on birds, especially on their populations and conservation status, and what can be done about it. Birds are widespread in their distribution and occur in almost all environments. People enjoy watching them and many are easy to observe. As a result, they have long been studied by both amateur naturalists and professional scientists and they are amongst the best understood group of organisms. Data exist on the migration of birds from ringing (banding) studies and the direct observation of arriving and departing individuals, on their historical distribution from museum specimens, archaeology, literary and other sources, and on the timing and success of their breeding from nest recording that span many decades, or in the case of museum specimens, over a century. More recently, quantitative counting and mapping techniques have provided up to 50 years of standardised population and distribution data collection (Møller & Fiedler 2010). The internet is now being used to collect millions of sightings from bird watchers every year, whilst recent technological advances allow almost real-time tracking of migrating birds. These data provide an unparalleled opportunity first to understand the relationship between climate and species distributions and populations, and second to document changes in those distributions and populations occurring as a result of climatic change. Critically reviewing and documenting these kinds of evidence and what they tell us about the impacts of climate change on birds is one of the main purposes of this book, covered in Part 1.

Unfortunately, popular as they are, many bird species and populations are under threat. Of the 10 064 bird species identified around the world, some 13% are regarded as threatened by extinction within the next 100 years. Another 880 species are near-threatened (BirdLife International 2012a). Populations of habitat-specialists and shorebirds are in particular decline (Butchart *et al.* 2010). The threat of extinction which these species face is a real one; 103 species have been lost forever during the last 200 years. There is an urgent need for effective bird conservation to halt these trends. Whilst there have been significant conservation successes, these have only slowed, rather than halted, global rates of biodiversity loss (Butchart *et al.* 2010; Hoffman *et al.* 2010). Conservationists are winning occasional battles, but seem to be losing the war.

Although the majority of threats facing bird populations are attributed to habitat loss and degradation, exploitation and impacts of invasive species (BirdLife International 2000), climate change is regarded as likely to become an increasingly significant threat to birds and other biodiversity during the course of this century (e.g. Thomas *et al.* 2004, Bellard *et al.* 2012, Warren *et al.* 2013). In the second part of the book, we therefore use our knowledge of the effects of climate change on birds to suggest how conservationists should respond. We also consider some of the potential indirect effects of climate change on birds mediated through human responses to the threat, such as through the expansion of renewable energy generation, and how best to minimise these effects. However, before we immerse ourselves in bird biology, in this introductory chapter we aim to set the scene by briefly summarising the most relevant parts of what is now known about the climatic change that we currently appear to be facing.

For more than a decade, of the many environmental issues of concern, the issue of climate change has most captured the attention of the public and policy-makers. Whether someone is persuaded by the science, or is a climate change sceptic, almost everyone has something to say about the matter. We come from the UK, where the temperate oceanic climate means that the weather varies so much from day to day and year to year that talking about it is a famous national foible. Global climate change now gives such conversations an extra edge. Not surprisingly, given the potentially huge impacts of climatic change on human beings and the economic consequences of efforts to limit them (Stern 2007), many of these conversations are about whether rapid global climatic change is really happening and, if so, whether it is driven by human activity. At least part of the reason for this debate is that climate change can be difficult for us as individuals to perceive. How do we know that the climate is changing?

1.2 Climate change observed from close up

The question is a challenging one for us to answer from our own personal experience. So much of our understanding of the world is based upon recent perception compared to an imperfectly remembered or recorded past. This makes it very difficult for us to grasp long-term trends in the climate hidden within the short-term fluctuations of our weather. Hence, measurements of climatic conditions with scientific instruments, such as thermometers, are of great importance. The longest running direct temperature measurement time series in the world comes from England and stretches back to 1659 (Figure 1.1). This graph of annual averages illustrates these fluctuations from one year to the next, which sometimes exceed 3 °C in magnitude. However, when running averages are used to smooth the graph, we can begin to see patterns emerging. The Little Ice Age during the seventeenth century, when temperatures were consistently 1 °C lower than the 1961–1990 average, can be identified. During the nineteenth century there were periods of several years with unusually cold conditions in England: sufficient for the River Thames in London to freeze in winter, which it has hardly ever done during our lifetimes. Most striking of all, though, is the recent warm period since about 1985, which is warmer than any other period since measurements began. Is this enough to convince us of a recent unusually rapid and sustained increase in average temperature in England?

Not really, because the graph shows other periods with consistent sustained trends as well as this one, such as very rapid warming at the end of the Little Ice Age, when the temperature rose by in excess of 1 °C during 10 years. We cannot be sure what is happening from this information alone, long-term and detailed though it is. We need to take a bigger view, and can do that in two ways. We first need to examine a much wider area than just England, even though the weather-obsessed British have the longest

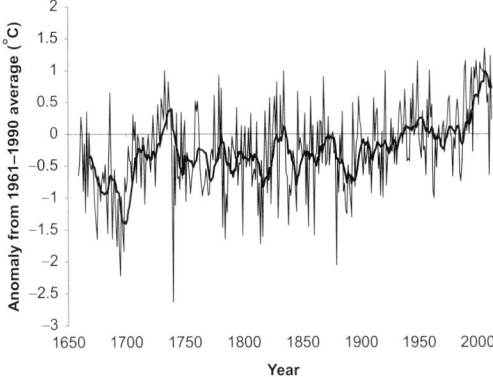

Figure 1.1 Annual variation in the average temperature in Central England, UK, 1659–2010, as measured as an anomaly relative to the 1961–1990 mean (thin line), alongside a 10-year running mean (thick line). Data from www.metoffice.gov.uk/hadobs as published by Parker *et al.* (1992).

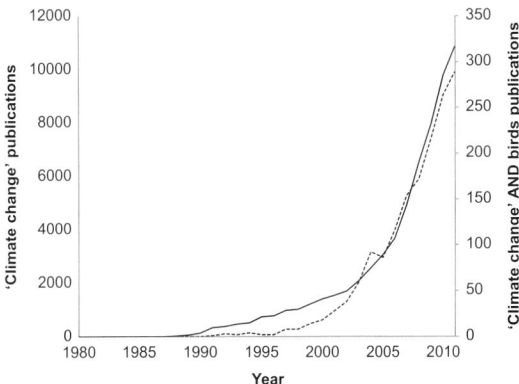

Figure 1.2 Annual variation in the number of scientific papers that have 'climate change' as a keyword (solid line, y-axis) compared to those which additionally include 'bird' as a keyword (dashed line, z-axis).

run of measurements. We also need to look further back in time than 1659. Although this is difficult, as it pre-dates the thermometer record, it is not impossible. We will have considerable help in doing this. As illustrated by a rapidly rising, almost exponential growth in the numbers of peer-reviewed scientific articles published annually about climate change (Figure 1.2), there has been an unprecedented global scientific effort, stimulated, supported and summarised since its establishment in 1988 by the Intergovernmental Panel on Climate Change, to take both the wider and the longer views.

1.3 A wider view of climate change

The equivalent graph of instrumentally measured global average temperature on land (Figure 1.3) to that for central England only starts in 1850 but demonstrates that recent rapid warming is not just local but also a global phenomenon (Brohan *et al.* 2006). Both

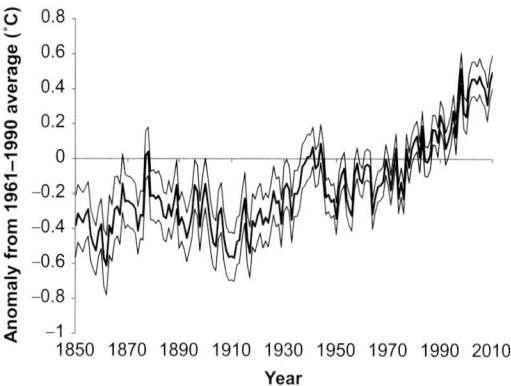

Figure 1.3 Time series of global temperature, 1850–2010 (thick line) based on analyses of data from a range of recording stations, alongside with 95% confidence intervals (thin lines). As in Figure 1.1, temperature is presented as an anomaly relative to the 1961–1990 average. Note the contraction in the level of uncertainty (confidence intervals) through time as the number of recording stations has increased. Data from www.metoffice.gov.uk/hadobs as published by Brohan *et al.* (2006).

the English and global time series show a strong upturn in temperature during the 1980s. Both graphs also suggest the rate of warming may have slowed recently, in response to changing solar insolation, a change in the Southern Oscillation and increasing sulphur emissions (Kaufmann *et al.* 2011), or because more heat is being absorbed by the oceans (Otto *et al.* 2013). Mean global surface temperature is now about 0.7–0.8 °C warmer than it was a century ago (IPCC 2007b). Despite considerable annual fluctuations in the record, 13 of the 14 warmest years in the 160-year time series have occurred since 1995. Sea-surface temperature has increased by 0.7 °C over the same period (Rayner *et al.* 2006).

As a result of changes in atmospheric and oceanic circulation, rates of temperature increase have not been uniform (Figure 1.4). The most rapid temperature increases have occurred at high latitudes in the Northern Hemisphere, particularly in northern Canada and Scandinavia, and around parts of the Antarctic, although there is greater uncertainty associated with these high-latitude trends than for other global trends because they are based upon data from a small number of isolated stations (IPCC 2007b). They are supported by sea surface warming trends, which have been greatest in the north Atlantic, particularly since the mid 1980s, and the north Pacific, associated with phase shifts in ocean circulation (Baines & Folland 2007).

Warming at the poles has occurred particularly during the respective winter periods in each hemisphere (December–February in the Arctic and June–August in the Antarctic; Figure 1.5), which is at least partly related to a positive feedback loop known as Arctic amplification (Serreze & Francis 2006). As the amount of winter sea ice decreases, less incoming radiation is reflected back into space. Heat absorption by the Arctic Ocean is thereby increased, so that ice formation in the autumn, which normally insulates the Arctic Ocean, is delayed. This promotes continued upwelling of warm water to the surface, thus heating both the sea surface and the lower troposphere. The associated reduction in snow cover on the land further reduces albedo and increases heat absorption. This warms the lower atmosphere further, exacerbating the loss of sea ice.

1.3 A wider view of climate change · 5

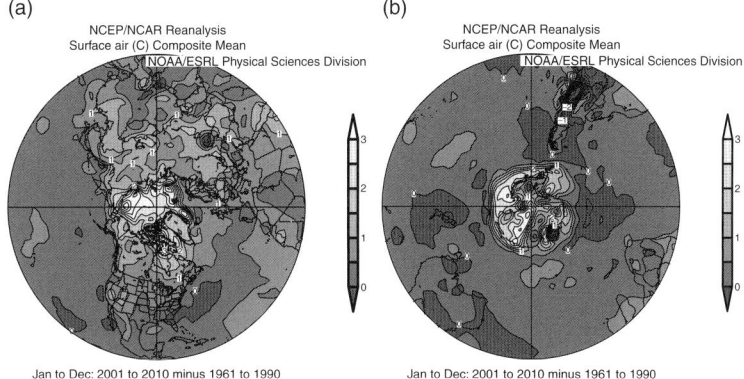

Figure 1.4 Spatial variation in mean annual temperature (2001–2010) relative to the 1961–1990 global average across the Northern Hemisphere (a) and Southern Hemisphere (b). Light areas indicate the areas of greatest warming. Contours denote 0.5 °C intervals. Image provided by the NOAA/ESRL Physical Sciences Division, Boulder, Colorado, from their website at http://www.esrl.noaa.gov/psd/ and based on Kalney et al. (1996).

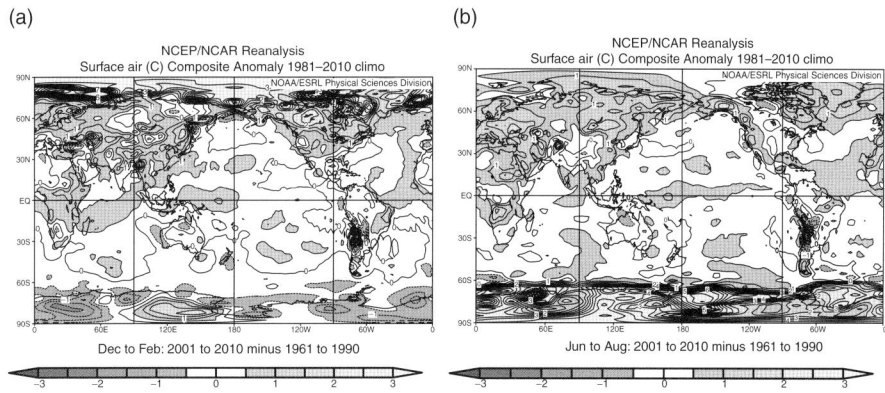

Figure 1.5 Spatial variation in December–February warming (a) and June–August warming (b) as indicated by the (2001–2010) anomaly of mean temperature relative to 1961–1990. White areas indicate stable climates (< 0.5 °C change). Light grey indicates increasing levels of warming, whilst dark grey colours indicate cooling. Contours denote 0.5 °C intervals. Image provided by the NOAA/ESRL Physical Sciences Division, Boulder, Colorado, from their website at http://www.esrl.noaa.gov/psd/ and based on Kalney et al. (1996).

Summer warming in the Northern Hemisphere has been greatest in Europe and North Africa, Mongolia and eastern Siberia, Alaska and north-eastern Canada. These trends have led to increased frequency of heat waves, for example in China (Wang *et al.* 2012), the Mediterranean (Kuglitsch *et al.* 2010) and southern states of the USA (Gershunov *et al.* 2009). Temperature increases in the Tropics and Southern Hemisphere have been more moderate, but they are still statistically significant in many areas (IPCC 2007b).

As a result of increasing temperatures, there have been significant reductions in the extent of snow and ice cover in the Northern Hemisphere where a 5% reduction in cover

6 · Birds and climate change

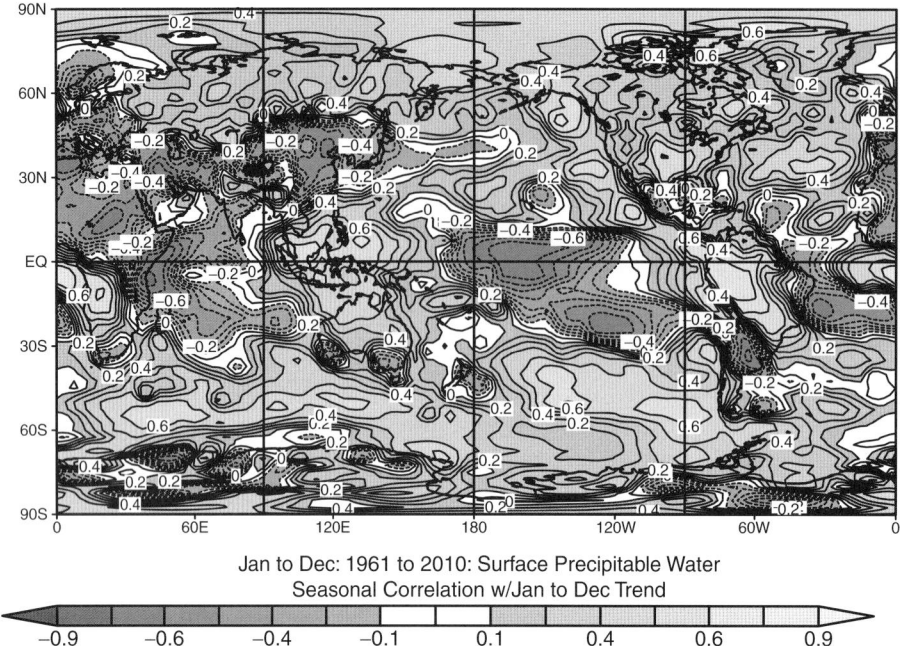

Figure 1.6 Spatial variation in the strength of the correlation between annual variation in precipitation and year, 1961–2010 as a measure of trend. Areas in white show little trend ($-0.1 > r < 0.1$). Annual precipitation increased in light grey areas, but declined in dark grey areas. Contours indicate intervals of $r = 0.1$. Image provided by the NOAA/ESRL Physical Sciences Division, Boulder, Colorado, from their website at http://www.esrl.noaa.gov/psd/ and based on Kalney et al. (1996).

has occurred since the late 1980s. The extent of ice in glaciers and ice caps has also reduced over the same period, particularly in Patagonia, Alaska, the Rocky Mountains and the Himalayas, whilst tropical glaciers have declined in extent by 80% or more since 1900. This has had significant impacts on flow rates in ice-fed rivers (Sorg et al. 2012). Arctic sea ice has contracted in extent by 2.4% per decade from 1978 to 2004, although no overall change in Antarctic sea ice extent has occurred over the same period. Here, the rate of warming has been limited by strong circumpolar winds which reduce the transfer of heat from the tropics to the poles. Largely as a result of the thermal expansion of seawater associated with warming, there has been a 7.5 cm rise in mean sea level between 1961 and 2003 (IPCC 2007b; Hurrell & Trenberth 2010; Serreze 2010).

Although there have been no strong trends in global precipitation during the last century, there have been fluctuations between wet decades such as the 1950s and 1970s and dry decades such as the 1990s. There has also been considerable regional variation in precipitation trends (Figure 1.6). Western Amazonia, south-east Asia, equatorial West Africa and much of North America have experienced significant increases in precipitation over the last 50 years (IPCC 2007b). Conversely, a continuous band from the Mediterranean and North Africa, through central Europe, the Middle East, East Africa,

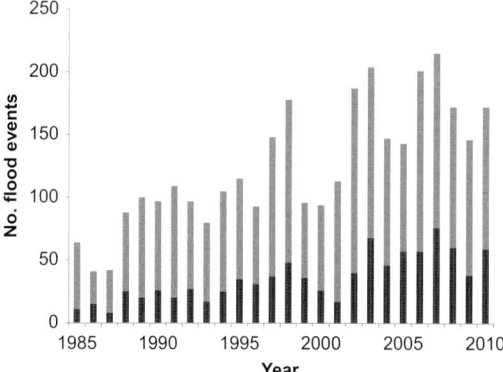

Figure 1.7 Increases in the frequency of severe (grey bars) and very severe (dark grey bars) floods in recent years. Flood magnitude is calculated from a severity class (based on the likely recurrence interval and equals 1 for events with a 10–20 year interval, 1.5 for a 20–100 year interval and 2 for a > 100 year interval), duration (days) and the size of the affected area (km^2). Magnitude = Log (severity*duration*area). A flood with an M>4 is listed as severe, and an M>6 is very severe. These data were collated by the Dartmouth Flood Observatory (Brakenridge 2012).

southern India and China has suffered significant reductions in precipitation levels, which can be linked to changes in tropical sea-surface temperatures (Dai 2010). Combined with the increases in temperature, these changes mean that areas of drought have increased significantly, with central North America, the Cerrado of Brazil, the Mediterranean, Central Africa, the Middle East, China and Western Australia having experienced higher frequencies of drought in the last decade, relative to 1961–2000 (IPCC 2007b).

Given that the water holding capacity of the atmosphere increases by 7% for every 1 °C rise in temperature (the Clausius–Clapeyron relation), increased global temperature has led to more intense precipitation events when they occur. As a result, there have been increases in the frequency of heavy precipitation events that have contributed to a rise in severe flood events around the world during the last 25 years (Figure 1.7). Related to this, there has been a significant increase in the intensity and duration of tropical storms since the 1970s, although such storm events are strongly related to El Niño fluctuations. Thus, there has been a 75% increase in the number of category 4 and 5 hurricanes, particularly in the North Atlantic, Indian and south-west Pacific oceans (IPCC 2007b). Although there has been no overall trend in the frequency of extreme snowfall events, there have been some significant regional trends, with increases in heavy snowfall in parts of northern and eastern United States (Kunkel *et al.* 2009), northern and eastern China (Sun *et al.* 2010) and Europe, which appear to be related to declining Arctic sea ice (Liu *et al.* 2012).

To conclude, warming has been widespread both on land and at sea, and particularly apparent at high latitudes, resulting in significant changes in ice extent, most obviously in the Arctic. There have been significant and interrelated changes to ocean and atmospheric circulation systems which influence the spatial pattern of warming and precipitation change. The main change at lower latitudes has been an increased frequency of drought risk, particularly in the Mediterranean and parts of northern and east Africa and the Middle East. Other parts of the globe have suffered an increased risk of severe rainfall events causing flooding and increased frequencies of tropical storms. The climate has changed in our lifetimes, but is this change significantly different from what has occurred before?

1.4 A longer view of climate change

The idea of past large cyclical changes in global mean temperature, including cold ice ages of global scope, was first proposed in 1837 by the Swiss scientist Louis Agassiz, as a consequence of his geological observations. Since then, much remarkable evidence has been amassed about their magnitude, frequency and causes, which lie in cyclic variations in the Earth's orbit and rotation, amplified by changes in greenhouse gas concentrations. If large changes in global mean temperature have occurred in the past, then perhaps the recent increase in global mean temperature does not require any special explanations or warrant concern.

To place the directly measured changes in global mean temperature of recent centuries into a longer term context at first seems impossible because thermometers were not invented until the sixteenth century. However, palaeoclimatologists have found a wide variety of proxies for air and water temperatures that allow the temperature record to be constructed back in time over thousands and sometimes millions of years. Some of these involve studies of the growth rates of living organisms or the evidence of growth left within their fossilised remains, that can be related to temperature, such as growth lines in trees and marine corals. Variation in the growth of plankton populations can also be related to temperature and measured by the thickness of annually deposited layers in sediments. Alternatively, modern data linking the geographical distribution of different closely related species to temperature can again be used to infer long-term temperature records from the identification of the most prevalent species amongst the remains of pollen, plankton or midge mouthparts preserved in bog, lake or marine sediments.

The validity of these reconstructions depends upon the critical assumption that the biotic relationships with temperature that we measure now have not changed from those in the distant past. Although apparently reasonable, we cannot be certain of this due to potential effects of other environmental changes upon these species, or evolutionary adaptation altering the physiological and ecological responses of species to temperature. To guard against this, proxies of many different types are often used, since it is unlikely that very different types of organisms would all change their responses in similar ways.

An even better method is to use proxies that depend upon chemical or thermodynamic principles that do not change over time. Some of these also involve living organisms. Proportions of different stable isotopes of oxygen incorporated into the skeletons of planktonic foraminifera and marine corals vary with temperature because of well-established effects of temperature on isotope ratios in the water around the living organisms as they grow. By measuring the isotopic composition of preserved remnants of the skeletons, past temperatures can be estimated. However, the best known palaeoclimatic temperature reconstructions do not involve living things at all. Proportions of the different stable isotopes of oxygen and hydrogen in annually deposited layers of ice drilled from the ice caps of Greenland and Antarctica provide information on the temperature of the seawater that gave rise to the vapour that eventually became the snow that fell onto the ice cap. Painstaking measurements of isotope ratios from ice cores and dating of the layers from which the samples came allows a biology-free proxy record of past temperatures to be constructed. In the case of the EPICA ice core from Antarctica, this record extends back 800 000 years before the present (Lambert *et al.* 2008). Combined, these records of the palaeoclimate indicate that temperatures in the past few decades are high relative to any other period in recent centuries (e.g. Alley *et al.* 2010). In the Northern Hemisphere, for which temperature reconstructions are best developed, it is likely that the average temperature in the last 50 years is higher than in any other 50-year period in the last 1300 years (IPCC 2007b).

Looking further back, during the last interglacial (130 000–116 000 years ago; Kulka *et al.* 2002), the Earth may have been warmer than at present. As a result, there was also probably less glacial ice then than there is now (Stirling *et al.* 1998). While the rate of current climate change during the twentieth century was thought likely to be ten times greater than the 4–7 °C warming which occurred at the end of the Last Glacial Maximum (21 000 years ago; IPCC 2007b), more recent evidence suggests that this may not be the case. High-resolution ice-core data from Greenland suggests temperature changes occurred at a rate of 2–4 °C per year during this period also, leading to a shift in polar atmospheric circulation in less than 4 years (Steffensen *et al.* 2008; see also Brauer *et al.* 2008; Bakke *et al.* 2009).

Change has therefore long been a feature of our planet's climate. Previous climates have been warmer than at present, and may also have warmed at least as rapidly at present. What then is unique about our current 'climate change'? The answer is the origin of the recent warming. There is considerable evidence to suggest that the change that we are currently experiencing is anthropogenic in origin. We are warming the planet, and therefore if such warming continues, there is considerable potential for future climate change to be much greater than experienced in the recent past, or even in the palaeological past. For example, a further 2 °C rise in global temperature would mean that world climate would be warmer than that experienced for 2.5 million years (Williams *et al.* 2007).

1.5 The causes of recent rapid global climate change

To understand the causes of recent global change, we need to first understand the tools used by climatologists to answer this question and examine what is known as attribution, the process of establishing the most likely causes of change. In particular, climatologists use detailed computer models of the atmosphere, oceans and, increasingly, also the biosphere, to examine the extent to which predictions from their current understanding match the changes which have been observed. Based on a good understanding of the mechanisms responsible for our weather and climate, built up over decades of observation and research, these General Circulation Models (GCMs) seek to incorporate, at as fine a spatial scale as computer power permits, the physical processes which drive global climate and as many of the interactions between those processes as possible. The main elements of a GCM are therefore an atmospheric model coupled with models of ocean circulation, the land surface and sea ice. The validity of the model is then rigorously tested by examining how well it can reproduce both the instrumental record of recent climate and the palaeoclimate proxies of past millennia. Different research groups have developed

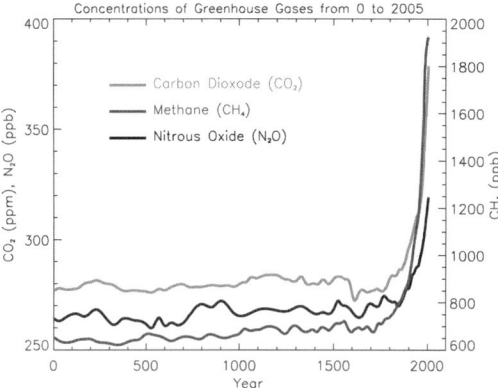

Figure 1.8 Atmospheric concentrations of important long-lived greenhouse gases over the last 2000 years. Increases since about 1750 are attributed to human activities in the industrial era. Concentration units are parts per million (ppm) or parts per billion (ppb), indicating the number of molecules of the greenhouse gas per million or billion air molecules, respectively, in an atmospheric sample. The figure is taken from *Climate Change 2007: The Physical Science Basis*. Working Group I Contribution to the Fourth Assessment Report of the Intergovernmental Panel on Climate Change, FAQ 2.1, Figure 2. Cambridge University Press (IPCC 2007b).

different GCMs and often each has several variants. None of the models describe (retrodict) observed climate or proxies perfectly, and they can vary considerably in the ways in which they fail to match observations. To allow for these differences, a frequently used approach is to average results from several GCMs with contrasting assumptions. This 'ensemble' approach to modelling means that the extent of agreement between outputs of the different models can be used to assess the probability that a particular outcome is robust.

Having developed models with outputs that approximate observed past climatic change reasonably well, they can then be run with different levels of various potential drivers of climate change in order to attribute the most likely cause of the recent warming observed. Special attention has been given to the effects of changes in the concentrations of greenhouse gases. It is well known that increased concentrations of a greenhouse gas in the atmosphere lead it to absorb more of the infrared radiation that is emitted from the surface of the Earth, and that would otherwise be lost to space. Hence, the atmosphere becomes warmer. Careful long-term measurements of greenhouse gases in the atmosphere show that concentrations of carbon dioxide (CO_2) have increased by 38% over the last 150 years, levels of methane (CH_4) by 148% and nitrous oxide (N_2O) by 9% (Figure 1.8). These changes are far in excess of the natural variability in these concentrations measured in bubbles of air trapped in Greenland and Antarctic ice over the last 20 000 years, and are in large part due to human actions. Carbon dioxide has increased because it is released by the burning of fossil fuels and the clearing and burning of forests; methane because of increased rice cultivation and livestock production; and nitrous oxide because of vehicle exhausts and fertiliser application to farmland.

The greenhouse gases vary in their initial concentrations and tendency to absorb radiation, so the scale of the increases does not on its own tell us the likely impacts on

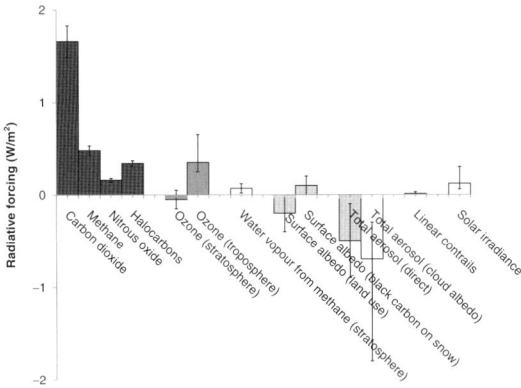

Figure 1.9 Global average radiative forcing in 2005 (best estimates and 5–95% uncertainty ranges) with respect to 1750 for CO_2, CH_4, N_2O and other important agents and mechanisms. Estimates are shaded by the level of scientific understanding (dark grey, high; mid-grey, medium; light grey, medium-low; white, low). Aerosols from explosive volcanic eruptions contribute an additional episodic cooling term for a few years following an eruption. The range for linear contrails does not include other possible effects of aviation on cloudiness. Adapted from *Climate Change 2007: The Physical Science Basis*. Working Group I contribution to the Fourth Assessment Report of the Intergovernmental Panel on Climate Change, Figure SPM.2. Cambridge University Press (IPCC 2007b).

climate. The effect of gas concentration changes on the Earth's energy budget are expressed in terms of their effect on radiative forcing – the difference between the amount of radiation energy per unit time coming in from space and the amount going back out, measured in watts per m^2. The best estimates of radiative forcing suggest that the majority of warming is attributable to increases in atmospheric CO_2 concentrations, followed by increases in CH_4 and N_2O (Figure 1.9). Some other anthropogenic drivers, such as aerosols produced through atmospheric pollution by sulphur dioxide and smoke, counteract the warming effects of greenhouse gases by promoting cloud formation that reflects more incoming radiation back into space. Combining these man-made effects, there is still a positive net radiative forcing caused by humans of 1.6 W/m^2. When these various man-made effects are included in runs of GCMs, alongside other changes like the effects of volcanic eruptions and fluctuations in solar output, they reproduce the observed recent global warming quite well. When the man-made drivers are taken out the model outputs show little or no warming (Figure 1.10). Hence the IPCC concluded in their Fourth Assessment Report that recent global warming is very likely to be caused by human actions – a conclusion which by the time of publication is likely to be reinforced by the IPCC Fifth Assessment Report.

1.6 Future projected climate change

Having tested them against past climates and human influences, the GCMs can also be run to look into the future, with varying assumptions about changes in greenhouse gas emissions, aerosol formation and forest clearance. Put simply, these simulations indicate

12 · Birds and climate change

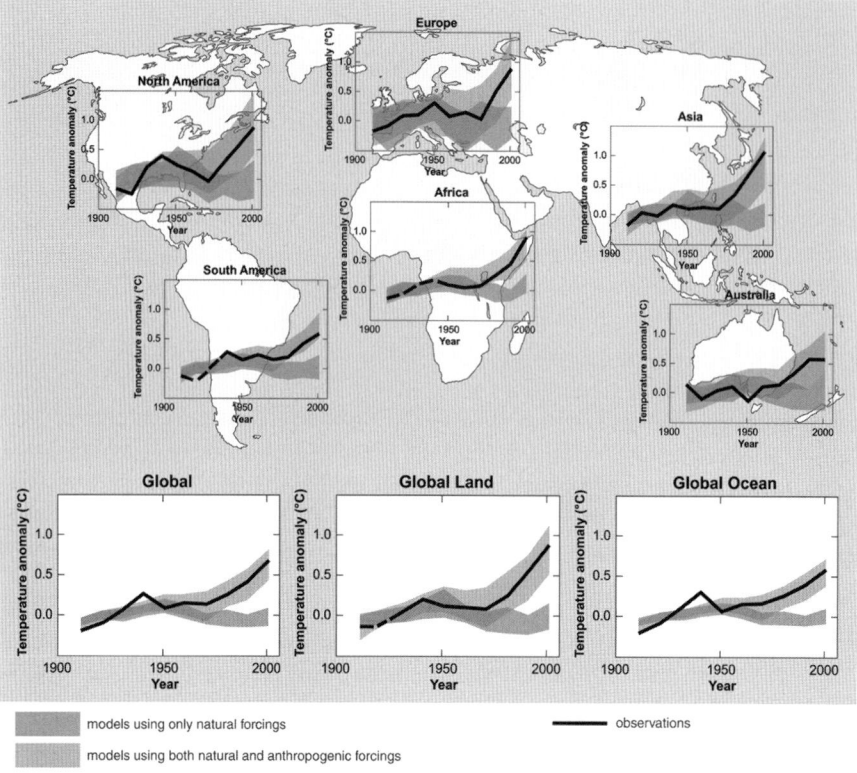

Figure 1.10 Comparison of observed continental- and global-scale changes in surface temperature with results simulated by climate models using natural and anthropogenic forcings. Decadal averages of observations are shown for the period 1906–2005 (black line) plotted against the centre of the decade and relative to the corresponding average for 1901–1950. Lines are dashed where spatial coverage is less than 50%. Dark shaded bands show the 5–95% range for 19 simulations from 5 climate models using only the natural forcings due to solar activity and volcanoes. Light shaded bands show the 5–95% range for 58 simulations from 14 climate models using both natural and anthropogenic forcings. The figure is taken from *Climate Change 2007: Synthesis Report*. Contribution of Working Groups I, II and III to the Fourth Assessment Report of the Intergovernmental Panel on Climate Change, Figure 2.5. IPCC, Geneva, Switzerland (IPCC 2007a).

that continued emissions will cause continued warming, thus magnifying and extending the climate trends already observed. Further, the degree of warming is likely to be made worse by feedbacks between the warming atmosphere and the biosphere (living things) whose effects are increasingly being incorporated into the models (Moss *et al.* 2010). Although the biosphere models within GCMs are relatively crude, there is general agreement that increases in temperature are likely to reduce the ability of CO_2 to be removed from the atmosphere by natural ecosystems (Friedlingstein *et al.* 2006). As a result, estimates of the ceiling on anthropogenic greenhouse gas emissions required to stabilise concentrations at a given level have become lower over time as the biosphere components of the models have been developed (Anderson & Bows 2008). It is now

1.6 Future projected climate change

thought that stabilisation of greenhouse gas concentrations at 450 ppm CO_2 equivalent (CO_{2e}; the concentration of CO_2 required to produce the summed degree of forcing of the various greenhouse gases) would require limitation of total emissions to about three-quarters of the level that was estimated before the biosphere feedbacks were incorporated (IPCC 2007b).

A second cause for concern is that much of the recent development of climate change policy has been based on modelled rather than observed rates of emissions after 2000. This means that the required rate of emission reductions in order to stabilise greenhouse gas concentrations at a particular level is now greater than was previously assumed, because both the atmospheric concentration of greenhouse gases and current rate of emissions are actually larger than the previously assumed values (Anderson & Bows 2008). The later we act to reduce emissions, the greater the pain of such reductions, which means they become less and less feasible to achieve. For this reason, given the lack of widespread action to reduce anthropogenic greenhouse gas emissions, Anderson and Bows (2008) provide a sobering assessment that a global agreement is unlikely to achieve the radical reversal in emission trends required for stabilisation at 450 ppm CO_{2e} and suggest that stabilisation at much below 650 ppm is improbable. An increase in greenhouse gases of this magnitude would have a 50% chance of driving an increase in global average temperature of 3.5 °C above pre-industrial levels, and 10% chance of exceeding 6 °C of warming (Rogelj *et al.* 2012), although there is some recent evidence that the rate at which these temperatures may be reached is slower than previously thought (Otto *et al.* 2013).

Probably the greatest uncertainty associated with future projections is human behaviour. The amount of future climate change is largely dependent upon the magnitude of greenhouse gas emissions, and therefore dependent upon the long-term consequences of international policies and treaties established now and in the future. To account for this uncertainty and assess the likely consequences of different potential societal options, climatologists have developed a range of different emissions scenarios based upon different models of economic growth, population growth and technological development (IPCC 2000). These are then used to underpin simulations conducted with the different GCMs. It is this combination of scenarios and GCMs that allows the quantification of the potential uncertainty associated with future projections of climatic change. We are pretty much guaranteed a further 1 °C of global warming from 2000 by 2040, as a result of existing greenhouse gas concentrations and similar future emissions pathways over the next few years (IPCC 2007b). Beyond 2040, future projected scenarios presented in the Fourth Assessment Report show greater divergence in trajectory by 2100, with a mean rise of 1.8 °C from 1980–1999 levels projected under the lowest (B1) emissions scenario, and a 4 °C rise projected under the highest (A1FI) scenario, although even greater temperature rises are within the bounds of uncertainty (Figure 1.11).

These scenarios are being revised for the next (fifth) IPCC assessment report (Moss *et al.* 2010), which will be available by the time this book is published. Sets of emission scenarios, greenhouse gas concentrations and land-use trajectories will be combined into what will be termed representative concentration pathways (RCPs). These will be based on published scenarios and selected to be representative of the range of plausible possible futures, for example ranging from RCP 2.6 with low or even negative emissions likely to stabilise CO_{2e} at 400 ppm by 2100 to RCP 8.5 with a CO_{2e} of in excess of 900 ppm by

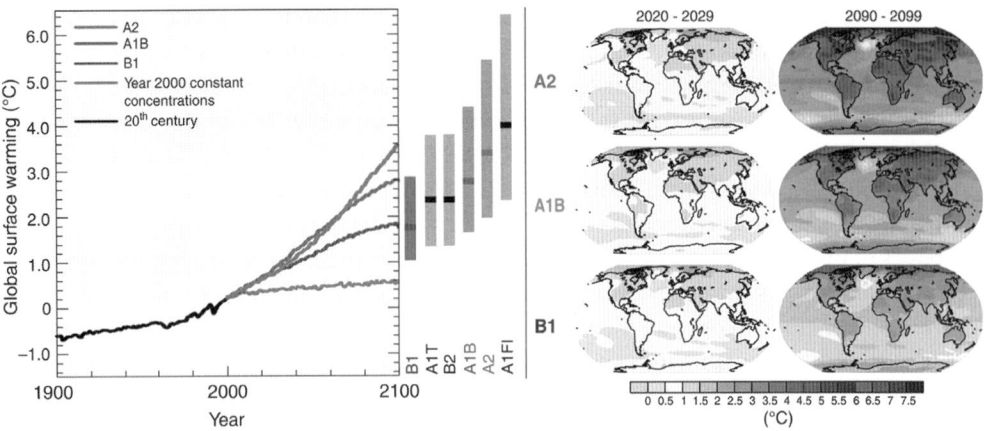

Figure 1.11 Left panel: Solid lines are multi-model global averages of surface warming (relative to 1980–1999) for the SRES scenarios A2, A1B and B1, shown as continuations of the twentieth-century simulations. The lower grey line is for the experiment where concentrations were held constant at year 2000 values. The bars in the middle of the figure indicate the best estimate (solid line within each bar) and the likely range assessed for the six SRES marker scenarios at 2090–2099 relative to 1980–1999. The assessment of the best estimate and likely ranges in the bars includes the Atmosphere–Ocean General Circulation Models (AOGCMs) in the left part of the figure, as well as results from a hierarchy of independent models and observational constraints. *Right panels*: Projected surface temperature changes for the early and late twenty-first century relative to the period 1980–1999. The panels show the multi-AOGCM average projections for the A2 (top), A1B (middle) and B1 (bottom) SRES scenarios averaged over decades 2020–2029 (left) and 2090–2099 (right). The figure is taken from *Climate Change 2007: Synthesis Report*. Contribution of Working Groups I, II and III to the Fourth Assessment Report of the Intergovernmental Panel on Climate Change, Figure 3.2. IPCC, Geneva, Switzerland (IPCC 2007a).

the same time (van Vuuren *et al.* 2011). With negative emissions, which means there is a net removal of greenhouse gasses from the atmosphere resulting from significant technological advance, the RCP 2.6 would be likely to limit warming to below 2 °C, a limit that, as just discussed, is unlikely to be attained otherwise. Alternatively, the RCP 8.5 would lead to frightening median projections of a 4.9 °C global temperature increase by 2100 and 8 °C by 2300 (Meinhausen *et al.* 2011; Rogelj *et al.* 2012). It is hoped that these RCPs may be used to help society decide the future that we want, and then work out how we need to alter our current behaviour in order to help us get there.

1.7 Regional differences in projected climate change

Given the complexities of different atmospheric circulations and interconnections between the climatic processes in different parts of the globe (such as the El Niño–Southern Oscillation – Hurrell & Trenberth 2010), increases in temperature are likely to result in very different rates of warming and other climatic effects around the globe. This is already evident in the global variation observed in recent temperature and precipitation trends (Figures 1.4–1.6). Despite the different assumptions underpinning the different GCMs, they are consistent in many of the changes they predict and how they are likely to vary globally, particularly in relation to warming (Figure 1.11). The most striking pattern of future temperature change is the projected warming of the Arctic, particularly during the Northern Hemisphere winter. This results from Arctic amplification, where temperature increases in excess of 7 °C above 1980–1999 levels are projected by 2100, even under a medium-emissions scenario (e.g. A1B). Milder winters may be associated with projected increases in precipitation through increased levels of water vapour, and therefore may lead to snowier winters across boreal regions. The projected degree of warming in the Antarctic winter of some 3–5 °C is again likely to reduce the extent of sea ice, but not by the same degree as in the Arctic, and some increases in snow cover may also occur. Elsewhere, most continental areas are projected to experience some 3–5 °C warming by 2100 under the A1B (medium-emissions) scenario. Significantly milder winter weather is likely at temperate latitudes, particularly across North America and central Asia, along with anticipated increases in precipitation. Temperature increases during the summer are likely to be particularly high in the interior of North America, the Mediterranean, Middle East and central Asia, where summer reductions in precipitation are also anticipated, thereby significantly increasing drought risk.

Although future precipitation patterns are more difficult to assess than temperature trends, with less agreement between different GCMs (IPCC 2007b; Solomon *et al.* 2009; Dai 2013), there is general consistency between models of significant reductions in summer precipitation in western and southern Europe and North Africa, extending eastward to some of the central Asian republics. Thus, under an A1B scenario, the Mediterranean region is projected to experience significant reductions in rainfall through most of the year, but particularly during the summer, increasing the frequency of summer drought (Solomon *et al.* 2009). Levels of projected warming at equivalent southern latitudes are likely to be much less, at 1–3 °C. Most models predict significant reductions in rainfall along the coast of Chile, potentially exacerbating drought conditions there. The magnitude of warming in the south of the Pacific, Atlantic and Indian oceans is projected to be lower than most other parts of the globe, at less than 2 °C for the A1B scenario.

In the tropics there is considerable heterogeneity in projected climate trends. Rates of warming are likely to be greatest in central South America and the Sahara and Kalahari deserts. Reductions in summer precipitation are projected for much of the USA, Central America and the Caribbean. Significant reductions in rainfall are also projected during the dry seasons of eastern South America, southern Africa, parts of south-east Asia and Western Australia. Conversely, significant increases in the frequency of rainfall from December to February are projected closer to the equator, along with a projected increase in the intensity of monsoon rainfall in southern India, Himalayas and parts of south-east Asia. Thus, increases in temperature are largely accompanied by increases in precipitation for most tropical forest regions, with the potential (and vitally important) exceptions of parts of Central America, the Amazon and the Atlantic forests of Brazil. Potential impacts of increasing drought conditions on the existing rainforests in these regions are therefore a cause for significant concern, particularly as they may be associated with significant carbon loss to the atmosphere, providing a potential positive feedback that would accelerate the rate of climate change (da Costa *et al.* 2010; Fisher *et al.* 2010).

16 · Birds and climate change

1.8 The consequences of climate change for species

Having described the potential magnitude of climate change, let us now consider the likely implications of such change for the species with which we share this planet. There are strong links between the climate and the organisms, populations, ecological communities and habitats which occupy a particular location. Starting with individuals, the weather, which through time reflects local climate, can affect the lives of organisms directly and indirectly in a variety of ways. For organisms that do not generate internal body heat (ectotherms), the ambient temperature directly influences the rate of their metabolism and the chances that they will be killed or damaged by high or low temperatures. Animals that generate internal body heat (endotherms), such as birds, have to spend more energy, and therefore find more food, to regulate their body temperature within safe limits when the ambient temperature is unusually high or low. In addition the amount of moisture in the environment can affect the growth, reproduction and survival rates in a similar way. In addition to these direct effects of weather on an organism's immediate environment, populations are strongly influenced by interactions with other species living in the same ecosystem. Effects on a species' food, predators, competitors and

> **Box 1.1** · *How variation in demographic parameters and individual movement operate to determine species' distribution and abundance*
>
> In a hypothetical example, a species occupies a series of potential habitat patches (circles) with the degree of movement between them (e.g. natal dispersal), indicated by arrows. Patches vary in quality from high (black) to low (white) from the centre of the species' range, or location of optimal environmental conditions (bottom), to the edge of the range (top). High-quality patches are characterised by high productivity and survival, and therefore produce emigrants which colonise poor-quality patches with low productivity and survival, which otherwise would not be maintained. It is this combination of varying productivity and survival, and the degree of dispersal between patches, which will determine local abundance (measured by circle size). As a result of these processes, a gradient of high to low patch quality, potentially as a result of climate, drives a gradient of high to low abundance across a species' range (see Martínez-Meyer et al. (2013) for a recent cross-taxa analysis of these patterns). Note that in response to density-dependent natal dispersal, the decline in abundance towards the edge of a species range may lag behind the decline in quality.
>
>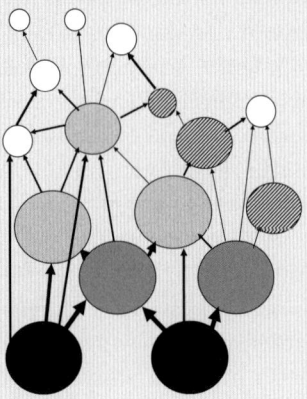

pathogens may all impact its populations indirectly (e.g. Mustin *et al.* 2007; Greyer *et al.* 2011; Cahill *et al.* 2013).

Impacts of weather on populations can scale-up to determine the climatic limits of species' distributions. In some cases, range boundaries may simply reflect limits beyond which individuals of the species cannot occur because of their ecology. For a terrestrial species this kind of boundary might be the shore of an ocean or the bank of a river. For a species that must live in trees it might be grassland. In other instances, the boundary may not have an obvious cause, but may exist because of variation in the ecological conditions that affect populations via variation in reproductive and death rates, and the probabilities of emigration and immigration. If you were able to measure these demographic rates along a transect from the middle of the species' range, or a place of optimum environmental conditions, towards the range boundary, you might find that the reproductive rate exceeded death rate deep within the range, but that the difference became smaller with increasing proximity to the range boundary. Eventually the death rate would exceed the reproductive rate at the fringe, where the species would die out were it not for wandering individuals moving in from deeper within the range (Box 1.1). You might also find that, even in areas near the edge of the species' range where the population is stable even without immigration, the population density is regulated at a level below that in the core of the range because ecological conditions there are less favourable. Although there is considerable debate about the extent to which these simplified gradients of environmental suitability and abundance within a species' range apply to a wide range of species (Gaston 2003), the principles of how climate may scale-up to affect abundance and distributions will still hold in other contexts.

1.9 Climate change and a real bird species

Having suggested how climatic conditions and climate change may affect the distribution and abundance of a species in theory, let us now consider how these ideas might work out in practice for a real bird. The willow grouse, or willow ptarmigan, *Lagopus lagopus*, is a species that has a Holarctic distribution across Scandinavia, northern Russia, Canada and the USA, but has a subspecies, the red grouse, *Lagopus lagopus scoticus*, which is endemic to Great Britain and Ireland. It is probably only in the last 10 000 years that red and willow grouse ranges have been separated by the North Sea (Yalden & Albarella 2009). However, a comparison of the DNA of Scottish red grouse and Scandinavian willow grouse shows that they are likely to have been genetically distinct since before the end of the last ice age, between 12 500 and 125 000 years before present (Bp), and are well on the way to being separate species (Quintela *et al.* 2010). The red grouse even looks different: it has brown not white wings, and does not change to a white plumage in winter. These are evolutionary adaptations to the less snowy winters experienced in the British Isles, probably driven by changes in moult pattern (Skoglund & Höglund 2010). The willow/red grouse provides an interesting example with which to start thinking about the role of climate in determining species population density and range boundaries and in driving speciation and global patterns of species distribution.

Most willow grouse subspecies feed upon buds and catkins of willow (*Salix* spp.) and birch (*Betula* spp.) and the berries of dwarf shrubs like bilberry (*Vaccinium myrtilus*).

18 · Birds and climate change

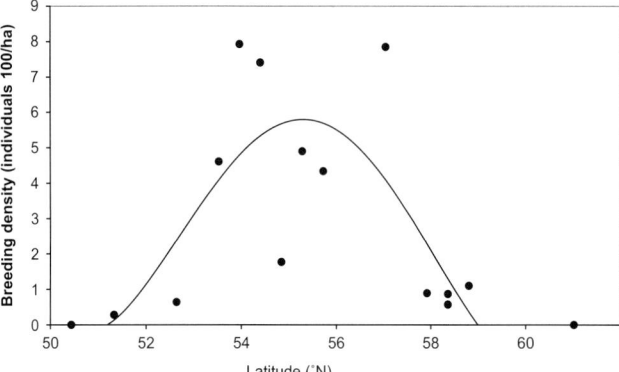

Figure 1.12 Latitudinal variation in the mean breeding density of red grouse in a range of UK upland regions (data from Grant & Pearce-Higgins, 2012).

However, red grouse mainly eat shoots of heather (*Calluna vulgaris*), which forms the predominant vegetation cover of much of the uplands of Britain and Ireland. Here the patterns of red grouse distribution and abundance are closely tied to the availability of heather, with which it shows a widespread association (Pearce-Higgins & Grant 2006; Pearce-Higgins *et al.* 2009a). Red grouse are also amongst the most heavily managed of all wild birds. They are a popular game bird and many populations are maintained for sport shooting on areas of heather moorland known as grouse moors. This involves the implementation of predator control, rotational burning management of the heather to promote young, nutritious heather shoots, and the provision of medication to reduce the incidence of the nematode parasite *Trichostrongylus tenuis* (Hudson 1992). In response to such management, grouse densities can attain exceedingly high levels, although when they do, varying parasite burdens and territorial behaviour often drive dramatic population cycles (Seivwright *et al.* 2005). Surprisingly, despite this intensive management, the species shows a very simple relationship between abundance and latitude across its range in the UK, as expected from the idealised relationship of Box 1.1. Grouse occur at low densities in the south, low densities in the north and both low and high densities in between (Figure 1.12). This is the classic pattern of how species abundance varies across a species range, as described above.

How is this pattern maintained? As already outlined, the species is closely tied to heather moorland, and on that moorland, the productivity and nutrient status of the heather (Watson & O'Hare 1979). Although heather has a widespread distribution, it occurs extensively only in the cool, oceanic climate of the UK uplands and southern tip of Norway (Thompson *et al.* 1995). In the far west and north of the UK, the extent of heather cover is limited by rainfall, whilst wind restricts heather growth on Shetland. As a result, red grouse densities in these areas are extremely low.

In the south, the English Channel is the natural limit of the species' range margin and, although the climate in the European Alps resembles that in parts of the range of willow grouse, neither the willow grouse nor the red grouse occur there. The fact that red grouse populations introduced into Belgium were not self-sustaining suggests that perhaps it is not just the English Channel that prevents the species from breeding further south (Watson & Moss 2008). In some parts of the red grouse range, such as Exmoor, it is likely that a sparseness of heather as a result of high levels of grazing limits densities, whilst in other areas it may be high numbers of predators (Fletcher et al. 2010), or higher summer temperatures reducing the amount of invertebrate food for their chicks (Pearce-Higgins et al. 2010) that limit productivity (Park et al. 2001; Fletcher et al. 2013), and therefore density.

In combination, these factors mean that conditions are optimal for this species in the centre of the UK's range (Figure 1.12), where heather grows well and there are sufficient invertebrates to support the chicks. For example, when modelling red grouse density in southern Scotland, between 55° N and 56° N and therefore within the latitudinal optimum, the most significant correlate in the absence of information about vegetation condition was rainfall. The highest grouse densities occurred in the relatively dry east. However, when information on vegetation characteristics, including heather cover, was included in the model, rainfall was no longer a significant predictor; the variation was better explained by field-based measures of the vegetation (Pearce-Higgins & Grant 2006). The influence of climate was therefore largely mediated through habitat (heather) quality. But this does not mean that all areas within this range will support high densities of grouse. It is within this zone that the grouse moors are located, where conditions are optimised for the species through management. Thus, even accounting for vegetation cover in models of red grouse abundance, there were additional positive effects of the intensity of grouse moor management and negative effects of predator numbers upon grouse densities (Tharme et al. 2001; Pearce-Higgins & Grant 2006). But equally, there were some regions within this range where grouse densities were low or absent because of other limiting factors such as the loss of heather through livestock grazing (Thirgood et al. 2000; Pearce-Higgins & Grant 2006) and habitat fragmentation by commercial forestry (Hancock et al. 2009). Variation in soil type and fertility may also affect heather quality and therefore grouse densities (Watson & Moss 2008), and indeed, potentially interact with climate to influence population cycles (e.g. Watson et al. 2000).

Our appraisal is striking in that it suggests that climatic conditions appear to play a significant role in limiting the distribution and population density of red grouse, despite this being a species subject to a high degree of human management. More widely, the range limits of the willow grouse throughout its distribution correlate well with particular combinations of climatic conditions (Huntley et al. 2007). If climatic conditions play such a major part in determining the distribution of red and willow grouse today, then we would expect their ranges to have been very different during the most recent ice age. On the basis of climate reconstructions for this period, the species is predicted to have occupied refugia as far south as northern Spain, southern France, the Balkans and Carpathian mountains. Comparison of reconstructions of the climatic conditions in those areas at that time (Singarayer & Valdes 2010) with the climatic conditions within the willow/red grouse range now show a good match (Huntley & Green 2011). In support of this, abundant fossilised bones of willow grouse have indeed been found in deposits in caves laid down during the last ice age at many sites across southern Europe and Russia (Tyrberg 1995; Tyrberg 1998; Yalden & Albarella 2009; Figure 1.13).

20 · Birds and climate change

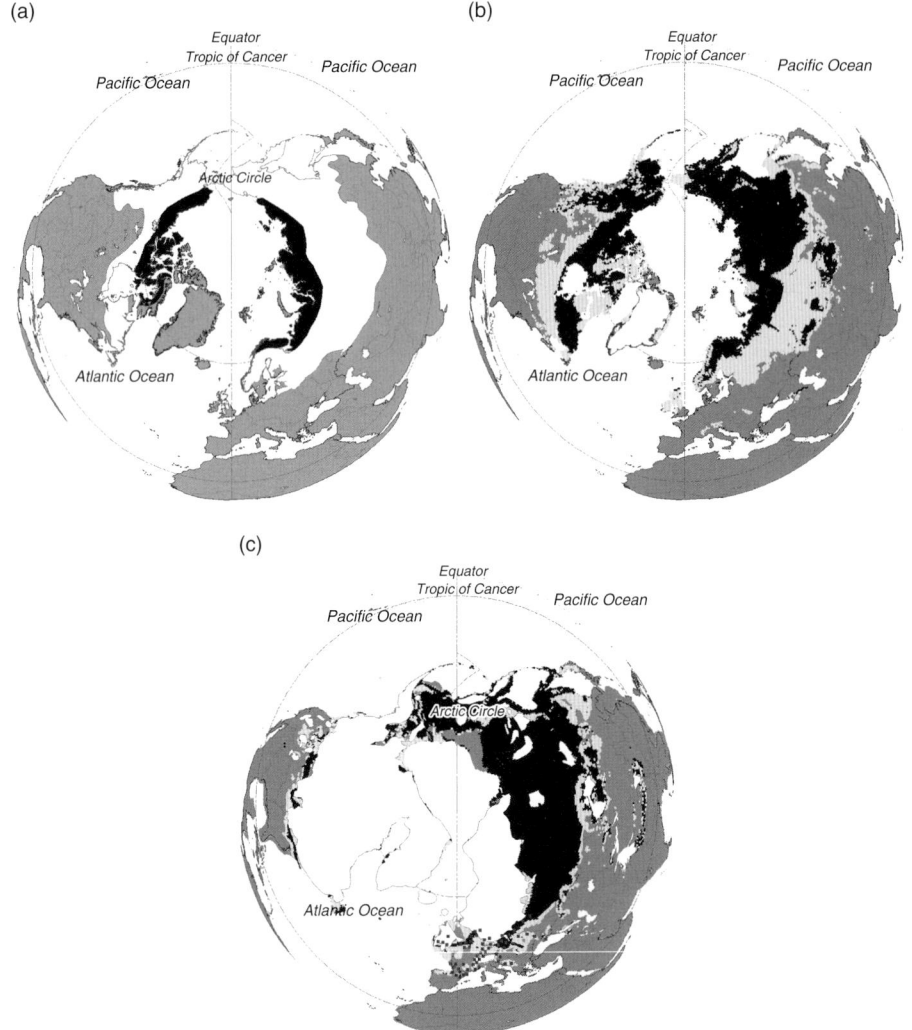

Figure 1.13 The current distribution of the willow grouse (a) which can be well simulated by a climate envelope model (b). That model can then be used to simulate the likely distribution of willow grouse during the last glacial maximum (21 000 yrs BP) (c) which can be compared to the presence of late-glacial palaeontological records (dots). In (a) white indicates where the species is resident and black, where it is migratory. In (b) and (c), black show areas where the species is simulated present with a high probability (0.8 < P_{occ}) and light grey with a moderate probability of occurrence (0.564 < P_{occ} < 0.8). White land areas show the extent of ice caps, and dark grey, ice-free land. Grouse projections from Huntley & Green (2011) and palaeontological records from Yalden & Albarella (2009).

1.10 The task ahead

Many bird populations are in trouble. Although in the majority of cases this is not a result of climate change which has occurred, given the ultimate importance of the climate in driving the abundance and distribution of bird species around the world, we would expect future climate change to have a significant impact on the abundance and distribution of those species, just as past climate change has driven previous species' range shifts. In Part I of the book we explore in detail the ways in which these impacts may occur, from phenological change in Chapters 2 and 3, further mechanisms of population impact in Chapter 4 and how those changes scale up to influence species distributions and bird community structure in Chapter 5.

It is difficult to project what the future holds, but climatologists are developing increasingly sophisticated models to describe and understand how our climate works. Although the current magnitude and rate of warming around the globe is unusual and outside of the range experienced for many centuries, it is not yet unprecedented in a timescale measured in millennia. However, given that this recent warming is very likely caused by humans (IPCC 2007b), some of us may well experience climates in our lifetime outside of that which the world has known for some 2.5 million years. The impact on our children, and our children's children, may be much worse. If realised, such rapid and severe climate change will surely pose a significant threat to many bird populations around the world, particularly when combined and interacting with other threats. Appraising the likely future magnitude of this threat, and the potential for conservationists to reduce the severity of that threat through appropriate intervention and management, will form the focus of the second part of the book. Based upon the potential severity of this threat to society, as well as to the natural world, there is an urgent need to reduce the magnitude of future climate change by reducing greenhouse gas concentrations in the atmosphere. However, depending on how this is achieved, this may also cause significant population-level impacts on birds, which in some cases may be more severe than the direct effects of climate change itself. We will therefore end the second part of the book with a consideration of this additional complication.

Much has been written, and is being written, about this topic (Figure 1.2). And yet there remains much that we do not know. Our purpose in writing this book is to summarise and synthesise the wealth of material which exists, alongside some new analysis which hopefully will increase scientific knowledge by at least a little. We hope that by doing so, we have made it easier for others both to understand the extent of the likely impacts of climate change on birds and to identify appropriate conservation responses, which will help ensure that the birds with which we share this planet have the best chance of surviving the climate change we may inflict on them.

1.11 Summary

- Birds are among the best studied and monitored of organisms, yet many are under significant threat of extinction. This book documents the impact of climate change on bird populations in Part I before suggesting conservation solutions in Part II.
- The longest running temperature time series, from central England, shows evidence of significant warming during the last century, and particularly since 1985, which is matched by global trends. Warming has been greatest at high latitudes, particularly during the winter months, whilst continental areas have experienced an increased frequency of heat waves. Snow and ice cover has generally decreased.
- There are no strong global trends in precipitation, although significant regional patterns exist. Droughts have become more frequent and intense, particularly at lower

latitudes, whilst rainfall intensity has also increased, leading to more frequent flood events and greater storm intensity.
- During the last 150 years, greenhouse gas concentrations in the atmosphere have risen beyond natural variability, largely as a result of human actions. These gases absorb solar radiation and warm the atmosphere. In 2007, the IPCC concluded that recent warming was 'very likely' caused by human actions.
- Current trends of greenhouse gas emissions are likely to continue into the near future, leading to probable further global warming of up to 5.0 °C by 2100. Warming is projected to be particularly marked in the Arctic, where rises in excess of 7 °C during winter months may occur. Future changes in precipitation are more uncertain, although a number of regions appear at risk of future drought.
- These changes are likely to impact the abundance and distribution of species, as illustrated with reference to the red grouse, a subspecies of the willow grouse endemic to the UK.

Part I
Impacts

2 · *Altered timings*

2.1 What is phenology and why does it matter?

We are all familiar with the changing seasons of the natural world around us.

At medium and high latitudes, spring is characterised by budburst, leaf growth and the flowering of many plants, the arrival of long-distance migrants and breeding of most bird species, and the emergence of adult stages of many insects. Autumn is signalled by the departure of long-distance migrants and leaf fall of deciduous plants. In both freshwater and marine environments, spring warming stimulates first phytoplankton and then zooplankton blooms which provide food for higher predators, influencing the timing of fish and bird breeding seasons. In the humid tropics, where temperature regimes vary less throughout the year, seasonality is often determined by predictable variation in rainfall, which then stimulates a flush in plant growth, flowering and fruiting, animal emergence and breeding. In the dry tropics, many organisms adjust their life cycles to the unpredictable arrival of rains or fires, which then lead to a pulse of growth and biological activity. Phenology is the study of the timing of these events.

Changes in such biological timing provide some of the most obvious and widely reported examples of climate change (Parmesan & Yohe 2003; Root *et al.* 2003; Thackeray *et al.* 2010). Around the world, spring events have become, on average, 2.8 days earlier per decade from 1951 to 2001 (Parmesan 2007). These include the timing of spring bird migration (reviewed in Lehikonen *et al.* 2004; Rubolini *et al.* 2007; Lehikoinen & Sparks 2010) and bird breeding (reviewed in Dunn 2004; Dunn & Winkler 2010). Before we examine these changes in more detail, it is worth asking why they are important.

Many birds live in seasonal environments and match the timing of particularly demanding stages of their life cycle with peaks of resource availability, usually the abundance of food. The timing of their migration has evolved to track seasonal patterns in resource availability, allowing migrants to exploit geographical variation in the availability of the resources they require at different times of the year (Berthold 1996). For example, migrants that travel in the spring from equatorial zones to higher latitudes are able to take advantage of the long days and high primary productivity of the summer for energetically demanding and time-consuming breeding activities without incurring potential costs associated with harsh winter weather (Alerstam & Högstedt 1982). In tropical areas, migratory or nomadic species similarly track patterns of rainfall and the resulting flush in plant growth and associated food resources. Thus, the ability of individual birds to follow changes in resource abundance in time and space is critical if they are to survive and breed successfully.

Given that many seasonal changes in resource availability vary on an annual basis with temperature or precipitation, climate change has the potential to alter and disrupt the ability of birds to time their migrations and breeding appropriately. In this chapter we will review the evidence that climate change has affected the timing of bird migration and breeding. As the situation for migrants clearly is particularly complex, due to their exposure to different patterns of climate change in different parts of their range, we examine how species' phenological responses vary with respect to migratory behaviour. Because very few birds are actually truly resident throughout their range, we compare patterns among long-, medium- and short-distance migrants, including what may traditionally be regarded as 'resident' species in this final grouping. This discussion is a precursor to the next chapter, in which we examine the population consequences of these phenological responses, or lack of them, in a changing climate.

2.2 How do birds respond to seasonality?

Most bird species which breed at medium and high latitudes only show migratory behaviour for short periods in the spring and autumn. Similarly, breeding usually only occurs at certain times of year when the sex organs (gonads) become enlarged and capable of producing eggs and sperm. This suggests that birds are able to predict and anticipate improving environmental conditions before they happen. Experimental evidence indicates that day length (photoperiod) is the key factor which determines the timing of these processes. Increasing day length in the spring initiates the departure of long-distance Palaearctic migrants from their African wintering grounds, weeks before conditions are suitable on the breeding grounds (Gwinner 1996; Dawson et al. 2001; Coppack et al. 2003). For species which winter south of the equator, such as barn swallows *Hirundo rustica* in South Africa, declining day length performs the same function. The change in day length experienced by migrating individuals as a consequence of poleward movement further moderates their behaviour (Lambrechts & Perret 2000; Helm & Gwinner 2005). After the breeding season, declining day-length contributes to the initiation of post-breeding moult, gonadal regression and autumn migration (Berthold 1996; Dawson et al. 2001; Wingfield 2005). Although most studies demonstrating these effects have involved species that breed in the northern temperate zone, even tropical species may detect and respond to small variations in day length (Hau et al. 1998). Photoperiod therefore appears to be the ultimate driver of avian phenology that sets the seasonal boundaries within which appropriate behaviour may occur.

This is important because it prevents the occurrence of inappropriate behaviours out of season in response to short-term weather fluctuations and ensures that individuals are ready to breed or migrate at the right time, as soon as conditions become favourable. However, within the times of year when photoperiodic control triggers migration and breeding, the precise timing of both migration and reproduction can vary in response to environmental factors, including weather. These effects are the basis of birds' phenological responses to climate change, which we describe in the rest of this chapter. Before we review these responses, however, it is necessary to briefly describe how changes in phenology are measured and the limitations imposed by different kinds of phenological information.

Table 2.1 *Sources of potential bias in first arrival dates (FAD)*

Bias	Explanation	References
Sample size	Because FAD measures the earliest arriving individuals detected, FAD will tend to advance with an increasing number of samples, whether through greater observer effort or increased population size.	Sparks (1999); Tryjanowski & Sparks (2001); Lee *et al.* (2011b)
Behaviour of earliest individuals	FAD is a measure of a population extreme, being dependent on the response of a small number of individuals, which may not represent changes in the entire population.	Ahola *et al.* (2004); Tryjanowski *et al.* (2005)
Detectability	Species with a low detectability will have less certain estimates of FAD, a more scattered FAD through time and reduced power to detect statistically significant trends.	Tryjanowski *et al.* (2005)
Volunteer behaviour	Many FAD measures are derived from volunteer networks. Changes in observer behaviour and effort may influence FAD estimation. For example, the overlap between weekends and migrant arrival will influence FAD recording date.	Tryjanowski *et al.* (2005), Sparks *et al.* (2008)

2.3 Some methodological considerations

For a migratory bird species which is absent from a location for some of the year, the simplest phenological measure is the earliest report of its return: the first arrival date (FAD). Because many birdwatchers note the date of such events every year, FADs form the majority of data in studies of migration phenology and have developed into various 'citizen science' initiatives to record changes in phenology through time (e.g. UK Phenology Network, www.naturescalendar.org.uk; European Phenology Network, van Vliet *et al.* (2003); USA National Phenology Network, www.usanpn.org). Recording FADs has long appealed to human nature and it has been possible to extract historical figures from notebooks and diaries, providing information on phenological changes extending back two centuries (Sparks & Carey 1995; Leihikoinen *et al.* 2004; Ellwood *et al.* 2010). Recently, annual compilations of local or regional bird records have begun to include this information as standard (e.g. Sparks *et al.* 2007). However, this measure has drawbacks which must be considered when interpreting such phenological change (Table 2.1).

A more robust measure of the timing of migration or breeding than the first reported date is the median or mean date of arrival or egg-laying, which records the timing of a typical individual within a population. However, estimating means or medians reliably requires intensive and standardised observations, which are not easy to obtain. Is the second sighting of a species during a season another record of the first individual seen, or second bird? Because of these difficulties, most data on median or mean arrival dates (MAD) are derived from the observation or trapping of individuals at bird observatories, where there is a similar detection effort made on each day and there are no or few resident individuals (e.g. Hüppop & Hüppop 2003; Stervander *et al.* 2005). However, as bird

Box 2.1 · *Analyses of published trends in spring migration phenology*

We collated published information on trends in spring arrival times of migrant birds throughout the world to the end of 2010, providing a database of 2062 reported changes in FAD from 79 studies and 444 changes in MAD from 29 studies. These were analysed within a mixed-model framework, in which study was specified as a random effect, to account for the potential non-independence of multiple data from individual locations. Only a small proportion (4%) of the variation in FAD trends was accounted for by differences between studies, whereas study accounted for a large proportion (39%) of the variation in MAD trends. As a result, our estimates of MAD trends were subject to a greater degree of error because of this significant between-study variation, whereas changes in FAD were much more consistent between studies, and therefore are better estimated.

In order to examine effects of both start- and end-year upon the trends, we included species and continent as fixed factors, and start- and end-year of each time series as covariates in the models. The dependent variable was the estimated rate of advance over time for each species from each study. There was significant variation in FAD trend due to both species ($F_{356, 1517} = 7.03$, $P < 0.0001$) and continent ($F_{1, 440} = 3.96$, $P = 0.047$), but this was not the case for MAD trend (species, $F_{137, 191} = 0.67$, $P = 0.99$; continent, $F_{1, 42.4} = 0.97$, $P = 0.33$). There was a significant effect of start-year on trends in FAD ($F_{1, 283} = 12.51$, $P = 0.0005$) and both start-year ($F_{1, 303} = 10.39$, $P = 0.0014$) and end-year on trends in MAD ($F_{1, 303} = 44.11$, $P < 0.0001$). Subsequent analyses of variation in FAD were conducted using models that accounted for variation in start-year, whilst models of variation in MAD also included end-year.

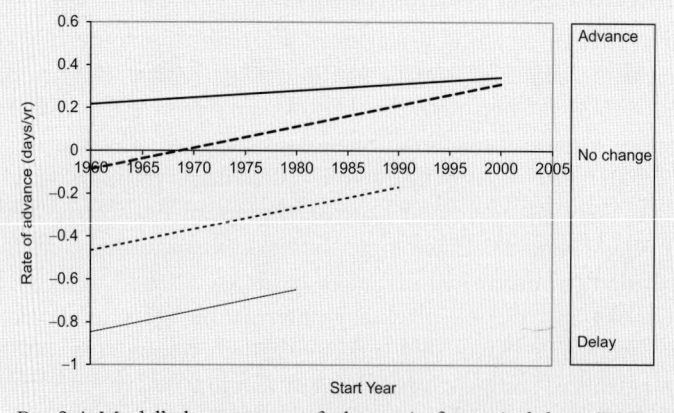

Box 2.1 Modelled mean rates of advance in first arrival dates (FAD, solid line) and mean arrival dates (MAD, dotted lines) over time in relation to the initial year of the study. There was no significant effect of end-year upon the magnitude of change in FAD, but this did affect variation in MAD between studies. The magnitude of advance in MAD was greater in studies that ended later (end year = 2010 for thick dotted line, 2000 for medium dotted line and 1990 for thin dotted line).

observatories tend to be located at places where migrating birds are concentrated, such as in a mountain pass or at a narrow isthmus, the individuals recorded may originate from, and be migrating to, a wide variety of locations. Hence they are likely to derive from a large number of breeding localities and/or overwinter in different regions, and therefore

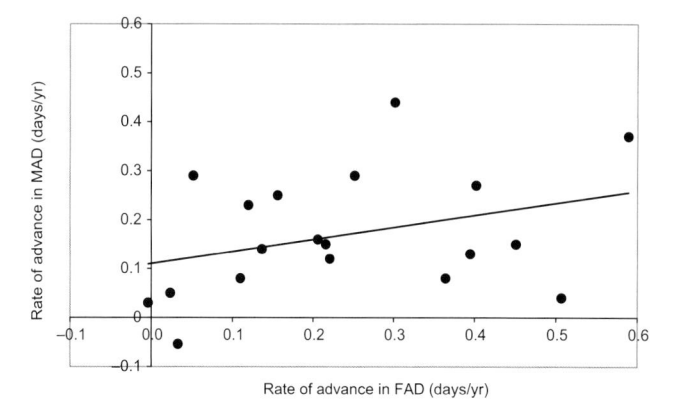

Figure 2.1 The estimated rate of advance of mean or median spring arrival date (MAD) in days per year in relation to the equivalent advance rate for the date of the first report (FAD). Each point represents a species. FAD and MAD were each averaged across at least five studies for 19 species (data from Tables S2.1[*] and S2.2[*]). Trends in MAD and FAD are only weakly correlated ($r = 0.36$, $n = 19$, $P = 0.13$).

the timing of migration might be influenced by conditions at an uncertain mixture of locations. This mixing may mask important differences between populations (Both *et al.* 2006b).

For laying dates, mean or median values for a population (MLD) can be obtained from the frequency distribution of the date of first eggs (FED) being laid in nests found by observers. Unlike arrival dates based upon unmarked birds, MLD is easy to relate to demographic rates measured for the same population. In species where females lay one clutch of eggs in a season, the MLD is likely to be reliable if observers search for nests consistently and with similar effectiveness throughout the breeding season. However, females of some species lay more than one clutch of eggs during a season and it is often difficult to know whether a particular clutch is the female's first of the season, a replacement or subsequent clutch. This is important because a year in which females laid more replacement or second and third clutches would have a later MLD, based upon all nests found, than one with fewer subsequent clutches, even if the timing of egg-laying of first clutches in the two years was identical. This problem can be overcome if females are individually identifiable, or by statistical methods (Etheridge *et al.* 1997; Cornulier *et al.* 2009).

Despite these potential sources of error, temporal trends in FADs and MADs are significantly positively correlated with one another across six of seven time series where this has been assessed (Sparks *et al.* 2005; Rubolini *et al.* 2007; Miller-Rushing *et al.* 2008; Miller-Rushing & Primack 2008; Lehikoinen & Sparks 2010). Based on a collation of estimates of FAD and MAD across Europe for 19 species for which both estimates have been derived from five studies or more (Box 2.1), we found a weak, non-significant, correlation between trends derived from the two measures of arrival phenology (Figure 2.1). This suggests that the two metrics provide slightly different information. Years with an early first arrival relative to the mean tend to be characterised by an

---

[*] See online material.

elongated and protracted arrival distribution, with relatively small numbers of individuals arriving very early that slowly build up through the spring. Years with an early mean arrival, relative to FAD, tend to be characterised by a more protracted arrival of late arriving individuals (Sparks *et al.* 2005). By measuring both, a considerable amount of information about the phenology and influence of the weather upon spring migration timing can be gained (Ahola *et al.* 2004).

A final consideration when comparing or correlating results from different studies is to ensure that the time periods over which trends are measured are similar to one another. This is important because the rate of climate change has not been constant over time. When comparing between studies, it is therefore important to account for variation in the timing and duration of any study (Box 2.1). We used linear regression to model trends in FAD from the published literature, which indicated that spring arrival has advanced (become earlier) by an average of 0.22 days per year for a study started in 1960 and ending in 2010, and 0.34 days per year for a study started in 2000, although based on a shorter, 10-year time series. Trends in egg-laying (measured by MLD) were similarly affected by the start-date of a study, with equivalent advancement rates of MLD being 0.14 and 0.37 days per year for studies started in 1960 and 2000 respectively (see Box 2.8). Average trends in MAD varied with both start- and end-date, being most likely to show an advance in studies with a late start (post-1970) and end (post-2000). The rate of phenological advance has therefore increased significantly through time, at least to 2010.

2.4 Spring migration phenology

2.4.1 General patterns

There is considerable similarity between the results of different studies that have examined changes in the timing of spring bird migration (reviewed by Parmesan & Yohe 2003; Root *et al.* 2003; Lehikoinen *et al.* 2004; Jonzén *et al.* 2006; Rubolini *et al.* 2007; Gordo 2007; Parmesan 2007; Lehikoinen & Sparks 2010). We analysed collated trends in FAD across 1437 published time series to 2010 from Europe, which indicated a mean advancement ($\pm$ SE) of 0.24 $\pm$ 0.02 days per year has occurred. Correcting for the non-independence of data from individual studies and accounting for variation in start-year (see Box 2.1) altered this estimate only slightly, to 0.24 $\pm$ 0.04 days per year. Equivalent mean advancement rates in MAD across 294 published time series averaged 0.15 $\pm$ 0.02 days per year. This also remained largely unchanged in magnitude after accounting for variation in both start- and end-year and the non-independence of studies at 0.14 $\pm$ 0.15, but with a much greater standard error due to the high variability in trends in MAD between studies. These estimates are therefore within the range published previously for Europe of 0.22–0.37 days per year for FAD and 0.10–0.16 days per year for MAD (Lehikoinen *et al.* 2004, Rubolini *et al.* 2007, Lehikoinen & Sparks 2010).

The rate of advance in MAD has been less than that for FAD (see also Figure 2.1). This has been suggested to result from a greater sensitivity to spring weather of the individuals which migrate earliest (Lehikoinen *et al.* 2004; Sparks *et al.* 2005; Rubolini *et al.* 2007). Based on our analysis, the earliest arriving individuals of a typical bird species in Europe in 2010 arrived some 7 days earlier than they would have done in 1980, whilst the 'average' individuals in a population arrived about 5 days earlier. Spring arrival periods have therefore become marginally more extended over time (Sparks et al. 2005).

Using a mixed model to account for variation between studies resulting from different start-years, and the non-independence of data from the same study, the average rate of advance in FAD for spring arrival of species that breed in North America has been marginally slower than that observed for Europe, at 0.17 ± 0.05 days per year (Box 2.1). Although the rate of change in MAD in North America was also slower than observed for Europe at 0.08 ± 0.03 days per year, when accounting for the non-independence of different studies, this estimate changed to a mean 0.09 ± 0.33 day delay per year, again with wide standard errors. It is therefore difficult to assess the extent to which there has been a significant change in MAD in North America because of the wide variation in trends between studies. Overall, our analysis suggests that there was no statistically significant difference in MAD between the two continents (Box 2.1).

Only three published studies have examined changes over time in arrival dates of migratory species in Australia and with contrasting results. Chambers (2008) detected few consistent trends in south-west Australia, although the arrival of migrants most comparable with Northern Hemisphere spring migrants had advanced by 0.63 ± 0.58 days per year. Beaumont et al. (2006) found evidence for advancing FADs in 36% of species in the south-east of the country, although these included a mix of long-distance migrants arriving from high-latitude Northern Hemisphere breeding grounds, and medium- and short-distance austral migrants which breed in Australia. The mean arrival time of 17 medium- and short-distance spring migrants breeding in Australia has advanced by 0.31 ± 0.08 days per year. There was no significant advance in the arrival of two summer visitors to Eyre Bird Observatory, Western Australia (Chambers 2005). When combined in a mixed model, with both study and species as random effects, there has been an estimated mean rate of advance in FAD of Australian migrants of 0.44 ± 0.27 days per year. Despite the apparently large rate of advance, there is too much variation between the three studies and particularly between species, for a consistent pattern to be apparent.

Across all studies, including also data from a small number of species from Asia and Antarctica, there has been a consistent advance in FAD of 0.20 ± 0.02 days per year and a mean advance in MAD of 0.12 ± 0.02 days per year, based on a simple average. Accounting for the non-independence of data from the same study and the effects of start-date and end-date as appropriate, altered these estimates to 0.22 ± 0.03 and 0.14 ± 0.14 for FAD and MAD respectively, again increasing the uncertainty associated with the latter. These values are similar to, but slightly lower in magnitude than, those from the global database of Lehikoinen & Sparks (2010) of 0.28 days per year advancement in FAD and 0.18 days per year advance in MAD.

2.4.2 Spatial variation

Average global patterns may mask considerable variation between regions and species. However, when assessed at the country level, after accounting for variation in species composition and start-year, there was no significant variation in FAD trends between different European countries (Box 2.2). Although there were insufficient data to repeat

Box 2.2 · *Spring migration phenology in relation to taxonomic group and location*

Analysis of country-specific variation in arrival date trends was conducted for 14 European countries for which there were at least 10 estimates of change in FAD. Only five European countries met this threshold with respect to MAD. Following the mixed model of Box 2.1, with study as a random effect, trend in FAD was modelled as a function of species and start-year as nuisance variables, and country. Estimates of change in FAD did not differ significantly between countries ($F_{13, 25.6} = 0.86$, $P = 0.60$).

Secondly, we looked for evidence for latitudinal variation in arrival trends across the Northern Hemisphere, using the same mixed-model framework (Box 2.1), with species, continent and start-year included as nuisance variables for FAD and end-year additionally included in the model for MAD. When included in this model, there were significant effects of latitude on both changes in FAD (latitude, $F_{1, 68.9} = 6.05$, $P = 0.016$; latitude^2, $F_{1, 73.4} = 5.83$, $P = 0.018$) and MAD (latitude, $F_{1, 67.1} = 4.77$, $P = 0.033$; latitude^2, $F_{1, 80.6} = 6.36$, $P = 0.014$). These effects were hump-shaped, indicating that advancement rate was highest at intermediate latitudes (Figure 2.2). These differences were not a result of variable proportions of long-distance migrants at different latitudes (Chapter 5) because the model incorporates species as a factor, and therefore examines residual variation once differences in species composition between sites have been accounted for. Replacing the species term in the model with a term for migratory distance also did not affect the results.

The mixed model of Box 2.1 was also used to examine the statistical significance and magnitude of variation in both FAD and MAD trends between different levels of phylogenetic detail (order, family, genus and species), although the continent term was excluded as few species were common to both Europe and North America. There was significant variation in FAD trends across all taxonomic levels, which was greatest at genus and species levels, but no significant variation across taxa in MAD trends, probably because of the greater degree of variation in MAD trends between studies of the same species.

Table 1 *The significance of variation in first arrival date (FAD) and mean arrival date (MAD) trends between different levels of phylogeny.*

	FAD	MAD
Order	$F_{20, 1945} = 4.15$, $P < 0.0001$	$F_{6, 149} = 0.77$, $P = 0.60$
Family	$F_{65, 1931} = 6.97$, $P < 0.0001$	$F_{28, 316} = 0.99$, $P = 0.49$
Genus	$F_{208, 1756} = 7.48$, $P < 0.0001$	$F_{80, 302} = 0.63$, $P = 0.99$
Species	$F_{356, 1484} = 7.02$, $P < 0.0001$	$F_{137, 183} = 0.91$, $P = 0.71$

this analysis for MAD, given the greater variation between studies, we might expect there to be stronger differences between countries in MAD than FAD.

Spring temperatures have increased most in central latitudes of both Europe (Menzel *et al.* 2006) and North America (Strode 2003). Correspondingly, Rubolini *et al.* (2007) estimated that rates of advancement in FAD were also greatest at intermediate latitudes (55–60° N), but found no significant relationship between the rate of advance in MAD with latitude. We repeated these analyses combining data across both Europe and North America and found evidence for significant latitudinal gradients in time trends of both

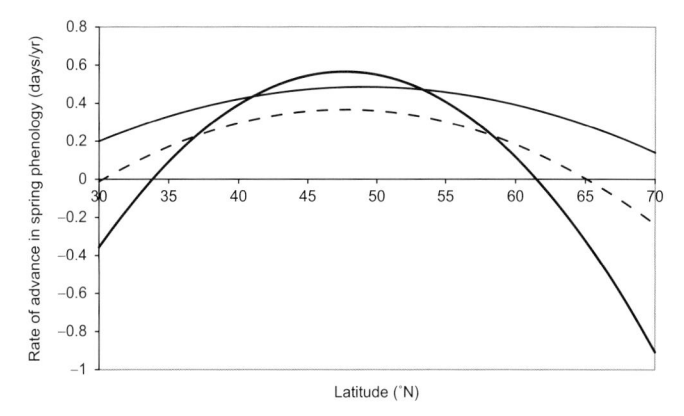

Figure 2.2 Mean rates of advance in first arrival date (FAD; thin solid line), mean arrival date (MAD; thick solid line) and mean laying date (MLD; dashed line) with latitude, as predicted by modelling latitude and latitude^2 in the mixed models of Box 2.1. To standardise the effects of start- and end-year, predictions are for a study that starts in 1975 and finishes in 2005.

FAD and MAD, even after accounting for variation in species composition (Box 2.2). It therefore appears that rates of phenological advance have been greatest at intermediate latitudes of the Northern Hemisphere, peaking around 45–50° N (Figure 2.2). Interestingly, average FAD appears to have advanced to different degrees across the entire range of latitude, whilst MAD has only advanced at mid-latitudes. This pattern contrasts with the apparent tendency for stronger advancement at higher latitudes across a range of taxa reported by Parmesan (2007), although both studies are based upon rather few data.

2.4.3 Differences between species

There is considerable variation that can be attributable to phylogenetic differences between species, particularly at higher taxonomic levels (Rubolini *et al.* 2007). This is supported by our analysis of trends in FAD (Box 2.2), where there was much variation at the species, genus and family levels (Table S2.1).[*] Of the 17 orders for which we analysed at least five time series, 10 (59%) showed a statistically significant mean rate of advance in FAD, with the strongest evidence for arrival being earlier apparent for Podicipediformes (grebes), Procellariiformes (shearwaters, petrels and albatrosses), Pelecaniformes (gannets, pelicans and cormorants) and Anseriformes (wildfowl and their relatives), each of which have advanced by in excess of 0.5 days per year. Across 42 families, 23 (55%) showed a statistically significant mean rate of advance, which was greatest amongst the Anatidae (wildfowl), Ciconiidae (storks), Threskiornithidae (ibis), Gruidae (cranes), Alaudidae (larks), Corvidae (crows), Pelecanidae (pelicans), Phalacrocoracidea (cormorants), Podicipedidae (grebes), Hydrobatidae (storm petrels) and Procellariidae (shearwaters and petrels). Of 101 genera, 39 (39%) showed a significant rate of advance and of 94 species for which there were sufficient data to present trends, 38 (40%) had advanced significantly.

---

[*] See online material.

Box 2.3 · *Correlations between spring migration timing and the North Atlantic Oscillation*

Many studies have examined how the timing of spring arrival varies in relation to North Atlantic Oscillation (NAO). We applied the mixed-model framework of Box 2.1 to these results, focusing on 576 time series from Europe in relation to FAD and 254 series in relation to MAD. Because some studies present information only on the slope of the relationship between NAO and arrival date, whilst others present information only on the correlation coefficient, in order to make maximal use of the data, we examine what we term correlation scores. A study was scored as -1 if there was a significant ($P < 0.05$) negative correlation between NAO and arrival date, 1 if there was a significant positive correlation, and 0 if there was no significant correlation. There was significant variation in the mean values of these correlation scores between FAD and NAO in relation to migratory distance ($F_{2,\,569} = 89.6$, $P < 0.0001$), but not MAD ($F_{2,\,248} = 1.24$, $P = 0.29$).

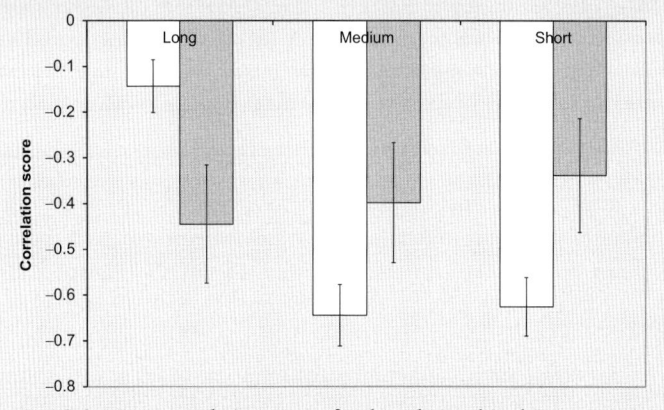

Box 2.3 Mean correlation scores for the relationships between NAO and both first arrival dates (FAD, white) and mean arrival dates (MAD, grey) in relation to migratory distance of European migrants. The more negative the score the stronger the tendency for arrival to be early when NAO is high. Vertical lines represent ±1 SE.

The trends of those species covered by five or more time series are presented in Table S2.1.[*]

In contrast to the analyses of first arrival dates, estimates of the rate of advance in mean arrival date (MAD) varied much more between studies than between species (Box 2.1). Given strongly contrasting trends in MAD between studies in different locations and with time (e.g. Sokolov *et al.* 1998), as shown by analyses in Boxes 2.2 and 2.3, this is perhaps unsurprising, but does mean that where studied, relatively few species have shown consistent trends. This contrasts with the inference of analyses of Rubolini *et al.* (2007) and Møller *et al.* (2008) who quantified trends in mean arrival data for 100 European migrant species. Our estimates of the rate of advance in MAD through time (Table S2.2)[*] hardly correlate with those published by Møller *et al.* (2008) for the same species ($r = 0.07$,

---

[*] See online material.

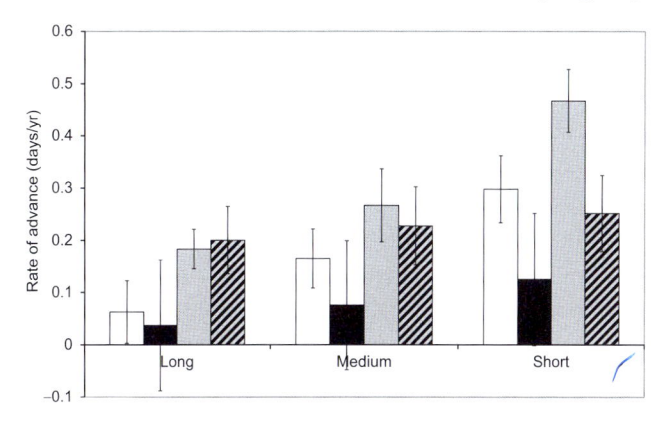

Figure 2.3 Mean rates of advance (± 1 SE) in first arrival date (FAD; open) and mean arrival date (MAD; diagonal stripe) of long-, medium- and short-distance migrants in North America (white background) and Europe (grey background). Estimates are standardised predictions from a mixed model (Box 2.1.).

$n = 20$, $P = 0.76$). Part of the reason for this difference could be because the phenologies of Rubolini and Møller were largely based upon data from a much narrower geographical area (concentrated in central Europe and southern Fennoscandia) with more similar warming trends than the wider array of locations used in our analysis.

It has been suggested that the degree to which migratory bird species have advanced their spring arrival date in Europe is related to how widely separated their breeding and wintering grounds are (Sokolov *et al.* 1998; Žalakevičius 2001; Tryjanowski *et al.* 2002; Végvári *et al.* 2010), although other studies failed to detect this effect (Hüppop & Hüppop 2003; Stervander *et al.* 2005; Jonzén *et al.* 2006). Even meta-analyses of data from multiple sites and studies show contrasting findings. Rubolini *et al.* (2007), in an analysis of published studies and unpublished data, particularly from central Europe and Scandinavia, found consistent evidence for a more rapid advance in the arrival of short-distance than long-distance migrants. Gienapp *et al.* (2007), however, did not, but did find evidence for such a contrast in data from North America, which is supported by the results of individual studies (e.g. DeLeon *et al.* 2011). As a result of these discrepancies, Knudsen *et al.* (2011) concluded that no firm pattern of differential (phenological) response to climate change according to migratory distance has been established so far, and that case studies and meta-analyses should more properly account for confounding factors and effects of study design. After accounting for some of these confounding factors, particularly variation in start- and end-years between studies (Box 2.1), we did find significant variation in FAD with migratory distance ($F_{2, 1846} = 16.63$, $P < 0.0001$), but not in MAD ($F_{2, 241} = 0.10$, $P = 0.90$; Figure 2.3).

Although our analyses suggest that migration distance may affect the rate of advancement of spring arrival, there are a number of other variables that correlate with migration distance and which might also account for these species differences. These include diet, with more generalist species having showed a greater advancement in phenology, breeding strategy, with reduced advance in single-brooded species, and moult strategy (Møller *et al.* 2008; Végvári *et al.* 2010). Evidence suggests, however, that mating system, nest type or age of reproduction are probably not significant covariates of change (Gienapp *et al.* 2007;

Végvári *et al.* 2010). More detailed studies are therefore required to more specifically tease apart the ecological factors and traits which determine why some species have advanced their timing of arrival, but others have not, particularly as this may influence species' sensitivity to potential demographic impacts of climate change (Chapter 3).

2.4.4 The impact of climate change

It is difficult to relate advances in spring arrival to climate change, because migrants experience a range of different conditions whilst they are away from the breeding grounds. Are they responding to altered conditions on the wintering grounds, on migration or on or close to the breeding grounds? Because of the large number of weather variables for different localities which could be included in such analyses, many studies have correlated annual variation in FAD or MAD with large-scale summary measures of variation in the climate that describe conditions across extensive geographical areas, such as the North Atlantic Oscillation (NAO; the difference in atmospheric pressure at sea level between the Icelandic low and the Azores high pressure areas). Annual variation in NAO has been correlated with many aspects of weather conditions in the areas that breeding birds of Europe visit during their migrations to Africa (Hurrell 1995; Hurrell *et al.* 2001, 2003; Hurrell & Trenberth 2010).

The timing of arrival of migrants to the German island of Helgoland (Hüppop & Hüppop 2003), and further north in Scandinavia (Vähälato *et al.* 2004; Stervander *et al.* 2005; Jonzén *et al.* 2006), is negatively correlated with annual variation in NAO. Positive values, indicative of warm, wet winters in northern Europe, but cool, dry conditions in the Mediterranean and North Africa, are associated with early arrival, particularly of long-distance migrants. Conversely, analysis of data from Lithuania (Žalakevičius *et al.* 2006) and the Czech Republic (Hubálek 2003), failed to find strong negative effects of winter NAO on the spring arrival dates of long-distance migrants, but instead detected strong effects on FAD of short- and medium-distance migrants. Studies across Europe emphasise that the relationship between winter NAO and the timing of migrant arrival is spatially variable (Jonzén *et al.* 2006), which also appears to be the case in North America (e.g. MacMynowski & Root 2007; Miller-Rushing *et al.* 2008; DeLeon *et al.* 2011).

Across all studies, accounting for variation in the start-year, our analyses found significantly more negative correlations (more evidence of advancement) between FAD and NAO for medium- and short-distance migrants than long-distance migrants (Box 2.3). There were no such differences apparent for MAD, with consistently negative relationships between MAD and NAO for all migrant types. Thus the timing of first arrival of medium- and short-distance migrants has been more strongly and consistently negatively correlated with NAO than the arrival of long-distance migrants. The timing of MAD across all species groups also appears to have been advanced by positive NAO values.

Benign winter weather in northern Europe associated with positive NAO values is therefore likely to have caused the arrival times of short-distance migrants that winter in central and Western Europe to advance. It is intriguing that medium-distance migrants (species wintering in southern Europe and north Africa) also show the same relationship because in the places where they winter, positive NAO values mean cold and dry conditions, which are likely to be less favourable to the birds involved. One potential explanation is that these NAO effects may act on arrival times by influencing conditions in central and northern Europe during migration, rather than through conditions on the wintering grounds.

The mechanisms by which the spring arrival of long-distance migrants wintering south of the Sahara might be related to winter NAO are similarly unclear, as they may experience contrasting weather responses between Africa and northern Europe in relation to the same NAO phase. Our analysis suggests that NAO has weaker effects on the FAD of long-distance migrants than on the MAD (Box 2.3). It is unlikely NAO may influence arrival times through correlations with conditions in Africa, because correlations between NAO and African conditions only extend to coastal West Africa and the Sahara northwards (Wang et al. 2005; Hurrell & Trenberth 2010). It is possible that NAO may influence the timing of migration through its effect on wind direction or strength; positive phases of NAO are associated with south-westerly winds favourable in providing tail winds for migration, whilst negative phases are characterised by north-westerly winds in the Mediterranean. However, given that most studies correlate winter NAO (which is averaged from December to March) to arrival times in April and May, it is difficult to see how the two might be directly linked through this mechanism. Therefore it is perhaps most likely that migrants have responded to changes in conditions in Europe that reflect the climate during the previous winter. Positive values of NAO are related to drier and potentially unfavourable conditions in the Mediterranean, which may slow migration, but warmer, wetter conditions in central and northern Europe that are likely to increase migration speed through association with earlier spring conditions. In accordance with this idea, the arrival of migrants to Capri (Italy) was positively correlated with NAO (and therefore birds arrived later when NAO values were positive), but, northern Europe arrival was negatively correlated with NAO (Jonzén et al. 2006). Given that most European studies are from central and northern Europe, this may explain why the effects of NAO upon arrival times are, an average largely negative, so advancement occurs with more positive NAO.

Other studies have examined more direct effects of temperature or precipitation in influencing the speed of migration and timing of arrival. For example, the MAD of 11 of 12 short-distance migrants and 7 of 12 long-distance migrants were significantly negatively correlated with (advanced by) temperature at the Helgoland observatory (Hüppop & Hüppop 2003). Across all species, the timing of arrival is probably influenced by weather conditions on the wintering grounds and during migration. For short-distance migrants, temperature near the area where arrival is measured is likely to be a fairly good indicator of conditions on the breeding and wintering grounds, particularly given the strong degree of spatial autocorrelation typical of temperature data. Therefore short-distance migrants have tended to show a stronger correlation with temperature in the area where arrival is measured than long-distance migrants, in relation to both FAD and MAD (Box 2.4).

The arrival of long-distance migrants is influenced by a greater range of conditions than for short-distance migrants because of the spatial separation of the wintering and breeding grounds and the distance over which passage occurs. Thus the timing of departure from wintering areas may be determined by local conditions and the speed of migration determined by a combination of temperature and wind speed along the migration route (Ahola et al. 2004; Žalakevičius et al. 2006, 2009; Sinelschikova et al. 2007; Both 2010a). As a result, annual variation in FAD may be correlated with both large-scale climatic

Box 2.4 · *Correlations between spring migration timing and temperature*

We used the mixed-model framework of Box 2.1 to examine common patterns of variation in spring migration phenology in relation to temperature at the same location, focusing on 1236 FAD time series and 292 MAD time series. There was significant variation with migratory distance in the relationship between temperature and both FAD ($F_{2, 853} = 3.38$, $P = 0.035$) and MAD ($F_{2, 184} = 13.98$, $P < 0.0001$). Short-distance migrants showed significantly stronger relationships between arrival date and temperature than long-distance migrants.

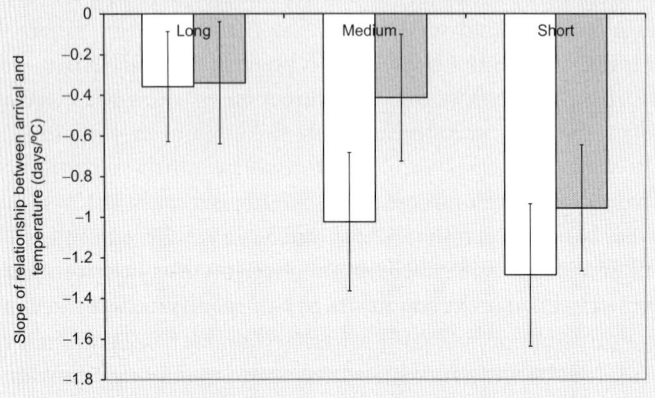

Box 2.4 Average slopes between arrival date and local temperature for first arrival dates (FAD, white) and mean arrival dates (MAD, grey) in relation to migratory distance. The more negative the score the stronger the tendency for arrival to be early when temperature is high. Vertical lines represent ±1 SE.

processes, such as NAO, and local temperature at the arrival site. Whilst these effects of local temperature on arrival times appear to have been greatest for short-distance migrants, they also appear important for the earliest migrating individuals in short- and medium-distance migrating populations (Box 2.4), probably because it is at this stage that variation in temperature will have had the greatest fitness consequences (Tøttrup *et al.* 2010); discussed in Section 3.3.

The precise timing of departure from the wintering grounds also appears under environmental control, and therefore likely to respond to climate change. Some of the best evidence comes from detailed studies of of individually marked waterfowl which show that wind direction and air pressure are important stimuli influencing departure (Evans 1979). Indeed, because of the risk of mortality during severe weather conditions, swans tend to travel under conditions of high and rising pressure (Griffin *et al.* 2010), although long periods of harsh weather can force birds to depart into headwinds (Jenni & Schaub 2003). As a result, spring and autumn migration phenologies of species such as the snow geese *Chen caerulescens* can be strongly affected by large-scale atmospheric processes, and the occurrence and track of storms (Smith & Hayden 1984).

Wader migration appears under similar control with departures of both long-distance migrants from New Zealand and short-distance migrants from the Pacific coast of North America being influenced by rising pressure and wind direction (Battley 1997; Butler *et al.*

1997), although individuals also appear to show a high degree of consistency in their departure decisions between years (Battley 2006). The departure decisions of migrant passerines in Europe are also strongly related to local wind and temperature conditions, but may be less influenced by variation in atmospheric pressure (e.g. Lack 1960; Erni *et al.* 2002; Sinelschikova *et al.* 2007). Thus, the timing of departure of migrants undergoing major sea crossings is strongly influenced by the occurrence of tailwinds and rising pressure, as they attempt to reduce the risk of encountering storm conditions en route. Individuals undertaking shorter distance flights may be influenced by local conditions but be less sensitive to large-scale pressure variation because they will more easily be able to find shelter in the event of bad weather.

Limited data suggest that departure dates from wintering grounds have been advanced by recent climate change. Two of three long-distance migrant waders have advanced their departure from their Australian wintering grounds by in excess of 1 day per year (Beaumont *et al.* 2006). Further, the timings of the departure of both pied flycatchers *Ficedula hypoleuca* (Both 2010a) and barn swallows (Altwegg *et al.* 2012) from their African wintering grounds have also become earlier, potentially in response to changes in rainfall patterns. Recent data from individually marked raptors and waders indicate that there may be consistency in individual departure decisions between years (Battley 2006; Vardanis *et al.* 2011), which suggests that phenological advances may be driven by earlier departure of new recruits to the population rather than behavioural plasticity of individual departures as a function of local climatic conditions (Gill *et al.* 2014). Clearly, more work is required to tease apart the relative importance of climate change and individual characteristics upon departure decisions, particularly as most of this work on individual decisions has been conducted on large migratory shorebirds or raptors. It is also unclear how well this work may relate to small migratory passerines with very different life history strategies, such as pied flycatcher or barn swallows, whose arrival times in the breeding areas appear to correlate with local weather conditions in the African wintering grounds or subsequently on migration (Both 2010a).

Although understanding how weather and climate change influence departure and migration speed is difficult, recent technological advances, such as satellite tags and geolocators, which now enable the day-by-day tracking of individuals on migration, should make studies easier. Such information has already been used to variously identify migratory routes that were previously unknown because of insufficient ring (band) recovery data (e.g. Osborne *et al.* 1997; Qian *et al.* 2009), and to link particular breeding populations to specific wintering or foraging areas for conservation purposes (e.g. www.seabirdtracking.org). We therefore expect there will be major advances in this area over the next few years, which will provide a much greater insight into the mechanisms by which changes in migration timing occur at the individual level. Given potential impacts of climate change on global circulation systems, storm tracks and wind direction (Hurrell & Trenberth 2010), increasing our understanding of these effects will be important in developing an improved ability to observe and predict the effects of climate change on migrants. However, in the meantime, the following is probably a reasonable summary of the role of weather in driving variation in the timing of spring migration.

The initiation of spring migration in a typical Western Palaearctic migrant wintering south of the Sahara is endogenously controlled. Small changes in day length increase migratory restlessness and the sensitivity of the individual to environmental conditions (Berthold 1996), although the exact timing of departure varies with local weather conditions, such as precipitation (Saino *et al.* 2004) and temperature (Rodriguez-Teineiro *et al.* 2005). As a result, the spring arrival of migrants in the Mediterranean region is strongly influenced by African weather (Jonzén *et al.* 2006), particularly rainfall (Gordo *et al.* 2005; Gordo & Sanz 2006; Both 2010a). Such effects are likely to operate through variation in food availability and adult condition (Tøttrup *et al.* 2008; Robson & Barriocanal 2011).

Once on migration, and particularly when travelling through higher latitudes, the speed of movement is determined by the temperature in the area through which the birds are travelling (Ahola *et al.* 2004; Hüppop & Winkel 2006; Žalakevičius *et al.* 2006, 2009; Both *et al.* 2006b), and wind speed (Sinelschikova *et al.* 2007). Temperature during the spring is a good proxy for local food availability, and migrants can suffer if they advance their migration too much relative to weather conditions (Section 3.3). Variation between studies in the rate of advance of arrival dates across Europe therefore probably results from different warming trends experienced by different populations on migration (Both *et al.* 2006b; Both 2010a). Thus, the timing of arrival of migrants in central Europe is influenced by temperature in southern Europe (Sparks & Tryjanowski 2007), whilst arrival dates in Scandinavia are more strongly correlated with temperature in north-central Europe (Ahola *et al.* 2004; Hüppop & Winkel 2006; Jonzén *et al.* 2006). So far, this whole pattern is best understood for the pied flycatcher (Box 2.5), but the same principles probably also apply to other migratory species such as geese (Box 2.6). In general, photoperiod and temperature combine to cause the initiation of spring migration northwards, enabling individuals to track improving spring conditions and increasing food resource availability, although precise departure and migration decisions may also be influenced by the weather through variation in wind speed and direction, rainfall and storm events, particularly at sea crossings.

Box 2.5 · *The spring migration of pied flycatchers*

Pied flycatchers winter in the dry tropical forests to the south of the Sahelian region of West Africa and breed in woodland across Europe. The initial departure from the wintering grounds in spring is triggered by day length (Gwinner 1996) and it has generally been thought that the ability of pied flycatchers to advance their arrival in Europe is constrained as a result (Both & Visser 2001; Both *et al.* 2006a). However, recent analysis of the timing of spring recoveries in North Africa of pied flycatchers that were ringed as nestlings in Europe has shown that the mean date of spring passage through North Africa has advanced significantly by about 10 days since 1980, perhaps as a result of recent increases in Sahel rainfall (Both 2010a). The most important determinant of arrival times to central and northern European breeding grounds, however, appears to be conditions experienced by the birds during the spring migration. There has been no significant warming in southern and central Europe during the period of spring passage of central European pied flycatcher populations. As a result, the rate of advance in arrival time of individuals from these populations to Europe is limited. Scandinavian breeding birds, on the other hand, migrate slightly later, at a time when there has been a significant warming in central Europe, and have consequently advanced their arrival (Ahola *et al.* 2004; Both *et al.* 2004; Both 2010a).

Box 2.5 (cont.)

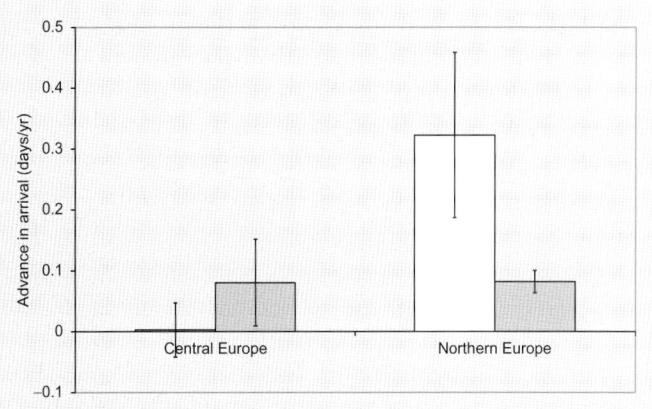

Box 2.5a Mean (± 1 SE) rates of advance in spring arrival times of pied flycatchers from published studies. There has been significant advance in FAD (white) and MAD (grey) for arrival in northern Europe (Sweden and Finland), but not central Europe (Holland and Germany). The difference is particularly pronounced in relation to the earliest arriving individuals (FAD), as increasing temperatures have resulted in a protracted arrival distribution in Scandinavia (Ahola *et al.* 2004).

Box 2.5b Temperature on migration plays an increasingly important role in driving pied flycatcher arrival time with increasing latitude. Photograph by Ben Darvill.

Box 2.6 · *The spring migration of pink-footed geese*

The timing of spring migration of waterfowl from northern Europe to their Arctic breeding grounds has been studied in detail using individually marked birds. This allows individual departures and arrivals from and to various staging posts en route to the breeding grounds to be tracked. Pink-footed geese *Anser brachyrhynchus* breed in Arctic and subarctic areas with a short breeding season, making the timing of their arrival critical. If they arrive too early they may suffer high mortality in cold weather. If they arrive too late there will be insufficient time to raise a brood. The timing of departure from the wintering grounds in Western Europe is determined by both day length and temperature. The two variables interact so that the effects of temperature are enhanced when day length is long, which means that, as spring progresses, the birds respond more strongly to warming. Once migration has been initiated, day length becomes relatively unimportant, and the timing of migration is determined by temperature alone. This results in the geese being able to track variation between years in the rate of improvement in feeding conditions at different stopover sites. It is not certain whether the birds respond directly to temperature, or indirectly through the growth of grass – their main food in spring, which is also temperature-related. Because inter-annual variation in spring temperature at a given staging site is broadly correlated with that at other sites along the birds' route, conditions at one site allow the geese to predict conditions further north. Getting the timing right and ensuring adequate food resources on migration, particularly at staging posts close to the breeding grounds, means that the birds are able to arrive in good condition. This improves their subsequent breeding success (Drent *et al.* 2003; Bauer *et al.* 2008a, 2008b).

Box 2.6 In the spring, migrating pink-footed geese time their movements according to temperature to ensure there is sufficient grass for then to eat. Photograph by Ben Darvill.

Although most of the discussion so far has been on the Africa–Europe flyways, the same factors also appear to affect migration in the New World, where some intensive and detailed studies have been conducted on specific populations. The timing of spring departure of American Redstarts *Setophaga ruticilla* wintering in Jamaica is negatively correlated with March rainfall, so that departure is earliest in wet springs. In such years, arthropod abundance is increased, and it appears to be this increase in food resources which has allowed an earlier departure (Studds & Marra 2007, 2011). Indeed, this correlation is supported by experimental switching of females from invertebrate-poor scrub habitats to invertebrate-rich forest habitats. This led to an improvement in female body condition during the winter relative to the birds remaining in scrub, and ultimately resulting in an earlier departure (Studds & Marra 2005). Thus, there is a clear link between precipitation and temperature patterns, food abundance and the timing of departure and migration.

Once on migration, the rate of advance northwards across the continent is dependent upon spring phenology, as the migrants rely upon arthropods being available for food (Marra *et al.* 2005; Box 2.7). Studies of yellow warbler *Dendroica petechia* indicate that the timings of arrival and clutch initiation in a population breeding in southern Manitoba, Canada, are strongly correlated with the degree of spring warming, with little impact of weather conditions on the wintering grounds (Mazerolle *et al.* 2011). For high latitude populations, the speed of migration appears to be the main determinant of the timing of arrival, rather than the timing of departure from the wintering grounds. Thus, as demonstrated for pied flycatchers (Both 2010a), with increasing distance from the wintering quarters, the role of conditions on the wintering grounds in driving arrival phenology will decline relative to the role of the conditions experienced during migration. Although Swedish breeding marsh harriers *Circus aeruginousus* show considerable individual consistency in spring migration phenology between years, this consistency declines with increasing distance north from their Sahelian wintering grounds, further emphasising the role of conditions on migratory routes influencing migratory speed (Vardanis *et al.* 2011).

To summarise, the advance in spring arrival of short- and medium-distance migrants is likely to have been caused by spring warming across the mid and high latitudes which these birds winter in and travel through. As a result, there is likely to be a close link between observed advances in spring migration and increases in spring temperature across many parts of the world for these species, although recent evidence suggests for some species that advances in breeding phenology may also have contributed to earlier migrant phenology at the population level by driving earlier phenologies of new recruits (Gill *et al.* 2014). Changes in the climate in the tropics and Southern Hemisphere may also have affected departure times of long-distance migrants to the Northern Hemisphere, although the arrival times of these species, particularly to high latitude breeding areas, is more strongly influenced by changes in the conditions experienced during migration. Greater variation in the degree and direction of climate change experienced over these longer passage routes may have caused the less consistent phenological response of long-distance migrants to climate change than is apparent for the other species. Alternatively, given the evident importance of body condition,

Box 2.7 · *The spring migration of New World warblers*

A wide range of New World wood warblers (Parulidae) breed in central and northern North America and winter in the Caribbean, Central and South America. On migration northwards in the spring, they feed on arthropods, whose abundance is related to the timing of tree budburst and flowering. As a result, migrant populations closely track tree phenology, and may use tree budburst or flowering to select suitable food-rich stop-over locations on migration (McGrath *et al.* 2009). Spring warming has led to an advance in the timing of budburst (Marra *et al.* 2005), which may partly account for the link between temperature and warbler migration speed across the continent. For every 1 °C rise in temperature, five species of wood warbler took 0.94 days less to migrate across the country (data from Marra *et al.* 2005). Temperature therefore has a strong effect on the timing and speed of movement of North American migrants in the spring, probably as a result of the direct effects of food resource availability upon warbler decisions to stop or migrate.

Box 2.7 Migrating yellow warblers track the timing of tree flowering and leafing on their northward migration in the spring. Photograph by Neil Calbrade.

and therefore food resource availability, in influencing departure dates, it is possible that deteriorating environmental quality on the wintering grounds, for climatic or other reasons, may also limit the opportunity for long-distance migrants to advance their migration phenologies. This possibility has been little studied and would be worth further research.

2.5 Breeding phenology

2.5.1 General patterns

As discussed earlier, long-distance migrant birds which breed in northern temperate and boreal regions are able to take advantage of the spring flush of food resources in those environments, particularly for feeding their chicks (Alerstam & Högstedt 1982). Therefore, the main biological effect of variation in the timing of migration, at least at the population level, may be to affect the timing of breeding, which we will discuss in Section 3.4. Medium- and short-distance migrants in the same regions also exploit these food peaks and attempt to time their breeding accordingly. As with the initiation of spring migration (Section 2.2), photoperiod controls the time window within which breeding can begin, but weather, particularly temperature, is also important (Lack 1966). Egg production is costly for females, with clutch weights exceeding female body weight in some species (Perrins 1970). Therefore, for income breeders, which use recently consumed food resources to produce their eggs, scarcity of food at the start of the breeding season, generally caused by poor local weather conditions, can delay the initiation of egg-laying (Perrins 1970; Svensson & Nilsson 1995).

Advancement of the date of breeding of such species by warm spring temperatures is therefore generally mediated through effects of temperature on the food available to females prior to egg-laying (Buse *et al.* 1999; Nilsson & Källander 2006). Direct effects of temperature on breeding phenology have also been recorded (Silverin *et al.* 2008; Visser *et al.* 2009a), potentially through reductions in thermoregulatory costs when conditions are warmer. At high altitudes and latitudes, spring warming may also provide snow-free ground on which birds can nest (Byrkjedal 1980; Meltofte *et al.* 2007b). Although experimental provision of supplementary food in early spring allows egg-laying to occur earlier than it would otherwise do, the magnitude of this effect diminishes at higher latitudes. This suggests that the relative importance of local conditions and photoperiod varies; food availability appears the key determinant of laying at low latitudes, but at higher latitudes, photoperiod appears most important (Schoech & Hahn 2008). This probably results from the shorter duration of the breeding season at high latitudes and raises the question of whether female birds take greater risks there to ensure that they can breed by beginning egg-laying early even when food availability is limited.

Given the changes in the timing of spring migration in recent decades and the role of temperature in determining laying dates, it is unsurprising that there have been significant changes in the timing of breeding of both migrant and resident birds. This was first highlighted by Crick *et al.* (1997) who showed that 20 of 65 UK bird species had significantly advanced their timing of mean egg-laying date (MLD) by an average of 8.8 days from 1971 to 1995 (0.37 days per year). Crick and Sparks (1999) followed this by demonstrating that 19 of 36 species showed significant long-term trends in laying dates, which became later during the 1960s and 1970s, but then advanced in the 1980s and 1990s. These contrasting trends were related to temperature trends, which were negative during the first period and positive during the second. A similar pattern was found in a detailed long-term study of the timing of egg-laying of great tits *Parus major* at Wytham Wood,

Box 2.8 · *Analysis of published trends in egg-laying dates*

The statistical significance and magnitude of variation in trends in mean laying date (MLD) were examined using the mixed-modelling approach of Box 2.1 to account for the non-independence of multiple data from the same study by specifying the study as a random effect. Given the non-random distribution of species between studies, species was specified as a fixed effect. As with MAD, a large proportion of the variance in MLD was attributed to study (71%), again resulting in a high degree of error associated with the species-specific estimates because they vary so much between locations. There was a significant effect of start-year upon the trend in MLD ($F_{1, 206} = 6.12$, $P = 0.015$, slope $= 0.0057 \pm 0.0023$), indicating that the rate of advance has increased through time, as found for arrival dates (Box 2.1).

There was significant latitudinal variation in the rate of advance in MLD (latitude, $F_{1, 110} = 3.54$, $P = 0.063$; latitude^2, $F_{1, 109} = 4.47$, $P = 0.0037$), with the rate of advancement greatest at intermediate latitudes. These results therefore replicated those of Box 2.2 for arrival dates, and are also illustrated in Figure 2.2.

Estimates of MLD varied significantly between both orders and families, but decreased in significance with increasing phylogenetic subdivision.

Table 2 *The relative importance of terms describing different taxonomic subdivisions in accounting for variation in mean laying date (MLD)*

	F	P
Order	$F_{7, 108} = 2.61$	0.0157
Family	$F_{29, 117} = 1.51$	0.065
Genus	$F_{48, 86.3} = 1.22$	0.21
Species	$F_{66, 79.2} = 0.95$	0.58

near Oxford in the UK (McCleery & Perrins 1998). Updated trends in MLD for 56 species of UK birds showed a significant mean advancement rate of 0.19 days per year between 1976 and 2005 (Thackeray et al. 2010).

In a review of 14 papers covering changes in the timing of breeding of 75 bird populations (Dunn 2004), 49.3% showed evidence of significant advancement in the timing of breeding in recent decades. This was updated by Dunn & Winkler (2010) who showed that 40 of 68 species covered by published studies exhibited significant advances in MLD through time of 0.13 days per year, similar to the rate of change described previously for MAD. We have examined 256 time series of 90 species, 104 of which show a significant advance in laying date, 24 a significant delay and half (128), no significant change. Averaged across these studies, the timing of laying has advanced significantly by an average ($\pm$ SE) of 0.24 ± 0.07 days per year. As we also found for FAD trends, there was a significant effect of the timing of the start of the study on this estimate. Studies that started more recently exhibited an increased rate of advance (Box 2.8). Rates of advance in MLD were also greatest at mid-latitudes (Figure 2.2), where the greatest spring warming has occurred. Thus, between 40° N and 50° N, there has been an average advance in MLD of about 3 days per decade from 1970 to 2010.

A review of these trends across studies has shown that the rate of advance in MLD varied significantly among taxonomic groups (Box 2.8). The greatest difference in MLD trends was among orders. Passeriformes (songbirds) in particular showed a greater rate of advance (0.30 ± 0.075 across the 169 time series contributing to this analysis) than other taxa. Six passerine families and five passerine species for which there were five or more time series showed significant rates of advance (Table S2.3).[*]

Our analysis highlighted that there was substantial variation in the rates of advance measured at different localities for the same species. This is illustrated by an analysis of long-term trends in MLD in pied flycatcher across Europe, which vary from 0.25 days delay per year at Gunnebo, Sweden, to 0.49 days advance per year at Lingen, Denmark (Both *et al.* 2004), or by variation in the rates of advance in blue and great tit populations which range for great tits from 0.10 days advance per year change at Oosterhout, the Netherlands to 0.67 days advance per year at Boswachter, Belgium, and for blue tits *Cyanistes caeruleus* from 0.09 days advance per year change at Vlieland, Netherlands to 0.59 days advance per year change at Boswachter (Visser *et al.* 2003). Given that such variation occurs within the same species over relatively short distances (Sweden to Denmark, or the Netherlands to Belgium), it is unsurprising that relatively little of the variation in mean laying date was attributed to species, with most being found among studies (Box 2.8).

It has been suggested that rates of change in the timing of breeding might be greater for residents than migrants and greater for short- than long-distance migrants, because short-distance migrants have advanced arrival times more rapidly than long-distance migrants (Both & Visser 2001). However, for the woodland species studied by those authors, there was no difference in the rate of advance in the timing of laying of pied flycatchers (a long-distance migrant) when compared with three resident tit species breeding in the same locations (Both *et al.* 2009). More widely, Crick *et al.* (1997) also found no systematic difference in the rate of advance of MLD between long- and short-distance migrant and resident species. However, a recent analysis using ringing data to estimate variation in breeding phenology found that short-distance migrants advanced their timing of breeding more rapidly than long-distance migrants (Moussus *et al.* 2011).

Given these contradictory findings, we analysed results from various studies with the start-year of the study as a covariate (Box 2.8), to test for differences in rates of phenological change in laying dates between short-, medium- and long-distance migrants. There were no significant differences in the rate of change in MLD between North America and Europe ($F_{2, 87.8} = 0.25$, $P = 0.78$), and also no overall difference in the trend in MLD with migratory distance ($F_{2, 234} = 1.51$, $P = 0.22$; Figure 2.4). Given the inconclusive nature of our results, and the contradictory results from other studies, more work is required to understand the implications of the observed differences in the rate of advance in arrival times in relation to migratory distance (Figure 2.3) for changes in the timing of breeding of those species. Our results do suggest, however, that there is not the strong link between the two that has sometimes been assumed.

---

[*] See online material.

48 · **Altered timings**

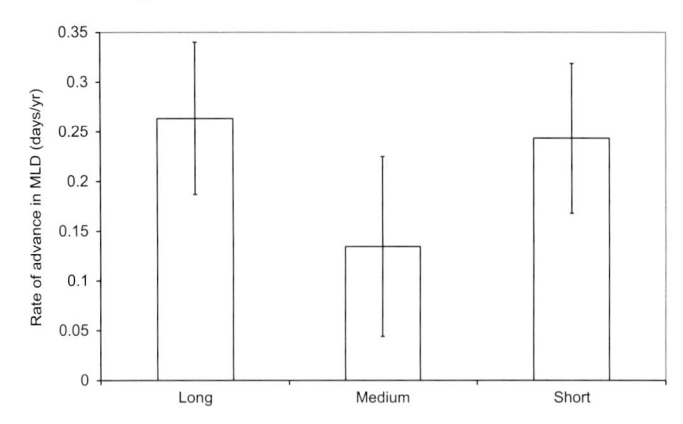

Figure 2.4 Mean rates of advance (± SE) in mean laying date (MLD) for long-, medium- and short-distance migrants. Estimates are standardised predictions from a mixed model (Box 2.8).

2.5.2 The role of climate change

Changes in the timing of egg-laying appear to be correlated strongly with temperature (McCleery & Perrins 1998; Sokolov & Payevsky 1998; Crick & Sparks 1999), at least in the Western Palaearctic where sufficient data exist to examine this question. This means that it is recent climate warming which has been largely responsible for the significant advancement in laying dates over time. Further, this also suggests that the considerable variation in the rates of advancement in breeding phenology of individual populations of a particular species (Visser *et al.* 2003; Both *et al.* 2004) may be at least partly caused by different temperature trends in different places.

As mentioned, the relationship between egg-laying date and temperature is thought to be more complex for long-distance migrant species than short-distance migrants. Most work on this has been conducted on pied flycatchers, whose rate of advance in laying dates has been shown not just to depend upon temperature on the breeding grounds after arrival, but also the timing of arrival, and therefore (Box 2.5), conditions on migration (Ahola *et al.* 2004). Thus, the restricted ability of pied flycatchers breeding in the Netherlands to advance their timing of breeding appears to have been caused by conditions during migration, whilst the delay in the timing of laying in northern Scandinavian populations appears to result from reductions in temperature at the time of arrival (Both & te Marvelde 2007; Both 2010a). The lack of advance in pied flycatcher laying does not appear to be limited by arrival time at all locations, however. The 27-day mean interval between arriving and egg-laying at a site in Wales (Goodenough *et al.*), compared to a 12-day interval in Finland (Ahola *et al.* 2007), adds weight to the suggestion that laying dates do not closely track arrival dates in at least some locations (Section 3.4.2). Spatial variation in the trends of pied flycatcher nesting phenology through time are not due to variation in the relationship between temperature and laying date at each site, but spatial variation in the temperature trends (Figure 2.5), as outlined above for the tits. Similar patterns are also apparent for the common starling *Sturnus vulgaris*, which has advanced its laying in eastern Europe, but delayed MLD in southern Europe (Both & te Marvelde 2007).

The strength of the relationship between local temperature and arrival time varies in relation to migratory distance. Therefore, we might expect that the relationship between local temperature and MLD also varies with migratory distance. This is the case (Box 2.9),

2.5 Breeding phenology · 49

Box 2.9 · *Timing of egg-laying in relation to local spring temperature*

We applied the mixed-model framework of Box 2.8 to look at differences in the relationship between MLD and local temperature with respect to migratory distance. Given that 90% of the data were from Europe, we did not examine differences in this pattern between North America and Europe, but simply examined mean relationships across all species studied. As expected, there was significant variation in the relationship between temperature and MLD with migratory distance ($F_{2, 126} = 5.56$, $P = 0.0049$), with the greatest degree of advancement in relation to temperature being for short-distance migrants.

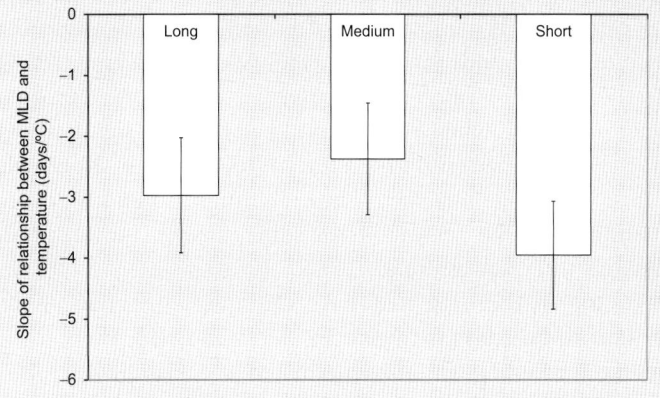

Box 2.9 The effect of migratory distance on the slope ($\pm$ SE) between mean laying date (MLD) and local temperature.

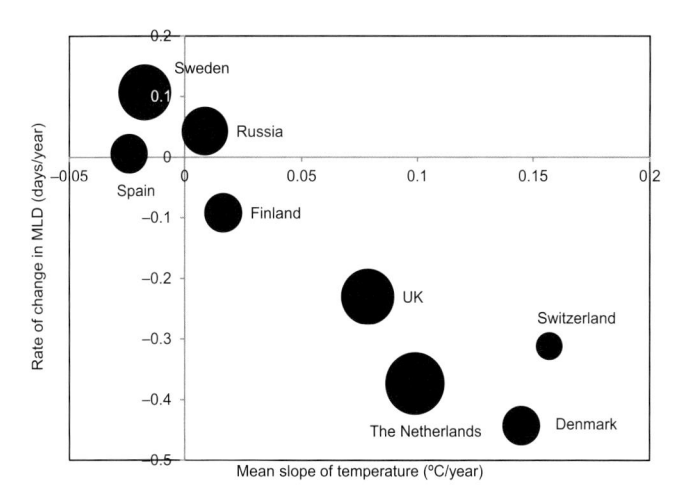

Figure 2.5 Spatial variation in the trend in mean laying date (MLD) of pied flycatcher populations between European countries is negatively correlated with mean spring temperature trend. Warmer temperatures lead to an advance (negative value) in MLD. The size of the circle indicates the number of studies in that country, which range from 1 (small) to 5 (large). Adapted from Both *et al.* (2004).

with the laying dates of short-distance migrants most strongly related to temperature. The magnitude of the relationship between local temperature and MLD (a 3–4 day advance per °C rise in temperature) is much greater than the 0.4–1.3 day advance in FAD and <1 day advance in MAD per °C increase in temperature (Box 2.4). This means that the effects of climate change on laying dates are likely to be of greater magnitude than the effects on arrival times, potentially accounting for the previous observation that rates of advance in MLD exceed those of MAD.

Despite the effect of migratory distance upon the relationship between MLD and temperature, the importance of local temperature upon the timing of breeding of long-distance migrants far outweighs the importance of potential carryover effects of climatic conditions on the wintering grounds for most species (Ockendon *et al.* 2013). National estimates of MLD in the UK were significantly correlated with spring temperature in that year for 13/19 migrant passerines, whilst precipitation in Africa was significantly correlated with laying dates for only three (barn swallow, Eurasian reed warbler *Acrocephalus scirpaceus* and northern wheatear *Oenanthe oenanthe*). Thus, although potential carryover effects from wintering conditions can be important for some species, they appear to be the minority of long-distance migrant passerines.

Advances in the timing of breeding may have multiple consequences for the birds involved. An earlier start to breeding may give an increased opportunity for multiple or replacement clutches if the breeding season is lengthened (e.g. Halupka *et al.* 2008; Wright *et al.* 2009). Multi-brooded species appear to have increased the length of their breeding season by an average of 0.43 days per year in response to earlier nesting. This suggests that as a result of recent warming, multi-brooded species may now attempt to raise more young in a season. This contrasts with the response of single-brooded species, whose breeding season has contracted in length by 0.44 days per year (Møller *et al.* 2010). An exception to this may occur if advances in the start of breeding increase the likelihood that females of a usually single-brooded species lay replacement clutches after nest loss. For example, the duration of the breeding season of Eurasian golden plovers *Pluvialis apricaria* at the southern edge of their range in the UK is positively correlated with March temperature, the key determinant of first egg-laying dates. Warming has lead to greater opportunities for failed breeders to produce replacement clutches (Pearce-Higgins *et al.* 2005). Climate warming and changes in breeding phenology may result in complex life-history decisions for individuals to make, the outcomes of which may influence their phenological response to increases in temperature (Visser *et al.* 2003). These issues will be explored in more detail in the next chapter.

It has long been recognised that clutch size is negatively correlated with laying date in many species; early laying females tend to produce larger clutches (Klomp 1970; Crick *et al.* 1993), at least in single-brooded species. Earlier breeding in response to warmer temperatures may therefore be expected to result in an increase in clutch size. As expected, recent advances in breeding phenology are associated with increases in clutch size (Cresswell & McCleery 2003; Schaefer *et al.* 2006), whilst delays have caused reductions in clutch size (Laaksonen *et al.* 2006). Thus, warming may simultaneously result in increased opportunities for birds to advance the timing of breeding, have longer breeding seasons in multi-brooded species, increased numbers of breeding attempts and larger clutches being laid. These positive effects on demography need to be balanced against potential negative effects of phenological change, and other impacts described in the next two chapters.

2.6 Autumn migration phenology

Fewer studies have examined changes in the timing of departure from the breeding grounds, or arrival to the wintering grounds, than have examined variation in spring migration phenology. This does not mean that autumn migration is of less interest. In fact, the results of these studies suggest that patterns of autumn migration are generally of greater complexity than in the spring because they involve the movement of both adults and juveniles which in many species migrate at different times. It can be argued that a greater range of pressures may influence the timing of autumn migration, due to inter-relationships between the timing of breeding, the number of breeding attempts, moult strategies, photoperiod and climate.

One of the strongest drivers of the timing of autumn departure from the breeding grounds is the timing of breeding (e.g. Ellegren 1990; Sokolov et al. 1999). Most obviously, the timing of juvenile migration is strongly dependent upon when young birds become old enough, or developed enough, to begin to migrate. This is probably the explanation for negative correlations between winter NAO conditions and the timing of autumn passage of European waders (Anthes 2004; Adamík & Pietrusková 2008). Thus, following a mild winter it is likely that earlier snowmelt in spring will advance the timing of breeding in those species (Pearce-Higgins et al. 2005; Meltofte et al. 2007b), which tend to be single brooded and therefore are likely to terminate the breeding season correspondingly early (Sokolov et al. 1999). However, as we shall show below, this does not appear to be a general pattern across all species, and many studies show that the timing of autumn departure and the timing of breeding have not advanced together.

Firstly, if the timing of breeding affects the length of the breeding season, then the link between breeding and autumn migration phenologies may be disrupted. Whilst this may occur through increased propensity to lay additional clutches, variation in the rate of breeding failure may also influence breeding season length and therefore the timing of migration. Studies of Arctic breeding curlew sandpipers *Calidris ferruginea* show that in years with poor breeding success, adult birds depart significantly earlier than in other years (Barshep et al. 2011).

Secondly, any delay in migration is not necessarily directly proportional to the delay in the termination of breeding, as studies on a Russian population of great tits show (Bojarinova et al. 2002). Here, the departure date of juveniles from first broods was related to their hatching date, with individuals departing at a constant age, whilst juvenile birds from second broods migrated at an increasingly younger age with later hatch date, resulting in a relatively constant migration date for the later brood young. This speeding up of departure, relative to age, may be a result of the ultimate control of photoperiod in limiting migration (Berthold 1996; Gwinner 1996; Wingfield 2005). Such interactions between photoperiod and the timing of breeding are not restricted to juvenile birds, with the migration of adults also under some degree of endogenous control that interacts with the termination of the breeding season (Berthold 1996; Sokolov et al. 1999; Coppack et al. 2001).

Thirdly, moult strategies after breeding may also influence the response of autumn migration phenology to warming, as moult plays an important part in the control of migratory behaviour (Carlisle et al. 2005). Adults of many species undergo a complete pre-migratory moult of flight feathers, beginning during or after breeding. The extent of overlap between breeding and moult varies considerably with latitude, and therefore climate (Ginn & Melville 1983). Moult is costly and time consuming (e.g. Klaassen 1995; Rubolini *et al.* 2002), not just because of the resources required to produce the feathers, but also the additional energetic costs associated with thermoregulation and flight with reduced feathering (Ginn & Melville 1983). The timing of moult may therefore interact with, and influence, migratory phenology, as individuals attempt to minimise conflicts between moult, breeding and migration. Such interactions are also likely to be complex and to vary between species in relation to their differing moult strategies, which vary from a complete post-breeding moult prior to migration, such as common redstart *Phoenicurus phoenicurus* (Snow 1969), suspended moult during migration, such as European turtle dove *Streptopelia turtur* (Mead & Watmough 1976; Swann & Baillie 1979) or delayed moult until the birds are on the wintering grounds in *Acrocephalus* and other warblers (Pearson 1973). Therefore, depending on migration strategy, earlier migration may occur if climate change results in an advance in the end of the breeding season and the start of moult. If the end of breeding is delayed because of climate change and if there is a strong selection pressure against overlapping moult with either breeding or migration (e.g. Hall & Fransson 2000; Hemborg *et al.* 2001), then species may delay migration in order to complete moult before departure (Coppack & Pulido 2004).

Changes in the timing of autumn migration may have fitness consequences later in the year. Some migrants face considerable competition for territories on the wintering grounds (Greenberg 1986; Sherry & Holmes 1996), so arriving there early or late may have implications for overwinter survival and reproduction in the subsequent breeding season (Norris *et al.* 2004). Therefore, there may be strong selection on long-distance migrants in particular to depart as early as possible to maximise their chances of claiming a high-quality winter territory. Conversely, for short-distance migrants that may migrate in response to deteriorating weather conditions, recent amelioration in climatic conditions may delay their timing of autumn migration. There is increasing evidence to support this. Of 30 species of short-distance migrants in Germany, there has been an increasing tendency towards reduced migration distance in nine species, and a tendency to winter at higher latitudes in ten species (Fiedler *et al.* 2004). The occurrence of birds in eastern Poland in winter is negatively related to the severity of snow cover (Golawski & Kasprzykowski 2010), as in very cold and snowy winters, these birds travel further west and south. Studies of wildfowl in both North America and Europe (Cooke *et al.* 1995; Svažas *et al.* 2001; Gunnarsson *et al.* 2012; Lehikoinen & Jaatinen 2012), Eurasian blackbirds (van Vliet *et al.* 2009) and blue tits (Smallegange *et al.* 2010) have all shown evidence for reduced migratory tendency in recent years, which impacts upon departure phenology.

Given this discussion, perhaps unsurprisingly there appears to be considerable variation between studies of changes in autumn migration phenologies, both temporally (e.g. Sokolov *et al.* 1999) and spatially (Sparks & Mason 2001; Cotton 2003; Sparks *et al.* 2006; Sparks *et al.* 2007). As a result of this strong variation between locations and species, we found no consistent trend in either mean (MDD) or last departure dates (LDD) through time (Box 2.10). Thus, the mean ($\pm$ SE) rate of change in MDD across all studies was 0.07 $\pm$ 0.04, and LDD 0.01 $\pm$ 0.09.

This is not the whole story, however. When examined in relation to migratory distance, there was strong variation in the rate of change in MDD ($F_{2,\,278} = 9.34$, $P = 0.0001$), but not

Box 2.10 · *Analyses of autumn migration dates*

We applied the same approach that we used for the analysis of spring migration (see Box 2.1) to published information on mean departure/passage (MDD) dates for autumn migration from nine studies covering 405 time series, and on last departure dates (LDD) from 14 studies covering 321 time series. Each data point was a published trend. There were no significant effects of continent, start-year or end-year upon trends in autumn migration phenology. There was a significant tendency for species differences to occur in LDD ($F_{188,25.7} = 2.24$, $P = 0.0089$), but not in MDD ($F_{145,188} = 0.86$, $P = 0.83$). Species variation in departure dates is shown in Table S2.4[*].

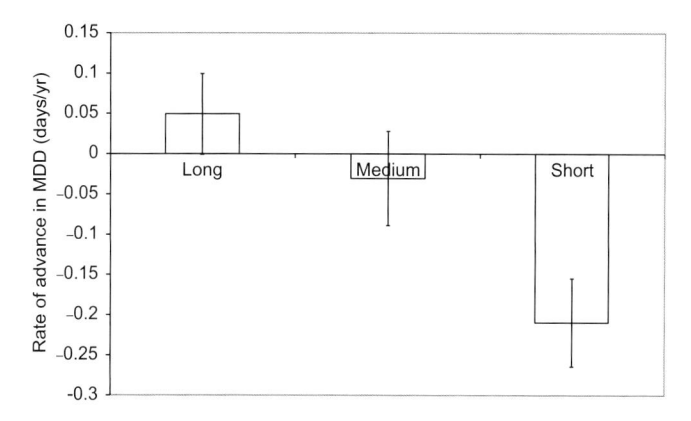

Figure 2.6 Mean rates of advance ($\pm$ 1 SE) in mean departure dates (MDD) of long-, medium- and short-distance migrants. Estimates are standardised predictions from a mixed model (Box 2.10).

LDD ($F_{2, 98.3} = 0.13$, $P = 0.88$). Short-distance migrants have significantly delayed mean departure dates by an average of 0.21 days per year (Figure 2.6) in both the Nearctic and Palaearctic regions. This contrasts with the general pattern of largely unchanged phenology of medium- and long-distance migrants. As discussed above, part of this delay for short-distance migrants may be associated with increasing numbers of females laying more than one clutch as a result of a lengthened breeding season (Jenni & Kéry 2003) or related to milder weather conditions reducing the tendency of individuals to undertake cold weather–induced movements (Fiedler *et al.* 2004, Lehikoinen & Jaatinen 2012). Jenni & Kéry (2003) also suggest that long-distance migrants may be more likely to depart earlier because of the pressure they are under to cross the Sahel before the onset of the dry season, although this may only be a significant pressure during particular drought years (see Chapter 4).

Comparing the trends in mean arrival dates and mean departure dates for the same species from Tables S2.2[*] and S2.4[*], there was a weak negative association between the two ($F_{1, 15} = 8.91$, $P = 0.092$), after accounting for variation in migratory distance ($F_{1, 15} = 14.77$,

---

[*] See online material.

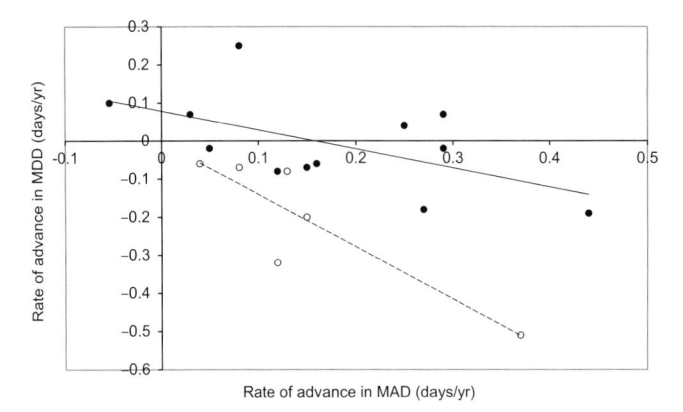

Figure 2.7 Relationship between the rates of advance in mean arrival date (MAD) and mean departure date (MDD) for species with five or more studies of such trends in both (data from Tables S2.2* and S2.4*). Species are separated by migratory distance (short-distance, open circles and dashed line; medium- and long-distance, closed circles and solid line).

$P = 0.0016$). Although based upon a relatively limited sample of species, this suggests that, contrary to the naïve expectation, species with the greatest rate of advance in spring migration were likely to experience the greatest delay in autumn departure (Figure 2.7). A number of possible hypotheses may account for this correlation. Firstly, variation in species' sensitivity to temperature may mean that the most sensitive species, particularly the short-distance migrants, are most likely to advance their arrival time in the spring in response to milder spring weather, and also most likely to delay their autumn departure in response to delayed onset of winter. Alternatively, the species with the most rapid advance in arrival time are among those most likely to increase the number of breeding attempts within a season in response to the earlier onset (Visser *et al.* 2003). As expected, multi-brooded species have tended to increase the duration of their breeding season, whilst this has shortened in single-brooded species. The rate of advance in the onset of breeding is strongly correlated with the rate of increase in breeding season length (Møller *et al.* 2010). Both factors may be important, although more work is required to understand the drivers of change in autumn migration phenology.

2.7 Tropical species

Most of this chapter has focused on birds breeding in medium to high latitude northern temperate and boreal zones, reflecting the geographical bias in the studies undertaken. Whilst the available evidence suggests largely similar responses occur across Europe and North America, and therefore probably also in boreal and temperate biomes of Asia, there is much less information available about the likely effects of climate change on the timing of migration or breeding in tropical areas, from which there have been virtually no long-term studies. This should be a high priority for future monitoring. Here, it is again likely that phenologies will be driven by food resource availability, as at higher latitudes. Thus, frugivorous species are likely to undergo movements to track spatial and temporal variation in the flowering and fruiting of trees, granivorous species will similarly track

---
* See online material.

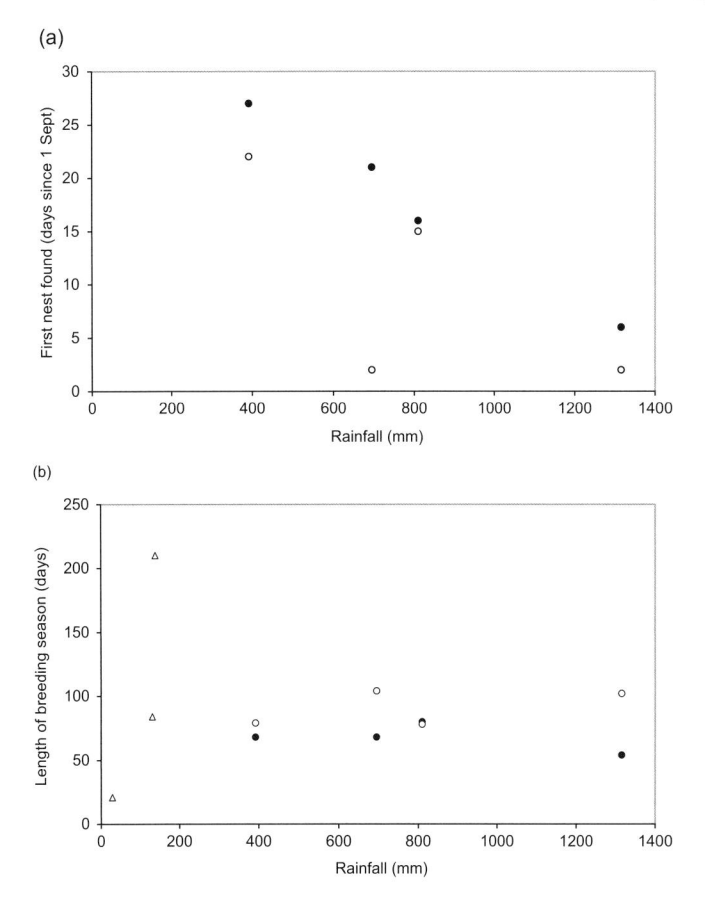

Figure 2.8 Variation in (a) date of finding the first nest and (b) the duration of the breeding season of the Kurrichane thrush *Turdus libonyanus* (filled circle), white helmet shrike *Prionops plumatus* (open circle) and grey-backed sparrow-lark *Eremopterix verticalis* (open triangle) in relation to rainfall. Data from Vernon (1978, 1984) and Maclean (1970), given by Dean *et al.* (2009).

the availability of seed and invertebrate feeders will likely track peaks in invertebrate prey availability. One of the key determinants of these events in the tropics is likely to be rainfall, rather than temperature, as it is often moisture which limits primary productivity at low latitudes (Chapter 5) and therefore affects the survival and productivity of tropical species (Chapter 4). We might therefore expect the migratory and breeding phenology of tropical species to be related to the timing of rainfall events, rather than temperature.

The effect of the wet season on avian phenologies is neatly demonstrated by a comprehensive study of variation in the timing of breeding and moult of birds in Venezuelan semi-arid thorn scrub and forest (Poulin *et al.* 1992). Here, June to August rains stimulate a peak in plant flowering, fruit availability and arthropod abundance. In response to this boom in a variety of food resources, nectivorous, frugivorous and insectivorous species all concentrate their breeding activity after the rains. Primary moult then follows breeding. The same patterns are also apparent in arid environments (Dean *et al.* 2009), where the amount of rainfall is also related to the timing of breeding (Figure 2.8a).

Studies of ground finches *Geospiza* spp. in the arid Galapagos show that gonadal development is stimulated by rainfall rather than photoperiod or temperature (Hau 2001), and therefore the onset of breeding in these species is heavily dependent upon precipitation (Gibbs & Grant 1987; Grant *et al.* 2000). The same pattern is apparent in zebra finches *Taeniopygia guttata* in central Australia, where the timing of hatching of first clutches after a rainfall event matches the first availability of grass seeds (Zann *et al.* 1995). The response of three species of *Columbina* ground dove breeding in Venezuelan savanna to rainfall is also driven by seed availability. These doves tend to breed primarily in the dry season, when seed resources peak, although each has different sensitivity to rainfall cues and photoperiod (Bosque *et al.* 2004). The importance of the wet season as a determinant of bird breeding holds across other tropical savanna and dryland habitats and species (Marchant 1959; Ahumada 2001; Marini & Durães 2001; Jansen & Crowe 2005; Repenning & Fontana 2011), and also extends to semi-tropical and Mediterranean dryland environments (Brown *et al.* 1999; Chase *et al.* 2005).

The breeding of Mexican jays *Aphelocoma wollweberi* in Arizona is similarly advanced by rainfall, but indirectly, by monsoon rainfall nine months in advance of breeding, as well as by mild winter temperature. Early breeding is promoted by greater food availability, mediated through the lagged effect of precipitation on invertebrate and seed abundance, and hence female condition. Although many species in these drylands breed during the late summer monsoon rains (Short 1974), jays actually provision their chicks during the driest time of the year in early summer. However, this is the time with the greatest invertebrate biomass, such as of emerging cicadas, whose abundance is likely to be related to the preceding wet season, and so the jay's strategy makes sense in light of their main prey resource.

In the most extreme examples, species occupying the most arid of habitats tie their breeding to periodic rainfall events. Thus the banded stilt *Cladorhynchus leucocephaus* in Australia breed in large colonies only when rainfall causes water to flood the salt pans of the interior of the continent (Burbridge & Fuller 1982; Robinson & Minton 1989). The magpie goose *Anseranas semipalmata* of north Australia also requires heavy rain as a precursor for nesting (Whitehead & Saalfeld 2000). When there is long-term drought, these species are unable to breed.

Few long-term monitoring data exist for these areas and species, although some have been analysed as part of the multi-species studies from Australia described in Section 2.4.1. Here, it is clear that the arrival of breeding waterbirds to the Mediterranean-type climate of south-western Australia is particularly linked to variation in precipitation, which was an important predictor of both arrival and departure dates for ten of 19 species, more than the number of species whose phenology was significantly affected by temperature (Chambers 2008). The timing of breeding of the Australian magpie *Gymnorhina tibicen* is similarly advanced by cool, moist conditions, which tend to occur at high values of the Southern Oscillation Index. These conditions also led to an increase in the proportion of individuals breeding during any one year (Gibbs 2007). Variation in precipitation is also linked to the movement of budgerigars *Melopsittacus undulatus* and purple-crowned lorikeets *Glossopsitta porphycrocephala*, probably through variation in food resources, triggered by the flowering of eucalyptus trees (Chambers 2005; Higgins 1999).

Some species breeding in arid environments are affected by temperature. Cold weather delays trumpeter finch *Bucanetes githagineus* breeding in Spain as a result of delays in the germination of a key food plant during the spring (Barrientos *et al.* 2007). Similarly, the timing of monk parakeets *Myiopsitta monachus* breeding at around 32° S in Argentina is more strongly advanced by warm temperatures than by rainfall (Navarro & Bucher 1992). These are, however, rare exceptions to the general rule that precipitation drives the phenology of tropical and Mediterranean-type climates.

Not only does rainfall trigger the start of breeding, but providing that it is wet enough, many species continue breeding, taking as much advantage of the beneficial conditions as possible (Wyndham 1986; Yom-Tov 1987; Grant *et al.* 2000; Dean *et al.* 2009; Figure 2.8b). In the Galapagos, in an El Niño year when it is wet, female ground finches can produce as many as eight broods in a single breeding season! Similarly, the length of the breeding season of the critically endangered helmeted honeyeater *Lichenostomus melanops cassidix*, which breeds in swamp forest in Victoria, Australia, is extended by rainfall (Chambers *et al.* 2008). A reduction in rainfall has therefore led to a recent decline in the numbers of eggs produced per year, probably mediated through changes in food resources. This may have serious consequences for the continued persistence of this subspecies of the yellow-tufted honeyeater.

Most of these studies have been of dry and arid-zone species whose breeding is perhaps not unexpectedly, closely tied to rainfall. The same principle also appears to hold in tropical rainforest habitats, although here, birds may anticipate the wet season, rather than directly respond to it. For example, spotted antbirds *Hylophylax naevioides* breeding at 9° N in Central America use variation in photoperiod to enter breeding condition prior to the wet season. The subsequent level of rainfall then determines the duration and intensity of breeding (Wikelski *et al.* 2000). Gonadal development in this species is therefore highly sensitive to photoperiod, but fine-tuned by information about food abundance (Hau *et al.* 1998; Hau 2001).

Other studies of neotropical forest birds similarly suggest that breeding activity increases at the end of the dry season (Skutch 1950; Wikelski *et al.* 2003; Johnson *et al.* 2012). This is clearly seen in seasonal patterns of brood patch occurrence in understory passerines near Manaus, Brazil, where the strongest positive correlations between mean monthly rainfall and the proportion of species with brood patches occur some three to four months in advance of the rainfall (Figure 2.9). Unlike arid habitats, the smallest proportion of individuals in breeding condition occurs some two to three months after the peak rainfall. This potential difference between dry and wet tropical habitats may reflect the longer breeding season in the latter, where some species may breed all year round (Johnson *et al.* 2012), or different temporal patterns of food resource availability in relation to rainfall (cf. Yap *et al.* 2007). For example, in central South America, nectivorous hummingbirds nest at the start of the dry season when flowers are most abundant, whilst granivorous birds nest later in the dry season, when seeds are most available (Skutch 1950).

It is clear that much more research is needed on variation in the phenology of tropical birds, although the available evidence suggests that species will closely track resource availability, both as a cue for migratory or nomadic movements and as a cue for breeding, and will continue breeding as long as sufficient food remains available. Where temperature or photoperiod is a cue for the timing of breeding, any changes to the phenology or

58 · **Altered timings**

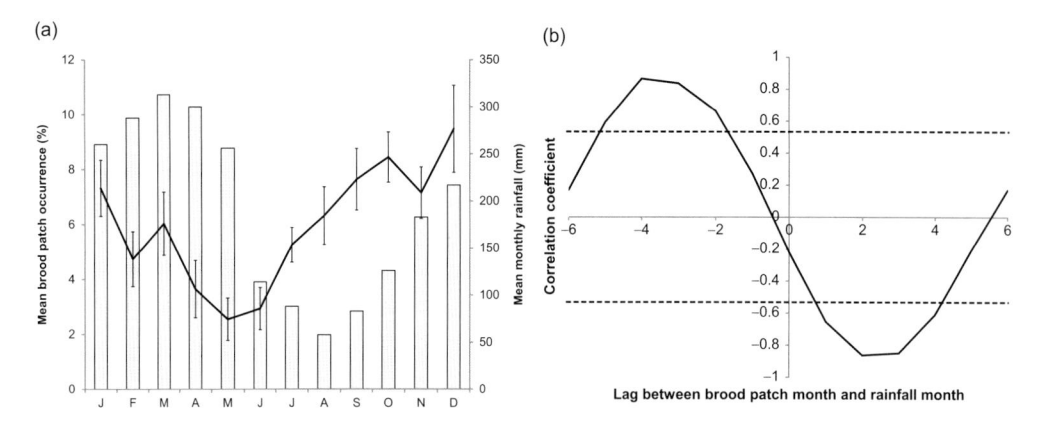

Figure 2.9 The link between the timing of breeding in tropical understory passerines and rainfall. (a) Monthly variation in the proportion of species with a brood patch averaged across 31 species (solid line ± SE) in relation to mean monthly variation in rainfall from Manaus, Brazil 80 km away (bars). (b) Correlation coefficients (r) between the proportion of species with a brood patch and monthly rainfall based on different lags between mean monthly rainfall and brood patch occurrence (negative values of the x-axis indicate the brood patch month is in advance of rainfall, whilst positive values indicate the reverse). A zero lag indicates the same months are used for both. The threshold for statistical significance ($P < 0.05$) is denoted by the solid dashed line. Data from Johnson *et al.* (2012).

pattern of rainfall may cause mismatch effects on the reproduction of these tropical species (see Chapter 3). However, given that it is food abundance which appears to fine-tune the precise timing and duration of the breeding season for many tropical birds, it may be that they actually have greater flexibility to respond to changes in the phenology of their environment than species breeding in higher latitudes with a more constrained breeding season. If true, this could be because some tropical species already experience, and have had to adapt to, a high degree of between-year variation in the amount and timing of precipitation dependent upon the El Niño Southern Oscillation. The seasonality of their environments is inherently less predictable than those of higher latitudes, although the link between precipitation and timing of breeding in rainforest habitats may be more complex in wetter than in drier tropical habitats, where individuals appear to respond more closely to precipitation events stimulating an increase in food resources. This may be because in rainforests there is a greater availability of resources through the year, or a weaker link between resource availability and precipitation (Yap *et al.* 2007).

Much more monitoring and research should be conducted in both tropical humid and dryland habitats to test these hypotheses and monitor the impacts of climate change. There is insufficient long-term monitoring of these phenologies to assess any temporal trend in the timing of movement and breeding in tropical birds; changes which have been some of the most apparent signals of climate change at higher latitudes (Parmesan & Yohe 2003; Root *et al.* 2003; Parmesan 2007; Thackeray *et al.* 2010). In the absence of such data, based on the best available evidence, we tentatively suggest that any significant impacts of climate change upon the phenology of tropical species will occur largely through changes in precipitation patterns rather than temperature. We will return to this

2.8 Conclusions

issue in Chapter 4, when we examine in more detail the demographic consequences of variation in precipitation on tropical bird species.

Despite the fact that bird migration and breeding is under strong endogenous control, there is clear evidence for significant impacts of recent climate change upon the timing of both. Thus, the arrival of the first spring migrants to northern latitudes has advanced by about 2 days per decade since the 1960s, whilst the arrival of the average individual has advanced by 1–1.5 days per decade. These changes have been most apparent in short-distance migrants, although many long-distance migrants are now also arriving earlier than they used to. Increases in temperature have been the main cause of these changes, although demonstrating this for long-distance migrants is difficult because they are affected by climatic change over a wide area. Such effects probably occur through temperature-driven increases in resource abundance along migratory routes in response to earlier spring plant growth and flowering, although reductions in the risk of mortality directly caused by cold may also be a factor. The mechanisms underpinning relationships between the arrival dates of long-distance migrants and NAO also require further explanation. Because of the complex changes in the climate which may occur along the route of long-distance migrants, they may be most vulnerable to negative effects of phenological change. This issue is examined in more detail in Chapter 3.

The timing of breeding of the average individual of a northern latitude population has recently advanced by about 2 days per decade as a result of warming. In fact, the rate of advance in breeding is greater than that for migration, probably because breeding phenology may be more sensitive to temperature than migratory behaviour, particularly for medium- and long-distance migrants (compare Box 2.4 and Box 2.9). By implication, this suggests that the length of time between migrant arrival in spring and breeding has decreased, which may occur because migrants are under greater pressure to breed early because of their later arrival, because conditions when they arrive have improved, or because changes in arrival and breeding phenologies are determined by different mechanisms (see Chapter 3).

Given potentially complex relationships between the timing of breeding, the likelihood of multiple brooding and the production of replacement clutches, advances in the onset of laying do not necessarily result in advances in the end of the breeding season. In particular, it appears that as a result of climate change, multi-brooded species now have longer breeding seasons than they used to. The relationship between the timing of breeding and migratory departure varies in relation to migratory distance and moult strategy. Although mean and last departure or passage dates in the autumn have not changed significantly across the range of species studied, they have tended to become delayed in short-distance migrants, associated with reductions in the distance travelled by such species. Clearly, however, there is considerable variation between species in the patterns of phenological change through time (Box 2.11).

In contrast to medium and high latitudes, where consistent warming patterns have driven phenological change, variation in the phenology of tropical species is likely to be driven by changes in rainfall patterns. These are much more spatially variable (see Figure 1.6), and therefore it is likely that phenological responses of tropical forest

60 · **Altered timings**

Box 2.11 · *Changes in the phenology of pied flycatchers and barn swallows through time*

The averaged estimates of the rate of change in both pied flycatcher and barn swallow arrival, egg-laying and departure dates across Europe based upon our meta-analysis of published studies (Tables S2.1* to S2.4*), illustrate how the patterns of occurrence and breeding of these two long-distance migrants has changed over the last 40 years in response to climate change.

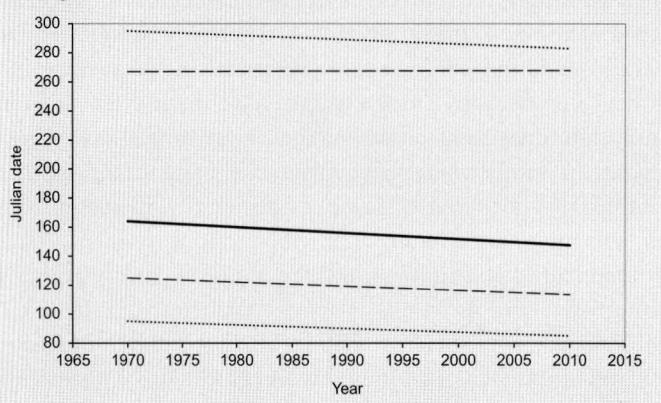

Box 2.11a Advances in the spring first and mean arrival times (FAD, bottom dotted line; MAD, bottom dashed line) of swallow have been reflected in advances in the timing of mean laying date (MLD, solid line). There has been little change in mean departure dates (MDD top dashed line) whilst the apparent advance in last departure dates (LDD, top dotted line) is non-significant. The apparent increase in the time swallows spend on the European breeding grounds is matched by a decline in the duration of their stay in the South African winter quarters (Altwegg *et al.* 2012).

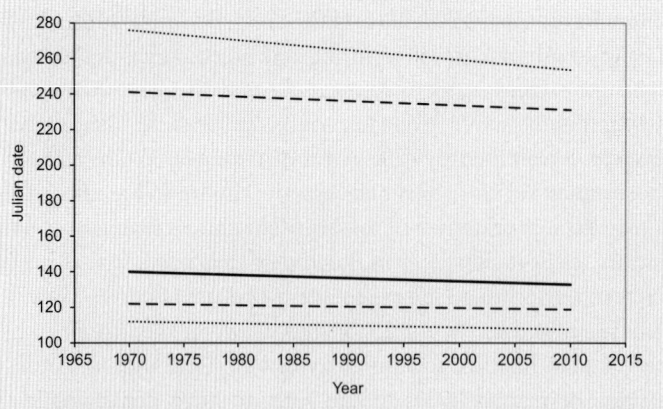

Box 2.11b There has been little shift in the arrival times of pied flycatchers to Europe overall, with an advance in mean laying dates indicating a decrease in the already narrow interval between arrival and the onset of laying. The strongest rates of advance are in relation to autumn departure dates, resulting in a reduced period of occupancy of the breeding grounds over time.

---

* See online material.

species through time similarly vary across the tropics. Unfortunately, the lack of monitoring and published long-term ecological studies of phenological change means that we cannot test this.

In summary, most phenological events appear strongly determined by resource availability. Therefore, as scientists and conservationists, if we want to understand the drivers of phenological change in a system, then we also need to understand the phenology of the key resources for the birds involved, the seasonality of those resources and how they have, and will, respond to climate change. This should be an important focus for future research around the globe, because only then will it be possible to assess the implications of changes in phenology for the ecology and populations of birds (Visser & Both 2005). This is of key interest from a conservation perspective, and has been the subject of much research. In the next chapter, we will consider if altered timings may translate into significant population responses of conservation importance.

2.9 Summary

- Changes in the timing of seasonal events are one of the most widely reported impacts of recent climate change. Around the world, the timing of spring events has advanced by some 0.28–0.39 days per year. These trends may disrupt the ability of birds to match their timing of breeding and migration to periods of peak resource availability in the environment.
- Although day-length is the ultimate driver of phenological events in birds that sets the seasonal boundaries within which appropriate behaviour may occur, there is considerable potential for changes in climate to affect the precise timing of those behaviours.
- There is a wealth of data available to study this, particularly from countries with a history of biological recording. Many observers report first sightings of particular events, such as first arrival dates (FAD) of migrants, although this measure is subject to some biases. A more robust measure is that of median or mean arrival (MAD) or laying dates (MLD), but this requires more intensive and standardised observations.
- Migrant FADs have recently advanced in Europe by an average of 0.24 days per year, compared to a 0.15 advance in MAD. In North America, rates of advance appear slightly less, at 0.17 days per year for FAD and 0.09 days for MAD. Globally FADs have advanced by 0.22 days per year, and MADs by 0.14 days. Rates of advance have increased through time and have been greatest at intermediate latitudes between 45° N and 50° N. Short-distance migrants have tended to advance their arrival times more rapidly than long-distance migrants.
- Trends in migrant arrival, particularly of short- and medium-distance migrants, can be explained by large-scale climatic indices, such as North Atlantic Oscillation (NAO). These effects are likely to result from positive-phase NAO being indicative of warm weather on the wintering grounds. The arrival time of long-distance migrants is the product of weather conditions on the wintering grounds to influence departure time, and during migration. The influence on arrival time of conditions on the wintering grounds declines with increasing migratory distance.
- The timing of egg-laying has recently advanced by 0.24 days per year, a rate which has also accelerated in recent years. The magnitude of advance has also been greatest at

intermediate latitudes, matching trends in arrival times. There are no consistent differences in the rate of advance in MLD in relation to migratory distance.
- Advances in the timing of laying appear strongly correlated with changes in temperature, at least in the Western Palaearctic, where most data originate. Such effects are stronger than for arrival, particularly for medium- and long-distance migrants. Significant within species spatial variation in MLD trends result from variation in warming trends between different locations.
- Depending upon whether a species is multi-brooded and on its moult strategy, advances in the timing of breeding may either advance or delay the timing of autumn departure from the breeding grounds. Short-distance migrants have significantly delayed their mean departure dates by an average of 0.21 days per year, but there has been no overall trend in departure dates for medium- and long-distance migrants.
- In the tropics, the timing and duration of rainfall events is a crucial determinant of migration and breeding phenology, and the length of the breeding season. This suggests that it will be through changes in precipitation patterns, rather than warming, that climate change may affect the phenology of tropical species, although there is little long-term monitoring data to test this.

3 · The impact of altered timings

3.1 Why timing matters

In the previous chapter we saw that many bird species have altered the timing of their migration and breeding as a result of recent climate change. At first sight, the amounts of change seem trivial, averaging 2–3 days advance per decade, but cumulatively they mean that over the last 30 years, birds may now be arriving or breeding a week earlier than they used to. This is important because in many bird species, the timing of these events has evolved to match the timing of peak resource requirements, and therefore any disruption in that timing may affect birds' breeding success or survival. Most obviously, the time at which birds are rearing their young and need a lot of readily available food often coincides with the greatest abundance of that food. Tits (Paridae) breeding in oak woodland try to maximise the availability of caterpillars, particularly of the larvae of moths such as the winter moth *Operophtera brumata*, and *Tortrix* species at the time when nestlings are being reared (Visser *et al.* 2006; Both *et al.* 2009). Linked with this, sparrowhawks *Accipiter nisus*, which find recently fledged tits easy prey, time their reproduction so that the peak abundance of tit fledglings coincides with their own nestling period (Newton 1986; Nielsen & Møller 2006; Both *et al.* 2009). On the coast, many seabirds breed when large numbers of small fish are maximally available (Durant *et al.* 2004a, 2004b, 2005). Arctic and upland nesting waterfowl and waders time their breeding to fit in the narrow window of snow-free conditions on the ground, and when there is a superabundance of invertebrate prey (Pearce-Higgins *et al.* 2005; Meltofte *et al.* 2007a). The breeding of many tropical species is triggered by rainfall and timed to match peaks in invertebrate or seed resources (Section 2.7).

It is not the change in the timing of bird migration or breeding itself which may affect populations, but rather the change in timing of arrival or breeding *relative* to the change in the timing of weather events or peaks in resource availability (Visser & Both 2005; Visser *et al.* 2012). If the timing of both great tit egg-laying and peak caterpillar availability advanced at the same rate, then the condition and survival of the great tit chicks would not be affected. Similarly, if the rate of advance in the arrival of breeding purple sandpipers *Calidris maritima* to Spitzbergen matched the rate of advance in the beginning of snow-free conditions, then there would be no alteration in sandpiper survival rates. Instead, difficulties may arise when the change in the timing of bird migration or the commencement of breeding differ from the change in timing of peak resource availability or favourable weather conditions. When this occurs, there is a mismatch between the period of the birds' peak demand and optimal environmental conditions. Mismatched timing to environmental conditions may also occur if the selection pressures in favour of matched timing are

Box 3.1 · *The potential consequences of mismatch for breeding golden plovers*

Eurasian golden plover *Pluvialis apricaria* chicks hatched on peatlands in the UK forage on adult craneflies (Diptera: Tipulidae) amongst other invertebrate prey. The chicks grow more rapidly and survive better when craneflies are abundant (Pearce-Higgins & Yalden 2004). Craneflies emerge in a short period in May and June, around the time when golden plover chicks hatch. Based on the relationship between cranefly abundance and chick survival rates, and after simplifying seasonal distributions of both golden plover laying and cranefly emergence by using fitted normal distribution curves (Pearce-Higgins *et al.* 2005), it is estimated that a 15-day mismatch between the peak hatching of golden plover chicks and peak cranefly emergence reduces plover breeding productivity by about 30%.

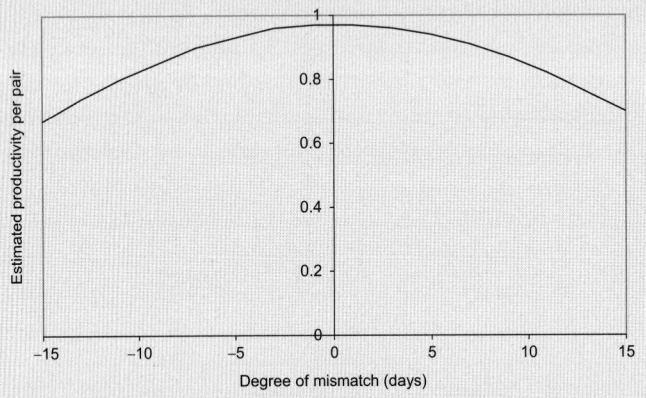

Box 3.1 The modelled effect of mismatch between the timing of cranefly emergence and the timing of hatching of first clutches upon the number of golden plovers fledged per breeding pair in a season. Full details of the underlying model are given in Pearce-Higgins *et al.* (2005) and Pearce-Higgins (2011a).

outweighed by other constraints which force individuals to breed earlier or later than ideal. These mismatches, or asynchronies, are of concern to conservationists if they have consequences for demographic rates, population size and species' distribution (Box 3.1).

3.2 Are birds becoming too early or too late?

In recent decades there has been an average annual advance in the date of the last spring frost across the Northern Hemisphere by 0.15 days per year, and advance in plant phenology by some 0.10–0.12 days per year (Schwartz *et al.* 2006a). These compare to our estimates of an advance in first spring arrival dates (FAD) of 0.24 days per year for Europe and 0.17 days for North America, and suggest that the earliest arriving migratory birds to these continents are arriving earlier than would be expected from the change in environmental conditions. It should be noted, however, that the estimates of Schwartz include data from across Asia where rates of warming have been much less than that in the areas from which most of the bird data come. The estimated shift in the rate of advance in

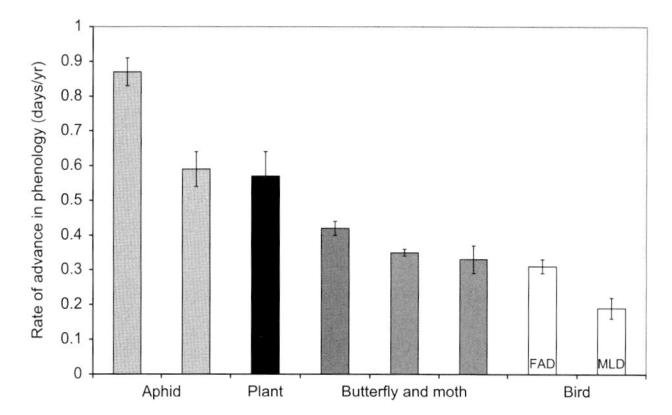

Figure 3.1 Mean rates of advance (± SE) in the phenology of aphids (light grey), plants (black), butterflies and moths (dark grey) and birds (white) in the UK, 1976–2005. Rates of advance are from Thackeray *et al.* (2010). Bird data are from the BTO nest record scheme (mean laying dates, MLD) and from county bird reports (first arrival dates, FAD).

mean arrival date (MAD) is much closer to the advancement rate for spring environmental conditions, at 0.14–0.15 days per year for Europe and 0.08–0.09 days per year for North America. Based on these figures, it may be that, with the exception of the earliest arriving individuals, birds are on average shifting the timing of their spring migration at about the same rate as changes in their environment.

However, because of considerable spatial variation in these trends, comparable data are required from the same locations in order to examine this fully. For example, in the UK which has some of the most comprehensive phenological time series the rate of advancement of migratory bird FAD of 0.31 days per year is slower than the rate of advance in aphid first flight (0.87 day advance per year), butterfly first flight (0.42 days) and plant first flowering (0.57 days; Thackeray *et al.* 2010). This suggests that although it has advanced, the timing of bird migration to the UK may not have kept pace with the advance of spring, as indicated by these plant or insect phenologies (Figure 3.1). A similar pattern is shown by analyses from North America, where summer migrant FADs have advanced at about one-third the rate of the change in spring conditions and tree budburst (Strode 2003; Marra *et al.* 2005; Miller-Rushing & Primack 2008; Ellwood *et al.* 2010). Nearctic summer migrants now may also no longer arrive on their breeding grounds at the optimal time relative to the timing of improvement in spring conditions, assuming that is what they did previously.

We estimate that mean egg-laying dates (MLD) in the Northern Hemisphere have advanced by 0.24 days per year (Chapter 2), similar to the 0.19 days per year advancement rate for MLD for the UK from 1976 to 2005. Again this is noticeably lower than the equivalent rate of advance in mean butterfly flight dates of 0.35 days advance per year, and median moth catch dates of 0.33 days per year (Thackeray *et al.* 2010; Figure 3.1). Thus, using either first dates for migration or mean dates for laying, there is potential for some birds in some areas to have suffered mismatch as a result of climate change. However, the extent to which individual populations may be matching or mismatching the phenology of their environment is not clear from these crude averages. Given the high degree of variation in phenological trends between studies, even of the same species (Box 2.2), analyses at fine spatial scales are required to understand the changes that have occurred, and to examine their significance. It is therefore to such assessments that we now turn. We will review the evidence for mismatches occurring in response to recent climate change, and the extent to which they have affected bird population processes, focussing first on bird migration and then on breeding success.

3.3 Phenological mismatch in the timing of migration

As we saw in Chapter 2, the timing of migration to and from high latitudes is strongly affected by temperature. The survival of birds during migration and upon spring arrival is likely to be either directly affected by temperature, such as when cold spring or autumn weather increases the risk of mortality, or indirectly, through effects on food abundance (Section 2.4.4). The timing of migration in the tropics is generally more sensitive to rainfall, as it is water availability, not temperature, which is the main indirect driver of food abundance (Section 2.7). Negative impacts of mismatch on migrants to high latitudes would be expected to occur through increased exposure to severe weather conditions or reduced food availability. If there are mismatch impacts at low latitudes, mismatch is likely to cause increased mortality through reduced water and food availability.

There are occasional examples of high spring mortality of migrants associated with arriving too early on the breeding grounds, relative to prevailing weather conditions. In 1981, unusually late snowfall in the Peak District, England, caused the death of about 60% of adult common sandpipers *Actitis hypoleuca* when they returned from their African wintering grounds (Holland & Yalden 1991; Pearce-Higgins *et al.* 2009c). Examples of similar high mortality events in response to late snowmelt or snowstorms have also been recorded affecting Arctic breeding waders and waterfowl further north (Meltofte *et al.* 2007b; Mallory *et al.* 2009). Many of these species are income breeders rather than capital breeders (Klaassen *et al.* 2001; Morrison and Hobson 2004) and arrive in spring with limited fat reserves. They must rely on food being available on the breeding grounds in order to recover from migration and prepare for breeding, and can only survive for a few days should they get this wrong (Tulp *et al.* 2009). Although the timing of shorebird arrival to the Arctic breeding grounds is closely related to the timing of snowmelt (Niehaus & Ydenberg 2006; Meltofte *et al.* 2007b), and birds are able to tune their arrival time to local conditions, they may still be caught out by unusually late storms.

In response to rapid warming there has been a considerable advance in the spring arrival times of Arctic breeding waders. The advancement in spring arrival of dunlin *Calidris alpina*, sanderling *C. alba* and ruddy turnstone *Arenaria interpres* in Zackenberg, Greenland has been slightly slower than the rate of advance in the date of snowmelt over the last decade, suggesting that the birds have responded in such a way that they are slightly less at risk of encountering severe spring weather than they were previously (Høye *et al.* 2007). Similar advances are seen in bird species which breed in upland and alpine areas at lower latitudes. In the Rocky Mountains of Colorado, spring warming has advanced the arrival time of American robins *Turdus migratorius* by 14 days over 25 years (Inouye *et al.* 2000). However, here the timing of snowmelt has not changed because of an increase in the depth of the snowpack during the winter. As a result, the birds might suffer reduced survival due to the lack of bare snow-free ground for foraging. This indicates the potential for a difference between the environmental driver of arrival time (often temperature) and the driver of foraging conditions or thermoregulatory costs at the breeding site (often snow cover or severe storms) to lead to a mismatch when values of environmental drivers change at different rates over time. Whilst this has resulted in some examples of catastrophic mortality, evidence is not available for enough species and regions to indicate whether climate change has reduced, increased or had little impact on the frequency of these events. Given the rapid climatic changes which are occurring at high latitudes and high elevations, collecting and analysing such data is a high priority.

As outlined in Chapter 2, migrating species often track changes in the availability of food resources through space (Boxes 2.6 and 2.7). Whilst any relative delay in food availability may have significant consequences for such species, where this has been most studied, the rate of advance of bird arrival has generally been less than the rate of advance in spring, as measured by either temperature, plant phenology or invertebrate phenology (Section 3.2). This means that phenological changes are unlikely to have negatively impacted upon the survival of these species during migration, leaving aside potential increases in the frequency of severe weather events. Instead, individuals are likely to have experienced improved conditions as a result of advanced spring conditions at these higher latitudes. There may, however, be different implications of these trends for the success of breeding, as we shall now examine.

3.4 Mismatch in the timing of breeding

We have already outlined how increasing temperatures may advance the timing of bird breeding; directly, through increased food resources, and at high latitudes, increased availability of snow-free ground (Section 2.5). Where there are differences in the environmental factors that determine the timing of breeding, and those that affect the timing of peak resource availability later, and where climate change affects those factors at different rates, there is potential for mismatch to occur (Durant *et al.* 2007). Where the timing of breeding has advanced, but the timing of peak food availability for the chicks has remained unchanged, the eggs may hatch too early, relative to the peak in food resources (Box 3.2); they have advanced too much. Conversely, when the timing of arrival and breeding has not been advanced much by spring warming but the timing of peak resource availability for breeding has become earlier, the birds may breed too late for the main peak of food, resulting in reduced breeding success. These birds have advanced too little. Hence warming could cause too much or too little advance in the timing of breeding, according to its effects on the timing of the food peak. Whether a particular species or population has advanced too much, too little or by the right amount will depend on the relative importance and rate of change in different drivers of predator and prey phenology. This issue has been best studied in relation to four bird species of European temperate woodland, a highly seasonal habitat with a pronounced spring peak in invertebrate food. The species are two tits, the great tit and blue tit, and two long-distance migrant flycatchers, the pied flycatcher and the collared flycatcher *Ficedula albicollis*. Both tits and the collared flycatcher have shown significant advances in egg-laying date in recent decades across Europe, whilst the trend for pied flycatchers has been weaker and less consistent across studies (Figure 3.2).

68 · The impact of altered timings

Box 3.2 · *Simulating the effects of mismatch on productivity*

To simulate the effects of mismatch, we used a simple model in which daily variation in both food resource abundance and food demand were symmetrically distributed around a date of peak abundance and date of peak demand. An index of overall match or mismatch was simply the integral of the product of the two curves on a daily basis, and was assumed to reflect overall productivity (although probably not linearly, as the likely rate of increase in productivity associated with an increase in the match index (I) will probably be high at low levels of the index, but minimal above a certain threshold). Where peak food abundance and food demand were matched, productivity in our example was likely to be maximised ($I = 19.1$; a). However, $I = 10.9$ if a five-day advance in the timing of peak demand relative to peak food abundance was introduced (b), or five-day advance in the timing of peak food abundance relative to peak demand (c).

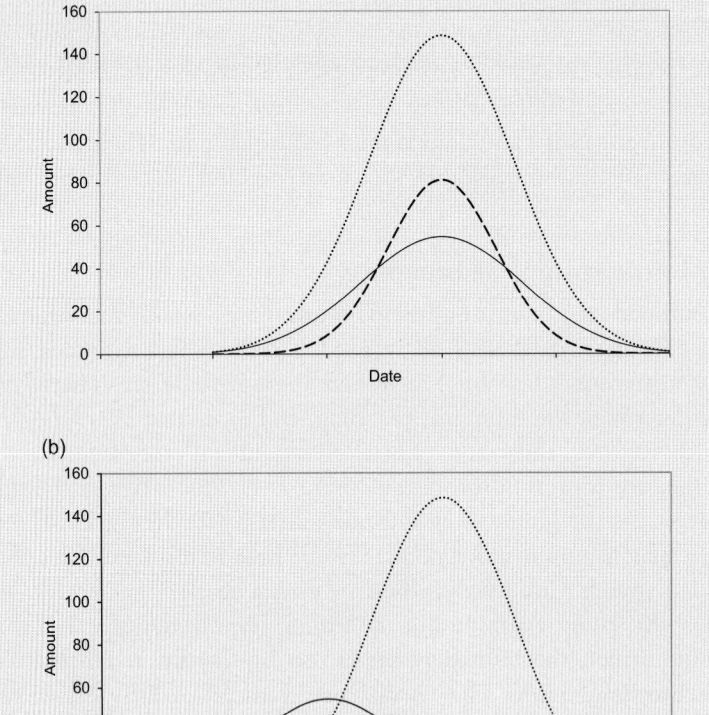

Box 3.2 Theoretical relationships between resource abundance (dotted), the timing of peak resource demand (solid) and variation in the extent of match (dashed) for a situation of phenological match (a), too much advance (b) and too little advance (c) in the timing of bird breeding.

Box 3.2 (cont.)

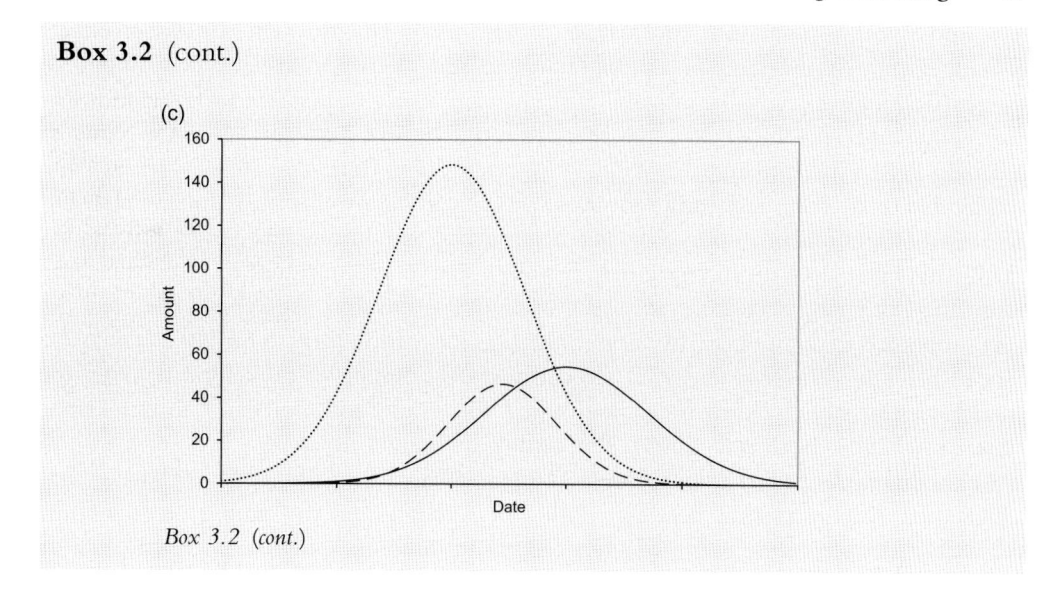

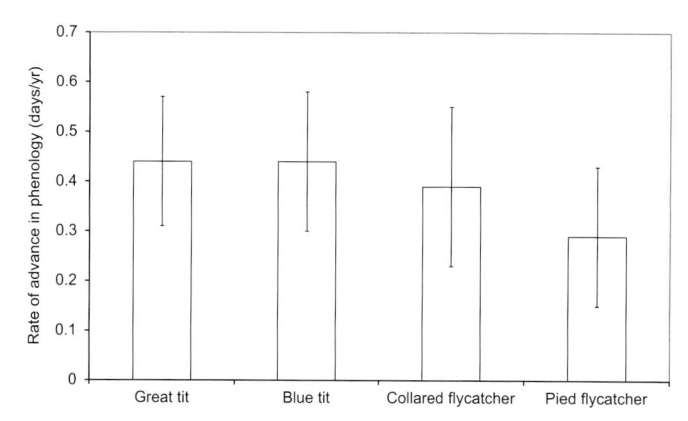

Figure 3.2 Mean advancement rates (± SE) in the mean laying dates of four woodland passerines in Europe, from analysis in Box 2.8.

3.4.1 Tits

Across Europe, breeding has significantly advanced in 13 of 26 great tit and 7 of 17 blue tit populations studied and at rates that vary considerably between locations. For example, by the late 1990s, great tits had shown significant advancement in the timing of their breeding in England (McCleery & Perrins 1998) and Germany (Winkel & Hudde 1997), but not in the Netherlands (Visser *et al.* 1998), although the latter had shown significant advancement ten years later (Both *et al.* 2009).

As outlined, the main prey of these tits in oak woodland are a few caterpillar species, whose abundance at least partly determines the condition of great tit fledglings and their subsequent chances of recruitment to the adult population (Wilkin *et al.* 2009). The timing of caterpillar abundance is strongly affected by temperature, partly as a result of the link between the timing of the emergence of oak leaves, upon which the caterpillars rely, and spring temperature (Buse *et al.* 1999), and partly through the direct effects of temperature on the rates of lepidopteran egg and caterpillar development (Topp & Kirsten 1991). Peak caterpillar availability at one particularly well-studied woodland site in the Netherlands, the Hoge Veluwe, has advanced by 0.7 days per year as a result of warming in March, April and early May (Visser *et al.* 2006; Both *et al.* 2009). The tits have also tended to lay their eggs earlier in years with an early caterpillar peak, indicating some degree of adaptation in response to advancing spring conditions. However, this rate of change has been less than that required. For each day of advancement in peak caterpillar abundance, tit laying dates have advanced by only 0.4–0.6 days. As a result, the great tits have attempted to compensate by shortening their incubation time to further advance the date of hatching (Visser *et al.* 1998). Nevertheless the timing of peak food demand for great tit nestlings has become less synchronised with peak food availability through time (Visser *et al.* 2006; Both *et al.* 2009). The birds now breed too late.

At another well-studied population at Wytham Wood, England, great tits have maintained their synchronisation between timing of hatching and the timing of peak food availability, despite a similar rate of advancement in caterpillar phenology to that seen in the Netherlands. Counter to the Dutch example, female great tits breeding in Wytham Wood have advanced their laying dates more rapidly than the peak caterpillar availability has shifted. The tits have avoided breeding too early by subsequently increasing their clutch size and delaying the start of incubation. They have maintained the match between peak food availability and peak brood demands through time (Cresswell & McCleery 2003).

Matching the expectation of Box 3.1, the number of great tit fledglings produced per pair in both populations is dependent upon the relative timing of hatching and peak food availability. The food requirements of a great tit brood are greatest when the nestlings are about 11–12 days old. The chicks which are at this age when caterpillars are most abundant, grow most rapidly and survive best (Visser *et al.* 2006). As a result of the increasing mismatch between the timing of peak caterpillar availability and peak chick requirements in the Hoge Veluwe, there has been a significant reduction in great tit fledgling success. The reduced survival of an increasing number of late-hatching chicks has meant that overall, fewer fledglings have subsequently recruited to the breeding population (Visser *et al.* 1998; Visser *et al.* 2006). At Wytham Wood in England there has been an increase in the degree of hatching synchrony. A greater proportion of the great tit broods now coincide their period of peak food demand with the period of high caterpillar availability, which has resulted in an increase in tit productivity through time (Cresswell & McCleery 2003).

These contrasting effects of climate change on two great tit populations have been caused by different patterns of spring warming at the two sites (Figure 3.3). At Wytham Wood, temperature increases during the period before egg-laying have been double those at the Hoge Veluwe, resulting in a more rapid advance in the timing of breeding (McCleery & Perrins 1998). Conversely, rates of warming during incubation have been much greater in the Dutch wood, resulting in a more rapid caterpillar growth than at Wytham. Climate change has so far been advantageous to the English great tits, reducing the cold-weather stress they experience early in the season which previously forced females to lay later than the optimum (Cresswell & McCleery 2003). However, the slower increase in early spring temperatures in the Netherlands (Visser *et al.* 2003; Both

Wytham Wood   **Hoge Veluwe**

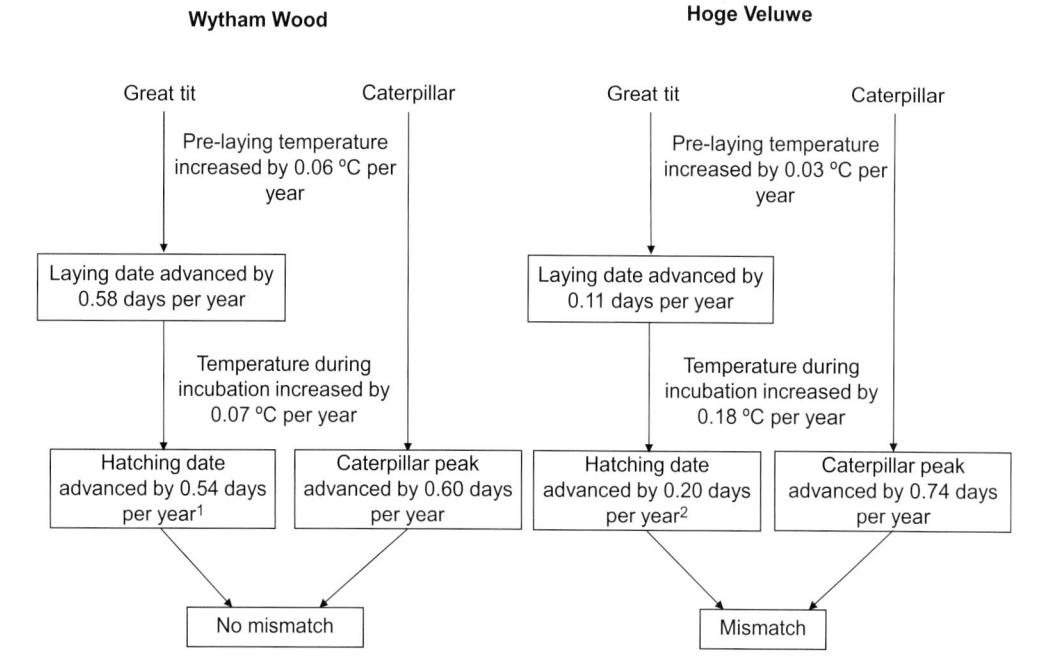

Figure 3.3 Schematic to illustrate how contrasting patterns of spring warming in Wytham Wood (England) and Hoge Veluwe (Holland) affect the degree of mismatch between the timing of great tit breeding and peak caterpillar abundance. Data extracted from Creswell & McCleery (2003), Visser *et al.* (1998, 2003).
[1] Delay in hatching relative to laying due to increasing clutch size and delayed onset of incubation.
[2] Advance in hatching relative to laying due to decrease in incubation period.

et al. 2009) has meant that any female great tit at the Hoge Veluwe attempting to advance its egg-laying time to match the advance in caterpillar availability has had to form eggs at lower temperatures, thus costing more energy and potentially reducing her subsequent chance of survival (Stevenson & Bryant 2000; Chapter 4). Despite their best efforts, the Dutch great tits have therefore been forced by changing conditions to breed too late relative to the food peak (Visser *et al.* 1998). More broadly, there is considerable variation in the trends in great tit phenology across Europe. For example, at a third study location in the Czech Republic, changes in the timing of oak budburst, peak caterpillar abundance and great tit laying dates all show similar phenological trends, with no suggestion of increased mismatch through time (Bauer *et al.* 2010).

Although much of this variation among widely separated areas can be attributed to variation in the degree of spring warming (Figure 3.4), there remains considerable variation in the rates of breeding advancement over relatively small spatial scales. Tits breeding in woodlands less than 50 km apart in the Netherlands and Belgium exhibit very different phenological trends, whilst the contrasting effects of mismatch on Dutch and Czech great tits do not appear to result from very different temperature trends or phenological responses (Figure 3.4). It has been suggested that this localised variation is due to differences in the frequency of double brooding (Visser *et al.* 2003). Populations which have advanced their

72 · The impact of altered timings

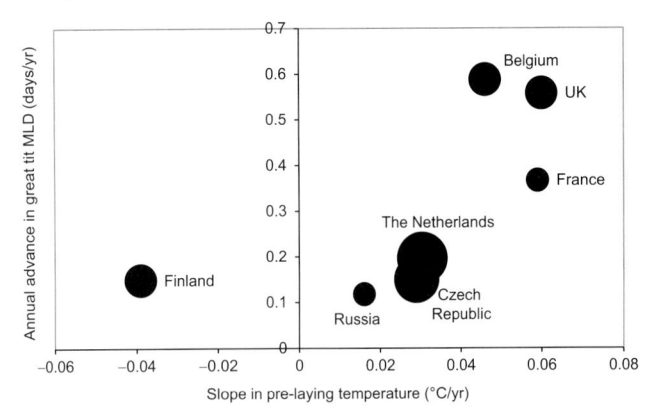

Figure 3.4 Correlation between the country-specific slope in pre-laying temperature in relation to year and the mean rate of advance in great tit mean laying date (MLD) in that country (adapted from Visser *et al.* 2003, and including Czech Republic data from Bauer *et al.* 2010). The size of the circle indicates the number of studies in that country, which range from 1 (small) to 5 (large).

egg-laying most appear to be those where the proportion of double brooding has remained constant, such as in England where nearly all females only lay one clutch, whilst populations where the proportion of second broods has declined have tended not to alter their phenology. It is argued that double-brooded pairs hatch the first brood in advance of the main peak of food abundance to increase the likelihood that their second brood will be able to take advantage of the latter part of the food peak (Crick *et al.* 1993). However, this means that neither the first nor second brood is well synchronised with peak prey availability. As a result of this trade-off between the demands of the first and second broods, a decline in the proportion of pairs that produce two broods would be expected as they become increasingly unprofitable through time. This would result in a slower rate of advance in the mean laying date of first broods relative to their prey than in a single-brooded population, leading to an increase in the degree of match between the first brood and the food peak (Visser *et al.* 2003; Both *et al.* 2009). If this hypothesis is correct, the slower advance in laying date relative to the advance in the food peak shift in the Netherlands may actually be adaptive.

Some support for this 'adaptive hypothesis' comes from a study in beech woodland in Belgium, only 150 km from the Hoge Veluwe, where great tits have significantly reduced the frequency of double brooding, leading to an increase in the synchrony of nesting attempts so that most individuals now maximise the overlap of their first clutches with peak food resources (Matthysen *et al.* 2011). Previously there was much greater variation in laying dates. However, other strands of evidence do not match with the hypothesis. Firstly, there has not been a reduction in the duration of the food peak associated with an advanced phenology (Visser *et al.* 2006). This means that any lack of shift in tit phenology cannot be purely adaptive, as great tits now breed on average five days too late relative to the caterpillar peak (Both *et al.* 2009), but instead must imply some degree of constraint. If the timing of first laying dates had kept pace with the timing of the food peak, there would have been no shift in the value of second broods and therefore no need for an adaptive reduction in the frequency of double brooding. Secondly, caterpillars are not the primary food of great tit chicks from second broods (Verboven *et al.* 2001), suggesting that their success may be less closely related to the degree of match with peak caterpillar availability than first broods. It is therefore worth considering other potential explanations for the observed correlations.

An alternative 'constraint hypothesis' can be proposed to account for the observed reduction in double brooding. This hypothesis states that the additional effort required by the adult tits to rear a mismatched first brood, compared to one that is matched with peak food availability, has a negative effect on female condition. This makes it difficult for the female to produce a second clutch of eggs without compromising future survival prospects. This hypothesis is supported by recent evidence that the energetic demand of foraging great tits increases when food availability declines (te Marvelde *et al.* 2011), and the fact that mistimed females experience lower survival (Reed *et al.* 2013b). The energy expended by females breeding early is less than that expended by late breeding females mismatched with peak caterpillar abundance. These results cannot be explained by differences in energy expenditure during laying (te Marvelde *et al.* 2012) but probably result from the fact that when caterpillar availability is high, adult tits make fewer visits to the nest per hour because of the high profitability of caterpillars relative to other prey (Wilkin *et al.* 2009; García-Navas & Sanz 2010). Consistent with the potential link between energy expenditure and probability of producing a second brood, great tits that nest early or in close proximity to oak trees rich in caterpillars are more likely to produce a second brood than those with access to fewer prey (Verboven *et al.* 2001). Further, the probability of double brooding in great tits is negatively related to the extent of mismatch between the timing of the first clutch relative to peak caterpillar abundance (Husby *et al.* 2009; Reed *et al.* 2013a). Although experimental food supplementation to great tit pairs did not lead to a significant increase in the frequency of double brooding (Verboven *et al.* 2001), supplementary feeding of great tits did reduce the interval between clutches.

A significant recent decline in the number of recruits produced from second clutches over time apparently supports the initial adaptive hypothesis that in a changing climate, females should increasingly switch to a single-brood strategy, and time their first laying dates accordingly. However, this does not take into account the fact that, although the benefit of second clutches has declined with increasing temperature, the reproductive output from double-brooded females still exceeds that of single-brooded females. Despite recent warming, females should still attempt to lay two clutches where possible. With no apparent loss of survival associated with double-brooding, the balance of evidence reviewed above therefore suggests that the correlation between the rate of decline in double-brooding and the advance in tit breeding may be a consequence, and not a cause, of the lack of the initial phenological mismatch, as least in some locations. We therefore suggest that the observed results may be best explained by the constraint hypothesis.

Neither hypothesis explains why woods in close proximity show different trends in laying date and in the rate of change in the frequency of double-brooding. One fruitful area of research to explore this further would be to consider the potential for habitat differences between the woods to account for this fine-scale variation. Whilst large-scale variation in the timing of peak caterpillar abundance can be related to temperature, it also appears closely related to the habitat characteristics of each site (Smith *et al.* 2011). Both the species of tree, particularly the contrast between deciduous and coniferous species (Pimentel & Nilsson 2007; Veen *et al.* 2010), and tree size

(Visser *et al.* 2006) affect the phenology and abundance of caterpillar prey, leading to subsequent impacts on tit productivity. Great tit broods raised near oak trees receive a greater proportion of caterpillars in their diet, and fledge at a greater weight than those reared further away from oak trees (Wilkin *et al.* 2009). As a result of variable trends in resource availability, individuals breeding in good-quality areas may therefore be more likely to produce second broods and show differential trends in laying date to individuals breeding in other habitats. These potential habitat effects should be explored further as habitat may interact with temperature to affect at a small scale the sensitivity of populations to climate change. For example, in a wood with a mix of tree sizes or species, there is likely to be a greater temporal spread of caterpillar availability, reducing the potential negative effect of any phenological mismatch upon tit productivity. Although the most seasonal habitats may be the most productive when food resources and food requirements are matched, an increasing degree of phenological mismatch may reduce the quality of these habitats to below those of habitats with a wider, but less pronounced, food peak (Box 3.3).

To summarise, recent warming has resulted in great tits in the Hoge Veluwe in the Netherlands breeding too late relative to the peak of food availability. This has reduced the productivity of first clutches which rely on the seasonal peak in caterpillars. An accompanying reduction in the number of recruits from second clutches and the number of females laying second clutches may be partly adaptive, but perhaps more likely result from constraints on females imposed by the mismatch. The different responses of great tit populations in woods separated by only a few kilometres may result from variation in the quality of those sites, although this hypothesis requires testing. It is possible that the highest quality sites, which have the greatest peak in caterpillar abundance, are also the most seasonal. If so, climate change may reduce the quality of these good but highly seasonal habitats, but have less impact on other poorer quality, but less seasonal habitats, and therefore potentially alter the relative quality of different habitats for particular species.

Although we have focussed on great tits, there is good reason to believe that the same processes also affect blue tits. Blue tit populations have undergone similar changes in the timing of laying to great tits (Figure 3.2), and similar reductions in the frequency of double-brooding in populations which have not advanced their laying as much as others (Visser *et al.* 2003; Matthysen *et al.* 2011). They appear to have suffered the same degree of mismatch as great tits (Both *et al.* 2009). Fledgling condition and overall blue tit breeding success is linked to caterpillar availability in the same way as for great tits (Tremblay *et al.* 2003), and the degree of mismatch is likely to also affect the costs of breeding.

The potential effects of mismatch on blue tits are illustrated by studies of a population breeding in evergreen oak woodland in southern France. These tits breed too early relative to the food supply available to them because they have originated from nearby populations adapted to breeding in deciduous oak woodland (the commoner habitat locally) where caterpillar phenology is earlier than in evergreen oak. As a result, the adults that attempt to rear their young before the caterpillar peak has occurred incur higher costs during chick rearing. However, an isolated blue tit population on the island of Corsica has been able to adapt to breeding in evergreen oak woodland. These birds breed much later and match the period of maximum food demand with the time of peak food availability,

3.4 Mismatch in the timing of breeding · 75

Box 3.3 · *Simulating the effects of variation in food peak width upon productivity*

We extended the simulation of Box 3.2 to examine the extent to which the width in food peak may affect both productivity, and the sensitivity of productivity, to mismatch. Firstly, we examined the effect of doubling or halving the duration of food availability through the breeding season whilst keeping the overall amount of food resource the same. A doubling of the width of the peak meant that food resources were likely to be spread too thinly through the breeding season and the match index (I) was reduced from 19.1 (Box 3.2 a) to $I = 12.5$ (Box 3.3a). Halving the width meant that more of the resources were concentrated during the period of greatest demand, and led to an increase to $I = 23.7$ (Box 3.3b).

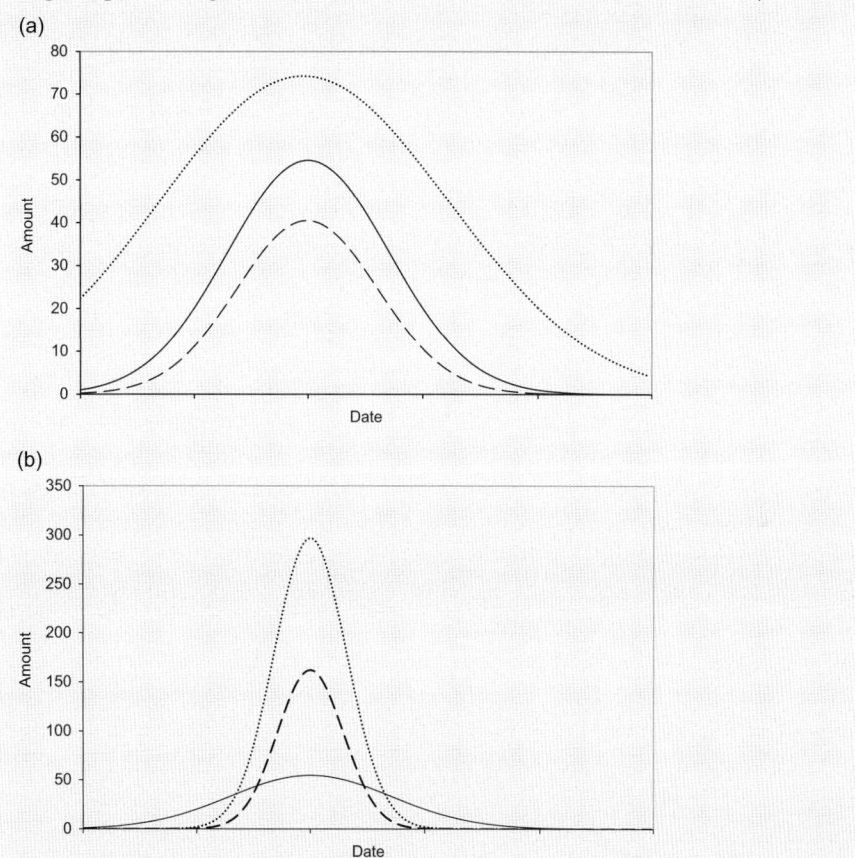

Box 3.3a,b Theoretical relationships between resource abundance (dotted), the timing of peak resource demand (solid) and variation in the extent of match (dashed) for a situation with a wide food peak (a), and narrow food peak (b). Note the different y-axis scales.

Variation in the width of food peak (the seasonality in food abundance) can have a significant impact on overall breeding success. The greatest productivity will occur when all the food resources are available at the time most required by the birds, the situation approximated by the narrow food peak, simulating a highly seasonal habitat. What about the effects of mismatch however? We combined the variable food peak widths with the extent of mismatch to test whether food peak width may influence the sensitivity of populations to mismatch (Box 3.3c, d).

In this instance, the magnitude of the drop in productivity associated with mismatch was greatest for the narrow food peak ($I = 10.2$, a 56% reduction), and smallest for the wide

Box 3.3 (cont.)

food peak ($I = 10.0$, a 20% reduction). Indeed, if the severity of mismatch was extended to 10 days, then $I = 0.8$ only for the narrow food peak, much less than the figure for the wide food peak of $I = 5.0$.

Overall, this indicates that in our example, the most suitable breeding conditions were likely to occur in highly seasonal habitats with a matched synchrony. However, such habitats appeared particularly vulnerable to phenological mismatch because a significant shift in peak food resources relative to peak demand led to very few resources being available for breeding. In contrast, habitats with a wide food peak were modelled not to be as productive during matched years, but more resilient to phenological mismatch.

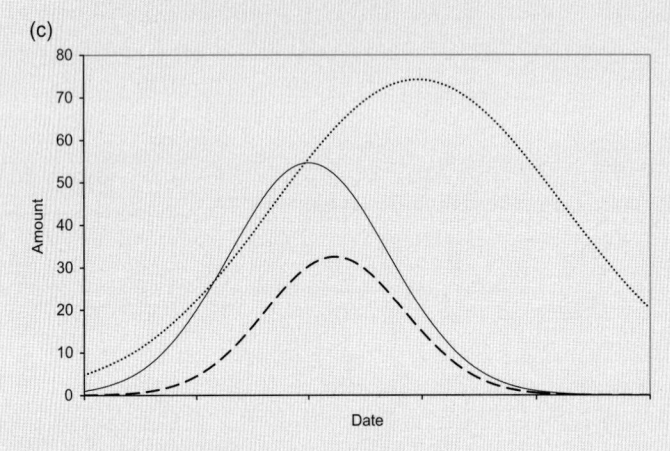

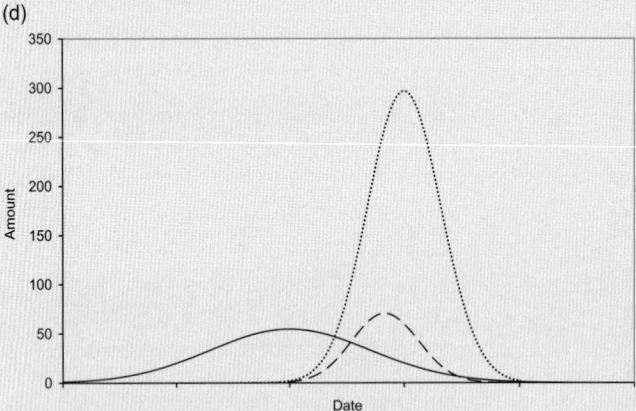

Box 3.3c,d Theoretical relationships between resource abundance (dotted), the timing of peak resource demand (solid) and variation in the extent of match (dashed) for a situation with five days of mismatch and a wide food peak (c) or a narrow food peak (d).

Table 1 *Variation in the match index (I) as a measure of simulated productivity in response to variation in the width of the food peak and whether there is a match or mismatch in the timing of peak food availability and peak food requirements*

	Match	Mismatch
Narrow food peak	23.4	10.2
Normal food peak	19.1	10.9
Wide food peak	12.5	10.0

by tracking the phenology of oak budburst. As a result, they incur lower energetic costs in brood rearing than the mismatched population (Thomas *et al.* 2001; Visser *et al.* 2004; Bourgault *et al.* 2010).

Late-hatching blue tits breeding in montane oak forest near Madrid, Spain are forced to switch their diet from large noctuid to small tortrix caterpillars, leading to an increased foraging rate as the adults have to work harder to gather less profitable prey. Breeding success per nesting attempt is also reduced. This system has many similarities to that of the Dutch great tits. Although there has been significant warming in April that has advanced laying dates, warming in May, after the blue tits have laid their eggs, has been more rapid. As expected, after accounting for variation in clutch size, the number of fledglings produced per nest is negatively correlated with May temperature. However, unlike the Dutch great tits, the negative effects of mismatch have been outweighed by the increase in clutch size associated with earlier breeding. Somewhat surprisingly, in this study there has been an overall increase in the number of young fledged per nest from 1984 to 2008 (Potti 2009; García-Navas & Sanz 2010).

As with great tits, there are also important habitat differences between woodlands which affect blue tit ecology. As outlined, adults breeding in higher quality deciduous and mixed woodland nest earlier, produce larger clutches and more fledglings of higher quality, and lay second clutches with a greater frequency, than those nesting in low-quality evergreen woods with fewer, and later emerging, caterpillars (Fargallo 2004; Lambrechts *et al.* 2004).

Irrespective of the uncertainty regarding the precise underlying mechanisms, there is good evidence that in some tit populations (particularly Dutch great tit populations of the Hoge Veluwe) spring warming has resulted in a mismatch between brood requirements and peak food availability. This appears most likely to have occurred where the rate of spring warming between the onset of incubation and the period of peak energetic demand of the broods has been most rapid. This has given breeding birds limited opportunity to respond to the more rapid advancement in food availability than in breeding phenology. Despite these impacts of mismatch in influencing the success of individual breeding attempts, the extent to which they have resulted in population level effects in either species appears limited. This is because any reduction in breeding success is compensated by density-dependent improvements in overwinter survival, which is the key driver of population change in these species (Grøtan *et al.* 2009; Reed *et al.* 2013a, b). We will examine the potential effects of climate change on these other parameters in the next chapter.

3.4.2 Flycatchers

As discussed in Chapter 2, the arrival times of pied flycatchers are most strongly affected by climatic conditions during spring migration (Ahola *et al.* 2004; Both *et al.* 2006b; Both 2010a). Annual variation in the timing of breeding in pied flycatchers is correlated with the timing of spring arrival in some populations (Potti 1998; Both *et al.* 2005), but as they are largely income breeders arriving with limited body reserves (Silverin 1981), the ability of females to attain sufficient body condition for egg-laying is most strongly affected by local conditions on the breeding grounds (Ockendon *et al.* 2013). This is illustrated by the

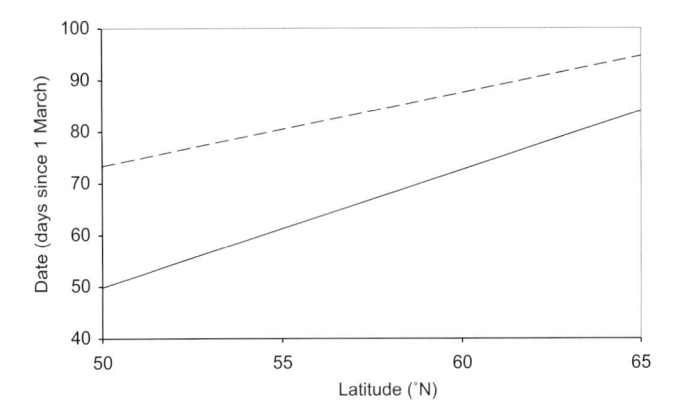

Figure 3.5 Mean arrival date (continuous line) and mean laying date (dashed line) of pied flycatchers vary in relation to latitude. Lines based on regression equations from Both (2010a).

considerable between-site variation in the interval between arrival and laying between studies, which ranges from 12 days in Finland (Ahola *et al.* 2004) to 27 days in the Forest of Dean, England (Goodenough *et al.* 2011). Part of this variation may be related to latitude (Figure 3.5), which, as we shall discuss later, may reflect variation in prey phenology and abundance, but part may also be explained by local variation in habitat quality.

Let us look at what these processes mean in practice for specific flycatcher populations across Europe. The timing of breeding of pied flycatchers in the mountains of the Iberian Peninsula, close to the southern margin of their global range, has not advanced because of a lack of spring warming prior to arrival (Sanz 2003; Sanz *et al.* 2003). Further north, in the Netherlands, pied flycatcher laying dates advanced by 8 days between 1980 and 2004 (Both & Visser 2005), as have those in central Europe (Both & te Marvelde 2007), although limited warming during the period these birds cross southern Europe has prevented a greater rate of advance through time (Both 2010). Slightly later migrating pied flycatchers breeding further north in Scandinavia have benefitted from increasing temperatures in central Europe and therefore have advanced their arrival times more rapidly than those in the Netherlands and central Europe (Ahola *et al.* 2004, Laaksonen *et al.* 2006, Both 2010a; although see Nilsson 2008). However, despite a correlation between the timing of laying and local spring temperature, and a warming trend between arrival and laying, laying dates in Norway and Sweden do not appear to have advanced (Ahola *et al.* 2004; Laaksonen *et al.* 2006; Both & te Marvelde 2007; Nyholm 2011), the reasons for which are discussed later. Overall, the timing of breeding in 19 of 23 well-studied pied flycatcher populations was significantly correlated with local temperature (Chapter 2), with local warming having led to a significant advance in MLD in nine (Both *et al.* 2004; Figure 2.5).

Pied flycatchers incubate their eggs in May and early June (Figure 3.5). May temperature has increased significantly across Europe (Sanz 2003; Sanz *et al.* 2003; Both *et al.* 2004, 2005; Laaksonen *et al.* 2006), resulting in a significant advancement in the timing of peak caterpillar abundance as described in the previous section. This rate of advance in prey phenology has exceeded the most rapid advances in pied flycatcher breeding phenology (Sanz *et al.* 2003; Both & Visser 2005; Both *et al.* 2006a); pied flycatchers are now breeding too late relative to the peak in caterpillar food for their nestlings. This has had two important consequences.

Table 3.1 *Summary of the demographic changes in pied flycatchers across Europe in response to recent climate change.*

Country	Trend in arrival date	Trend in laying date	Trend in clutch size	Trend in breeding success	Population Trend	References
Spain	0	0	0	–		Sanz *et al.* (2003)
The Netherlands	–	–	+	–	–/+/∪[a]	Both & Visser (2005); Both *et al.* (2006a); Both (2012); Sovon (2012)
Finland	–	0	–	–	∪	Ahola *et al.* (2004, 2012); Laaksonen *et al.* (2006)
Norway / Sweden		0	0	0	–	Thingstad *et al.* (2006)
Norway				0		Veen *et al.* (2010)
Sweden	0	0	0	0	0	Nilsson (2008)
Sweden		0	0	∪	–	Nyholm (2011)
UK	0	0	0	–	–	Goodenough *et al.* (2009, 2011)

[a] The direction of population change depends on the scale at which it is observed, with declines in deciduous woodland, increases in mixed woodland and a nonlinear decrease and increase at the national scale.
– indicates a significant reduction in that parameter has occurred through time (for arrival and laying date trends, this is an advance); + indicates a significant increase in that parameter has occurred through time; ∪ indicates a nonlinear decrease and then increase; 0 indicates no significant change in that parameter. Blank cells indicate that no data were presented.

First, this has driven changes in female investment to each breeding attempt. Within a season, pied flycatcher clutch size follows the expected decline with later laying date (Lundberg & Alatalo 1992). In the Netherlands, where the timing of breeding has advanced significantly in response to localised warming, there has been an increase in clutch size. However, where there has been little or no advancement of breeding, clutch size has declined as the timing of breeding has actually become later relative to the timing of the food peak (Table 3.1). Limits to prey abundance at the start of the breeding season may account for the reduced clutch size and failure to advance laying in Scandinavia (Laaksonen *et al.* 2006; Ahola *et al.* 2012), and reductions in egg size in response to warming in Spain (Potti 2008).

A second consequence of pied flycatchers breeding too late is that the adults now have to work harder to provision their chicks, leading to a decline in breeding success and subsequent recruitment rates of young, a problem first noted in the montane oak woodland of central Spain (Sanz *et al.* 2003). Because of the increased cost of reproduction in a mismatched environment, the condition of breeding females has also declined (Potti 2008), with possible consequences for subsequent survival.

As with great tits, even where the timing of egg-laying has advanced markedly, pied flycatchers still face problems. The eight-day advance in pied flycatcher laying date at the

80 · The impact of altered timings

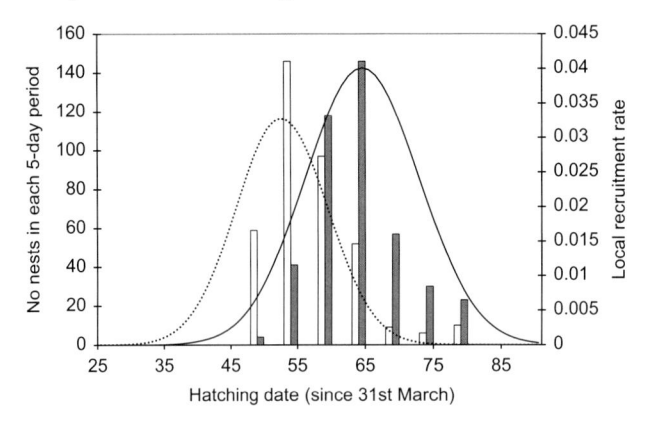

Figure 3.6 Modelled changes in the local recruitment rate of fledgling pied flycatchers breeding at Hoge Veluwe, the Netherlands, as a function of hatching date, and described by normalised curves for 1980–1984 (solid line) and 1996–2000 (dotted line). The shift in selective advantage of nesting early is reflected by the advance in hatching date 1996–2000 (white bars) relative to 1980–1984 (grey bars). From data in Both and Visser (2005).

Hoge Veluwe in the Netherlands has been insufficient to keep pace with the more rapid advance in the timing of peak caterpillar abundance (Both & Visser 2005). By the early 2000s only the earliest breeding flycatchers were able to raise large numbers of fledglings, whereas 20 years earlier flycatchers that bred in the middle of the season were most successful (Figure 3.6). Productivity averaged over the whole population has therefore fallen, even though clutch size has increased. Across the Netherlands, populations of pied flycatchers have declined in woods, with the earliest peak of caterpillar abundance and slowest rate of advance in pied flycatcher MLD (Both *et al.* 2006a). Given that pied flycatchers exhibit significant dispersal away from their natal woods (Paradis *et al.* 1998; Thomson *et al.* 2003; Both *et al.* 2012), with many populations comprised largely of immigrants (Stenning *et al.* 1988; Artemyev 2008), it is unclear how much such fine-scale variation in population trends is related to local fledgling success, and how much may be driven by the movement of individuals away from poor or declining quality sites. As the adults tend to be site-faithful, it is possible that rates of natal dispersal are greater away from poorer quality sites, potentially contributing to some of the trends in population size observed in these studies. Recent evidence supports this, with young more likely to disperse long distances if they experience significant mismatch when being raised (Both 2012). Thus, the observed patterns of population trends in the Netherlands may be more indicative of pied flycatcher redistribution between sites than large-scale population reductions resulting from climate change. Such effects could occur through interactions between conditions experienced during the nestling phase and subsequent dispersive behaviour (e.g. Duckworth 2009), although this remains to be specifically tested in this species.

As with the tits discussed earlier, it is likely that fine-scale variation in the magnitude of advance in the timing of woodland caterpillar peaks between sites is driven by habitat variation. Sites with the earliest caterpillar peaks tend to be those dominated by large deciduous trees (Visser *et al.* 2006; Pimentel & Nilsson 2007) rather than mixtures of deciduous and coniferous trees. Reflecting these local differences in the Netherlands, mixed and coniferous forests in Scandinavia and elsewhere in northern Europe also support a greater spread in timing of invertebrate prey than deciduous woodland. Even in oak woodlands, sites in the west and the north of the UK appear to have later and more extended peaks in caterpillar abundance than those in the south-east (Smith *et al.* 2011), and may therefore be more suitable for breeding pied flycatchers. This may explain the current distribution of pied flycatchers in the western and northern part of the UK (Gibbons *et al.* 1993).

Phenological mismatch may switch the relative quality of these different habitats (Box 3.3), leading to a redistribution of the species. As a result of earlier food peaks, pied flycatcher populations in the Netherlands breeding in pure deciduous woods have suffered the greatest degree of mismatch and their populations have declined more than those in mixed oak and pine woodland, where populations have either increased or remained stable (Visser *et al.* 2004; Both 2012). If this pattern was apparent across Europe, we might expect there to be a latitudinal gradient in the response of pied flycatchers to warming, with a greater degree of mismatch between birds and prey in the more seasonal woodlands of the south than the north. Through time, this alone could drive the northward range shift of this species across Europe projected from climate envelope models (Huntley *et al.* 2007), a topic we shall discuss in Chapter 6.

Further evidence of the importance of such spatial variation in habitat quality comes from the fact that pied flycatchers breeding in oak woodlands have experienced a much greater decline in the contribution that caterpillars make to the diet of broods through the season than flycatchers breeding in other deciduous and coniferous habitats (Burger *et al.* 2012). The extent of this decline has been greatest in warm years, when mismatch would be expected to be most severe. Although pied flycatchers take alternative prey when caterpillars are unavailable, this change in diet has a negative effect on chick condition. Further work is needed to explore the potential interactions between habitat and mismatch, and potential impacts on populations.

Overall, the Dutch pied flycatcher population declined from 1990 to 2002, when much of this work was conducted, but interestingly, has subsequently recovered and therefore may be regarded as stable during the last 20 years (Sovon 2012). As the contrasting phenological trends between caterpillars and flycatchers have continued through much of the 2000s (Both *et al.* 2009; Both 2012), this apparent improvement in the species' prospects does not appear to be a result of reduced mismatch in recent years. Instead, the relatively stable national trend may be due to redistribution of pied flycatchers away from deciduous to mixed woodland, although it is possible that other changes, for example on the African wintering grounds, may have contributed to the recovery (see Box 4.8). Elsewhere, pied flycatcher populations have declined in abundance in England and Scandinavia, which fits the expectation from the effects of mismatch-related decline in breeding success, although again, factors on the wintering locations may also be involved (Thingstad *et al.* 2006; Goodenough *et al.* 2009).

The collared flycatcher is closely related to the pied flycatcher, and has been relatively well-studied because it also takes well to nest boxes. As with the pied flycatcher, the breeding success of individual collared flycatchers is closely tied to the relative timing of breeding compared to peak availability of caterpillars. Detailed studies of collared flycatchers on the Swedish island of Gotland have shown that early nesting individuals are more likely to be successful than late nesters, because the time when they are feeding chicks in the nest tends to be most closely matched to peak caterpillar availability (Sheldon *et al.* 2003; Brommer *et al.* 2005). Despite this, there has been no significant change in laying date through time, suggesting that some other pressures are constraining the ability of the collared flycatchers to advance their breeding. Given that there is no evidence of a decline over time in the breeding success of the Gotland population (Sheldon *et al.* 2003), it is unclear the extent to which phenological mismatch is affecting the population, particularly as the population has increased recently (Vallin *et al.* 2012). A similar conclusion was reached by a detailed study of collared flycatchers breeding at three sites in the Czech Republic. Replicating the multi-trophic approach of Both *et al.* (2009), Bauer *et al.* (2010) compared phenological trends in oak budburst, peak caterpillar abundance and first and mean laying dates from 1961 to 2007. Here, there was evidence for an advance in laying date through time (matching the overall conclusions of studies of this species; Figure 3.2), but no evidence for mismatch because the phenological trends of all three trophic levels were similar. Similar results were found by a second Czech study (Weidinger & Král 2007).

To summarise, there is evidence that individuals of all four species may suffer detrimental effects of mismatch, although only in the pied flycatcher have these effects been related to local population trends. Even for this species, the extent to which national population declines may be driven by such mismatch remains unclear. We need to broaden our examination of the literature, and test the extent to which there is more evidence for effects of mismatch upon other bird species.

3.4.3 Mismatch in other woodland birds

Durant *et al.* (2007) suggested a number of criteria that must be fulfilled in order for mismatch between predator and prey to occur:

1. A predator must exhibit a strong seasonal peak in food demand and its prey must also have a strong peak in abundance.
2. The recruitment or survival of predators must be largely determined by prey abundance.
3. The phenology of predators and prey must be determined by different environmental or climatological drivers which change over time in different ways.

Visser *et al.* (2012) elaborated on criterion 3 and outlined two potential hypotheses to explain why climate change may lead to mismatch.

1. The cues hypothesis refers to the cues being used by the predators to time their breeding in order to match peak resource availability. It the cue used no longer accurately predicts the resource peak, then mismatch will occur.
2. The constraint hypothesis refers to the fitness costs to the predator of starting reproduction too early being substantial and greater than the potential fitness benefits of timing reproduction to match the resource peak.

As outlined in the introduction, most bird species fulfil some of Durant's criteria. The breeding success of many species is dependent upon food availability (e.g. Arcese & Smith 1988; Marshall *et al.* 2002; Pearce-Higgins & Yalden 2004), whilst the resource requirements of birds tend to peak markedly during the breeding season. There are also strong seasonal peaks in the abundance of food for many bird species, especially in protein-rich foods such as insects and rapidly growing young plant leaves needed by female birds forming eggs and by growing chicks. The literature contains examples both of the cues hypothesis, where the effects of weather on the phenology of peak bird requirements and the timing of food peaks differ, and the constraints hypothesis, where breeding too early is detrimental for survival, despite potential advantages for reproductive success. Tits and flycatchers breeding in Dutch oak woodland fulfil all criteria. The availability of their prey (caterpillars) is highly seasonal, and the magnitude of late-spring (May) warming, which determines caterpillar phenology, has been greater than warming in March and April, the driver of bird breeding phenology. Individuals which breed too early may suffer reduced breeding success, be subject to increased energetic costs during the breeding season and experience reduced survival probabilities afterwards.

Does this mean that other woodland insectivorous birds have the potential to be affected by mismatch? Both *et al.* (2010) compared the population trends of resident, short-distance and long-distance migrants in woodland and wetland habitats in Holland. Based on the supposition that woodland habitats are highly seasonal, whilst wetland habitats provide a more even distribution of food resources during the breeding season, the authors expected that population declines would be greatest in woodland. They also expected that long-distance migrants would be most likely to have suffered recent population declines, following their observations of the effects of mismatch on pied flycatchers. Accordingly, long-distance migrants breeding in woodland were the species group with the greatest rate of recent population decline, whilst other species all appeared to have increased in abundance. Further, populations of three long-distance migrants which occurred in both habitats had increased in wetlands but declined in woodland. Population trends were also more negative for the same long-distance migrants in the temperate deciduous woodlands of western Europe than the less seasonal boreal forests of northern Europe with a wider food peak. The evidence in support of the vulnerability of long-distance migratory woodland birds to mismatch appears strong from this study. Similarly, in England, populations of long-distance migrant woodland birds have declined, whilst resident species have increased in abundance (Figure 3.7), although these trends have been regarded as more likely to be attributable to changes on the wintering grounds than mismatch (Hewson & Noble 2009).

What evidence is there from detailed studies of other woodland species to support these correlations? We have assessed the literature and compared studies against Durant's three criteria. Thus in order for a species to be classified as vulnerable to mismatch, there must be evidence for seasonality in resource availability which influences breeding success, and importantly evidence for differential trends in phenologies of predator and prey through time, or differential fluctuations of those phenologies in relation to climatic drivers. Finally, for our assessment, there must also be evidence of an impact of mismatch upon demographic processes in that population, such as breeding success or population change.

The wood warbler *Phylloscopus sibilatrix* is a rapidly declining long-distance migrant to Europe which, like the pied flycatcher, has shown little advance in spring arrival dates (FAD advance $= 0.04 \pm 0.10$ days per year when averaged across studies; Box 2.2).

84 · The impact of altered timings

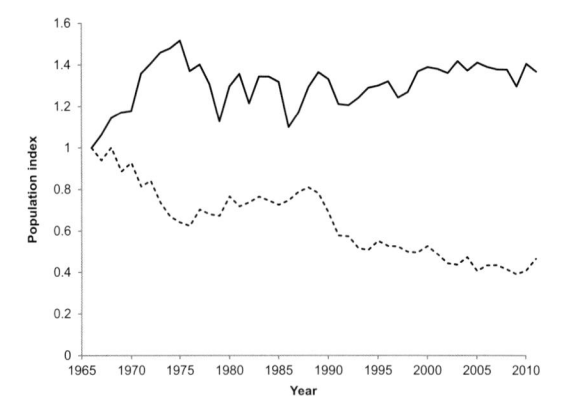

Figure 3.7 Average population trends of resident (solid line, n = 15) and long-distance migrant (dashed line, n = 16) woodland bird species in England from 1966 to 2010.

Hence, it is a good candidate to be another woodland migratory insectivore likely to be declining as a consequence of phenological mismatch (Møller *et al.* 2008). A study of wood warbler breeding performance in Bialowieza National Park, Poland, showed that, as expected for a seasonal species, clutch size was negatively correlated with laying date; the earliest laid clutches tended to be the largest. However, despite the limited advance in arrival date, there was an apparent advance in the timing of laying in response to spring warming through time, and, contrary to expectation, no significant reduction in breeding success. This was because predation, rather than food limitation, was the main proximate cause of nest failure (Wesolowski & Maziarz 2009). Wood warblers in Bialowieza did not therefore appear to be suffering the expected reductions in productivity as a result of mismatch. Limited evidence from the UK also suggests that mismatch may not be responsible for declines there (Mallord *et al.* 2012).

There is also no evidence of a negative effect of mismatch from a study of willow tits *Parus montanus* breeding in the forests of Finland (Vatka *et al.* 2011). Here, the timing of breeding advanced more rapidly than the timing of peak food abundance, which actually improved the degree of match between the timing of breeding and peak food abundance. Breeding success increased through time in a manner similar to that of great tits at Wytham Wood.

Also in boreal Finnish woodland, rapid warming in early spring has advanced the timing of black grouse *Tetrao tetrix* and buzzard *Buteo buteo* egg-laying dates. The rate of this advance has again exceeded the rate of change in conditions later in the breeding season, when the birds have chicks. However, in contrast to the willow tits, this appears to have led to mismatch. Due to a lack of warming in early summer (June), when the chicks of both species hatch, the advanced breeding phenology means that both species are now breeding too early relative to ambient conditions. As a result, their chicks now experience colder temperatures than before, reducing breeding success and contributing to observed population declines (Ludwig *et al.* 2006; Lehikoinen *et al.* 2009). Although it is not clear whether such mismatch is a result of variation in food peak phenology, or more direct effects of weather conditions, both studies are persuasive that negative mismatch effects have occurred.

3.4 Mismatch in the timing of breeding

In the case of black grouse, and the ecologically similar western capercaillie *Tetrao urogallus*, females ideally lay their eggs so that the period of peak food requirements, at 2 to 3 weeks of age, roughly matches the time of peak biomass of their invertebrate prey of caterpillars and sawfly larvae (Wegge & Kastdalen 2008). As chick survival is positively related to prey abundance (Picozzi *et al.* 1999), there is the potential for differences in the cues that determine bird breeding phenology and peak prey occurrence to cause mismatch (although see Wegge *et al.* 2010). In Scotland, it has been suggested that a subtle change in the pattern of spring warming has reduced capercaillie breeding success. It is hypothesised that this may have occurred through delayed spring plant growth which decreased the quality of food available to females attempting to gain condition for egg-laying (Moss *et al.* 2001). Other factors, including rainfall during chick rearing also affect breeding success, and more research is needed to disentangle these effects.

Studies in North America suggest that differential patterns of warming along the spring migration route may prevent long-distance migrants, such as New World wood warblers (Parulidae), keeping pace with the advance of spring on the breeding grounds. They may therefore suffer some of the same problems as pied flycatchers in Europe. Strode (2003) showed that despite significant warming above a latitude of about 40° N, a lack of warming, or even cooling, further south prevented most warbler species from advancing their arrival times to the breeding grounds. As a result, as outlined at the start of this chapter, the rate of advance of arriving North American migrants was slower than the rate of advance of spring plant phenology (Marra *et al.* 2005; Miller-Rusking & Primack 2008; Ellwood *et al.* 2010; see Box 2.7). However, as yet there is no evidence that this has led to reductions in their breeding success.

For example, a detailed study of five insectivorous woodland birds in high altitude forest in central Arizona (albeit south of 40° N), found that although warming had driven significant phenological changes, breeding success was not correlated with the rate of advance in egg-laying date, May temperature, or, crucially, the interaction between them (Martin 2007). Similarly, annual variation in populations of American redstarts across the species' range did not fluctuate in response to spring temperature, as might be expected if they were strongly affected by mismatch (Wilson *et al.* 2011). Indeed, there is some evidence to suggest that Neotropical migrants may have considerable flexibility to adjust their breeding phenology to match spring temperature conditions (Mazerolle *et al.* 2011), and that it is variation in prey population size, rather than phenological mismatch, which may have been the most important determinant of productivity in these New World insectivorous migrants in recent years (Holmes 2007). This will be discussed in more detail in Chapter 4. However, more studies are required, particularly in the higher latitude forests of North America, where significant spring warming has occurred, to test the extent to which mismatch may be a problem for these insectivorous migrants.

Turning to a resident North American species, declines in the abundance of grey jays *Perisoreus canadensis* at the southern edge of their boreal forest range in North America also appear unrelated to the timing of breeding, which has advanced in response to warmer late-winter temperature. Instead, population declines appear to result from increasing autumn temperatures, potentially because warming may increase the perishability of stored food which the birds rely on over the winter (Waite & Strickland 2006).

We started this chapter by illustrating a possible trophic cascade in European deciduous woodlands from oak leafing to moth caterpillars to tits to sparrowhawks. Has the altered breeding phenology of woodland passerines affected their sparrowhawk predators through phenological mismatch? There is potential for an effect of mismatch because sparrowhawks have failed to advance their hatching dates in response to the 0.43 days per year advance in tit and flycatcher hatching dates at the Hoge Veluwe. This has caused a significant increase in mismatch because in 2004 sparrowhawks nested and hatched 10 days later relative to the timing of passerine laying dates than in 1985 (Both *et al.* 2009). This and a similar lack of shift in sparrowhawk egg-laying dates in Denmark might be expected to have reduced sparrowhawk productivity through time, given the negative correlation between laying date and sparrowhawk breeding success (Nielsen 2004; Nielsen & Møller 2006). This does not, however, appear to have been the case, as annual variation in the breeding success of the Danish population is positively correlated with early spring (February–April) temperature, the reverse of what we might have expected were mismatch important. Further, the population has increased in abundance through time (Nielsen & Møller 2006).

To summarise, aside from the well-studied examples of great and blue tits and pied and collared flycatchers, there are a number of additional examples of mismatch between changes in the timing of environmental conditions and woodland bird requirements, particularly for more northerly distributed woodland species such as black grouse. Of these species, only studies on pied flycatchers (Both *et al.* 2006a) and black grouse (Ludwig *et al.* 2006) have specifically linked mismatch to changes in population size, and in each case, other factors may also be responsible or, even more important, drivers of decline, such as changes in the African humid-zone wintering ground of the pied flycatcher (Thaxter *et al.* 2010), increasing rates of predation (Summers *et al.* 2004) and changes in large-scale forest management and drainage (Ludwig 2007; Ludwig *et al.* 2008) affecting black grouse. The evidence that long-distance migrants may be particularly vulnerable to negative effects of mismatch is not apparent from the admittedly small number of detailed species-specific studies reviewed above. In Europe and North America, populations of many long-distance migrant woodland insectivores are declining, but more work is required to assess the extent to which phenological mismatch may have contributed to these declines (Knudsen *et al.* 2011).

3.4.4 Mismatch in wetland species

What about birds in wetland habitats? If Both *et al.* (2010) are correct; there should be little evidence of mismatch affecting insectivorous wetland species in temperate latitudes, given the greater spread of food resources during the breeding season in such habitats. The limited data available suggest this does appear to be the case. Studies from central Europe, an area of potential mismatch due to the magnitude of late spring warming (cf. Both 2010a), show both Eurasian reed warbler *Acrocephalus scirpaceus* and great reed warbler *A. arundinaceus* have significantly advanced the timing of their breeding, leading to an increase in breeding success. This increase may be due to either an increase in clutch size, associated with the earlier breeding, an increase in the number of nesting attempts, or an improvement in weather conditions (Schaefer *et al.* 2006; Halupka *et al.* 2008). Tree swallows *Tachycineta bicolor* in North America forage primarily over wetlands where the availability of flying insect prey increases through the breeding season, and therefore shows little seasonality. As a result, there is no evidence of phenological mismatch in this species either, which has also advanced its laying date through time. Indeed, as with the reed warblers, earlier breeding has been associated with greater productivity, apparently driven by an increase in clutch size (Dunn *et al.* 2011).

Common sandpipers occupy upland streams and lakesides, which may therefore be more seasonal than the eutrophic reedbed habitat of the reed warblers, although sandpiper chicks are not necessarily reliant on aquatic invertebrate prey for food (Yalden 1986). Being long-distance migrants, sandpipers may also be limited in their ability to respond to any advance in the timing of any peak of abundance of invertebrate prey. Despite this potential for mismatch, detailed analysis of the demography of a declining population in the Peak District, England, found no evidence for a reduction in productivity through time (Pearce-Higgins *et al.* 2009c). More specifically, annual variation in productivity was not related to May temperature (a strong determinant of breeding phenology; Dougall *et al.* 2005), or the interaction between May and June (the chick rearing period) temperature, as a crude index of phenological mismatch, but was instead positively correlated with June temperature. In this example, there was again no evidence for climate change having caused the decline in this long-distance migrant, which probably resulted from reductions in annual survival. Warming in the UK may even have increased productivity.

A number of studies have been conducted on the breeding success of boreal and Arctic breeding waterbirds, which might be expected to exhibit a greater degree of seasonality than those breeding in temperate wetlands. For example, the breeding success of eider ducks *Somateria mollissima* in the Canadian Arctic shows a strong humped relationship with laying date. The chicks which hatch just before the disappearance of residual winter ice survive best, whilst those which hatch too early, or too late, are less likely to survive. Although this suggests these ducklings may be vulnerable to mismatch, it appears that advances in both snowmelt and the timing of laying in response to spring warming may have increased productivity. In an early spring, poorer quality females were able to gain sufficient condition to breed, which led to an overall positive effect of warming on productivity (Love *et al.* 2010). Warming therefore appears to have been beneficial because the eiders have continued to time their breeding appropriately.

Snow geese *Chen caerulescens* in the Canadian Arctic breed in the same seasonal environment, with the start of breeding constrained by snow cover, whilst late breeding is penalised because of insufficient time for goslings to prepare for autumn migration (Lesage & Gauthier 1997). In this case, breeding success peaks at intermediate values of summer Arctic Oscillation, being low when cold, probably through direct effects of chilling, and low when warm. In addition, gosling condition is negatively related to spring temperature. This may be a sign of mismatch, with a more rapid response of plant growth to warmer temperatures than goose laying dates, reducing the quality of plant forage for the goslings. Alternatively, such a result may also occur as a result of density dependence, with a greater proportion of geese breeding in warm springs than are able to breed when snowmelt is delayed (Dickey *et al.* 2008).

Drever and Clark (2007) found little evidence of phenological mismatch affecting the hatching success of ducks breeding in Saskatchewan, Canada. In contrast to the other studies reviewed in this chapter, the authors focussed on variation in hatching success, mediated through nest predation. They argued that this could be related to mismatch reducing resource availability for incubating females, impacting upon rates of nest

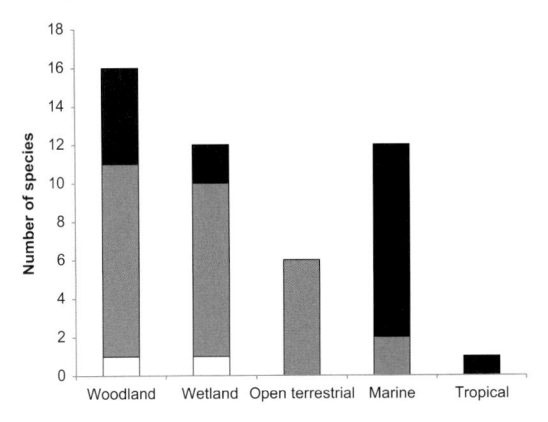

Figure 3.8 The number of species for which at least one study has highlighted evidence of a negative impact of phenological mismatch upon demography (black) compared to those with no such evidence (grey) or potential increases in match leading to demographic benefit (white), varies by habitat.

attendance. This was not the case, with little evidence for such mismatch across the five species studied, with the possible exception of northern pintail *Anas acuta*. It could be argued that this study did not consider what may have been the primary way these ducks would be vulnerable to mismatch, that of mismatch between duckling food requirements and peak invertebrate abundance (Cox *et al.* 1998). A larger-scale study of Canadian waterfowl potentially included these wider mismatch effects by comparing population trends of breeding scaup *Athya* spp. and scoters *Melanitta* spp., which have fixed breeding phenologies determined by photoperiod, with those of mallard *Anas platyrhynchos* and American wigeon *Anas americana*, which are more likely to have advanced MLD in response to warming (Drever *et al.* 2012). Scaup and scoter populations have declined through time, but mallard and wigeon populations have not, which may be because the latter have been able to adapt to changing environmental phenologies. However, as more detailed information on productivity was not presented, and the patterns may potentially be explained by other hypotheses, we do not include this study in our summary (Figure 3.8). We must therefore conclude that the extent to which mismatch may be affecting Arctic breeding waterbirds relying on highly seasonal wetlands, remains unclear, although the results of some studies are suggestive that mismatch effects could occur here.

3.4.5 Mismatch in open terrestrial habitats

A smaller number of studies have looked at the potential effects of phenological mismatch upon non-woodland terrestrial habitats, ranging from farmland to heathland and upland peatland to Arctic tundra (in addition to the studies of waterfowl just outlined). In the case of Eurasian golden plovers, we have already described how breeding success is linked to the abundance of craneflies, which form a critical food resource for young chicks (Box 3.1). The timing of first and mean golden plover egg-laying dates is strongly advanced by warm March and April temperatures, whilst the timing of the emergence of craneflies is positively correlated with May temperature (Pearce-Higgins *et al.* 2005). Although the strengths of these two temperature effects are similar, the degree of recent warming in March and April in the UK has been greater than the degree of warming in May, which has probably caused a slight tendency for golden plover laying dates to have advanced more rapidly than the timing of cranefly emergence, although by only about 0.1 days per year. Crucially, however, there is no evidence that this degree of mismatch has been sufficient to result in significant reductions in productivity of a southern range margin population in the Peak District, UK since 1972 (Pearce-Higgins *et al.* 2010). Phenological mismatch has therefore not significantly impacted upon this population, despite the potential highlighted by Pearce-Higgins *et al.* (2005), although any differential warming between early and late spring in the future does have the potential to cause phenological mismatch. Other, more northerly distributed wader species may also be vulnerable to mismatch. For example the growth rate of Baird's sandpiper *Calidris bairdii* chicks is similarly dependent upon their synchrony with the peak in cranefly abundance, which has led to the suggestion that increasing temperatures in the Arctic may reduce the degree of synchrony between bird breeding and peak prey availability (McKinnon *et al.* 2012).

In the British uplands, a study of the potential impacts of climate change on declining ring ouzel *Turdus torquata* populations found no link between breeding phenology and productivity (Beale *et al.* 2006a), although the phenology of prey availability (earthworms) was not specifically examined. Two strands of evidence further support the contention that mismatch-mediated reductions in breeding productivity have not driven the observed population decline. Firstly, the main cause of ring ouzel breeding failure was found to be density-dependent nest predation, not chick starvation. Secondly, a comparison of productivity between a stable and a declining population found no difference in productivity between the two (Burfield 2002), suggesting that the causes of decline were occurring outside of the nesting and chick-rearing period, such as in response to low juvenile and adult survival rates (Sim *et al.* 2011).

Away from the uplands, increasing temperatures have advanced laying dates of both Ortolan buntings *Emberiza hortulana* and red-backed shrikes *Lanius collurio* in central Europe. A significant correlation between temperature and MLD of woodlarks *Lullula arborea* breeding in Thetford Forest, England is also indicative of earlier breeding in warmer springs, although there has been no overall trend in laying date through time due to inter-annual variation in the temperature (Wright *et al.* 2009). As a result of increases in clutch size with earlier breeding in red-backed shrike (Hušek & Adamík 2008), and the potential for a greater number of woodlark nesting attempts in warm years, significant spring warming is likely to have benefited both species. However, the Thetford woodlark population has declined for other reasons (Wright *et al.* 2009). Changes in nesting phenology appear to have been neutral for Ortolan Bunting, which may have declined in response to hunting-related reductions in overwinter survival (Lang 2007).

To conclude, there is no evidence for phenological mismatch affecting populations of any of the open-ground terrestrial breeding species described, either because warming has been beneficial, because other drivers may be more important determinants of population change or, in the case of golden plovers, probably because the magnitude of difference in the trends in bird and environmental cues has been small relative to other factors. In addition to studies investigating potential mismatch effects on productivity, there has been much discussion about the potential for mismatch between arrival times and host laying dates to affect populations of the common cuckoo *Cuculus canorus*, an obligate brood parasite. Although recent changes appear to have influenced the relative importance of different brood hosts, there is again no evidence that recent population declines have been caused by such mismatch (Box 3.4).

3.4.6 Mismatch in the marine environment

The breeding success of piscivorous seabirds around the world is positively related to the abundance of the fish on which they prey, as is discussed in much more detail in the next chapter (Section 4.6). Thus, the productivity of seabirds breeding off the east coast of Scotland is positively correlated with the abundance of lesser sandeels *Ammodytes marinus* (Rindorf *et al.* 2000; Frederiksen *et al.* 2006). The success of Atlantic puffins *Fratercula arctica* breeding in Norway is positively related to the abundance and size of herrings *Clupea harengus* (Durant *et al.* 2003), the productivity of common guillemots *Uria aalge* breeding in California is related to the abundance of rockfish *Sebastes* spp. (Mills *et al.*

Box 3.4 · *The special case of cuckoos*

Common cuckoos are long-distance migrant brood parasites which depend upon other bird species, both residents and migrants, to rear their nestlings. They may therefore be significantly impacted by changes in migration and nesting phenology in complex ways. Cuckoo first arrivals (FAD) have advanced by about 0.1 days per year (Table S2.1[*]), which is a weaker advance than many of their migrant hosts, particularly those which are short-distance migrants such as the dunnock (hedge accentor) *Prunella modularis* and meadow pipit *Anthus pratensis* (Saino *et al.* 2009). As a result, there is potential for reductions in the rate of brood parasitism on those host species, relative to long-distance migrants. Matching this expectation, the rate of parasitism of Eurasian reed warblers, a key long-distance migrant host, increased up to the 1980s, whilst parasitism of short-distance migrant species has declined. However, these changes appear to have commenced before the start of significant spring warming (Brooke & Davies 1987).

Detailed analysis of phenological changes shows the expected reductions in the likely overlap between the nests of three key short-distance migrant hosts (dunnock, meadow pipit and pied wagtail *Motacilla alba*) and the main period of cuckoo egg-laying. Advances in reed warbler laying dates have increased the proportion of nests vulnerable to cuckoo parasitism (Douglas *et al.* 2010). As would be expected from these trends, there has been a reduction in the proportion of nests of resident and short-distance migrant hosts parasitised by cuckoos. Further, these reductions are greatest in areas with the most rapid spring warming (Møller *et al.* 2011). By differentially affecting the arrival and laying dates of different host species, climate change has therefore affected the patterns of brood parasitism in cuckoos across Europe. Although cuckoo populations are declining rapidly (e.g. 49% decline in the UK between 1995 and 2010; Risely *et al.* 2012), there is, crucially, no evidence to date that the decline is strongly related to changes in host phenology (Douglas *et al.* 2010).

---

[*] See online material.

Box 3.4 (cont.)

Box 3.4 There has been a reduction in the proportion of dunnock nests parasitised by cuckoos as a result of a more rapid advance in dunnock nesting phenology than cuckoo arrival time. However, there is no evidence to date that this has caused declines in cuckoo populations. Photograph by Andy Musgrove.

2007; Reed *et al.* 2009) and that of rhinoceros auklet *Cerorhinca monocerata* in Japan related to the availability of anchovies *Engraulis japonicus* (Watanuki *et al.* 2009). Given the strong, temperature-driven seasonality of these environments, the timing of fish reproduction is an important determinant of food availability for seabirds. The survival of fish larvae is a function of the match between the timing of their hatching and peak primary productivity (Cushing 1982; 1990). Therefore there is the potential for changes in sea temperature to result in complex changes to the phenology of fish and their food resources, depending on the relative timing of the peak bloom of phytoplankton, peak abundance of zooplankton and the peak requirements of fish larvae (Burthe *et al.* 2012). These are not just features of medium and high latitude cool water systems, but also of the feeding grounds of tropical seabirds, where changes in ocean currents associated with El Niño events may also reduce food resources and delay seabird breeding (Surman *et al.* 2012). These issues are examined in more detail in Section 4.6, but mean that seabirds may be vulnerable to the effects of phenological mismatch, particularly where the phenology of seabird breeding and prey availability are determined by different environmental cues.

One of the ways in which these cues may differ in the marine environment is through the influence of ocean currents to transport prey (often small fish) close to seabird colonies. These currents are driven by large-scale climatic processes and subject to variation according to atmospheric pressure and wind direction, whilst the timing of seabird laying dates is often more closely related to local temperature. Two good examples illustrate this principle: rhinoceros auklets breeding at Teuri Island, off Hokkaido, Japan, and Atlantic puffins breeding on the Norwegian coast.

The auklets breeding on Teuri Island are an interesting example because they experienced a shift from a cold- to a warm-water regime in the early 1990s, leading to a switch in prey from sardines *Sardinops melanostictus* to anchovies. The availability of anchovies is determined by the Tsushima current, a flow of warm water from the southern Japan Sea whose strength is correlated with atmospheric pressure over the North Pacific. Variation in the laying date of these burrow-nesting auklets is negatively correlated with local March air temperature, directly linked to low pressure in the Arctic. These two climatic processes are uncorrelated (Watanuki *et al.* 2009; Watanuki 2010). Because auklet productivity is closely linked to the phenology of the warm-water current, in years in which auklet breeding phenology and the timing of this current are not matched, success is low. The same processes also seem to affect Japanese cormorants *Phalacrocorax filamentosus*, but not black-tailed gulls *Larus crassirostris*, which prey primarily on sandeels, whose availability is unrelated to the Tsushima current and instead linked to local conditions. Although years with mild spring temperatures and a weak Tsushima current do occur and cause low auklet productivity, there is no evidence that climate change has so far driven an increase in the frequency of such events. Thus, although sensitive to mismatch, there has been no overall trend in either auklet laying dates or the timing of the Tsushima current through time (Watanuki & Ito 2012).

More widely, rhinoceros auklets appear vulnerable to warming across their range. In British Columbia, reductions in the abundance of their main sandeel prey as a result of increases in sea-surface temperature have reduced breeding success (Hedd *et al.* 2006), either as a result of phenological mismatch or perhaps more importantly, reductions in the sandeel population. Cooler conditions also benefit the species breeding in California where they rely on rockfish. Here, colder water increases primary and secondary productivity, leading to greater abundance of rockfish (Thayer & Sydeman 2007). Again, the main effects of warming appear to be mediated through variation in prey abundance, rather than phenology, although the two processes are difficult to disentangle. The effects of climate change on seabird populations mediated through reductions in prey abundance are covered in detail in Section 4.6.

Spawn produced by herrings along the Norwegian coast drifts northwards in the Norwegian coastal current, the speed of which varies from year to year in response to wind speed and direction (Sætre *et al.* 2002). The productivity of puffins nesting at colonies along the coast is dependent on the degree of synchrony between the timing of their breeding and peak herring availability. The availability of herring to the puffins is therefore determined by large-scale climatic drivers, whilst puffin breeding phenology is correlated with local temperature (Barrett 2001; Durant *et al.* 2004a, 2005). Although the absolute size of the herring stock is the main influence on puffin breeding success, accounting for 20% of the variation in productivity between years, phenological mismatch contributes an additional 11% of the inter-annual variation. There is therefore the potential for mismatch to drive changes in puffin productivity through time, with delayed herring arrival reducing the growth and survival of puffin chicks. It is not clear, however, whether climate change has driven an increasing trend for mismatch, and therefore whether puffin productivity has declined through time.

Secondly, seabird colonies associated with productive shallow coastal seas rely on an extremely seasonal environment and may also be vulnerable to mismatch. Here, rapid spring warming produces a bloom of phytoplankton, and then zooplankton. That in turn provides food for small fish, such as sandeels. Around the North Sea, where lesser sandeels are a key prey for many seabird species (see Section 4.6), increasing temperatures have advanced the timing of sandeel spawning (Rindorf *et al.* 2000), although due to slower sandeel growth rates, the date at which 0-class fish reach an appropriate length for foraging seabirds has actually become later over time (Frederiksen *et al.* 2011; Burthe *et al.* 2012). During this period, seabird egg-laying dates have remained largely unchanged, or have even become later. Through time, there has been a reduction in the length of sandeels available to a range of seabird species, including common guillemot, razorbill *Alca torda*, European shag *Phalacrocorax aristotelis*, black-legged kittiwake *Rissa tridactyla* and Atlantic puffin (Frederiksen *et al.* 2006; Burthe *et al.* 2012), causing a decline in productivity of a number of these species. However, the statistical link between this decline and mismatch is actually fairly weak (Burthe *et al.* 2012) due to covarying effects of sandeel phenology, quality and abundance (examined in more detail in Section 4.6.1), which have made it difficult to disentangle the effect of mismatch from those of other factors. In addition, the productivity of species, such as kittiwake and puffin, is also correlated with the abundance of older 1+ class sandeels, whose availability has also declined, at least partly in response to warming (Frederiksen *et al.* 2004b, 2006; Burthe *et al.* 2012). Despite these analytical challenges, declines in the breeding success of guillemots, razorbills and shags do appear related to slower sandeel growth which we regard as an indication of vulnerability to mismatch, although the evidence for kittiwake and puffin breeding success is less clear.

Away from the North Sea, the breeding success of Cassin's auklet *Ptychoramphus aleuticus* in British Columbia is closely related to temperature, because the phenology of their copepod prey is strongly advanced by warming, whilst the timing of auklet egg-laying is independent of temperature, potentially under the control of photoperiod or winter prey abundance. Warm years are characterised by early copepod availability, causing a reduction in the proportion of copepods in the diet, and negative effects on the condition and survival of auklet chicks (Hipfner 2008). There is similar evidence that climate-driven delays in breeding may also reduce the productivity of tropical seabirds, including roseate terns *Sterna dougallii* breeding on Aride Island, Seychelles (Ramos *et al.* 2006; Monticelli *et al.* 2007) and a range of species breeding at Houtman Abrolhos, Western Australia (Surman *et al.* 2012).

A third mechanism through which mismatch may affect seabirds is through variation in the timing of sea ice breakup, which will influence the accessibility of high latitude breeding species to open water (Gaston *et al.* 2005). This is illustrated by Brünnich's guillemot (thick-billed murres) *Uria lomvia* breeding at Coat's Island in Hudson Bay, Canada, where the timing of sea ice breakup (as measured by the date of 50% ice cover) has advanced significantly since 1990, and at a greater rate than the advance in guillemot hatch dates. As peak food availability is closely linked to sea ice breakup, this has increased mismatch over time. As a result, the growth rate of guillemot chicks has declined, which may have reduced their survival (Gaston *et al.* 2009), although the population-level consequences of this mismatch remain unclear.

For many seabirds, the potential effects of phenological mismatch are compounded by the significant reductions in the abundance of prey that have also occurred at the same time as recent mismatches in phenology (Section 4.6). The two effects interact to the detriment of many species. Increases in sea temperatures simultaneously advance plankton and fish phenology whilst reducing their abundance. As the timing of seabird breeding is correlated with food availability, warm years with earlier fish availability but reduced fish abundance are likely to also be years with the greatest mismatch, because the shortage of food for adult female seabirds may delay egg-laying. As a result, ten of the seabird species studied may be detrimentally affected by mismatch to some degree, although as with most other species, we are not aware of a single study which clearly links climate change to increasing rates of mismatch that then leads to a reduction in productivity and a negative population trend.

3.4.7 Mismatch in the tropics

We are aware of only one study of the demographic impacts of phenological change in the tropics. Increased August rainfall at the end of the austral winter has delayed the timing of egg-laying in the Mauritius kestrel *Falco punctatus*. This delay has increased the risk that breeding attempts will suffer from high rainfall in December associated with the start of the cyclone season when chicks are in the nest (Senapathi *et al.* 2011). Although rainfall is usually regarded as likely to advance the timing of breeding in tropical species (Section 2.7), in the case of raptors such as this kestrel, it may cause delay by reducing adult hunting efficiency, and therefore limiting adult condition (Chapter 4). This delay results in increased later exposure to adverse effects of high rainfall late in the breeding season, and therefore constitutes a mismatch effect.

3.4.8 Concluding remarks

This short review provides some support for the contention of Both *et al.* (2010) that birds breeding in seasonal woodland environments will be more vulnerable to mismatch than less seasonal wetland environments, and also appear more vulnerable than species occupying other terrestrial habitats. However, there is less evidence that it is long-distance migrants which may be most vulnerable to such effects. More detailed studies of long-distance migrants breeding in woodland habitats are required. Instead, our analysis suggests that seabirds may be the most vulnerable group of species to mismatch (Figure 3.8) due to the high seasonality of their environment, the critical importance of prey availability in driving productivity, and in many cases, the differential drivers of predator and prey phenology. However, even for seabirds, the evidence that such mismatch is having population-level effects through time remains largely equivocal (e.g. Burthe *et al.* 2012).

The complexities of the marine environment mean that it is particularly difficult to differentiate effects of mismatch from concurrent reductions in prey quality and abundance, and also to formally attribute such effects to climate change. Further, being long-lived, *k*-selected species, there is a long lag between reductions in breeding success translating into effects on breeding population size, which further compounds the challenge of correctly diagnosing the causes of change.

The species in which such mismatch effects appear most detrimental are those with the greatest difference in the magnitude of shift in the food peak (or environmental conditions) and shift in bird breeding phenology (Visser *et al.* 2012). Of the terrestrial species which fulfill this criterion and where long-term estimates of annual variation in productivity are available, only the pied flycatcher has shown a trend for reduced breeding success and fitness; the situation for the great tit appears more equivocal (Reed *et al.* 2013b). The degree of match in trends between laying date and breeding phenology is much greater for the remaining studies presenting long-term variation in productivity (Pearce-Higgins *et al.* 2005, 2010; Nielsen & Møller 2006; Charmantier *et al.* 2008; Matthysen *et al.* 2011), and accordingly, these studies show little evidence of negative effects of mismatch. There appears to be much greater discrepancy between the trend in prey phenology and breeding phenology for seabirds than for terrestrial species, which for a number of species have been related to annual variation in productivity. However, to our knowledge, no seabird studies present clear evidence for long-term declines in productivity that can be specifically related to mismatch.

3.5 Mismatch or not?

To summarise, a number of authors have attempted to detect and describe the potential effects of phenological mismatch upon avian breeding success and populations. The topic has received considerable attention in the scientific literature. In our review of 47 species, there was evidence that phenological mismatch has caused some reduction in the productivity of at least one population of 14 species during some years of poor matching (pied flycatcher, common buzzard, black grouse, European shag, Japanese cormorant, black-legged kittiwake, rhinoceros auklet, Cassin's auklet, Atlantic puffin, common guillemot, Brünnich's guillemot, razorbill, roseate tern and Mauritius kestrel), whilst evidence for a further four was more equivocal (northern pintail, western capercaillie snow goose and great tit), but still contributed to the results shown in Figure 3.8. In addition, there are probably potential effects of mismatch on blue tits and collared flycatchers which have yet to be empirically demonstrated, and Arctic breeding scoters and scaup (Drever *et al.* 2012). These negative effects must be balanced against positive effects of reduced mismatch as a result of warming on populations of two species (willow tit and eider), as well as in some tit populations, and wider benefits of a longer breeding season to a range of birds (Møller *et al.* 2010).

Although nine of the populations reviewed have declined in abundance through time, in only Dutch pied flycatchers and Finnish black grouse have these declines been quantitatively linked to phenological mismatch. In each of these examples, there is evidence that other processes may have been equally or more important in driving the observed declines. Detailed species-specific studies therefore provide limited evidence for phenological mismatch as a result of climate change having been the cause of population declines in birds (Knudson *et al.* 2011; Visser *et al.* 2012). This lack of evidence from detailed species-specific studies (with significant effects apparent from only about one-third of species examined) on terrestrial habitats must be balanced against the results of correlative studies which suggest that the detrimental effects of mismatch may be widespread. We have already highlighted that long-distance migrants breeding in seasonal deciduous woodland habitats have tended to decline, relative to other species, and relative to populations in other, less seasonal, habitats (Both *et al.* 2010). An increasing number of other multi-species correlative studies have been used to support the contention that phenological mismatch may be an important cause of bird population declines (Table 3.2).

Variation among recent (1990–2000) population trends of European migrant bird species is correlated with the rate of change in their spring arrival date (MAD) (Møller *et al.* 2008), mean spring arrival date (van Turnhout *et al.* 2010), average laying date (Salido *et al.* 2011), migratory distance (Jones & Cresswell 2010) and an estimate of the degree of mismatch based on accumulated temperature (Saino *et al.* 2011). Species which have suffered the greatest population declines are those with slow, or even negative, spring arrival advancement rates and longer migration distances. Indeed, migrants wintering furthest from the breeding grounds (trans-Saharan migrants) are those least likely to have advanced their timing of migration (data from Møller *et al.* 2008; $r = 0.42$, n = 100, $P < 0.05$; see also Figure 2.3). These species have suffered the greatest 'thermal delay' through time, measured as the increase in accumulated winter and spring temperature (degree days above $0\,°C$) at the date of MAD across four observatories on the southern edge of Scandinavia. Species-specific variation in this value is significantly negatively correlated with the population trend of those migrants across the seven Scandinavian countries they breed in, suggesting that at least part of the decline may be attributed to mismatch (Saino *et al.* 2011). Similarly, population trends of North American migrants are correlated with the difference in temperature trends on the breeding and wintering grounds as an index of mismatch (Jones & Cresswell 2010).

Long-distance migrants are suffering significant population declines in both Europe (Sanderson *et al.* 2006; Thaxter *et al.* 2010; van Turnhout *et al.* 2010) and North America (Holmes & Sherry 2001). This general pattern of decline is certainly consistent with the expected impacts of phenological mismatch (Table 3.2) on the assumption that long-distance migrants are constrained in their ability to advance their timing of breeding to match the advance in spring conditions on the breeding grounds (although we find limited evidence for this; Figure 2.4). They are certainly experiencing warmer temperatures on arrival to their breeding grounds than previously (Saino *et al.* 2011). Declines in populations of insectivorous migrants likely to be vulnerable to mismatch appear to be greatest following mild winter and spring weather on the breeding grounds, when mismatch would be most likely (Cormont *et al.* 2011).

The results of these multi-species correlative studies are certainly suggestive that mismatch is a widespread and important phenomenon, particularly for long-distance migrants, and particularly when combined with the detailed studies on pied flycatchers which illustrate how mismatch may work in practice. However, the lack of widespread evidence from detailed species-specific studies examining the evidence that mismatch has driven population declines in such migrants is notable. The fact that migrant population

Table 3.2 Summary of studies describing greater declines in long-distance migrants than other species, and where presented, the evidence that those declines are linked directly to phenological mismatch, wintering location (which may also be linked to vulnerability to mismatch in some circumstances) or other factors.

Study	Location	Species	Link to phenological mismatch	Link to wintering location	Link to other factors
Holmes & Sherry (2001)	Hubbard Brook, USA	24 woodland species			Habitat change leading to population declines in early successional species.
Ballard et al. (2003)	California, USA	31 species	Some large-scale climatic effects on migrant trends, although the mechanism is unclear.		Greater population declines in woodland species, cowbird hosts and species with high nests.
Sanderson et al. (2006)	Europe	121 long-distance migrants		Declines in populations of 8 long-distance migrants greater than for residents.	
Gregory et al. (2007)	Europe	57 woodland species		Population declines of 15 long-distance migrants from 1980 to 2003 greater than for partial migrants, although 13 resident species also declined.	
Heldbjerg & Fox (2008)	Denmark	62 passerines	Population decline greatest in species without advanced MAD.		
Moller et al. (2008)	Europe	100 migrant species		Timing of population declines varies between wintering location.	
Hewson & Noble (2009)	England	49 woodland birds			Populations of understory species declining most. Some effects of diet on trends.
Yamamura et al. (2009)	Japan	140 species		Declines in populations of 36 long-distance migrants occupying mature forest, whilst resident and short-distance migrants increased in abundance.	Local habitat change leading to population declines in early successional species. Migrant population declines attributed to habitat loss in south-east Asia.
Both et al. (2010)	The Netherlands	57 passerines		Declines of long-distance migrant populations in deciduous woodland but not wetland habitats. Resident and short-distance migrant populations stable.	

Table 3.2 (cont.)

Study	Location	Species	Link to phenological mismatch	Link to wintering location	Link to other factors
Jones & Creswell (2010)	North America	53 species	Population declines greatest in species with greatest contrast in temperature trends between breeding and wintering grounds.		
Jones & Creswell (2010)	Europe	83 species		Population declines greatest in species migrating the furthest distance.	
Thaxter et al. (2010)	England	59 species		Contrasting population trends between different overwintering zones.	
Van Turnhout et al. (2010)	The Netherlands	170 species, 54 long-distance migrants		Population declines greatest in long-distance migrants, particularly in those arriving late to the breeding grounds.	
Saino et al. (2010)	Europe	117 species	Population declines greatest in species suffering 'thermal delay' in MAD.		
Salido et al. (2012)	UK	50 passerines	Population declines greatest in late breeding migrants and migrants with least advance in FAD.		Population declines greatest in habitat specialists and invertivores.
Cormont et al. (2011)	The Netherlands	77 species	Population declines in insectivorous long-distance migrants after warm winter/spring weather.		
Ockendon et al. (2012)	UK	26 migrants		Contrasting population trends between different overwintering zones.	
Morrison et al. (2013)	UK	46 passerines		Contrasting population trends between different overwintering zones.	Population trends more positive in Scotland than England.

declines may also be strongly correlated with migratory distance and wintering habitat suggests that, at least for European birds, it is possible that changes in conditions in Africa may also be a contributory factor or more important than mismatch (Table 3.2). That a recent multi-species review failed to find any evidence for changes in breeding phenology being correlated with population trends from 1990 to 2000 across Europe and North America, as would be expected were these declines caused by mismatched breeding attempts (Dunn & Møller in press), adds weight to this suggestion. The potential for environmental change in the wintering grounds to be the main cause of these problems is illustrated by declines in long-distance migrants in Japan which have been attributed to habitat loss in south-east Asia associated with the spread of oil palm plantations (Yamaura *et al*. 2009; see Chapter 8). These declines have been greatest in species occupying mature forest, and therefore potentially mirror the results of Both *et al*. (2010), but have been attributed to a different cause. Such reductions in the quality of overwintering habitats may also limit the ability of migrants to gain condition for their return migration to their breeding grounds, potentially accounting for the observed links between trend in arrival time and population trend. There is an urgent need for research to concentrate on understanding these potential linkages between breeding and wintering habitats, and potential interactions between environmental changes in both, to further reduce this uncertainty. The current literature may neglect the possibility that the apparent increase in phenological mismatch of long-distance migrant populations is a symptom, rather than the cause, of a population decline that results from wider environmental degradation on the wintering grounds.

We therefore agree with Knudsen *et al*. (2011) that the evidence in support of population declines in migrant birds being caused by increased trophic mismatch on the breeding grounds as a result of recent climate change is limited. Continued monitoring of productivity in these environments should remain a priority in order to better attribute any changes to climate change. We would particularly urge workers to investigate mismatch in other declining long-distance migrants, particularly those in deciduous woodland or other seasonal environments, to add to our understanding. Our review perhaps suggests that although issues of phenological change and phenological mismatch have somewhat dominated the climate change literature over the last decade or so, they may not be the most important issues for those concerned about the impacts of climate change on bird populations and bird conservation. Phenological mismatch is only one of a number of mechanisms through which climate change may affect bird species, and it is to an examination of these other mechanisms that we turn in Chapter 4, in order to identify the species and habitats which appear to be most vulnerable to the impacts of anthropogenic climate change.

3.6 Summary

- Changes in the timing of migration or breeding will be of interest to conservationists if they result in a mismatch with periods of peak resource availability or with benign environmental conditions. Studies from the UK and North America suggest the rate of advance in arrival time and laying date for birds has been less than that observed for plant and invertebrate phenologies.

- Although mistimed migrant arrival may result in reduced survival, and can lead to catastrophic mortality events, there is little evidence that climate change has increased the likelihood of these occurring.
- At the Hoge Veluwe, the Netherlands, advances in great tit laying date have been insufficient to keep pace with advances in the timing of peak caterpillar availability, the main prey given to chicks. At Wytham Wood, England, early spring warming has improved the ability of great tits to maintain synchrony with advances in caterpillar timing, leading to increases in breeding success.
- Different warming trends between locations have led to variable trends in tit breeding phenology between populations, with divergent consequences for breeding success. Whilst some responses may be adaptive, the balance of evidence suggests that mismatch may be constraining the ability of females to rear two broods of chicks. Despite this, mismatch has not led to tit population declines.
- Rates of advance in MLD of pied flycatchers vary among populations in response to the degree of local warming. In many populations, this rate of advance has been less than the rate of advance in peak caterpillar availability, reducing clutch size and chick survival, and potentially also compromising adult survival. As a result, some local populations appear to have declined, although the link to larger-scale population declines remains unclear.
- For trophic mismatch to be an issue, birds must exhibit seasonal peaks in food demands which are linked to survival or breeding success. The availability of prey must also vary seasonally. The timing of peak demand and availability must be determined by different drivers with divergent trends through time. Birds may additionally be constrained if the fitness benefits of maintaining a match with prey phenology are outweighed by the costs.
- Birds breeding in highly seasonal habitats are expected to be particularly vulnerable to negative effects of mismatch. In support of this expectation, long-distance migrants breeding in deciduous woodland have tended to exhibit recent population declines. Detailed studies of five of 16 woodland breeding species have found some evidence for mismatch reducing productivity. Fewer species occupying wetland and open habitats appear affected by mismatch.
- Seabirds appear to be the group most likely to be vulnerable to mismatch effects, as a result of variation in breeding phenology and prey availability often being caused by different mechanisms. However, as these processes may also affect overall prey abundance, it has proved difficult to link mismatch to recently observed declines in seabird breeding success.
- Negative impacts of mismatch are most apparent where trends in the timing of food peaks have diverged from trends in the timing of bird breeding. Across 47 species reviewed, we found evidence for mismatch reducing productivity in at least one population of 14 species, and weaker evidence for an additional four. In two species was there some evidence that mismatch may be linked to population decline.
- There is good correlative evidence from multi-species studies that declining long-distance migrants have failed to advance their timing of arrival, and therefore have

been most likely to suffer phenological mismatch. This apparent contradiction between the limited support for mismatch from species-specific studies and strong circumstantial support from large-scale multi-species correlations may be explained if both lack of advancement of migratory phenology and declining population trends are symptoms of the same deterioration in environmental quality, rather than being cause and effect. This hypothesis requires thorough testing.

4 · *Further mechanisms of population impacts*

4.1 Introduction

As we explained in Chapter 1, environmental variables, including the weather and climate, can only influence bird populations if they alter demography: the reproductive or mortality rates and, for the subdivided parts of a closed population, immigration and emigration as well. In the previous chapter we discussed the effects of phenological mismatch on bird populations, but that is just one of the ways in which climate change can have an impact on demography (Table 4.1). These other mechanisms are the focus of this chapter. We will not restrict ourselves only to studies of climate change impacts, but also review the wider range of studies which have looked at the relationships between bird population processes and temperature, precipitation and other weather variables. Whilst many of these will really be examining the effects of annual variation in the weather (as opposed to long-term trends in climatic averages), they may still be useful in helping us understand the impact of climate change upon bird populations in the future.

Long-term studies are necessary in order to adequately describe how populations respond to annual fluctuations in the weather, and especially to see how population size is affected by longer-term changes, including recent climate change (which we regard as a long-term change in those weather variables, ideally over a minimum 30-year period, although many studies putatively demonstrating impacts of climate change span shorter periods). One of the longest such studies is that of the annual heronry census, coordinated by the BTO since 1928, which has been used to demonstrate the sensitivity of grey heron *Ardea cinerea* populations to cold winter weather (North 1979; Reynolds 1979). The impact of severe winters can be clearly seen leading to periodic population declines, but in response to a run of mild winters from the late 1980s to late 2000s, the population remained high and stable (Figure 4.1). Such large-scale population monitoring programmes are now widely established across Europe and North America, and often use the observations of amateur ornithologists, collected using standardised methods (e.g. Anders & Post 2006; Gregory *et al.* 2009; Moller & Fiedler 2010) to deliver large-scale monitoring for the production of robust population trend estimates (van Strien *et al.* 2001; North American Bird Conservation Initiative, US Committee 2011). However, for many species and countries elsewhere, these annual monitoring data do not exist, which is an obstacle to scientific understanding and effective conservation action (Amano & Sutherland 2013).

As an alternative, individual studies of particular populations can provide more precise data than large-scale abundance indices. However, such counts may suffer from greater effects of chance variations in local conditions, and may also be affected by net emigration or immigration, which can be important influences on local populations (Lampila *et al.*

Table 4.1 *Potential ways in which climate change may impact upon bird populations (adapted from Mustin et al. 2007; Geyer et al. 2011)*

Changes in competitor populations
Changes in disease populations
Changes in dispersal rates
Changes in immune function
Changes in physiology
Changes in predator populations
Changes in prey populations or food abundance
Changes in vegetation structure
Changes to the rate or frequency of migration or breeding events
Disruption in synergistic relationships
Loss of suitable habitat
Mortality associated with extreme events
Phenological mismatch

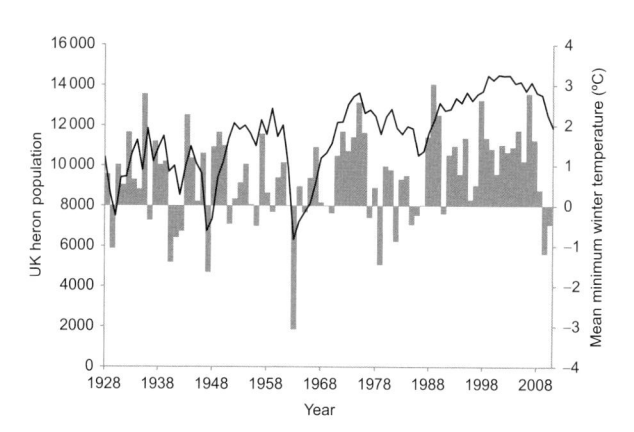

Figure 4.1 Fluctuations in the UK grey heron population (line) in response to winter severity (grey bars).

2006; Pearce-Higgins *et al.* 2009c). To provide information about the demographic mechanisms underlying population changes, reproductive and mortality rates may be measured and related to environmental variables, including those describing the weather (e.g. Thompson & Ollason 2001; Sæther *et al.* 2006). More elegantly, simulation models may be developed to allow the effects of environmental changes and density dependence to be combined to reveal how they act together to cause population change (e.g. Grøtan *et al.* 2009; Pearce-Higgins *et al.* 2009c, 2010; van de Pol *et al.* 2010b; Eglington & Pearce-Higgins 2012). However, even a model which has a good fit to the observed data may not necessarily provide a good prediction of the future (Box 4.1).

In this chapter, we review the array of studies which have related variation in population growth, survival or productivity, to variation in the weather experienced by populations, in order to document the changes which have occurred, and to identify the sorts of species most likely to be vulnerable to future climatic change. Although many of these studies have been conducted in the absence of explicit consideration of climate change,

Box 4.1 · *Models may have limited ability to predict future population changes*

Yalden & Pearce-Higgins (1997) published a simple model of the breeding population of Eurasian golden plovers at a site in the Peak District, UK, located towards the southern margin of the global range. The model used annual data on plover population size and weather variables known or believed to affect demographic rates for the period 1972–1994. The logarithms of annual values of population multiplication rate (λ) were modelled as being linearly related to the size of the population in the previous year (N_{t-1}) and winter temperature (T_W), which was thought to affect survival. Population multiplication rate was given by the following equation:

$$\lambda = \exp(-0.1813 - 0.0437 N_{t-1} + 0.2108\ T_W).$$

A second model updated the earlier model of annual multiplication rate using data to 2005 (Pearce-Higgins *et al.* 2010), over which period August temperature (T_A) was the most important predictor:

$$\lambda = \exp(1.7852 - 0.0205 N_{t-1} - 0.0755\ T_A).$$

These models can be used to produce free-running predictive population models from 1972 that can be compared with observed counts as a stringent test of performance. Although both models have a similar ability to predict population growth to 1994 (correlation between observed and predicted log ratios of change from 1972–3 to 1993–4: T_w model, $r = 0.63$, $P < 0.0001$; T_A model $r = 0.62$, $P = 0.0001$), the winter temperature model of Yalden and Pearce-Higgins performs much less well from 1994 onwards (correlation between log ratios from 1994–5 to 2004–5: T_w model, $r = 0.08$, $P = 0.65$; T_A model $r = 0.44$, $P = 0.01$). In this case, there was an apparent switch in the relative importance of winter and summer temperatures in driving population change during this period which reduced the efficacy of the original model through time (Pearce-Higgins *et al.* 2010). The poor prediction in 1981 was due to snowfall in late spring.

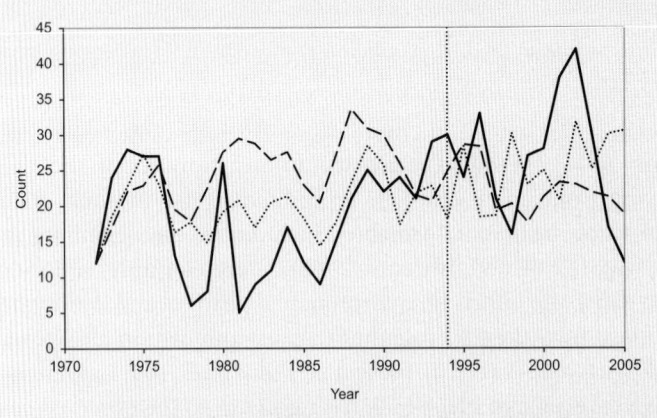

Box 4.1 Changes in the golden plover population at Snake Summit through time. The observed population is given by the solid line, the predicted population trend from the Yalden & Pearce-Higgins (1997) T_w model by the dotted line, and the predicted population trend from the Pearce-Higgins *et al.* (2010) T_A model by the dashed line. The vertical dotted line indicates the limit of the data analysed by Yalden & Pearce-Higgins (1997).

we assume that their results are useful to help us consider the potential implications of climate change on a population or species. For example, if the population growth of a particular species is positively related to temperature through enhanced adult survival, then we might expect climate warming to result in an increase in the size of that species' population, at least in the short term. This pattern is shown by the grey heron population in Figure 4.1. Conversely, for a population of a species whose productivity is negatively impacted by drought, for example through reductions in the abundance of their prey, if climate change were to result in an increased frequency of drought, that population would be more likely to decline.

4.2 Broad patterns

Before we look in detail at the different ways in which bird populations may be affected by climate change, we first describe some broad patterns in how the sensitivity of different species to temperature and precipitation, which are the two most widely available climatic variables, varies around the world. We do this having collated the results of published studies that have examined effects of weather and climate variation upon survival, productivity and population size (Box 4.2). Because changes in population size, at least for a closed population, may be a result of changes in either survival, productivity or both, and in many cases (although not all, as we will illustrate later), the same weather condition may have equivalent effects on different demographic parameters, this analysis provides an overall assessment of the general relationships between these measures of the weather and demography. Within these general patterns, however, there is much detail and variation, which is unpacked from Section 4.3 onwards.

4.2.1 Temperature

The majority of studies that we reviewed indicated a positive effect of increased temperature on avian demographic processes. When the results of all studies were averaged, the mean temperature effect ($\pm$ SE) was 0.36 ± 0.05. Therefore, if we take all these studies at face value and adequately representing the overall effect of temperature upon birds, warmer temperatures are likely to result in larger bird populations through either increased survival or reproductive rates. This is a very simplistic picture, however, as it appears that the strength of this relationship varies between terrestrial and marine environments, and with latitude (Box 4.2). There was a strong positive relationship between latitude and the effect of temperature on populations, with populations at high latitudes being much more likely to respond positively to temperature than those close to the equator. In addition, seabirds tended to show a consistently more negative relationship between demography and temperature than terrestrial species. This means that at low latitudes, temperature was more likely to have a negative effect on seabird population size, whilst at low latitudes on land there appeared to be a similar proportion of studies which showed positive or negative relationships between temperature and demography.

Effects of temperature differed between breeding and non-breeding seasons. For land birds, a strong positive non-breeding season mean temperature effect suggests that on average, populations of many terrestrial species were likely to benefit from increasing

106 · Further mechanisms of population impacts

Box 4.2 · *Variation in the response of populations to temperature*

We collated the results of 152 studies of a total of 147 species, covering 468 individual cases (many studies are multi-species and many species are covered by multiple studies) published to early 2011. We combined studies of the effects of variation in temperature on productivity, survival or abundance (including population multiplication) to maximise sample size. Studies of temperature also included variables describing frost or snow cover, indicative of cold and severe winter weather. Changes in abundance will reflect changes in productivity and/or survival rates, and often a reduction in the quality of conditions as a result of changes in temperature will affect both productivity and survival. Unlike the review of phenological studies in Chapter 2, there was no common currency for measuring changes in these different rates. Therefore, we simply classified the relationship between demography and temperature (temperature effect) as being either significantly ($P < 0.05$) positive (1), significantly negative (-1), or non-significant (0). Following the methods of Chapter 2, analyses were conducted in a mixed-model framework to account for the potential non-independence of data from the same study, with study identity as a random effect.

There was a close to significant effect of species on the temperature effect ($F_{107, 28.5} = 1.68$, $P = 0.06$), although very few species actually demonstrated significant, consistent positive or negative temperature effects across all studies. With species and study as random effects, there was a weak correlation between the temperature effect and latitude ($F_{1, 133} = 8.11$, $P = 0.051$) and a significant difference in temperature effect between marine and terrestrial environments ($F_{1, 99.1} = 23.06$, $P = 0.0001$).

Of the studies which specifically tested non-breeding (i.e. autumn and winter for temperate latitudes) or breeding (i.e. spring and summer) season effects (423 of the 468 studies), temperature effects varied weakly between breeding season and non-breeding season periods ($F_{1, 344} = 3.23$, $P = 0.073$) and in different ways between terrestrial and marine environments ($F_{1, 226} = 7.25$, $P = 0.0076$). Although most studies of breeding season temperature were on productivity, and non-breeding season temperature were on survival, this was not necessarily the case because of studies which accounted for lagged effects, as some of the examples described in this chapter make clear. Insufficient data existed to separately examine interactions with latitude within this breakdown.

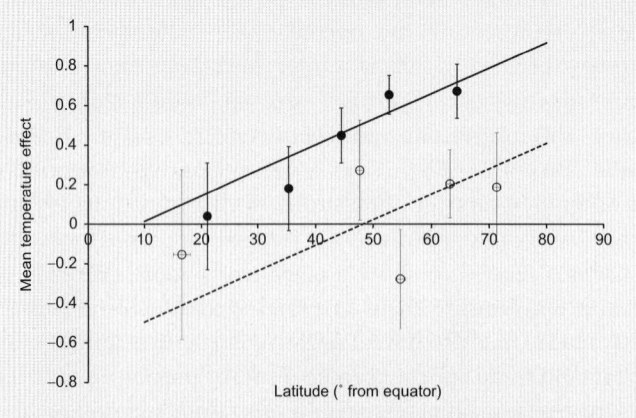

Box 4.2a Correlation between latitude (both hemispheres combined) and mean temperature effect for terrestrial species (black symbol, solid line) and seabirds (open symbol, dashed line). Symbols represent data when binned into 10° categories (amalgamating bins

Box 4.2 (cont.)

Box 4.2a (cont.) with < 10 cases) along with standard error bars. A value of one would indicate that all studies demonstrated a significant positive effect of temperature on demography, whilst −1 would indicate that all studies showed a significant negative effect.

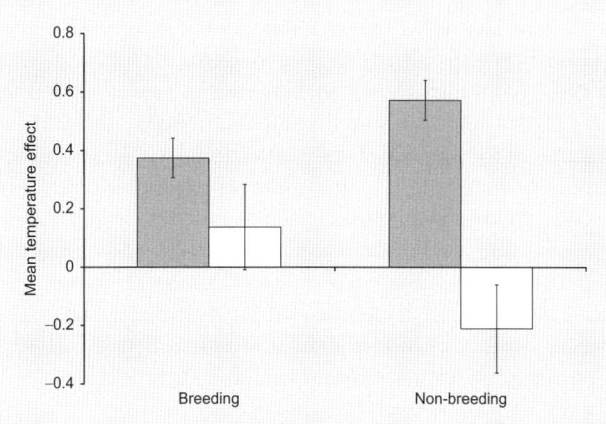

Box 4.2b Mean effects (± SE) of breeding and non-breeding season temperature upon populations of terrestrial species (grey) and seabirds (white). A value of one would indicate that all studies demonstrated a significant positive effect of temperature on demography, whilst −1 would indicate that all studies showed a significant negative effect.

autumn and winter temperatures. The same effect was apparent during the breeding season, but to a lesser degree, suggesting that a greater proportion of studies showed either negative or no effect of breeding season temperature. As outlined previously, effects of temperature upon seabird populations were less positive than for terrestrial species, and particularly tended to be negative in relation to non-breeding season temperature (Box 4.2).

We examined these relationships further by comparing the response of different taxa and testing the effects of ecological factors (Box 4.3). Populations of Accipitridae (eagles and hawks), Charadrii (shorebirds), Paridae (tits), Troglodytidae (wrens) and Turdidae (thrushes) each showed generally consistent positive effects of non-breeding season temperature upon them. This pattern was also apparent in eight of 11 temperate European species covered by five or more studies (Table S4.1[*]) and is suggestive of population-level benefits of increases in winter temperature. The sensitivity of species to non-breeding season temperature was related to diet, but not migratory status. Carnivorous, omnivorous and invertivorous (those which prey on invertebrates) species were most sensitive to cold weather, whilst piscivorous species appeared relatively insensitive to temperature.

Different taxonomic groups showed consistent positive effects of breeding season temperature upon their populations (Table S4.2[*]). Such effects were most marked in Anatidae (ducks and geese) and Tetraonidae (grouse), with no evidence for a

[*] See online material.

Box 4.3 · *Variation in the response of populations to temperature in the non-breeding season and breeding seasons*

Following the mixed-model framework of Box 4.2, the effect of non-breeding season temperature on bird demography did not vary significantly with order ($F_{11,63.4} = 1.26$, $P = 0.27$) or family ($F_{35, 14.2} = 1.52$, $P = 0.20$), but did between genera ($F_{62, 41.8} = 1.94$, $P = 0.013$) and species ($F_{79, 23.1} = 1.85$, $P = 0.048$). Estimates of mean temperature effects are listed for taxa with more than five time series (Table S4.1[*]). In contrast, the effect of breeding season temperature varied with order ($F_{13, 60.3} = 1.84$, $P = 0.057$), but not consistently with family ($F_{36, 32} = 0.97$, $P = 0.54$), genus ($F_{62, 17.8} = 1.25$, $P = 0.31$) or species ($F_{81, 7.56} = 1.32$, $P = 0.36$), although there were some differences between particular taxa which have been the subject of most studies (Table S4.2[*]).

With species and study as a random effect, there was no significant effect of migratory distance upon the effect size of either non-breeding ($F_{2, 65.6} = 0.95$, $P = 0.39$) or breeding season temperature ($F_{2, 82.7} = 1.03$, $P = 0.36$). There were, however, significant differences in the mean non-breeding season temperature effect in relation to non-breeding season diet ($F_{4, 33.9} = 3.32$, $P = 0.021$). Although there was not an overall difference in the mean breeding season temperature effect in relation to breeding season diet, ($F_{4, 70.9} = 1.13$, $P = 0.35$), piscivores again showed the weakest response to temperature.

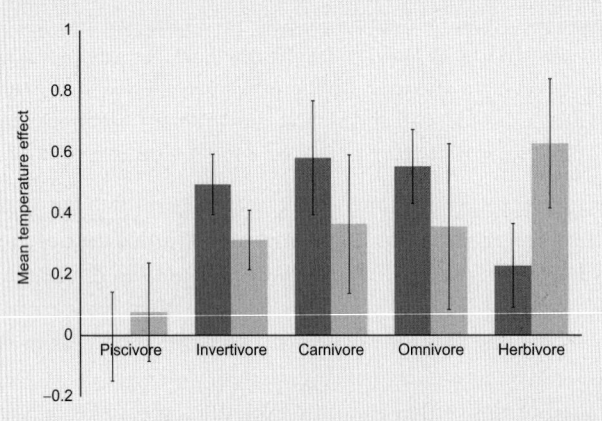

Box 4.3 Mean effects (± SE) of non-breeding season temperature upon populations varies with non-breeding season diet (dark grey) and breeding season temperature in relation to breeding season diet (light grey). A value of one would indicate that all studies demonstrated a significant positive effect of temperature on demography, whilst −1 would indicate that all studies showed a significant negative effect.

unidirectional effect of temperature in other groups, including passerines, which were the subject of the greatest number of studies. There were no consistent differences between the temperature sensitivity of species and migratory distance or diet, although invertivores and herbivores tended to show the most positive relationships between their populations and breeding season temperature (Box 4.3).

[*] See online material.

4.2.2 Precipitation

Variation in precipitation appears to have had a mixed effect on bird populations (mean precipitation effect = 0.04 ± 0.071), although as with temperature, this varied significantly with latitude (Box 4.4). Crucially, our analysis suggests that in contrast to temperature, precipitation has had a positive effect on populations in the tropics, but a more mixed effect on intermediate and high latitude populations. Unlike temperature, there was no

---

Box 4.4 · *Variation in the response of populations to precipitation*

We collated the results of 110 studies which quantified the effects of variation in precipitation on the productivity, survival or abundance of 167 species, yielding 331 individual cases of analysis. In the same way that we analysed temperature effects (Box 4.2), we classified the effects of precipitation upon bird demography as either significantly positive (1), significantly negative (−1), or non-significant (0), using $P < 0.05$ as the threshold of significance. Analyses were conducted in a mixed-model framework to account for the potential non-independence of data from the same study, which was listed as a random effect.

There was some variation in the response of species to precipitation ($F_{154, 48.3} = 1.40$, $P = 0.086$). With species and study as random effects, there was a strong negative correlation between the precipitation effect and latitude ($F_{1, 87.8} = 8.97$, $P = 0.0036$), which did not differ between marine and terrestrial environments ($F_{1, 74.6} = 0.68$, $P = 0.41$).

Of the studies that specifically tested non-breeding (i.e. autumn and winter for temperate latitudes) or breeding (i.e. spring and summer) season effects (316 cases), precipitation effects appeared much more likely to be positive outside of the breeding season (mean precipitation effect = 0.34 ± 0.98) than during the breeding season (mean effect = −0.14 ± 0.073), leading to a significant contrast between the two ($F_{1, 275} = 16.09$, $P < 0.0001$). Note that as in Box 4.3, not all studies of the effects of breeding season precipitation were on productivity, and not all studies of non-breeding season precipitation were on survival.

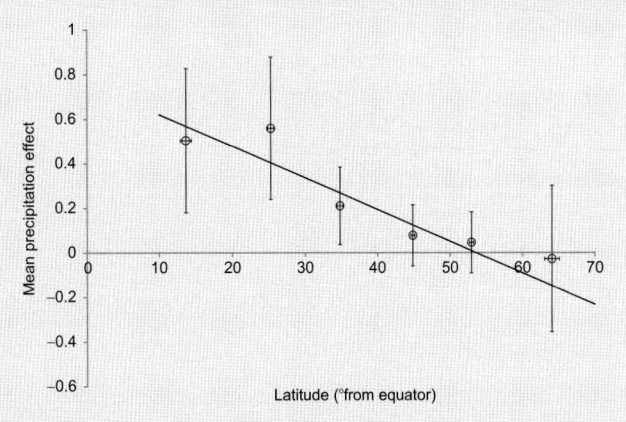

Box 4.4 Correlation between latitude and mean precipitation effect for all species. Symbols represent data when binned into 10° categories (amalgamating bins with < 10 cases) along with standard error bars. A value of one would indicate that all studies demonstrated a significant positive effect of precipitation on demography, whilst −1 would indicate that all studies showed a significant negative effect.

significant contrast between terrestrial and marine species in the effect of precipitation upon bird populations.

Precipitation effects differed between the breeding and non-breeding seasons. Breeding season rainfall tended to have a negative effect on populations, but a more positive effect during the non-breeding season (Boxes 4.4 and 4.5). Accipitridae (hawks and eagles) and Tetraonidae (grouse) appeared particularly sensitive to breeding season rainfall, a topic we shall return to later in the chapter (Section 4.4.2), whilst some passerine groups, such as thrushes, appeared to benefit from wet weather during the breeding season (Table S4.4[*]). There were only weak effects of diet and migratory distance on sensitivity to breeding season precipitation.

In contrast, effects of non-breeding season precipitation varied significantly in relation to migratory distance. Populations of long-distance migrants which winter primarily in tropical areas showed consistent positive effects of precipitation upon their populations (Box 4.5), matching the latitudinal gradient in precipitation effects of Box 4.4. Thus, taxa such as storks and herons (Ciconiformes), New World and Old World warblers (Parulidae and Sylviidae), the majority of which are migratory, all appeared to benefit from wetter conditions in the wintering grounds of the Sahel and tropical zones of Africa, or the Caribbean and northern South America (Table S4.3[*]). The precise climatic influences on migrant populations are discussed in detail later in the chapter (Section 4.4.1). In our analysis, winter precipitation appeared to have the most positive effects on piscivorous and invertivorous species. The former is unsurprising, as such species will rely most on wetland habitats which are in many areas temporary and maintained by highly seasonal rainfall, whilst many invertebrate groups preyed upon by birds are sensitive to drought (e.g. Pearce-Higgins 2010).

4.2.3 Conclusion

In combination, this brief analysis of the published literature suggests that the majority of studies showed generally positive effects of temperature, and particularly non-breeding season temperature upon bird populations. These effects were strongest for carnivorous, omnivorous and invertivorous species, and much weaker for seabirds, a number of which appeared to suffer negative effects of increasing temperature upon their populations. Conversely, effects of precipitation were mixed, with generally positive effects of non-breeding season rainfall on wetland and piscivorous species and particularly long-distance migrants wintering in tropical areas, but negative effects on breeding season population processes at higher latitudes. As will be apparent later, the vast majority of these studies examined relatively direct and short-term effects of temperature and precipitation upon bird populations, rather than investigating potential lagged effects. This means that the generally positive assessment that temperature increases are likely to result in positive impacts on bird populations may not tell the whole story. It also means, as we shall again discuss, that the majority of these responses reflect more direct effects of these variables on survival and productivity, rather than more indirect, biotic effects, that may turn out to be more important (Cahill et al. 2013).

---

[*] See online material.

Box 4.5 · *Variation in the response of populations to precipitation in the non-breeding season and breeding seasons*

Following the mixed-model framework of Box 4.2, the effect of non-breeding season precipitation did not vary significantly with order ($F_{10, 39.6} = 1.12$, $P = 0.37$), family ($F_{29, 42.3} = 1.01$, $P = 0.47$), genera ($F_{55, 18.7} = 1.20$, $P = 0.34$) or species ($F_{70, 9.53} = 1.19$, $P = 0.42$), although there was a tendency for some taxa subject to the greatest number of studies to exhibit positive demographic effects of precipitation. In particular, populations of Ciconiformes (storks and herons) and Passeriformes (songbirds) both appeared to show consistent positive effects of non-breeding season precipitation (Table S4.3[*]). The effect of breeding season precipitation varied significantly with order ($F_{13, 74.2} = 2.29$, $P = 0.013$) and family ($F_{37, 43.6} = 1.86$, $P = 0.025$), but not genus ($F_{79, 5.98} = 1.44$, $P = 0.34$) or species ($F_{104, 13.7} = 1.49$, $P = 0.21$). Accipitridae (raptors) and Tetraonidae (grouse) appeared subject to consistent negative effects of breeding season precipitation, whilst Turdidae (thrushes) apparently benefit from breeding season precipitation (Table S4.4[*]).

With species and reference as a random effect, some of the (weak) differences in the response of populations to non-breeding season precipitation between species were strongly related to migratory distance ($F_{2, 102} = 7.39$, $P = 0.001$). Populations of long-distance migrants showed a strong tendency towards benefitting from wet conditions on the wintering grounds, whereas the effects were much weaker for medium- and short-distance migrants. Conversely, there were no differences in the response of species to precipitation on the breeding grounds with migratory distance ($F_{2, 90.6} = 0.08$, $P = 0.92$).

There were no overall significant differences in response between species in relation to winter diet ($F_{4, 57.7} = 1.61$, $P = 0.18$), with most species apparently benefiting from wet non-breeding season conditions, with the exception of carnivores. Carnivores were again different from other species by showing the strongest mean negative breeding season precipitation effect on populations, although again, there was no overall difference in species' responses to precipitation in relation to summer diet ($F_{4, 109} = 1.16$, $P = 0.33$).

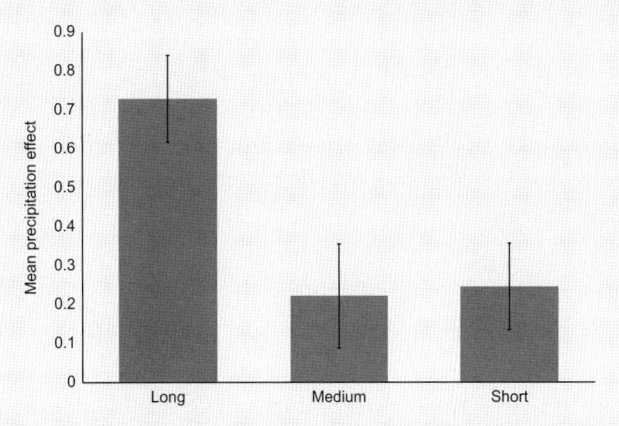

Box 4.5a Variation in the effects (± SE) of non-breeding season precipitation in relation to migratory distance. A value of one would indicate that all studies demonstrated a significant positive effect of precipitation on demography, whilst −1 would indicate that all studies showed a significant negative effect.

---

[*] See online material.

Box 4.5 (cont.)

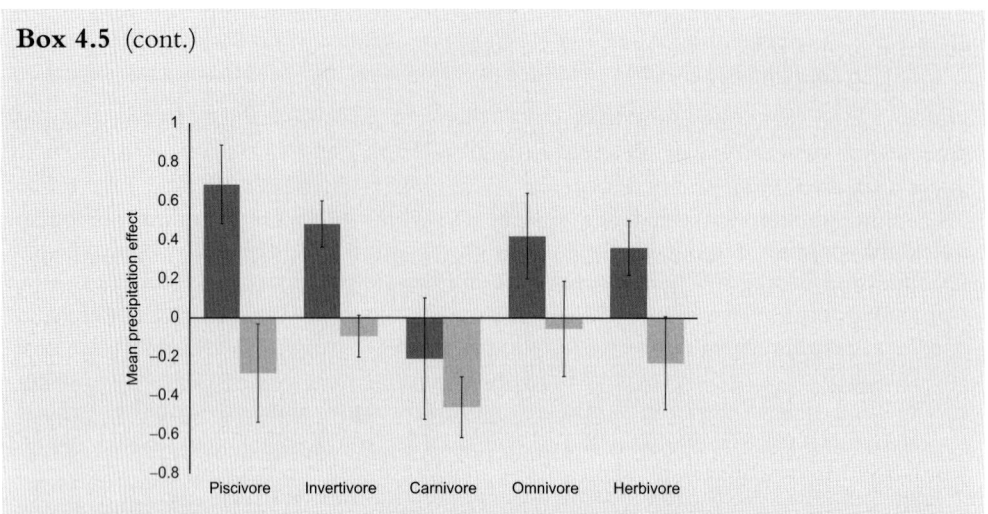

Box 4.5b Mean effects (± SE) of non-breeding season precipitation upon populations varies with non-breeding season diet (dark grey) and breeding season precipitation in relation to breeding season diet (light grey). A value of one would indicate that all studies demonstrated a significant positive effect of precipitation on demography, whilst −1 would indicate that all studies showed a significant negative effect.

Given these differences with respect to latitude, migratory strategy and between the marine and terrestrial environment, we will now examine in much more detail the ways in which variation in temperature, precipitation and other climatic and weather variables affect bird populations around the world. To do this, we therefore split our examination of evidence into four parts, examining separately the drivers of change in mid- to high-latitude species occupying Arctic, boreal and temperate zones, long-distance migrants that breed in such areas but winter in subtropical or tropical habitats, resident species of subtropical and tropical habitats and finally, seabirds. Based on the analysis we have just conducted, we would expect each of these categories of birds to face differing challenges from fluctuations and long-term changes in weather, and therefore to be subject to differing impacts of climate change.

4.3 Arctic, boreal and temperate regions

4.3.1 Survival

Polar, boreal and temperate terrestrial environments above about 40° latitude are characterised by cold winter weather conditions, accompanied by significant periods of snow cover and sub-zero temperatures, which are particularly severe where a continental climate prevails. In addition day length is short at high latitudes in winter. These conditions pose special challenges for species which remain in these zones during the winter. Indeed, increasing winter severity at high latitudes means that, towards the poles, most species tend to be at least partially migratory (Newton & Dale 1996; Carnicer & Diaz-Delgado 2008), although populations of many such species remain within the temperate zone. Long-distance migrants which winter in Mediterranean, subtropical and tropical zones will be covered in Section 4.4.

One of the best-studied resident species which has to survive the northern temperate winter is the great tit which, as already described in the previous chapter, has been the subject of many long-term population studies across Europe. These have not only looked at breeding productivity, but also provided a considerable amount of information on survival rates. A brief review of these studies indicates that the magnitude of annual fluctuations in population size varies significantly in relation to winter severity in 11 of 17 studies, although the exact measure of winter severity that best correlates with changes in abundance differs between them. For example, annual fluctuations in great tit abundance in detailed studies at a small geographic scale in the UK, Holland and Finland have been most strongly correlated with late-winter or early-spring temperatures (Kluijver 1951; Slagsvold 1975; Orell 1989), whilst analyses of data collected at the national level in the UK indicates that fluctuations in both population size and survival rate are better correlated with snow cover than temperature (Greenwood & Baillie 1991; Robinson et al. 2007a). These temporal patterns of sensitivity to snow and temperaure provide a clue as to the likely mechanisms involved.

At least part of the negative effect of adverse winter weather on survival rates appears to arise because such weather reduces the availability of food. In many woodlands, particularly in continental Europe, wintering great tits feed predominantly on fallen beech *Fagus sylvatica* seeds (mast) taken from the forest floor, the abundance of which is a strong determinant of adult survival (Perdeck et al. 2000) and changes in population size (Grøtan et al. 2009). This probably explains the susceptibility of these European populations to heavy snow cover, which reduces their access to this food. Beech mast is probably a less important driver of survival in the UK because much artificial food is provided in winter in gardens, and accordingly, adult great tit survival rates appear relatively constant at about 50%, regardless of conditions (Robinson et al. 2007a). Juveniles, however, appear more susceptible to poor conditions, and even in the UK, their annual survival varies from 40% in snow-free winters to 25% in the most snowy winters (30 days of snow cover). Given that the survival of adult great tits remains sensitive to mast abundance after accounting for winter weather effects (Perdeck et al. 2000), there are also likely to be interactions between the effects of weather and food abundance upon great tit survival.

In addition to the effects of snow, great tits are also sensitive to temperature, particularly towards the end of the winter and early spring, when they become more territorial and prepare for the breeding season (Section 3.4.1). At this stage, individuals are likely to be under additional stress, as males attempt to establish or maintain breeding territories, whilst females produce a large clutch of eggs. Cold weather at this time will both increase the costs of thermoregulation and reduce the availability of invertebrate prey. Food becomes progressively scarcer during the second half of the winter (Gibb 1960), yet is crucial for the onset of breeding (Chapter 3). It is notable that a number of studies identify cold weather during this so-called hungry gap in early spring when natural food resources are at their minimum, as the strongest determinant of survival, with a peak number of significant correlations between population growth, abundance or survival, and temperature in March (Figure 4.2).

114 · Further mechanisms of population impacts

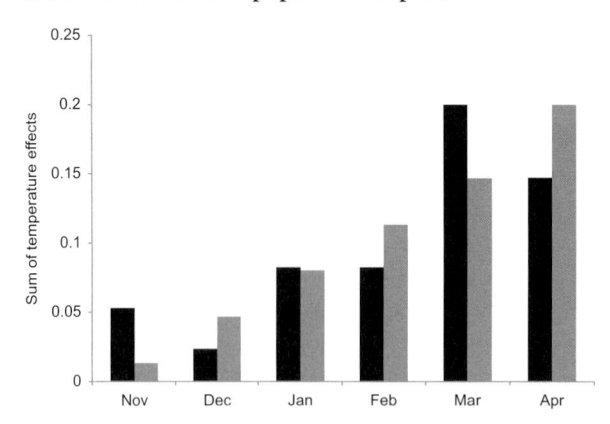

Figure 4.2 Monthly variation in the response of populations of great tits (black) and blue tits (grey) to severe winter weather. The sum of temperature effects is an average of the contribution of each month across all populations studied for that species (n = 17 for great tits and n = 15 for blue tits), where the contribution is weighted by the reciprocal of the number of months which that study found to be important for that species.

These broad-scale patterns may be obscured at finer spatial scales by strong buffering effects as a result of territoriality and density dependence (Kluijver & Tinbergen 1953; Clobert *et al.* 1988). Interactions among individuals mean that increasingly unfavourable habitats are occupied with increasing population size as individuals are displaced from preferred areas because of agonistic interactions and depletion of food by competitors. Given likely interactions between habitat quality, food abundance and climate, the survival of individuals occupying a poor-quality habitat, such as farmland, in a cold winter is likely to be much lower than that of individuals in woodland (Greenwood & Baillie 1991). These processes may also result in significant flows of individuals between locations and habitats. Juvenile great tits tend to leave woodland breeding areas during cold winters to escape from dominant adult male territory holders and to find more accessible food. They often move to gardens where they take advantage of artificial food provision (Slagsvold 1975; Orell 1989; Perdeck *et al.* 2000). The distance travelled by these dispersing individuals is likely to affect their likelihood of return, and hence the rates of local recruitment (Bulmer & Perrins 1973; Orell 1989), whilst the ability of any returning recruits to successfully gain a territory will depend upon the number of surviving resident birds (Slagsvold 1975). As a result of these processes, population fluctuations at some sites may be strongly buffered by density dependence (Newton *et al.* 1998), whilst at others, variation in winter survival may appear the most important driver of change (Sæther *et al.* 2002; Grøtan *et al.* 2009).

This detailed discussion of great tit demography complements our appraisal of the role of phenological mismatch in driving variation in great tit breeding productivity (Section 3.4.1). These studies suggest that the main cause of population change in this species is variation in the mortality of full-grown birds, rather than in breeding success (Grøtan *et al.* 2009). Thus, whilst mismatch may be an important driver of individual reproductive output and fitness, it is not a strong determinant of population change (Reed *et al.* 2013a). Density-dependent compensation is so important that any reductions in great tit breeding productivity as a result of mismatch are offset by subsequent increases in overwinter survival rates due to reductions in competition (Reed *et al.* 2013b). This buffers the population from potentially detrimental consequences of climate change on productivity. The best available evidence is that, despite Dutch great tits being one of the emblematic examples of climate change impacts on birds (Chapter 3), the population has not declined as a result of recent warming.

How widely can these conclusions about great tits be applied? Blue tits appear to follow a similar pattern (Figure 4.2). It is thought that blue tits may be more sensitive to cold, wet weather than they are to snow (Grosbois *et al.* 2006; Robinson *et al.* 2007a), potentially because of their more arboreal foraging habits than great tits. As might be expected from the pattern of regional variation in great tit response to winter severity described by Sæther *et al.* (2003), the survival of blue tits in the Mediterranean region is more strongly affected by summer conditions, with reduced survival of adults in warm, dry summers (Grosbois *et al.* 2006). This suggests that the latitudinal gradients in the effects of temperature and rainfall on species populations observed in Section 4.2 are not just restricted to between-species comparisons, but probably also operate within species, although more research is required to establish this. In addition, coal tit *Parus ater* survival is positively correlated with January to March temperature, linked to the reduction in invertebrate prey availability resulting from cold weather at this time (Gibb 1960). The survival of willow tits in Scandinavia, particularly juveniles, is also reduced by cold winter weather, but this can be countered by the artificial provision of food, demonstrating again that the likely mechanism of these effects is through a reduction in food availability rather than hypothermia (Lahti *et al.* 1998).

How consistent are these effects across other temperate and boreal bird species? Population changes of other European woodland birds also appear driven by a combination of winter severity and food availability. For example, the annual survival rates of wood nuthatches *Sitta europaea* in populations across Europe are reduced by cold winter weather, but increased by the size of the beech mast crop (Nilsson 1987; Wesolowski & Stawarczyk 1991; Zang & Kunze 2007), effects which appear stronger for first-year than for adult nuthatches (Matthysen 1989). As with great tits, territoriality and immigration also play an important part in the regulation of nuthatch populations (Enoksson & Nilsson 1983; Zang & Kunze 2007). Thus nuthatches, which occupy similar habitats and eat a similar range of foods to great tits, also appear similarly sensitive to weather variables. The abundance of lesser spotted woodpeckers *Dendrocopos minor* has been positively correlated with winter temperature in two of three studies in Scandinavia (Nilsson *et al.* 1992; Saarri & Mikusiński 1996; Steen *et al.* 2006). The survival of two small woodland passerines, winter wren *Troglodytes troglodytes* and Eurasian treecreeper *Certhia familiaris*, is also strongly reduced by cold weather (Peach *et al.* 1995; Newton *et al.* 1998). Because of this, an index of the wren population was adopted by the UK government as a climate change bio-indicator (Figure 4.3). It would appear from this brief review that in general, the effects of winter weather severity upon populations of small woodland birds appear relatively widespread.

This conclusion is supported by a multi-species analysis of national trends of the abundance of 13 widespread bird species in the UK derived from the Common Bird Census (CBC) with measures of winter weather (Greenwood & Baillie 1991). When analysed in a single model, the population trends of these species in woodland varied

116 · **Further mechanisms of population impacts**

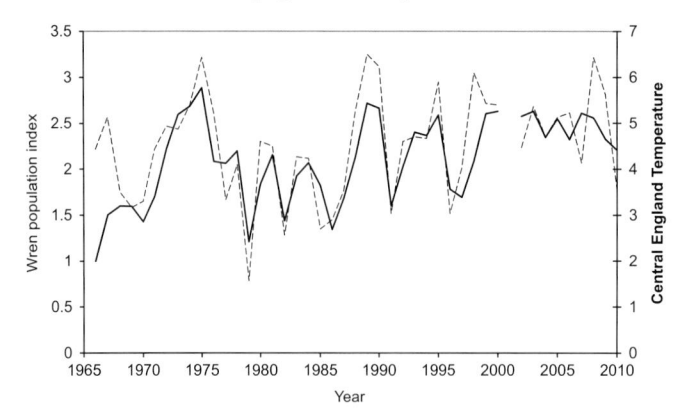

Figure 4.3 Fluctuations in an index of the breeding population of the winter wren in England (solid line) in relation to winter temperature (mean for December–February) prior to the season in which the population index was measured (dashed line). The wren index was derived by combining CBC and BBS surveys. Temperature data are for Central England from www.metoffice.gov.uk/hadobs, as published by Parker *et al.* (1992). The break in the data in 2001 reflects a year of limited surveyor access to the countryside due to the foot-and-mouth disease outbreak.

significantly in relation to winter snow cover, with individual correlations reaching statistical significance for five (winter wren, dunnock (hedge accentor), common starling, European robin *Erithacus rubecula* and song thrush *Turdus philomelos*). Interestingly, the effects of winter severity on farmland populations of the same species were greater, suggesting that these more marginal populations of species that prefer woodland and scrub were more vulnerable to severe weather, potentially as a result of the buffer effect described above. Accordingly, woodland populations were more strongly regulated by density-dependent processes. These findings are complemented by a more detailed analysis of the survival rates of ten UK woodland species using ringing data (Robinson *et al.* 2007a) which detected significant effects of winter severity in six species. The fit of Greenwood and Baillie's models is correlated with the magnitude of the winter weather effect upon survival described by Robinson *et al.*, emphasising that it is over-winter mortality which causes the large-scale fluctuations in these populations (Figure 4.4).

Variation in the magnitude of the adverse effect of the cold 1978–1979 winter among species of resident birds in the UK was found to be correlated with the species' average body weight. Small-bodied species, especially those weighing less than 20 g, suffered the largest declines (Cawthorne & Marchant 1980). This pattern may arise because small birds have higher metabolic rates and higher rates of heat loss than large birds and may also have proportionally smaller body reserves to tide them over a period with restricted opportunities to feed.

Combined with the results of studies on populations of non-woodland passerines (e.g. Sæther *et al.* 2000; Hogstad *et al.* 2003), it appears that many species are detrimentally affected by cold winter weather, which has a concomitant effect on population size – reinforcing the results of our previous analysis (Box 4.3). These species might therefore be expected to benefit from a reduction in the severity of winter weather as a result of climate

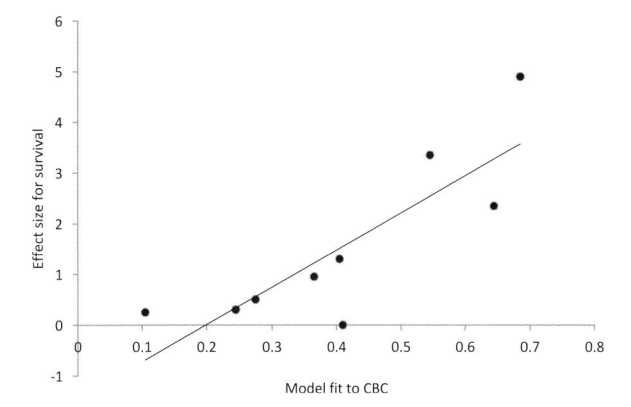

Figure 4.4 The correlation, across nine species of birds resident in the UK, between the effect of winter NAO (as a single measure of winter weather) on survival rates obtained by Robinson *et al.* (2007a) and the effect of winter weather on year-on-year population change from Greenwood & Bailllie (1991). The effect size of Robinson *et al.* (% survival rate caused by 1 SD of NAO) is the average of effects for adult and first-year birds (y-axis), whilst the r^2 value of Greenwood & Baillie is the average of the effects for farmland and woodland CBC plots (x-axis). The ordinary least squares regression, shown by the line, is $y = -1.46 + 7.34x$, $r = 0.84$.

change. For many north temperate resident species, cold winter temperatures, or the duration of periods of snow cover, are currently likely to be limiting the northern extent of the geographical range, and therefore recent warming and amelioration of winter temperature may have facilitated population increases and range expansion (Chapter 5). The pattern of population fluctuations shown for grey heron in Figure 4.1 may be widespread, suggesting that one of the most widespread impacts of recent warming on bird populations may have been population increases in many residents and short-distance migrants across mid- and high latitudes.

The negative effects of cold winters on bird populations in this region are widespread. Annual changes in abundance or annual survival rates of a wide range of shorebirds (Charadrii) are also positively correlated with winter temperature (Table S4.1[*]). Thus, variation in northern lapwing *Vanellus vanellus* (Peach *et al.* 1994; Catchpole *et al.* 1999), common redshank *Tringa totanus* (Insley *et al.* 1997) and Eurasian golden plover (Piersma *et al.* 2005) annual survival rates in north-west Europe are linked to winter weather. It is likely that the mechanism for increased mortality during cold winters is again through reduced access to food resources, which in the case of shorebirds are generally surface-active or subsurface invertebrates, many of which are detected by sight. For example, both lapwing and golden plover feed on soil invertebrates such as leatherjackets (tipulid larvae) and earthworms (Pearce-Higgins *et al.* 2003b; Gillings & Sutherland 2007), which become inactive or burrow deeper when the ground is frozen. Similarly, the reduction in redshank survival in cold, wet winters probably occurs as a direct result of the mudflat surface freezing, or because rainfall reduces the foraging efficiency of intertidal shorebirds

---

[*] See online material.

(Goss-Custard 1970; Kelly *et al.* 2002). Immature birds are again particularly sensitive to these effects, because they have smaller fat reserves (Swann & Etheridge 1989; Insley *et al.* 1997) and may be excluded from the best foraging areas by dominant adults (Groves 1978; Goss-Custard 1980). Cold and hungry birds may also be forced to forage in more dangerous habitats than at other times, in order to maximise food intake, leading to increased risk of predation (Creswell & Whitfield 2008).

Waterfowl can be similarly affected by cold temperatures and icing of water bodies and intertidal areas, although perhaps not to the same extent as shorebirds (Table S4.1[*]). The abundance of five of ten species of waterfowl that breed in south-west Finland was significantly reduced by cold winter weather, whilst four of the remainder showed similar non-significant tendencies (Rönkä *et al.* 2005). The survival of common coot *Fulica atra* in the Netherlands was negatively correlated with the number of ice days (Cavé & Visser 1985), which reduced access to underwater plant and animal food, and caused starvation (Visser 1978). We have already described the effects of winter cold on grey heron populations in the UK (Figure 4.1). These effects are not restricted to sub-surface feeders reliant on access to open water. Even the survival of some geese, which feed on terrestrial plants, may be reduced by poor winter weather (Kéry *et al.* 2006).

Raptors and owls also tend to suffer reduced survival during severe winters, with an overall significant positive effect of non-breeding temperature upon both Accipitriformes (hawks and eagles) and Strigiformes (owls) (Table S4.1[*]). Again, the main mechanism for these effects appears to be through snow cover reducing access to prey. Thus, the survival rates of barn owls *Tyto alba* in Switzerland were negatively correlated with the number of days of deep (> 5 cm) snow cover in a winter which reduced their access to their small mammal prey. Barn owl populations crash severely after harsh winters because of the combined effects of low levels of recruitment of young birds and very high losses of territorial adults (Altwegg *et al.* 2006). Similar detrimental effects of cold snowy weather have been found in common kestrels *Falco tinnunculus* for the same reasons. Although larger common buzzard *Buteo buteo* and northern goshawks *Accipiter gentalis* appear to be less sensitive to winter weather effects, severe winter weather may still affect their demography if it reduces prey populations (Kostrzewa & Kostrzewa 1991; Fairhust & Bechard 2005; Moser & Garton 2009). Survival rates of spotted owls *Strix occidentalis* are reduced during cold, wet springs, which reduces hunting efficiency at a time of high energetic demands (Franklin *et al.* 2000). Thus, effects on owls and raptors can occur through either the direct effect of snow in preventing the access to prey on the ground, by other effects of weather on hunting success or efficiency or indirectly by severe weather reducing prey abundance.

Birds are not entirely at the mercy of the weather, because they have a number of strategies available to them to cope with severe conditions. Most widespread of these is the use that individuals make of fat reserves as an insurance against periods of low food availability caused by bad weather. As might be expected, the size of these reserves, as measured by weight, tends to be greatest at high latitudes (Castro *et al.* 1992) and to show short-term increases in response to cold weather, at least while food resources remain

---

[*] See online material.

available (Pienkowski *et al.* 1979; Lima 1986; Summers *et al.* 1992; MacLeod *et al.* 2005). Not only does fat provide additional insulation against the cold, but also buffers individuals against the effects of starvation in the event of prolonged inaccessibility to food. However, the fact that individuals do not continually maintain maximal fat reserves during the winter suggests that there are disadvantages to being fat, or that some may be unable to do so. In some species the risk of being caught by a predator is increased by high body mass because of reduced agility in flight (MacLeod *et al.* 2007). They face a trade-off between being fat enough to insure against starvation in cold weather and agile enough to escape predators (Gosler *et al.* 1995; MacLeod *et al.* 2005). Conversely, 'interrupted foraging species' appear vulnerable to predation-related disturbance which reduces their ability to maintain adequate body weight in cold weather. These species tend to exhibit increases in body mass in response to higher predation risk as additional insurance against cold weather. The adoption of these strategies may vary with environmental quality (MacLeod *et al.* 2007), and therefore with future climate change.

An alternative strategy of ensuring adequate food reserves is through food hoarding, where stored food is preserved by cold temperatures and accessed during extended periods of food inaccessibility. This strategy is employed particularly by species living at high latitudes with cold winters, as in the case of the Eurasian pygmy owls *Glaucidium passerinum*, which are too small to penetrate deep snow to catch small mammals, but cache prey in advance of heavy snow (Halonen *et al.* 2007). Although it works well in the cold, such hoarding species may be vulnerable to climate change impacts, as warmer winter weather may increase the perishability of cached food. As a strategy, it is particularly prevalent in tits and corvids. The loss of cached food in warm autumns has been implicated in a decline of grey jays at the southern edge of its range (Waite & Strickland 2006). It is interesting to speculate whether similar effects may occur in a wider range of hoarding species. Alternatively, with milder weather, these species may adapt their behaviour and rely less on cached food.

Instead of staying put during cold weather and relying on body reserves or cached food for survival, individuals may alternatively undertake cold-weather movements in an attempt to find areas where food resources are less restricted. Such movements are widely employed, particularly by a range of short- and medium-distance migrants (e.g. Kirby & Lack 1993; Burton 2000). However, they are likely to be energetically expensive and therefore can only be undertaken successfully by individuals in good condition.

It is clear from this assessment of the current literature and our previous analysis (Box 4.3) that a wide range of species are at risk of high mortality during cold winter weather, whilst others are less vulnerable. If the long-term trend towards warmer winters in Europe (e.g. Jenkins *et al.* 2008) continue as expected, the species and populations most vulnerable to population limitation through winter mortality may be amongst those most likely to benefit from future warming. The survival rate of many high-latitude residents is strongly determined by overwinter conditions, and particularly the effects that such conditions have upon food availability. This provides the causal mechanism that underpins the generally positive link between temperature and bird populations at high latitudes (Box 4.2).

Although much of the mortality of resident and short-distance migrant species that breed at temperate and high latitudes occurs during the winter, for some species, the breeding season can also be a difficult time. The food of song thrushes in the UK includes soil-dwelling earthworms (Gruar *et al.* 2003), whose availability is strongly determined by soil moisture (Peach *et al.* 2004a). Under dry conditions, the worms tend to be inactive or too deep in the soil to be available to the thrushes. Spatial variation in a decline in song thrush populations in the UK has been attributed to the extent of under-field drainage on farmland, which promotes the rapid drying of soils (Peach *et al.* 2004b). Variation among years in the survival of adult and young song thrushes was found to be negatively affected by the occurrence of summer droughts which makes their prey less available (Robinson *et al.* 2004; Robinson *et al.* 2007a). Reductions in first-year survival, and perhaps also adult survival, were associated with a decline in population size (Robinson *et al.* 2004; Baillie *et al.* 2009). Although the long-term population changes were not closely related to changes in the weather, it is likely that an increasing trend to warmer, drier summers will be detrimental to survival rates and population size of this species. Eurasian blackbird survival rates have also been similarly reduced by summer drought (Robinson *et al.* 2007a), whilst a similar correlation exists between annual fluctuations in ring ouzel populations and summer temperature (Beale *et al.* 2006a), probably mediated through reductions in adult or first-year survival (Sim *et al.* 2011). Thrushes which feed on subsurface invertebrates may therefore be vulnerable to drought, accounting for the generally positive relationship between breeding season precipitation and thrush demography identified by our meta-analysis (Table S4.4[*]).

4.3.2 Productivity

We will now examine the climatic factors which influence breeding success, and the effect this has on population size. To begin, we return to the woodland passerines with altricial young, like the great tit. Many of these are insectivorous during the breeding season, preying particularly on caterpillars (Krištín & Patočka 1997), and tend to produce most chicks when such prey are most abundant (Hogstad 2005). As previously described in Section 3.4.1, the condition and survival of great tits is positively correlated with caterpillar abundance (Visser *et al.* 1998; Visser *et al.* 2006). Aside from the detrimental effects of phenological mismatch associated with warming, which reduces prey availability, the fledgling success of both blue and great tits tends to be positively correlated with May temperature, when they are provisioning their broods (Solonen 2001). This positive effect of spring temperature on productivity is also seen for a range of other insectivorous birds (Sokolov 1999). For example, the growth and survival of Eurasian chaffinch nestlings is increased by dry, warm weather (Cramp & Perrins 1994; Leech & Crick 2007). Indeed, in 2012 where April and June rainfall in England and Wales was the highest on record, chaffinch productivity fell by 58% compared to the previous five years (British Trust for Ornithology 2012), Similarly, the productivity of both middle-spotted

---

[*] See online material.

Dendrocopos medius (Pasinelli 2001) and white-backed *D. leucotos* (Hogstad & Stenberg 1997) woodpeckers is also related to weather conditions during chick rearing.

Despite these specific effects, Bradbury *et al.* (2003) argued that in general, the magnitude of weather effects on the breeding success of altricial passerines may be quite small except in years with unusual weather, because the adults can compensate for poor conditions by working harder to raise their young. In these species, which tend to have moderately low annual adult survival rates, there is a trade-off between adult survival prospects and current reproductive success. It may be worth the parents investing more effort foraging to buffer their young against low temperatures and poor weather conditions during the breeding season, even at the potential cost of a reduced chance of surviving to the next year.

In contrast, there is a wealth of literature on the importance of weather in determining the breeding success of precocial species with mobile chicks. For example, the growth rates of red knot *Calidris canutus* (Schekkerman *et al.* 2003), Eurasian golden plover (Pearce-Higgins & Yalden 2002), northern lapwing, common redshank, black-tailed godwit *Limosa limosa* (Beintema & Visser 1989), Eurasian dotterel *Eudromias morinellus* (Thomson 1994) and corncrake *Crex crex* (Tyler & Green 2004) are all positively correlated with daily measures of temperature, whilst measures of productivity of common sandpipers (Pearce-Higgins *et al.* 2009c), dunlin (Beale *et al.* 2006b), red knot and ruddy turnstone (Meltofte *et al.* 2007c), mallard (Krapu *et al.* 1983), Eurasian wigeon *Anas penelope* (Gardarsson & Einarsson), black grouse (Zbinden & Salvioni 2004), rock ptarmigan (Watson *et al.* 1998) and western capercaillie (Moss *et al.* 2001) are each positively correlated with temperature across the breeding season. On average, studies of Charadriiformes (shorebirds, gulls, terns and auks) and Galliformes (gamebirds), which have precocial or semi-precocial young, provide evidence for stronger positive effects of breeding season temperature and negative effects of breeding season precipitation on population processes than do studies of passerines with their altricial young (Table S4.2[*]).

Rainfall during the breeding season may have a similar detrimental effect on breeding productivity to that of cold temperatures, although the two effects are often difficult to disentangle. Negative effects of rainfall on productivity are particularly apparent for grouse species (Moss *et al.* 2001; Summers *et al.* 2004; Novoa *et al.* 2008), ducks such as mallard (Krapu *et al.* 1983), common eider (Mendenhall & Milne 1985) and Eurasian wigeon (Gardarsson & Einarsson 1997) and corncrake (Tyler & Green 2004), again supporting the consistent negative effects of breeding season precipitation on these taxa (Table S4.4[*]).

This weather-related variation in breeding success may occur through a range of mechanisms. Firstly, there may be direct effects of weather on chick condition, as individuals are likely to have to spend more energy on thermoregulation during periods of cold and wet weather. Secondly, and related to this, during cold and wet conditions, chicks will require more brooding from the parents, reducing the time available for the adult to forage (in altricial species) or for the chicks to feed for themselves (in precocial species). This will lower the rate of food intake by the chicks. Thirdly, as the activity and

[*] See online material.

Table 4.2 *Summary of the likely mechanisms which reduce the productivity of bird species during cold, wet weather, and an assessment of whether parental compensation is likely*

	Hypothermia	Reduced foraging time	Reduced prey abundance	Parental compensation?
Precocial insectivore	X	X	X	
Precocial piscivore	X	X		X
Semi-precocial	X	X		X
Semi-altricial	X	X		X
Altricial insectivore		X	X	X
Altricial granivore		X		X

apparent abundance of a range of invertebrates is enhanced during warm weather (Pearce-Higgins & Yalden 2004; Høye & Forchhammer 2008); cold and wet weather may reduce prey availability and again lower foraging efficiency. Fourthly, cold and hungry chicks may be more vulnerable to predation, either because they are more vocal or the adults less attentive (e.g. Mendenhall & Milne 1985), although as predation is the proximate cause of many breeding failures, this interaction is difficult to disentangle.

Examining these mechanisms helps us understand the differential effects of breeding season weather on different species. We might expect that species in which the chicks eat invertebrate prey would be more strongly affected by poor weather conditions than those with other diets because the abundance and availability of invertebrates is more directly affected by weather (Table 4.2). For example, wood nuthatch productivity is enhanced by weather conditions that increase the abundance of caterpillars, their main prey during chick rearing (Wesolowski & Stawarczyk 1991), whilst the productivity of the blue-throated black warbler, which also feeds on caterpillars, is reduced during periods of heavy rain (Rodenhouse & Holmes 1992). The foraging success of great tits feeding on spiders is reduced during cold weather because of the spiders' reduced activity (Avery & Krebs 1984), whilst the productivity of snow buntings *Plectrophenax nivalis* is positively related to temperature as a result of increased invertebrate activity (Hoset *et al.* 2004). An example of interactions between food availability and predation is illustrated by Evans *et al.* (1997), who studied the cirl bunting *Emberiza cirlus*. Nestlings which were in poor body condition because of food shortage were more likely to be taken by nest predators than those in good condition.

Precocial chicks appear even more vulnerable to these processes, (Table 4.2) particularly when young (e.g. Pearce-Higgins & Yalden 2002). Because they forage for themselves, they are more directly exposed to ambient weather conditions than altricial nestlings. Precocial chicks must rely on their own, relatively unpractised foraging capabilities and therefore have less capacity to avoid or adapt to adverse weather. They are also highly vulnerable to predation and the interactions between predation and weather (e.g. Grant *et al.* 1999; Summers *et al.* 2004). Finally, precocial chicks have a higher metabolic requirement than equivalent altricial chicks (Schekkerman & Visser 2001), due to the costs of locomotion. These differences probably account for the greater sensitivity of the productivity of precocial charadriiform and galliform birds to temperature than altricial passeriformes (Tables S4.2*, S4.4*). Such impacts from weather are best seen in Arctic breeding shorebirds which breed successfully within the short summer, despite the cold temperatures. The chicks have high metabolic requirements in order to grow rapidly and maintain body temperature in the cold (Schekkerman et al. 2003). They survive by virtue of good insulation and thermoregulatory capabilities and by achieving thermal independence at a younger age than their temperate counterparts (Koskimies & Lahti 1964, Steen et al. 1989). These requirements are fuelled by the super-abundance of invertebrate prey in the Arctic summer (Schekkerman & Visser 2001). These birds breed on the edge of physiological and environmental constraints, and therefore it is unsurprising that the growth and survival of Arctic breeding shorebird chicks remain particularly vulnerable to unusually poor weather (Schekkerman et al. 2003). They are also likely to be particularly vulnerable to any future reductions in invertebrate abundance as a result of climate change (see below).

Semi-altricial raptor chicks, which have limited mobility and require parental nourishment and attendance, might be expected to be relatively impervious to weather effects by virtue of their size, and the fact that the mother attends the nest to brood and guard them. However, they appear to experience reduced survival in cold and wet weather. For example, the productivity of both common kestrels and northern goshawks breeding in Germany is positively correlated with temperature, whilst that of buzzards is negatively correlated with rainfall. These effects are greatest during the first two weeks after hatching, when chicks are covered in down and have the lowest thermoregulatory capabilities (Kostrzewa & Kostrzewa 1990; see also Village 1986). The effects of poor weather during breeding upon reproductive success have also been documented in red-tailed hawks *Buteo jamaicensis* (Adamcik et al. 1979), lesser kestrels *Falco naumanni* (Rodriguez & Bustamante 2003), American kestrels *F. sparverius* (Dawson & Bortolotti 2000), black kites *Milvus milgrans* (Sergio 2003), hen harriers *Circus cyaneus* (Redpath et al. 2002) and bald eagles *Haliaeetus leucocephalus* (Swenson et al. 1986). These effects can vary within a species, with northern populations tending to benefit from relatively warm and dry conditions, whilst in more southerly Mediterranean-type climates, extremes of high temperature and drought are detrimental to productivity (Steenhof et al. 1997; Watson 1997; Redpath et al. 2002). Thus, the latitudinal gradients described at the start of the chapter are again not just apparent between species, but also within a species' range.

Given that raptors in northern and temperate zones forage more actively in warmer weather, at least part of the benefit is likely to relate to improved foraging conditions, particularly for soaring species which benefit most from the existence of strong thermals. However, wet weather reduces the ability of a wide range of raptor species to forage, including black kite, American kestrel and hen harrier (Dawson & Bortolotti 2000; Redpath et al. 2002; Sergio 2003), which is likely to have considerable implications for the provisioning and survival of their chicks. Therefore, despite there probably being little direct effect of cold or wet weather upon the abundance of mammalian or avian prey, the breeding success of raptors appears vulnerable to such weather. This may be partly as a result of direct chilling effects on young chicks, though the mother is usually available to

---

* See online material.

Box 4.6 · *Modelling potential effects of catastrophic events on populations*

We used a simple population model of female birds in which survival (s) varied randomly from 0.5 to 0.74 with a logit-normal distribution to examine the potential impact of catastrophic events on populations. Female recruitment to the breeding population (r) in year t_{+1}, per adult female in year t, varied randomly with a normal distribution from 0 to 1.25. Population growth was then given by $n_{t+1} = n_t s + n_t r$. The model was free-running and fluctuated randomly from a starting population of 100 (the baseline). From this baseline, where the probability of extinction ($n_t < 1$) was $< 1\%$ over 50 years, we then compared the consequences of reducing the starting population by 80% to 20, introducing randomly occurring catastrophic events which meant there was absolute breeding failure with a 20% probability in any one year, and a combination of the two. The population exposed to a high frequency of catastrophic breeding failure was much more likely to experience extinction than the small population. The greatest probability of extinction was however associated with both a small initial population and high frequency of catastrophic breeding failure, indicating that potential interactions between anthropogenic pressures on populations and increased frequency of severe events as a result of climate change may exacerbate the threat faced by bird populations.

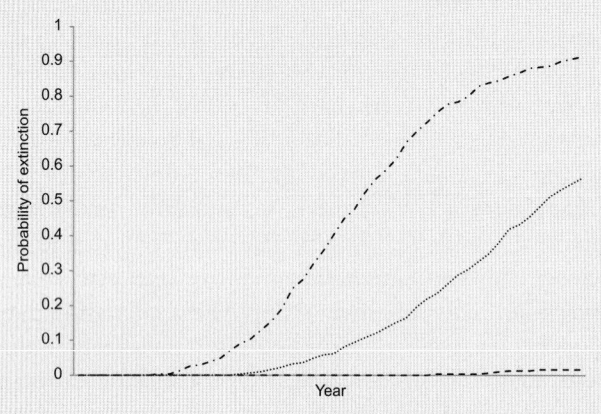

Box 4.6 The probability of extinction of a population under the three scenarios of reduced population size (dashed line), catastrophic breeding failure (dotted line) and both combined (dashed and dotted line) over 50 years.

brood them, at least early in life. The effects of weather on foraging opportunities for their parents is probably the more frequent mechanism (Table 4.2).

Aside from these effects of mean temperature and rainfall on breeding success, birds may also be vulnerable to extreme events during the breeding season (e.g. Holland & Yalden 1995; Boyd & Piersma 2001). Although most populations are able to cope with such periodic weather perturbations, catastrophic events can cause extinction in already small populations. The increased potential for extreme weather to occur as a result of climate change may therefore interact with other pressures to increase the likelihood of entire populations being lost (Box 4.6).

An example of this principle is given by an analysis of great bittern *Botaurus stellaris* populations in the UK, which had been so reduced by freshwater wetland habitat loss and deterioration that only 11 territorial males were present across seven sites in 1997 (Wotton *et al.* 2009a). The most productive three sites, responsible for two-thirds of breeding attempts, were on the Norfolk and Suffolk coast (Smith & Tyler 1993), and extremely vulnerable to saline inundation associated with rising sea levels and increased frequency of storm surges. Indeed, repeated storm surges in December 2005, November 2006 and November 2007 resulted in significant saline inundation of these coastal reserves, changes in habitat and fish populations and subsequent reductions in bittern productivity. Depending on the frequency and severity of such inundation, population models indicated that storm surges could further drive the long-term decline of the species were it to remain so restricted in range (Gilbert *et al.* 2010). Inundation during the breeding season may also flood nests; five were lost at Minsmere on the Suffolk coast in 2008 in response to heavy rain.

Flooding of nesting attempts as a result of heavy rainfall has also been a problem for black-tailed godwits breeding on lowland wet grassland in the UK. Their main breeding site was the Ouse Washes, where wet grassland of high conservation value has been maintained under low-intensity management. The grassland has been protected because it acts as a temporary store of storm water to protect valuable agricultural land from flooding. A marked increase in the frequency of spring and summer flooding has caused repeated breeding failure on the site, leading to population decline and forcing birds to breed on poorer quality farmland habitat nearby (Ratcliffe *et al.* 2005). The breeding population of this species increased at a nearby site where summer flooding was infrequent. We shall return to these examples in Chapter 7 when we consider potential conservation responses to these impacts.

In addition to flooding, storms may cause catastrophic habitat damage, which may lead to the loss or abandonment of particular breeding sites. For example, Hurricanes Rita and Katrina caused significant damage to heronries in the southern United States in 2005. This resulted in a significant redistribution of birds, with the abandonment of sites that suffered high wind speeds and losses of trees. However, in contrast to the example of the small population of bitterns in the UK, there existed an extensive network of colonies in the area, and individuals were able to move from damaged to undamaged colonies. Hence, some colonies vanished or declined, although others expanded (Leberg *et al.* 2007). Although the consequences of the hurricanes appeared locally catastrophic for particular sites, when examined on a larger scale there was little overall impact on heron populations in the wider area. This example further emphasises the fact that large populations distributed across an extensive network of sites will tend to be more resilient to locally catastrophic events than small and highly fragmented populations (Box 4.6), a point emphasised from a conservation perspective in Sections 7.5 and 7.7.

4.3.3 General effects summarised

To summarise our appraisal for Arctic, boreal and temperate species so far, reduced food availability appears to be a key determinant of reduced chick survival during periods of cold, wet weather, although less foraging time, increased thermoregulatory demands and increased predation risk may also contribute to this. The most vulnerable species to cold and wet weather are likely to be those whose food abundance or foraging ability is heavily weather dependent (such as insectivorous species which experience reduced prey activity or abundance in response to poor weather, and raptors unable to hunt their prey during wet conditions). Given their additional energetic requirements and reduced ability to compensate, precocial species appear to be the most susceptible to these pressures. In terms of mortality, the species which appear to suffer the greatest losses during cold winter weather are ground-feeding species for which frost and snow reduce access to their food (Box 4.3). Many studies also highlight a particular high risk of mortality associated with cold weather in early spring, just prior to breeding. On the basis of this review it would appear that the majority of species therefore experience both higher survival rates in mild, snow-free winters and greater productivity in warm, dry summers but yet occupy cooler climates. We shall attempt to solve this conundrum in the next section.

4.3.4 How warming can be detrimental

The issue is well illustrated by a review of the literature documenting correlations between the demography or abundance of bird species which occur in the UK uplands (Pearce-Higgins 2011b). Eighteen of the 28 studies collated found significant evidence for positive effects of temperature on population processes, with only four appearing to show significant negative effects. Why, then, do upland birds tend to occupy cold environments but apparently benefit from warmer than average weather?

Some of the answer comes from studies which show evidence of a hump-shaped relationship between productivity and temperature. For example, annual variation in the productivity of Arctic breeding dunlin peaks at a mean temperature of around 11 °C within a range of values from 8 °C to 13 °C (Beale *et al.* 2006b). The growth of lapwing chicks, although most rapid on warm and dry days, is reduced by long spells of dry weather, which cause earthworms, the main prey of large chicks in the Dutch meadows, to become unavailable (Beintema & Visser 1989; Beintema *et al.* 1991). Because avian productivity is so strongly linked to food abundance (Arcese & Smith 1988; Marshall *et al.* 2002), understanding the links between weather, climate and food ability, as illustrated by the example of lapwing chicks above, is likely to be necessary to accurately predict the likely effects of climate change upon populations. We hypothesise that the effect of climate upon food availability is likely to be an important factor influencing a species' sensitivity to climate change.

This possibility is well illustrated by the Eurasian golden plover, which has a northern Palaearctic distribution, occupying open heaths, peatlands and tundra habitats from the UK northwards and eastwards to western Russia. As with many of the examples outlined above, the growth and survival of golden plover chicks is enhanced by warm temperatures during the growing period of the chicks (Pearce-Higgins & Yalden 2002). It is also affected by the abundance of invertebrate prey, especially adult craneflies (Tipulidae) (Pearce-Higgins & Yalden 2004). In good years, these insects are superabundant for a short period in May and early June (Box 3.1), particularly on warm days, and golden plovers breed most successfully when they are able to synchronise their breeding with this food peak (Pearce-Higgins *et al.* 2005). On average, the survival of chicks over the first 10 days of life is low, at about 20% (Pearce-Higgins & Yalden 2003a), but is higher if chicks hatch during warm, dry conditions, for all the reasons outlined above. They will require less brooding, spend less energy keeping warm and there will be more food for them to eat. It would therefore seem that increasing summer temperatures as a result of climate change would be sure to benefit the golden plovers.

4.3 Arctic, boreal and temperate regions · 127

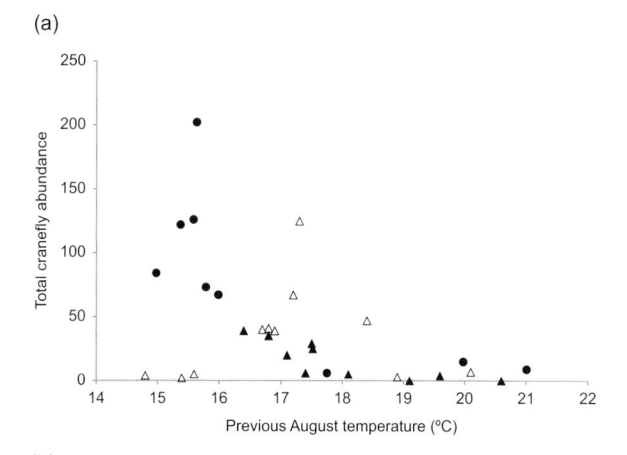

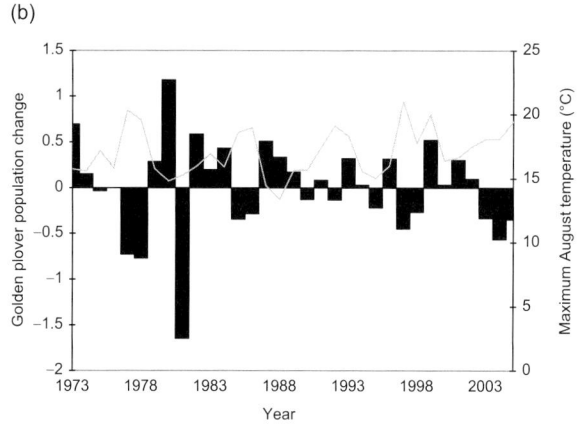

Figure 4.5 (a) Correlations between cranefly abundance (y-axis) and August temperature in the previous year (x-axis) for three upland areas in the UK denoted by different symbols. Dark symbols indicate blanket peatland sites, triangles indicate Scottish sites sampled by pitfall traps and circles, Pennine sites sampled by line-transects. (b) The log-ratio of change in the golden plover population at Snake Summit (black bars) compared with maximum August temperature (grey line) with a two-year lag ($r^2 = 0.14$ or 0.37 if the outlier from 1981 is removed). Figures redrawn from Fig. 1 and Fig. 2 of Pearce-Higgins *et al.* (2010) respectively.

However, after emergence, adult craneflies lay their eggs in the top layer of the soil. The eggs hatch during July into young larvae, which require moist conditions to survive. If the weather in late summer is hot and dry, the surface layer of the soil dries out, and many of the larvae die (Coulson 1962). Surviving larvae overwinter in the soil, pupate and hatch the following spring, when spatial patterns in emergence are also closely related to soil moisture (Carroll *et al.* 2011). As a result, there is a strong negative effect of August temperature on the abundance of craneflies that subsequently emerge (Figure 4.5), with up to a 95% reduction in cranefly abundance in springs that follow the hottest Augusts (Pearce-Higgins *et al.* 2010). Because of the close link between cranefly abundance and golden plover productivity, at least in peatland habitats, warm conditions in August will reduce golden plover breeding success in the following year, and lead to a subsequent decline in the population in the year after that because of a lack of new recruits (Figure 4.5b). This example illustrates that, despite the immediate positive effects of increasing spring temperature upon both cranefly activity and golden plover chick growth rates, as well as the effect of warm winters on golden plover overwinter survival rates (Piersma et al. 2005), increasing temperatures are likely to ultimately limit golden plover populations as a result of detrimental effects on their food supply.

In the case of the golden plover, the negative effects of warming as a result of reductions in prey abundance may be extended over longer time periods through gradual reductions in habitat suitability. In the UK, golden plovers mostly breed in habitats that are maintained as open areas with low ground vegetation and few bushes or trees by grazing by domesticated livestock and deer and fires deliberately set by humans (Pearce-Higgins & Grant 2006; Grant & Pearce-Higgins 2012). However, across much of the species' global range, golden plovers breed in open habitats, such as tundra and alpine heaths, in which climatic conditions are largely responsible for preventing the invasion of bushes and trees. Current climatic change is expected to cause the spread of scrub and forest into alpine heath and tundra, for example through reductions in the magnitude of lemming cycles (see below; Oloffson et al. 2009). Golden plovers avoid forested areas and have suffered population declines near to artificially planted forests in the UK (Amar et al. 2011). Hence, the spread of scrub and forest into tundra will probably lead to the loss of golden plover populations in areas where it occurs. This may be because of effects of forest spread on demographic rates, but too little is known about the effects of nearby forests on golden plover survival and reproduction to be sure how this would happen. One possibility is that forests may harbour higher densities of plover egg and chick predators, such as foxes and crows, and provide perches from which avian predators can hunt (Fletcher et al. 2010). If this is the case, the spread of forests and scrub into tundra might reduce productivity below the level required to sustain the local population. Adults may also avoid breeding close to trees or in areas with high predator populations.

The golden plover example illustrates the likely complexities of climate change impacts on birds, and the need for a good ecological knowledge. Relevant studies include investigations of lagged or long-term effects of climatic change on other species which provide birds with food and cover, or deprecate them or their eggs and young. Although there are few other documented examples of such multi-trophic effects on terrestrial birds as yet (in contrast to the marine environment discussed in Section 4.6), this is likely to be an important avenue for future research. For example, given the widespread importance of craneflies to a wide range of other northern and upland bird species (Buchanan et al. 2006; Pearce-Higgins 2010), the effects outlined above for the food supply of golden plover chicks are likely to apply to other species too. The growth and survival of red grouse (Park et al. 2001) and snow bunting (Hussell 1972) chicks, and the condition of adult Eurasian dotterel (Holt et al. 2002), are all positively correlated with cranefly abundance. Annual fluctuations in red grouse breeding success are also negatively correlated with August temperature in the previous year, as expected were they related to cranefly availability for their chicks (Fletcher et al. 2013). More broadly, recent trends in upland bird populations in the UK are most negative for species which rely on drought-sensitive prey such as craneflies (Pearce-Higgins 2010). Similarly, red-billed chough *Pyrrhocorax pyrrhocorax* populations breeding on the west coast of Scotland may also be limited by cranefly abundance, although here, the choughs feed primarily upon cranefly larvae in the soil (leatherjackets). The first-year survival of choughs is strongly linked to winter leatherjacket abundance (Reid *et al.* 2008), variation in which is a key determinant of population growth rate (Reid *et al.* 2004). These craneflies are larger species than those on blanket bog and emerge later in the summer. As a result, their abundance is positively correlated with autumn soil moisture, which is affected by rainfall, again matching the period when they exist as early larval instars and are vulnerable to dessication (McCracken & Foster 1995; Reid *et al.* 2008).

It seems as if an understanding of the effects of climate change on a species cannot always be derived from simple short-term correlations between temperature, rainfall and other weather variables with estimates of survival, productivity or population growth. This is a limitation of our analysis in Section 4.3, which included the results from many such studies. Given the potential importance of lagged effects of climatic change on food resources and other factors affecting productivity and survival, an understanding of species' ecology is required in order to account for potential effects and interactions between those same weather variables and the abundance of other species. Especially important are likely to be effects on prey populations and the availability of food. Where correlations between those resources and weather are opposite to direct correlations between weather and demography, the latter analysis may be misleading and fail to detect potentially important effects, as illustrated for the golden plover.

Another example where warming may reduce food availability for a bird species is the South Hills crossbill, part of the red crossbill *Loxia curvirostra* species complex endemic to southern Idaho in the United States. Recent studies revealed a 60% population decline in the population as a result of low adult survival. Survival was strongly negatively correlated with temperature, and it appears that recent warming has reduced the availability of an important food, lodgepole pine *Pinus contorta* seeds (Santisteban *et al.* 2012). If such warming continues, then the long-term persistence of this population may be threatened, because as with other crossbills, it appears tied to this one seed crop.

Changes in the abundance of food resources are not the only way in which negative effects of climate change will occur. There are many other alternative mechanisms by which climate change may impact upon species, as we outlined at the start of the chapter (Table 4.1). Let us now examine the evidence for some of these other mechanisms being important.

Continuing the theme of trophic interactions, it is possible that impacts of climate change on the abundance or behaviour of predatory species may also have a significant effect on populations of their prey. In the absence of climate change, there are examples where increased rates of predation have been implicated in declines of bird species of conservation concern, whether a result of introduced non-native mammal species (O'Donnell 1996) or increasing populations of generalist predators (Grant *et al.* 1999). Indeed, predation has been suggested to be one of the ecological factors which determines the lower latitudinal limit of species' ranges (Pienkowski 1984), and therefore climate-driven changes in predation rates, either in response to changes in the abundance or behaviour of predators may affect the distribution of a species.

Earlier sea ice breakup in the Hudson Bay has led to a shift in the foraging behaviour of polar bears *Ursus maritimus* away from spring sea ice, where adult bears previously focussed on ringed seal *Pusa hispida* pups, to foraging onshore. This means that they now impact the breeding of birds at Cape Churchill on the edge of Hudson Bay. This has resulted in

130 · Further mechanisms of population impacts

significant predation events on both snow geese and Brünnichs guillemots in the area (Rockwell & Gormezano 2009; Smith *et al.* 2010). Similar changes in bear behaviour have also occurred on Svalbard and have adversely affected brent goose *Branta bernicla* productivity (Madsen *et al.* 1998). If sustained, the magnitude of this predation is such that it is likely to have a significant impact upon the long-term survival of these colonies. For example, in the absence of other changes, snow goose productivity at Hudson Bay is projected to decline sufficiently to cause a 90% population decline over 25 years (Rockwell *et al.* 2010). However, in addition to this change in foraging behaviour, the Hudson Bay polar bear population has also suffered recent population declines which are projected to continue as a result of future warming (Stirling *et al.* 1999; Regehr *et al.* 2007; Molnár *et al.* 2011). In the long term, future polar bear population declines may potentially counteract any likely increase in predation as a result of changes in bear distribution.

Climate change may have wider impacts on predation in the Arctic system, where some of the most rapid warming has occurred in recent years. The tundra ecosystem is classically characterised by three- to five-year cycles in lemming (*Lemmus* spp. and *Dicrostonyx* spp.) populations. These cycles and their underlying causes have been long studied in the scientific literature, and appear largely under top-down control by predators (Box 4.7), potentially moderated by additional interactions with the quality of plant food (Ims & Fuglei

---

Box 4.7 · *Climate change, lemming cycles and Arctic birds*

There is good evidence for some lemming species of top-down control by predators (Gilg *et al.* 2003; Ims & Fuglei 2005). Although the precise details vary between systems and species, this may work as follows. In years when lemmings are abundant, they provide a super-abundant food for resident mammalian predators such as the stoat and Arctic fox and birds such as long-tailed skuas, all of which are present in most years. These species usually eat a wide variety of prey, but when lemmings are plentiful they switch to feeding mainly on them (the functional response). High lemming densities also attract predators from elsewhere to settle, such as snowy owls (year *a* in the figure). These establish air superiority around their nests and chase away or deter both avian and mammalian predators, providing incidental protection for waterfowl and shorebirds nesting nearby. In good lemming years, predators feed almost exclusively on lemmings and reproduce very well. This leads to especially marked population increases of stoats, whose populations closely track the lemming population, but with a time lag (the numerical response). The increase in the stoat population, exacerbated by increased predation from the other species as they cue in on lemmings as an abundant food source, driven by their functional response, imposes top-down control on the lemming population (year *b*). In response, the lemming population then crashes. Snowy owls are forced to leave the area because of the lack of food, and the other predators switch back to alternative prey, such as breeding waterfowl (particularly in the case of Arctic foxes) and shorebirds (in the case of skuas and stoats). These nests are no longer protected by snowy owls (year *c*). As a result of the combined effects of high numbers of foxes and stoats, which built up during the good lemming years and dietary switching to other prey, waterbirds and shorebirds suffer significant nest and chick predation in these years of low lemming abundance (Summers & Underhill 1987; Blomqvist *et al.* 2002). Predator populations, particularly of stoats, then decline due to a lack of food as the biomass densities of migratory breeding shorebirds and ducks do not match those of good

Box 4.7 (cont.)

lemming years, and are only available for a short window of time in the summer, whilst the functional response of the other species also means they increasingly focus on other non-lemming prey. This allows the lemming population to recover, and the whole process repeats itself again (year *d*).

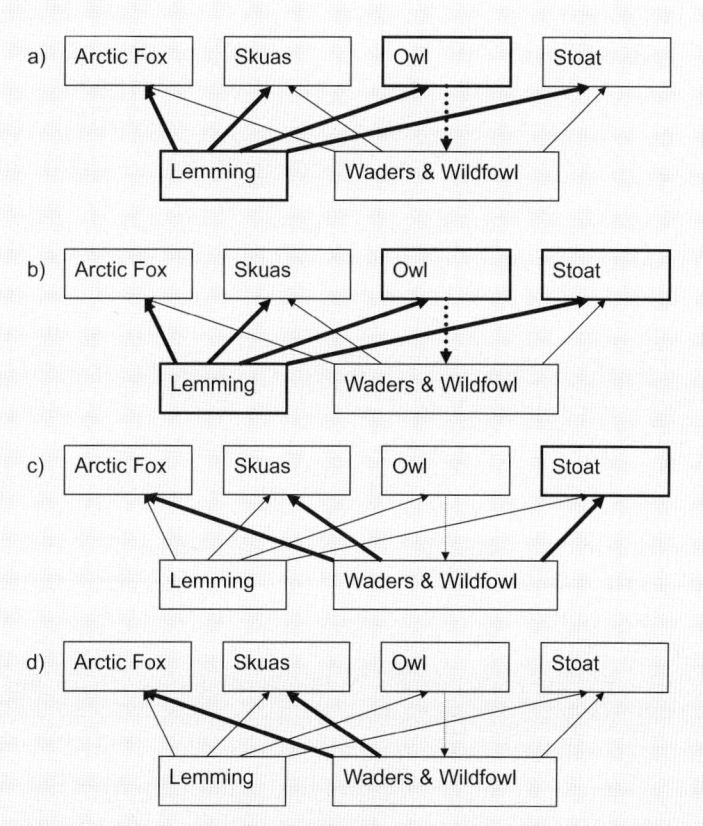

Box 4.7 Schematic diagram of a four-year lemming cycle. Years of high abundance are denoted by boxes with thick lines. Years of high predation are denoted by thick arrows. Because of their longevity, there is little short-term change in shorebird and waterbird populations, but in year c, they suffer low productivity. Potential benefits from snowy owls offering protection to nearby nesting shorebirds and waterfowl are indicated by the dotted down arrow.

2005). Recent work has identified that climate also plays a crucial role. Sustained periods of deep snow cover provide protection and shelter and facilitate continued lemming population growth through the winter, leading to larger lemming peaks during the increase phase of the population cycle (Kausrud *et al.* 2008). If climate change results in milder, less severe winters and earlier snowmelt in spring, then the cycles may decline in amplitude, with fewer large peaks, and lengthening in periodicity, ultimately leading to unstable dynamics. Indeed, in response to recent warming, changes of this kind have been

132 · **Further mechanisms of population impacts**

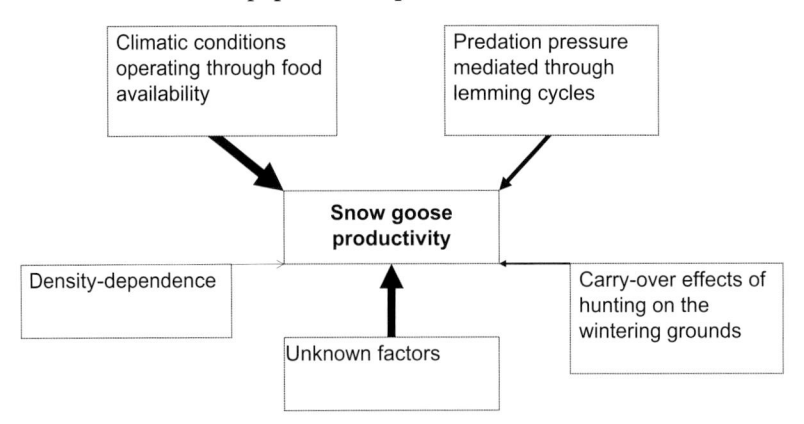

[Diagram: Boxes labeled "Climatic conditions operating through food availability", "Predation pressure mediated through lemming cycles", "Density-dependence", "Carry-over effects of hunting on the wintering grounds", and "Unknown factors" all with arrows pointing to a central box "Snow goose productivity". The arrow from "Climatic conditions" is thickest.]

Figure 4.6 The relative strength of factors affecting greater snow goose productivity in Arctic Canada. The width of the arrows represents the amount of variation (r^2) in annual breeding productivity explained by each factor(s). Adapted from Morrissette (2010).

detected in small rodent population cycles across Arctic, boreal and even temperate regions (Ims *et al.* 2008). For example, long-term studies in north-east Greenland indicate a lack of lemming peaks since 2000, in a system which previously exhibited a regular four-year cycle. The lack of a superabundant food peak of lemmings every four years has meant that no snowy owls *Bubo scandiacus* have bred in one study area since 2000 and overall owl productivity has declined by 98%, stoat *Mustela erminea* populations have crashed at one site and the breeding success of long-tailed skuas *Stercorarius londicaudus* and Arctic foxes *Vulpes lagopus* have also declined markedly (Meltofte & Høye 2007; Gilg *et al.* 2009; Post *et al.* 2009; Schmidt *et al.* 2012).

As yet, it is unclear what the consequences of these changes have been for breeding waterbirds. In one study of snow goose populations in the Canadian Arctic, the effects of weather on vegetation growth rate and the food supply were stronger than the top-down effects of predation (Figure 4.6), suggesting that this population would be relatively insensitive to a climate-induced collapse in lemming cycles (Morrissette *et al.* 2010). Conversely, there is evidence that the recent stabilisation of the previously increasing dark-bellied brent goose *Branta bernicla bernicla* population that winters in the Netherlands but breeds in the Taimyr peninsula, may be caused by the dampening of the lemming cycle since 1988 (Nolet *et al.* 2013). Brent goose breeding productivity was formerly cyclic and related to the lemming cycle, but has recently declined since lemming peaks have become less frequent. Declines in red knot could also be at least partly related to disrupted lemming cycles in the Canadian Arctic (Fraser *et al.* 2013). It would be valuable to repeat this type of analysis for other Arctic breeding waterbirds, and particularly for shorebirds for which the effects of spring and summer weather on invertebrate food abundance may also be important (see above). Although there is no evidence that their breeding success has been chronically reduced in response to low lemming abundance, it is possible that the general lack of lemmings may mean a more constant, and an average higher, level of nest predation in all years, which may be detrimental in the long term. The situation in the Arctic may also be further complicated by the spread of the red fox *Vulpes vulpes*, which is expanding its range in response to climate-induced higher plant productivity and consequent increases in small mammal densities, and seems to be outcompeting the Arctic fox (Hersteinsson & MacDonald 1994; Killengreen et al. 2007). It is unclear what impact this will have on ground-nesting waterfowl and shorebirds, but given the role that red foxes play in limiting populations of boreal grouse (Lindström et al. 1994) and shorebirds (Grant et al. 1999), this may be an additional mechanism by which Arctic ground nesting species are likely to suffer future range contractions and population declines in response to climate change (Chapter 5).

More widely, there has been a general trend for a collapse in vole cycles in boreal and northern temperate zones in recent years (Ims et al. 2008), which in a number of cases appears related to longer growing seasons and shorter winters (e.g. Yoccoz et al. 2001; Hörnfeld 2004; Bierman et al. 2006). The survival and productivity of many raptors and owls are linked to vole and lemming abundance (Francis & Saurola 2004; Lehikoinen et al. 2009), as are those of predatory mammals. Many of these predators feed on birds as well as small rodents, and switch between prey types in response to changes in rodent abundance. Hence, these trends are likely to have wide implications for the dynamics of northern ecosystems, and illustrate the complex way in which climate change may affect current ecosystem functioning and processes.

Another well-studied cyclical system that may also be affected by climate change is that of red grouse on managed moorland in the uplands of the UK, already described in Chapter 1. Instead of predation, grouse cycles that occur at high density managed populations are driven by cycles in the abundance per bird of the nematode parasite *Trichostrongylus tenuis*. The infestation of grouse with this worm increases with grouse density (Hudson 1992). In the absence of the nematode, warm temperatures during the breeding season have a positive effect upon productivity, and wet weather a detrimental effect (Tables S4.2*, S4.4*). However, the weather also affects the intensity of nematode infestation, which is enhanced by wet summer weather, particularly in May and July, exacerbating the negative effect of the same conditions upon the chicks, and by warm May and July temperatures (countering any potential benefit of warmer temperatures on foraging time and thermoregulation costs of grouse chicks). Dry May weather reduces the survival of parasite eggs and early larval stages, whilst cold July weather further reduces parasite development, synchronising grouse cycles (Figure 4.7; Cattadori et al. 2005). Ultimately, increasing temperatures are expected to increase infection rates, potentially destabilising these cycles, and increasing the frequency of large disease outbreaks, despite the initially positive effects of temperature upon grouse growth and survival (Hudson et al. 2006).

Managed red grouse populations in the UK may also be susceptible to louping ill, a tick-borne disease. There is a strong altitudinal and temperature gradient in the abundance of ticks (Gilbert 2010), which suggests that red grouse may also be negatively affected by climate change in the future through an expansion and increase in tick populations in upland areas, and a consequent spread in louping ill. Despite the high degree of management of this species for shooting, including the medication of wild grouse to control the nematodes, the prevalence of these diseases may be an increasingly important mechanism through which populations may be affected by climate change, aside from any impact of changes in insect prey populations described above (Fletcher et al. 2013).

* See online material.

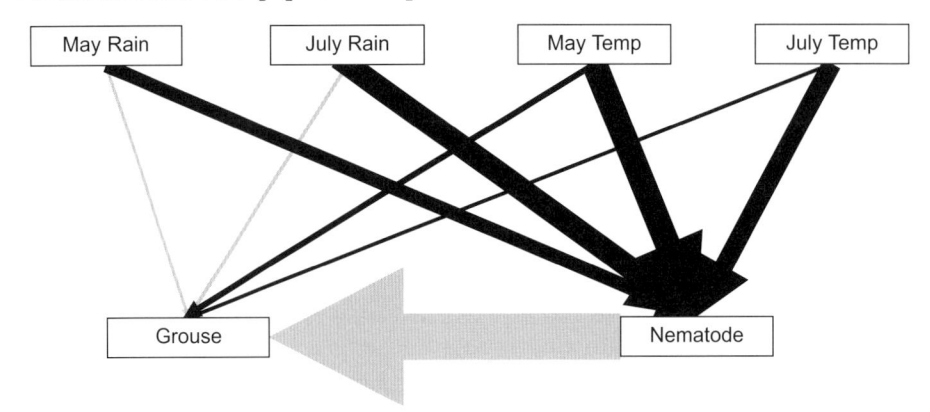

Figure 4.7 The average strength of the effects of May and July rainfall and temperature upon red grouse population dynamics directly, and indirectly through the nematode parasite *Trichostrongylus tenuis*. The size of the arrow represents the magnitude of effect, averaged across parts of the population cycle with both increasing and decreasing grouse populations. Black arrows indicate positive and grey arrows negative effects. Data are summarised from Cattadori *et al.* (2005).

Aside from the red grouse, there are relatively few well-documented examples of links between climate change, disease and bird populations in temperate and boreal areas. Avian disease has recently gained a high public profile because of the spread of avian influenza (H5N1 virus) from eastern Asia across to Western Europe through the migration of waterfowl (Kilpatrick *et al.* 2006) and the spread of West Nile virus in North America (Kilpatrick *et al.* 2007). Both diseases have significant human health implications. However in both cases, there appears to have been little impact of climate change upon their spread or prevalence, although potential shifts in migratory patterns in response to variation in the climate may result in new and unpredictable disease outbreaks in the future (Gilbert *et al.* 2008; Koenig *et al.* 2010).

Although there is no evidence that tick burdens or West Nile virus contributed to the decline in South Hills crossbills already described in this section (Santisteban *et al.* 2012), disease can be a significant limiting factor for some bird populations and in some outbreaks. West Nile virus has caused significant declines in the abundance of American crows *Corvus brachyrhynchos* (Koenig *et al.* 2010) amongst other North American species (LaDeau *et al.* 2007), whilst the infection of the introduced population of house finches *Carpodacus mexicanus* in the eastern USA by a novel strain of the bacterium *Mycoplasma gallisepticum*, illustrates how a novel pathogen may limit population distribution and abundance (Hochachka & Dhont 2000). In this case, there may be a hint of climatic influence on the prevalence of *Mycoplasma* infection. The degree of aggregation between individuals influences the prevalence of disease through time, leading to strong seasonal patterns in infection rates that also vary with latitude (Hosseini *et al.* 2004). On this basis, one might expect climate-driven changes in seasonality or winter conditions to affect the sensitivity of the population to *Mycoplasma*, depending on how concentrated individuals are at feeding stations. The emergence of *trichomoniasis* as a newly virulent pathogen affecting finches in the UK has already caused significant population declines in European greenfinches *Carduelis chloris* and Eurasian chaffinches *Fringilla coelebs* (Robinson *et al.* 2010; Lawson *et al.* 2012).

Although these outbreaks do not appear driven by climate change, they do highlight the potential for avian disease to have significant population level impacts, particularly when a novel disease impacts upon a naïve population. However, with the exception of the few cases outlined above, there is a lack of knowledge about the effects of disease on wild bird populations. Given that climate change is likely to result in significant shifts in the distribution of species, and changes to migratory routes, as well as increased stress to individuals, there is significant potential for species to be infected with pathogens that they have not been much exposed to in the recent past. As a consequence, new disease outbreaks may increasingly affect species or populations with limited immunity to that disease.

4.4 Long-distance migrants

4.4.1 Survival

Many species avoid the severe winter weather of high and temperate latitudes by migrating to subtropical and tropical zones. Within the Western Palaearctic region, migrants either winter in the Mediterranean region or cross the Sahara desert to the Sahel, a dry subtropical zone of scrub and forest north of the equator, or further south to the humid forest and savannas of tropical Africa. Many Nearctic migrant birds winter in the southern United States, Central America and the Caribbean, whilst others travel further to tropical South America and beyond. Eastern Palaearctic species travel south to central and southern Asia, or even Australasia, and there are some southerly distributed species in South America which similarly migrate north during the austral winter. We will examine in this section the influence of weather and climate on the demographic rates and population processes of these species, as a contrast to their less migratory relatives that remain at higher latitudes, focussing again on Western Palaearctic and Nearctic migrants because these have been studied in most detail.

Within the UK, research into the causes of population change in long-distance migrant birds was given a particular urgency in the late 1960s, when a number of trans-Saharan migrant bird species breeding in the UK underwent large-scale population crashes (Figure 4.8). Analyses of population changes of these species (Marchant 1992), alongside demographic data obtained from large-scale ringing programmes (e.g. Peach *et al.* 1991; Pratt & Peach 1991; Baillie & Peach 1992), have now established a good picture of the causes of these declines which were the result of drastically reduced overwinter survival.

It was soon apparent from this research that annual variation in the survival of these species was closely related to rainfall in the main wintering areas. Sand martins *Riparia riparia*, sedge warblers *Acrocephalus scheonobaenus*, common whitethroats *Sylvia communis* and common redstarts *Phoenicurus phoenicurus* each winter in the Sahel region of Africa, and as a result, studies in the UK have highlighted strong correlations between both survival rates and changes in population size, and Sahel rainfall (Cowley 1979; Peach *et al.* 1991; Baillie & Peach 1992; Marchant 1992; Robinson *et al.* 2008). Similar correlations have also been documented for populations of these species breeding in central Europe

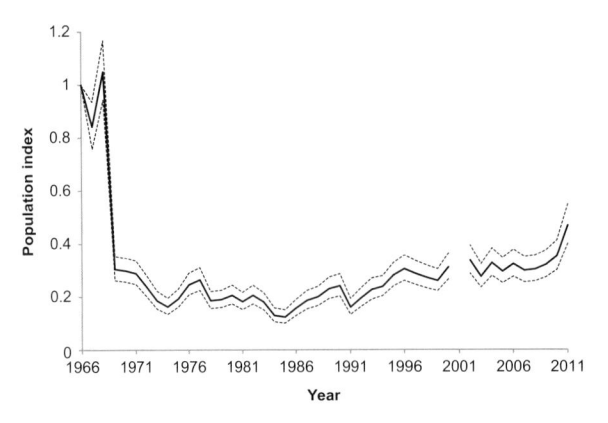

Figure 4.8 An index of the breeding population of whitethroats in the UK derived by combining CBC and BBS surveys, bounded by 95% confidence intervals. Between the summers of 1968 and 1969, the whitethroat suffered a two-thirds decline in numbers. There has been only a slow and incomplete recovery after the population crash; the population is now just under half of that in 1966. Note the 33% increase in 2011 in response to one of the wettest seasons in the Sahel zone of West Africa since the 1950s.

(Berthold *et al.* 1986; Szép 1995; Foppen *et al.* 1999; Pasinelli *et al.* 2011), indicating that the pattern is widespread. Baillie and Peach (1992) hypothesised that the carrying capacity of the Sahel region for these species is strongly related to the amount of rainfall during the wet season of the previous summer (May–October). For species such as sedge warblers and sand martins, there is a clear mechanism for this, as these birds use both temporary and permanent wetland habitats in the winter in much the same way as they do in the breeding season. For non-wetland species, rainfall will stimulate vegetation growth and therefore winter invertebrate and fruit abundance across the entire Sahel region (Schaub *et al.* 2005). As a result, annual variation in Sahel rainfall is a good proxy for annual variation in food available for many overwintering species whether they rely on wetland habitats or not. For this reason, Newson *et al.* (2009) advocated the use of variation in the abundance of these Sahelian migrants as a potential indicator of climate change impacts on the ecology of the region (Box 4.8).

The survival or abundance of the many European migrant waterbirds, which also winter in the Sahel, show similar correlations with wet-season rainfall (Figure 4.9). The decline of the little bittern *Ixobrychus minutus* in France from 1968 to 1990 matches drought periods on their wintering grounds of west Africa, with a subsequent recovery in the late 1990s corresponding to an increase in rainfall levels at that time (Marion *et al.* 2006). Fluctuations in purple heron *Ardea purpurea* populations in the Netherlands correlate with a measure of annual rainfall in their West African wintering grounds, due to low survival rates of adult birds during drought years (Den Held 1981; Cavé 1983), although population trends in north Italy do not appear to follow the same pattern (Fasola *et al.* 2010). Changes in French and Italian populations of black-crowned night heron *Nycticorax nyctucorax* and Squacco Heron *Ardeola ralloides* also appear to be at least partly caused by variation in Sahel rainfall (Den Held 1981; Fasola *et al.* 2010). These correlations partly account for the apparently strong positive effect of non-breeding season

Box 4.8 · *Using migrants to indicate ecological responses to climate change*

Newson *et al.* (2009) proposed that changes in the relative abundance of trans-Saharan migrant birds on their breeding grounds could be used to measure the impact of climate change on this group of species. To illustrate the potential of this approach, we collated the population trends in England of seven arid-zone trans-Saharan migrants (as classified by Thaxter *et al.* 2010); yellow wagtail *Motacilla flava*, lesser whitethroat *Sylvia curruca*, common redstart, sedge warbler, common whitethroat, Eurasian reed warbler and common chiffchaff *Phylloscopus collybita*. These species are expected to respond positively to high rainfall in the Sahel zone immediately to the south of the Sahara desert, where they winter. We calculated a geometric mean across the seven species of population ratios for successive pairs of years to generate a multi-species population index. This was significantly positively correlated with the rainfall total in the Sahel in the period of the year immediately before the migrants arrive there from the north ($r = 0.61$, $n = 39$, $P < 0.001$). Similarly, annual variation in the mean log ratio of population change across all species was correlated with rainfall ($r = 0.46$, $n = 38$, $P = 0.0037$). This supports Newson's suggestion that there is the potential to develop an indicator of the ecological consequences of climate change on this group of species. This index shows no evidence of a significant population change over the last 40 years, but does indicate population reductions of 20–30% occurred during the drought years of the 1970s and early 1980s.

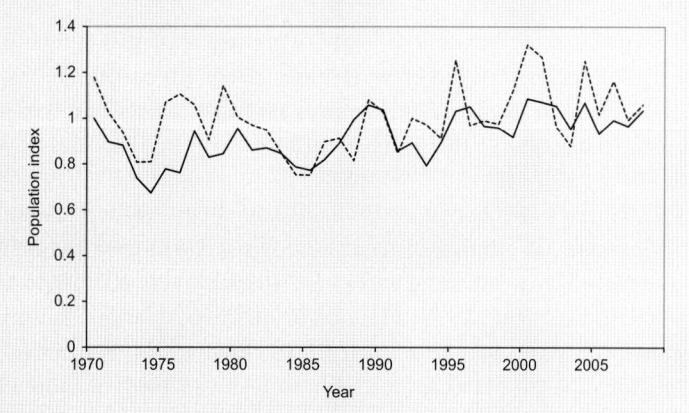

Box 4.8 Annual variation in Sahel rainfall (dotted line) in the previous year compared to a multi-species population index of arid-zone trans Saharan migrants (solid line). Sahel rainfall has been standardised to be the ratio of the annual value to the mean, so that it can be plotted using the same axis as the bird index. The population index is calculated from the geometric mean of natural log-collated population trends of each species, standardised to 1 in 1970.

precipitation on the demography of stork and heron (Ciconiidae and Ardeidae) populations (Table S4.3[*]). As described for sedge warblers, the mechanism most likely to

---

[*] See online material.

138 · Further mechanisms of population impacts

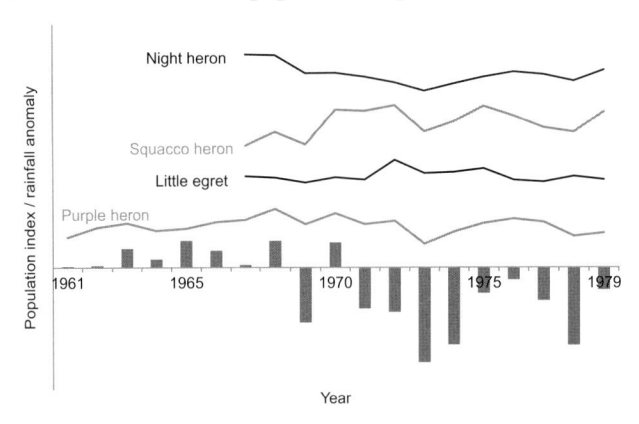

Figure 4.9 Variation in the abundance of a range of migrant heron species from locations in western Europe France and the Netherlands. Bars show the anomaly (deviation from the long-term mean) of rainfall in the Sahel zone for the period June–October in the year before the heron count (they are therefore advanced by a year). Population counts are from Den Held (1981), offset by varing amounts for easy visualisation. Changes in the abundance of Night Heron, Squacco Heron and Purple Heron were significantly positively correlated with Sahel rainfall.

underpin these correlations is that rainfall is a good predictor of the extent of suitable wetland habitat for these species. For larger waterbirds, these effects may be exacerbated by increased hunting pressure in dry years, when birds are most concentrated in dwindling wetland areas. This may particularly affect some migratory wildfowl species (Zwarts *et al.* 2009).

The species for which these effects of Sahel rainfall have been studied in most detail is the white stork *Ciconia ciconia*. Western European populations winter in the Sahel, and as a result, the survival rates of birds breeding in France are positively correlated with wet-season Sahel rainfall (Barbraud *et al.* 1999; Nevoux *et al.* 2008). Eastern European stork populations winter in eastern and southern Africa, and fluctuate in relation to measures of rainfall in those regions (Sæther *et al.* 2006), although the survival of individuals from these populations is also affected by rainfall in the Sahel, which remains an important staging area for individuals en route further south (Schaub *et al.* 2005). Thus, eastern European storks use the eastern Sahel as a food-rich staging area in October and November following the main wet season there, before continuing on to eastern and southern Africa where rainfall occurs from November onwards. Here the rainfall is less predictable and the birds are nomadic. Western European storks that remain in the Sahel experience a drying out of the landscape during the winter, and therefore food availability in late winter is strongly dependent upon the magnitude of the previous rains. The survival of western European storks is directly related to rainfall in the western Sahel, whilst that of eastern European populations appears to be affected by rainfall both on Sahelian staging grounds and in the wintering grounds further east and south. With an increasing tendency for storks from western Europe to winter in the Mediterranean region of Europe (Archaux *et al.* 2004), the importance of Sahel rainfall as a driver of stork populations in western Europe appears to be declining (Nevoux *et al.* 2008). This provides yet another example of how climate change may alter the relative importance of different climatic drivers through time.

Thus, in contrast to their resident competitors, whose survival and abundance are heavily influenced by winter cold and, to some extent, snow, the survival of Western Palaearctic long-distance migrants that winter in tropical zones is more heavily influenced by rainfall, accounting for the difference in sensitivity of long- and medium/short-distance migrants to rainfall (Box 4.5). It is also worth noting that, unlike the winter severity effects, these rainfall effects are largely indirect because the main period of rainfall occurs before the arrival of most migrant species, and therefore must occur in response to habitat modification and changes in food availability. Because these effects are indirect, it is possible that human modification of waterways, such as the construction of dams or diverting of water for irrigation, may alter the relationships between precipitation and habitat quality for the birds through time (Zwarts *et al.* 2009).

There is evidence that effects of weather on winter food availability may also affect survival rates of ring ouzels wintering in Morocco (Beale *et al.* 2006a), whilst a relationship between NAO and common sandpiper survival may be driven by conditions on the wintering grounds (Pearce-Higgins *et al.* 2009c). It is less clear whether populations of migrants overwintering in the humid forest zones of tropical Africa are also sensitive to fluctuations in precipitation. Some suggestion that they are is derived from common fluctuations in the survival of sand martins, Northern house martins *Delichon urbicum* and barn swallows in relation to rainfall, despite the fact that each of these winters in different locations in Africa (Robinson *et al.* 2008).

Variation in wet-season rainfall on the wintering grounds also appears to influence populations of Nearctic migrants, of which a small number of species have been studied in detail. The overwinter survival of both black-throated blue warblers and yellow warblers *Dendroica petechia* is positively correlated with the Southern Oscillation Index, with low survival rates during dry El Niño years (Sillett *et al.* 2000; Mazerolle *et al.* 2005). The effects on black-throated blue warblers were only apparent from studies conducted during the winter in Jamaica, and not from a breeding population in New Hampshire, where survival rates were relatively stable. This was attributed by Sillett *et al.* to the fact that individuals from a breeding population were likely to be spread across the Caribbean winter range, and that the relationship between the Southern Oscillation Index (SOI) and weather also varied across that range, potentially masking any effects. However, the relationship between yellow warbler survival and SOI was derived from a breeding population, which by the same logic suggests that the wintering grounds of this population, likely to be located in southern Central America or northern South America, may suffer drought on a wider spatial scale during El Niño years. Variation in the strength of migratory connectivity between breeding and wintering populations will influence the ease with which these climatic relationships may be detected and the spatial scale at which such signals will be visible (Webster *et al.* 2002).

It is clear that the survival of a significant number of both Nearctic and Palaearctic migrants is negatively affected by drought. Both Parulidae and Sylviidae show positive associations between non-breeding season precipitation and demography

(Table S4.3*). The similarity of this pattern is particularly noteworthy because the former tend to occupy forest habitats in the Caribbean, Central or South America, whereas many of the Palearctic migrants studied inhabit scrub and wetland habitats in drier regions. The mechanism underlying these relationships is likely to be the same in both continents, of drought-induced reductions in vegetation growth decreasing both the abundance of arthropod prey and fruit available to overwintering warblers.

This has been demonstrated by studies of American redstarts *Setophaga ruticilla* (Studds & Marra 2007), in which body condition was positively related to invertebrate abundance, and therefore is also likely to have influenced survival rates (Johnson *et al.* 2006). Using an experimental approach, female American redstarts were found to switch habitats from invertebrate-poor scrub to high-quality invertebrate-rich mangrove forest when dominant males were removed from the forest (Studds & Marra 2005). Individuals that shifted habitat maintained their body mass during the winter but those that remained in scrub habitats lost condition. As a result, the females in the mangrove forest departed earlier to the breeding grounds and a larger proportion of them returned in the following winter because they survived better. Early departure on spring migration might also have reduced phenological mismatch on the breeding grounds (see Chapter 3). Eastern American redstart populations which winter in the Caribbean therefore tend to increase in abundance following winters with high plant productivity. However, this same pattern was not apparent for western populations which winter in Mexico (Wilson *et al.* 2011). Studies of ovenbirds *Seiurus aurocapilla* showed similar results (Brown & Sherry 2006). It therefore appears that wet years in the tropics lead to greater availability of food for wintering migrants, which may increase their body condition and survival, and might even have a positive impact on productivity on the breeding grounds. For black-throated blue warblers, much of the annual mortality is thought to occur during migration, rather than overwinter (Sillett & Holmes 2002), although this was assessed by inference, rather than empirically. If correct, such mortality may be affected by the birds' body condition prior to departure, providing an additional mechanism by which weather conditions in the non-breeding season can affect annual survival.

Returning to the Western Palaearctic, there is evidence for negative correlations between white stork population changes and winter rainfall in parts of south and east Africa (Sæther *et al.* 2006) and between barn swallow survival rates and March rainfall in South Africa (Møller 1989). These correlations may reflect poor foraging conditions during periods of wet weather, reducing the ability of individuals to gain condition prior to the return flight. Poor conditions during migration itself may also have a detrimental effect on survival rates, as suggested for Northern house martins (Stokke *et al.* 2005).

Aside from the direct negative effects of heavy rain, studies in the Caribbean have also found negative correlations between rainfall during the spring and summer before autumn arrival, and the survival of American Redstarts (Dugger *et al.* 2004). This counterintuitive relationship was suggested to result from greater competition with resident species that are more numerous after wet years. The amount of spring rainfall is positively correlated with

---

* See online material.

changes in the abundance of resident insectivorous birds (Faaborg *et al.* 1984; Faaborg & Arendt 1992; see below) which may increase the competition arriving migrants may face for food. Given the competition between male and female American redstarts in winter already outlined, it seems feasible that birds of different species but similar food requirements might also compete. Whether competition from resident birds of other species is sufficient to have a significant effect on demographic rates of migrants is likely to depend upon the degree of prey depletion by residents. This in turn will depend upon the similarity of the foraging niche of the species. Dugger *et al.* (2004) suggested that survival of migrant American redstarts might be affected by competition from the abundant resident Adelaide's warbler *Dendroica adelaidae*, which is similar in size and foraging behaviour. More widely, without detailed ecological knowledge, it is difficult to predict which species might be most susceptible to competition with residents. Many studies have not been designed to detect lagged climatic correlations or to look for competition between species. Hence, effects of competition between resident and migrant species may have been overlooked.

High levels of rainfall on the wintering grounds may either be advantageous to Nearctic migrants by increasing winter food resources and survival rates, or detrimental if it enhances competition with resident species or reduces foraging efficiency. Indeed, both processes may operate on the same species. Recent rainfall trends in Jamaica are towards less, and less predictable, winter rainfall (Studds & Marra 2007), whilst future predictions are for declines in rainfall throughout the Caribbean region (Neelin *et al.* 2006). The future for many North American migrant birds may therefore be bleak. Future rainfall predictions for the Sahel region are uncertain (Solomon *et al.* 2009; Dai 2013), and there is an urgent need to develop the same mechanistic understanding and detailed demographic monitoring across the Africa–Europe flyway that has been undertaken in the Americas. However, climatic drivers of survival are only part of the demographic story, and conditions on the breeding grounds must also be accounted for to fully appraise the likely effects of global climate change upon long-distance migrants.

4.4.2 Productivity

Before focussing on conditions during the breeding season, it is worth considering the possibility of carry-over effects between winter and breeding seasons that may affect breeding productivity. Earlier, we mentioned the fact that individuals wintering in food-rich habitats depart for the breeding grounds earlier than their conspecifics wintering in poorer quality habitats (Studds & Marra 2005). This change in timing in response to winter conditions may be widespread and affect subsequent timing of breeding (Chapter 2). Earlier arriving individuals may be less susceptible to any negative effects of phenological mismatch (Chapter 3). Positive carryover effects as a result of high food abundance on the wintering grounds may therefore result in improved breeding success the following breeding season, as demonstrated by the detailed studies of the American redstart (Norris *et al.* 2004), and hinted at by correlations for some Palearctic long-distance migrants breeding in Europe (Saino *et al.* 2004; Zwarts *et al.* 2009). Such effects are not restricted to passerines. The departure dates of wintering black-tailed godwits to Iceland are earliest in individuals wintering in the best quality habitats, conferring significant advantages when they breed (Gunnarsson *et al.* 2006). However, much more work on this is required in order to explore the prevalence of carry-over effects, and to quantify whether these effects are of sufficient magnitude to be important at the population level. Indeed, whilst some studies have identified significant carry-over effects on breeding success in some species, recent work suggests that the magnitude of carry-over effects across migrant species in general may be quite small (Ockendon *et al.* 2013).

Weather during the breeding season has strong effects on the breeding productivity of long-distance migrants similar to those described for resident species (Section 4.3.2). For example, the productivity and mean fledgling mass of black-throated blue warblers is positively correlated with SOI, such that in an El Niño year, productivity is low. These effects appear attributable to effects of weather on prey availability, as the abundance of caterpillars, a key food for this species, is reduced during El Niño years (Sillett *et al.* 2000). Food manipulation experiments, where pairs were provided with extra food, resulted in an increased frequency in the production of two broods, and greater overall productivity, indicating that food was otherwise limiting (Nagy & Holmes 2005). Further, there are strong interactions between population size and climate, with density-dependent reductions in productivity being much greater during El Niño years, when food supplies are low (Sillett *et al.* 2004). The effect of weather on food availability therefore strongly limits both fecundity and population size, making this species sensitive to climatic variation (Sillett *et al.* 2000). Given similar correlations between caterpillar availability and the abundance of six other long-distance migrant species (Jones *et al.* 2003), food availability is likely to be a key determinant of long-distance Nearctic migrant productivity.

In the same way, fluctuations in yellow-billed cuckoo *Coccyzus americanus* populations in North America are correlated with weather (Anders & Post 2006). These cuckoos specialise in eating caterpillars, and their breeding success is positively related to caterpillar abundance. The relationship between changes in cuckoo abundance and fluctuations in the both NAO and SOI varies between regions because of variation in the association between these large-scale climate indices and temperature. Changes in cuckoo populations from one year to the next are negatively correlated with breeding season temperature in the first of the two years. This relationship with temperature is strongest in regions with the most rapidly declining cuckoo populations. It therefore appears that warming is negatively affecting the abundance of this species, which the authors suggest may be mediated through reduced frequency of caterpillar outbreaks following warm winters (Myers 1998).

As outlined in Chapter 3, there is evidence for changes in productivity underlying declines in some populations of long-distance Palaearctic migrants. Fine-scale geographical variation in recent changes in pied flycatcher populations in the Netherlands appears to relate to the degree of phenological mismatch, and hence the availability of caterpillars when parents are attempting to feed chicks (Both & Visser 2005), although the magnitude of the impact of mismatch upon national populations remains uncertain. Although attributed to phenological mismatch, presumably pied flycatchers and other similar woodland species would also be sensitive to large-scale reductions in caterpillar populations in response to climate change. There have been population declines in many moth species in southern England (Conrad *et al.* 2006) which may be expected to affect populations of our migrant birds. The extent to which these declines have been driven by changes in the climate, as opposed to the wide range of possible other factors, is uncertain. Whilst climatic change has been implicated in the decline of one species, the garden tiger moth *Actia caja* (Conrad *et al.* 2003), whose caterpillars are prey of adult common cuckoos, it is possible that land-use change and agricultural intensification will also have been equally or more important drivers of change for many species.

Changes in prey availability may not be the only problem pied flycatcher populations face. There is evidence that increases in the collared flycatcher population on the Swedish islands of Öland and Gotland in the Baltic has had a detrimental effect on the co-occurring pied flycatchers. This location is at the northern edge of the collared flycatcher range; both species are sympatric across much of central and eastern Europe. Both nest naturally in tree cavities but take to nest boxes, and have similar feeding ecologies, although as noted in Section 3.4.2, collared flycatchers are more reliant on caterpillars than pied flycatchers (Qvarnström *et al.* 2005, 2009; Veen *et al.* 2010). Accordingly, they compete for nesting resources, leading to male pied flycatchers being excluded from establishing new territories in areas of high collared flycatcher abundance (Sætre *et al.* 1999). This increases the risk of hybridisation between the species. The net result of this is that pied flycatchers now only occupy relatively poor-quality coniferous woodland on Öland (Vallin *et al.* 2012). Whilst it is unclear why collared flycatchers are increasing in abundance across Europe (Gregory *et al.* 2007), the colonisation of the Baltic Islands is consistent with a climate-mediated northward shift (Huntley *et al.* 2007). Although other factors may be responsible, the observed effects are relevant to understanding potential impacts of climate change on sympatric closely related species. Interestingly, the observed outcome of this expansion and competition for pied flycatchers is the same as that resulting from phenological mismatch outlined in the previous chapter, of altered habitat association away from what were previously the highest quality areas.

There is also evidence of similar competitive processes between great tits and pied flycatchers breeding in south-west Finland (Ahola *et al.* 2007). Here an increasing overlap between the timing of laying in response to warming has increased competition for nest boxes, leading to a rise in the number of fatal takeover attempts by male pied flycatchers. Competition between the range-expanding western bluebird *Sialia mexicana* in response to the provision of nest boxes has similarly led to displacement of mountain bluebirds *S. currucoides* (Duckworth & Badyaev 2007; Duckworth 2006, 2008).

Such observations of competition are not restricted to studies of species in nest boxes for which nest sites tend to be limiting. Virginia's warblers *Vermivora virginiae* are displaced from their preferred, humid forest habitats by orange-crowned warblers *Vermivora celata*. In wet years, when orange-crowned warblers are abundant, Virginia's warblers are forced to occupy drier forest habitats, where they suffer greater rates of predation (Martin 2001). Further habitat changes as a result of climate-driven changes in browsing intensity have reduced the extent of nesting habitat for both species, leading to greater competition for nesting locations between the two species and a third, the red-faced warbler *Cardellina rubrifrons*. Combined, this has led to further increases in nest predation rates, which for each species are positively correlated with the extent of overlap with nesting territories of the other species (Auer & Martin 2013). Interspecific competition therefore appears to influence productivity, although as shall be seen later, additional climatic impacts on the system are more important (Section 4.8). Although relatively rarely studied, competition between species may influence the fine-scale distribution and abundance of less-dominant species. Based on these findings, we would therefore expect any climate-mediated expansion in the distribution or abundance of dominant competitors to have detrimental impacts on other species, and advocate research on ecologically similar closely-related species to test this, particularly at range boundaries where the distribution or abundance of one species may be increasing at the expense of the other (see also Section 5.2.1).

4.4.3 Conclusions

The results of our assessment might be taken to suggest that populations of Palearctic migrant birds are less strongly affected by variation in productivity than by variation in survival (Baillie & Peach 1992), although this contrasts with the implications of other studies (e.g. Both *et al.* 2006a, 2010). One potential explanation for this discrepancy is that the Baillie and Peach study did not include data beyond the late 1980s, and that increasing effects of mismatch-related declines in productivity may have increased the importance of productivity in driving population trends. Yet there remains considerable uncertainty about the magnitude of the effect of any changes in breeding success upon populations (Chapter 3). Alternatively, these contrasting results may be a function of the difference scales of the two studies; impacts of variation in survival may be more apparent across larger spatial scales.

Figure 4.10 summarises how variation in the weather can affect both survival and productivity, although currently there is insufficient evidence to assess fully how vulnerable migrants are to climate change (Knudsen *et al.* 2011). Both breeding season and winter weather may be important in driving population change (for example as shown by studies of white stork; Sæther *et al.* 2006). Further, we know almost nothing about how changing conditions on migration or at stopover locations may influence migrant populations, and yet it may be during such migration periods that most mortality occurs (Sillett *et al.* 2000). When considering the likely vulnerability of migrants to climate change, it is therefore important to incorporate potential impacts at all stages of the life cycle by taking account of migratory connectivity between specific breeding, wintering and migratory locations (Small-Lorenz *et al.* 2013). As many long-distance migrants are declining (Section 3.5), there are many conservation reasons to replicate the integrated long-term studies on the demography of black-throated blue warblers conducted at Hubbard Brook for other species, not just in North America, but also in Europe and elsewhere. Such detailed population studies are needed for elucidating the mechanisms by which climate change impacts upon a species.

4.5 Birds of Mediterranean, subtropical and tropical regions

The preceding discussion of the drivers of population change in long-distance migrants suggests that rainfall is the key determinant of avian demography within their Mediterranean, subtropical and tropical wintering grounds. There are fewer studies of the effects of climate upon resident species which occupy the same habitats, but the available evidence from these supports these conclusions. This explains the lack of consistent effect of temperature on bird populations in low latitudes which contrasts

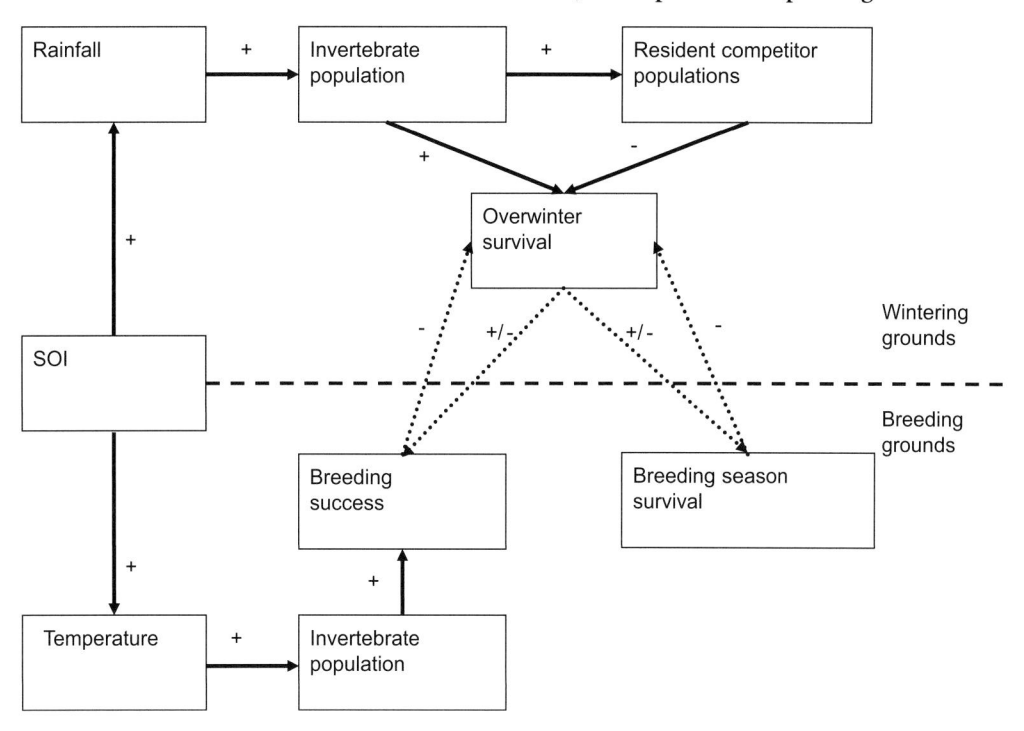

Figure 4.10 Schematic diagram illustrating how variation in the climate (SOI) may affect both breeding and wintering population processes in a Nearctic migrant to the Caribbean. Diagram based upon the studies of Sillett *et al.* 2000, 2004, and Sillett and Holmes 2002 on the black-throated blue warbler and Studds and Marra 2005, 2007, 2011 on the American redstart. Given that both species experience strong density-dependence of demographic rates on the breeding and wintering grounds, high overwinter survival tends to increase the spring population which can have a negative effect on breeding productivity in the following summer. High breeding success has a similar effect on overwinter survival.

with the more positive effect of temperature at high latitudes (Section 4.2.1), and the suggestion that such populations are more strongly driven by a positive effect of precipitation upon demographic parameters (Section 4.2.2). The fact that studies of the populations of tropical birds are amongst those most likely to show negative effects of warming and drought adds evidence to the suggestion that tropical species may be among some of the most vulnerable species to climate change (Şekercioğlu *et al.* 2012).

There are many published studies examining annual variation in the demography of tropical and subtropical raptor or owl species, covering examples from four continents, although for only one of these studies (Krüger *et al.* 2002) does the data span 10 years or more. Of 23 examples, there were positive effects of rainfall in 12 species, negative effects in two, and no or mixed effects of rainfall in the remainder. Interestingly, the positive effects of rainfall were largely (10 of 12 cases) lagged effects of rainfall during the preceding winter or year. It is worth noting that not all rainfall effects were positive, and in common with raptors breeding at higher latitudes described above, periods of heavy rain during the breeding season may have direct negative impacts on productivity and survival (McDonald *et al.* 2004; Senapathi *et al.* 2011).

In a wide-ranging analysis, Krüger *et al.* (2002) examined variation in the abundance of 15 raptor species in the Kalahari Desert as a function of rainfall. They found that in general, the species which benefited most from high rainfall were those that relied upon the largest prey items, such as white-backed *Gyps africanus* and lappet-faced vultures *Torgos tracheliotos*, bateleur *Terathopius ecaudatus* and tawny eagle *Aquila rapax*, whilst populations of smaller, more rapidly breeding species, particularly falcons, exhibited the strongest negative effects of population density. The authors suggest that this finding results from the fact that the abundance of prey in semi-arid systems tends to be closely related to precipitation (Sinclair & Arcese 1995), with greater rainfall resulting in more abundant prey and greater breeding success (Wichmann *et al.* 2003). They argue, however, that the lack of effect for smaller raptors is an artefact of their higher reproductive and mortality rates, and that they are also likely to respond to rainfall effects on prey populations in a similar way.

Other examples of lagged links between rainfall, prey abundance and raptor populations in arid or semi-arid areas are provided by studies of the Aplomado falcon *Falco femoralis* in Mexico (Macías-Duarte *et al.* 2004), ferruginous pygmy owl *Glaucidium brasilianum* in Arizona (Flesch 2007) and barn *Tyto alba* and magellanic horned owls *Bubo magellanicus* in northern Chile (Lima *et al.* 2001). In each case, the mechanism for the lagged rainfall effects appears to have been greater grass seed production during wet years, which increased the populations of granivorous birds (prey of the Aplomado falcon) or rodents (food for owls), and hence boosted falcon or owl productivity in the following year. In a semi-arid area of Chile, high rainfall increased the productivity and abundance of the leaf-eared mouse *Phyllotis darwini*, leading to a rise in avian and mammalian predators (Jaksic *et al.* 1997), particularly of barn and horned owls, and also of raptors (Box 4.9). The resulting high rates of predation, particularly by owls, then appeared to subsequently limit the mouse population (Lima *et al.* 2001). The authors suggest that the cycle is initially driven from the bottom up. El Niño events stimulate heavy rainfall which causes rapid vegetation growth and seed production which increases mouse fecundity. In response to the rapidly increasing mouse population, density dependence and then owl predation increasingly suppress population growth, exacerbated by a reduction in food resources associated with a return to dry conditions. The mouse population decline during the down phase of a cycle therefore occurs in response to both bottom-up and top-down processes. Kestrel–vole dynamics in the Mediterranean region follow a similar pattern (Fargallo *et al.* 2009) where wet weather increases vole abundance, leading to a population increase in kestrels. High kestrel predation then reduces vole abundance. These systems are therefore conceptually and functionally very similar to the lemming cycles described in the previous section, but instead of being driven by snow cover improving overwinter survival and allowing rodents to continue to breed during the winter, they are driven by surges in plant productivity in response to rainfall.

In the same way, high rainfall is associated with increased breeding success in a range of North American scrub breeding species, including Brewer's sparrows *Spizella breweri*, sage sparrows *Amphispiza belli* and song sparrows *Melospiza melodia* (Rotenberry & Wiens 1991; Chase *et al.* 2005), Mexican jays *Aphelocoma wollweberi* (Li & Brown 1999), and wild

Box 4.9 · *Mechanisms of El Niño-driven changes in raptor populations in Chile*

Rainfall in the semi-arid scrub zone of northern Chile is strongly influenced by the El Niño–Southern Oscillation. In wet years, seed production is promoted, which in turn increases small mammal populations and then the abundance of the raptors and owls which feed upon them. Data from 1989 to 1994, albeit from one El Niño cycle, indicate a strong correlation between rainfall and seed production with no time lag. There was high seed production in the two wet El Niño winters of 1991 and 1992.

High seed density increased the small mammal population in the following year. The time lag arose because of the time needed for the mammals to accumulate food and for successive generations to breed successfully.

The abundance (frequency of sightings within a 750 ha study area) of diurnal, small mammal feeding raptors (Falconiformes) correlated well with small mammal density, but with a six-month lag (this produced a marginally better fit compared with an immediate response). The short duration of this lag suggests that this is due to the immigration of birds into the area in response to increasing mammal populations.

Thus, changes in raptor populations appear to be driven by rainfall events 18 months previously through a trophic cascade effect.

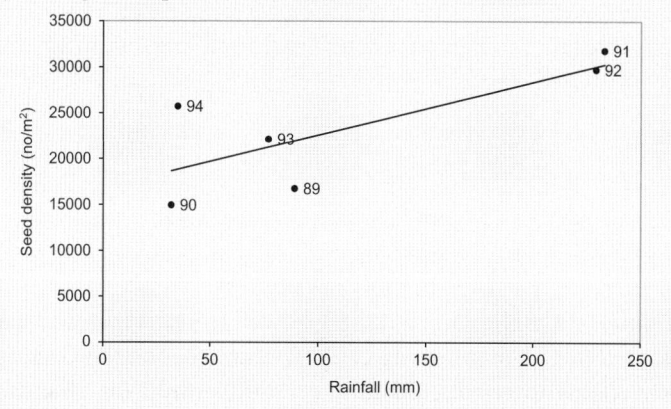

Box 4.9a Correlation ($r = 0.78$) between rainfall and the density of perennial and ephemeral seeds in a semi-arid zone of northern Chile (data from Jaksic *et al.* 1997). The numerical value denotes the year.

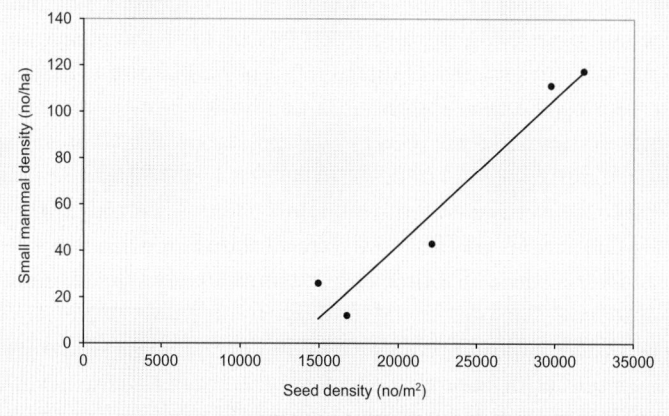

Box 4.9b Correlation ($r = 0.97$) between the density of seeds in a semi-arid zone of northern Chile (from the previous graph) and subsequent small mammal abundance in the following year (data from Jaksic *et al.* 1997).

Box 4.9 (cont.)

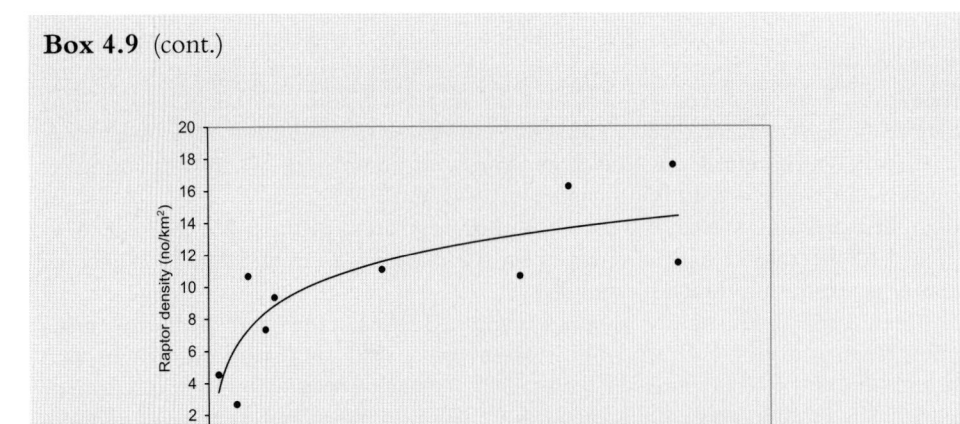

Box 4.9c Correlation between the density of five species of raptor (red-backed hawk *Buteo polyosoma*, American kestrel, black-chested buzzard-eagle *Geranoaetus melanoleucus*, Chimango caracara *Milvago chimango* and Harris's hawk *Parabuteo unicinctus*) and small mammal density in semi-arid zone of northern Chile. Here, data are presented for six-monthly seasons, rather than the annual summaries of the previous two graphs (data from Jaksic *et al.* 1997). The fitted line is a logarithmic curve ($r = 0.83$).

turkeys *Meleagris gallopayo* (Schwertner *et al.* 2005), as well as little bustards *Tetrax tetrax* in Spain (Delgado *et al.* 2009). The productivity of Darwin's finches on the Galapagos Islands is strongly positively related to rainfall (Grant *et al.* 2000), whilst the abundance of cirl buntings *Emberiza cirlus* in Spain (Ponz *et al.* 1996), tropical birds in Puerto Rico (Faaborg 1982; Faaborg *et al.* 1984; Faaborg & Arendt 1992; Dugger *et al.* 2000), and house wrens *Troglodytes aedon* in California (Verner & Purcell 1999) are each also positively related to precipitation. As with the raptors, it is likely that for at least some, if not most of these examples, the mechanism underlying these effects is greater food abundance after rainfall.

The example of the Darwin's finches *Geospiza* spp. on the Galapagos Islands is worthy of further comment. During the breeding season, these finches prey upon caterpillars and other arthropods, and feed them to their young. The abundance of such prey (Figure 4.11) is dramatically enhanced during wet El Niño years, which lengthens the breeding season of Darwin's finches, and can even enable individuals to breed when only three months of age (Gibbs *et al.* 1984; Gibbs & Grant 1987). High food abundance in a wet year results in large first clutches, and when these first breeding attempts are completed, adults produce second and third clutches. The success of individual breeding attempts declines in successive clutches as a result of rising temperatures and greater costs of territory defence against the increasing number of juveniles. Even so, the greater frequency of breeding attempts in an El Niño year leads to an increase in overall productivity and population size. Outside of the breeding season, populations of Darwin's finches are driven by variation in survival determined by seed availability. For example, populations of the

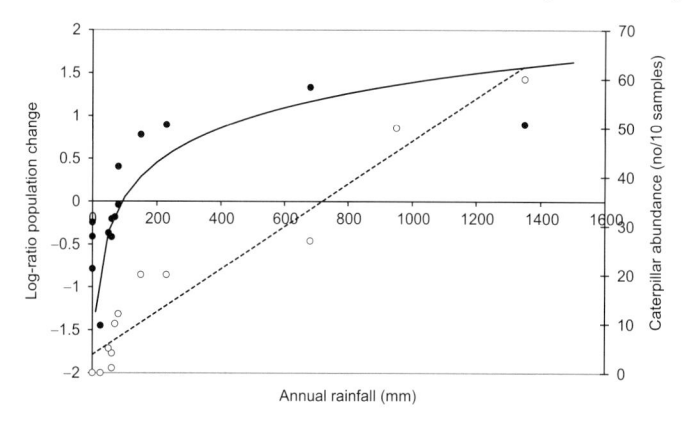

Figure 4.11 The correlation between caterpillar abundance and rainfall in the same year (open circles, dotted line) on the Galapagos island of Daphne Major ($r = 0.96$). Changes in the breeding abundance of four species of Darwin's finches on the same island between the year in which the rainfall was recorded and the following year are shown by filled circles and the solid line and described by a logarithmic curve ($r = 0.68$). Data are from Grant *et al.* (2000).

cactus finch *G. scandens* declined following exceptionally heavy rainfall which led to the *Opuntia* cactus it feeds on being smothered by faster growing plant species, whilst the more generalist medium ground finch *G. fortis* survived better (Grant & Grant 1993).

A beneficial effect of rainfall operating through food abundance has also been found to increase the length of both song sparrow and Mexican jay breeding seasons (Chase *et al.* 2005; Li & Brown 1999). In wet years, species breeding in arid environments tend to produce more clutches and therefore have greater productivity (Dean *et al.* 2009). Additionally, greater moisture availability in arid environments may also increase the amount of time birds can spend foraging without having to look for, or travel to, water (Molokwu *et al.* 2010). Thus, not only may rain increase food abundance, but it can also make it easier for that food to be exploited. Song sparrows also appear to benefit from reduced rates of nest predation during wet years, although the mechanism underlying this effect is unclear (Chase *et al.* 2005).

One of the best studied responses to rainfall is that of the red-billed quelea *Quelea quelea*, as this species is a major agricultural pest in the interior of southern Africa. Outside of the breeding season, the birds forage on small grass seeds and at the start of the rainy season, move ahead of the rain front which causes these seeds to germinate. Once grass seeds have germinated across the species' range, the birds return to the start of the rain front, where new seed and copious invertebrates (primarily caterpillars and Orthoptera nymphs) are available, and commence breeding. As soon as their young fledge, adults then repeat their initial movement along the direction of the rain front, but this time, breeding wherever rainfall has stimulated sufficient grass growth. Breeding ceases when 6 weeks have passed since rain has fallen across the species' range, and the birds then move nomadically to track grass seed availability until the next rainy season (Ward 1971; Cheke *et al.* 2007). As with the species mentioned above, population size and distribution across the range is therefore

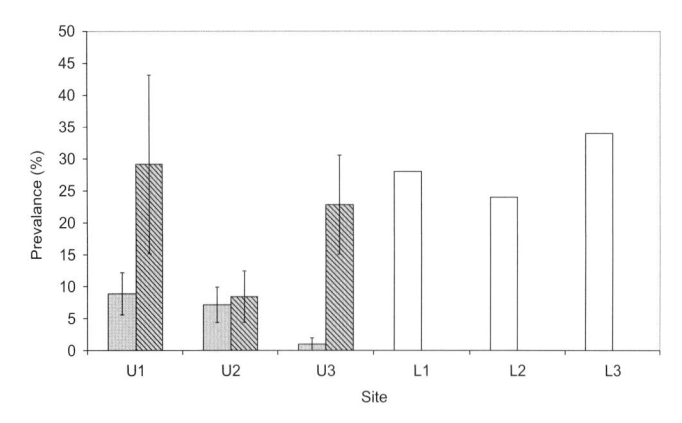

Figure 4.12 Prevalence of avian malaria (detected from blood smears) in eight species of native birds caught at three upland sites (U1, U2, U3) on the Alaka'i Plateau, Kaua'i (data from Atkinson & Utzurrum 2010), and in amakihi *Hemignathus virens* populations at three lowland sites (L1, L2, L3) close to the Mauna Loa Volcano (from Woodworth *et al.* 2005). Data from the upland sites are from 1994–1997 (grey bars) and 2007–2009 (striped bars), whilst the samples from the lowland sites are from 2002 (white bars). Standard error bars for the upland sites are given based on the variation in prevalence between species.

dependent upon the magnitude and location of precipitation, knowledge which may be used to generate predictive models of breeding distributions to inform pest control (Cheke *et al.* 2007). With sufficient data, similar models could be developed for species of conservation concern, and may be used in a climate change context to identify species and areas likely to be particularly vulnerable in the future (Chapter 6).

Although we have again focussed on the role of climate in limiting populations through food resources, let us not neglect other potential mechanisms. For example, it is well-established that previous introductions of new host species of birds and of insect disease vectors have led to disease outbreaks and population extinctions in some tropical species, particularly of isolated species on islands. This is most notably the case for endemic Hawaiian passerines which have been adversely affected by the spread of avian malaria and avian pox. The vector of avian malaria in the islands is the mosquito *Culex quinquefasciatus*, which was introduced in 1826. House sparrows *Passer domesticus*, great tits, and blackcaps *Sylvia atricapilla* are among the introduced hosts of malaria, but are less susceptible to malaria than native species (van Riper *et al.* 1986). Mosquito larval development is only successful in the warm temperatures found at low elevations, so populations of some endemic birds have persisted at high altitudes. However, if warming allows mosquitoes to extend their elevational range in future, there may be more extinctions (Benning *et al.* 2002). Indeed, the frequency of avian malaria has increased in some upland areas in recent years, and now matches that previously recorded in some lowland areas (Figure 4.12). There is a ray of hope, however, as it appears that at least some populations of native species may be able to co-exist with the malaria parasite (Woodworth *et al.* 2005).

There is worrying evidence that arid-zone species may be affected by an increasing frequency of heat waves (Albright *et al.* 2010a,b; McKechnie *et al.* 2012). Historical evidence of the mortality of thousands of budgerigars *Melopsittacus undulatus*, zebra finches *Taenopygia guttata* (Finlayson 1932) and parrots (McGilp 1932) during severe heat waves in Australia has been repeated. Heat waves in January 2009 and 2010, when temperatures exceeded 45 °C, killed not only many budgerigars and zebra finches, but more than 200 endangered Carnaby's black cockatoos *Calyptorhynchus latirostris* (Saunders *et al.* 2011; Low 2011; McKechnie *et al.* 2012). Although birds require up to double the amount of water than normal during hot weather (McKechnie & Erasmus 2006; McKechnie & Wolf 2010) these mortality events appear to have occurred not as a result of dehydration, but as a direct result of physiological heat stress. Despite their physiological adaptations to arid environments, which include effective insulation, low rates of evaporative water loss and high heat tolerance (Weathers 1997; Weathers & Greene 1998; Weathers *et al.* 2001; Seavy 2006), given the upper critical temperatures of zebra finches are 40–42 °C and budgerigars, 41 °C (Burton & Weathers 2003; Low 2011), such mortality is perhaps not surprising. With future warming associated with an increasing likelihood of such extreme events occurring, there is considerable potential for heat stress to threaten already rare and endangered bird species in tropical arid environments (McKechnie & Wolf 2010; McKechnie *et al.* 2012).

This brief review of existing studies suggests that rainfall is the most important short-term determinant of the demography of subtropical and tropical birds, with the abundance of food directly or indirectly linked to the increase in vegetative growth which rainfall produces. The strength of that link and its underlying mechanism determines the magnitude of any effect, and duration of any lag before it is apparent. However, severe weather during the breeding season, both in terms of high temperatures or heavy rainfall (Grant *et al.* 2000; McDonald *et al.* 2004; Chase *et al.* 2005) is also likely to depress productivity, just as it does at high latitudes and in the temperate zone. Although the evidence in support of these general conclusions is strong (Section 4.2), it is based upon few detailed examples, and in particular, relatively few studies which have examined the mechanisms underlying the observed responses. Although we have focussed largely on the effects of rainfall on the food supplies of birds, which appear to underpin most effects, more detailed studies might reveal other mechanisms, such as in response to competition, invasive species and disease (Şekercioğlu *et al.* 2012), as found for higher latitude populations. Recent observations of catastrophic mortality events in response to recent heat waves also give cause for concern. Given that the majority of biodiversity occurs in tropical areas, there is an urgent need to initiate and continue long-term ecological studies of species in these ecosystems which are vulnerable to change.

4.6 Seabirds

4.6.1 Productivity

Most seabirds are long-lived, with low fecundity (often laying a single clutch of one egg per year) and late maturity. As a result, population fluctuations might be expected to be most strongly affected by variation in adult survival rates (Sæther & Bakke 2000). To minimise such fluctuations, adult seabirds tend to operate a 'bet-hedging' strategy, which means that they will attempt to reduce the impact of poor environmental conditions upon their survival, and therefore sacrifice a year or two of reproduction if that ensures they can survive to attempt to breed when conditions are more favourable (Jenouvrier et al. 2005a). This means that it is breeding productivity which is usually most sensitive to adverse weather effects. There are probably more studies of annual variation in seabird productivity which have highlighted many effects of weather than of annual variation in seabird survival, although such studies of productivity are also generally easier to conduct than long-term ringing studies.

The majority of seabirds feed on fish or marine invertebrates such as plankton or krill which also form an important food source for fish. As fisheries scientists have long collected data on both fish populations and the abundance of their prey in order to improve fisheries management, there are extensive datasets available on both temporal and spatial variation in a number of key seabird food resources. The existence of such long-term data on variation in the abundance of various components of the marine food chain has arguably allowed a deeper understanding of the likely effects of climate change to be attained for many seabird populations than has been possible for most of the terrestrial breeding birds that we have considered so far.

One of the best studied examples of the effect of variation in weather conditions on seabird populations comes from the North Sea coast of the UK. This is a shallow continental shelf sea < 200 m in depth, which means that strong winds and low levels of sunlight during the winter ensure that the water column is well mixed. In spring, as wind speeds drop and the water warms, this stratifies into a warm upper layer that overlies cooler, deeper water, resulting in a spring bloom of diatoms at the warm surface which feeds an April flush of zooplankton (Miller 2004; Scott et al. 2006). This in turn feeds juvenile (0-class) fish, such as lesser sandeels. Sandeels spend most of the year buried in the sand, but emerge to spawn during the winter, and again to feed on the zooplankton in the spring. It is during these periods that they become most available to foraging seabirds. As the spring plankton bloom declines in proportion to the depletion of nutrients in the warm surface water, the adult sandeels return to the seabed by June, reducing their availability to foraging seabirds. At this point, when most parent birds are feeding chicks, 0-class sandeels become the main prey, as they remain in the water column for longer (Harris & Wanless 1985; Lewis et al. 2001).

In a normal year this process ensures a plentiful supply of small, energy-rich fish for millions of breeding seabirds. However, the ecosystem is vulnerable to a number of climate-related disruptions. Firstly, there is some evidence of phenological mismatch between peak phytoplankton availability and peak zooplankton demands (Edwards & Richardson 2004), which has the potential to reduce the magnitude of the spring flush of zooplankton (Scott et al. 2006; Sharples et al. 2006). Secondly, there has been replacement of cold water zooplankton species, such as the copepod *Calanus finmarchicus*, by warm water species, such as *C. helgolandicus*. This is important for seabirds because *C. finmarchicus* is a spring emerging species, and a key food source for many larval fish, including sandeels, whilst *C. helgolandicus* is an autumn emerging species whose abundance has little impact upon sandeel populations. As a result, there has been an overall reduction in spring copepod biomass (Beaugrand et al. 2002, 2003; Reid et al. 2003) which has reduced the size of 0-class sandeel larvae (Frederiksen et al. 2004a; Wanless et al. 2004). Thirdly, the increase in annual average sea temperature has

Table 4.3 *A range of studies have related metrics of sandeel availability to the breeding success of seabirds at specific seabird colonies around the UK*

Species	Sandeel measure	Reference
Arctic tern	Abundance	Uttley et al. (1989)
Atlantic puffin	Biomass of 0-class sandeels with 1-year lag	Burthe et al. (2012)
Atlantic puffin	Biomass of 0-class sandeels with 1-year lag	Frederiksen et al. (2006)
Black-legged kittiwake	Biomass of 0-class sandeels with 1-year lag	Burthe et al. (2012)
Black-legged kittiwake	Biomass of 0-class sandeels with 1-year lag	Frederiksen et al. (2006)
Black-legged kittiwake	Phenology and size of 0-class sandeels	Lewis et al. (2001)
Black-legged kittiwake	Abundance and phenology	Rindorf et al. (2000)
Common guillemot	Sandeel growth rate	Burthe et al. (2012)
Common guillemot	Size of 1-class sandeels	Frederiksen et al. (2006)
Common guillemot	Abundance and phenology	Rindorf et al. (2000)
Common guillemot	Size of sandeels	Wanless et al. (2005)
Common tern	No effect of abundance	Uttley et al. (1989)
European shag	Biomass of 0-class sandeels with 1 year lag	Burthe et al. (2012)
European shag	Biomass of 0-class sandeels with 1 year lag	Frederiksen et al. (2006)
European shag	Abundance and phenology	Rindorf et al. (2000)
Razorbill	No effect of size or biomass	Frederiksen et al. (2006)

increased the metabolic cost of wintering sandeels, further reducing their growth rate, fecundity and survival (Scott et al. 2011).

The productivity of a wide range of seabird species around the UK is positively correlated with the abundance and availability of sandeels (Table 4.3), although with subtle differences between species which can be related to their ecology. Therefore, any impacts of climate change on sandeel populations would be expected to affect the demography of these seabirds. For example, the breeding success of common guillemots on the Isle of May, south-east Scotland, is dependent upon the size of 1-class sandeels, which hatched in the previous year (Rindorf et al. 2000; Wanless et al. 2004; Frederiksen et al. 2006). Although guillemots have the advantage of being able to dive deeply, enabling them to access these adult sandeels throughout the season instead of relying on juvenile fish in the upper parts of the water column, they are only able to carry one fish at a time back to the breeding colony from the capture location, usually 40–80 km away (Thaxter et al. 2012). The abundance of sandeels of this age has declined significantly since the 1980s (Harris et al. 2005b), impacting guillemot breeding success (Frederiksen et al. 2004a). The same principles apply in the Baltic Sea, where guillemot productivity is linked to the size of the sprats with which they are able to provision their chicks (Österblom et al. 2006).

Seabirds that capture prey at shallower depths than the guillemot are more likely to be affected by the availability of juvenile, 0-class sandeels which frequent the upper strata of the water column. For this reason, the productivity of black-legged kittiwakes is dependent upon the abundance and particularly the size of juvenile sandeels (Wright 1996; Lewis et al. 2001), which means that they are likely to be particularly sensitive to the climate-related disruptions to populations of zooplankton upon which the young fish feed (Wanless et al. 2004). Kittiwake productivity is also affected by the abundance of 1-class

Figure 4.13 Trends in the productivity of kittiwakes in six UK coastal regions from 1986 to 2002 from Frederiksen *et al.* (2005). The length and orientation of the arrow indicates the magnitude direction of the trend, whilst the width of the arrow indicates mean productivity over the whole period.

sandeels, accounting for a negative correlation between breeding success and winter temperature with a one-year lag (Frederiksen *et al.* 2004b, 2006). This suggests that the abundance of adult sandeels determines the condition of kittiwakes at the start of the breeding season, which then impacts upon subsequent productivity. The productivity of kittiwakes may therefore be sensitive to both the availability of 1-class sandeels, which they feed upon during April and May, and 0-class sandeels, which become important as food for their chicks in June (Rindorf *et al.* 2000). They are therefore one of the seabird species whose demography can be most closely related to recent climate change (Frederiksen *et al.* 2004b). Spatial variation in kittiwake productivity can also be explained by these processes (Frederiksen *et al.* 2005). Major crashes in kittiwake productivity as a result of sandeel shortages have only occurred on Shetland and the eastern North Sea coasts (Figure 4.13). In Shetland, changes to the advection currents which transport larval sandeels to the islands from Orkney (where productivity has remained fairly high) have been responsible for at least some of the decline, along with the presence of a local sandeel fishery. Kittiwake populations in East Scotland and England have been most affected by the climatic changes outlined above. On the western coasts of the UK, sandeels are a less important component of kittiwake diet. Accordingly, productivity in these areas tends to be low, but has not declined (Furness & Tasker 2000; Frederiksen *et al.* 2005). More generally, effects of climate change on seabird populations on the west coast of the UK, such as in the Celtic Sea, appear weaker than those observed in the North Sea (Cook *et al.* 2011). This may be a result of a less clear link between climate and plankton communities than that found in the North Sea (Laura *et al.* 2012).

Similar processes also appear to be affecting Atlantic puffin and European shag populations on the Isle of May. Despite being heavily reliant on juvenile sandeels to feed their young, the productivity of both seabird species is strongly positively related to the biomass of juvenile sandeels in the previous year, a proxy for 1-class fish abundance in the year of interest (Rindorf *et al.* 2000; Frederiksen *et al.* 2006). As with kittiwakes, the availability of these 1-class fish is likely to affect the condition of adult seabirds at the start of the breeding season, and impact on their breeding success through adult behaviour and the amount of energy they are prepared to invest in a breeding attempt. These species will also suffer dramatic crashes in productivity when class-0 fish are lacking and there are simply not enough fish to feed their chicks.

There is reasonable evidence that climate change has resulted in significant shifts in the plankton–sandeel–seabird food web around the northern North Sea, resulting in declines in the productivity of a range of sandeel specialists breeding at some seabird colonies on the eastern coasts of England and Scotland, although the links between climate and seabird demography are probably most fully developed for kittiwake. Are similar changes happening elsewhere? Sandeels (or sandlances) *Ammodytes* spp. are also the key prey for seabirds in the north-eastern Pacific, where the California current and wind interact to drive the timing and size of planktonic blooms in a similar way. In this ecosystem, the productivity of rhinoceros auklets *Carorhinca monocerata* is positively correlated with the predominance of 0-class sandlances in the diet of chicks, which is negatively related to sea temperature (Hedd *et al.* 2006). Similar effects are apparent in tufted puffins *Fratercula cirrhata* (Gjerdrum *et al.* 2003). In a manner that is similar to the changes observed in the North Sea, recent warming in the eastern Pacific has advanced the timing of plankton availability (Bertram *et al.* 2001), leading to a reduction in the availability of Pacific sandlance *Ammodytes hexapterus* later in the season. Cassin's auklet *Ptychoramphus aleuticus* lives in the same area as rhinoceros auklet, but feeds instead on zooplankton. For this reason, it is most sensitive to subtle changes in the timing and strength of planktonic blooms (Wolf *et al.* 2009). Further north, the productivity of zooplankton-feeding least *Aethia pusilla*, whiskered *A. pygmaea* and crested auklets *A. cristatella* in the Bering Sea are also affected by variation in sea-surface temperature through effects on their euphausid and copepod prey (Bond *et al.* 2011). Detrimental effects of warming upon plankton and sandeel populations leading to a cascade of effects on seabird populations may therefore be widespread. But are they confined to shallow-water sandeel-dominated systems?

Where the same seabird species rely on different species of fish, they may be affected by climate in markedly different ways, depending on the way in which climate change affects their prey. Annual variation in the breeding productivity of the 660 000 Atlantic puffin pairs breeding at Røst on the Norwegian coast, close to the continental shelf, is positively correlated with the abundance of larval 0-class herring (Sætre *et al.* 2002; Durant *et al.* 2003). Unlike sandeel abundance, the availability of herring to the puffins increases with increasing temperature, leading to a positive correlation between winter temperature and subsequent puffin productivity. This may be explained by the transport of *C. finmarchicus* to the Norwegian and Barents seas by warm water flows from the Atlantic, which increases the food supply available to juvenile herring (Toreson & Østvedt 2000; Sætre *et al.* 2002; Durant *et al.* 2003, 2006). In addition, the strength and direction of the Norwegian coastal current determines the rate of transport of 0-class herring from the spawning grounds past the puffin colonies, and influences the degree of synchrony between herring availability and the peak in puffin food requirements (Durant *et al.* 2003, 2005), as described in Chapter 3. Persistent northerly winds during puffin chick-rearing may push the 0-class herrings away from the coast, reducing their availability (Sætre *et al.* 2002). Warming may therefore be expected to benefit Norwegian coastal puffin colonies as a result of the positive effects of temperature upon herring abundance.

Despite this, the colony at Røst is currently declining as a result of low and variable productivity (Harris *et al.* 2005a) due to the effects of wind upon herring transport (Durant *et al.* 2005). Given the uncertainties over how such currents and winds will change in future, it is difficult to predict what the overall consequences of climate change will be for this and many other seabird populations which depend upon the maintenance of particular oceanic circulatory systems and weather patterns.

Alcid (auk) populations elsewhere are similarly sensitive to variation in sea temperature and oceanic currents. Reductions in sea-surface temperature in the north-west Atlantic associated with a major perturbation during the 1990s resulted in a significant mortality of large, early spawning capelin *Mallotus villosus*, and seaward shift in the distribution of the remaining fish (Carscadden *et al.* 2002). In a scenario familiar to seabird biologists in the North Sea, common guillemots breeding at Funk Island off Newfoundland delayed their breeding, were unable to maintain the quality of prey being provided to their chicks, which starved (Davoren & Motevecchi 2003). The chicks of Atlantic puffins breeding on the Gannet Islands, off Labrador, also suffered reduced growth rates and breeding success, although the adults appeared to partially compensate for the lack of capelin by switching to sandeels (Baillie & Jones 2004). Black-legged kittiwake populations in this area also suffered reduced productivity as a result of the changes in capelin availability (Hipfner *et al.* 2000), but gannets were relatively unaffected (Montevecchi & Myers 1997). Further south, a reduction in the abundance and quality of 0-class herring around Machias Seal Island in the Bay of Fundy resulted in significant declines in the productivity of both Arctic *Sterna paradisaea* and common terns *Sterna hirundo*, although Atlantic puffins and razorbills *Alca torda*, being deeper foragers and less reliant on juvenile fish, were less affected (Diamond & Devlin 2003).

At the highest latitudes, the extent of sea ice is a major constraint upon seabird populations. The productivity of Brünnich's guillemots (thick-billed mures) nesting in the high Arctic is negatively correlated with the extent of sea ice during the breeding season. In cold years with a late ice breakup, the timing of breeding at these northern colonies is delayed, and productivity reduced (Gaston *et al.* 2005). At these northern range margins, there is sometimes too little open water free of ice during the brief summer for birds to breed successfully. However, the reverse applies to more southern colonies of the same species, where productivity is positively correlated with sea ice extent, and chick condition is reduced in warmer years. As might be expected from the previous text, this effect can only be understood by examining the relationship of food supplies to sea temperature and ice extent (Gaston *et al.* 2005). Brunnich's guillemot prefer to feed on Arctic cod *Boreogadus saida* (Gaston & Nettleship 1981), whose distribution is closely tied to that of sea ice (Mehlum & Gabrielsen 1993). In warm years when this species is less available, the guillemots switch to the less profitable and smaller capelin and sandeels (Gaston *et al.* 2005). As a result of recent warming trends, in accordance with expectations based on this ecological understanding, northern Brunnich's guillemot populations have increased with increasing access to open water, whilst southern populations have declined in line with reductions in prey abundance and quality (Irons *et al.* 2008). The extent of sea ice has similar contrasting effects on a variety of other alcid populations in the north-west Pacific. Cold years with delayed ice retreat favour planktivorous crested and parakeet auklets *Aethia psittacula*, whilst warmer years favour piscivorous horned *Fratercula corniculata* and tufted puffins. This contrast is not due to the direct effects of sea ice extent but to shifts in the abundance of plankton associated with these changes in water temperature. Macro-zooplankton, the prey of the auklets, are favoured by cold water, whilst meso-zooplankton, favoured by warm water, are too small for the auklets to feed on, but constitute the main prey of pelagic juvenile herring and sandeels (Kitaysky & Golubova 2000). In the same way, the expansion of sandeels into the Canadian Arctic as a result of warming has led to significant northwards colonisation by razorbills (Gaston & Woo 2008).

Climate change is therefore likely to have considerable effects upon seabird populations across the Northern Hemisphere, where warming may benefit species associated with herring and capelin systems in Norway and Canada or northern colonies limited by the extent of sea ice, but may have negative effects on more southerly populations associated with sandeel-dominated food webs. A recent shift in seabird populations in response to warming on the California shelf summarises these processes. Warming since the late 1980s has reduced primary productivity, leading to a decline in the abundance of wintering sooty shearwaters *Puffinus griseus* by 90% as a result of the reduced degree of nutrient upwelling and corresponding reduction in zooplankton abundance (Veit *et al.* 1997; Sydeman *et al.* 2001; Hyrenback & Veit 2003). These declines were also mirrored by population trends in both Cassin's and rhinoceros auklets, although at least one warm-water species, the pink-footed shearwater *Puffinus creatopus*, became more common. These effects have been largely sustained through time although they may also be partly related to increasing baleen whale populations (Ainley & Hyrenbach 2010).

Overall, the mechanism underlying these changes appears to be largely related to food availability or abundance, a key determinant of seabird productivity. Put simply, there appears to be a north to south gradient in the main foods for northern seabirds, from Arctic cod and capelin in the north to herring and then sandeels in the south. It appears that the southern populations relying on sandeels are those most vulnerable to negative changes, because there are fewer profitable fish prey to replace them. However, northern populations of sandeel specialists may expand further north. It may currently be the availability of sandeels which limits the southern range of many northern seabird species, such as common guillemot, Atlantic puffin and black-legged kittiwake, although heat stress may also be a factor (e.g. Oswald *et al.* 2008). Thus, there is considerable variation in the relationship between temperature and seabird productivity with latitude (Sandvik *et al.* 2008), which provides the ecological explanation to the latitudinal gradient in the effects of warming described in Box 4.3.

4.6.2 Survival

There is increasing evidence that seabird survival rates are related to climate (Thompson & Ollason 2001; Sandvik *et al.* 2005; Harris *et al.* 2005a; Crespin *et al.* 2006), although because of the mobility of seabirds outside the breeding season, and uncertainties over their ranges and diet during these periods, such effects can be difficult to measure and interpret. However, attempting to do so is crucial because even small changes in mortality rates of long-lived seabirds can have large effects on their populations.

The survival of adult northern fulmars *Fulmaris glacialis* breeding on Orkney, north Scotland, is negatively correlated with winter NAO, although the precise details differ between the sexes (Grosbois & Thompson 2005). This matches negative effects of NAO upon both the probability of adult fulmars breeding, which is dependent upon their body condition, and on subsequent breeding productivity (Thompson & Ollason 2001). Increasing values of the NAO index in the winter, which in the north-east Atlantic is associated with increased sea-surface temperature (Sandvik *et al.* 2008), are likely to reduce both survival and productivity as a result of reduced lesser sandeel abundance (Arnott & Ruxton 2002). Both black-legged kittiwake (Oro & Furness 2002) and great skua (Ratcliffe *et al.* 2002) survival also co-vary with sandeel abundance. For kittiwake the probable negative effects of warming on survival will be additive to the effects of temperature upon productivity. Adult survival in least auklets breeding in the Aleutian Islands, Alaska, is similarly related to the North Pacific Index in summer, with the mechanism likely to be reductions in zooplankton abundance (Jones *et al.* 2002).

Atlantic puffin survival rates at five colonies around the north-east Atlantic are each correlated with sea temperature. Although the directions of these correlations differ, they do so in ways explained by differences in their prey. The main prey of Atlantic puffins from Skomer, the Isle of May and Fair Isle is sandeels, and as expected, puffin survival at these colonies is negatively correlated with temperature. A similar but weaker correlation is found for Atlantic puffins breeding on Hornoya, where both sandeel and capelin are taken, whilst at Røst, where herring are the main prey, puffin survival is positively correlated with temperature (Harris *et al.* 2005a). These individual relationships produce a hump-shaped quadratic correlation between sea-surface temperature and survival rate across the species' entire latitudinal or temperature range, from the warm south at Skomer, where warming is detrimental, to the cold north of Røst, where warming is beneficial (Grosbois *et al.* 2009).

The survival and condition of adult seabirds are not just related to prey abundance. Weather can have direct effects. Stormy conditions during late winter, when mortality is highest, can have a significant impact on the annual survival rate of European shags. Such weather not only reduces the ability of birds to forage through increased turbidity, but also causes hypothermia. European shag populations can crash during particularly stormy years, but they have the potential to produce large numbers of young during years of high food abundance (Harris *et al.* 1994; Frederiksen *et al.* 2008). Tern populations may also be vulnerable to high winds reducing foraging efficiency (Becker & Specht 1991) and causing inundation of nests (such as of tern colonies nesting on coastal shingle banks).

4.6.3 The Southern Ocean

The same processes and patterns seem to be apparent across northern latitudes of both the Pacific and Atlantic Oceans, but what about seabird populations in the Southern Ocean, where the marine ecosystem has a very different prey base? Here, the food web is largely driven by Antarctic krill *Euphausia superba*, whose abundance and distribution is in turn strongly linked with the extent and distribution of sea ice (Kawaguchi & Satake 1994; Siegel & Loeb 1995; Loeb *et al.* 1997; Trivelpiece *et al.* 2011). Larval krill rely on the algae found on the under-surface of the ice to survive the winter (Daly 1990). In turn, krill provide an important food source directly for a range of seabird species, and for fish which are then eaten by seabirds.

Accordingly, variation in the extent of Antarctic sea ice has had significant effects on the survival and productivity of a range of seabird species. The extent of sea ice prior to breeding is positively correlated with the numbers of both Adélie *Pygoscelis adeliae* and chinstrap penguins *Pygoscelis antarcticus* arriving to breed in the South Orkney Islands, suggesting that the ability of these long-lived seabirds to gain breeding condition is related to winter food availability (Trathan *et al.* 1996). Recent declines in Adélie penguin populations on the South Shetland Islands appear to result from reductions in overwinter survival, particularly of juveniles. Mortality of juvenile Adélie penguins is inversely related to krill abundance, but it is unclear whether reduced survival results mainly from starvation or through increased predation, such as by leopard seals *Hydrurga leptonyx* (Hofmann *et al.* 1977). Although there is no evidence of recent reductions in the reproductive output of Adélie penguins, the duration of Adélie penguin foraging trips is negatively correlated with krill density. Warming may therefore be reducing food abundance in the breeding season, but the effect of this on penguin productivity may be buffered by greater parental effort (Fraser & Hofmann 2003; Hinke *et al.* 2007; Carlini *et al.* 2009).

Farther south, on the western Antarctic Peninsula, the climate has shifted from a continental to maritime climate, leading to a reduction in sea ice cover that contrasts with an overall increase across the Southern Ocean. This is one of the most rapidly warming parts of the world, having experienced a 2 °C rise in mean temperature since 1950 and 6 °C rise in mean winter temperature (Ducklow *et al.* 2007). Adélie penguins do not hunt at night, and therefore in the Antarctic winter rely on the ice margin being close to upwellings of warm water where krill and fish are concentrated. The significant contraction in sea ice extent has therefore reduced the penguins' ability to access areas of peak prey availability at these upwellings, particularly in winter, in a manner similar to that affecting the South Orkney population.

In addition, Adélie penguins require dry, snow-free areas to nest, and it appears that an increase in frequency of spring blizzard events associated with the switch to a maritime climate, has significantly increased rates of breeding failure through flooding and chilling of eggs and chicks (McClintock *et al.* 2008). Combined, these two factors have driven a 65% decline in the population breeding at the Palmer research station from 1975 to 2003 (Ducklow *et al.* 2007), a decline which has continued since (Figure 4.14). It is no wonder that David Ainley termed this species the 'bellweather of climate change' (Ainley 2002).

Although declines in Adélie penguin populations towards the northern range margin appear to be caused by recent warming, rising temperatures may have a more mixed effect on high latitude populations in the Ross Sea and Pointe Geologie Archipelago. Here, the survival of individuals, particularly juveniles, is reduced in years of extensive winter sea ice cover that limit their access to the productive waters on the margin of the Antarctic Polar Front. Survival may also be reduced in very warm years with little sea ice due to a lack of good foraging habitat (Wilson *et al.* 2001; Jenouvrier *et al.* 2006; Ballerini *et al.* 2009). Thus, as with Northern Hemisphere alcids, there is evidence for differential effects of warming upon lower latitude populations, where warming reduces prey abundance, and high latitude populations, where warming may increase accessibility to rich feeding areas, at least in the short term. However, future changes in sea ice extent in the winter, and the

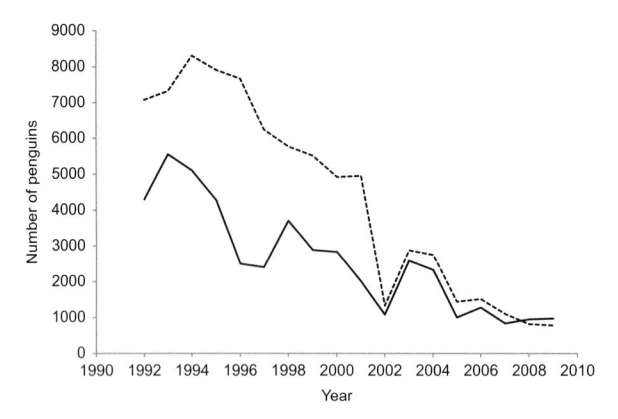

Figure 4.14 The decline in the number of pairs of breeding Adélie penguins (solid line) and chicks (dashed line) recorded at Palmer Station, Antarctica from 1991/2 to 2008/9. Note the drop in reproductive rate from 2001/2 onward. Data from the Palmer LTER data repository were supported by Office of Polar Programs, NSF Grants OPP-9011927, OPP-9632763 and OPP-0217282.

potential reductions in the overlap between winter sea ice, prey-rich zones of upwelling and areas of twilight required by the birds to forage, may limit the ability of these populations to expand further south in a warming world (Ainley *et al.* 2010; Ballard *et al.* 2010).

The response of Adélie penguin populations to catastrophic events is illustrated by the impact of two large icebergs measuring many kilometres across, which broke away from the Ross Ice Shelf and settled against Ross Island in 2001. They disrupted the normal circulation and flow of sea ice around the Island, reducing primary productivity and increasing the distance which penguins at nearby breeding colonies had to travel in order to forage. As a result of these impacts, penguin breeding productivity was significantly reduced by some 75–80% (Arrigo *et al.* 2002; Ainley *et al.* 2004), but with little impact upon adult survival (Lescroël *et al.* 2009). These long-lived seabirds compromised breeding productivity in order to minimise the effects of environmental perturbation on their survival. Similarly, Cresswell *et al.* (2008) illustrate for macaroni penguins *Eudyptes chrysolophus* how changes in female foraging behaviour can compensate for reductions in krill abundance to a certain point, beyond which productivity, and then survival, may be compromised.

Emperor penguins *Aptenodytes forsteri* have responded to recent warming in a similar way to Adélie penguins. The survival of individuals breeding at colonies in Terra Adélie is reduced by rising temperatures, presumably as a result of reduced food abundance. However, the hatching success of eggs is negatively correlated with the extent of sea ice, as this increases the distance walked by adults between the colony and the sea during foraging trips (Barbraud & Weimerskirch 2001a). Therefore, the same climatic process (warming) increases hatching success but reduces adult survival. For the long-lived emperor penguin, the net result of anomalous warming during the 1970s has been negative, as indicated by a 50% population reduction from 1952 (Jenouvrier *et al.* 2005b). Increases in temperature detrimentally affect both productivity and survival of the closely related king penguins *A. patagonicus* nesting on the Crozet Archipelago. These effects appear to be mediated through negative effects of warming cascading through the food chain to impact upon their lantern fish (Myctophidae) prey (Le Bohec et al. 2007, 2008). Emperor and Adélie penguin populations have declined widely as a result of contractions in sea ice extent reducing the productivity and survival of krill, resulting in a poleward contraction in their northern range margin, whilst the ice-intolerant gentoo *Pygoscelis papua* and chinstrap penguins *P. antarctica* have expanded their ranges southwards (Croxall 2002; Forcada & Trathan 2009; Carlini et al. 2009).

Climatic changes in the Southern Ocean have not just affected penguins. Reductions in krill abundance have also affected populations of southern fulmars *Fulmarus glacialoides* and snow petrels *Pagodroma nivea*. The adult survival of fulmars is negatively correlated with winter sea-surface temperature and positively related to winter sea ice cover (Jenouvrier et al. 2003). Snow petrel productivity is positively related to winter sea ice extent for the same reasons of increased krill abundance. However, the likelihood of adult snow petrels breeding is negatively correlated with winter sea ice cover, probably because in the coldest years, sea ice may be sufficiently extensive to prevent access to their prey, although not by enough to reduce adult survival (Barbraud & Weimerskirch 2001b; Olivier et al. 2005; Jenouvrier et al. 2005b). The net result of these processes is the snow petrel is anticipated to decline as a result of future warming.

Changes in Antarctic conditions are not only affecting seabirds that breed in and around the continent, but also species which breed further afield in the sub-Antarctic zone. The survival of thin-billed prions *Pachyptila belcheri* breeding in the Kerguelen Islands (48° S) is positively affected by warming, being negatively correlated with the extent of Antarctic winter sea ice. This may be because in cold years, extensive sea ice may restrict access to their prey. Prion breeding success is, however, negatively correlated with sea temperature, and in the long term, future increases in temperature are likely to be detrimental (Nevoux & Barbraud 2006). In contrast to the prions, the survival of blue petrels *Halobaena caerulea*, which also breed on the Kerguelen Islands, is negatively affected by warming, particularly when the population is high, indicative of strong density dependence. A long-lasting warm anomaly from 1994 to 1997 resulted in a 40% population decline in the species (Barbraud & Weimerskirch 2003). The productivity of the Antarctic foraging light-mantled albatross *Phoebetria palpebrata* is similarly negatively affected by warming (Inchausti et al. 2003). Rising temperatures are therefore predicted to have a widely detrimental effect on most southern seabird species that rely upon krill for food, despite some potential benefits where reductions in winter sea ice may increase access to prey.

A large number of albatross species nest within the sub-Antarctic zone, but tend to forage further north, between about 30–50° S. Many of these are declining in response to longline fisheries (Inchausti & Weimerskirch 2001), but may also be impacted by climate change. The survival of one of the rarest, the Amsterdam albatross *Diomedea amsterdamensis*, is negatively affected by warming in the south and south-western Indian Ocean, which may push this extremely endangered seabird, with a current breeding population of only 25 breeding pairs, towards extinction (Rivalan et al. 2010). In contrast, breeding success in the black-browed albatross *Thalassarche melanophrys* is positively related to sea-surface temperature in spring around the breeding colonies, but negatively correlated with sea-surface temperature in Tasmanian waters in the winter. However, the winter effect is less marked, suggesting that warming might be beneficial if it were evenly spread

(Rolland *et al.* 2009). Similarly, the productivity of both the wandering albatross *Diomedea exulans*, which feeds in the sub-Antarctic zone, and sooty albatross *Phoebetria fusca* found in the subtropical zone, is enhanced by higher sea-surface temperatures (Inchausti *et al.* 2003). For some of these threatened species, climate change may therefore help their populations recover from the threats associated with longline fishing, whilst for others, warming may exacerbate the current conservation problems they face. Clearly more work is required to identify which species are most vulnerable to these changes, in order to assist with the future prioritisation of conservation action (Chapter 7).

4.6.4 The tropics

Warming may also be detrimental to seabirds in the tropics, although there is typically less published literature on this. For example, the productivity and survival of Galapagos penguins *Spheniscus mendiculus* are negatively correlated with temperature. A severe El Niño event in 1982/3 increased sea temperatures and reduced adult survival, particularly of females. The effect of this was sustained and led to continued poor breeding productivity for several years afterwards (Boersma 1998). During the warm phase of the El Niño event, the degree of upwelling was reduced, limiting the nutrients available for the plankton bloom, and therefore detrimentally affecting the abundance of juvenile fish which form the penguins' food supply. Similar events were associated with reductions in blue-footed booby *Sula nebouxii* productivity off the Pacific coast of Mexico. The main mechanism for this was a switch in adult diet from herring to less profitable anchovies associated with warm water (Ancona *et al.* 2012), and for every 1 °C of warming, the number of fledglings produced per nest declined by 0.45 (Ancona *et al.* 2011). This reduction in prey abundance in warm years may also account for a decline in first-year survival from more than 80% in the coolest years, to less than 60% in the warmest years (Oro *et al.* 2010).

In the Indian Ocean, breeding conditions for roseate terns on Aride Island in the Seychelles also decline in warm years, mediated through reductions in the intensity of phytoplankton blooms (Ramos *et al.* 2006; Monticelli *et al.* 2007). The productivity of four species of seabirds at Houtman Abrolhos, along the Western Australia coast, is reduced during El Niño events (Surman *et al.* 2012). Here, however, such effects were mediated by a reduction in the strength of the warm water Leeuwin Current responsible for transporting tropical prey southwards down the west coast of Australia.

4.6.5 Conclusions

There are widespread effects of warming upon seabirds in both the Northern and Southern hemispheres. Where the extent of sea ice currently limits foraging opportunities, future warming may be beneficial, resulting in the poleward expansions of some breeding species. Where the growth and survival of fish prey species is also enhanced by high temperatures, then seabird populations that prey upon those fish are also likely to benefit from warming. However, where seabirds prey upon fish or plankton species in highly productive cold water systems (which appears to be the majority of those studied), these are likely to be detrimentally affected by warming. We can therefore account for the significant latitudinal trends in the sensitivity of seabird populations to temperature on the basis of this ecological understanding, whether auks in the Northern Hemisphere or penguins in the south.

These effects on prey populations probably underlie the negative effects of non-breeding season temperature on seabird populations, which contrasts with the apparently strongly positive short-term effect for terrestrial species (Box 4.2). The implication of these findings is that it is likely to be largely through climate-driven reductions in food abundance that seabird populations will decline and their distributions change. For many populations, future conditions will also depend upon changes in the strength and direction of oceanic currents which can be difficult to predict. It is clear that many seabird populations are highly sensitive to climatic disruption, whether in response to periodic El Niño events, occasional regime shifts or even longer-term climate change. They may therefore be amongst the most vulnerable bird species to climate change.

4.7 Conclusion

Global climate change is likely to result in increases in temperature and significant changes to precipitation patterns around the world. Whilst variation in the strength and direction of temperature and precipitation trends will have a significant effect on the exposure of particular species and populations to climate change, our review has highlighted that the intrinsic vulnerability of populations to climate change varies considerably between species and populations, much of which can be related to their ecological characteristics.

There are strong latitudinal gradients in the response of bird populations to temperature. At medium and high latitudes there appear to be relatively consistent positive correlations between temperature and productivity, survival and population growth. The positive effect of temperature appears strongest outside of the breeding season, and can be clearly explained with reference to many temperate and boreal species whose populations fluctuate strongly in relation to the severity of winter conditions. Such cold weather particularly affects species which prey on small mammals and surface and subsurface invertebrates whose availability is likely to be restricted by snow or frost, and small-bodied species with limited capacity to endure long periods of cold. The breeding productivity of most species in these environments is also enhanced by warm weather during the breeding season, which reduces thermoregulatory costs for the chicks and generally increases food availability. The species most sensitive to cold, wet weather during the breeding season are precocial or semi-altricial species whose food availability is most heavily affected by such conditions.

At lower latitudes, populations appear more strongly affected by variation in precipitation, with more equivocal effects of temperature. Thus, where studied, tropical species, particularly across arid and semi-arid habitats, appear to be negatively affected by drought and high temperatures. Similarly, the survival of long-distance migrants which winter in tropical habitats also varies with changing rainfall patterns. Thus, there is relatively consistent evidence that rainfall affects the demographic rates of bird populations in the tropics much more than temperature. The species most likely to benefit from winter precipitation are wetland and fish-eating species such as storks and herons, and insectivorous migrants, such as Old and New World warblers. By implication, it is therefore the effects of climate change on rainfall patterns in tropical areas which may be of most concern for the conservation of such tropical and long-distance migrant birds. There is likely to be greater spatial variability in changes in precipitation around the world than changes in temperature, and we are much less certain about these trends for specific locations than for temperature (Solomon *et al.* 2009). Importantly, this suggests that the effects of climate change on tropical species and long-distance migrants may be much harder to predict than on medium- and short-distance migrants breeding at medium and high latitudes, where patterns of warming are likely to be more uniform and predictable.

The ecological mechanisms by which variation in temperature and precipitation will affect bird populations are varied. Whilst positive effects of warming on high latitude populations appear largely related to short-term increases in survival and productivity in response to improving ambient conditions reducing the risk of chilling and hypothermia, there is increasing evidence that longer-term effects of warming may be more detrimental. Detailed studies of particular species strongly suggest that where increasing temperatures are associated with reductions in the abundance or availability of prey, those populations are likely to be vulnerable to warming. The strongest evidence for this comes from the marine environment, where long-term data on plankton and fish populations collected by fisheries scientists can be related to long-term variation in seabird productivity and survival. Multiple studies from most ocean systems demonstrate the importance of the climate in determining marine productivity either directly, or influencing the strength of ocean currents that transport prey, which then determine the abundance of particular prey species to seabirds. Seabird demography is closely tied to food availability, and there are many examples where disruption to oceanic systems, for example associated with El Niño events, has led to significant reductions in seabird productivity and survival. Where longer-term regime shifts have occurred, these have had correspondingly longer-term consequences for the populations of seabirds affected. Now, there is increasing evidence that consistent warming trends are detrimentally affecting some seabird populations, particularly towards the low latitude margins of their range, whilst some higher latitude populations may benefit from warming. Although the mechanisms linking climate and seabird populations are perhaps more strongly developed than for other taxa, these results support other studies which suggest that it is in the marine environment where the impacts of climate change may be most apparent and serious (Belkin 2009; Cheung *et al.* 2009; Sunday *et al.* 2012). We therefore identify seabirds as likely to be particularly vulnerable to future climate change.

There is some evidence that climate-mediated variation in prey populations may also affect terrestrial bird species, although based upon analyses of far fewer long-term time series of prey populations. It is likely that species which feed on prey vulnerable to climate change, such subsurface invertebrates vulnerable to warming and drought, or caterpillars exhibiting significant phenological changes or climate-driven reductions in population size, may be particularly at risk (e.g. Pearce-Higgins 2010). Changes in precipitation patterns in Mediterranean and tropical climates may lead to a cascade of effects along an ecological food chain affecting granivorous and frugivorous birds through rapidly altering plant productivity, insectivorous species through lagged effects on insect populations and raptors and owls through effects on small mammal and bird populations.

The potentially widespread importance of variation in prey availability as a key mechanism potentially influencing the vulnerability of species and populations to climate change is probably one of the main messages of this chapter. This has not previously been identified, although the results of a recent review suggest that most extinctions resulting from climate change are likely to result from altered interactions between species, such as disrupted food resources (Cahill *et al.* 2013). Research should therefore prioritise the identification of keystone prey species within every environment, and then, as with the marine environment, long-term monitoring of the abundance and availability of such species should be instigated. The monitoring of populations of plankton and relevant small energy-rich fish species around seabird colonies provides time series which can be consistently related to the productivity of those populations. In the same way, it is likely that the long-term monitoring of key, energy-rich invertebrate groups, fruit and seed production and small mammal populations around the world would go a long way to significantly improving our understanding of the drivers of terrestrial bird populations, and their likely vulnerability to climate change. In short, when attempting to understand the likely effects of climate change upon bird populations, there is no substitute for good ecological knowledge based upon autecological studies, and long-term monitoring data, neither of which are easy to fund, but are incredibly useful to develop the understanding required to manage global climatic change (Part 2).

As well as variation in food resources, there is some evidence that climate-mediated changes in predation pressure may also affect some populations, particularly in the Arctic. It has been suggested that predation can limit the low-latitude range margin of some bird populations (Pienkowski 1984) and many ground-nesting bird species such as wildfowl, waders and gamebirds appear particularly vulnerable to increasing generalist predator populations (Gibbons *et al.* 2007a). Where climate change causes increases in predator populations, we would therefore expect their potential avian prey may be vulnerable to population decline. There is a hint that this may be affecting some Arctic wildfowl species, but predation, as yet, does not yet appear to be a major driver of climate-related change in bird populations.

Inter-specific competition between species may similarly be responsible for climate-mediated impacts on particular populations. Models of speciation suggest that competition may be a key ecological process at species' range margins (Bridle & Vines 2007) and therefore could be expected to be a particular feature of climate change impacts on species interactions. Although there is some limited evidence that variation in the climate may be associated with changes in the balance of reproductive success between species (e.g. Martin 2001; Ahola *et al.* 2007; Şekercioğlu *et al.* 2012; Vallin *et al.* 2012) and may affect migrant survival rates (Dugger *et al.* 2004), the number of such studies is relatively small, given the evidence for significant changes in species distributions and avian communities reviewed in Chapter 5. This may be because competition is a difficult process to study, and we therefore advocate that to test this specific studies be established along dynamic range boundaries between closely related species that appear to be shifting in response to recent warming.

There are few examples of disease and parasites limiting bird populations. However, those that do exist, whether West Nile virus in the USA (LaDeau *et al.* 2007; Koenig *et al.* 2010) or trichomoniasis in the UK (Robinson *et al.* 2010), demonstrate the potential for novel disease outbreaks to have a rapid and potentially catastrophic impact on the populations in which they occur. Although there is no clear link between climate change and disease incidence in bird populations, there is a good theoretical basis to suggest that where the distribution and abundance of particular pathogens, alternative hosts, vectors or parasites may be limited by climate, particularly temperature, then warming is likely to result in an expansion in the incidence of that pathogen, with likely negative impacts on its hosts. Thus, avian malaria may threaten an increasing proportion of Hawaiian bird species as warming increases its altitudinal range (Benning *et al.* 2002), whilst red grouse in the UK may be affected by expanding tick populations and increased prevalance of *Trichostrongylus tenuis*. Whilst we do not anticipate that climate change will necessarily lead to widespread losses of bird populations as a result of disease in the same way that it may be doing for amphibians (Pounds *et al.* 2006; Lips *et al.* 2008; Blaustein *et al.* 2010), this is a topic which requires continued monitoring and research.

Climate change is also likely to be associated with an increased frequency of catastrophic weather events and storms. For species whose populations appear negatively affected by heavy precipitation, such as raptors and gamebirds, increased intensity of rainfall events may pose a long-term threat. Coastal breeding species may be particularly vulnerable to storm surges and saline inundation, potentially exacerbated by rising sea levels, whilst riparian and freshwater breeding species may also be affected by rapid changes in water level that may inundate nesting attempts. Extreme weather events may potentially affect any species and population, but with a rising frequency of flood events through time (e.g. Figure 1.7), as well as increased risk of extreme heat waves and fire outbreaks, climate change-driven catastrophes may increasingly threaten rare species with small populations concentrated within a limited geographical area.

It is clear from this review, and the range of examples presented in the preceding pages, that the mechanisms by which climate change can impact upon species may be complex, even in ecosystems with relatively few species, such as Arctic tundra, peatlands and deserts. These results can also be used to identify the sorts of species most vulnerable to climate change. It is noteworthy that in many cases, interactions between species will mean that climate change may have the opposite effect on a species' demography than might initially be expected from direct correlations between temperature or precipitation and demographic measures. This principle is neatly illustrated by studies on upland birds in the UK and provides a cautionary note for conservation scientists and climate researchers to take care with the inferences they draw from correlations. It is essential to develop a good ecological understanding of a particular system in order to be able to identify these potential linkages and direction of effects, in order to fully assess the likely sensitivity of particular populations and species to climate change (Chamberlain & Pearce-Higgins 2013). Indeed, multiple factors can potentially affect the same populations and result in contrasting demographic effects in response to a change in the climate (e.g. Mustin *et al.* 2007). In order to identify some of the main drivers for particular species and populations, long-term monitoring data, detailed ecological information, demographic modelling and even experimentation may be required. We conclude with two examples that best illustrate these approaches.

The first describes the potential effects of climate change on a population of Eurasian oystercatchers *Haematopus ostralegus* breeding on salt marshes around the Wadden Sea. These birds are likely to suffer reduced breeding success in response to climate change, due to sea level rise causing an increased risk of nests on salt marsh being flooded. Such flooding, coupled with winter warming, also reduces the availability of nereid ragworms, their key prey. Climate change is therefore likely to decrease oystercatcher breeding success as a result of reductions in prey abundance and increased frequency of catastrophic flooding events, two of the mechanisms outlined above by which climate change is likely to detrimentally affect populations. However, these two negative impacts need to be balanced against the strong positive correlation between winter temperature and overwinter survival for this long-lived species (Duriez et al. 2009). The population is currently declining, but models indicate that projected future increases in overwinter survival rates in response to climate change might slow or even reverse this trend (van de Pol et al. 2010a, b). This example therefore contrasts with that outlined for Eurasian golden plovers (Section 4.3.4). Although both waders are characterised by positive effects of warming on overwinter survival and negative effects of warming on food resources leading to a reduction in productivity, the projected outcomes of climate change are different. In the case of the oystercatchers, improvements in survival may outweigh reductions in productivity, whereas in the case of golden plovers, the reduction in breeding productivity is likely to outweigh the benefit associated with higher survival rates.

The second example is Thomas Martin's long-term study of warblers in high altitude (2400 m) forests in Arizona. Here, there is evidence that changes in precipitation have led to shifts in the distribution of species along a gradient of dry forest at the highest sites to moist forest on the lower slopes. Some of these changes are direct, but others are indirect. We have already described how Virginia's warblers appear displaced from their preferred, moist habitats by orange-crowned warblers, leading to an increase in predation rates (Martin 2001). More important, however, appears to be the effects of climatic change on the warblers' habitats. Normally, heavy winter snow would cause elk *Cervus canadensis* to move to low altitudes, protecting the dry montane forests from winter browsing. However, recent reductions in snowpack have led to increased browsing of deciduous plants by elk, despite an overall decline in the size of the elk population. This has led to a reduction in the cover of understory vegetation, which has reduced the concealment of warbler nests and further increased competition between species, which combined has led to increased rates of nest predation and declines in overall breeding success. Mammals are the main nest predators, and reduced snow cover and increased frequency of summer drought may also have reduced the abundance of their alternative prey, further exacerbating these losses. As a result of these changes, populations of five migrant warbler species which nest on the ground or in the vegetation understory have declined significantly through time (Martin 2007; Auer & Martin 2013).

At this point, being a largely correlative study, impacts outside the breeding season may also have been implicated in contributing to these trends. To address this issue of whether correlation between demographic parameters and climatic variables signifies causation, which bedevils almost all of the published literature in this area, Martin and Maron (2012) uniquely extended their work through the experimental exclusion of elk from replicated treatment plots. Within these exclosures, elk browsing was eliminated, thus simulating the effects of deep winter snow that previously forced the elk to lower levels. As expected, the exclosures reduced elk browsing and restored shrub density, and led to a concomitant increase in migrant populations within the experimental plots (Martin & Maron 2012). This study is therefore an extremely rare but valuable example that goes beyond correlation to demonstrate experimentally at least one of the underlying causes of the ecological effects of recent climate change on this system, which then can be used to inform a potentially adaptive management response (Section 7.6).

For a climatologist, climate is measured over at least a 30-year timespan. Therefore, meaningful climate change can only really be described over a 30-year trend or more. It is worth finishing with a cautionary note that the majority of studies covered in this chapter do not span this duration (only 24% did, whilst 56% were shorter than 20 years in duration), and indeed, cannot really be said to describe the effects of long-term climate change. Instead, they document relationships between annual variation in the weather and bird populations. This does not render this chapter irrelevant with respect to understanding climate change impacts. Far from it. These studies provide our best understanding of the likely causal mechanisms by which climate change will impact on bird populations around the world, and the sorts of species which may be most vulnerable to them. But it is important to recognise their limitations, and to once again emphasise the need to establish long-term monitoring of bird populations around the world to address this gap. Ideally, such monitoring should not just focus on the birds but should also collect relevant environmental variables, particularly relating to the key resources those birds rely on, their predators and competitors. Only then will we have the widespread understanding required to best appraise and track the potential impacts of an increasing magnitude of climate change on the bird populations around us. Such information will usefully inform our conservation response that we outline in the second part to this book. But first, let us consider in the next chapter how impacts of climate change on individual populations may scale up to affect species' distributions and the structure of communities.

4.8 Summary

- Birds are some of the best monitored organisms, providing relatively long-term data with which to examine how they respond to fluctuations in the weather and changes to the climate. These come from large-scale standardised monitoring programmes which may use volunteers to collect data at national or continental scales, or from site-specific count data. Where demographic data exist to estimate survival and productivity, they may provide additional information about the mechanisms underpinning any observed change.

- Across published studies, most high latitude populations appear to increase in response to warmer temperatures and drier conditions, whilst at low latitudes, populations appear limited by drought, with more equivocal effects of temperature. Effects of temperature appear to be more mixed for seabirds than terrestrial species. Populations tend to fluctuate most in response to variation in non-breeding season temperature. Negative effects of precipitation upon populations are more apparent during the breeding season, but tend to be positive outside of the breeding season, particularly for long-distance migrants wintering in the tropics.

- Populations of many medium to high latitude species may naturally be limited by severe winter weather, either in response to reductions in food availability during the winter or cold weather in the spring, when birds are preparing for the breeding season.

The survival of a smaller number of other species, particularly those which rely on subsurface prey such as thrushes, may be reduced by summer drought.
- Free-ranging precocial chicks appear more sensitive to variation in temperature and precipitation than altricial chicks. This probably results from their greater exposure to ambient conditions, greater energetic requirements and limited potential for adult behaviour to buffer the chicks to poor conditions. Semi-altricial raptor and owl chicks also appear vulnerable to poor weather which reduces the ability of their parents to forage.
- Catastrophic weather events can cause large-scale loss of breeding attempts, or high rates of mortality. The population level consequences of such events are greatest when they impact upon small populations concentrated in a limited number of sites.
- Although the effects of temperature upon medium and high latitude species tends to be positive, negative effects of warming are more apparent when the effects on interspecific interactions such as reductions in food availability and prey populations, vulnerability to predation and increasing parasite and disease prevalence are examined. As climate change is likely to affect individual populations through multiple mechanisms, conservation biologists can use demographic models to identify the most important factors for a given situation.
- The survival of most medium- and long-distance migrants which winter in the Sahelian region of Africa or the Caribbean fluctuates in response to annual variation in precipitation in those areas. For many species, wet rainy seasons maximise the food resources available for overwintering birds. There is some evidence that declines in migrant breeding productivity, for example associated with a reduction in prey availability, may be responsible for some recent population declines.
- Demographic studies from arid tropical and Mediterranean climates confirm the importance of precipitation in driving variation in both breeding productivity and survival rates, largely by affecting food resources and prey abundance. Climate change may also increase the frequency of extreme events, such as storms or heat waves which can cause widespread and sudden mortality. Climate-related increases in disease prevalence may also impact vulnerable populations.
- Variation in seabird productivity appears consistently linked to prey availability, providing a widespread mechanism through which they have been impacted by recent warming and oceanic regime shifts. It is in seabirds that the effects of climate change mediated through prey abundance have been best described. Some seabirds may additionally be affected by heat stress, although at high latitudes, retreating sea ice may boost productivity at some colonies. Seabird survival rates also appear sensitive to climate-mediated reductions in prey availability. Some seabird species may also be vulnerable to severe storm events, which can cause catastrophic mortality.
- There is perhaps the greatest evidence for climate change to impact species through direct changes in the risk of hyperthermia and heat stress, and indirect effects of variation in prey availability and abundance. Biotic factors associated with altered species' interactions may be the most important mechanisms associated with increased extinction risk due to long-term climate change.

- A minimum 30-year period is generally regarded as required to properly describe climate and climate change. Relatively few avian studies span that duration. Robust long-term monitoring of bird population and relevant environmental variables, such as the abundance of keystone prey species, should be established globally in order to properly track, attribute and understand the population level impacts of climate change on birds.

5 · *Effects of climate change on distributions and communities*

5.1 Introduction

Preceding chapters have illustrated how temperature, precipitation and other climatic factors affect the breeding productivity, survival and abundance of individual bird species through a variety of mechanisms. As a result, the geographical ranges of species can frequently be well described by the climate, as illustrated with reference to the red grouse in Chapter 1, although that descriptive ability does not show for certain whether the climate has a direct influence, an indirect influence or no real influence at all on species' distributions (Gaston 2003). There are plenty of examples of biotic factors such as prey availability (Koenig & Haydock 1999; Banko *et al.* 2002), competition (Terborgh 1985; Emlen *et al.* 1986; Gross & Price 2000) and predation (Pienkowski 1984; Dekker 1989) being the main proximate factor limiting species' ranges, but of course, the distribution of many of those other species may also be affected by climate. For example, the northern limit of the distribution of the red fox, which is thought to restrict the range of some wader species (e.g. Pienkowski 1984), is determined by resource (food) availability and therefore ultimately determined by climate (Hersteinsson & Macdonald 1994). The northern limit of Hume's leaf warbler *Phylloscopus humei* which feeds on arthropods in tree canopies, is limited by cold temperature, as this causes leaf loss and therefore reduces food availability (Gross & Price 2000). Climate is therefore often regarded as the ultimate determinant of species' distributions and abundance, even though the precise mechanisms causing the limitation may be unclear (Huntley *et al.* 2007).

Of course, there are factors other than climate that influence species' distributions, as becomes especially apparent when distributions are viewed on a global scale. Equivalent climates occur on different continents, but only a few bird species are widespread enough to occupy those climate niches wherever they occur. Many are therefore also limited by where they originated, where they were able to disperse to and the competitors, predators, parasites and food organisms they encountered along the way. More recently, human activity and pressures have become an increasingly important restriction on species' distributions. The influence of humans has, in many cases, weakened associations of bird distributions and climate because human distribution itself is only weakly related to climate. For example, human persecution has historically limited the distribution of many large raptor species in the UK (e.g. Evans *et al.* 2012), weakening the link between climate and occurrence for these species (Anderson *et al.* 2009b). The drainage and conversion to agriculture of wetland areas across Europe has caused the contraction and fragmentation of the ranges of many waterbird species (Shrubb 2003). Many island endemic bird species have been lost or suffered extreme range limitation in response to the introduction of non-native predators (Reaser *et al.* 2007; McGeoch *et al.* 2010). These pressures can pose significant challenges to analysts attempting to describe the climatic determinants of species ranges and predict the future consequences of climate change, as we shall see in Chapter 6.

Assuming that climate is in many respects the ultimate determinant of bird distributions, we would expect those distributions to shift in response to climate change. This would be the logical outcome of the potential positive effects of climate change on some populations, and negative impacts on other populations, described in Chapter 4. We examine the evidence for this in the first part of this chapter. Species do not exist in isolation, but as part of ecological communities, the term we use to describe the groupings and aggregations of populations and species at a particular location. Changes in the distribution and abundance of species, for either the climatic or anthropogenic reasons outlined above, will have an impact on the structure of those communities. Secondly, we appraise the evidence for the link between climate and avian communities before thirdly, reviewing the evidence that recent climate change has caused detectable changes to these communities.

5.2 The consequences of climate change for species distributions

5.2.1 Heading poleward

There is increasing evidence that one of the most widespread impacts of climate change on biodiversity has been to alter species' distributions. At mid- to high latitudes, there is increasing evidence that the poleward range margin of a wide range of taxa has shifted closer to the poles, and that the magnitude of this shift is related to the degree of climate change (Hickling *et al.* 2006; Chen *et al.* 2011). These patterns are also apparent in birds. Across mid- to high latitudes, there has been a generally consistent poleward shift in avian distributions ($\pm$ SE) of 0.76 ± 0.27 km per year (Table 5.1), a mean shift of 15 km over a 20-year study (Box 5.1). In addition, there is evidence from South Africa that a number of bird species have also extended their range southwards towards cooler climates, presumably again in response to climate warming, whilst other species appear to have shifted westward, potentially in response to land-use change (Hockey *et al.* 2011). It is worth noting that in the tropics, where precipitation may be the most important determinant of populations (Section 4.5) and communities (Section 5.3), climate change may not necessarily be expected to cause poleward species' shifts (VanDerWal *et al.* 2013).

It appears that the latitudinal shift of poleward (leading) range margins for birds (1.2 ± 0.3 km per year) may exceed that for equatorial (trailing) range margins (Box 5.1), although a greater number of studies are required to test this fully. It is possible that this may be a methodological artefact, as colonisations are generally easier to detect than extinctions at the scale of most studies (Thomas *et al.* 2006a), or as a result of variation in observer effort through time (Kujala *et al.* 2013). Alternatively, this may indicate more rapid latitudinal advances at the leading rather than trailing edges. Consistent with this pattern, Beale *et al.* (2013) found, in an analysis of Tanzanian Bird Atlas data from two time periods (1960–1989 and 2000–2006), that sites colonised by savanna birds by the second time period had improved in climate suitability for those species, whilst the probability of extinction was unrelated to climate suitability. Thus, climate change had

Table 5.1 *Summary of studies of birds documenting recent shifts in the geographical range boundaries of birds.*

Location	No. species	Study duration	Shift type	Mean absolute shift	Reference
Latitude					
UK	69	20 yrs	Leading	18.8 ± 6.5* km	Thomas & Lennon (1999)
UK	42	20 yrs	Trailing	4.5 ± 9.0	Thomas & Lennon (1999)
UK	22	20 yrs	Leading	29.0 ± 20.0	Hickling et al. (2006)
Finland	116	12 yrs	Leading	18.8 ± 6.1*	Brommer (2004)
Finland	116	12 yrs	Trailing	16.9 ± 14.8	Brommer (2004)
USA	29	26 yrs	Leading	61.1*	Hitch & Leberg (2007)
USA	26	26 yrs	Trailing	28.4	Hitch & Leberg (2007)
Great Plains, USA	5	25 yrs	Mean	46.0 ± 51.7	Peterson et al. (2003)
New York State, USA	41	20 yrs	Leading	9.6 ± 5.2	Zuckerberg et al. (2009)
New York State, USA	44	20 yrs	Trailing	11.4 ± 3.1*	Zuckerberg et al. (2009)
Altitude					
UK	22	20 yrs	Leading	2.1 ± 13.1 m	Hickling et al. (2006)
France	29	25 yrs	Mean	19.3 ± 12.0	Archaux et al. (2004)
Italy	56	11 yrs	Mean	29	Popy et al. (2010)
Czech Republic	50	20 yrs	Mean	30.5 ± 11.8*	Reif & Flousek (2012)
New York State, USA	129	20 yrs	Leading	5.7 ± 9.4	Zuckerberg et al. (2009)
New York State, USA	129	20 yrs	Trailing	11.6 ± 7.7	Zuckerberg et al. (2009)
Lassen, California, USA	78	80–100 yrs	Trailing	36.5 ± 25.1	Tingley et al. (2012)
Lassen, California, USA	78	80–100 yrs	Leading	97.2 ± 46.0*	Tingley et al. (2012)
Yosemite, California, USA	78	80–100 yrs	Trailing	19.3 ± 40.0	Tingley et al. (2012)
Yosemite, California, USA	78	80–100 yrs	Leading	203.7 ± 57.5*	Tingley et al. (2012)
Southern Sierra, California, USA	73	80–100 yrs	Trailing	129.7 ± 46.9*	Tingley et al. (2012)
Southern Sierra, California, USA	73	80–100 yrs	Leading	143.7 ± 78.6	Tingley et al. (2012)
Peru	55	41 years	Mean	49.0 ± 17.3*	Forero-Medina et al. (2011)

Note that both Thomas and Lennon (1999) and Hickling et al. (2006) present estimates of range shift from the same data sources; between the 1968–1972 breeding bird atlas (Sharrock et al. 1976) and the 1988–1991 atlas (Gibbons et al. 1993). Where available, standard error margins are presented for individual estimates. An asterisk denotes studies where the shift is of statistical significance.

Box 5.1 · *Analyses of range change in birds*

Six multi-species studies have described recent latitudinal range shifts in birds, in comparable ways. An additional seven studies examined altitudinal change (Table 5.1). In order to summarise the main effects from these studies, we analysed the magnitude of average latitudinal and altitudinal shifts between studies after standardising the results of each study to the mean horizontal or vertical distance moved per year. To account for the non-independence of data from the same study, analysis was conducted using a mixed-model framework, with study as a random effect (including the two studies which compare changes in the distribution of British birds from the same sources as a single random effect level). The contribution of each study was weighted by the reciprocal of the standard error of the estimate of each shift, to reduce the influence of estimates with the greatest uncertainty. No estimates of error were presented by Peterson (2003), so we used the error estimate for this study from Chen *et al.* (2011).

We compared the strength of latitudinal shifts in the five leading range margins where this was documented (in this context, the poleward margin estimates) with those for the four trailing range margins (the equatorial margin) and found, despite the small sample size, a close to significant difference ($F_{1,\,7} = 3.39$, $P = 0.11$) in shift between the two.

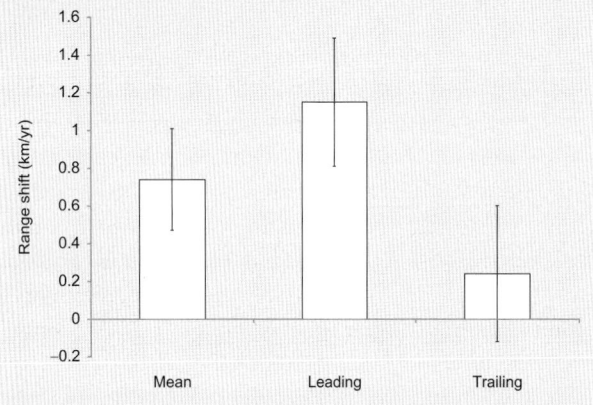

Box 5.1 Average ($\pm$ SE) range shifts across all measures (mean) and for leading and trailing range margins only.

facilitated range expansions but not caused range contractions. If true, a net result of this would be that recent climate change has generally increased the latitudinal range of species' distributions; in other words, it has resulted in an expansion of species' range extent.

Such recent expansion has been documented in terrestrial ectotherms (Sunday *et al.* 2012) and attributed to recent warming relaxing the thermal limits which directly limit populations at the leading range margin. Detrimental effects of warming at trailing range margins are suggested to occur through more complex biotic interactions such as variation in predation rates, prey populations or habitat availability (Chapter 4; Cahill *et al.* 2013), which are likely to require a longer time to take full effect. If these contrasting processes at leading and trailing range margins are confirmed in birds, this would suggest that the short-term effects of climate change may be more positive than the long-term projections suggest (Chapter 6), at least in some locations. Alternatively, such differences may be an artefact of the dispersal of individuals between patches in a meta-population (Anderson *et al.* 2009a). Clearly more work is required to examine this fully, and particularly to document evidence for population change and range contraction at the trailing margin of species' ranges.

This does not mean that there is no evidence that species are suffering range contractions in response to recent warming. One potential example is the rusty blackbird *Euphagus carolinus* which was once widespread across the boreal region of North America, but has contracted its southern range boundary northwards by some 140 km from 1967/1977 to 1998/2008, which the authors attribute to a lagged response to fluctuations in the Pacific Decadal Oscillation (McClure *et al.* 2012). The precise mechanisms underpinning this relationship are unclear, and although this shift is consistent with a potential climate-related range contraction, we suggest that further work is required to validate this conclusion fully.

A second example of recorded distribution shift and poleward range contraction in line with the expectation from climate change is that of the willow warbler *Phylloscopus trochilus* in the UK, which has strongly declined in abundance across southern and eastern England, whilst populations in Scotland have increased in size (Morrison *et al.* 2010), a pattern apparent in a wider range of species (Ockendon *et al.* 2012; Morrison *et al.* 2013). Although no mechanism has been identified to link this pattern to climate change, the willow warbler might be regarded as one of the species potentially vulnerable to warming. For example, it is one of the migrants regarded by Møller *et al.* (2008) as having little advanced the timing of its arrival across Europe, and therefore being potentially vulnerable to phenological mismatch (although see Tables S2.1[*] and S2.2[*]). Alternatively, it is plausible that willow warblers may be vulnerable to competition with the closely related congeneric chiffchaff which is a medium- rather than long-distance migrant, and has increased substantially in abundance during the same period (Figure 5.1). Chiffchaffs are absent or scarce in the areas of Scotland where willow warblers have not declined. There is no evidence, to our knowledge, of such competitive effects having been demonstrated between these species, but this is the sort of pattern we might expect to see were competition driving the changes. As mentioned in Chapter 4, we would advocate detailed research on potentially competitive sibling species such as these, at their range boundaries, to test this.

5.2.2 Going up?

In contrast with the strong evidence for latitudinal shifts in range margins, there is less evidence for a significant and consistent upwards altitudinal shift in bird distributions in response to recent warming (Table 5.1), with a mean shift of 0.33 ± 0.30 m per year of elevation, equivalent to only a 6.6 m shift in 20 years (Box 5.1), and not significantly different from zero. Although some studies have found evidence for significant upward shifts in altitudinal distribution, the majority have not, and have tended to find as many species exhibiting downward shifts. For example, although Maggini *et al.* (2011) showed

---
[*] See online material.

176 · Effects of climate change on distributions and communities

(a)

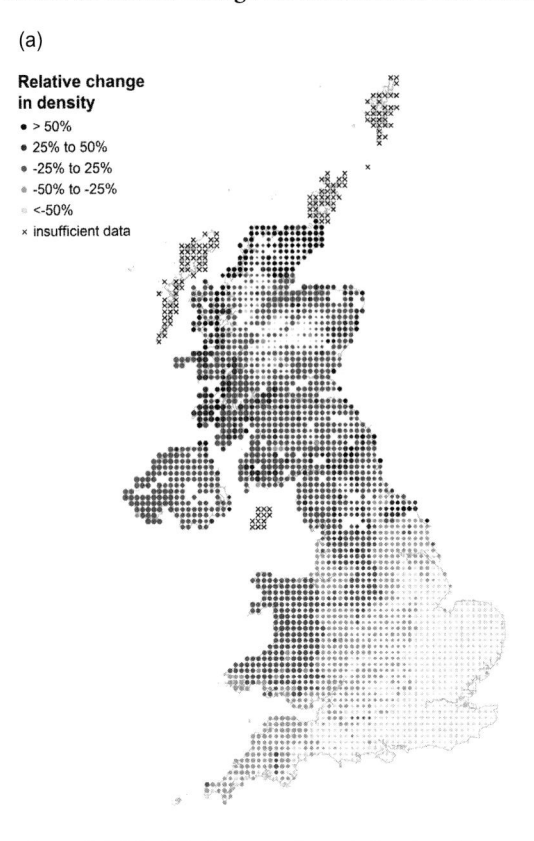

Relative change in density
- > 50%
- 25% to 50%
- -25% to 25%
- -50% to -25%
- <-50%
× insufficient data

Figure 5.1 Modelled fine-scale variation in willow warbler (a) and chiffchaff (b) population trends, 1994/1996–2007/2009. Spatial models for each time period describe density as a function of habitat and additional spatial variation, and are used to generate local measures of population change (see British Trust for Ornithology 2013 for more details). The size of each circle indicates mean density

that 33/95 species in the Swiss Alps exhibited a significant upward trend in distribution from 1999–2002 to 2004–2007, a further 28 species showed evidence of a significant downward shift, and the overall response probably did not differ significantly from zero. Although some UK upland breeding birds have tended to suffer population declines at low altitudes, as might be expected in response to warming, these are not clearly linked to climate change and may be a consequence of other changes at those altitudes (Box 5.2).

Conversely, four studies have found evidence for significant altitudinal shifts in distribution in response to climate change. The first study documented changes in Peruvian forest bird communities at five sites along an altitudinal gradient from 690 m to 2220 m from 1969 to 2010 (Forero-Medina *et al.* 2011). Of the 55 species studied, 36 showed evidence for an upward shift in abundance and 12 a downward shift. The mean 49 m shift upward, after correcting for survey effort, is less than the 152 m expected from the 0.79 °C warming over a similar period, suggesting that the bird response lagged behind that of the climate. Also comparing the occurrence of birds at points along altitudinal transects, Reif and Flousek (2012) found 40/51 species shifted upward from 1996/1998 to 2006/2008 in

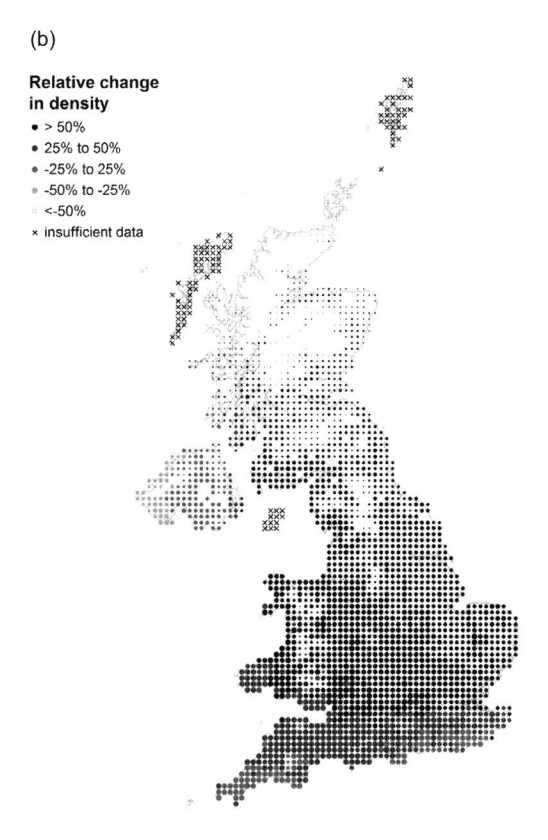

Figure 5.1 (cont.)

Box 5.2 · *Altitudinal shifts in UK upland birds*

Several correlative studies of changes in the abundance of declining upland birds suggest that population declines have been most apparent at low altitude, once habitat variation has been accounted for. Declines in ring ouzel populations have been most apparent below about 400 m (Buchanan *et al*. 2003; Sim *et al*. 2007), whilst black grouse population declines in Scotland were greatest below 300 m (Pearce-Higgins *et al*. 2007b). Population declines in five breeding wader species did not, however, appear closely related to altitude (Amar *et al*. 2011). Both ring ouzel and black grouse are believed to be vulnerable to detrimental effects of warming (Beale *et al*. 2006a; Ludwig *et al*. 2006), and therefore these changes might be expected to signal an impact of climate change. However, this would ignore the fact that both species are also sensitive to other environmental changes, such as changes in grazing management (Burfield 2002; Calladine *et al*. 2002) and predation rates (Summers *et al*. 2004). These other factors, which are not measured easily across large spatial scales, are also likely to be correlated with altitude and probably more important causes of the observed patterns than climate change in these instances, although a full analysis is required to test this properly.

the Giant Mountains, Czech Republic, although there was little overall change in distribution during the previous decade. This upward shift was statistically significant, and averaged 30 m, a similar magnitude to the shift in species composition recorded by Popy *et al.* (2010) in the Italian Alps.

Taking a cruder approach, Peh (2007) compared the upper and lower altitudinal limits of 485 resident species in south-east Asia given in two field guides (King *et al.* 1975 and Robson 2000) compiled decades apart. Despite the potential methodological biases in such data, there was greater evidence for an upward shift in the upper (leading-edge) margin (129 species) than for downward shifts (66 species), and much less evidence than for shifts in the lower (trailing edge) margin (12 species show an upward shift compared to 42 showing a downward shift). Whether these shifts are due to increased recorder effort, climate change, or the extensive habitat destruction which has occurred in the region is difficult to judge, although two lines of evidence suggest habitat destruction may not be responsible. Firstly, greater losses at lower altitudinal limits would probably be expected were the changes driven by the loss of lowland forests, and secondly, the shifts were not affected by the habitat specificity of the species involved.

The complexities of the link between climate and altitude which these contrasting results suggest are well illustrated by detailed studies of changes in the abundance of bird species in the Sierra Nevada, California. Here, long-term changes along four altitudinal transects first surveyed from 1911 to 1929 and re-surveyed between 2003 and 2008 have been documented and related to climate change (Tingley *et al.* 2009, 2012). Whilst a summary of the species' specific changes suggests that there were consistent upward shifts in the leading range margins at Lassen and Yosemite, and significant downward shifts in the trailing range margin at Southern Sierra (Table 5.1) overall, only 51% of the shifts were upwards (Tingley *et al.* 2012). Despite this apparently weak overall response, some 82–91% of species shifted their distribution in the expected direction in response to changes in temperature and precipitation between the two time periods. Species occupying low altitudes, where precipitation is limiting, responded particularly to changes in rainfall, whereas at high latitudes, species responded to warming, presumably accounting for the more consistent evidence for upwards movement in the upper (leading) range margins. This variation reflects the relative contribution of both variables to primary productivity (see Section 5.3). Thus, during the course of the twentieth century, it appears that shifts in the distribution and community structure of these mountain species responded in the expected way to climate change, providing support for the potential for models which link bird distributions and populations to climate to be able to predict future changes, providing that they are not just based on temperature, a point we shall return to in Chapter 6.

Overall, there appears to have been a greater latitudinal shift in bird distribution than altitudinal shift, although evidence is mounting from some recent studies that upward shifts in altitude have occurred. Based on a more extensive review across all taxa, Chen *et al.* (2011) concluded the same. Should this difference indicate that latitude and altitudinal shifts may occur at different rates in response to warming, montane species, widely regarded as highly vulnerable to climate change (Şekercioğlu *et al.* 2008; Chamberlain *et al.* 2012), may be more resilient to change than currently thought because they are less affected by climate change than expected. Alternatively though, they could be argued to be more vulnerable, because they are failing to keep pace with the climate change that has occurred. Such discrepancies between warming and range change may occur because latitudinal shifts may be closely related to temperature whilst altitudinal shifts may not, potentially because of a greater role for wind speed, variation in topography (slope and aspect) or soil type in limiting species' altitudinal ranges, whilst the likely greater importance of precipitation in determining species' distributions in the mountains is clearly illustrated by the work of Tingley *et al.* (2012). The magnitude of altitudinal shifts may also be masked by the more complex microclimates that occur in mountainous areas, which may complicate the link between altitude and temperature when measured at large scales. Studies on this to date suggest that the importance of microclimate in affecting bird distributions is mixed (Bradbury *et al.* 2011; Calladine & Bray 2012). Alternatively, this difference may simply be an artefact of the much more limited altitudinal shift (tens of metres) to be expected from a given increase in temperature than the tens of kilometres' shift in latitude the same temperature increase would cause, making the former more difficult to detect. More work to disentangle these potential explanations would be valuable, as would establishing detailed long-term studies of demographic rates in bird populations along an altitudinal gradient, to examine the processes underpinning such change (Chamberlain *et al.* 2012; Chamberlain & Pearce-Higgins 2013).

5.3 Global patterns of species richness

If species distributions around the world are very much influenced by climate, how is this reflected in patterns of avian richness? Why do some parts of the world support many species, whilst others hold relatively few? Global patterns in avian species richness are now readily accessible because BirdLife International has compiled maps, in digital form, of the breeding and non-breeding ranges of virtually all the world's bird species. When these species distribution maps are overlaid to give species numbers at any particular point, some strong patterns are evident (Orme *et al.* 2005). Most obviously, there is a strong latitudinal gradient in local species richness, with the largest number of species per unit area occurring at low latitudes and richness declining with increasing distance polewards (Figure 5.2). This pattern is even more pronounced when examining the same pattern for only species with small global ranges of less than 50 000 km^2, or for just endemic species (Dynesius & Jansson 2000; Orme *et al.* 2005). Given strong latitudinal gradients in climate, a causal link between climate and richness might seem plausible. A large number of hypotheses have been put forward to link climate to richness, which are reviewed in detail elsewhere (Currie *et al.* 2004; Evans *et al.* 2005a, b; Clarke & Gaston 2006). We explain them briefly below because they can help us understand how bird communities may respond to climate change.

5.3.1 Hypotheses to do with temperature

Some explanations of the species richness pattern directly link temperature to species richness. Put simply, polar environments are colder and harsher than tropical ones. Thermoregulatory costs of warm-blooded birds are higher where it is cold and many

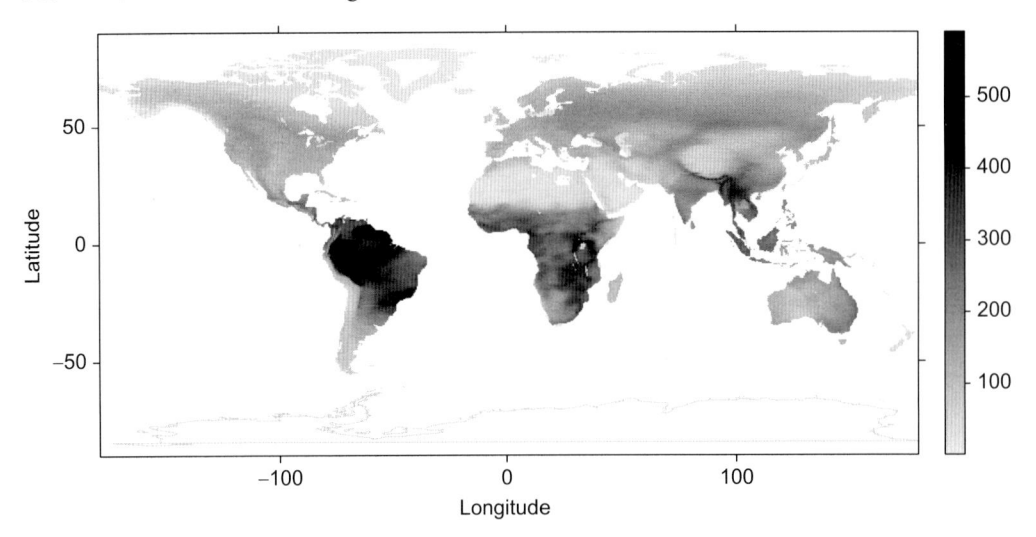

Figure 5.2 Spatial variation in species richness across the globe (shading), based upon the overlap of species' geographical ranges within 1° latitudinal grid cells.

species die if the average temperature falls too low for too long. The poleward boundary of the distributions of many species may therefore be limited by their inability to survive freezing temperatures (the 'freezing tolerance' hypothesis or the 'physiological tolerance' hypothesis). Indeed, we have already shown how populations of many species at high latitudes are limited by cold (Section 4.3). However, based on the analysis of Chapter 4, this hypothesis should presumably only drive variation in richness across temperate, boreal and polar environments, and should not affect subtropical and tropical biomes where populations are much less sensitive to temperature (Section 4.5). It is also unclear why temperature, per se, should limit richness; if one species may adapt to tolerate cold temperatures, why not many (Hutchinson 1959; Currie 1991)? A number of tests of this hypothesis have been published and generally suggest that, although climate or temperature does limit many species' distributions, other factors are also important (Currie *et al.* 2004).

Another idea, related to the physiological tolerance hypothesis, involves a link between metabolic rate and temperature (Clarke & Gaston 2006). In places with high temperatures it is possible for species to employ a greater range of metabolic rates and therefore a greater diversity of ecological 'lifestyles', which leads to greater richness of species (the 'metabolic niche hypothesis'). There is good evidence for strong links between richness and temperature in a range of ectothermic (cold-blooded) animals, including fish (Clarke & Johnston 1999), butterflies (Turner *et al.* 1987) and reptiles (Schall & Pianka 1978; Rodriguez *et al.* 2005). This pattern seems unsurprising for ectotherms, but a similar correlation between the range of metabolic rates and temperature is also exhibited by endotherms (birds and mammals; Anderson & Jetz 2005), which lends some support to this hypothesis.

Next, it has been suggested that the rate at which new species appear in a region by speciation may be temperature dependent. This is the 'evolutionary rates' hypothesis of

Rohde (1992) and may occur through positive correlations between temperature and either mutation rates or generation time. There is weak evidence that higher temperatures may promote mutation (Evans & Gaston 2005). In addition, biological rates are rapid at high temperatures (Brown *et al.* 2003) which can shorten generation times, particularly of ectotherms (e.g. Yamamura & Kiritani 1998). This would, however, be unlikely to directly affect endotherms with relatively constant body temperatures (Storch 2003) and so is unlikely to be an important driver of bird richness. Although both the metabolic niche and evolutionary rates hypotheses are more likely to have stronger effects on ectotherms than endotherms, they may still drive variation in endotherm richness, including birds, through variation in richness at lower trophic levels. However, there is no strong evidence for the clear link between bird diversification rate and latitude which would be expected under this hypothesis (Jetz *et al.* 2012).

Yet another hypothesis proposes that species richness is influenced not by mean temperature but by the seasonality of temperature. Tropical climates are much more stable than polar climates, where there are much greater contrasts between winter and summer conditions (Clarke & Gaston 2006). It is argued that stable temperatures in the tropics facilitate greater climatic specialisation, because individuals are exposed to a narrower range of temperatures during their life cycle than at higher latitudes. As a result of this specialisation, species have much more localised ranges than at high latitudes (Stevens 1989; Orme *et al.* 2006). Indeed, a better fit to global patterns of avian species richness is obtained from regression models which include the statistical interaction between temperature variability and mean temperature than from simply temperature alone (Gaston & Chown 1999). For example, areas of high bird endemism in Africa tend to be characterised by low seasonality (Jetz *et al.* 2004). Further support for this hypothesis comes from the weak but statistically significant negative association between species range area and species richness when examined globally across a 1° grid (Orme *et al.* 2006). However, contrary to expectation, species range size declines from the Arctic to the Antarctic, rather than declining from the Arctic to the tropics and then increasing again, suggesting that Steven's hypothesis is not general to both hemispheres, but a function of the fact that, at a given latitude, the Southern Hemisphere tends to have less landmass than the north, resulting in smaller ranges of terrestrial bird species because there is simply less land available for them to occupy (Jetz & Rahbek 2001).

As an extension of the temperature variability hypothesis, Martin *et al.* (2009) suggested that the degree of spatial synchrony in environmental phenology may drive speciation rates. It is argued that at high latitudes, the synchrony of seasonality across different areas is high. Large areas of the Arctic warm at the same time in response to increasing day length in the spring. This synchrony promotes genetic mixing between populations because their breeding seasons are similar, reducing the level of speciation. Conversely, in the tropics, seasonality is more commonly driven by precipitation (Section 2.7), which shows a much more spatially varied pattern. Asynchrony between populations is likely to reduce the degree of hybridisation between them, particularly as any offspring are less likely to be locally adapted. Two nearby rufous-collared sparrow populations separated by the Andean divide are genetically divergent with differently timed breeding seasons which can be related to variation in the climate (Moore *et al.* 2005) and therefore match the expectation from this hypothesis, although further evidence is required.

To conclude this section, cold temperatures on their own may play some direct part in limiting the richness of species at high latitudes, although the evidence for this is relatively weak and the relative importance of the various plausible mechanisms is uncertain.

5.3.2 Hypotheses to do with energy

Closely related to these temperature hypotheses are a range of further hypotheses linking species richness to climate loosely linked under the umbrella-term of the species–energy hypothesis (Evans *et al.* 2005a, 2005b; Clarke & Gaston 2006). The growth of plants requires solar energy which provides light and warmth, and water, and so more energy potentially leads to a greater degree of plant growth, plant biomass and plant diversity, particularly where water availability is not limiting (Francis & Currie 2003). Indeed, a combination of soil moisture or precipitation, and temperature or potential evapotranspiration, can explain plant richness patterns across the world pretty well (O'Brien 1998). At high latitudes, temperature or solar energy appear to be most limiting (often summarised by potential evapotranspiration, PET), whilst a combination of energy and water availability appear to best describe productive energy at low latitudes (summarised by actual evapotranspiration, AET; Hawkins *et al.* 2003). Thus, a better description of energy that is relevant to birds than solar energy alone is a measure of the solar energy which is converted into plant biomass (productive energy), such as net primary productivity (NPP) or the normalised difference vegetation index (NDVI) which is closely related to plant biomass.

Why do a greater abundance of resources, whether of solar energy and water, plant productivity or prey, translate into a greater richness of species, rather than simply more or larger individuals of the same species (Clarke & Gaston 2006)? One possibility is that a greater number of individuals resulting from the greater availability of resources buffers populations against extinction, leading to reduced rates of species loss and therefore more species in warmer areas (Wright 1983). This is termed the 'more individuals' hypothesis. It implies a dynamic equilibrium between the speciation rate and the extinction rate. The more individuals hypothesis supposes a low extinction rate because of high abundance of typical species in places with high primary productivity or solar energy, without there necessarily being a higher speciation rate. However, empirical evidence suggests that the link between mean species' abundance and temperature is weak (Evans *et al.* 2008).

Alternatively, and very simply, a greater number of individuals may be associated with a greater richness within a given small area through the random allocation of those individuals to species (the sampling hypothesis; Evans *et al.* 2005b, 2008). Thus, as environmental energy increases, and plant biomass and the abundance of individuals of higher trophic levels increases, there is a greater probability of at least one individual of a rare species occurring, thus increasing local richness. This hypothesis has some support, at least at the fine spatial scale of the 1 km squares used in the UK Breeding Bird Survey (Evans *et al.* 2008).

Thirdly, high energy and consequent high plant productivity may lead to greater competition between plants driving greater plant richness. This, in turn, leads to greater animal richness, although the evidence for covariance in both plant and animal richness is weak (Hawkins & Porter 2003). Alternatively, greater plant productivity may lead to greater richness in habitat structure, which in turn increases the diversity of ecological niches and therefore drives a greater diversity of species to fill them (Lee & Rotenberry 2005). This is termed the habitat heterogeneity hypothesis. Analysis of the form of species–energy relationships using UK atlas data found the strongest relationships (greatest slope between energy and occurrence) for specialist species with narrow ecological niches, as would be expected if energy increases avian richness by maximising the number of ecological niches available (Evans *et al.* 2006a). However, this effect did not translate into a stronger relationship between energy and species richness for specialist than generalist species (Evans *et al.* 2005a). Instead, the reverse was true, with the species–energy relationship being strongest for generalist species. Further work is therefore required to test this hypothesis more fully.

Individual studies therefore provide some support for a number of these mechanisms underpinning potential links between temperature, precipitation or other related climate variables and species' richness. Across the range of studies which have formally examined the link between spatial variation in climate and spatial variation in avian richness, there is generally strong evidence for correlations between the two.

5.3.3 Hypotheses to do with history

Current bird distributions are often a product of history (e.g. Porzecanski & Cracraft 2005; Yalden & Albarella 2009). Hawkins *et al.* (2007) argued that the high avian richness in the tropics has been partly a consequence of the relative climatic stability of these regions. In particular, the persistence of the oldest bird taxa (termed 'basal clades') in tropical areas is a function of this stability. At higher latitudes, more frequent climatic change, such as cooling and drying during the Oligocene period, is suggested to have led to the extinction, or reduced diversity and abundance, of these early bird families. Bird communities at higher latitudes therefore tend to consist of more recently evolved families (e.g. Mayr 2005), as severe fluctuations in temperatures between glacial and interglacial periods would have promoted change. Latitudes above about 50° in Europe and 40° in North America have only been occupied by their current species assemblage for a few thousand years (e.g. Yalden & Albarella 2009). Restriction of species to refugia during past glaciations is likely to fragment species' distributions and increase the likelihood of allopatric speciation. However, rapid changes in total population size due to glacial cycles may also have increased extinction rates. Whilst rates of speciation do not differ latitudinally, it appears that the relative stability and extent of tropical forests have led to the long-term accumulation and persistence of a greater richness of species than other environments (Jetz & Fine 2012; Jetz *et al.* 2012).

A considerable amount of allopatric speciation in tropical environments appears to have occurred as a result of a few individuals crossing geographical barriers, such as mountains or rivers, to disperse and found new isolated subpopulations (Cheviron *et al.* 2005) or by fragmentation of a previously continuous population in forest refugia during drier glacial periods (Keast 1985). Within the Neotropics, the areas of highest richness are the humid forests of the Andes, which harbour many species with small range sizes due to the narrow climatic zones and disjunct habitat distributions (Rahbek & Graves 2001; Rahbek *et al.* 2007). In Africa, most centres of endemism are also mountainous (Jetz *et al.* 2004). Although at a fine scale, bird richness decreases with altitude (McCain 2009), the degree of topographical variation within an area is an important correlate of avian species richness globally, with significant associations between elevational range and species richness in five of six biogeographical regions (Davies *et al.* 2007), the exception being Australasia. Mountainous areas contain many physical barriers (e.g. ridges and valleys) within relatively small geographical areas, promoting allopatric speciation, whilst the wide climatic range, also over relatively small distances, promotes diversity of habitats and geographical differences in breeding phenology. Island archipelagos are also associated with high species richness because of rapid allopatric speciation in isolated subpopulations. The best example of this is the diversification of white eyes (Zosteropidae) across the islands of the Indian and Pacific Oceans (Moyle *et al.* 2009; Jetz *et al.* 2012).

5.3.4 Hypotheses reviewed

The general thrust of the many theories put forward to explain patterns of bird richness across the world is that the tropics have high richness as a result of the productive warm, wet environments which they contain, and their relative climatic stability, both seasonally and across millennia. These support more plants, larger plants and a more diverse array of plants, which provides a diverse array of food and ecological niches for the birds. Thus, productive energy appears the most important correlate of species richness across studies, and better accounts for spatial variation in richness than either temperature or precipitation on its own (Box 5.3). This matches the conclusions of Field *et al.* (2009) who conducted a meta-analysis of the main determinants of species-richness patterns across all taxa, and found that measures of climate or vegetation productivity were the strongest correlates, although different climatic variables were not seperated. Similarly, McCain (2009) examined the correlates of spatial variation in bird richness in relation to elevation and found the most frequently recorded determinant of richness was the interaction between temperature and precipitation, as a measure of plant productivity. These three reviews therefore provide strong, consistent evidence of the importance of climatic drivers of plant productivity as the main cause of variation in species-richness gradients around the world.

> **Box 5.3** · *Relative importance of climate in determining spatial patterns of avian diversity*
>
> To assess the importance of climate in determining global patterns of species richness, we reviewed the results of 29 studies comprising 70 separate multivariate analyses. Studies correlated diversity with a range of predictor variables that relate to the different hypotheses proposed in the literature. In relation to the role of climate, studies examined variation as a function of temperature, precipitation and actual or potential productive energy (primary productivity including both PET and AET (Rosenzweig 1968), NDVI or field assessments of vegetation structure). In terms of non-climatic variables, studies considered measures of topography, habitat heterogeneity (as measured by the range of different land covers or habitats present) and historical constraints.

Box 5.3 (cont.)

The results of each study were ranked so that the least important variable considered was scored 0 and the most important received the maximum score given for that study. Hypotheses which were not covered by a study were not scored. These ranks enabled the support that each study gave a hypothesis to be modelled as a proportion of the maximum rank score possible, using a binomial error structure. The model output assigned each hypothesis an estimated proportion of the maximum possible rank achieved which ranged from 0 (always ranked last) to 1 (always ranked first). The mean importance was assessed independently for each variable using a generalised linear mixed model, in which both study and biogeographical region were included as random effects. Across the studies considered, productive energy was generally ranked as the most important variable, followed by historical constraint, whilst the remaining predictor variables were similarly ranked.

Studies assessed bird diversity at a range of different scales from individual sites up to grid squares 1000 × 1000 km across. As the drivers of diversity may vary with spatial scale (van Rensburg *et al.* 2002), the natural log of grid-square length was included in the analyses as a covariate. The importance of precipitation was negatively correlated with scale ($F_{1,12.77} = 9.23$, $P = 0.0097$) and tended to be the most important predictor (proportional rank > 0.8) up to grid squares of 16 × 16 km in size (2.8 on the x-axis), but was ranked in the bottom half of variables when considering diversity with a resolution of greater than 60 × 60 km squares (4.1 on the x-axis). This variation probably reflects the spatially variable nature of the precipitation data. Conversely, the importance of productive energy was significantly positively correlated with scale ($F_{1, 27.83} = 6.87$, $P = 0.014$), being ranked as having less than average importance at spatial scales of less than 2.2 × 2.2 km (0.8 on the x-axis), but the most important predictor at around 25 × 25 km grid squares or larger (3.2 on the x-axis).

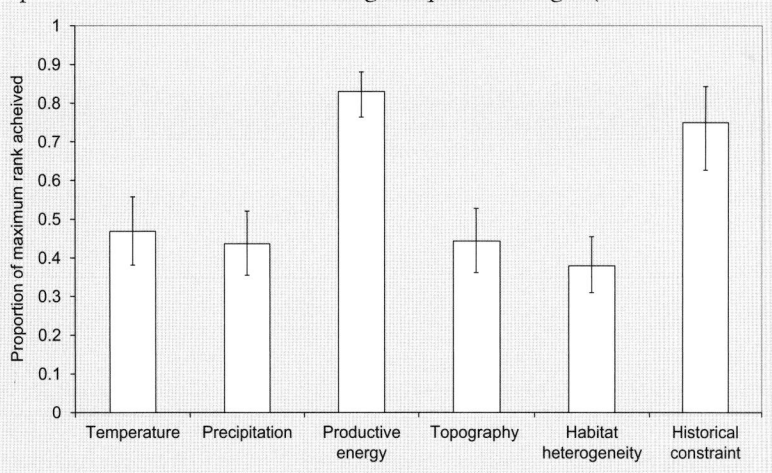

Box 5.3a Mean (± SE) relative ranking of different predictor variables of global patterns of avian diversity.

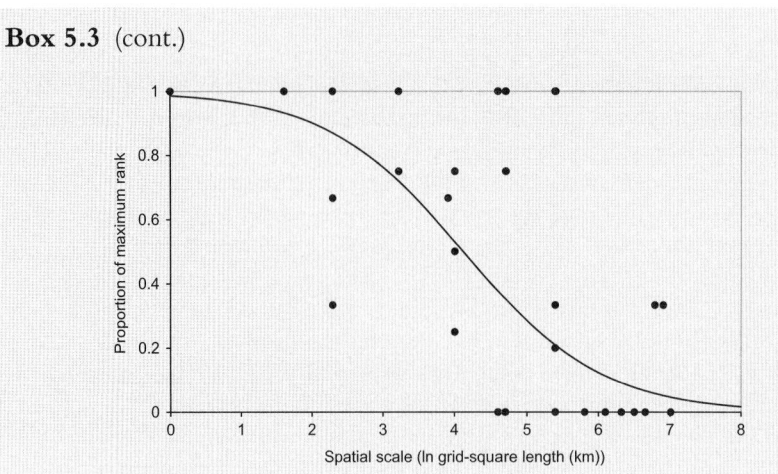

186 · Effects of climate change on distributions and communities

Box 5.3 (cont.)

Box 5.3b The importance of precipitation in determining spatial variation in avian diversity decreases with increasing spatial scale.

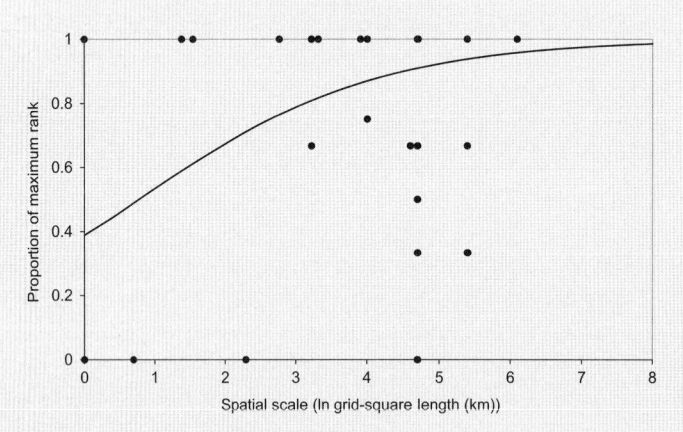

Box 5.3c The importance of productive energy in determining spatial variation in avian diversity increases with increasing spatial scale.

Beyond this main effect, we found that the importance of different variables varied with spatial scale. Spatial variation in precipitation was the most important predictor of species richness at the smallest scales, whilst the importance of productive energy increased with spatial scale, being the most important predictor across grid squares of 25 km^2 or greater (Box 5.3). The importance of climate as a driver of species-richness patterns across taxa was similarly found to increase with spatial scale by Field *et al.* (2009).

In addition to these climate effects, there also appeared to be strong effects of evolutionary and biogeographical history upon richness (Box 5.3), although this was based upon only seven studies that formally attempted to examine this, and contrasts with the conclusions of Field *et al.* (2009) across taxa, where this was the least important predictor of species richness gradients. If true, this suggests that drivers such as the recent climate change associated with the last ice age, or the greater long-term stability of the tropics facilitating greater persistence of older, basal, families (Hawkins et al. 2007) have played a significant role in the current patterns of avian richness. Recent evidence from the newly completed phylogeny of all extant bird species supports these conclusions, and emphasises the importance of both climate and history in driving current patterns of avian richness (Jetz et al. 2012).

The greatest hotspots of avian richness are in tropical South America, particularly the eastern Andes, Guyanian Highlands, Amazon and Atlantic forests, the Rift Valley in tropical Africa and tropical areas of south-east Asia and the eastern Himalayas (Hawkins et al. 2007); areas which combine high plant productivity, topographical complexity and historically stable climates. A significant component of the richness of the African and Asian areas mentioned comes from more derived and recently speciated clades (Hawkins et al. 2007; Jetz et al. 2012). Tropical desert and savanna areas tend to support fewer species because of their more limited primary productivity and simpler habitat structure. For example, only 8% of neotropical bird species occur in savanna habitats (Stotz et al. 1996), and within these habitats, species richness is linked to vegetation complexity (Pearce-Higgins 2000). Outside of the tropics travelling polewards, increasingly harsh climatic conditions limit the growth and diversity of plants, first through summer drought in Mediterranean-type climates, and then by winter cold in temperate, boreal and Arctic zones, where high wind speeds may also reduce structural diversity. High latitude environments have also experienced repeated glaciation and therefore the current species distributions are a consequence of dispersal from glacial refugia only 10 000 years Bp (Yalden & Albarella 2009). The relationship between climate and richness changes subtly across the globe, such that at high latitudes, temperature is the predominant driver, whilst in the tropics where cold is not limiting, it is moisture availability that is important (Hawkins et al. 2003); the water–energy hypothesis of O'Brien (1998). These findings closely match the latitudinal patterns we have identified in the role of temperature and precipitation in driving populations and demographic rates of individual bird species (Section 4.2).

We have described overall patterns of species richness, but how do these differ between species groups? There is good evidence for contrasting trends in the richness of migrants and resident species in particular. Across both North America and Europe, the richness of migrants tends to be greater in the north, in contrast to resident species (Lemoine & Böhning-Gaese 2003; Schaefer et al. 2007; Carnicer & Díaz-Delgado 2008). Migratory species breeding in a given area may be able to better exploit seasonal variation in resource availability (i.e. the highly productive high latitude summers) than resident species (Evans et al. 2006b). Conversely, the richness of resident species is strongly positively related to winter temperature and therefore greatest at lower latitudes. A neglected area of research is the potential importance of interspecific competition between resident and migrant species. An example of where this may be important in explaining patterns of species richness is in the differences in richness at the same latitude in the Northern and Southern hemispheres. A factor which may be involved in explaining the different patterns in the two hemispheres, as described above, is that in the temperate regions of the Northern Hemisphere, many migratory birds from the boreal and Arctic regions arrive to spend the winter. However, in the temperate zone of the Southern Hemisphere there is little land further poleward from which migrants can come to winter. The different patterns of competition which result from these hemispheric differences in landmass distribution warrants further investigation.

5.4 The consequences of climate change for bird communities

What are the implications of these patterns for our understanding of the likely effects of climate change on bird communities, as measured by species richness? Given the pivotal role of climate in driving spatial patterns of avian bird richness, we would expect the current spatial variation in bird communities to change with climate change, reflecting the summation of all the individual relationships between climate and species' populations already elaborated on in previous chapters. Because the warmest, wettest climates support the highest richness of birds, through the impact these variables have upon plant productivity, we would expect general patterns of increasing local species richness with warming, particularly at high latitudes where water availability is not limiting. However, in the tropics, the precise direction and magnitude of change at any one location is likely to be strongly influenced by changes in water availability. Here, areas projected to suffer future droughts as a result of climate change may experience reductions in species richness. Beyond these general patterns, we might expect changes in temperature to have variable consequences on species depending on their biogeographic affiliation, migratory status and guild (Schaefer *et al.* 2007; Carnicer & Díaz-Delgado 2008; Moreno-Rueda & Pizarro 2008).

Is there any evidence that these projected changes and patterns are already occurring? Most of the work examining patterns of change in bird communities in response to climate change has been conducted at higher latitudes, and particularly in Europe, where there is increasing evidence of a detectable signature of climate change on bird communities. Unfortunately, this means that the patterns outlined below may not necessarily translate directly to tropical areas where the majority of avian richness is found.

5.4.1 Changes in richness, diversity and specialisation

As expected, species richness and bird diversity across Europe have increased significantly over the period from 1990 to 2008 (Le Voil *et al.* 2012), which was a period of significant warming. More detailed analysis of data from Britain has linked this increase in diversity specifically to temperature (Davey *et al.* 2012). From 1994 to 2006 there was a significant 8% increase in mean diversity of birds recorded from Breeding Bird Survey (BBS) squares, as measured by the Simpson's diversity index, a trend mirrored in species richness. In Sweden, similar changes appear to have occurred as a result of the range expansion of common generalist species (Davey *et al.* 2013).

Unfortunately, not only have bird communities increased in diversity, which sounds like good news, but they have also suffered a reduction in community specialisation (CSI), a measure designed to indicate the extent to which species and communities exhibit a wide or narrow habitat distribution (Le Voil *et al.* 2012). In France, these changes have been driven by declines in the abundance of the most specialised species (Jiguet *et al.* 2007) and attributed to landscape degradation and fragmentation (Devictor *et al.* 2008a, 2008c).

However, as we will examine in more detail below, disentangling the effects of climate and land-use change upon these community metrics is not easy (Clavero *et al.* 2011; Barnagaud *et al.* 2012). In Britain (Davey *et al.* 2012) and Sweden (Davey *et al.* 2013), such changes in communities have been linked to warming. Populations of generalist species have increased most in response to climate change, whilst populations of specialist species have increased at a slower rate, or indeed, have declined in abundance.

In summary, as the temperature has warmed, the diversity of birds in the British countryside has increased, as expected from previous studies (e.g. Lennon *et al.* 2000). The greater increase in the abundance of generalist species relative to specialists is also to be expected, given the fact that the species–energy relationship in the UK is stronger for common bird species with broad niches than for rare, specialists (Evans *et al.* 2005a, 2005b). Given the latitudinal gradient in bird diversity, which is also apparent in the BBS data from Britain, these results are suggestive of a simple northwards shift in the distribution of species, although the data suggest the greatest increases in diversity have actually been in the west (Davey *et al.* 2012).

5.4.2 Changes in thermal association

An alternative approach to describing changes in the composition of bird communities in response to climate change uses the thermal association of each species, based on the mean temperature averaged across the whole of the geographical range it occupies. These species-specific measures (species temperature index; STI) are combined for the species within a community to give a single value known as the community temperature index (CTI), which is the mean thermal association of the species present at a site, and can be weighted by abundance. The work of Devictor *et al.* (2008b) has shown firstly a strong latitudinal gradient in CTI across France of about $1\,°C$ from south to north. Secondly, in response to $0.68\,°C$ warming per decade from 1989 to 2006, the CTI at a typical site has increased by an average of $0.06\,°C$ per decade. Given the $0.12\,°C$ reduction in CTI for every 100 km distance northward, this is equivalent to a 91 ± 11 km northwards shift in bird community composition over 17 years.

The trends observed by Devictor *et al.* in France have been replicated across Europe, where a general increase in CTI of $0.026\,°C$ per decade has been observed, equivalent to a 37 ± 3 km northward shift in bird community composition from 1990 to 2008 (Devictor *et al.* 2012a). This was driven by statistically significant increases in CTI in France, the Netherlands, Czech Republic, UK and Sweden, and a non-significant increase in Catalonia. These changes represent the differential effects of warming on populations, combined across species. At 5.4 ± 0.6 km per year across France (Devictor *et al.* 2008b) or 2.0 ± 0.2 km per year across Europe (Devictor *et al.* 2012a), they, intriguingly, appear more rapid than the observed species-specific shifts in species' range margin (Table 5.1), which is difficult to explain.

The relationship between these changes in communities, shifts in distributions and impacts of climate change upon populations can be explained by spatial variation in the response of populations to warming. Bird populations located near the species' high latitude range margin, which previously experienced low temperatures relative to those in the core of the species' range, have tended to increase in response to warming. However, populations located near the species' low latitude range margin, which previously experienced

190 · Effects of climate change on distributions and communities

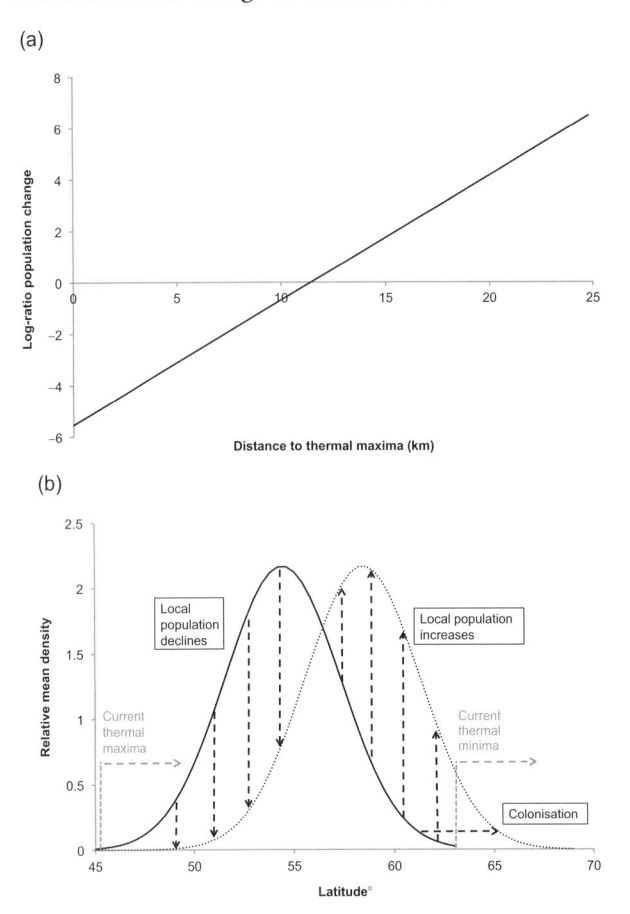

Figure 5.3 (a) Simplified relationship between the distance to the thermal maximum of a population and the likely future population change in a changing climate. (b) The effect that the relationship will have on a simplified species density-latitude curve (solid line) in response to climate change (dotted line). Text in boxes summarises the underling population processes whose direction is given by the black dashed arrows. The grey lines and text indicate the position of the thermal range limits and the grey arrows, their magnitude of change.

high temperatures relative to those in the core of the species' range, have tended to decline (Jiguet *et al.* 2010). In Europe, warming thus appears to have caused population declines in southern populations of a species but driven population increases in the north of its range, leading to poleward range shifts; a general pattern that simplifies much of the detail of individual population responses to temperature outlined in Chapter 4 (Figure 5.3).

Davey *et al.* (2012) documented apparently rapid shifts in community structure in response to warming, with correlations between community structure and temperature in the year of the bird survey. This suggests that the responses may not be entirely caused by variation in demographic parameters, but influenced by variation in settlement patterns. Conversely, changes in CTI appear to track changes in temperature but with a 1- to 3-year lag (Lindström *et al.* 2013). Generally, these changes appear slower than might be expected from the degree of warming. The geographical location of a particular temperature regime in France has shifted northward by an estimated 273 ± 53 km between 1989 and 2006 (Devictor *et al.* 2008b), or 249 ± 27 km northward across Europe between 1990 and 2008 (Devictor *et al.* 2012a). Hence, bird communities are tracking climate warming, but not perfectly. Community metrics related to temperature are lagging behind the change in climate. As a result, populations are now occupying on average a slightly warmer climate than they would have done 20 years ago. This suggests that these bird populations may now be incurring a 'climate debt', and that they may be vulnerable to longer-term negative consequences of warming, although these consequences have yet to be empirically demonstrated. Alternatively, this debt may simply reflect the need for climate changes to be matched by equivalent habitat changes in order to facilitate large-scale range shifts (Barnagaud *et al.* 2012).

Devictor *et al.* (2012a) also used the same approach to document changes in CTI for butterflies across Europe, which they suggested have shifted by some 114 ± 9 km from 1990 to 2008; less than the degree of temperature change, but a greater movement than was observed in birds. This, they suggest, may be a sign of future ecological disruption as a result of warming. Whilst Devictor's CTI has been criticised for not incorporating uncertainty in the degree of association between temperature and distribution (Rodríguez-Sánchez *et al.* 2012), it does appear to be relatively robust. Estimates of STI derived from different data sources, such as atlas or BBS-type data, tend to be strongly correlated, whilst measures of change at both local and national scales also appear similar (Devictor *et al.* 2012b; Lindström *et al.* 2013). Further work is required to investigate the constraints on the ability of communities to respond to warming, and the ecological consequences for a species to 'keep pace' with climate change. Parallel studies are also needed on the effects of changes in precipitation upon communities.

5.4.3 Disentangling the effects of climate change from those of other drivers

Disentangling the effects of climate change from other factors in causing changes in community composition is difficult, particularly as measures of both STI and SSI vary among habitats (Julliard *et al.* 2006; Clavero *et al.* 2011), and are correlated across species (Barnagaud *et al.* 2012). Forest species tend to be more cold-adapted whilst farmland species are associated with warmer climates. Habitat specialists also appear to have a narrower thermal tolerance than more generalist species. This means that habitat change unrelated to climate change could cause significant changes in CTI (Clavero *et al.* 2011). Care needs to be taken when attributing some of the observed changes outlined above specifically to climate warming. Indeed, there may be a weak negative correlation across countries between the rate of change over time in CTI and that of CSI (Figure 5.4). For example, Sweden shows the largest reduction in CSI and the largest increase in CTI.

The potential difficulties in definitively attributing community change to climatic change can be illustrated by an analysis of farmland bird community changes. As outlined at the start of this section, the reduction in CSI in farmland habitats reflects the loss of specialised farmland species, such as skylarks *Alauda arvensis*, corn buntings *Emberiza calandra* and grey partridges *Perdix perdix*, which are most exclusively associated with farmland. Long-term reductions in the abundance of many farmland birds, and particularly the most specialised species such as these, can be closely related to changes in the

192 · Effects of climate change on distributions and communities

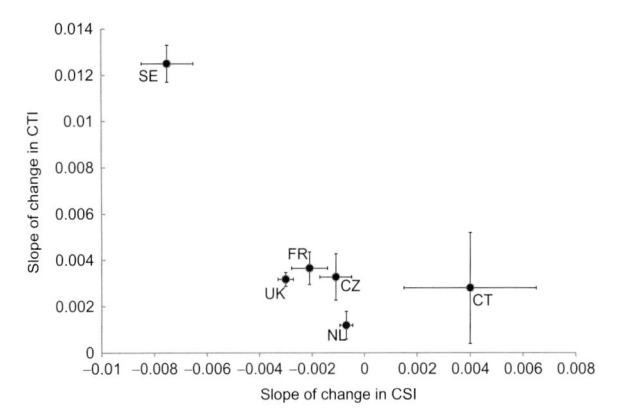

Figure 5.4 Relationship between country-specific changes in the degree of habitat specialisation CSI (from Le Voil *et al.* 2012) and in the degree to which species are characteristic of warm geographical ranges CTI (from Devictor *et al.* 2012a). The slope of the annual trend in each is presented ± SE. Although based on limited data, the two appear negatively correlated ($r_s = 0.77$, $0.1 > P > 0.05$).

intensity of agricultural management, which appear to have benefitted a few generalists which also use other habitats (Chamberlain *et al.* 2000). Indeed, detailed analysis of the role of climate change in driving population trends of individual farmland bird species in the UK suggests that for the majority, recent climate change has been relatively unimportant compared to agricultural intensification (Eglington & Pearce-Higgins 2012). Because farmland specialists in the UK tend to be continental grassland or steppe species with high STI values compared with the mean temperature in the UK, declines in their populations caused by changes in farming practice might be expected to lead to a decline in CTI on farmland, rather than the increase expected from recent warming (Clavero *et al.* 2011; Barnagaud *et al.* 2012). This alone may contribute to the explanation of why observed changes in CTI are less than expected from the magnitude of warming. Effects of this kind may also cause differences in trends in CTI between habitats. Recent changes in community composition on Dutch farmland, where there has been a significant decline in CTI, support this suggestion (Kampichler *et al.* 2012). Changes in farmland bird communities appear not to have been strongly driven by recent climate change.

In contrast, coastal, forest and heathland bird communities in the Netherlands have exhibited increases in CTI as a result of population increases in species with a high STI rather than declines in species with a low STI. Together, these results suggest that the impact of climate change may be more apparent in natural and semi-natural habitats than in intensively managed habitats, although even here, community change may be partly driven by other environmental changes such as in forest management or nitrogen deposition (Kampichler *et al.* 2012). Although we do not think that the same analysis has been repeated elsewhere, Davey *et al.* (2012) also found interesting differences between habitats in the changes in bird communities in the UK (Figure 5.5). Upland habitats experienced the greatest increase in diversity but the smallest decline in CSI. In this case, increases in temperature may have facilitated the expansion of 'lowland' species into upland areas,

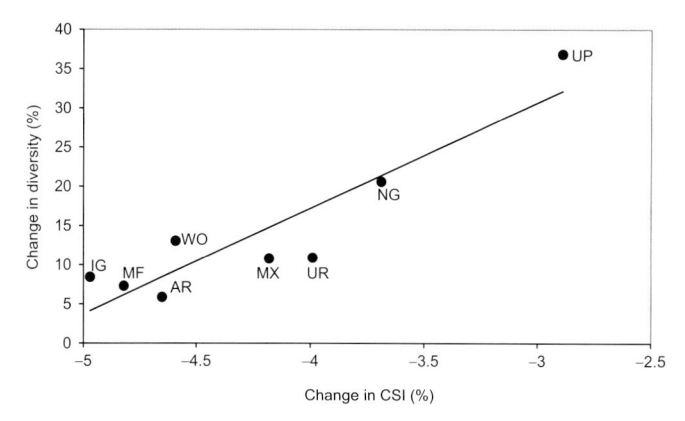

Figure 5.5 Habitats where bird communities have experienced the greatest reduction in the degree of habitat specialisation (CSI) have tended to show the smallest increase in diversity (data from Davey *et al.* 2012). Habitats are abbreviated as follows: arable (AR), mixed farmland (MF), improved grassland (IG), mixed (MX), urban (UR), woodland (WO), semi-natural grassland (NG), and upland (UP).

as recorded for one of the most southerly upland areas in the UK, the Peak District (Pearce-Higgins *et al.* 2006). Lowland agricultural habitats experienced the greatest decline in CSI and smallest increase in diversity, probably because of the loss of specialised farmland birds outlined above.

More research is required to disentangle the relative importance of climate and land-use change in driving changes to the structure of bird communities in different habitats, as there is evidence that both can be important. The current analysis suggests significant changes have occurred, although perhaps they raise at least as many questions regarding the underpinning mechanisms and causes as they answer. The climate change signal may be greater in more natural habitats, because changes due to climate are masked or counteracted by land-use change in intensively managed habitats subject to rapid changes in management practices, such as farmland (Eglington & Pearce-Higgins 2012; Kampichler *et al.* 2012). Further, in these more managed habitats, reductions in the average level of specialisation may be greatest (Figure 5.5). More work is required to examine the extent to which the widespread losses of specialist species (Le Voil *et al.* 2012) are climate-related (Davey *et al.* 2012), the result of other anthropogenic pressures or due to interactions between the two (Devictor *et al.* 2008a; Kerbiriou *et al.* 2009; Doxa *et al.* 2012; Eglington & Pearce-Higgins 2012).

Despite these uncertainties, detailed studies from Europe provide strong evidence for detectable shifts in bird communities consistent with expected responses to recent warming over a relatively short time frame. This conclusion is supported by additional analysis summarising species' population trends from a number of other European countries which also show a general trend towards more negative population trends in more northerly distributed species – even, in some cases, when accounting for potentially confounding habitat associations and variation. Thus, in Finland, species with northern distributions have declined in abundance by an average of 21% over a 10–20 year period, whilst populations of species with southern distributions have increased by an average of

29% (Virkkala & Rajasärkkaä 2011). Population trends of rare breeding birds in the UK are correlated with their mean European latitude, such that species with a southern European distribution have tended to increase, but more northerly species have declined (Green et al. 2008). On the Swiss/German border at Lake Constance, where a breeding bird atlas has been conducted on a decadal basis since 1980, population trends of species with a high latitude distribution were more negative than those with a southern distribution from 1990 to 2000, after accounting for habitat variation (Lemoine et al. 2003). Interestingly, no such difference was apparent between 1980 and 2000, suggesting that any putative effect of climate change on community composition has only been apparent more recently. This is consistent with a tendency for more rapid warming in Europe from the mid 1980s onwards (Gregory et al. 2009). In central Europe, negative population trends of northerly distributed species in the Czech Republic from 1982 to 2006 contrast with positive population trends of species with a central or southern distribution in the country (Reif et al. 2008). However, the strongest effects were for species not affected by habitat changes, suggesting that habitat loss may limit the ability of species to track their climate optima (Reif et al. 2010). Breeding bird surveys in Catalonia from 1996 to 2004 showed that species occupying areas with higher June temperatures and greater spring rainfall have also tended to increase in abundance more than species occupying cooler and drier areas, after accounting for habitat variation (Seoane & Carrascal 2008).

5.4.4 Changes in migratory propensity

Given that a greater proportion of bird species breeding in cool areas tend to migrate away during the winter, we might expect warming, particularly in the winter, to reduce the number and proportion of migrant breeding bird species within a community. The evidence for this appears to be weak, with small increases in the proportion of long-distance migrants being recorded across Europe from 1972–1976 to 1988–1992 (Lemoine & Böhning-Gaese 2003; Lemoine et al. 2007). However, this was before the period of major warming across Europe, and therefore this study may have had limited power to detect significant effects of breeding season climate change. Further, during this period, there are likely to have been large effects of variation in climate on the wintering grounds. After a previous decline, increases in Sahel rainfall may have increased populations of many long-distance migrants to Europe by 26% (Box 4.8).

Although evidence from migrant breeding populations is weak, there is stronger evidence for significant changes in the distributions of wintering birds and their community composition. There is a strong positive correlation between temperature and the richness of wintering bird communities, which means that in response to winter warming, there has been a significant increase in species richness in North America (La Sorte et al. 2009). The slope of this effect (2.4 ± 0.08 species per °C) is significantly greater than that detected for breeding birds in the UK by Davey et al. (2012) of 1.2 ± 0.06 species per °C. As with work on European breeding bird communities, there is evidence, however, that these changes lag behind that expected on the basis of observed warming by about 35 years (La Sorte & Jetz 2012). Recent warming has also led to a significant increase in the CTI of wintering wader assemblages in Europe and Africa by 0.3 °C per decade (Godet et al. 2011), indicating that species are shifting their wintering distributions polewards at about

20 km per year. The size of this effect is about five times that observed for breeding birds in France (Devictor *et al*. 2008b) and, like the study of La Sorte, suggests that wintering bird communities may be responding more rapidly to climate change than breeding bird communities. Further, there is robust evidence of significant north, or north-easterly shifts in the wintering distribution of estuarine waders around the UK (Austin & Rehfisch 2005) and Europe (Maclean *et al*. 2007), and in the distribution of wintering waterfowl in Europe (Gunnarsson *et al*. 2012; Lehikoinen *et al*. 2013). Such a contrast between rates of change in wintering and breeding bird communities is perhaps to be expected because of the probable lower level of fidelity of individual birds across years to wintering sites than to breeding sites which would allow individuals to more closely track changes in winter conditions than they do during the breeding season. More studies of the effects of warming on both breeding and wintering bird communities are required to test this formally, however.

5.4.5 Effects of drought

Based on previous chapters and our conclusions in Section 5.2, we would expect bird communities within tropical areas and arid zones to be much more affected by changes in water availability or precipitation patterns, rather than temperature. Unfortunately, there are too few relevant studies to test this rigorously. However, what studies there are do indeed suggest that following periods of drought, the richness of bird communities is reduced in arid and semi-arid habitats, such as the Kalahari desert (Herremans 2004) or the Great Plains of North America (George *et al*. 1992). Large-scale reductions in the abundance of dry-forest bird species in Puerto Rico following a three-year drought (Faaborg 1982) would probably also have been reflected in changes in community structure if the drought had been extended.

Detailed studies from the central North American plains show that it is species in dry habitats which are most sensitive to drought and vulnerable to decline (Albright *et al*. 2010a). This may be driven by the association between many North American prairie species and the presence of small wetlands (Niemuth *et al*. 2008). In response to drought and the loss of these wetlands, these species move elsewhere to track water resources, leading to a relatively rapid reduction in local abundance and diversity. However, such mobility highlights the adaptive capacity of these species, which means that dryland bird communities also respond relatively quickly to the return of precipitation (George *et al*. 1992; Verner & Purcell 1999), presumably through re-colonisation from other areas. Further work is required to identify the species which may be most vulnerable to drought, but Albright *et al*. (2010) suggest that long-distance migrants may be amongst the species most detrimentally affected, perhaps because they are particularly dependent on peaks of spring invertebrate abundance emerging from wetland habitats, or feeding on plant growth stimulated by rainfall. Longer-term monitoring of the consequences of climate change in these environments is required in order to detect and understand these changes more widely, and particularly to identify the extent to which the length of a drought affects the severity of the ecological consequences. Given future projected increases in drought severity in some arid regions (Solomon *et al*. 2009; Dai 2013), this research is a high priority.

5.4.6 Concluding remarks

Some of the clearest impacts of climate change on birds have been detectable at the community level. The use of citizen science and volunteer bird survey data from hundreds or thousands of sites provide the power to detect even relatively small changes. These changes represent the combined effect of impacts on populations of individual species, as described in Chapter 4. Overall, increases in temperature have been associated with increases in abundance at locations towards the poleward range limit of species, but declines in abundance towards the low latitude range margin. As a result of these changes, there appears to have been an overall shift in community composition poleward which is apparent both across Europe as a continent, and also at the scale of individual countries. Where this has been studied, within any defined area, populations at lower latitudes occupying warmer environments have tended to exhibit more positive population trajectories than higher latitude populations. Given the latitudinal gradient in bird diversity, this is likely to be leading to an overall increase in species diversity at individual sites, particularly in high and temperate latitudes, as has been demonstrated empirically for Britain.

The rapidity of these community responses is noteworthy. Bird populations of species which have done well across Europe have tended to increase overall by some 20% since the mid 1980s, but those which have declined in response to climate change have declined by about 10% on average (Gregory *et al.* 2009). Although community changes associated with warming have been observed, their magnitude is less than expected from the change in temperature, leading to the suggestion that communities will increasingly experience a climate debt which may bring about harmful future changes which these communities are already committed to (Devictor *et al.* 2008b, 2012a). There is no evidence yet that this debt is associated with a risk of population declines of most species, and it may instead represent lags caused by the slow pace of climate driven habitat change (Barnagaud *et al.* 2012). Some recent studies suggest that at least some of these signals may also be potentially confounded with or masked by land-use change, at least in some habitats. Hence, care is required when specifically attributing these changes to climate change – although current observations are generally consistent with the anticipated effects of warming.

There are no long-term studies documenting changes in the structure of tropical forest bird communities, yet we would expect climate change to also produce detectable effects on these communities. By way of illustration, this could occur through changes in precipitation patterns which may affect the phenology or amount of fruiting by trees which could significantly affect the diversity and abundance of frugivorous birds at particular forest sites (Valdez-Hernández *et al.* 2010; Pomara *et al.* 2012). Any changes to the ecology of forest army ants in response to climate change may affect the many obligate ant followers found in the understory bird community (O'Donnell *et al.* 2011). Despite concerns that climate change may be causing significant impacts on tropical forest bird communities in South America (Nores 2009), there is so far little evidence that this is the case (Stouffer *et al.* 2011), although this finding is based on limited data. The establishment of robust long-term monitoring across the tropics, as established in Europe and North America in recent decades, is urgently required to fill this gap, in order to document the population and community changes which may already be occurring.

5.5 Conclusions

Recent climate change has altered the timing of both migration and breeding in birds (Chapter 2) and this may affect the breeding productivity and survival of some species (Chapter 3). More widely, changes in temperature and precipitation have significant effects on populations and demographic rates of bird species through a wide variety of mechanisms (Chapter 4). As we have shown in this chapter, these effects have translated into detectable impacts on bird distributions and communities. There is good evidence for poleward shifts in species' distributions and community composition in Europe. Indeed, it is these changes in bird communities and distributions which provide some of the most compelling evidence that climate change is already having a significant and detectable impact on bird populations.

Although few bird species appear to be facing immediate conservation threat as a result of climate change, there is good reason to suspect that, as the magnitude of climate change increases, it is likely to have an increasing impact upon bird populations, distributions and communities. The evidence to date suggests that it will be specialist species, such as those with the most restricted habitat requirements or diet, and species which are already threatened by other factors, which may be under the greatest threat from climate change. There is an urgent need to consider the implications of climate change for bird conservation and to identify priorities for remedial efforts. Conservationists then need to outline potential solutions in order to reduce the magnitude of these impacts. We also need to consider the best ways of reducing the magnitude of climate change in order to limit the level of climate stress which bird populations are likely to face. These are the topics which are the focus of the second part of this book.

5.6 Summary

- The geographical ranges of species' are frequently limited by climate, either directly or indirectly through biotic interactions. Therefore we might expect the structure and composition of bird communities to be similarly affected by climatic variation, and therefore sensitive to change in response to climate change.
- There is good evidence for species' ranges shifting polewards in response to warming, at least at intermediate and high latitudes, at an average of 0.8 km per year. There is much weaker evidence for consistent altitudinal shifts in range extent, which average some 0.3 m per year, although a number of studies do describe significant shifts. Reasons for this discrepancy are discussed, which may relate to variation in the importance of temperature in driving latitudinal and altitudinal range limits.
- The evidence published to date suggests that leading range margins may have shifted poleward more rapidly than trailing margins. If true, this suggests that birds have experienced a short-term range expansion in response to recent climate change.
- Such changes in distribution are likely to affect the structure of bird communities. Across the globe, species richness appears most strongly explained by spatial variation in productive energy, a combination of climate that links most closely to plant productivity. At high latitudes this is closely related to temperature or solar energy, but at lower latitudes, it is a combination of energy and water availability. Productive

energy appears most important at larger spatial scales above a grain of 25 km², although precipitation may be more closely related to richness at small spatial resolutions. In addition to these climatic factors, there is evidence that historical constraints may also limit richness, whether related to long-term climatic stability in the tropics, past glaciation at higher latitudes, or isolation by physical barriers.

- The diversity of migrant species is greatest in northern high latitudes where productivity during the summer months is greatest, but winter cold limits the number of resident species. The tendency for the proportion of migratory species to increase poleward is less well marked in the Southern Hemisphere, and it seems possible that the hemispheric difference in the latitudinal distribution of land masses may cause this difference.
- Based on these relationships of species richness to climate, warming is expected to promote increased diversity at high latitudes, but decrease the proportion of migrants, whilst at low latitudes, changes in precipitation should be the main driver of change. Supporting this expectation, warming in the UK and Sweden has been associated with an increase in bird diversity. At the same time, the proportion of habitat specialists in bird communities has declined, either because warming has had more of a beneficial effect on populations of generalist species, or because specialists are more vulnerable to wider environmental changes.
- Bird communities in Europe have become increasingly composed of species associated with warmer temperatures so that average community composition is now typical of what it was 37 km further south two decades ago. This is much less than the 249 km northward shift expected if community changes had exactly matched temperature changes. Attributing these changes to climate change is difficult because of other potentially confounding and masking environmental changes that have also occurred.
- More widely, there is consistent evidence from a range of countries and regions across Europe that species with predominantly northern distribution have exhibited more negative population trends than species with more southerly ranges, matching the expectation of shifting communities in response to warming.
- The proportion of migratory species in communities has also changed in response to warming. On the breeding grounds, so far these effects seem relatively weak, but when examining winter bird communities in Europe and North America, the degree of migrant community response appears to be considerably larger than that observed for breeding birds.
- In the tropics, changing rainfall patterns are likely to be the main driver of community change. There is evidence that drought causes reduction in the abundance and diversity of bird communities in arid and semi-arid habitats, although this is partly related to the tendency of individual birds to move elsewhere. Hence, the changes could be short-term and related to the adaptive capacity of these species to cope with change.

Part II

Conservation responses

6 · *Using models to predict the effects of climate change on birds*

6.1   Introduction

Having described the impacts that climate change has already had upon birds, their populations, distributions and communities, in this second part of the book, we look now at what can be done to reduce the negative impacts of current and future climate changes on birds. The first stage in attempting to do this is to predict what the consequences of future climate change will be for the conservation status of wild species and populations. Although there are many impacts of climate change which have been documented, few clearly demonstrate a current and urgent threat to particular populations or species. For most species, it is not the climate change which has occurred so far that is the problem, but the magnitude of climate change to come. In this chapter, we attempt to quantify the likely size of that future problem – how severe is the impact of climate change on birds likely to be?

This is not a simple question to answer. The foregoing chapters documented the complexity of the effects of climate and climatic change on reproductive and mortality rates of birds, which are the mechanisms by which climate affects their distribution and abundance. Given this complexity, it might be thought that any attempt to predict the effect of climate change on a bird species would require a detailed knowledge of how its demographic rates will be affected, in both the short and the long term. Such knowledge can certainly be very helpful as we shall see later in this chapter, but realistically, is only available for a handful of the 10 000 bird species on Earth. To make an assessment that will be widely applicable, we need to consider alternative approaches, which require less detailed information, to predicting the effects of climate change on bird species. Building on the role of climate in delimiting species' distributions (Sections 1.8 and 5.2), the most widely used approach is to build a statistical model of geographical variation in the distribution or abundance of a species in relation to climatic and sometimes also to other environmental variables. The spatial association between a species and climate described by that model is then used to make future projections of the impact that climate change may have on that species' distribution or abundance.

These statistical models are called bioclimate models or climate envelope models and are a special case of species distribution models (SDM) or ecological niche models, which have been developed over recent decades to relate differences between locations in the occurrence or population density of a species, to features of the landscape, such as habitat type and quality, or elevation (Franklin 2009). Once the climate envelope model has been built, it can be used to quantify potential future changes in the distribution of a species in response to climate change, on the assumption that the current relationship between climate and that species will continue to hold in the future. The changes are called 'potential' to recognise that they may not occur at all if other factors prevent them happening, or they may occur only slowly because of lags and delays.

Climate envelope models remain the most widely applicable tool for making future projections relevant to bird conservation and so we use much of this chapter to describe the ways in which these models have been used to document observed patterns of bird distribution and what they say about the likely effects of future climatic changes. We examine the reliability of the predictions of climate envelope models, the ways in which they can be checked and the circumstances when they may not be expected to work perfectly, or sometimes not at all. Then we turn to recent developments in the methods used to predict the effects of climatic change on birds and particularly the prospects for the development of more detailed models which incorporate effects of climate on demographic rates.

6.2 What is a climate envelope model?

Climate envelope models are statistical models of the geographical distribution of species. At its most simple, a climate envelope model requires mapped locations at which the species has been recorded as well as measurements of meteorological variables at those places. Such records are normally available for defined spatial units, such as map grid squares or cells, with each cell being classed as having the species known to be present or not. It is useful, though not essential, to have records of definite or probable absence of the species from other spatial units, where field observers recorded that they looked for the species and did not find it. Values of climate variables are collected for the same spatial units from which the bird data are available. These may be averages of a particular quantity, such as annual mean temperature or annual mean precipitation, over multiple years or several decades (30 years often being the standard required to adequately describe climate). They can also be measures of short-term variability or frequencies of extreme events, such as storms, droughts or severe frosts.

For some applications, particularly for modelling the distribution of montane species, species distributions can be described as a function of elevation (height of the land above sea level) rather than climate (e.g. Şekercioğlu et al. 2008). Here, elevation is being used as a surrogate for a suite of climatic variables and other ecological factors influenced by them. In particular, mean air temperature is well known to decrease with increasing elevation, though the rate at which it does do so, known as the lapse rate, varies geographically, being greater at high latitudes (Stone & Carlson 1979). If the lapse rate is assumed to be the same in future or can be predicted, then the species' potential geographical distribution under a future climate can also be predicted. However, the accuracy of the predictions are likely to depend upon how much the elevational limits of the species are linked to temperature and how much they are influenced by other climatic variables, such as precipitation or wind speed, or other non-climatic measures, such as land use, which may also vary with altitude, but less predictably than temperature (see Box 5.2).

The next step in building a climate envelope model is to fit a mathematical model describing the observed geographical distribution. This usually represents a species' probability of occurrence in a grid cell as a mathematical function of a combination of climate variables.

Box 6.1 · *Climate envelope models simplified*

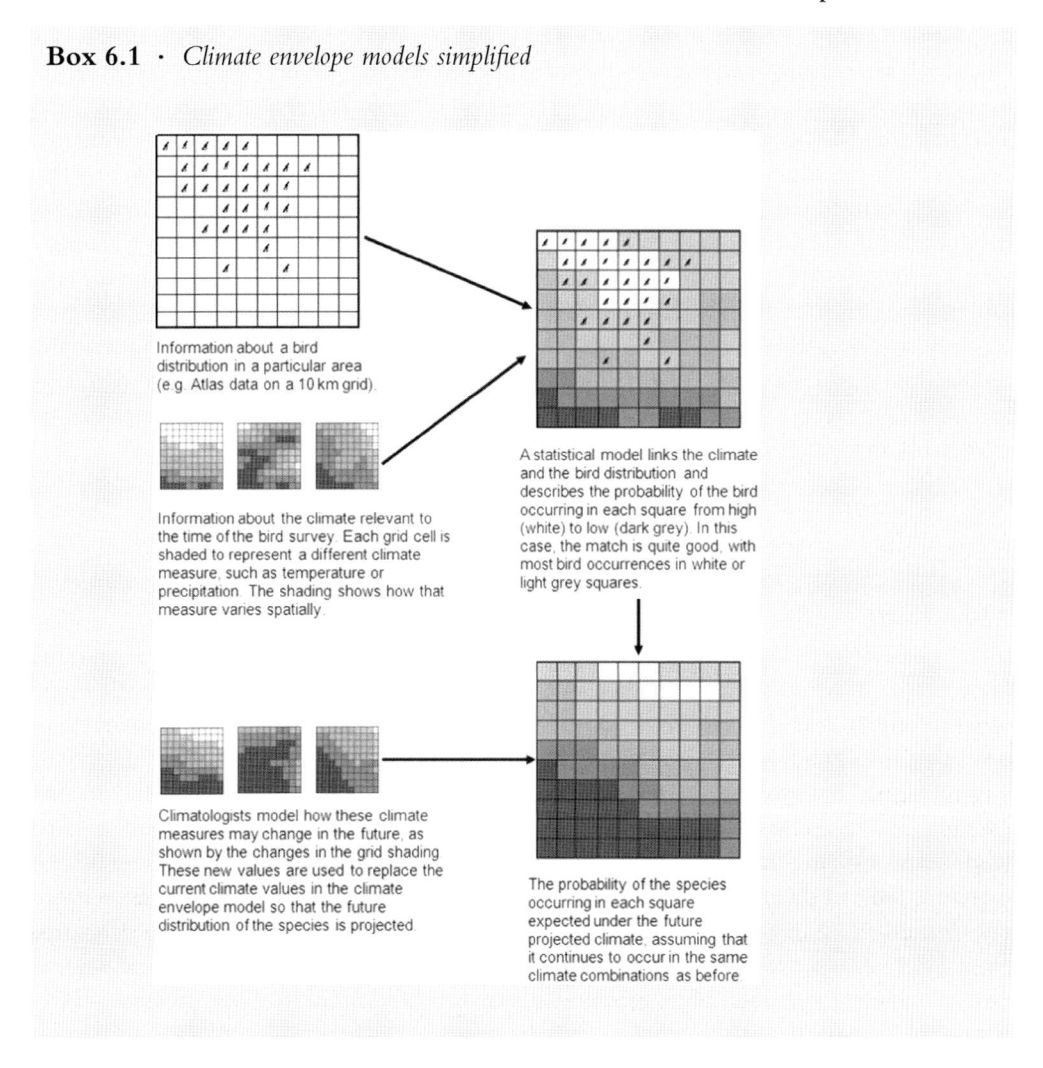

Information about a bird distribution in a particular area (e.g. Atlas data on a 10 km grid).

Information about the climate relevant to the time of the bird survey. Each grid cell is shaded to represent a different climate measure, such as temperature or precipitation. The shading shows how that measure varies spatially.

A statistical model links the climate and the bird distribution and describes the probability of the bird occurring in each square from high (white) to low (dark grey). In this case, the match is quite good, with most bird occurrences in white or light grey squares.

Climatologists model how these climate measures may change in the future, as shown by the changes in the grid shading. These new values are used to replace the current climate values in the climate envelope model so that the future distribution of the species is projected.

The probability of the species occurring in each square expected under the future projected climate, assuming that it continues to occur in the same climate combinations as before.

Once the model has been fitted, it can be used to calculate the expected probability of occurrence in grid cells separated from the area where the data were collected. Or it might be used to do this for grid cells in the same area but at a different time in the past or the future (Box 6.1). This requires that values of the environmental variables in the model are available for these grid cells in different places or at different times. Current climate is reasonably well known from recent meteorological observations, with good time series available for most parts of the world, though the spacing of recording stations and the frequency of observations vary. A number of different datasets provide such data on a gridded basis, based on interpolations between recording stations, such as the high-resolution CRU datasets for the globe (Mitchell & Jones 2005) or country-specific datasets, such as that produced by the UK Climate Impacts Programme (UKCIP; Perry & Hollis 2005). Hence, predicting the current distribution of a species in a region outside that for which the model was constructed is often feasible. For many areas, meteorological observations also extend back in time for decades, and sometimes for centuries. As long as instruments and recording methods have not changed, or the effects of any changes can be removed, reconstructions of the past distribution of the species can be made using the climate envelope model fitted to recent observations. The same approach can be used to make predictions for the future, and to reconstruct distributions for the distant past before instrumental or proxy data on climate were available (Figure 1.13). This requires models of the climate, such as General Circulation Models (GCMs), which can be used to calculate the probable values of climatic variables at another time. Many research groups are engaged in attempts to make projections of future climate (Section 1.6) and there has also been considerable progress recently in the use of GCMs to simulate climates in the distant past (Singarayer & Valdes 2010).

This preliminary outline of climate envelope modelling and its applications has glossed over many important details which are considered in the next sections.

6.3 The bird data

6.3.1 Types of data

Many types of bird data have been used for climate envelope modelling. At one extreme there is a set of records of a species known to be at certain localities, but with little or no other information (e.g. Reside *et al.* 2010). Entries in the field notebook of a naturalist or collection localities from the labels on bird skins in museums are examples of this type of information. They are useful because, as long as the identifications and the locality information are accurate, they allow the grid cells from which the observations came to be declared as being definitely occupied by the species during the period concerned and therefore help to describe the climatic conditions the species can tolerate. A little more information would allow more refined inferences to be made. For example, if records were kept of whether birds were singing, defending breeding territories, nesting or feeding dependent young, then specific climate envelope models of the breeding distribution of the species could be made (museum records of nests, eggs or nestlings also provide this). Information on abundance or the proportion of years in which a species was recorded as present can be used to screen out aberrant records, such as those of vagrant migratory birds.

These simple lists of records are examples of a class of bird distribution data known as 'presence-only data'. This means that, although definite presences were recorded, the absence of a species from identified localities was not recorded during the field-work. Given the difficulty of proving a negative, how could absence be inferred reliably? This is usually done by the field observers recording the amount of effort they put into searching for the species in each locality visited, or requiring that they put in a specified minimum level of effort at all sites. This approach is typical of that often used in reporting results of bird atlas studies in which each species is mapped as being present or absent in each grid cell. There have now been a large number of bird atlas studies worldwide and they provide valuable resources for climate envelope modellers (Gibbons *et al.* 2007). If the amount of effort expended searching for a species in a grid cell is judged to be sufficiently high, then it might seem reasonable to declare the species absent from that cell. It might also be reasonable to assume that a focal species is absent if it was not found even though many other equally elusive species were recorded, and a number of methods have been developed to do this. Of course, this is less certain than the evidence of presence obtained from definite records from a grid cell. There is a danger of committing the logical fallacy of argument from ignorance, in which lack of positive evidence of presence is assumed to be firm evidence of absence. The greater the search effort, the less likely this error is, but it cannot be excluded completely. Although many studies do not consider this issue, or are based on sufficiently robust data that it is not a problem, there are two potential ways to deal with this problem should it exist.

The first is available if the fieldworkers made several searches of each locality, each search being conducted in a comparable way. The data for each species then consists of a sequence of recorded detections and recorded failures to detect it. If the species can reasonably be assumed to be present throughout the sampling period at a locality where it was recorded at least once, even if it was not detected on all visits, then these data can be used to calculate, from the number of visits, the probability that a species would be detected in a grid cell if present, even in those localities where it was never recorded. The necessary calculations are performed using occupancy models (MacKenzie *et al.* 2006) which treat the bird survey data as if each search of a locality was like a trapping session in a mark-recapture study. In the same way that mark-recapture models estimate the probability that a marked individual is really alive and present, even if it is not captured, and also its average probability of recapture per session, the occupancy model estimates the probability that a species is present in a locality and its probability of being detected per search, given that it is actually present. This can be used to get at its corollary, the probability that an apparent absence is real. Occupancy models can be used with data collected on standardised searches in which methods and time in the field are strictly controlled, but they can also cope with surveys of variable length or thoroughness by observers with different levels of skill, by making these covariates of the modelled probability of detection. Hence, occupancy modelling allows the status of a species in a set of spatial units with particular characteristics to be specified as a probability that it was actually present, rather than the more widely used proportion of units with recorded presence.

Secondly, analysts may use the combined data for all the species covered by the survey work to fit species discovery curves for each locality or for sets of localities. Various types of species discovery analysis are possible, but they all involve examining the number of additional species detected for the first time at a given stage of the survey work at a locality in relation to the accumulated effort, number of individuals seen or number of other species detected up to that stage of the survey. As surveys proceed, the number of new species detected declines until, if enough surveys are done, there is eventually a full inventory of all the species present (e.g. Hill *et al.* 2011; Szabo *et al.* 2012). Some kinds of data of this type can be used to estimate the probability of detection of a particular species, if it is present, given the accumulated number of other species, individuals counted or survey effort (Szabo *et al.* 2010). As was the case with occupancy modelling, this can allow a probability to be assigned to the presence of a species in a spatial unit in which it was not detected.

The most detailed bird datasets available for climate envelope modelling include information on population density from censuses, line transects or point counts. An increasing number of standardised monitoring schemes, such as breeding bird survey data, provide a robust source of such information in a stratified fashion across an area. These data have the advantage of allowing abundance and not just presence/absence to be modelled in relation to climate variables (e.g. Renwick *et al.* 2012).

What is the most appropriate spatial scale for climate envelope models? It seems obvious at first that it should be the finest scale at which the bird data are available: if bird data are available by 1-km grid cells, surely the most useful model will be obtained by modelling the species' distribution at this scale? However, this may not necessarily be the case for various reasons. Firstly, in many bird species, individuals have large home ranges and it may be environmental conditions, including climate, averaged over a substantial area that determine whether a species is present or absent at a particular small locality, not just the conditions at that locality itself. Secondly, the presence or absence of the species at a fine spatial scale is especially likely to be affected by factors other than climate, such as habitat availability and quality. For this reason, studies of fine-scale variation in species' distribution also incorporate measures of land cover which often correlate well with species' occurrence (Pearson & Dawson 2003; Pearson *et al.* 2004). Such variables are, however, less useful at larger spatial scales, where climate is generally a better correlate of species' distribution (Thuiller *et al.* 2004). If quantitative data on non-climate variables are available, then a model can be made which includes them as well as the climate variables. However, data on the non-climate variables are sometimes not available or it may be undesirable to include them because of difficulties in predicting how they will change in future (see below). In that case, the adverse consequences of ignoring these influential variables may be reduced if the distribution of the species is modelled at a coarser spatial scale.

For example, suppose a species can only tolerate a certain set of climatic conditions, but it also requires rocky cliffs to provide safe nesting and roosting sites. If detailed information on topography is not available, then a model of the species' distribution in terms of climate variables alone is likely to be unreliable at the scale of 1-km grid cells because it will predict the occurrence of the species in many cells where the climate is suitable but where there are no cliffs. However, if a model with the same climate variables was fitted to the same bird data, but aggregated into larger grid cells, say 50 km instead of 1 km, it would probably give more reliable, though much coarser, predictions. This is because the specialised habitat needs of a species, in this case cliffs, are more likely to occur in at least a few places in a typical large grid cell in which climatic conditions are suitable for the species. Huntley and Baxter (2003) have illustrated that the ability of models to predict the features of species' distributions can be improved by including the effects of non-climate variables, but Luoto *et al.* (2007) showed that these improvements mainly affect the performance of the models at fine spatial scales. When predicting abundance rather than occurrence, which will be more closely determined by habitat quality and availability, the incorporation of non-climatic information is likely to be more important (e.g. Renwick *et al.* 2012).

Despite the widespread use of climate envelope models, or even more widely, SDMs for large-scale modelling, there is surprisingly little guidance about how best to decide on the scale to use (Elith & Leathwick 2009). In most studies, this is pragmatic and based upon the resolution of either the bird data or the climate data available. However, there do exist some statistical tools that can be used to best characterise scale, such as spectral analysis or wavelet-coefficient regression (Saunders *et al.* 2005), or examining the degree of spatial autocorrelation in the data (Schaefer & Mayor 2007). Further testing of the utility of these to better identify the scales at which such modelling should be conducted, which may also vary for different ecological processes, would be worthwhile. However, it should be recognised that the choice of spatial scale which gives the best performance in accurately modelling a currently observed bird distribution might not be the best for making future predictions when the climate or non-climate variables change. Tests of such predictions are also needed, and we will return to them later.

6.3.2 Time periods of data

Systematic surveys of bird distribution used to develop climate envelope models have mostly been conducted within the last few decades. This makes them subject to the effects of recent changes in distribution caused by factors unrelated to climate, such as persecution by humans, exploitation or pollution. Conversion to human land use of large continuous tracts of natural habitats such as wetlands and forest may also render previously occupied areas unsuitable for a species, especially if it is a species that requires large areas of undegraded habitat to persist. This can reduce the reliability of the fitted climate envelope model because some current range boundaries will be determined by factors unrelated to climate, and it can also make projections of future potential range expansion inaccurate because an apparently climatically suitable area in future may lack the species' required habitat. These problems are expected to be more likely to occur for large-bodied than small-bodied species (Huntley *et al.* 2007) because the former are more likely to be hunted for food, be persecuted as predators and to require larger tracts of suitable habitat than small species. Possible solutions are to obtain information on the distribution of the species before the range was modified by human activities (e.g. Evans *et al.* 2012), or to exclude from analysis those parts of the range where this is known to have occurred, although this may reduce the ability of the model to fully describe a species' climate space (Section 6.3.3).

Another consideration is whether climatic conditions have been stable for a long period up to and including the period in which the survey data were collected. If they have not, then the species' distribution is unlikely to be at equilibrium with regard to the climate measured during the period when it was mapped, even if the species' distribution is strongly influenced by climate (Section 5.2). If the climate has been changing, the species may not have reached the boundaries of the range of climatic conditions it can tolerate at the time when the survey was done, or it may still be present in an area where the climate is now unsuitable. Climate envelope models are then likely to give unreliable projections of future change for the same reasons as those given above concerning artificial modifications of the range caused by human activity. For this reason, climate envelope models should ideally be fitted to bird distribution data that precede the recent period of especially rapid anthropogenic climate change. In many parts of the world these changes have been especially marked since the 1980s.

6.3.3 The geographical extent of data

Ideally, climate envelope models should be fitted to data of uniform good quality from the entire extent of the species' global geographical range, though modelling the breeding and non-breeding ranges of migratory species separately is generally most appropriate. When a model is fitted to only part of a species' geographical range it might give misleading projections, because some of the limits of its distribution in climatic space may not be represented in the data available (Barbet-Massin et al. 2010). For example, if the data on the distribution of a species are not available at low latitudes, but they are actually present there, then the projections of potential range under a future warmer climate may erroneously indicate a greater poleward shift in the low latitude limit of the potential future range than is actually likely to occur. Hence, if global data on the distribution of the species cannot be obtained for practical reasons, it is advisable to extend survey coverage beyond apparent upper and lower climatic limits to the range in as many places as possible. Studies of the transferability of species distribution models suggest they may not work well in locations outside of the geographical area from which the data used to fit them were obtained (Randin et al. 2006). The same issue is likely to also affect climate envelope models.

6.4 The climate data

The first issues we address are the number and nature of the meteorological and climatic variables included in a climate envelope model. Some modellers begin with a long list of candidate variables, often without any *a priori* hypotheses about likely effects based upon information about the ecology of the species concerned. They then use a model selection procedure to identify a statistical model that best fits the observed distribution of the species. However, this approach runs the risks inherent in data dredging, which can select a model founded upon spurious correlations which are bound to emerge if a sufficiently large number of explanatory variables and their combinations are considered (Burnham & Anderson 2002). One way to avoid this problem is to define in advance a small set of appropriate bioclimate variables, based upon prior knowledge, that reflect processes of physiological or ecological relevance to the organisms being studied (Leathwick & Whitehead 2001). This approach involves having a working hypothesis about the mechanisms by which climate might directly or indirectly affect the demographic rates of a species (Chapter 4).

Based on our review of climatic drivers of variation in bird populations (Chapter 4) and bird communities (Chapter 5), we might expect various combinations of temperature and precipitation variables to be important, and this is indeed the case. There is good evidence that many populations, particularly at high latitudes, may be limited by temperature (Section 4.2.1), and so to represent this, many studies include a measure of winter cold, such as the mean temperature of the coldest month, or mean winter temperature, as a potential limiter of high-latitude or elevational range extent. A second important temperature-related variable is the overall warmth or solar radiation received at each location. This may have a number of ecological consequences, also being linked to variation in bird communities (Section 5.3), as well as wider impacts, such as being closely linked to the energy available or the length of plant growing seasons. For this reason, many climate envelope studies use a measure of the annual sum, in degree-days, of daily temperatures exceeding 5 °C, which approximates to the lower threshold temperature for plant growth, as a second bioclimatic variable (e.g. Huntley *et al.* 2007, 2008). Thirdly, we have already outlined the importance of variation in precipitation in affecting populations at lower latitudes (Section 4.2.2) or moisture availability in driving spatial variation in bird diversity patterns around the world, operating through variation in plant productivity (Section 5.3). For example, the ratio of actual to potential evapotranspiration (AET/PET) reflects the availability of soil water to terrestrial plants (Prentice *et al.* 1992); the lower this ratio is, the more likely that plant growth is limited by low moisture availability. This variable is known from studies of plant physiology to be a direct determinant of the ability of certain types of drought-tolerant plants to compete for space with other species which are less tolerant. Hence, the plant functional type and species composition of an area are likely to be influenced strongly by this bioclimate variable which we would expect in turn to affect the abundance and distribution of birds.

AET/PET might also be quite a good proxy for aspects of soil water balance that would be expected to influence birds more directly than indirectly via plants. For example, the availability of food to some bird species that feed on soil-dwelling invertebrates is strongly affected by soil moisture levels (Pearce-Higgins 2010). The average water content of surface soils is likely to be low during the plant growing season in areas with a low average AET/PET. Birds that depend for food on soil invertebrates which are most active at and near the soil surface when the soil is moist, would be expected to have a less reliable food supply in such areas. This is illustrated by a study of variation over time in the annual survival rate of song thrushes in the UK, which indicates that survival rates were lowest when there were long periods of drought in the summer (Figure 6.1a). It seems probable that the influence of drought on the availability of earthworms and other soil invertebrate foods is the mechanism underlying this correlation (Robinson *et al.* 2004). The other weather variable which was correlated with song thrush survival was the duration of periods of frost, which had a negative effect. Like drought, sub-zero temperatures during the winter reduce the activity of soil invertebrates and cause them to move deeper in the soil and hence to be less available to surface-feeding thrushes. Of course, cold weather also increases the cost of thermoregulation of birds, so an effect on food supply is not the only plausible mechanism by which this variable might affect song thrush survival (Section 4.3).

Climate envelope modelling of the European distribution of breeding song thrushes in terms of three bioclimate variables revealed that the limits of the distribution of the species were most strongly associated with the AET/PET, with the species rarely occurring where this ratio was less than 0.6, which indicates dry conditions. The influence of the mean temperature of the coldest month of the year was less strong, though song thrushes rarely occur in the small part of Europe where this is less than −20 °C. This bioclimate variable is a close proxy for the duration of periods of frost, which was found to be important in the study of annual survival rates, although as many populations in cold areas are wholly or partially migratory, this effect may also operate indirectly through other mechanisms. There was little effect on song thrush distribution of the third bioclimate variable considered, growing season warmth (Huntley *et al.* 2007). Hence, the ecologically

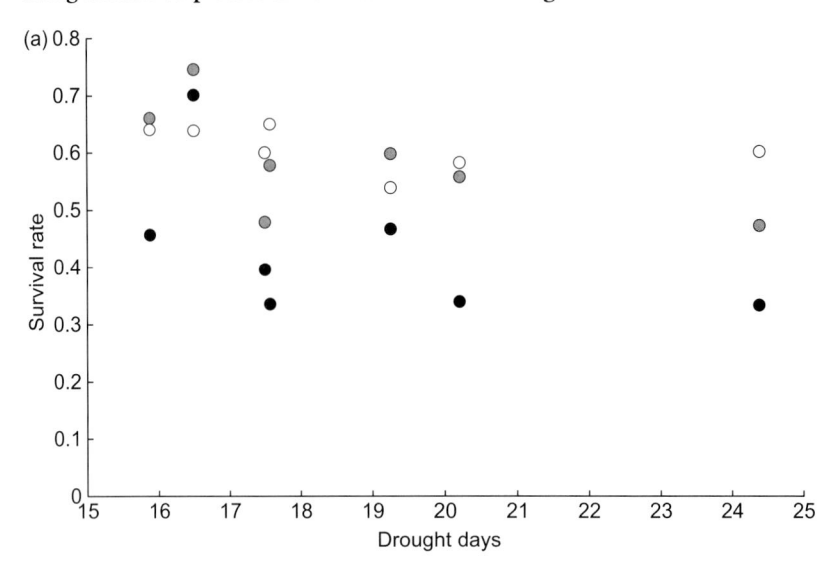

Figure 6.1 Relationships between moisture availability and the demographic rates and breeding distribution of the song thrush. (a) Survival of fledged song thrush young in the UK during the period of dependence on the parents (black circles) and annual survival of full-grown birds in their first year after independence (grey circles) and as adults (white circles) tend to decline with the increasing numbers of consecutive drought days between June and mid-August. Points represent averages for groups of consecutive years in which the population trend remained similar (reproduced with permission from Robinson *et al.* 2004). (b) Proportion of 50 km grid cells in Europe in which song thrush was recorded as a breeding species (intensity of shading) in relation to average values for 1960–1990 of three bioclimate variables, the mean temperature of the coldest month, the annual temperature sum above 5 °C, and moisture availability (the ratio of actual to potential evapotranspiration AET/PET). Song thrushes were rarely present when moisture availability was low (AET/PET < 0.6). Uniform pale shading at the edges of each panel represents parts of climate space not represented in Europe during this period. Reproduced from Huntley *et al.* (2007).

based working hypothesis that soil moisture content and ground frosts affect both the survival and distribution of song thrushes through effects on availability of their food is reasonably well supported by both studies of demographic rates and climate envelope modelling.

6.5 The use of non-climate variables

Including non-climate variables in species distribution models, such as soil type and land cover, can increase the realism of the models in describing current distributions, because real species distributions are obviously affected by some things which are neither directly nor indirectly influenced by the climate. However, doing so affects the ways the model can be used. Models using climate data alone can make projections about potential future

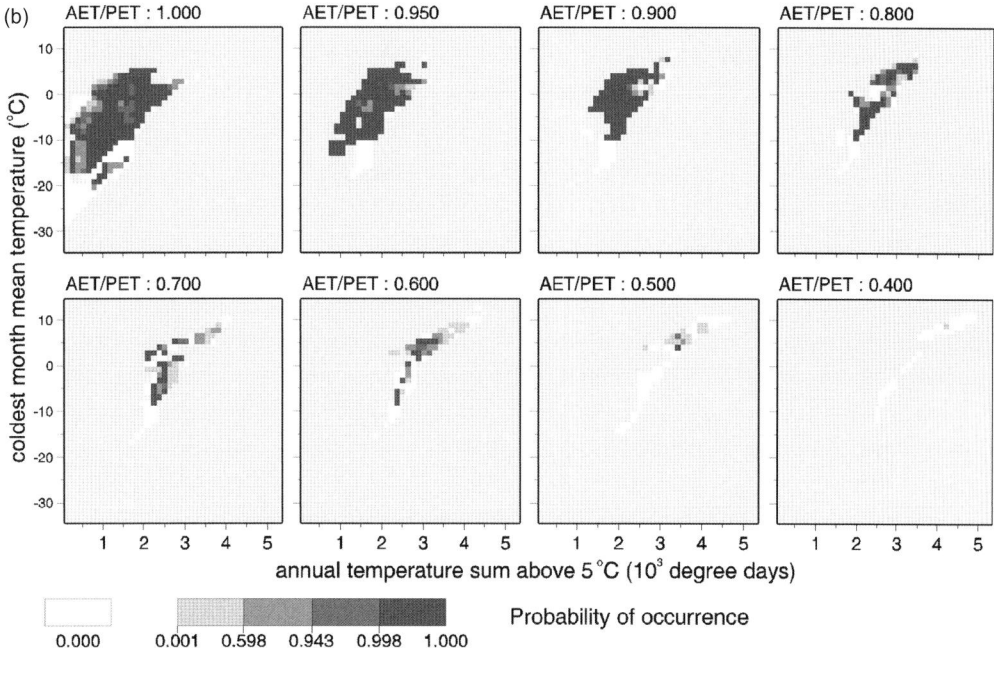

Figure 6.1 (cont.)

distributions based on well-parameterised GCM climate projections with greater confidence than models which are also dependent on projections of change in non-climate variables. Most of the studies using climate envelope models that we review in this chapter have taken this approach of linking large-scale variation in occurrence to climate and focussing on coarse-grain projections of distribution change for this reason.

Many habitats of importance to birds can potentially change in extent and distribution quite quickly. For example, in response to increasing human demand for land and resources, the extent of natural forest and wetland habitat can be rapidly reduced through logging, clearance for agriculture, land drainage and water abstraction. The distribution of particular types of crops and pastures, which provide habitats for many bird species, and the ways in which these are managed, can also change rapidly because of altered demand for agricultural products of different kinds and changes in technology. These changes are known to affect bird distribution and abundance strongly and by a wide variety of mechanisms (Wilson *et al.* 2009b), but are difficult to predict with confidence, introducing large and unquantifiable uncertainties about future values of these non-climatic variables and their impacts on bird populations. Future projections based from such models that also incorporate non-climate variables, such as land cover, should therefore be regarded as indicating how the suitability of the land cover for a species is likely to change in response to climate change (e.g. Renwick *et al.* 2012). These models may then be used to determine an optimum land cover in order to reduce potentially negative climate change impacts, or to explore the likely interaction between climate change and a number of alternative future land-use scenarios to inform future policy (e.g. Vos *et al.* 2008; Barbett-Massin *et al.* 2012).

6.6 Modelling methods

6.6.1 Presence/absence data

Climate envelope modellers make widely varying assumptions about the type of relationship between the probability of occurrence of a species in a locality and its climate. Some modelling approaches that have been used to fit climatic envelope models assume a particular underlying parametric form of the relationship between a species' probability of occurrence and the climatic variables. In other words, the probability of occurrence is determined by an equation from which its expected value can be calculated as a function of a set of explanatory climate variables. The type of function can be chosen to fit the data or to conform to theoretical constraints or expectations. Examples are the Gaussian or logistic functions. Statistical software packages which allow the fitting of Generalised Linear Models (GLMs) with various forms of parametric relationship and distributions of the errors around it have made the methods needed to fit such models widely accessible.

Parametric modelling approaches may assume that each climate variable affects the probability of occurrence of a species in its own way, with the effect of a change in one variable being unaffected by the values of the other variables. Alternatively, interactions among the climate variables in their effect on probability of occurrence can also be tested. This means that the magnitude of the effect of a change in one variable differs according to the values of the other variables. One problem with incorporating such interactions into climate envelope models is that models that have more than just a few climatic variables have large numbers of possible interactions among them, which require large amounts of data to describe. Models with large numbers of interactions also run the risk that spurious patterns will be identified simply because a large number of things were looked for at once. This is a similar problem to that of data dredging we mentioned earlier, where spurious patterns can emerge by chance just because a large number of potential explanatory variables were examined. Ideally, the inclusion of interaction terms in parametric climate envelope models would be based upon ecological or physiological prior knowledge about mechanisms that lead to that interaction being expected. In practice, prior ecological knowledge of many species is too vague for a sound basis for such expectations to be available.

Another approach is to smooth out an observed empirical relationship between the probability of occurrence and the climate variables. In practice, this is often done by fitting parametric models, as described above, but to subsets of the data within each of several limited ranges of each of the variables. The piecewise fitted curves are joined up to provide a smooth composite model. Generalised Additive Models (GAMs: Hastie & Tibshirani 1990; Wood & Augustin 2002) and Climate Response Surfaces (CRS), essentially do just this. Smoothing-based methods have the advantage of allowing the relationship to have a very flexible form and to incorporate interactions among variables, with a level of complexity determined by the data and the degree of smoothing applied. However, it is difficult with these methods to define an optimal level of smoothing in a completely objective way.

Regression trees and classification trees offer another modelling approach in which the data are partitioned into two sets based upon the value of a continuous climate variable or a categorical variable. Doing this repeatedly gives the models a tree-like dendritic structure, with branches separating at successive nodes (De'ath & Fabricius, 2000). A variant of the tree method is the Random Forest in which multiple tree models are built instead of just one, by using randomly selected sets of the observations and random subsets of the predictor variables. The predictions of occurrence probability are then averaged across the multiple models (Breiman 2001).

Finally, we mention several machine-learning methods which use complex computer algorithms to build descriptions of the relationships between values of climate variables and the presence of a species. These methods include maximum entropy modelling (Maxent; Phillips et al. 2006), artificial neural networks (Ripley 1996) and the genetic algorithm GARP (Stockwell & Noble 1992).

A wide variety of examples exist using these different methods (see Elith & Leathwick 2009; Franklin 2009). The method used will depend upon the precise requirements of the study. Where the form of the relationships between occurrence and climate are predictable from theory or ecological knowledge, parametric regression-based approaches such as GLMs may be favoured. Where more unpredictable complex and non-linear relationships are likely, the other modelling techniques may be useful.

6.6.2 Presence-only data

Modelling methods such as GLMs, GAMs and CRS require data on both presence and absence, such as that derived from systematic atlas studies and other surveys. As outlined above, much distribution data are derived from more opportunistic recording, and therefore in the form of presence-only data, with no definitive absences. These data can be modelled using these methods by regarding spatial units with no recorded presence as if they were absences (pseudo-absences). If the recorded presences constitute a representative sample of the places where the species is really present, this can result in a reliable index of probability of occurrence, though not the absolute probability of occurrence. Other modelling methods, such as Maxent, are specifically designed for use with such presence-only data. They use information on spatial variation in climate and other environmental factors throughout the area from which the presence data were drawn, including places where the species was not recorded (Phillips et al. 2006).

6.6.3 Abundance data

Most of the studies of climate envelope modelling have been of the distribution of species using presence/absence or presence only data, and therefore characterise the climatic limits of a species' range, and how the distribution of that range may change in response to a changing climate. Range size and trend in range size are important determinants of extinction risk, but it is population size and population trends which are most frequently used to assess conservation priorities. Species with small populations and those with negative population trends, even with an initially large population, are assigned higher conservation priority (Table 7.1). Population declines may occur before any reduction in range is observed (Chamberlain & Fuller 2001), making population size a potentially more sensitive measure of potential future change than range extent, particularly as it may then be used to assess future risk of extinction directly. This has been a largely neglected topic, but see Shoo et al. (2005), Renwick et al. (2012) and Johnston et al. (2013).

The modelling of abundance data poses different challenges to modelling occurrences. The detectability of birds during surveys is just as much an issue as it is with determining presence or absence, and ideally, surveys need to be designed to allow the proportion of birds detected in a survey area to be estimated so that population density can be calculated (Buckland et al. 2007). Even if absolute population density cannot be estimated, differences in detectability of birds in different habitat types should be allowed for by comparing relative abundance across survey locations. Residual variation in count data can follow a wide variety of statistical distributions, which will need to be accounted for in analysis by specifying appropriate error distributions. Birds are often more highly aggregated than is predicted by simple models. This may be because of flocking or colonial behaviour or simply because the model fails to take some important variables into account. This makes it necessary to account for over-dispersion of counts. Once the appropriate error distribution has been specified, then a similar range of modelling approaches can be used to those outlined previously, with GLMs and GAMs often being used to fit relationships between population density and climate.

Within a species' range, abundance is much more heavily influenced by variation in non-climate aspects of environmental or site quality than occurrence (Section 6.3.1). Climate alone therefore tends to explain a relatively small proportion of the variation among sites in bird abundance. For example, in regression models of the abundance of 17 breeding seabirds and 45 wintering waterbirds in Western Europe, temperature and precipitation variables accounted for only 1.4% and < 0.1% respectively of the fine-scale variation in abundance among sites. This was despite the same models accounting for 56% of the interspecific variation in population trends when scaled up across all the sites (Johnston et al. 2013). Climate was therefore a poor predictor of how many birds were found at a particular site, but a much stronger covariate of large-scale trends. For this reason, it may be desirable to also include additional non-climate explanatory variables that may describe habitat quality or availability in order to more accurately model abundance (Renwick et al. 2012). However, the same problems arise with this as for models of species occurrence: non-climate variables dependent on human activity are even more difficult to forecast than climate and this makes projections of future bird abundance that rely on these forecasts highly uncertain.

6.6.4 Combining different approaches

The greatest variation in the output from climate envelope models of the same data comes from the choice of statistical method used (Dormann et al. 2008; Diniz-Filho et al. 2009). This can account for some 30–50% of the variation in estimates of projected future range change, and 40% of variation in projected species turnover. As projections are made further into the future, the importance of the general circulation model and emissions scenario used increases, but these generally only account for about 20% of the variation in the magnitude of projected change (Buisson et al. 2010). For this reason, some recent studies have tended to employ an ensemble approach, where information from a range of statistical methods are collated and combined, to make predictions and future projections (Araújo & New 2007; Buisson et al. 2010; Barbet-Massin et al. 2012; Fordham et al. 2012b). The procedures used vary considerably and include averaging across alternative model formulations, selecting the best-fitting of several alternatives and identifying features of several different predictions which the different approaches all agree on. Ensemble approaches have the advantage of indicating the extent to which projections of future distributions are similar across a range of modelling approaches. However, it is uncertain whether they result in more accurate forecasts than would have been obtained by more careful selection of the most appropriate modelling technique and variables for the species concerned. Ensemble forecasting has the potential disadvantage that it can allow projections to be influenced by inappropriate and defective approaches.

Other ways exist for combining different modelling approaches. Using a hurdle model, it is possible to combine separate models of occurrence and abundance into a single output to predict both population and range changes in response to climate change (Mellin *et al.* 2012). There is considerable interest in the potential to combine outputs from climate envelope models with more mechanistic approaches (e.g. Keith *et al.* 2008), such as some of those discussed in Chapter 4. This area of current development has been best developed for plants (e.g. Fordham *et al.* 2012a) and mammals (Anderson *et al.* 2009a), and partly extended to birds, to incorporate dispersal (Barbet-Massin *et al.* 2012), but much more work is required. We shall return to this topic at the end of the chapter.

6.7 Making projections

The most frequent way in which climate envelope models are used for conservation purposes is to make projections of the future potential range of a species under a future projected climate. The future potential range is the range a species would be expected to occupy if its future probability of being present under a given combination of specified climatic conditions was determined solely and immediately by those conditions in exactly the same way as is described by its climate envelope model. The future projected climate is usually derived from a GCM under a particular assumed future greenhouse gas emissions scenario, or range of GCMs, usually for a set of coupled atmosphere–ocean GCMs (AOGCMs) for each emissions scenario.

Such projections are predicated on the assumption that the model, fitted for a past time period and for an area from which data were available, describes relationships between climate and occurrence which remain constant into the future (Box 6.1). A simple way to express the expected impact of climate change on a species is to calculate the ratio between the area of its future potential range and either the area of its current or recent range, or to account for any discrepancies in model fitting, the area of its range simulated using the climate envelope model under current or recent climatic conditions. If the future potential range is smaller than the current actual or simulated range, this may indicate a prospect of deteriorating conservation status for the species (Figure 6.2).

The future potential range would be the same as the realised future range of the species if its geographical distribution tracked the future changes in the location of the climatic conditions it tolerated in the past perfectly, with no delays or discrepancies. However, in reality, delays and discrepancies are both very likely (Section 5.4). We will look at the potential reasons for these in more detail later in this chapter, but for now we will explain how the outputs of climate envelope models are adapted to allow for one particular source of delay. Climate envelope models frequently identify areas of the future potential range which lie outside the current range but are simulated as being newly suitable for the species. For the

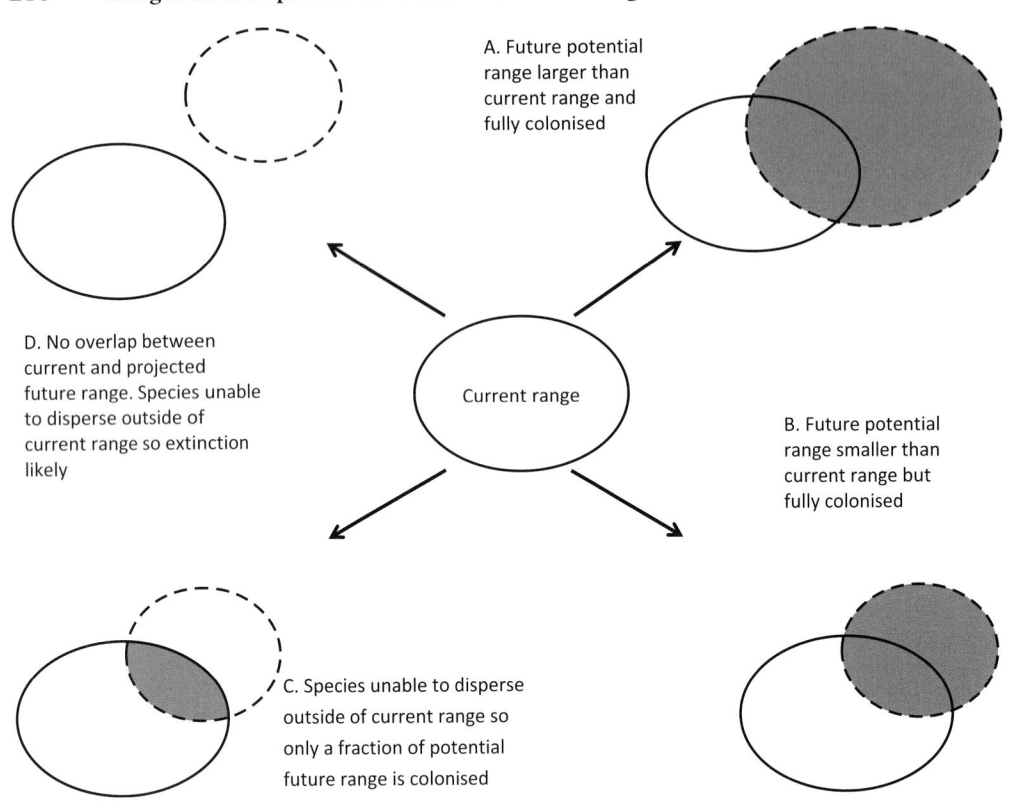

Figure 6.2 Cartoon of different outcomes of climate envelope modelling for a species based on the relative size and overlap of the current range (solid oval) and projected future range (dashed oval), with the realised future range indicated by shading. This varies according to the dispersal ability of the species, with an increasingly severe impact of climate change on the species from A (likely benefit) to D (likely extinction).

species to spread to these areas requires powers of dispersal and that the ecological conditions for the species become suitable immediately. A worst-case assumption can be made that the newly suitable part of the future potential range will not be occupied (Figure 6.2c, d). The future potential range is then modified by taking the area of overlap between the future potential range and the current range. The extent of this overlap zone can be expressed as a proportion of the area of the current range. This is a projection of the ratio of the future range to the current range if the species followed the model's predictions of range loss perfectly, but did not colonise any of the areas projected to become newly suitable for it under the future climate. Such projected ratios are often called 'no dispersal' projections because one way in which they might occur is if a species has no capacity to disperse to new areas, although failure to colonise new areas can be caused by other things than just low dispersal capacity. Such 'no dispersal' projections are useful worst-case assessments.

Attempts are now being made to include empirical information on dispersal when making climate envelope model projections of future range (Anderson *et al.* 2009a). This might allow more realistic predictions to be produced, for example to identify locations where habitat isolation may restrict future range expansion in response to climate change

(Vos *et al*. 2008), a topic to which we return in Chapter 7. The first systematic attempt to do this used ringing data (Paradis *et al*. 1998) to produce a probability distribution of natal dispersal which was used to modify the probability of range expansion into areas of potentially suitable climate into the future (Barbet-Massin *et al*. 2012). However, it should be borne in mind that demographic and ecological lags are also likely to contribute to failures of species to colonise areas in which the climate has recently changed to become suitable. These mechanisms for colonisation lags are discussed in detail in Section 6.10.2. Estimates of natal dispersal within the present range therefore only capture part of the probable set of mechanisms underlying colonisation lags.

All climate modelling approaches can run into difficulties when used to make predictions for climatic conditions at the edge of, or outside, the set of conditions in the observed dataset to which the model was fitted. Being able to make such predictions is especially useful in regions where expected future climate change is large, so that some areas have projected climates that are different from any found recently in the study area. For parametric models, such as GLMs, it is easy to use the estimated parameters of the fitted model to make predictions of probability of occurrence for any climatic conditions, including those outside the range of what has been observed. However, the reliability of the model's predictions obviously is increasingly doubtful the further one goes beyond what has been established from empirical observations (Elith & Leathwick 2009). As we argued regarding the choice of which climatic variables to include in models, the incorporation of prior knowledge of physiology and ecology of a species into the choice of the form of a parametric relationship or interactions among variables is likely to increase the reliability of such extrapolations. For example, if the probability of occurrence of a species declines with decreasing mean temperature of the coldest month within the range of values found in the existing empirical data, knowledge of the ecology or physiology of a species may make it reasonable to assume that the trend will continue beyond the observed range. This is perhaps easiest to do for ectotherms whose distribution may be relatively simply limited by climate (Sunday *et al*. 2012), and an example of this approach is given by Lee *et al*. (2009), but may be more challenging for many bird species whose ranges may not be closely limited by particular temperature or precipitation thresholds. The Ethiopian bush-crow, pictured on the front cover of the book, may be an exception whose distribution is strongly limited by temperature (Box 6.2). When smoothing methods, such as GAMs, are used, it is difficult to predict the probability of occurrence outside the range of climatic conditions found in the study area at the time that the observed distribution data used to fit the model were collected. This is often simply because the smoothing procedure cannot give expected values, or gives values markedly different to those within the range of observed values, when applied even just outside it.

6.8 Projected impacts of climate change on bird populations

6.8.1 A case study of European breeding birds

As an example of projected impacts of climatic change on bird distribution and abundance we first consider an assessment made for European breeding birds (Huntley *et al*. 2007, 2008). Three GCMs and two emissions scenarios were used to give six versions of the

Box 6.2 · *Temperature limitation of a globally threatened bird*

The globally threatened Ethiopian bush-crow *Zavattariornis stresemanni* occupies a very restricted geographical area at the southern edge of the Ethiopian Highlands. It lives in mosaics of grassland and acacia vegetation, such as those created by grazing, and is therefore associated with human settlements and their livestock. These habitats appear to be more widely spread than the bird is. The species' range is closely correlated with temperature and it does not occur outside the mean annual temperature range of 16.5–20 °C (Donald *et al.* 2012). During the heat of the day, the Ethiopian bush-crow pants and exposes an unusual patch of bare skin behind the eye, perhaps in an attempt to keep cool. As corvids are known to be particularly sensitive to high temperatures (Prinzinger 1976), given the apparent temperature limits on its distribution now, the Ethopian bush-crow may be particularly susceptible to future warming.

Box 6.2 Ethiopian bush-crow exposing the patch of bare skin behind the eye to cool down in the heat of the day. Photograph by Paul Donald.

projected climate during the period 2070–2099. Climate envelope models fitted to bird distribution data collected in the 1980s were used to obtain future potential breeding ranges for all of the species that breed in Europe, except some with very restricted ranges for which satisfactory models could not be obtained. The resulting models covered a total of 431 species. Averaged across all species, the extent of the future potential range was between 11% and 28% smaller than the current range, depending on the future climate scenario used, if future range was assumed to follow the climate envelope models' predictions perfectly as per Figure 6.2a and b. However, if no colonisation of new areas was assumed, then the average projected declines in range extent lay between 47% and

69% (Figure 6.2c and d). Only change in climate was assumed to affect bird ranges: other changes due to factors such as habitat modification by people were ignored. Based on the same Europe-wide dataset of bird distributions, Araújo *et al.* (2011) predicted that some 65–71% of bird species would occupy smaller ranges than they do at present, in response to a range of climate change scenarios.

To assess the potential effects of these range size reductions on the risk of extinction of European birds, Thomas *et al.* (2004) used power law methods derived from the species-area relationship to translate projected range size reductions from climate envelope models into risks of extinction. They did this for 34 species of endemic or near-endemic (>90% of the global range in the Western Palearctic) birds because the risk of global extinction can only be assessed if the effect of climate change on the global range can be modelled. Depending upon the details of the calculation used, they found that the proportion of these species committed to extinction by the climatic change expected by the mid twenty-first century under a warming scenario approximating to 3 °C global temperature rise, was 4–6% if future range was assumed to follow the climate envelope model predictions perfectly, and 13–38% if no colonisation of new areas was assumed. We emphasise that these calculations estimate the proportion of species expected eventually to go extinct if the modelled changes in range expected from climate change occur and then persist into the future indefinitely. They are not predictions of how many species will go extinct before 2050.

Barbet-Massin *et al.* (2010) extended the Huntley *et al.* predictions for 179 species that breed in Iberia and North Africa by including additional occurrence information from the full Western Palaearctic range, including parts of North Africa and the Middle East. This reduced the projected future range loss by 2050 for this subset of species under a range of GCMs and climate scenarios from 38%, when the model was fitted using Europe-only data, to 12%. At the same time, the authors also considered the potential for additional species to colonise Europe from North Africa, identifying 18 out of the 27 North African bird species modelled for which parts of southern Iberia were included in the future potential range and therefore may be suitable for colonisation. Species such as the red-rumped wheatear *Oenanthe moesta* and house bunting *Emberiza sahari* may therefore become European colonists in a changing climate. Interestingly, for one-third of the African species modelled, such as house swift *Apus affinis*, and cream-coloured courser *Cursorius cursor*, parts of Iberia were already predicted to be climatically suitable, but these species do not yet breed there. This emphasises the potential role of geographical barriers, such as the Mediterranean Sea, in reducing the ability of species ranges to shift in response to climate change.

These climate envelope models have been extended further by also incorporating relatively simple land-cover variables and using future land-cover projections to match the three different emissions scenarios (Barbet-Massin *et al.* 2012). Future probabilities of occupancy of potentially suitable areas of range were also limited by likely natal dispersal probabilities over a 50-year time frame, derived from ringing data. Under these constraints, a total of 71% of species were projected to have a 2050 future potential range smaller than their current range (very similar to Araújo's projection above). Incorporating limitations on dispersal had little impact on the overall projected rate of change for 75% of species, but in 5% of cases, reduced the extent of the future potential range by more than 20%.

Box 6.3 · *The likely importance of future climate change on breeding and wintering grounds in driving population trends of European long-distance migrants*

We compared the projected changes in the extent of the breeding range for 56 long-distance migrants from Huntley *et al.* (2007) with the equivalent changes in winter breeding ranges from Barbet-Massin *et al.* (2009). The median change in breeding range for these species was a 7% decline, compared with a 12% decline in non-breeding range, if the change was assumed to follow the climate envelope models' predictions perfectly. This small difference was not statistically significant (Wilcoxon matched-pairs test, $P = 0.83$). However, there was a larger and statistically significant difference between breeding and non-breeding range results if no colonisation of new areas was assumed (median breeding rate decline = 39%, median non-breeding range decline = 23% decline; Wilcoxon matched-pairs test, $P = 0.02$). Hence, there is less overlap between the current range and the projected late twenty-first century range for the breeding range than is the case for the non-breeding range.

Identifying the species for which dispersal may limit their potential to respond to climate change is likely to be crucial in terms of prioritising the species on which adaptation to promote range shifts should focus (Section 7.7). It should be noted, however, that, as mentioned in Section 6.7, limitations on colonisation are not likely to be caused by limitations of natal distance alone. Demographic and ecological lags are also likely to be important, as described in Section 6.10.2.

Long-distance migrants that breed in Europe and spend the northern winter in sub-Saharan Africa may also be vulnerable to climate change on the wintering grounds. Barbet-Massin *et al.* (2009) applied similar climate envelope modelling procedures to those described above for breeding ranges, using five GCMs and three emissions scenarios in order to estimate projected changes in the extent of the non-breeding ranges of 64 passerine species. Using an ensemble approach they estimated that by 2100, the median potential non-breeding range extent would be 13% less than the current extent of the range if future distribution was assumed to follow the climate envelope models' predictions perfectly, and would be reduced by 28% under a no-colonisation assumption. The magnitude of these changes is less than that predicted for the European breeding ranges of these species (Box 6.3), which suggests that climate change on the breeding grounds may have a greater impact on long-term population trends of these species than on the wintering grounds. Further, if the climate envelope models are correct, the ability to colonise areas with newly suitable climate conditions will be more important for the breeding range than the non-breeding range of these long-distance migrants. Since individual birds are usually less mobile within and between breeding seasons than they are within and between non-breeding seasons, colonising newly suitable parts of the range may be easier in the African non-breeding areas than in the breeding range.

In a similar study to that of Barbet-Massin *et al.* (2009), Doswald *et al.* (2009) fitted climate envelope models to both the breeding and non-breeding ranges of *Sylvia* warblers breeding in Europe. This group of small, largely insectivorous passerines is of special interest because it includes residents or short-distance migrants which winter close the breeding grounds, medium-distance migrants which spend the winter in southern Europe and North Africa, and long-distance trans-Saharan migrants. It was found that the distance between the centroids of the future potential breeding and non-breeding ranges in the late twenty-first century tended to be greater than the present distance, especially for long-distance migrants, suggesting that migration might require more time and energy in future. However, the projected outcomes varied considerably among species. For four species which are currently exclusive trans-Saharan migrants, the projections suggested that part of the population might in future be able to spend the non-breeding season in North Africa, if they were able to adapt their migration strategy, thus shortening future migratory distance.

6.8.2 Variation in projections of change

Climate envelope models have been used to make inferences about the likely impacts of climate change on European breeding bird species. A range of other studies do this for birds in other regions. Some are for large areas, such as continents, whereas others may deal with a single country. Some deal with one or a few species, whereas others deal with the entire bird species assemblage of the region, so far as the data allow. The outcomes of many of these studies are summarised by Warren *et al.* (2010), but are synthesised further in this section.

Characteristics of species projected to be at high risk vary between studies from different regions and using different methods. Consistent patterns for this have not yet emerged. There are some striking examples where future changes are anticipated to be rapid, such as a mean projected loss of 84% of the potential range of northern land bird species in Finland by 2100 under a 3.8 °C warming scenario and a 74% average loss for a 2.0 °C warming scenario (Virkkala *et al.* 2008). From 49% to 85% of endemic bird species in Queensland are projected to be committed to extinction by 2050 under a high climate change scenario (Thomas *et al.* 2004). As much as 57% of California is projected to be occupied by novel bird species assemblages by 2070, indicating the potential coincidence of species which are currently allopatric with unknown consequences for those communities (Stralberg *et al.* 2009).

Some authors have combined assessments of the impact of climate change on bird distributions with projected land-cover changes (Jetz *et al.* 2007; Şekercioğlu *et al.* 2008; Barbet-Massin *et al.* 2012), which as already outlined may introduce further uncertainty. For example, less than 1% of land birds were regarded by Jetz *et al.* (2007) to suffer 100% range loss by 2100. In this study, climate change impacts on species' distributions occurred through the conversion of one broad land-cover type to another which that species does not use. Given that only 15 natural and 3 human-transformed land-cover types were defined for the whole planet, this approach may well underestimate likely climate change impacts on species distributions, as direct and indirect effects of climate and of finer-grained habitat differences influencing the distribution of bird species within these broad categories were not considered.

These varying methods account for the wide range in projected impacts of climate change on extinction risk of birds (see also Bellard *et al.* 2012), which vary from 0.4% to 21.2% depending upon the methods used, or to 24.5% including the results of our meta-

Table 6.1 *Estimates of the proportion of terrestrial bird species at risk of extinction as a result of climate change from studies attempting to quantify some degree of global impact.*

Reference	Year (magnitude of change)	Proportion of species
Thomas et al. (2004)	2050 (1.9–3.3 °C rise)	18.1–21.2%
Jetz et al. (2007)	2100 (1.6–3.2 °C rise)	0.5–0.9%
Şekercioğlu et al. (2008)	2100 (2.8 °C rise)	4.7–6.5%
Warren et al. (2013)	2100 (4 °C rise)	0.4–0.7% with <1% existing range occupied
Foden et al. (2013)[a]	2050 (c. 2 °C rise)	24–50% 'highly vulnerable'
This study (Box 6.4)	(2–6 °C)	0.6–1.8% based on immediate extinction risk
This study (Box 6.5)	(2–6 °C)	10.2–24.5% based on risk of being committed to extinction

[a] Results from a trait-based assessment of climate vulnerability, rather than the results of bioclimate modelling.

analysis (Table 6.1). Methodological variation probably accounts for the much lower projected effect of climate change on extinction risk by Jetz et al. (2007) than Şekercioğlu et al. (2008), where species' distributions also shrink towards higher elevations in response to warming (see Section 6.10.3 below). Although the Thomas et al. (2004) study is based on climate envelope modelling, which better describes the relationship between range occupancy and climate, it does so for a restricted range of endemic species which may be most sensitive to climate change, having narrow geographical ranges (Schwartz et al. 2006b; Jetz et al. 2007; Ohlemüller et al. 2008), and may therefore not represent a true measure of average extinction risk due to climate change for all bird species. This issue is addressed by Warren et al. (2013), based upon climate envelope model projections for all bird species. However, unlike Thomas et al. (2004), they do not use power law methods to estimate extinction risk, but instead, present projected changes in range extent. For the purposes of Table 6.1, we classed species projected by Warren et al. (2013) to have <1% of the existing range occupied by the 2080s as being at risk of extinction. If we had used a 50% threshold of range contraction, this would have identified some 30–40% of species, whilst 2–4% of species were projected to lose 90% of their current ranges, depending upon the assumptions made about dispersal (Warren et al. 2013). Although not a formal assessment of extinction risk, it is worth also mentioning the approach of Foden et al. (2013), who adopted a trait-based approach to identify the bird species vulnerable to climate change. They estimated some 2323–4890 bird species (24–50% of the global total) as being highly vulnerable, having high exposure and high sensitivity to climate change, but low adaptive capacity.

There is clearly considerable variation in the anticipated magnitude of severity of climate change impacts between these studies. We add to these assessments using collated projected impacts of climate change from 36 published climate envelope studies (excluding Warren et al. (2013) and Foden et al. (2013) due to their recent publication date) in terms of overall projected changes in range extent (Box 6.4) and extinction risk (Box 6.5). Given the existing variation, this is an attempt to identify some general messages about the likely future magnitude of climate change impacts on birds. These included some regional studies, rather than just those focussed on global extinction, which means the results

Box 6.4 · *Projected impacts of climate change on species' range extent*

Most climate envelope modelling studies make projections about likely changes in the range extent of species in response to climate change. We summarised these studies using a mixed model to account for the non-independence of multiple data from the same study. Twenty-seven studies were identified which presented comparable data on change in range extent. The mean reduction in range extent from these was $22.7 \pm 6.7\%$ when weighting each study equally, or $26.8 \pm 4.3\%$ when weighting the contribution of each study by the number of species covered, to produce an estimate that is more likely to be relevant globally.

Given that the size of these changes is likely to vary with the magnitude of future climate change assumed, we examined how these estimates of range change correlate with the assumed magnitude of increase in global temperature. We included in the analysis a two-level factor identifying whether it was assumed that the species would occupy all areas identified as having suitable climate, according to the climate envelope model, or whether the worst-case assumption of no colonisation of newly suitable areas was made. We focus here on the outputs based on the regression weighted by species numbers, although similar results were obtained from the unweighted model.

Studies which assumed no colonisation projected significantly greater proportional reductions in range extent than those without ($F_{1, 139} = 115.67$, $P < 0.0001$), with an additional negative effect of the magnitude of global temperature on the projected amount of range change ($F_{1,141} = 8.33$, $P = 0.0045$). Thus, with increasing magnitude of warming, there were increasing rates of range loss projected. There was a weak interaction between whether a study assumed colonisation and the effect of temperature ($F_{1, 135} = 3.68$, $P = 0.057$), suggesting that the effect of temperature was much more severe when no colonisation was assumed.

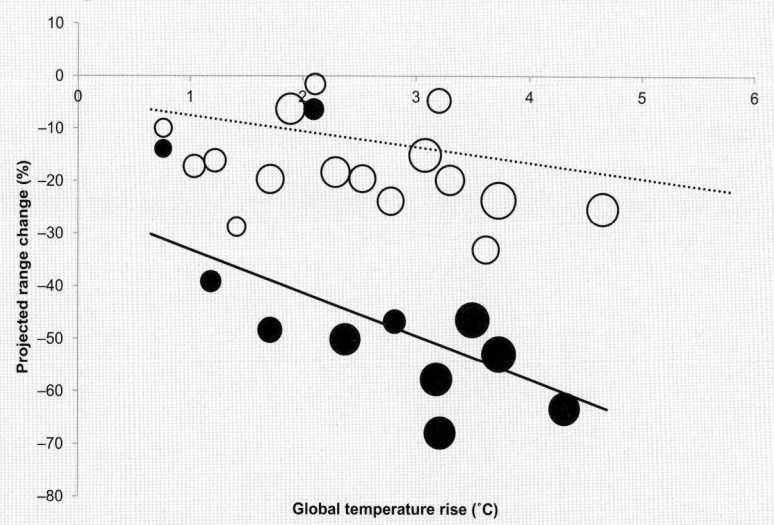

Box 6.4 Mean projected changes in species' range extent in relation to increases in global mean temperature. To summarise the observed data for display, the results of consecutive projections, when sorted in order of mean temperature rise, were aggregated into bins of six cases. The size of the circle is proportional to the number of species covered by the projections in each bin. The fitted line is the modelled slope from the analysis on the unaggregated data and covers the full range of data used for each model. The open circles and dotted line indicate projections in which colonisation is assumed and filled circles and solid line indicate projections with no colonisation.

should be less influenced by particularly sensitive narrow-range endemics. Although this means that some projected extinctions are likely to be regional, rather than global, as a result of the contribution of each study to the analyses being weighted by the number of species covered, this potential bias was minimised.

As already suggested, our analysis found a considerable amount of variation in the magnitude of range change projections among the studies we considered. Whether species were assumed to be able to colonise all newly suitable parts of the future potential range, or unable to disperse, had the greatest effect on the magnitude of projected climate change impact. After this, there was a significant negative effect of larger projected temperature changes upon future potential range size. Thus, in studies where species were assumed to disperse fully to occupy the future potential range, the projected magnitude of decline in range extent varied from 7% to 22% for 0.7–5.8 °C global temperature rise, whilst under a no-dispersal assumption, projected range decline averaged from 30% for a 0.7 °C warming scenario, to 63% under a 4.7 °C scenario of global warming (Box 6.4). This emphasises the need to understand the dispersal ability of species and the effects of demographic and ecological lags on the likelihood that they will occupy their future potential range, in order to fully assess their likely vulnerability to future change.

> **Box 6.5** · *Projected impacts of climate change on extinction risk*
>
> We summarised the probability of extinction in response to climate change across the 15 studies which present such information, using the same mixed-model approach as Box 6.4 to account for the non-independence of multiple data from the same study. Different studies used different methods to assess likely risk of extinction. Some assumed extinction if it had zero projected range extent in the future, particularly if no colonisation of newly suitable areas was assumed. We termed this immediate extinction risk. Others took a less conservative approach, and used IUCN criteria to identify species threatened with extinction, or the species-area power curve to estimate the likely proportion of species committed to extinction from the mean projected reduction in range extent (e.g. Thomas *et al.* 2004). There were insufficient studies to differentiate between these two approaches of what we term the risk of being committed to extinction. Because of the likely difference in the magnitude of risk of immediate extinction compared to the risk of being committed to extinction, we tested the importance of 'extinction-risk type' in the analysis. In addition, we included whether colonisation of newly climatically suitable areas was assumed possible or not, although as this showed a weak, non-intuitive, positive effect of allowing colonisation on the rate of extinction, this was dropped from the final model. We therefore modelled the proportion of species estimated to be at risk of extinction in each study as a function of global projected temperature rise and extinction-risk type, allowing for interactions between the terms. Models were constructed using a generalised linear mixed model with a binomial error distribution and logit link function.
>
> Extinction risk was greater if assessed using the risk of being committed to extinction rather than immediate extinction risk ($F_{1, 153} = 31.80$, $P < 0.0001$) and increased significantly with global temperature rise ($F_{1, 153} = 31.48$, $P < 0.0001$). There was no significant difference in the form of the slope with global temperature depending on the method used.

Box 6.5 (cont.)

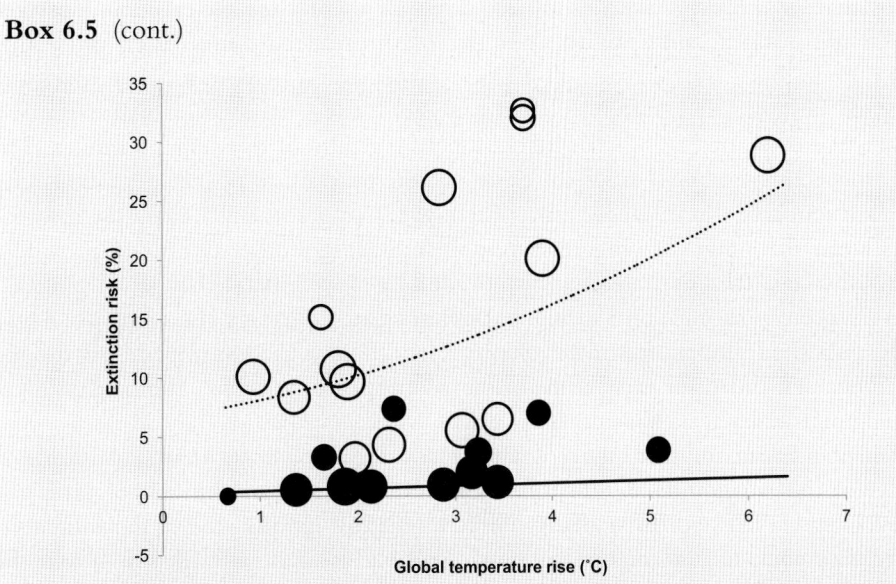

Box 6.5 Mean projected extinction risk in relation to increases in global mean temperature across all climate envelope model studies. Each symbol represents the mean extinction risk across a bin of six consecutive projections, when sorted in order of mean temperature rise. The size of the circle is proportional to the number of species covered by the projections in each bin. Black circles with a fitted solid line indicate projections of immediate extinction risk, whilst open circles and the dotted line indicate the risk of being committed to extinction.

Previous attempts to explain the variation among climate envelope studies or models in the magnitude of species' range change have shown that the modelling methods used and the GCM applied can account for 92% (Diniz-Filho *et al.* 2009), or 40–70% (Buisson *et al.* 2010) of variation in projections. From our analysis, a 2–6 °C mean global temperature rise was associated with a mean range extent decline averaged across species of 11–23%, assuming no restrictions on colonisation ability, and 41–74% mean range extent decline if no colonisation of newly suitable areas was assumed.

As described above, a number of studies have estimated the probability of species being committed to extinction from the projected change in the size of the potential future range. Our analysis of these extinction risk projections found a significant positive correlation between the projected extinction risk and the magnitude of temperature increase in the climate change scenario used (Box 6.5), after accounting for the method with which extinction was assessed. This provides additional support for the burning embers graph of the IPCC that shows increasing severity of climate change impacts on biodiversity with increased warming (IPCC 2007c). Mean projected extinction rates ranged from 0.6% to 1.8% across a 2–6 °C mean global temperature rise if extinctions were assumed to occur only when future potential ranges were zero (immediate extinction risk), which is a conservative approach. Using more indirect methods that assessed the likely number of species committed to extinction derived from the species-area curve, or the number of threatened species based on IUCN criteria (although see Akçakaya *et al.* 2006 for a discussion of potential considerations that should be associated with the latter approach), then estimates of extinction risk were much greater, at 10.2–24.5% across the same range of projected warming. The indirect methods may be regarded as relating to the proportion of species at long-term risk of extinction if the modelled potential range changes occur and persist into the future. Thus, the range of climate envelope modelling studies published provide a powerful message, that an increasing magnitude of global climatic change will threaten an increasing proportion of bird species with extinction, a message also emphasised by a recently published global assessment of projected climate change impacts on species' range extent that called for early climate change mitigation to reduce the magnitude of potential biodiversity loss (Warren *et al.* 2013).

Within this broad message, there is clearly considerable variation among studies in estimates of the magnitude of the threat. At relatively low magnitudes of projected climate change, there is a particularly marked variation among studies depending on whether they include colonisation of newly suitable areas or not (Box 6.4) and the method of assessing extinction risk (Box 6.5). Indeed, this difference among methods at low levels of warming is greater than the subsequent increase in threat associated with a high level of warming. For example, under a very low (0.5 °C) warming scenario, probably analogous to the current climate, estimates of projected range change from the 'no dispersal' models equal a mean 29% reduction (or 6% allowing full dispersal), with 7% of species threatened or committed to extinction (or 0.4% based on immediate extinction risk). Given the relative lack of species and populations for which there is strong evidence of population decline in response to climate change now, and the lack of documented climate change extinctions (Chapter 4), these models do not appear to be describing an immediate, or short-term, extinction response to climate change that has occurred. Instead, as argued by Thomas *et al.* (2004), these studies may represent the likely long-term consequences and potential size of an extinction debt associated with climate change. If this is the case, then these outputs would suggest that there is a significant extinction debt that biodiversity has already accrued in response to the climate change that has occurred so far. Whether this is true will become apparent in the longer term, but this uncertainty emphasises the importance of having a more detailed understanding of the effects of decreased habitat extent and population size, caused not only by climate change but also by other factors, on extinction probability. There is a need to consider the likely timescale over which any extinction events are likely to occur; what we have termed 'immediate extinction risk' may still take years or decades to be apparent. Improving such assessments is the objective of population viability models, and should be a priority for research. This uncertainty also emphasises the need to critically assess the performance of climate envelope modelling approaches, covered in detail in Section 6.9. Reassuringly, this assessment does provide some empirical support that they provide useful outputs.

Until more advanced models are available, it is probably a reasonable presumption that the spread of mean projected reductions in range extent of 7–22% under a full-dispersal scenario represents a best-case global scenario. Similarly, the projections of

0.6–1.8% of species likely to become extinct as a result of climate change may represent a best-case scenario of the proportion of species at risk of immediate extinction in response to climate change, but these estimates are likely to be unrealistic in the longer term because they assume that all areas with potentially suitable climate are colonised, ignore possible effects of climate on abundance and exclude the potential effects on extinction risk of extinction debt caused by reductions in population size and geographical range. The gap between these two methods of estimating extinction risk could be regarded as representing the species which are probably committed to extinction in the long term in response to climate change, should that climate change be sustained (Thomas *et al.* 2004), but which may take decades or longer to be realised, depending upon the degree to which lagged effects occur and the underlying mechanism involved.

6.8.3 Assessments based on altitudinal change

Many bird species are adapted to live in mountainous regions in a particular set of vegetation and climatic conditions found within certain limits of elevation above sea level. Because mountain areas with the required conditions for such species are often separated from one another by unsuitable lowland habitats, or have been separated prehistorically under past climates, different bird species often occupy similar elevational and ecological niches in neighbouring but separate mountain ranges (Section 5.3.3). For this reason, there is a large number of montane bird species; La Sorte and Jetz (2010) estimate 1009 high-elevation specialists (montane species with a lower elevational limit of 1000 m above sea level (a.s.l.) or higher).

La Sorte and Jetz (2010) used simulated changes in temperature from 1980–1999 to 2080–2099 from AOGCMs under the A2 emissions scenario and applied regional lapse rates (rates of change of temperature with increasing elevation) to estimate future elevation limits of montane species in 2080–2099 on the assumption that these correspond to the same mean temperatures as was the case in 1980–1999. The median projected temperature change examined was 4.8 °C. Having estimated future elevation limits, they used these to calculate the change in potential geographic range size based on topographical information. As discussed in Section 6.2, this approach is equivalent to a climate envelope model, but with elevation as a proxy for the only bioclimate variable, temperature.

If montane bird elevation limits were assumed to follow the envelope models' predictions perfectly within the mountain regions where they occur at present, then the projected median loss of range area was 27% of the current range, with 18% of species estimated to lose more than 50% of the present range and having a resulting range size of <20 000 km^2. However, under an assumption of no colonisation of new areas above the present upper elevation limit, median range sizes were projected to decline by 54%, with 32% of species estimated to lose more than 50% of the present range and having a resulting range size of <20 000 km^2. Under this scenario, 5% of montane species were anticipated to lose all of their range. Substantial negative changes were projected for all biogeographic realms but were especially severe for the Afrotropics and North America. We used method 2 of Thomas *et al.* (2004) to translate the median range extent losses into percentages of montane species committed to extinction by the late twenty-first century. This method uses the species-area power law relationship with an exponent z of 0.25

to estimate the proportion of species committed to extinction from a given expected reduction in the extent of their range. The resulting projected extinction rates were 8% if the species' potential distributions follow the models' predictions perfectly and 18% if no colonisation of new areas above the present upper elevation limit was assumed.

Şekercioğlu et al. (2008) used a different approach to estimate extinction rates directly from GCM projected climate changes, a global lapse rate and elevation limits for all landbird species. They did this for several climate change scenarios and assumed that species would shift to occupy the whole land area within their expected future elevation range limits except where prevented from doing so by habitat losses that were projected under Millennium Ecosystem Assessment scenarios. For the same projected temperature change as that used by LaSorte and Jetz (2010), the method of Şekercioğlu et al. (2008) gave an estimate of 13% of landbird species being committed to extinction and 26% at risk (threatened and near threatened). Shoo et al. (2005) applied a similar approach to model the potential changes on conservation status of rainforest birds in Australia, but extended this by converting change in altitudinal range into projected population change; a topic to which we shall turn to shortly (Section 6.8.5).

These approaches are dependent upon the assumption that climate change will drive predictable shifts to higher elevations in response to warming. As outlined previously (Section 5.2.2), there is relatively weak evidence of this to date (Chen et al. 2011), and recent evidence that at least in some mountainous areas, precipitation or wind speed may be as important as temperature in determining altitudinal limits. In these cases, depending on the direction of changes in precipitation, species ranges may shift down rather than up (Tingley et al. 2009; Tingley et al. 2012). Making accurate projections about the impacts of climate change on species in mountainous environments may therefore be particularly challenging, particularly given the uncertainties associated with future projections of precipitation and wind speed and direction (Chamberlain et al. 2012).

6.8.4 Assessments based on sea-level rise

In addition to effects of climatic change itself, there is concern that sea-level rise may threaten coastal and wetland habitats (Nicholls & Cazenave 2010), many of which are of considerable importance to birds. Much of the interest in this topic has focussed on likely changes to estuary and salt marsh habitats in temperate latitudes, which are particularly important for wintering waterbirds, such as Arctic breeding waders. As we will consider in Section 8.5.1, many of these sites support internationally important assemblages of migratory species at carrying capacity, and are therefore vulnerable to any reduction in their quality or extent. For example, losses of mudflats in response to reclamation, development or colonisation by invasive, non-native plants, have been shown to significantly reduce the numbers of birds they support (Evans & Pienkowski 1983; Goss-Custard & Moser 1988; Meire 1991).

Likely losses in response to sea-level rise are generally estimated by simply calculating the amount of currently available habitat that may be lost through inundation. For example, Galbraith et al. (2002) estimated under a conservative 2°C warming scenario, and based on 50% probabilistic sea-level rise projections from the mid 1990s, that habitat loss at four large North American Ramsar sites (Willapa Bay, Humbolt, Bay, San Fransico Bay and Delaware Bay) would range from 18–70% by 2100. The assumed relationships between sea-level rise and the amount of inter-tidal habitat lost were extremely non-linear and variable between sites. At Delaware Bay, an increasing magnitude of sea-level rise was projected to increase the extent of mudflat at the expense of salt marsh. At a fifth site studied, Bolivar Flats, on the Gulf of Mexico, the area of mudflat was also projected to increase with increasing sea-level rise, but due to the flooding of low-lying land.

The sensitivity of individual sites to such loss is clearly dependent upon micro-topography of the adjoining land, and the extent to which human intervention, such as the construction of seawalls, may be employed to prevent the inundation of low-lying land by the sea. The greater the defence of low-lying land by hard, coastal structures, the greater the likely magnitude of habitat loss to the birds. More detailed modelling of likely changes in the physical energetics of estuaries, based upon how their geomorphology is likely to change under different scenarios of sea-level rise, suggests that additional changes in sediment type and productivity will also influence the species composition and abundance of wintering waders on estuaries (Austin & Rehfisch 2003).

Above the open mudflats are vegetated salt marsh or mangrove habitats which may also be important to birds, as either breeding or wintering habitats. These may be amongst the habitats most threatened by climate change (Peterson *et al.* 2010), and particularly vulnerable to 'coastal squeeze' if the construction and maintenance of seawalls prevent their spread inland. However, if they are able to accumulate material through sedimentation, then they may have some adaptive potential to cope with a certain amount of sea-level rise in some situations (Hughes 2004; Gilman *et al.* 2007; Jagtap & Nagle 2007). For bird species breeding in these habitats, it is likely to be increases in the frequency of catastrophic inundation associated with sea-level rise, and an increase in storminess, which may have the greatest impact on their populations (van der Pol *et al.* 2010a, 2010b; Bayard & Elphick 2011). Globally, it is estimated that some 6–22% of coastal wetlands may be lost under a 3.4 °C warming scenario above pre-industrial levels, with the greatest losses likely in North America, the Baltic and Mediterranean (Warren *et al.* 2010). Climate change may also lead to the loss of 10–15% of mangrove forests (Alongi 2008).

Away from coastal wetland habitats, sea-level rise may threaten species which occupy and breed on other low-lying habitats, such as low-lying oceanic islands and atolls. For example, the Northwestern Hawaiian Islands support four endemic landbirds and 14 million seabirds of 18 species, including most of the world's Laysan albatrosses *Phoebastria immutabilis* and black-footed albatrosses *P. nigripes*, Tristram's storm petrel *Oceanodroma tristrami* and Bonin petrels *Pterodroma hypoleuca*. Projected losses range across 3–65% of island area under a 48 cm sea-level rise scenario, or 5–75% loss under an 88 cm rise, although greater proportions of the islands would be at risk of periodic inundation under spring tides. Impacts of these changes on birds are likely to be less severe than for some other taxa, but could affect some low-lying seabird colonies and translocated populations of the endangered Laysan finch *Telespiza cantans*, although the core population of Laysan Island should not be affected (Baker *et al.* 2006).

6.8.5 Assessments based on population change

As we have already outlined, information on population size and population trend are of special value for conservationists attempting to assess conservation status and extinction risk.

Although relatively few studies have examined this, there is increasing evidence that changes in population size will be of greater magnitude than changes in range extent (Shoo et al. 2005; Huntley et al. 2012), so the focus on change in range extent alone may underestimate potential future impacts of climate change on species and populations.

The study of Shoo et al. (2005) combined projected changes in altitudinal range as a result of warming with field information about species density and abundance in each altitudinal band. In a manner similar to Şekercioğlu et al. (2008), they found that warming was projected to significantly threaten an increasing number of rainforest bird species in Australia, particularly those which occupy high altitudes. By modelling population size, Shoo et al. converted their projections into estimates of likely change in IUCN threat status in response to warming. This indicated that 75–98% of species would be regarded as threatened under a mid-range scenario of 3.6 °C warming, depending upon the degree of colonisation of newly suitable habitat. Of these, some 67–89% of species were projected to be listed as endangered or critically endangered, based on a population decline of more than 50%.

Huntley et al. (2012) derived an index of abundance from the proportion of South African Atlas survey visits to a grid cell in which a bird species was recorded (reporting rate), and calculated changes in this index of abundance from climate envelope model projections of presence/absence. Overall, projected changes in abundance index were negative for more than three-quarters of species covered, and, in the absence of colonisation of newly suitable areas, were anticipated to result in 80% population declines for almost a quarter of species modelled. This novel approach to estimating changes in abundance from reporting rates could not be tested readily in South Africa because of limited availability of independent population estimates. However, the relationship between reporting rate and changes in abundance should be tested using survey data from other countries.

The study of Renwick et al. (2012) modelled relationships between population density, corrected for detectability, and climate for four UK breeding bird species, and used these to project likely future changes in population size. Projected population trends for two species with northern distributions in Europe (Eurasian curlew and meadow pipit) were negative, whilst those for two species with southern distributions (Eurasian green woodpecker *Picus viridis* and wood nuthatch) were positive. These projections match recent population trends for these species (Risely et al. 2012). Future projections of abundance for curlew were particularly negative, of the order of a 66% decline by 2080 under a high emissions A1F1 scenario of 3.9 °C global temperature increase, suggesting that the current decline of this species in the UK, which has contributed to its recent assessment in the IUCN Red List as near-threatened (BirdLife International 2012), may be exacerbated by future climate change.

It will be important to continue to develop methods to increase our ability to produce models which predict changes in population size, because such outputs may be more reliably translated into IUCN threat criteria and assessments of extinction risk, and to assist with protected area selection (see Section 7.4). In a recently published example, Johnston et al. (2013) achieved this for internationally important populations of breeding seabirds and wintering waterbirds in the UK, producing future projections that relate directly to the criteria used for protected area designation and conservation priority listing. Under a high A1FI emissions scenario to 2080, 7/17 seabirds and 24/45 waterbirds were projected to suffer sufficient population declines to warrant conservation listing.

6.9 Assessing the performance of climate envelope models

Climate envelope models give rise to concern about potential future impacts of climate change on bird populations and their conservation, yet there remains considerable uncertainty about the precise magnitude of this impact. Hence, it is important to assess how well they work. In the next sections we describe various ways in which this assessment has been done.

6.9.1 Testing model predictions with the data to which the model was fitted

Although there is some degree of circularity in calculating how well a statistical model fits the data that were used to build it, it can be a worthwhile check, as different models for the same species vary in this respect, as do models fitted in the same way to data for different species. Such a check usually consists of calculating observed and expected values and seeing how well they agree. For models of geographical distribution, the expected values are often expected probabilities of occurrence in a grid cell and the observed data are recorded presences and absences. A frequently used test is to convert the expected probability of occurrence in a cell from the model to a simulated presence or absence by assuming that the species is expected to be present if the modelled probability of occurrence exceeds a threshold value. Then a measure of agreement between observed and simulated distributions such as Cohen's kappa (Cohen 1960) can be calculated. A weakness of this approach is that the level of agreement depends upon the choice of threshold value of expected probability of occurrence, which is arbitrary. The threshold value can be chosen so that it gives the highest possible value of Cohen's kappa, or some other measure of agreement. Alternatively, the method involving calculation of the area under a receiver-operating characteristic curve (AUC ROC; Metz 1978; Kraemer 1988) has gained widespread acceptance as a useful measure of model performance (Fielding & Bell 1997; see also Peterson *et al.* 2008). The AUC ROC method avoids the use of a specific classification threshold completely. Instead, it uses the relationship between two different measures of the performance of a binary classification test, sensitivity and specificity, across the whole range of possible classification thresholds. Sensitivity is the proportion of actual presences which are correctly identified as such, whereas specificity is the proportion of absences which are correctly identified. A perfect predictive model would give an AUC value of one, whereas a model whose predictions were not better than chance would give an AUC of 0.5. Aside from not requiring the arbitrary definition of a threshold, AUC ROC has the additional advantage that it is less likely to be correlated with prevalence (the overall proportion of grid cells in which the species occurs) than some other measures of agreement (Manel *et al.* 2001), though AUC values still tend to be low for species with very low prevalence (Huntley *et al.* 2007).

Measures of agreement between observations and predictions from climate envelope models can be used in many ways. They can be compared across species with different body size and ecological characteristics such as habitat preference and trophic level (Huntley *et al.* 2004, 2007). Measures of agreement can be compared between fitted models and null models to test whether the climate envelope model is giving better predictions than are expected by chance (Beale *et al.* 2008). Null models are hypothetical distributions of a given species with a similar size and shape to the real distribution, but placed and oriented at random with respect to environmental variables. Measures of agreement can also be compared among different types of models fitted to the same data and can give some useful insights about the effects of the assumptions of the modelling method on the types of predictions the model makes (Lawler *et al.* 2006).

6.9.2 Testing the statistical significance of explanatory variables

Statistical tests of the significance of effects of variables in regression models are widely used in many fields of science, including ecology. Statistical testing involves calculating the probability that an association as large as one observed in some real data between the response variable of interest (usually probability of occurrence in climate envelope models) and some variable which might affect it (for example, a bioclimate variable) might have arisen by chance, rather than representing a real relationship. Statistical tests of regression models are subject to many pitfalls, including multiple testing, dependence of results upon the choice of variables in the model and spatial autocorrelation. These are all important considerations with regards to climate envelope models.

The problem of multiple testing parallels that of data dredging that we already mentioned. If you include enough variables in a statistical model, it is likely that according to a standard test, a few of them will have a statistically significant relationship with the variable you wish to predict, just because correlations occur by chance between two randomly generated variables with no real relationship to one another. There are several precautions that can be taken against this, including the selection of a small set of variables based upon prior ecological knowledge and the use of adjustments to the criteria for declaring significance to allow for multiple testing. The simplest and most widely used adjustment is the Bonferroni correction, in which the desired level of statistical significance is divided by the number of tests being performed.

Another problem with significance testing of climate envelope models is that of model specification. Frequently, the statistical significance of the effect of a variable differs according to which other variables are also included in the statistical model and which interactions among variables are considered. Modellers use various rules to reduce the number of explanatory variables from a sometimes large set of candidates. The aim is to remove those which seem not to contribute much to the ability of the model to predict the response variable. Although this application of the principle of parsimony seems good, it has the defect that model selection rules end up choosing one particular model, often based upon some quite minor differences between it and other models in how well they fit. That can lead to a variable which really does have an effect being left out of the selected model altogether. One solution to this is to use model averaging, in which predictions and estimated effects of variables are averaged across a set of several plausible models, with weighting of the results from different models according to the relative support each model receives from the data (Burnham & Anderson 2002).

The final important problem with significance testing of variables in climate envelope models is that of spatial autocorrelation (Beale *et al.* 2008). Statistical significance is affected by sample size. The more independent measurements you have, the more precisely you are likely to be able to measure the effect of an explanatory variable on a variable of interest and the more likely a test of statistical significance is to declare that variable to be significant. Datasets for climate envelope models often seem to have huge sample sizes: thousands or tens of thousands of grid cells, each with observed presence or absence of the species. However, the outcomes for grid cells that are close to one another may not be truly independent in the statistical sense. The occurrence of the species may be influenced by a variable which has not been measured or has not been included in the model, but which is correlated with a variable which is included. If high and low values of this unmeasured or excluded variable tend to occur in patches, then the apparent sample size will be erroneously inflated and there will be a risk of declaring statistical significance for a correlated variable with no real effect.

There are several advanced statistical techniques available for taking spatial autocorrelation into account when fitting climate envelope models and performing significance tests. These include autocovariate regression, spatial eigenvector mapping, conditional and simultaneous generalised least squares, autoregressive models and generalised estimating equations. These can be applied to cases where the response variable is binary (for example, presence or absence in a grid cell) or continuous (such as population density per unit area).

Methods which take spatial autocorrelation into account can be compared with ordinary regression methods, which ignore it, using simulated datasets in which the degree of spatial autocorrelation is controlled. There tends to be little difference in the estimates of the relationship of the response variable to the explanatory variables between the two methods. However, as expected, the ordinary methods assign statistical significance to effects of explanatory variables too often, whereas the spatial autocorrelation adjusted methods usually have an acceptably low rate of falsely declaring significance (Dormann *et al.* 2007; Beale *et al.* 2010). Hence, if the influential bioclimate variables affecting a species distribution can be identified accurately from prior ecological knowledge, a climate envelope model fitted by ordinary regression methods will provide a reasonably good description of the species distribution data. However, if the influential explanatory variables are being selected from a pool of candidates by testing their statistical significance and excluding some of them, then the ordinary methods will set too low a threshold for acceptance of effects into the final model which may then have an inappropriately large number of variables and give misleading predictions.

The use of null models of geographical distributions with similar spatial structure to that of the real distributions suggests that bioclimate modelling approaches in which significance testing is used to select variables may produce overfitted models of species' distribution. This has been proposed for European birds by Beale *et al.* (2008). Although concluding that 'most climate models are no better than chance associations', they actually found the goodness-of-fit statistic of the climate envelope model fitted to the real European bird distributions was as good or better than the best 5% of simulated null models in 32% of occasions, and as good or better than the best 10% of fits to the null models for 46% of species. Hence, the bioclimate models actually performed considerably better than chance for the average species. However, we agree with Beale and colleagues that statistical testing of effects in regression models of spatial data, including climate envelope models, needs greater care, especially with regard to spatial autocorrelation, than has often been taken in the past. To eliminate these problems, the statistical techniques which adjust for spatial autocorrelation mentioned above should be used when performing significance tests.

6.9.3 Significance testing summarised

The foregoing sections on significance testing illustrate a number of pitfalls, particularly associated with multiple testing and spatial autocorrelation. In our view, this means that it is best to avoid the use of significance tests to select bioclimate variables from a pool of candidates for inclusion or rejection in a climate envelope model. Instead, where possible, we advocate choosing a small set of bioclimate variables for a climate envelope model on the basis of prior ecological and physiological models. If it is desirable to use several models rather than just one, then averaging their predictions using model averaging methods (Burnham & Anderson 2002) is a valuable option. The appropriateness of the choices of variables and other details of models derived in this way still need to be tested, but we suggest that this should be done by model validation, which is testing the predictions the model makes about data different from those used to fit it.

6.9.4 Testing climate envelope model predictions using additional data

A better test of a climate envelope model than significance tests on the data used to fit it involves splitting the available observations. One part of the dataset, called the training set, is then used to fit the model, which is used to predict the probability of occurrence of the species for the grid cells of the other part of the data, which is called the evaluation set. Then the observed pattern of occurrences and absences for the evaluation set of cells can be compared with their expected probability of occurrence values. This is often done by fitting the model to a randomly chosen set of 70% of the available grid cells and evaluating it on the remaining 30%. Another widely used procedure is leave-one-out-cross-validation (LOOCV) in which the model is fitted to all but one of the grid cells and then used to predict probability of occurrence for the excluded cell. This is then repeated for each cell in turn so that every grid cell in the original dataset is in the evaluation set. Both of these procedures suffer from the important defect that the fitting and test datasets are not truly independent. This is because they were drawn at random from the same study area and many of the fitting and test cells are therefore close to one another. As we saw previously, spatial autocorrelation makes nearby cells non-independent. Hence, validation tests of this kind are over-optimistic.

This kind of validation test can be modified by extracting the training and evaluation data from larger contiguous geographical areas, consisting of many adjacent grid cells, instead of using individual grid cells. For example, Huntley *et al.* (2007) divided Europe into 98 large regions, each consisting of all the grid cells in a 6° longitude by 8° latitude block. A CRS climate envelope model was fitted to the data from all but one of the blocks and evaluation was performed by predicting probability of occurrence in the cells in the excluded block. This was done for each block in turn, and the evaluation statistics were calculated for all blocks combined. The goodness-of-fit statistics (AUC ROC) obtained from this evaluation were reasonably high, though lower than those obtained when the model using the same bioclimate variables was fitted to the full dataset. By making the evaluation areas large contiguous blocks, the leave-a-block-out procedure reduces the problems caused by spatial autocorrelation and is therefore an improvement in this regard over random splitting of small grid cells into training and evaluation sets and LOOCV.

However, some evaluation cells are still close to some of the training cells, so the method does not eliminate effects of spatial autocorrelation entirely. The problem of spatial autocorrelation becomes smaller as the size of the blocks in the leave-a-block-out procedure gets larger. However, if the blocks are made too large, many species with small geographical ranges only occur in one of the blocks, which makes using the other blocks as the training set impossible.

It is sometimes possible to fit a climate envelope model to data from one large study area and to evaluate its performance in an entirely separate large study area. This has been attempted most often for the native and introduced ranges of alien species and generally not for birds. In some cases the climate envelope model was fitted to the introduced range and evaluated using the native range (e.g. Beerling *et al.* 1995 for a plant introduced from east Asia to Europe) and in others the test was done the other way around (e.g. Duncan *et al.* 2009 for dung beetles introduced from southern Africa to Australia). In these tests the climate envelope models performed well for the plant and for some of the species of dung beetles, but poorly for the other beetle species. There are problems with this approach if it is treated as a test of the reliability of climate envelope models when applied to species in their native ranges. Introduced species often lack their natural enemies, diseases, competitors and prey organisms within the introduced range, so the way in which their geographical range is limited indirectly by climate in the native and introduced ranges will be different. This emphasises the role of biotic factors in linking populations and distributions to climate, rather than abiotic factors (Chapter 4), as the latter would tend to generate transferable models. This may also be the case when climate change causes a species to colonise a new area, but it is more probable that its enemies, competitors, etc., will colonise with it than is the case for long-distance artificial introductions. In addition, some introduced species may still be spreading and may not yet have reached the eventual boundaries of their future range. Some bird species have disjunct global ranges with separate native populations on two or more continents. Evaluating the performance on a different continent of a climate envelope model fitted to a species distribution on another continent would be an interesting exercise, though subject to the caveats mentioned above about differences in natural enemies, diseases, competitors and prey organisms.

It has been suggested that fitting a climate envelope model to data for a study area during one time period and evaluating it using data on geographical distribution for the same area, but for a different time period, constitutes an independent validation test of the model (Araújo *et al.* 2005a). However, the test is not really independent because the study area is the same and the bird population in it at one time gave rise to, or was derived from, the population at the other time. Hence, there is temporal autocorrelation which reduces the level of statistical independence. Multiple datasets for the same area at different times are more useful for another type of validation test, the prediction, using climate envelope models, of changes in bird distribution and abundance. We examine these tests in the next section.

6.9.5 Testing climate envelope model predictions using changes in range and abundance

The main value of climate envelope models in guiding conservation is to predict future changes in distribution and abundance of species of interest. Hence, it can be argued the most pertinent test of their performance is how well a model fitted to data collected during a period of little or no climatic change performs in predicting or retrodicting observed changes in distribution or abundance during a period of rapid climatic change. We think that this is a valid argument, though its validity depends upon the timescale over which observed and expected changes are compared, as we will see later. Relatively few direct tests of explicit climate envelope model predictions of this kind have been carried out. Some of the most detailed tests are for birds and we describe some of them here.

Miguel Araújo and colleagues fitted climate envelope models to distribution data collected in the period 1968–1972 on 116 species of breeding birds in Britain (Araújo *et al*. 2005b). They used four different approaches to fit the models, each of which included effects of six climatic variables which were averaged over the survey period and the year before it started, to account for potential one-year lags in the effects of weather upon distribution. The survey data were from an atlas of breeding bird distribution conducted by volunteers who recorded presence and absence in 10 x 10 km squares during the survey period (Sharrock 1976). These models were then used to predict the distribution of the same set of bird species in 1988–1991, when a similar atlas survey was carried out (Gibbons *et al*. 1993). They calculated the change in the number of grid squares in which the model predicted each species should be breeding between the two atlas surveys as their measure of expected change in distribution and then compared variation among species in observed changes in the numbers of occupied squares with the variation predicted using the models. Observations and predictions agreed best when all the data, rather than a subset from the first survey, were used to fit the model and when the maximum kappa method was used to make the predictions of square occupancy. However, provided those methods were used, predictions from all four of the different forms of the climate envelope models showed a significant tendency to be in approximate accord with observed changes (Figure 6.3), even though there was much scatter in the relationship. This is particularly impressive given the many environmental changes other than climatic change that are known to have affected bird numbers and distribution during this period, and, that climate changed by only a small amount between the two survey periods, compared with the much larger changes in bioclimate variables observed in Britain since then (Green *et al*. 2008).

More recently Rapacciuolo *et al*. (2012) analysed the same bird atlas data using similar methods, but drew a different overall conclusion; that climate envelope models had 'low predictive accuracy for range change'. However, this conclusion does not fully reflect their results, because they found correlations across bird species between observed and expected changes in the extent of the size of the geographical range between 1968–1972 and 1988–1991 which were highly statistically significant and broadly similar to those found by Araújo *et al*. (2005b). The reason for the contradictory negative conclusion of Rapacciuolo *et al*. (2012) was that, whilst climate envelope models predicted observed range changes of birds surprisingly well, given the short period and small climate change between the surveys, the same approach did not work well for the data on British vascular plants and butterflies, which they also analysed. There may be several reasons for this difference among taxonomic groups, including the quality of the atlas data, the effect of not using global or Europe-wide data to fit the models and possible differences in the duration of time lags in response to climate change. Suffice it to say that, for birds at least, the independent studies of Rapacciuolo *et al*. (2012) and Araújo *et al*. (2005b) concur in

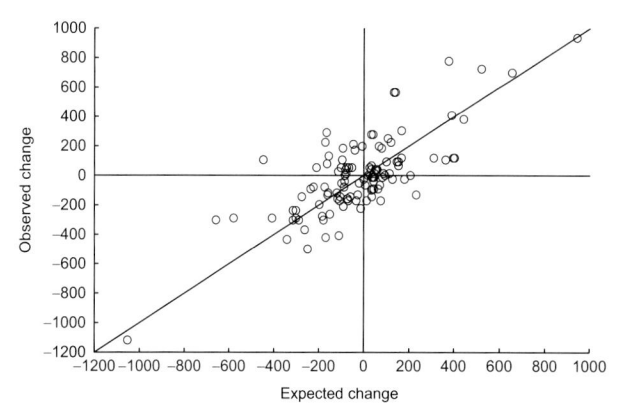

Figure 6.3 Observed change in the number of 10 x 10 km grid cells in Britain in which a species bred (vertical axis) between two atlas surveys in 1968–1972 and 1988–1991, in relation to the change expected from a climate envelope model fitted to data from the first of the two surveys (horizontal axis). The expected changes occurred because of differences in climate between the two survey periods. Each point represents a species. The diagonal line shows the average expectation if the observed and predicted changes agreed perfectly. Results are from Figure 1d of Araujo *et al.* (2005a) and are for climate envelope models fitted to all the 1968–1972 data using Generalised Additive Models with prediction of occupied squares by the maximum kappa method.

finding that climate envelope models made reasonably good predictions of the effects of recent climate change on changes in range extent of British birds.

Another test of climate envelope model predictions focussed on population changes, rather than distributional changes, of rare breeding birds (Green *et al.* 2008). In the UK, bird species right at the edge of their global geographical range tend to have small populations and therefore attract much attention from birdwatchers and conservationists because of their rarity. Trends in numbers of breeding pairs of these species were assessed from the records submitted every year by amateur ornithologists and nature reserve managers. Differences among species in the rate at which the numbers of records change over time are probably a reasonable indication of species differences in population trend, though the rates of change may not be entirely accurate in themselves because in most cases they are not based on systematic recording, but subject to variation in recorder effort. These observed changes were compared with assessments for each species of how the suitability of the climate in the UK had changed during the period for which population data were available. The climate suitability changes were calculated using climate envelope models fitted using CRS to the observed distribution of each species in 50 x 50 km squares across Europe recorded in an atlas survey undertaken in the 1980s (Huntley *et al.* 2007). The climatic data were 1961–1990 means of each of three bioclimate variables selected because of their ecological relevance to plant distributions. The trend in climate suitability was assessed using the climate envelope model of the species' European distribution and annual values for the bioclimate variables in each grid square in the UK to calculate the expected probability of occurrence of a species in each grid square in each year. Climate suitability trend was the trend over time in the average of these probabilities

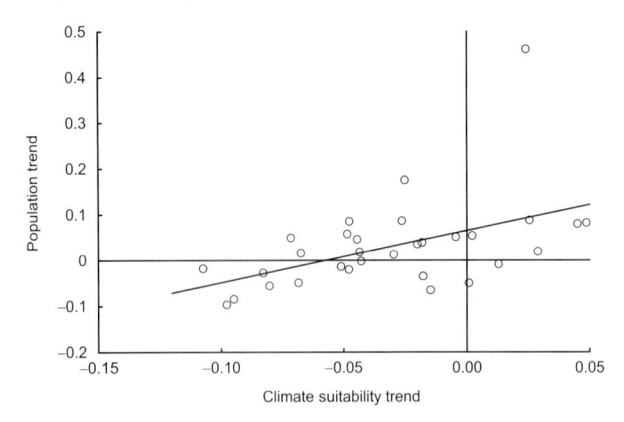

Figure 6.4 Observed rates of change in the breeding populations of 31 species of rare birds in the UK during the period 1980–2004 in relation to the trend in climate suitability for each species derived from a climate envelope model and annual meteorological data. Each point represents one species. The diagonal line shows the linear regression fitted to the points. Results are shown only for species with a mean annual population in the UK of five or more pairs. Data were taken from Figure 2 of Green *et al.* (2008).

of occurrence across all squares in the UK. Climate suitability changed quite markedly for some species over the period studied (1980–2002) because the UK's climate changed. In particular, a measure of the warmth of the growing season (annual sum of degree-days above 5 °C) increased because of spring and summer warming. The mean temperature of the coldest winter month also increased, but there was little change in moisture availability. Variation among species in the observed population trend was positively correlated with their climate suitability trend, especially for species with an average population of five or more breeding pairs per year (Figure 6.4). It may be that the very rare species showed less correlation because they were influenced more by chance events.

A Europe-wide analysis of abundance changes of common European breeding birds over a similar period found a similar pattern (Gregory *et al.* 2009). The bird survey data in this case came from the Pan European Common Bird Monitoring Scheme in which surveyors count breeding birds each year in sample plots using standardised methods. Observed rates of change in the combined breeding population across 20 European countries were analysed for all 108 species with eligible data during the period 1980–2005. Climate suitability trends based upon annual values of bioclimate variables and climate envelope models fitted to the European atlas data for the 1980s were calculated as described above for UK rare breeding birds. However, in this case the suitability trend was calculated across all the countries that contributed bird count data. There was a large amount of scatter for individual species (Figure 6.5), but an overall trend for species with negative climate suitability trends to be decreasing and those with positive suitability trends to be increasing was apparent. It was notable that although populations of 51% of species with increasing climate suitability trends were increasing in abundance, only 22% of species with decreasing climate suitability trends were increasing.

The most long-term assessment of the extent to which bird abundance and distribution are affected by changes in climate suitability was made possible by bird survey data

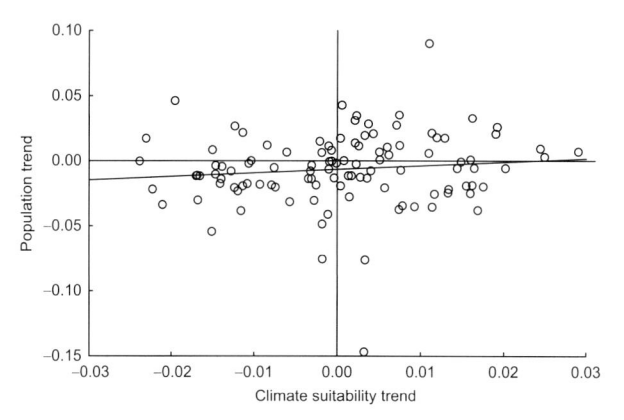

Figure 6.5 Observed rates of change in the breeding populations of 108 species of common birds in Europe during the period 1980–2005 in relation to the trend in climate suitability for each species derived from a climate envelope model and annual meteorological data. The analysis covers the period 1980–2002. Each point represents one species. The diagonal line shows the linear regression fitted to the points. Data are from Gregory et al. (2009).

collected on transects along elevational gradients in the Sierra Nevada mountains of California by Joseph Grinnell and colleagues in 1911–1929. Repeat surveys of bird populations at these sites in 2003–2008 showed some marked changes in bird numbers and distribution over this period (Tingley *et al.* 2009, 2012), as already described in Section 5.2.2. Some species disappeared or declined at some survey sites but increased at others. Averaged over all survey locations, mean temperature increased by 0.8 °C and annual precipitation increased by 5.9 mm, but there was considerable variation in the scale of the changes among sites. Models of the climatic niche of each bird species were fitted using the Maxent algorithm. Variation among sites in changes in distribution and abundance over the period between surveys tended to track changes in climate. Species were influenced most strongly by the changes in the climatic variable which the climate envelope model indicated that they were most sensitive to and changes tended to occur in the direction predicted by the model. The observed changes in distribution with respect to elevation were not just simple shifts to higher elevation, as would be expected if only temperature change was important. Although rising temperature tended to push species upslope, increased precipitation tended to pull them downslope. Overall, some 77–82% of altitudinal range shifts were in the direction expected from niche models, providing support for the importance of climate in limiting these altitudinal distributions. However, a detailed analysis indicated that, while 84% of species shifted their elevational distribution, only 51% of upper or lower range boundary shifts were upslope (Tingley *et al.* 2012). This study highlights the potential weakness of regarding changes in the elevational distribution of birds as being reliably predicted from expected changes in temperature alone (Section 6.8.3). Climate change may cause the distributions of some species to move downslope.

Many other studies have compared changes in the distribution and abundance of birds and other taxonomic groups with changes in climate. These studies show that, for the majority of species, observed changes over time in the boundaries of species' geographical ranges have tended to be in the direction predicted from observed recent climatic change, and often, of a similar magnitude (Parmesan and Yohe 2003; Chen *et al.* 2011). Thus, despite the caveats and uncertainties associated with the use of climate envelope modelling and the variation in the magnitude of their projected impacts depending upon the assumptions made and the methods used, there is an increasing amount of evidence that bird populations, and those of other taxa, have responded to recent climatic change in the ways that we would expect using these models. This does give us some confidence that the patterns of projected future impact reviewed and described in Section 6.8 are probably reasonable approximations of reality.

We have focussed here on the details of some examples of studies that compared explicit predictions of climate envelope models with observed changes. These are perhaps some of the best available tests of the climate envelope modelling approach. However, we do not claim that comparisons of observed changes with predictions from climate envelope models are entirely satisfactory as tests of the utility of climate envelope models. They have some important potential weaknesses, which we explain in the next section. There is much that remains to be done on this topic.

6.10 Why tests of the performance of climate envelope models in predicting change might be misleading

6.10.1 Spurious relationships between distribution and climate

The various potential problems with the reliability of climate envelope models we mentioned earlier also apply to their ability to make reliable predictions of change. These include the use in fitting the model of observed distribution data affected by recent human activity, such as hunting, persecution, pollution and habitat removal. These effects might lead a model to predict a pattern of change in distribution or abundance which is not observed when tested against data on observed change. There is also the general problem with models based upon potentially spurious correlations. For example, suppose that changes in the distribution or abundance of several species have really occurred because of some environmental changes that are independent of climate. However, our tests may detect a correlation across species of the observed changes with climate envelope model predictions because the geographical pattern of climatic change is itself associated with a similar pattern in the real causal factor. This has been an issue for some applications of the CTI measure of Devictor *et al.* (2008b, 2012a), as discussed in Section 5.4.2. The risk of such a mistake can be reduced in several ways.

One is to measure characteristics of the species and changes in the different environmental factors, other than climate, that are likely to affect them and to include these measurements in the analysis as covariates of the observed changes. This procedure may lead to the real causal factor being identified, but it also might not. If two potential explanatory variables are very highly correlated, it will be impossible to disentangle their relative importance by statistical analysis alone. It might also be that our knowledge of the species is not detailed enough for us to correctly identify the real causal factor at all, or we may have no measurements of changes in it, or measurements of such low precision that the real correlation is masked.

Another approach to this problem is to make tests with finer spatial resolution. For example, a large study area could be divided into regions, and correlations between observed and predicted changes in distribution or abundance examined across species within each region and across regions within each species. This approach may be limited by the availability of data. It requires large amounts of high-quality survey data collected in repeatable ways over long periods and a large area. Such data are beginning to exist for birds, because of the wider distribution of quantitative long-term bird population monitoring schemes.

6.10.2 Lagged effects of climate on distribution

The most fundamental problem with testing the predictions from climate envelope models by using observed changes in distribution or abundance is that there are many sound ecological reasons to expect that the responses of organisms to climate change may occur at a much slower rate than the climate change itself. Such time lags are expected for three main reasons: restricted dispersal which slows the spread of a species, long generation times which slow demographic responses and because the ecological changes induced by climatic change may involve biotic interactions with other organisms (Cahill *et al.* 2013), which take time to occur.

We have already identified the importance in modelling studies of the effect of assumptions about birds' ability to colonise newly suitable areas on the severity of impacts of climate change on range extent. Simulation models of hypothetical species distributions also provide clear illustrations of the effects of limited dispersal. Mustin *et al.* (2009) simulated the distribution of a species which lives in habitat patches and must disperse if new patches are to be colonised. The species could tolerate a certain range of climatic conditions. They assumed that demographic processes affecting the probability of extinction within a patch or colonisation of unoccupied patches were optimal in the centre of the initial latitudinal range of the species and declined towards the edges of the range. Having first simulated a stable geographical distribution under a stable average climate, but with annual fluctuations, the modellers then caused climatic conditions to change so that the location of the climate envelope changed latitude every year in the same direction and at a constant rate. The distribution of the species responded to this change by shifting in the same latitudinal direction as the climatic change. However, the annual rate of change of the position of the expanding edge of the species' distribution was initially much slower than the rate at which a given set of climate conditions were changing latitude. Variation in dispersal rates may also account for potential differences in the rate of shift in the leading and trailing range margin (Anderson *et al.* 2009b), with a slower rate of range contraction in species with greater dispersal capabilities, because declining range-limit subpopulations may be 'rescued' from extinction by dispersing colonisers from nearer the centre of the range.

The time taken for the rate at which the species shifted its range to catch up with the rate of movement of climate change was reduced when the species' simulated dispersal rate was increased, but, while the climate was changing, the expanding edge of the species' distribution always lagged behind the position of where the edge of the range would have been if the climate was stable. If the species' powers of dispersal were low relative to the rate of movement of its climatic window then its range started to shift, but was eventually overtaken by the climate window to such an extent that the rate of shift slowed and the population then crashed to extinction. It should be noted that the demographic rates of this species responded immediately to climatic change and that the lag was due entirely to delays imposed by the need for dispersal to occur before newly suitable patches could be colonised. The rate of movement of the expanding edge of the species' range speeded up through time because the edge came to lie in a zone of climate much nearer the optimum than was the case for the edge of the range under a stable climate. This improved the demographic rates in the patches at and near the range boundary and the capacity for colonisation. Thus, the lag in species' range movement itself eventually caused the rate of movement to catch up. The simulations showed that the movement of the contracting edge of the species' distribution also lagged behind the shift in the species' climate window, but to a smaller degree and with the rate of movement catching up with that of the climate window, much more rapidly. The hypothetical species matured one year after birth. Had the generation time been longer, additional delays would have occurred. For example, a long-lived tree or late-maturing bird might take a considerable time to shift its range in response to climate change, even if effects on its demographic rates occurred immediately.

The simulations showed that considerable delays could occur in the movement of the species' range even if the effects of climate change on its demographic rates were immediate. However, added to this are the delays imposed by indirect mechanisms by which species' demographic rates and range boundaries are influenced by climate. The simplest case can be imagined by re-using the simulations of Mustin *et al.* (2009). Suppose now that the hypothetical species affected immediately by climate is not the species of interest but that the species of interest feeds exclusively upon this modelled species. The species of interest is not affected by climate directly itself, but its shift in range is caused indirectly by climate change acting on its prey, and is delayed because the shift in the prey's distribution is delayed. A simple hypothetical example would be a seed-eating bird like a crossbill whose range shift would be delayed by the time taken for the coniferous tree species whose cones it is adapted to feed from to shift distribution. The same scenario could occur with the indirect effect arising through a plant which provides shelter or nest sites, a predator, a competitor or a disease. It is easy to imagine a whole food chain or food web across which range shift delays accumulate (Sheldon *et al.* 2011). Other mechanisms which could lead to additional delays are dependence of colonisation or death on infrequent extreme events such as fires, floods or drought. As discussed in Section 5.4, there is good evidence that observed changes in species' distributions and populations have lagged behind that expected from climate change. The challenge for ecologists is to work out why this has occurred, and what the consequences of this lag are.

Some idea of the duration of lagged effects of rapid climate change on the distribution of species can be obtained from the evidence of past vegetation changes preserved as pollen in lake sediments. It has also been shown that some species of chironomid midges, whose head capsules and mouthparts are preserved in lake sediments, respond rapidly to climate change measured using isotopes. So data on chironomid species composition can be used as a proxy for climate where oxygen isotope data are lacking. Williams *et al.* (2002) performed the first systematic and quantitative assessment of lags between climate change and changes in the distribution and abundance of plant species using time series of this kind. They analysed results obtained from lake sediment cores from North America and Europe that spanned a period from 14 000 to 9000 years Bp. This period includes a period of warming after the most recent glaciation, the Bølling–Allerød interstadial, and then a very rapid but short-lived cooling event known as the Younger Dryas stadial, which lasted only about 1200 years from 12 800 Bp, before warming resumed in the early Holocene.

Whilst some changes in the composition of vegetation in response to these marked and rapid climatic changes were virtually instantaneous, many others occurred after lags of 50–200 years and a few at longer lags of several hundred years. Because many bird species are strongly associated with certain types of vegetation and rely upon plants directly or indirectly for food and shelter, it seems likely that these measurements of lag give us some idea of roughly how long the delays in response to climate change might be for birds that are limited by habitat. Unfortunately, direct studies of lags in the response of the distribution and abundance of bird species to past climate change have not been successful because the fossil and subfossil record of birds is incomplete and highly discontinuous, and because of difficulties in species-level identification.

6.10.3 The consequences of delays in species' response to climate change

We have seen that the changes in distribution and abundance caused by climatic change can be rapid or may be delayed for decades or centuries after the climate change occurred. This has important consequences for the interpretation of tests of climate envelope models using comparisons of observed change with that expected from the models. Most of the quantitative data available on changes in bird distribution and abundance span just a few recent decades. Even the long-duration study in California mentioned above only covers a period of about 90 years. Regular bird population monitoring began in earnest from the 1960s onwards, but only in a few European and North American countries. Most countries still do not monitor their bird populations. Marked changes in climate have occurred since the 1980s, so the studies of observed and expected changes referred to above largely depend upon responses evident within a decade or two of the beginning of the change in climate. Hence, species which do not appear to have changed their distribution or abundance in the way expected from their climate envelope model may begin to do so in future. Their response might just be subject to a lag. We therefore expect to see a wide scatter in the relationship across species between observed population or distributional changes and those expected from climate envelope models, not only because many things other than climate affect bird populations, but also because of lags. Long-term monitoring is needed to look for lags and to assess their mechanisms and which kinds of species are most likely to be subject to long response lags. Paradoxically, it may be the species whose distribution and abundance does not respond quickly to climate change which are at the most risk from the effects of climate change, especially if they need to colonise areas with newly suitable climate in order to maintain their range and population. Species which do not shift their ranges quickly enough in response to climate change can be overtaken by rapid shifts in the location of their climate envelope and decline or become extinct (Mustin *et al.* 2009). These useful insights from simulation modelling require empirical testing using data from long-term observational studies.

6.11 Alternative approaches using population models

Although most of this chapter is about climate envelope models because they have quite simple requirements for data and can be applied to many species, where data exist on the effects of climate change on demographic rates, it may be possible to produce a simulation model of the demographic processes operating in the population in order to make projections about potential future impacts of climate change. This will only be possible for a relatively small number of well-studied cases, but for these, can provide an additional level of detail and accuracy. Some have even suggested that it is only through the development of such models that we can fully understand the likely impacts of climate change on species and populations (e.g. Chevin *et al.* 2010).

As outlined in Chapter 4 (Section 4.9), one of the best examples of this is Martijn van de Pol and colleagues' work modelling the effects of climate change on coastal breeding oystercatchers in the Netherlands. Using data from a 24-year colour-ringing study the authors measured variation in annual survival of four age classes, fecundity and the probability of transitions between breeding status categories (breeding in high- and low-quality habitat and non-breeding status) in relation to weather variables, food supply, the abundance of oystercatchers and the availability of vacant territories. Survival was positively correlated with winter temperature. Fecundity was negatively correlated with winter temperature, through effects on the abundance of ragworms, their main prey, and also affected by catastrophic summer flood events. Importantly, density-dependence was well-described. As a result of this wealth of data, van de Pol *et al.* (2010a) were able to build an age- and status-structured stochastic population model and to use it to make projections of future oystercatcher population size under various assumptions about future changes in climatic conditions. For that population, this is the most robust way of assessing the net effect of these contrasting and different climatic drivers. This showed that the current population decline, based on observed data, would consign the population to extinction if nothing changed. However, the net effect of climate change was projected to reduce the likelihood of extinction, by virtue of an overall increase in survival in response to warmer temperatures, providing the magnitude of sea-level rise was not too great (van de Pol *et al.* 2010a, 2010b). This model therefore usefully collated a range of potential climate change impacts in a single, robust framework in order to assess overall vulnerability. In addition, the model outputs could also be used to identify potential adaptive management solutions to reduce the magnitude of climate change impacts, a topic we shall return to in the next chapter.

A similar but less sophisticated model was developed for a southern range-margin population of Eurasian golden plovers in the Peak District, England. Here, as already outlined (Section 4.3.4), the population model included a negative effect of summer warming on the abundance of craneflies in the following year, which then reduced chick survival and overall breeding success. The model gave a good description of observed population trends. When used to extrapolate the population trajectory into the future, in the absence of climate change, the population fluctuated stochastically, but extinction was unlikely. However, when the observed August warming trend was extrapolated into the future, equal to a 5.2 °C rise above the 1971–2005 mean, this was projected to result in a significant population decline and 96% probability of extinction by 2100 (Pearce-Higgins *et al.* 2010). Being based on observable ecological processes, this model could then be used to inform potential adaptive solutions (Pearce-Higgins 2011a, 2011b). Interestingly, this golden plover model suggests that the two alternative projected population trends are unlikely to differ significantly until about 2055, as a result of the high degree of stochasticity in the population data, despite the high rate of climate change assessed. We are unlikely to detect a strong climate change signal on this vulnerable population using current monitoring until the middle of this century. There are clear challenges associated with the potential attribution of any future population decline to climate change.

Both studies demonstrate the value and potential of using population models to make future projections of climate change, to answer specific questions about the likely magnitude of future impacts, and to help inform potential adaptive management solutions.

There is considerable potential to extend these approaches to other species, where links between demographic parameters and climate have been quantified reliably. This has been done recently for a number of seabirds. Jenouvrier *et al.* (2009, 2012), used their demographic model of the emperor penguin colony at Terre Adélie to model the future population trajectory in a changing climate. Although breeding success is negatively related to sea-ice extent, adult survival is reduced by low sea-ice extent through reductions in prey abundance (Barbraud & Weimerskirch 2001a). This means that the overall effect of warming is negative (Jenouvrier *et al.* 2005b) with maximum population growth achieved at intermediate values of sea-ice extent (Jenouvrier *et al.* 2012). Under a future A1B scenario of warming, an increased frequency of warm years is projected to lead to an 81–93% population decline by 2100 with a 36–84% chance of quasi-extinction (a 95% decline in abundance; Jenouvrier *et al.* 2009). Sea-ice extent is difficult to project accurately; therefore this model was refined further by Jenouvrier *et al.* (2012) using five GCMs which best match the historical sea-ice cover to project future changes in sea-ice extent, on which the population model depends. These models projected a mean population decline of 81% by 2100, but with high uncertainty as future projections differed in their forecasts.

Similar models have also been presented for Amsterdam albatross, black-browed albatross and snow petrel populations breeding in the Indian, sub-Antarctic and Antarctic regions respectively (Barbraud *et al.* 2011). Matrix population models were used to incorporate effects of climate (sea-surface temperature and sea-ice extent) upon breeding success and survival, and to make future population projections under A1B, A2 and B1 scenarios. As in the case of the emperor penguin model, these models allowed for non-linearities in the relationships between climate and demography, particularly important for snow petrel (Barbraud & Weimerskirch 2001b; Olivier *et al.* 2005; Jenouvrier *et al.* 2005b). Future warming was projected to have little impact on the Amsterdam albatross population, but to drive a decline in black-browed albatross survival leading to projected population extinction by 2060. The snow petrel population was also projected to decline in response to a reduction in recruitment linked to a decline in sea-ice extent, but not sufficiently to cause extinction. Surprisingly, there was relatively little variation in trends between the three different future scenarios.

There is increasing recognition of the value of population models such as these to describe ecological change, to make future predictions and to inform management. Using current developments that enable multiple demographic data to be combined in a Bayesian framework using integrated population models (IPM), the estimation of formerly intractable demographic rates is possible (Schaub & Abadi 2011). This should further increase our ability to make meaningful projections of populations in the future. However, this will only ever be possible for a relatively small number of well-studied species, and is unlikely to replace the relatively simple approach of climate envelope modelling and regression modelling of abundance that can be applied widely.

6.12 The next steps in model development

Much current research effort is being devoted to develop models of species' responses to climatic change that incorporate information on species' abundance (Huntley et al. 2012; Renwick et al. 2012), demographic rates and dispersal (Barbet-Massin et al. 2012) and the direct and indirect effects of climate upon these (Huntley et al. 2010). Indirect effects of climatic change that act via effects on habitat (Midgley et al. 2010), predators, diseases and competitors can also be included within such models where feasible but there are formidable difficulties in doing this except for well-studied species. The ideal is to integrate climate envelope models and the population models just described. This would have the advantage of producing models that could predict not only the eventual future distribution of a species, but how long it will take to realise it, as well as future changes in its population size and geographical variation in its density. A key part of such models will be establishing robust causal links between weather and climatic variables and demographic rates, as described in Chapters 3 and 4. Inclusion of such effects in population models is currently made possible only by the existence of long-term datasets in which demographic rates have been estimated annually over a long period, within which weather fluctuations and preferably also climatic change have occurred. A few examples of these were given in the previous section.

Projections of range extent from a climate envelope model have been successfully coupled with a demographic model in order to assess the likely future abundance of a species within each part of the potential range (e.g. Hooten et al. 2007; Anderson et al. 2009a; Kearney & Porter 2009; Fordham et al. 2012a). However, at present, these coupled niche–population models tend to apply fixed demographic processes within the areas of suitable range, and therefore are largely used to provide biologically realistic rates of population growth and dispersal into areas of potential future range that are currently unoccupied. They also use variation in projected suitability from the climate envelope model to limit carrying capacity, which may then influence parameters in the model through density dependence. Such approaches are relatively simplistic, compared to the potential to link dynamic population models to climate envelope models in order to develop what perhaps may be termed coupled niche–dynamic population models. When doing so, it is important to appropriately link the different approaches, and particularly to ensure that model uncertainty is adequately propagated through the modelling system (Conlisk et al. 2013). Although coupled niche–population models have largely been developed for invertebrates and plants, these approaches have the potential to be extended and applied to birds for which we have good demographic and dispersal information.

This will be an exciting but challenging area of development that is currently only possible for a very small number of species which have been the subject of detailed population and ecological studies in several representative areas. Relationships between demographic rates and climatic and environmental variables will need to be generalised across large areas or established separately in various parts of the study area (e.g. Robinson *et al.* 2012). This will allow population processes to be simulated in sub-populations at different locations, enabling rates of distribution and abundance change to be modelled across a region as a function of climatic change. In an example that goes some way towards achieving this, detailed studies of the spotted owl *Strix occidentalis* in the USA have been used to develop models for three populations at different parts of the species' range. Those in Arizona and New Mexico were predicted to decline rapidly under three climate change scenarios in response to increasing temperature and drought, whilst improvements in spring weather conditions were predicted to increase the fecundity of the population in southern California (Peery *et al.* 2012). Dispersal rates should also be included in these models as they have a role in influencing the projected magnitude of climate change impact (e.g. Barbet-Massin *et al.* 2012). Perhaps the greatest challenge will be to model the duration of time lags in the response of a focal species to climate change caused by the time taken for other species, such as prey, to change in response to climate change. This will call for the development of linked multi-species models. Where multiple data exist, the ability of models to be validated on different populations will be useful, as many of the potential methodological challenges and problems discussed in this chapter in relation to climate envelope models apply also to demographic models and certainly will apply to coupled niche-population models.

We can therefore foresee an array of future modelling approaches being used to provide conservationists with the information required to inform the decisions they make. For rare well-studied species of conservation concern that occupy single or a small number of sites, population models that link climate to demographic parameters may form the best approach, that will also provide information about the likely underlying mechanisms associated with climate change impacts to inform future conservation management (Pearce-Higgins 2011a, 2011b). For more widely distributed species of conservation concern, dynamic population models or coupled niche–population models may be feasible, and could provide the most effective tools to inform conservation prioritisation and management, particularly if they can enable trade-offs between different conservation options to be quantified. However, for the majority of species, for which good long-term and demographic data will be lacking, simpler approaches that require fewer data will still need to be used. For these species, it is likely that the climate envelope approach will remain the most practical option to use.

6.13 Summary

- It is important for conservationists to estimate the likely magnitude of future climate change impacts on bird populations as a guide to the types of conservation action possible and their priority. The most widely used approach for doing this is climate envelope modelling.
- Climate envelope models describe associations between species' occurrence and climate during a specified period. Assuming these relationships will remain unaltered

over time, they can be used to predict past or future distributions based on climatic projections. Much work has been conducted to identify the most appropriate data to use, the time frame and geographical area over which data should be collected and the spatial scale at which analyses should be conducted.

- Whilst a wide range of potential bioclimatic variables may be used for such analyses, often a measure of winter cold, mean temperature, plant growing season warmth and moisture availability, such as AET/PET, adequately describe species' ranges, and closely link to the likely ecological mechanisms underlying species' distributions. The addition of non-climate variables into such models can improve their realism for describing current distribution, but may diminish their potential value for making future projections of change.
- The size of the future potential range relative to the current range provides a simple measure of the projected impact of climate change on that species. The ability of a species to occupy new areas of climatic suitability will be an important determinant of projected change. The magnitude of mean decline in range extent across the studies reviewed over a 2–6 °C gradient of global warming averages 11–23% if species are assumed to be able to fully colonise areas with newly suitable climate immediately, or 41–74% if colonisation was limited.
- Higher projected increases in temperature are likely to lead to larger reductions in range extent. This in turn is expected to increases extinction risk. Studies suggest that on average, some 0.6–1.8% of bird species may be at immediate risk of extinction over a 2–6 °C range of global warming, assuming that extinction only occurs when a species is projected to have no suitable range extent. A longer term evaluation of extinction risk is obtained from IUCN criteria or applying the species-area relationship to reductions in range extent or population. Such methods suggest some 10–25% of bird species may be committed to extinction over a 2–6 °C range of warming.
- All approaches provide a consistent message that increasing the magnitude of warming will threaten an increasing number of species with extinction, although the precise magnitude of this risk varies considerably with the assumptions made.
- Evaluating the performance of climate envelope models is difficult. A wide variety of techniques may be used to compare modelled against predicted distributions to identify the models most likely to produce meaningful projections. However, few of these fully take into account lack of statistical independence of data, even if they attempt to describe the distribution of a species in a geographical area not included in the modelling, or within a different time period.
- Given that climate envelope models are being widely used to make projections of likely future range and population change in response to climate change, the most meaningful tests of their performance are their ability to describe actual range and population changes during a period of climatic change. Where such tests have been performed, these tend to show that recent changes are correlated with observed changes. Thus, there is increasing support that climate envelope models may produce useful predictions of the likely direction of future change in response to climate change.
- There are good reasons why the observed rate of range change may be slower than that predicted from climate envelope models, because of limitations in species' dispersal ability, long generation times and lags in the ecological mechanisms that

links climate change to species' populations and distributions. Models suggest that species which show the slowest rate of range shift may be those most vulnerable to climate change impacts, although this has yet to be demonstrated by observation.
- Where demographic information linking population processes to climate is available, population models may be developed. These are being increasingly applied to produce predictions for particular populations, and provide additional information of value to conservationists.
- In future, models may be improved by explicitly incorporating dispersal within population models, and by linking demographic models from separate meta-populations across a species' range. It should also be possible to link demographic information to climate envelope model projections in dynamic models and coupled niche–population models in order to develop more spatially explicit projections. Whilst such tools may be particularly useful when developed for individual species, it is likely that, due to a lack of detailed demographic data for the majority of species, climate envelope models will remain the most effective approach to use for making future projections of climate change impacts.

7 · Conservation in a changing climate

7.1 Introduction

Climate change is anticipated to result in species shifting their distribution to higher latitudes and altitudes (Chapter 6), as has already been observed (Chapter 5). Changes to habitats, and the abundance of food organisms, predators, competitors, parasites and diseases, and the direct effects of climate will alter species' demographic rates and abundance (Chapters 3 and 4). In parts of the range where population density increases, this is likely to result in an increasing number of dispersing individuals being available to colonise areas of habitat beyond the current range margin. At the retreating range margin, conditions are likely to become increasingly unfavourable, resulting in reduced fecundity and/or survival. Initially, as population density declines, negative effects of climatic change on a particular demographic rate may be at least partially compensated for by density-dependent improvements in other rates. The population in this part of the range may then stabilise at a lower level for some time. However, progressive change will eventually cause population declines, fragmentation of the distribution, local extinctions and finally loss of range. Between the expanding and retreating margins, the same mechanisms may lead to shifts in the distribution of areas with high population density, and changes to the composition of communities (Chapter 5).

Observations of impacts of climate change, and concerns over the impacts projected to come, have stimulated increasingly detailed thinking about what conservationists can do to counter negative impacts through what is termed climate change adaptation: interventions to reduce the vulnerability of species and their habitats to actual or expected climate change effects. Recent advances in conservation science have provided an increased understanding of the precise requirements of species and the impacts upon them of threats such as habitat loss and degradation, overexploitation, persecution and pollution, all driven by expanding human populations and their increased demands for food, recreation and commodities. This understanding has underpinned some successful conservation programmes that have reversed population declines and range losses of some species. We therefore start this chapter with a summary of the tools that conservationists have found to be effective in countering these threats to birds, before considering how they may be adapted for use in the face of climate change.

7.2 The conservationist's toolkit

The various elements of species conservation interventions can be divided into six main tools (Green & Pearce-Higgins 2010), which are outlined below.

Table 7.1 *Summary of IUCN red list criteria (adapted from Butchart et al. 2005).*

Criteria	Red List category	Definition
Rapid population reduction	Critical	Decline $\geq$ 80% in 10 years or 3 generations observed, estimated or likely in near future, or decline $\geq$ 90% if the causes are reversible and have ceased.
	Endangered	Decline $\geq$ 50% in 10 years or 3 generations observed, estimated or likely in near future, or decline $\geq$ 70% if the causes are reversible and have ceased.
	Vulnerable	Decline $\geq$ 30% in 10 years or 3 generations observed, estimated or likely in near future, or decline $\geq$ 50% if the causes are reversible and have ceased.
Small range and fragmented, declining or fluctuating	Critical	Range $<$ 100 km^2 or occupied area $<$ 10 km^2, and present at only 1 location, population declining and/or extreme fluctuations in range or abundance.
	Endangered	Range $<$ 5000 km^2, or occupied area $<$ 500 km^2, and severely fragmented at $\leq$ 5 locations, population declining and/or extreme fluctuations in range or abundance.
	Vulnerable	Range $<$ 20 000 km^2, or occupied area $<$ 2000 km^2, and severely fragmented at $\leq$ 10 locations, population declining and/or extreme fluctuations in range or abundance.
Small population and declining	Critical	Population $<$ 250 mature individuals and declining or subject to extreme fluctuations.
	Endangered	Population $<$ 2500 mature individuals and declining or subject to extreme fluctuations.
	Vulnerable	Population $<$ 10 000 mature individuals and declining or subject to extreme fluctuations.
Very small population	Critical	Population $<$ 50 mature individuals.
	Endangered	Population $<$ 250 mature individuals.
	Vulnerable	Population $<$ 1000 mature individuals.
Very small range	Vulnerable	Area of occupancy $<$ 20 km^2 or $\leq$ 5 locations.

7.2.1 Prioritisation and planning

Not every species or area of habitat is under threat. With limited conservation resources, there is a clear need to prioritise where those resources are spent, and to plan what the most effective conservation strategies might be. The methods for identifying species at high risk of extinction are well established through the IUCN Red List (www.iucnredlist.org) and are used to assign species to categories of relative extinction risk, ranging from Least Concern to Extinct (Table 7.1; Mace *et al.* 2008). Under this system, 1253 bird species, some 12% of the total, are classified as threatened (i.e. in the categories of critically endangered, endangered or vulnerable) by BirdLife International (2012a). A further 843 bird species are close to meeting the thresholds for the category vulnerable and are listed as near-threatened.

Although prioritisation of species for conservation is important, so is the prioritisation of their habitats and the areas upon which they depend. Bird survey data are used for the identification of key sites and zones for species conservation such as Key Biodiversity Areas, Important Bird Areas and Alliance for Zero Extinction Areas. In many cases, these priority areas are accorded legal protection to prevent unrestricted damage through development or overexploitation. Agencies responsible for protected area establishment often aim to establish networks of protected sites and habitats for species, and to identify and fill unprotected gaps in such networks (Gaston *et al.* 2008), a good example of which is the Special Protection Area (SPA) network in the European Union. However, protected area networks are often not complete and interconnected enough to justify their name. Instead, they may only protect a small sample of isolated sites within a much more extensive complex of habitat patches critical for the future long-term persistence of a species. We term these patches 'core sites', whose protection is an important second tool for bird conservation.

7.2.2 Protection and creation of core sites

The protection of core sites, by means of nature reserves, national parks or areas of wider countryside managed for conservation has long been central to practical conservation (Reid & Miller 1989; McNeely *et al.* 1990). In order for the protection of core sites to be worthwhile, they should be identified with reference to the abundance of the species that they are intended to protect and support a significant proportion of a regional, national or international population. It is relatively easy to select a network of such sites where there are good data on species' abundance and distribution, and considerable research effort has been invested to design and produce algorithms to do this robustly (e.g. Pressy *et al.* 1996; Carroll *et al.* 2003; Nicholson *et al.* 2006). For a species with an existing high risk of extinction, or with a risk of extinction which decreases rapidly with increasing habitat area, the establishment of a single large reserve is likely to be more effective than multiple smaller reserves for the same cost, because populations in the many small reserves are individually at high risk of extinction in the short term. For less vulnerable species, the optimum population, and hence patch, size of a protected area should be established on the basis of the relationship between extinction risk and habitat area. The risk of extinction is therefore minimised when an increasing number of reserves are established which are at the optimum patch size (McCarthy *et al.* 2005). In the absence of climate change, if the goal is to minimise extinction risk, it is therefore advantageous to have a small number of large reserves that exceed the threshold required to maintain a viable population. The size of small reserves should be increased until they are of sufficient size to support a minimum viable population size.

In situations of high environmental stochasticity or risk of catastrophic loss irrespective of patch size, multiple reserves and the enhancement of connectivity among them should theoretically be favoured over patch size (Frank & Wissel 2002; Nicholson & Possingham 2007). The relative importance of increasing patch size or increasing connectivity should therefore be judged on the dispersal ability of the species concerned and the likely magnitude of environmental stochasticity. These same principles hold when considering an assemblage of species, although the situation is then more complex. In particular, there is added importance for prioritising areas of high endemism, where the ranges of several species with small global ranges overlap. This is likely to maximise the persistence of the greatest number of species (McCarthy *et al.* 2006) – see Section 7.5 below, although if more detailed information about the species concerned is available, then meta-population-based algorithms may be used to inform conservation planning (Nicholson *et al.* 2006). In reality, formal identification of protected area networks that maximise conservation objectives for many species is difficult, with the precise outcomes often dependent upon the specific objectives defined and the assumptions that are made (Nicholson & Possingham 2006; Van Teeffelen *et al.* 2006). Where bird survey data are sparse, as in many tropical countries, core sites may be identified and delineated using information on the distribution and quality of habitats thought to be important for bird species (Halpin 1997; Buchanan *et al.* 2008). This might introduce further uncertainty into the process because species' abundance can vary substantially within areas of apparently suitable habitat (Rompré *et al.* 2009).

The BirdLife International partnership of bird conservation organisations has identified a global network of over 10 000 core sites, the Important Bird Areas (IBAs), that contain habitats critical for the conservation of the world's birds. Identified nationally using globally standardised criteria, IBAs are delineated as actual or potential management units. At present, only 28% of IBAs lie completely within legally protected areas, and 49% are wholly unprotected (Butchart *et al.* 2012). Where species' declines have been associated with over-exploitation, the establishment of refuges that restrict or prevent hunting has allowed the successful restoration of previously declining populations (Balazs & Chaloupka 2004; Dutton *et al.* 2005; Shears *et al.* 2006). Where species have declined as a result of habitat destruction or degradation, or there was a threat of these processes impinging on their range, protected areas have sometimes acted to prevent or slow the loss of their habitat, although they may still be subject to degradation (Laurance *et al.* 2012). Habitat re-creation and restoration is implemented to a greater extent in protected than in unprotected sites because the considerable expense and difficulty of much restoration work would be a risky investment unless associated with the protection of the new habitat to avoid repeated loss or damage (Impey *et al.* 2002). Creating protected areas that cover a sufficiently large set of core sites may be adequate on its own to conserve the intended beneficiary species (Figure 7.1), though investment in staff to ensure that the habitat in the reserves and the species themselves are really protected is usually also needed (Laurance *et al.* 2012). However, more intervention than this is frequently required. For many species, just preventing direct negative human impacts is only one aspect of the role of protected areas for conservation. Often the habitats in such areas need to be managed to achieve the conservation objectives, which is the third tool that conservationists may employ.

7.2.3 Management of core sites

There is a well-established conservation science model which is often used to inform conservation management to benefit particular species (Gibbons *et al.* 2011). It involves monitoring of the distribution and abundance of species to detect population declines (see 7.2.1), followed by diagnosis of the causes of decline, using a range of comparative and experimental methods. These include comparisons among sites and time periods to identify external factors correlated with variation in the rate of population or distributional change. For example, variation in food supplies or predator abundance might be

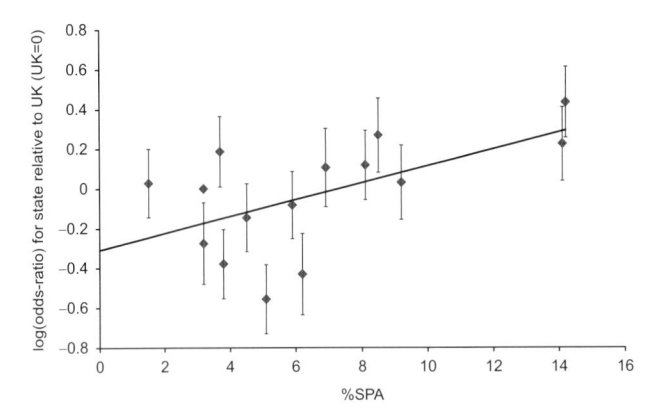

Figure 7.1 Large-scale protected area networks lead to more positive bird population trends. The percentage of land designated as SPAs within each European country is positively correlated with an index of bird population change having accounted for species-specific effects of migratory strategy and habitat. Change is referenced against the UK (the diamond with a value of 0 and no SE) using the odds-ratio. Reproduced with permission from Donald *et al.* (2007).

compared between regions with different population trends, or patterns of change over time in these potential external drivers might be compared with the temporal trends in the abundance of the focal species. Once a particular cause of decline has been identified, the next step is solution-testing to trial appropriate conservation action. These actions can be counteracting, aimed at arresting or reversing particular deleterious effects on a species, or compensatory, using the positive influence of particular managements on a population to compensate for other continued negative pressures (Wilcox & Donlan 2007; Green & Pearce-Higgins 2010). Where feasible, the interventions should be trialled experimentally. Fuller accounts of the potential advantages and pitfalls of this approach can be found elsewhere (Green 1995, 2002).

There are many options for the management of core sites. These range from other species management options, such as the promotion of the prey species providing the food supply of a focal species (e.g. Margalida *et al.* 2009) or the control of predator populations (Summers *et al.* 2004), to habitat management options, such as grazing or burning to reduce succession and promote habitat condition for open country species (Pons *et al.* 2003; Fuhlendorf *et al.* 2006), reduction of grazing or burning to favour species associated with tree and shrub cover, and hydrological management to maintain water levels (Milsom *et al.* 2002). As we will see, many of these options are likely to remain useful in a changing climate and can be used for adaptation (Green & Pearce-Higgins 2010; Pearce-Higgins 2011a, 2011b).

7.2.4 Habitat protection and creation in the wider landscape

The protection and management of populations of focal species within protected areas is desirable, but given that habitat loss and habitat degradation threaten some 1000 bird species (BirdLife International 2008), populations in protected areas are likely to become increasingly isolated and fragmented through time (e.g. Figure 7.2). The loss of certain

7.2 The conservationist's toolkit · 255

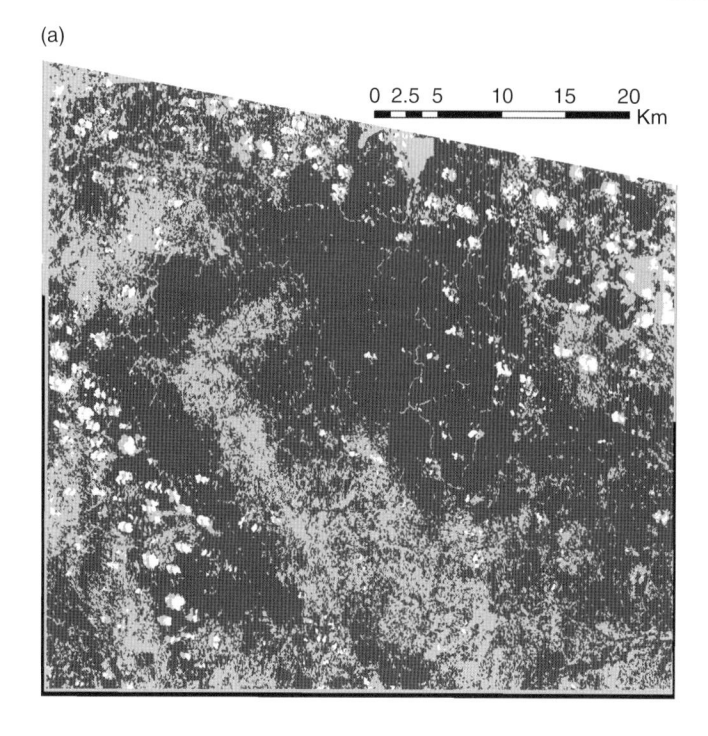

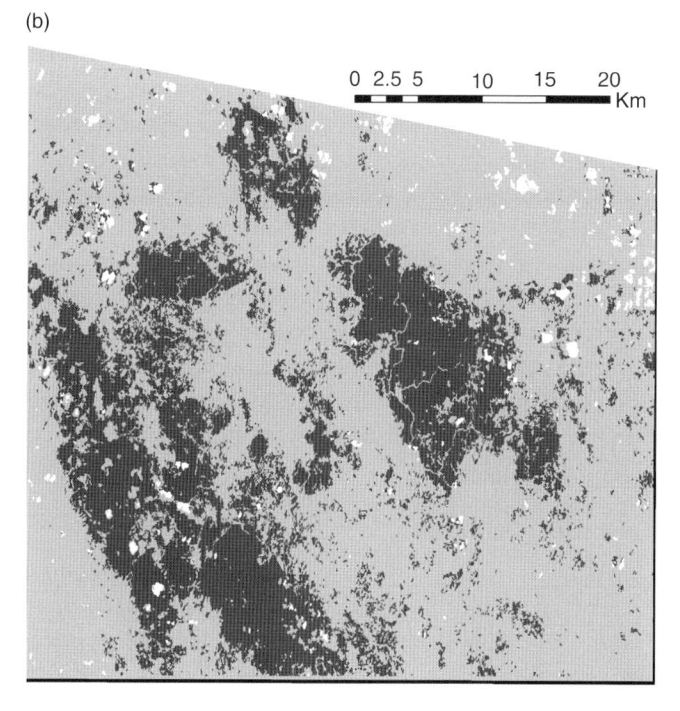

Figure 7.2 Mature forest cover (dark grey) in a part of Sumatra surrounding the Harrapan nature reserve in 1989 (a) and 2006 (b). Non-forest habitats are shown in light grey, and cloud in white. The Harrapan reserve covers most of the areas of forest cover outlined in the 2006 image, which had been part of a much larger area of continuous forest in 1989.

patches from a network can reduce the degree of connectedness among patches if the removed patches act as stepping stones to facilitate dispersal. Reduced connectivity can increase the chance of sub-population extinction due to stochastic events such as extreme weather, as these are not prevented by rescue re-colonisation or supplementation by dispersal from other patches. Further, the likelihood of re-colonisation of unoccupied patches is also reduced by fragmentation. Ultimately, the entire meta-population may decline to extinction even though a substantial area of habitat remains within the aggregate of surviving patches (Hanski & Gilpin 1997; Hanski 1999). There is good evidence from a number of bird species that habitat fragmentation is detrimental (Lampila *et al.* 2005). We review this subject in more detail in Section 7.7.

In response to deterioration in the connectedness of patches in meta-population networks, conservation efforts should aim to protect key patches to maintain connectivity. The isolation of suitable patches should be prevented in order to reduce the chance of extinction of sub-populations or groups of sub-populations. Additional emphasis has been put on the use of corridors to link habitats, or the creation of stepping stones to enable species to move between patches of habitat in easy stages (Henry *et al.* 1999; Jongman *et al.* 2004). Alternatively, the degree of connectivity between patches may be enhanced by reducing the hostility to the focal species of the matrix of land cover within which the patches of suitable habitat are placed. This approach assumes that it should be possible to manage the intervening landscape to lower mortality during dispersal between patches, to increase the chance that individuals attempt to disperse, or both (Donald & Evans 2006). Such management will be required for species and situations where dispersing individuals are unable to avoid temporarily utilising a hostile intervening land cover type on their way between more suitable patches. It is therefore most likely to apply to species with limited ability to rapidly move long distances in landscapes with widely separated suitable habitat patches (Gaston & Blackburn 2002; Hulme 2005; Donald & Evans 2006).

Despite the relatively limited evidence base for applying these approaches to birds, these principles do make good ecological sense as a means of reversing the detrimental consequences of habitat fragmentation. As a result, there is considerable conservation effort and policy focus, based largely on expert assessment, in increasing the connectivity of habitats across landscapes, leading to the development of ecological networks (e.g. Lawton *et al.* 2010). Given projected shifts in the distribution of species in response to climate change (Chapter 6), there is considerable interest in the application of these approaches to climate change adaptation, which will be discussed in detail in Section 7.7.

7.2.5 Management of the wider landscape

Many species are not restricted to core sites but occupy habitat so dispersed that the concept of core sites does not apply and the option of protecting most of their habitat in reserves is impractical. These have populations that are more likely to be affected by the management in the wider countryside than the management of a protected area network. Deterioration in the quality of these wider countryside habitats may therefore have large detrimental consequences for the birds they support. In Western European and North American landscapes dominated by agriculture and forestry, it is the types of forestry and agricultural practices used which have been the major drivers of population trends of many bird species (e.g. Chamberlain *et al.* 2000; Donald *et al.* 2001; Eglington & Pearce-Higgins 2012). In response to these declines, conservation science has again been applied in an attempt to guide conservation interventions.

The same types of management options may be applied across the wider landscape as are used on reserves. However, the quality of the management that can be achieved is sometimes lower than is possible on a core site devoted to conservation. Wider-countryside management has to be conducted alongside other demands on the land, and therefore may involve reduction in the intensity of such management, such as the edges of fields, or the introduction or maintenance of some small patches of natural or semi-natural habitats within the landscape. The implementation of such measures on farmland, through the promotion of agri-environment schemes, has attempted to reverse previous declines in farmland bird populations, with some limited benefit (Baker *et al.* 2012).

Changes in land use which affect the suitability of cropland, agricultural grasslands and forests as bird habitats are not the only threats to bird species in the wider countryside. There are other important anthropogenic threats such as deliberate killing, disturbance and pollution. These pressures have been responsible for declines of many bird species globally, with direct human exploitation, primarily for food or the caged bird trade, being the second most important threat for birds, affecting some 367 bird species (BirdLife International 2008). Other examples include poisoning of birds of prey by pesticides and veterinary drugs (Newton 1979; Oaks *et al.* 2004) and collisions of birds with man-made structures such as power cables and wind turbines (Drewitt & Langston 2006). These pressures will increase mortality rates or lower breeding productivity across the whole population unless they are completely compensated for by a density-dependent response. Even if they are principally a problem outside protected areas, they can turn the wider countryside into a sink habitat and reduce the total population size of the species. For example, because the birds range widely in search of carrion, populations of vultures in the Indian subcontinent have been greatly reduced by veterinary use of the toxic drug diclofenac on cattle, despite the continued availability of uncontaminated wild ungulate carcasses within national parks and other protected areas (Prakash *et al.* 2003, 2007).

7.2.6 Captive breeding, translocation and re-introduction

When all else fails, the pressures upon wild populations may exceed the capacity of *in situ* conservation and the size of the remaining population of a focal species may fall to such a low level that there is a significant risk of extinction before effective conservation measures can be identified and implemented. In this case, the only possible solution is to bring some or all of the remaining wild individuals into captivity in an attempt to establish a captive population for subsequent re-introduction into the wild (Conde *et al.* 2011). Although drastic and expensive, there are an increasing number of cases where this approach has led to successful re-introductions to the wild of species which would otherwise have been doomed to extinction. For example, captive breeding and release allowed the recovery of the Mauritius kestrel from four wild birds in 1974 to a hundred-fold larger population 25 years later (Jones 1998). In North America, the California condor *Gymngyps californianus* would have been extinct but for captive breeding, but several re-introduced wild populations now exist in the USA and Mexico.

An alternative approach to the release of captive-bred young is the translocation of individuals from one area, where they are threatened, to another which is less threatened and may be unoccupied. Perhaps the most famous example of this is the recovery of the kakapo *Strigops habroptilus*, which in the 1980s was found only in a few parts of New Zealand in which predation by cats and other introduced alien mammals made their long-term survival impossible. The remaining 61 individuals were captured and translocated to a number of predator-free offshore islands, leading to a stabilisation and subsequent increase of the population (Elliott *et al.* 2001). These individuals are still able to live relatively naturally in a similar environment to that occupied historically, which should make any potential future re-introduction to their historical range easier.

In the case of species which are not globally endangered, translocation of birds from a donor population is increasingly being used to restore populations of focal species in parts of their previous range from which they have been extirpated in historical times. In the British Isles, collection of eggs or young followed by captive breeding or rearing and release has been used in attempts to establish re-introduced populations of white-tailed eagles *Haliaeetus albicilla*, golden eagles, ospreys *Pandion haliaetus*, red kites *Milvus milvus*, black grouse, great bustards *Otis tarda*, corncrakes, common cranes *Grus grus* and cirl buntings to parts of their former range. The red kite and white-tailed eagle projects have been outstandingly successful (e.g. Evans *et al.* 1999, 2009), whilst for many others, the re-introductions are more recent and it is too soon to know whether they will succeed.

7.3 The climate change toolkit

Use of the tools described above may need to be refined when employed in support of climate change adaptation to reduce the negative impacts of climate change on the conservation of species. Much has been written about this topic, because it is of considerable policy relevance and interest, but at present, this discussion is severely limited by a lack of evidence and case studies of successful practical implementation of adaptation programmes. We do not have examples and experience of managing species through previous periods of rapid climate change that we can draw upon as models for action now. Instead, we are at the start of a new, unfamiliar and probably rapid environmental process and must make decisions based upon the best available evidence, which in many cases is very sparse. We are therefore forced to draw upon existing ecological principles and lessons learned from conservation success stories concerning other threats and apply those to the context of a changing climate (Green & Pearce-Higgins 2010). In the following text, we will make repeated reference to what we have learned from existing conservation practice in order to guide our understanding of how particular tools may be used in a changing climate. But before we do, let us first examine some general principles and consider how these different tools, if they work, may be used together.

Given the projected potential range shifts expected from climate envelope models (Chapter 6), much of the focus of climate change adaptation in the literature has been the management of changes in species' distribution and abundance through the creation or maintenance of effective ecological networks; patches of habitats that a species can utilise (Heller & Zavaleta 2009). The importance of this is highlighted by the fact that the ability of a species to colonise new areas of habitat that become climatically suitable is a key determinant of the projected magnitude of range change that species will undergo in response to climate change (Section 6.8.2). All other things being equal, climatic change is likely to render the lower latitudinal and altitudinal range limits of a species' current range less suitable for it, and the higher range limits more suitable – for which there is increasing evidence (Section 5.2), although in tropical areas, shifts in distribution may not be poleward (VanDerWal et al. 2013). To maintain or enhance the species' current total range extent and population size, conservation action could seek to slow or prevent the deterioration of conditions in the lower latitude or altitude parts of the range, to enhance population density anywhere in the present range and/or to facilitate the spread of the species at the high latitude or altitude margin of the current range (Pearce-Higgins et al. 2011a).

Unfavourable climate change at the lower latitudinal and altitudinal limits of a species' current range does not necessarily mean that the disappearance of the species from these areas is inevitable. It may be that expanding the network of sites with suitable habitat or special management of habitats or pressures on the species may allow it to persist in these areas, despite deterioration in aspects of suitability directly or indirectly affected by climate. This aspect of adaptation has generally been given less attention in the literature than efforts to facilitate the spread of a species into new areas of habitat where the climate has changed to be more favourable. If declines in range and population density at the retreating range margin cannot be avoided, then the way to maintain total population size at its current level is either to increase population density in other parts of the existing range or to facilitate range expansion into areas where climatic change results in newly suitable habitat (Figure 7.3).

Hence, an adaptation strategy to protect a species from adverse effects of climatic change requires several components. Patches of habitat required by the species and projected to remain suitable within the existing range (core sites) need to be identified and protected to prevent or reverse losses caused by adverse impacts not directly connected to climatic change, such as habitat loss, overexploitation, predation or competition from invasive alien species. This will be a 'no-regrets' or 'low-regrets' option that will provide benefit whatever the magnitude of climate change. It may also be necessary to expand the number or size of such patches by habitat creation or restoration. Management of habitats within core sites in the existing range may be needed to prevent, or slow, deterioration in their suitability for the species, whether caused by climatic change or other factors. Measures may be needed to increase the dispersal of birds among core sites to reduce the risk of local extinctions that often occur in isolated subpopulations. This can be done by adding core sites to the network to reduce distances between them or by adding small habitat patches or corridors of habitat to increase connectivity. Even if these small patches and corridors are not large enough for individuals to survive and breed permanently within them, they may be used to enhance the rate of movement between core sites and the survival of birds that attempt to move. This may also be achieved through modification of the surrounding habitat matrix.

Outside the existing range of the species, the protection or creation of patches of habitat may be needed in areas where climatic change is likely to significantly increase the suitability of unoccupied areas. This action is intended to promote the spread of the

260 · **Conservation in a changing climate**

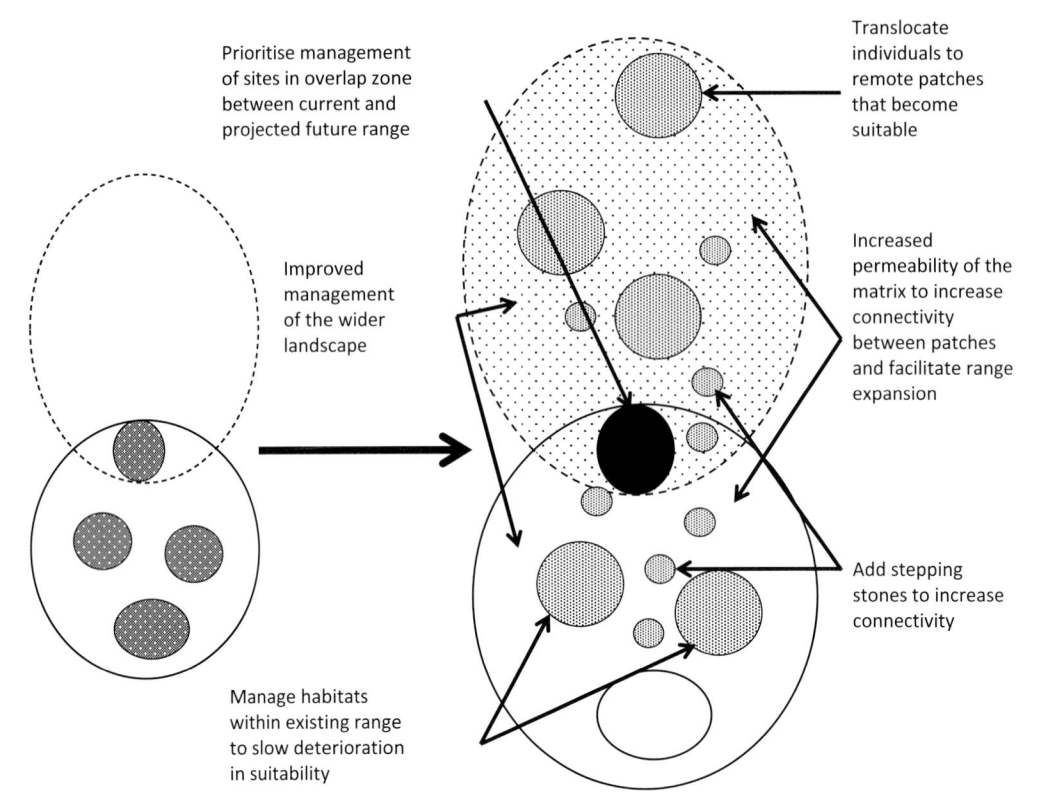

Figure 7.3 Schematic diagram of the potential for different adaptation options to assist the conservation of a particular bird species threatened by climate change. The current climatic range of the species is indicated by the closed circle where it occupies four protected areas (left). The future projected range in response to climate change is given by the dotted ellipse. Various actions on the right are suggested to improve the quality and abundance of the species at different locations. The intensity of shading indicates likely abundance or suitability for that species.

species into new areas. To make these additions to the network effective, similar consideration of the size and spacing of patches, based upon meta-population theory, will be needed. Beyond the range boundary, there will need to be enough patches of sufficient size and with suitable habitat, and sufficiently connected to their neighbours, to enable their colonisation by individuals originating from within the existing range. What is enough and sufficient in this regard could be determined by studies of metapopulation dynamics within the current range to describe dispersal parameters and the relationship between the probability of within-patch extinction to patch area and habitat characteristics. If a sufficiently large and connected network of patches beyond the leading edge of the range cannot be provided, then the translocation of individuals to these new areas (also termed 'assisted colonisation') may be an alternative means to enable species ranges to shift in response to climate change (Figure 7.3).

If future climate change matches current projections, the future distribution and abundance of bird populations is likely to be much changed from the present day (Section

6.8.2). Given the length of time required to plan for the creation of new habitats, it is important to consider how conservation priorities should be modified now in the light of these potential changes, in order to plan effectively for the future. In the next section, we will consider how this may be achieved, and the implications for conservation policy.

7.4 The role of conservation prioritisation, planning and policy

7.4.1 Conservation prioritisation

There is a considerable body of knowledge and existing practice concerning the prioritisation of species and the areas required to protect them. Although there is scope within the current IUCN criteria to prioritise species on the basis of likely near-future declines (BirdLife International 2000; Butchart *et al.* 2005), so far, the system has not incorporated projections of how future climate change will affect the risk of extinction, although this issue is being addressed. The most important information required for doing this is some assessment of the likely impacts of future climate change upon a species or population, which as described in the previous chapter comes largely from climate envelope modelling. As outlined in Section 6.8.1, this approach has been used for European bird species and showed that of 40 endemic or near-endemic species, four (Cory's shearwater *Calonectris diomedea*, Yelkouan shearwater *Puffinus yelkouan*, Audouin's gull *Larus audouinii* and spotless starling *Sternus unicolor*) are projected to suffer at least a 50% reduction in potential future range extent under an intermediate climate change HadCM3 scenario with full dispersal (Huntley *et al.* 2007). If it is assumed that the colonisation of future suitable range areas were not possible, and the likely future range is limited to areas within the current range, then the number of species projected to suffer a 50% reduction in range extent increases to 28. These endemic species are conservation priorities now, and should remain so into the future as they are likely to become increasingly threatened by climate change, and in particular may require connected landscapes in order to track likely future changes in the extent of suitable climate. More broadly, Huntley *et al.* (2007) also identified a number of more widespread European species simulated to suffer 90% reductions in range extent, including six: white-headed duck *Oxyura leucocephala*, Barbary partridge *Alectoris barbara*, Dupont's lark *Chersophilus duponti*, Berthelot's pipit *Anthus berthelotii*, trumpeter finch *Bucanetes githagineus* and Pallas' bunting *Emberiza pallasi*, projected to have no suitable areas of suitable climate in Europe by the late twenty-first century. Overall, of 76 species which may be identified as likely to be of conservation concern in Europe as a result of climate change on the basis of projected range contractions, only 35 are currently of conservation concern. Similar analyses have been carried out for African birds (Hole *et al.* 2009) and are in progress for birds of other regions.

The example for European birds illustrates how climate envelope models may be simply used to identify species for which future climate change may be of most concern and those for which adaptation actions may be most urgently required (Green & Pearce-Higgins 2010). This approach can be extended, however, to take account of other relevant information using a number of what may be termed 'vulnerability frameworks'. These generally compare the likely exposure of a species to future climate change with information about factors likely to influence its sensitivity to climate change, as well as

Box 7.1 · *Accounting for climate change in conservation prioritisation*

Thomas *et al.* (2010) present a framework which separates the potential threats of climate change, likely to cause population changes in the species' current range, from potential climate-driven population increases and range expansion. In order for the framework to be applied, recent distributional and population trend data need to be combined with the results of climate envelope, or similar, modelling, to produce a combined assessment of likely future risk as a result of climate change. Importantly, given the uncertainty, each assessment is weighted by an associated measure of confidence.

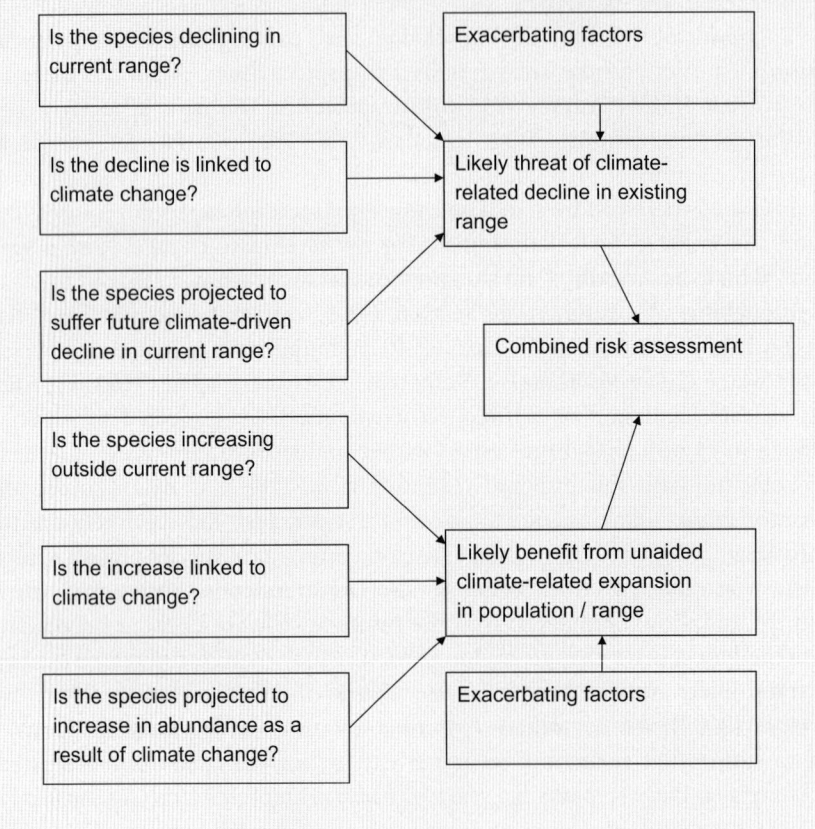

```
┌─────────────────────────┐           ┌─────────────────────────┐
│ Is the species declining │           │ Exacerbating factors    │
│ in current range?        │           │                         │
└─────────────────────────┘           └─────────────────────────┘
                                                │
┌─────────────────────────┐           ┌─────────────────────────┐
│ Is the decline is linked │──────────▶│ Likely threat of climate-│
│ to climate change?       │           │ related decline in       │
└─────────────────────────┘           │ existing range           │
                                      └─────────────────────────┘
┌─────────────────────────┐                     │
│ Is the species projected │                    │
│ to suffer future climate-│                    ▼
│ driven decline in current│          ┌─────────────────────────┐
│ range?                   │          │ Combined risk assessment │
└─────────────────────────┘          └─────────────────────────┘
                                                ▲
┌─────────────────────────┐                     │
│ Is the species increasing│                    │
│ outside current range?   │          ┌─────────────────────────┐
└─────────────────────────┘          │ Likely benefit from      │
                                      │ unaided climate-related  │
┌─────────────────────────┐──────────▶│ expansion in             │
│ Is the increase linked   │          │ population / range       │
│ to climate change?       │          └─────────────────────────┘
└─────────────────────────┘                     ▲
                                                │
┌─────────────────────────┐           ┌─────────────────────────┐
│ Is the species projected │           │ Exacerbating factors    │
│ to increase in abundance │           │                         │
│ as a result of climate   │           └─────────────────────────┘
│ change?                  │
└─────────────────────────┘
```

some consideration about the species' adaptive capacity, and are increasingly being adopted and used by various nature conservation organisations (e.g. Bagne *et al.* 2011; Young *et al.* 2011). One of the first such frameworks published in the peer-reviewed literature was that of Thomas *et al.* (2010), who developed a generic framework using information about recent and likely future changes in the extent or abundance of species in the existing range and potential, future suitable range which can be applied to any species (Box 7.1). Importantly, on the assumption that climate change is likely to result in species' declines within their current range that may be partially or wholly compensated for by expansion elsewhere, the approach of Thomas *et al.* (2010) separates climate change impacts on the current and future potential ranges. Greater confidence is attributed to projections for which there is observational evidence in support of the projected direction of change.

Box 7.2 · *Assessing the vulnerability of Californian birds to climate change*

Gardali *et al.* (2012) assessed the vulnerability of birds in California to climate change from the product of sensitivity and exposure scores. These were calculated from the sum of the scores for individual criteria as follows. Taxa with a score > 30 were classed as vulnerable to climate change, and those with a score of > 50 were listed as being of highest priority.

Table 1

Score	Criteria
Sensitivity	
Habitat specialisation	1 – Uses a wide variety of habitats
	2 – Tolerates some variability in habitat type
	3 – Uses only specific habitat types
Physiological tolerances	1 – No evidence of physiological sensitivity to climatic conditions
	2 – Some evidence of physiological sensitivity to climatic conditions
	3 – Strong evidence of physiological sensitivity to climatic conditions
Migratory status	1 – Resident
	2 – Short-distance migrant
	3 – Long-distance migrant
Dispersal ability	1 – High
	2 – Average
	3 – Low
Exposure	
Changes in habitat suitability	1 – Habitat suitability expected to increase or decrease by < 10%
	2 – Habitat suitability expected to decrease by 10–50%
	3 – Habitat suitability expected to decrease by > 50%
Changes in food availability	1 – Food availability likely to increase or be unchanged
	2 – Food availability likely to decrease
	3 – Major decrease in food availability
Changes in extreme weather	1 – No evidence of increased exposure to extreme weather
	2 – Some increase in exposure to extreme weather
	3 – Major increase in number and duration of extreme weather events

Thus, the species identified as being at high risk of climate change-driven declines are those which are declining in abundance now and are projected to continue to decline in future as a result of climate change in their core range, and that are also unlikely to benefit from compensatory increases facilitated by climate change outside of their current range. This approach has been applied to UK butterflies, suggesting that the majority are at low risk for climate change-mediated declines, with the exception of a small number of northern and montane species. Although not yet applied to birds, it is likely that at least for the UK, a similar pattern would also be apparent, with northern and upland birds showing the greatest evidence for recent population declines which can be linked to climate change (Green *et al.* 2008; Pearce-Higgins 2010; Pearce-Higgins *et al.* 2011b) that in the UK context will also have limited prospects for compensatory range expansion.

Gardali *et al.* (2012) applied a different approach to assess the vulnerability of Californian birds to climate change (Box 7.2) based on a combination of expert-based assessment

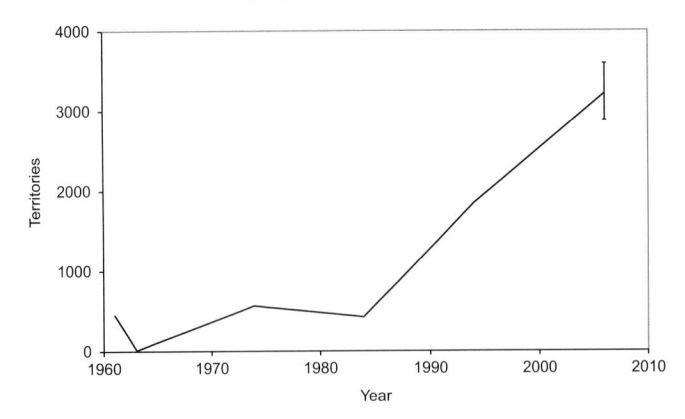

Figure 7.4 Increases in the Dartford warbler population in the UK from national surveys. Data from Robins and Bibby (1985), Gibbons and Wotton (1996), Wotton *et al.* (2009b). The final estimate for 2006 is bounded by 95% confidence intervals. Declines from 1961 to 1963 and 1974 to 1984 are attributable to cold winters.

of sensitivity using a number of ecological traits, and the results of climate envelope model projections and other analyses to infer the level of likely exposure to climate change. Of 29 species already classed as being of conservation concern, 21 were also classified as being vulnerable to climate change, further increasing their conservation prioritisation. The most vulnerable species tended to be Charadriiformes and Passeriiformes, and particularly birds of wetland habitats. A similar traits approach has been extended globally to a range of taxa, including birds, in order to assess the likely sensitivity, exposure and adaptive potential of species to climate change (Foden *et al.* 2013).

Each of these approaches (Huntley *et al.* 2007; Thomas *et al.* 2010; Gardali *et al.* 2012) highlights the need to reconsider the current predominantly national basis of conservation priority-setting, although clearly with an increasing array of methods and approaches available to do this, some degree of comparison and testing of these different methods would be desirable. An increasing population in one region or country may not be regarded as a conservation priority from the point of view of decision-makers in that region or country. However, if populations of that same species are declining because of climate change in other, lower latitude countries, then measures to maximise the compensatory increases at higher latitudes are essential at the larger international scale. A good example is provided by the Dartford warbler *Sylvia undata*, which is near-endemic to Western Europe. Dartford warbler populations in the UK have increased consistently during a period of warming since the 1980s (Figure 7.4). If conservation priorities in the UK were based only on population trends within the country, the species would no longer be a conservation priority. However, future projections of potential range for this species suggest that, in response to a moderate climate change scenario, more than 60% of the current European range may no longer be suitable by 2080 (Huntley *et al.* 2007), making growth of the UK component of the population increasingly important if its conservation status is not to deteriorate. In fact, the Dartford warbler is already amber listed in the UK because of its unfavourable conservation status elsewhere in Europe (Eaton *et al.* 2009), and in 2008, the global threat status of the species was uplisted by BirdLife International to Near-threatened on the IUCN Red List (BirdLife International

2012a), based on recent observed declines in Spain. Although covered by existing conservation prioritisation methodologies, the example of the Dartford warbler illustrates the importance of considering how local conservation priorities should be adapted in the light of the international context.

7.4.2 Conservation policy

As already outlined, the designation of areas for conservation is based upon assumptions that their characteristics and biota will remain quite stable over time. Crucially, the legal frameworks which underpin much conservation work and provide the imperative for many countries to undertake conservation action were drafted without consideration of the effects of climate change (Trouwborst 2011, 2012). This means that the establishment of static protected areas is a key component or mechanism for conservation. For example, both the Ramsar Convention, targeted at the conservation of wetlands, and the World Heritage Convention which protects a significant number of ecologically important sites, are clearly focussed on conservation within signatory territories. The Convention on Biological Diversity (CBD) also requires parties as far as possible to establish a system of protected areas where special measures must be taken to conserve biological diversity, and to develop guidelines for the selection, establishment and management of these. Similarly, the focus of the 1979 EU Birds Directive, whose success has already been outlined (Figure 7.1), is on EU Member States to designate SPAs for bird species listed in its Annex I and for (other) migratory bird species, 'in-so-far as these occur regularly in areas within their jurisdiction', whilst the EU Habitats Directive requires the designation of Special Areas of Conservation (SAC) to protect priority habitats and species. Although the original text of the Convention of Migratory Species (CMS) also makes no mention of climate change, by definition this agreement covers the conservation of species which cross state boundaries. As a result, CMS signatories already work together for the conservation of particular species, which should facilitate greater international cooperation with regards to trans-national climate change adaptation.

Whilst the focus of these agreements is very much on static conservation, their precise wording does allow for some flexibility with regards to climate change adaptation. For example, within the CBD there is provision for the management of species and habitats outside of these protected areas, which may provide some legal flexibility in relation to climate change adaptation. Similarly, together SPAs and SACs comprise the Natura 2000 network; 'a coherent European ecological network of protected areas', which may have the potential to effectively facilitate range expansion in the context of climate change by protecting sites important for a wide range of species (Johnston *et al.* 2013). In particular, as a result of the requirements of both the Birds and Habitat Directives to maintain species and habitats in favourable conservation status, there is greater potential to provide a mechanism for climate change adaptation than is currently realised (Dodd *et al.* 2010) through the following four elements:

1. The establishment of protected areas
2. Appropriate management inside and outside protected areas
3. The re-establishment of destroyed habitats
4. The creation of new habitats

Table 7.2 *Summary of outputs produced by international conventions or directives relevant to climate change adaptation. Relevant Conferences of the Parties (CoP) or communications (COM) to particular adaptation actions provide non-legally binding guidance on the interpretation and use of these conventions. Information summarised from Trouwborst (2010).*

	Consider climate change impacts	Prioritisation and planning	Habitat protection and creation in wider landscape	Management of core sites	Management of the wider landscape
Ramsar Convention	CoP 8.3			CoP 8.3	CoP 10.24
World Heritage Convention	29COM 7B.a			29COM 7B.a	
Convention on Biological Diversity		CoP 7.28	CoP 8.30	CoP 7.15 CoP 9.16	
Convention on Migratory Species	CoP 8.13 CoP 9.7	CoP 9.7	CoP 9.7	CoP 8.13	
European Union Birds and Habitats Directives	COM (2009) 147		COM (2006) 216	COM (2006) 216	COM (2006) 216

Recent case law establishes that member states are required to base their SPA networks on the best scientific knowledge available, and to ensure such knowledge is updated to determine the situation of Annex I and migratory species so that the most suitable sites are classified (Trouwborst 2011). This potentially provides the necessary flexibility for changes in response to climate change to be incorporated into the planning and protection of sites, as the best scientific knowledge changes.

In addition to using the existing legal flexibility within the original convention text, most international conservation conventions and directives are updated with additional texts agreed at Conferences of the Parties (CoP). Although these are not legally binding (Table 7.2), many promote the consideration of climate change as one of a number of potential impacts on the condition of core sites, and therefore identify the need to understand the potential for management of those core sites to increase resilience to climate change (Section 7.6). Few additional texts tackle the more difficult issue of accounting for and facilitating potential range shifts in response to climate change. At present it is not clear that these textual adjustments are leading to any changes in policy and practice on the ground, but that may come in time.

One of the best examples of the consideration of climate change in an international conservation agreement is the African-Eurasian Waterbirds Agreement (AEWA), which directs parties to, 'as far as possible, maintain the ecological character of the sites important for waterbird populations under changing climate conditions through appropriate management measures' and to 'provide wider habitat protection for species with dispersed breeding ranges, migration routes or winter ranges where the site conservation approach would have little effect, especially under climate change conditions'. In addition, the 4th Meeting of the Parties in 2008 requested the AEWA Technical Committee to 'assess whether the existing international networks of sites are sufficient for the protection of migratory waterbirds, including the projected climate change effects' and, if necessary, to indicate what complementary measures should be taken (MOP Resolution 4.14 adopted 19 September 2008). This has already been achieved for the Africa-Eurasian flyway (Maclean et al. 2007), including an assessment of species' vulnerability to climate change. Although relatively unsophisticated and with a number of shortcomings compared to the approach of Thomas et al. (2010), this provides an example of how a qualitative expert-based approach to prioritisation can be applied to situations with a relatively poor information base, at least at the whole flyway or species level.

To summarise, although approaches to conservation policy and prioritisation have been largely established in the absence of climate change, there is considerable potential for these approaches to be developed and adapted for a changing climate. In relation to policy, many of the required changes have been outlined through texts from CoP and other fora. However, these are not legally binding and it is unclear how important they will be in enabling better consideration of the needs for climate change adaptation in conservation policy and practice. Precisely how such practice should be adapted is the focus of the remainder of this chapter, starting with the protection of core sites.

7.5 The protection of a network of core sites

7.5.1 General points

As we discussed in Chapter 4, climate change is likely to add to existing pressures upon populations in protected areas, and indeed has led some to question the value of the entire protected area concept. It has been suggested that the current network of fixed protected areas needs to be replaced by a more fluid approach. This argument is superficially appealing because, as we have just discussed, the boundaries of protected areas have been identified, and their legal designation justified, using the recently observed distribution of species that are accorded special legal protection, including protection of the habitats upon which they depend. In addition, most of the theory underpinning conservation planning has been developed by relating a fixed spatial pattern of biodiversity to static threats (Pressey et al. 2007). Given the projected impacts of climate change upon the distribution of species and habitats, such a static assessment might be expected to become increasingly inappropriate over time. Protected areas may become increasingly climatically unsuitable for the species for which they have been designated (Opdam & Wascher 2004) and a static network of protected areas may, in future, be lacking in certain habitats required by newly colonising species or species for which a region has increased in international importance because of climate change.

In response, it has been proposed that protected areas may need to change from being static preservations of selected vulnerable species and habitats, to nodes within a landscape network of interconnected habitats (Opdam & Wascher 2004). Better connectivity is intended to fulfil two, linked, roles – that of linking subpopulations within a metapopulation to reduce their risk of extinction, and to facilitate the potential expansion of species distributions into new areas in response to climate change. Enhancement of connectivity may also require the intervening landscape between core patches of suitable habitat to become more favourable for the movement of species across that landscape. These topics are covered in Section 7.7. It may be possible to allow for likely future changes in the distribution of species when planning a protected area network; for example through using models to forecast the future boundaries of species' ranges and identifying a network that maximises conservation objectives in the future (e.g. Vos *et al.* 2008).

There are many sources of such uncertainty, which make the application of current conservation planning methods to projected future bird species distributions difficult to implement. One problem is that there are obvious reasons, presented in detail in Chapter 6, why climate envelope models of some bird species are unlikely to give a reliable picture of future change. For example, in the UK, the western capercaillie and corncrake are currently the focus of conservation programmes, but they are projected by climate envelope models to have no areas of suitable climate in the UK by the end of this century (Huntley *et al.* 2007). This could be used to suggest that conservation resources should no longer be directed towards such species because ultimately such conservation efforts will be futile. However, both species are among those for which such projections of future range are especially likely to be unreliable. This is because their recent ranges, which comprise the data used to fit the climate envelope models, are known to have been drastically modified in historical times by human activity: hunting and forest clearance in the case of capercaillie and mechanised grass mowing in the case of the corncrake.

Another source of uncertainty is that climate change is likely to alter the impacts of land use and other anthropogenic drivers of bird populations over time (van Rensburg *et al.* 2004; Pearce-Higgins & Gill 2010), a topic we will briefly consider in Chapter 9. Because predicting human responses to climate change is highly uncertain, this makes it even more difficult to plan for the future. Projecting future species distributions many decades hence based upon uncertain climate and land-use scenarios will therefore always be difficult (see also Section 6.5). Whilst undertaking such modelling work is useful and informative, specific results must therefore be used in a conservation planning context with caution, particularly in situations where the resulting conservation strategies differ radically from current strategies. Therefore, in addition to undertaking research to maximise the performance of these models (Pearce-Higgins *et al.* 2011a), conservationists should aim to use models alongside current information and best practice.

Although climate envelope model projections should be used with caution to inform specific decisions about the conservation of individual species, they can provide useful guidance on large-scale strategies for the planning of future protected area networks. Hole *et al.* (2011) implemented a procedure for identifying future priority areas for bird conservation in the face of climate change in sub-Saharan Africa, based on the IBA network. Their procedure used climate envelope models of a large set of species to assess proportions of species which would be expected to disappear from an IBA, to persist within it or to colonise it from elsewhere. The relative numbers of species within these categories were used to indicate the type of protection and management appropriate for a given IBA (Table 7.3). Model results also provided insights about regions where new protected areas would add value to the network by increasing the ability of species to maintain their current range extent under climate change, or at least to minimise losses.

Table 7.3 Climate change adaptation strategies at protected areas in relation to the likely persistence and turnover of species. Based on Hole et al. (2011), but adapted and amended to fit with the conservation toolkit presented in this chapter (conservation policy and prioritisation is not listed as this is overarching). The importance of each is given a score of 1 (high priority), 2 (desirable) or 3 (low priority).

Persistence	Colonisation	Core site protection	Core site management	Enhancing connectivity	Wider landscape management	Assisted colonisation
High	Low	1. Target refugia and areas of environmental diversity to maximise resilience. Expand protected area to maximise persistence	1. Manage within natural variability to maintain viable populations of persisting species	3. Unless required to maintain viable populations within protected areas	3. Unless required to maintain viable populations within protected areas	3. Unless losses become high
Low	Low	3. Unless to maximise conditions for emigrants	3. Unless to maximise conditions for emigrants	1. To facilitate dispersal and encourage colonisation of new sites	1. To facilitate dispersal and colonisation of new sites	1. To facilitate colonisation of new sites depending on habitat connectivity
High	High	1. Expand protected area to maximise resilience, persistence and colonisation	1. Ensuring that management for existing and colonising species is balanced	1. To facilitate dispersal and colonisation of new sites	1. To facilitate dispersal and colonisation of new sites	1. To facilitate colonisation of new sites depending on habitat connectivity
Low	High	1. To maximise source population of emigrants and chances of colonisation	1. Ensuring that management for existing and colonising species is balanced	1. To facilitate dispersal and colonisation of new sites	1. To facilitate dispersal and colonisation of new sites	1. To facilitate colonisation of new sites depending on habitat connectivity
Intermediate	Intermediate	2. Target refugia and areas of environmental diversity to maximise resilience. Expand area to maximise persistence.	2. Manage within natural variability to maintain viable populations of persisting species	3. Unless emigration or colonisation becomes significant	2. To help maintain viable populations and facilitate dispersal and colonisation	3. Unless emigration or colonisation become significant

Another potentially robust conclusion from climate envelope modelling for conservation planning is that the protection of natural and semi-natural habitats in areas that lie in the zones of overlap between current and modelled future potential ranges of species of conservation concern, or a group of species with similar habitats, is likely to be a sound investment for conservation under future climatic conditions. These locations will support important numbers of species now and, if the models are correct or have at least some degree of predictive power, then they are likely to continue to do so in the future. Even if the models are incorrect, then these locations are still good choices for protection because they support species of interest now. Because they contain natural and semi-natural habitats of conservation interest, they will also be good prospects for future colonisation by other rare species shifting their range in response to climate change (Thomas *et al.* 2012). Using bioclimate models to identify likely overlap zones between current and future projected ranges is therefore likely to be a sensible use of those models that should provide an effective strategy both for conservation now and for future climate change adaptation (Figure 7.3).

Given the many future uncertainties, conservation planning in a changing climate should follow a 'no regrets' principle. This means that the decisions which are made now to plan for future change should not be detrimental in the short term, and therefore if the projected future change does not happen, or does not happen as expected, the conservation actions undertaken will not have been wasteful or harmful. As already outlined, prioritising overlap zones between current distributions and projected future ranges is a good example of this. It is also important that uncertain conservation planning and action for the future does not take vital conservation funding away from important action now. The many current threats to biodiversity not related to climate change will continue to require significant and increasing amounts of conservation resources (BirdLife International 2008; Hoffmann *et al.* 2010). To illustrate the magnitude of the problem, a recent review of the conservation needs of endangered species in the United States identified 84% as requiring continued long-term management investment (Scott *et al.* 2010). If an increasing focus on climate change adaptation results in a significant shift in resources away from addressing current threats, it is likely to be extremely damaging to the short-term future of many species. There is clearly a balance to be struck between management for the future and protection of the present.

Conservationists making decisions about the location and implementation of protected areas must therefore make decisions which account for the current uncertainties about the future and do not take resources away from combating other conservation pressures. This is a very difficult task, but some general principles have been suggested which may help by increasing the synergy between current conservation needs and those of future climate change adaptation with respect to protected areas (Hodgson *et al.* 2009).

1. Maximise the extent of protected areas.
2. Enhance the protection of areas with high environmental heterogeneity.
3. Enhance the protection of areas that contain many species with small geographical ranges and/or high levels of threat.
4. Reduce the magnitude of other threats to biodiversity (covered in Section 7.8).

7.5.2 Increasing the extent of protected areas

There is a considerable advantage to having large areas of land under conservation protection for reasons unrelated to climate change. Large land areas tend to support larger numbers of species (Guilhaumon *et al.* 2008) and have a reduced risk of local extinction of the populations within them (Brashares *et al.* 2001; McCarthy *et al.* 2005). Under conditions of rapid climate change, where there is uncertainty over future climatic impacts on species, there may be additional advantages to large protected areas. If climate change is likely to have adverse effects on a species, then increasing its population size by expanding suitable protected areas may act as a buffer against extinction. Although population density may decline in future because of climate change, increasing the area suitable for a species could compensate for this and prevent the total population being reduced to a level where chance events could cause extinction.

There is a wealth of studies, across a wide range of habitats and locations, demonstrating that the diversity or persistence of bird species is positively correlated with the size of the area available to them (Table 7.4). About 40% of bird species respond negatively to habitat fragmentation and reduced patch size (Lampila *et al.* 2005). For some bird species, reductions in occurrence and population density in small patches are mediated through reduced productivity associated with higher brood parasitism and predation rates (see also Hinsley *et al.* 1999, 2006; Kurki *et al.* 2000; Chalfoun *et al.* 2002; Herkert *et al.* 2003) or reduced survival rates (Doherty & Grubb 2002; Hinsley *et al.* 2006; but see Pearce-Higgins *et al.* 2007a). Small habitat fragments support lower population densities as a result of the greater ratio of edge to interior, with edge habitat being of poorer quality for habitat specialists. Different habitats at patch edges encourage greater levels of incursion by brood parasites or predators from the surrounding landscape, turning such patches into population sinks. A widespread effect of fragmentation upon avian demography also appears to be that birds in small isolated patches are less likely to obtain a mate, perhaps because fragmentation limits dispersal (Lampila *et al.* 2005).

In general, the species which show the strongest associations with patch size, and therefore the largest negative effects of small patches, are habitat specialists (Schmiegelow *et al.* 1997; Bennett *et al.* 2004; Donnelly & Marzluff 2004), have large body size (Lindenmayer *et al.* 2002; Sodhi *et al.* 2004), and, in tropical forests, are frugivores or insectivores (Sodhi *et al.* 2004; Uezu *et al.* 2005; Mortensen *et al.* 2008). In the absence of climate change, the establishment of large protected areas is likely to benefit a wide range of bird species across all habitats. In the face of climate change, this principle will hold even more strongly for the following reasons:

1. Large sites are more likely to be resilient to other pressures and their potential interaction with climate change.
2. Large sites are more likely to be colonised successfully by species undergoing range shifts in response to climate change.
3. Populations within large sites are more likely to be resilient to extinction risk as a result of climate-driven reductions in abundance.
4. Populations within large sites are more likely to be protected from extinction caused by catastrophic climatic events.

Table 7.4 *Example studies of the effects of habitat patch size on bird persistence, abundance or demography*

Reference	Habitat	Location	Effect
Manu et al. (2007)	Tropical Forest	Nigeria	Only 1/62 species negatively affected by forest area but 12 species avoided edges and 20 were less common in isolated patches.
Şekercioğlu et al. (2002)	Tropical Forest	Costa Rica	Fragments contained 18% fewer species than continuous forest.
Stouffer & Bierregard (1995a)	Tropical Forest	Brazil	6/8 hummingbird species were more common following fragmentation.
Stouffer & Bierregard (1995b)	Tropical Forest	Brazil	Abundance of 28/33 insectivores declined following fragmentation.
Stratford & Stouffer (1999)	Tropical Forest	Brazil	Declines in abundance of 8/9 insectivores occurred following fragmentation
Pearce-Higgins et al. (2007a)	Tropical Forest	Bolivia	No difference in band-tailed manakin *Pipra fasciicauda* survival observed between forest fragment and continuous forest, but emigration rates from the fragment were lower.
Uezu et al. (2005)	Atlantic Forest	Brazil	Abundance of 3/7 species was related to patch size
Martensen et al. (2012)	Atlantic Forest	Brazil	Fragment size related to species richness and abundance, particularly in most fragmented landscapes.
Lindenmayer et al. (2002)	Eucalyptus Forest	Australia	34/90 species were less common in fragments than native forest
Santos et al. (2002)	Mediterranean Forest	Spain	Occurrence of all species was related to patch size
Donnelly & Marzluff (2004)	Temperate Forest	USA	9/20 species were absent from small (< 42 ha) patches
Hinsley et al. (1995b)	Temperate Forest	UK	Occurrence of 20/31 species was related to patch size
Trzcinski et al. (1999)	Temperate Forest	Canada	Occurrence of 25/31 species was related to forest area
Van Dorp & Opdam (1987)	Temperate Forest	The Netherlands	Occurrence of 26/32 species was related to patch size
Vergara & Armesto (2009)	Temperate Forest	Chile	9/20 species were negatively affected by fragmentation
Villard et al. (1999)	Temperate Forest	Canada	Occurrence of 12/15 species was related to forest area or configuration.
Davis (2004)	Savanna	Canada	Occurrence/abundance of 4/9 species related to patch size
Herkert (1994)	Savanna	USA	8/15 species affected by patch area
Johnson & Igl (2001)	Savanna	USA	Consistent effects of patch size apparent in 6/15 species, some evidence for 6 more

5. Large sites are more likely to contain a wider range of habitats and continue to accommodate species whose habitat preferences change in response to climate change.
6. Large sites will contain larger populations that will produce more dispersing colonists.

In developed countries, most protected areas are comprised of natural or semi-natural vegetation types which are rare in the wider countryside because they have been converted to farmland, urban areas or other human land uses. Their rarity and susceptibility to conversion are likely to be the main reasons that they are protected. For species largely dependent upon these scarce habitat types, these reserves are likely to become the main locations where they can exist. Given the projected growth of the human population and its per capita requirements for land, we envisage a continued increase in the extent of human land use and rates of habitat loss, so that this pattern will exist in more countries worldwide. Hence, protected areas are likely to become increasingly important for the conservation of species intolerant of human land use, because they will simply not be able to exist elsewhere in any numbers.

We have already noted that climate change is likely to result in significant redistributions of species and assemblages (Chapter 6). For species that depend upon habitats that are rare and susceptible to conversion to human use, the continued existence of protected areas outside their current ranges increases the chance that areas of suitable habitat will continue to persist, and that can be colonised in future. For example, if the distribution of a forest species in a heavily managed landscape has the potential to shift polewards as a result of climate change, then the only areas that it will be able to colonise will be reserves containing sufficiently large and closely spaced patches of forest in locations which become climatically suitable for it in the future. The protection of those forest areas now is therefore also of long-term value under a changed climate, beyond whatever value it has for the assemblage of species currently present. Thus the protection of large reserves of natural and semi-natural habitats now will benefit currently threatened species dependent on those habitats as well as providing habitat for future colonisation by other species with similar requirements. Having large reserves increases the likelihood of such colonisation occurring, and also increases the likelihood that a site can support sufficient individuals of colonising species to establish a viable population. Large populations in large reserves are also more likely to produce a greater number of potential colonists to other parts of the potential future range than smaller populations.

A specific example of this principle is the protection of wetland sites in the UK, where most large wetland areas, such as the fens, have been drained and converted into arable farmland in recent centuries, resulting in the widespread loss of many large wetland bird species (Shrubb 2003; Yalden & Albarella 2009). In an attempt to stem these losses, wetland nature reserves have been established, and new wetland sites created, including the conversion of arable farmland back to wetland (Figure 7.5). These have been valuable for the conservation and population recovery of a number of wetland bird species which had previously declined. For example, they have provided areas of healthy and accessible fish populations within reedbeds for the great bittern (Tyler *et al.* 1998; Gilbert *et al.* 2003), safe nesting and foraging habitats for western marsh harrier *Circus aeruginosus*, and the only available habitats for reedbed specialists such as the bearded parrotbill (bearded tit) *Panurus biarmicus* (e.g. Poulin *et al.* 2002).

Based upon climate envelope modelling (Huntley *et al.* 2007), it is anticipated that future climatic change will lead these sites to be colonised by other obligate wetland species which currently are only found on continental Europe. This has already occurred.

274 · Conservation in a changing climate

Figure 7.5 (a) Reedbed and wetland habitat created on what was once a carrot field to counteract the potential loss of coastal reedbed, now forms part of the RSPB nature reserve at Lakenheath Fen. (b) Part of the coastal reedbed at Minsmere RSPB nature reserve damaged by saltwater inundation during autumnal storm surges, where the long-term viability of breeding bittern populations is threatened. Note also the heathland on the ridge at the back of the photograph is one of the locations on the Suffolk coast recently colonised by Dartford warblers.

Wetland habitats in the UK have been colonised by a number of species from the south. These include the Cetti's warbler *Cettia cetti* (Robinson *et al.* 2007b) and little egret *Egretta garzetta*, which have probably previously been excluded by lower mean temperatures and frequent cold winters, although egret populations may also have been recovering from the consequences of historic persecution. In 2010, the first breeding records for both little bittern *Ixobrychus minutus* and purple heron *Ardea purpurea* in the UK were recorded on two wetland nature reserves on the south coast of England. These are also species whose ranges are projected to contract in southern Europe as a result of increasing temperature (Huntley *et al.* 2007). They only occur in wetlands, so the provision of wetland reserves in the UK is likely to increase the chances of a successful continuation of these initial colonisation events. Thus, the current conservation action to protect and enhance existing areas of rare natural and semi-natural wetland habitats in the UK provides current conservation benefit now, and will provide future conservation benefit in a changing climate, even if there is a change in the precise species assemblage utilising those habitats. It is a no-regrets option. Indeed, new wetland bird colonists to the UK have preferentially arrived at protected areas containing extensive wetland habitats, but then through time, have increasingly dispersed to other, non-protected wetlands in the wider countryside (Hiley *et al.* 2013).

The importance of protected areas being the first locations which range-expanding species tend to colonise is illustrated by analysis of more than 250 invertebrate species which have expanded their geographical range in the UK. Ninety-eight per cent of these were more likely to have colonised protected areas than other locations (Thomas *et al.* 2012). Of five habitat-specialist range-expanding bird species, three (great bittern, woodlark and Dartford warbler) also showed a significant preference for the colonisation of protected areas, whilst for a further two, the association was in the same direction, but non-significant (Figure 7.6a). On average across these five birds, the ratio of colonisation of protected areas to other locations was 3.76 ± 0.99. Thus, range-expanding bird species were almost four times more likely to colonise core sites designated as protected areas than random locations nearby in the landscape. This study provides important evidence of the long-term utility of protected areas in a changing climate, although additional work is required to identify why this is the case. Is it simply because these sites provide the only areas of suitable habitat for colonisation, or do they also tend to be managed more favourably? Tentative support for the former hypothesis comes from the tendency for species with a high proportion of recorded colonisations in protected areas to be more concentrated in semi-natural habitats (Figure 7.6b), although proactive management has certainly been important to enhance the expansion of the bittern (Wotton *et al.* 2009a). It is the fact that SPAs in Europe protect a network of sites of the same habitat designated for a wide range of species that ensures that they are likely to continue to be resilient to climate change effects in the future (Johnston *et al.* 2013).

As well as affecting the ideal total extent of protected habitat, climate change might also affect the ideal size of individual reserves. If increased climate variability is expected in the future, the optimum reserve arrangement might change from a few moderately sized reserves that most efficiently minimise extinction risk now, to one or a smaller number of large reserves. In that case, it may be only in large reserves that populations are large

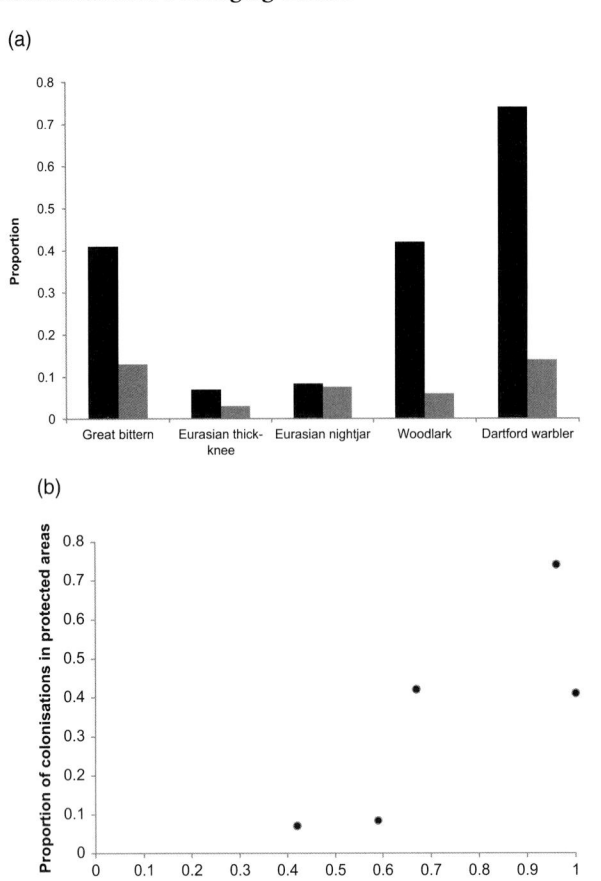

Figure 7.6 (a) The proportion of recorded colonisations of five species of range-expanding southerly distributed bird species in the UK which were on protected areas (defined as SSSIs; black bars) compared to the proportion of all land within colonised areas that was protected (grey bars). Drawn from data in Thomas *et al.* (2012). (b) The importance of protected areas for colonisation is related to the association of that species with areas of semi-natural habitat (heathland and wetland), as assessed for great bittern by Tyler *et al.* (1998), Eurasian thick-knee *Burhinus oedicnemus* by Green *et al.* (2000), Eurasian nightjar *Caprimulgus europaeus* by Conway *et al.* (2007), woodlark by Conway *et al.* (2009) and Dartford warbler by Wotton *et al.* (2009b).

enough to persist through periods of adverse weather. However, much depends upon the expected spatial extent of adverse weather events. If potentially catastrophic events are localised within small areas and occur at unpredictable locations, then it may become necessary to establish many smaller reserves to spread the risk and provide insurance against such extreme events.

If the tendency for higher population density of species to occur in the core of its geographical range compared with the edge is at least partly caused by climate (see Box 1.1), climate change is likely to alter the population density of a species at individual sites (see also Chapter 4 and Figure 5.3). This will have implications for estimating optimum protected area size for that species. In the case of a habitat specialist whose abundance is correlated with habitat quality, if climate change results in a reduction in the carrying capacity of a site, for example by reducing prey abundance, then this will reduce the chance of long-term persistence. Take a species that requires a minimum population of 50 pairs to be viable over a given time period. Were climate change to reduce the carrying capacity of a site by half, then currently viable sites which support 50 pairs will be exposed to a heightened risk of local extinctions as their carrying capacity declines to 25 pairs, notwithstanding the effects of any potential increase in climatic variability which may further increase the minimum number of pairs required for long-term population persistence. Climate change therefore increases the uncertainty associated with estimating the optimum protected area for a particular species within a reserve network (McCarthy *et al.* 2005). This means that the protection of as large an area as possible may become an appropriate insurance strategy. The need for caution in the face of a changing climate may result in decisions which might be seen as overly precautionary within a static paradigm. It is therefore crucial that models which are used for future conservation planning incorporate these uncertainties as much as possible, and are applied by practitioners and policy-makers who fully acknowledge and understand their limitations.

A further complication for conservationists is that species' habitat preferences may change as a result of climate change, making individual protected areas more or less important for particular populations or species. This again argues in favour of the protection of large sites in the face of climate change, as these are likely to support a greater range of habitats and micro-habitats than a small site. Although this phenomenon has largely been studied among invertebrates (e.g. Davies *et al.* 2006), the same principle may apply to birds. For example, common stonechats *Saxicola torquata*, by virtue of their sensitivity to cold winter weather, have long been associated with lowland and coastal heathland in the UK, which usually have mild winters (Gibbons *et al.* 1993). Heathland in England has been significantly reduced in area, degraded and fragmented as a result of afforestation, agricultural expansion and housing development (Rose *et al.* 2000). For this reason, stonechats had become increasingly associated with nature reserves and designated sites by the 1980s. However, climate warming during the next two decades had reduced the severity of winter weather effects on this species, enabling populations to expand into upland areas (Sim *et al.* 2005), where it occupied widespread areas of extensively managed heather moorland, largely outside nature reserves. Upland moorland now provides stonechats with habitat with similar vegetation structure to lowland heathland which the birds were previously unable to colonise because of cold winter conditions at higher elevation (Pearce-Higgins & Grant 2006), although this colonisation was then checked by severe winter weather in 2010 and 2011. The current expansion of the Dartford warbler away from southern coastal heaths of England follows a similar pattern (Wotton *et al.* 2009b), and probably has a similar underlying cause (Bradbury *et al.* 2011).

These examples illustrate the potential of climate change to increase the habitat niche breadth of some species, even though the climatic niche may remain similar. In some cases this may reduce their reliance on protected areas. However, other species may become more reliant upon nature reserves as a result of climate change. This is illustrated by the effects of agricultural development in the UK upon lowland wet grassland waders. Species such as common snipe *Gallinago gallinago*, common redshank and northern lapwing in lowland parts of the UK were formerly associated with extensively managed pastureland with wet soil or surface flooding which persisted into their spring and summer breeding seasons (e.g. Shrubb 2003). However, increasing intensification of grassland management, particularly artificial drainage, has reduced the abundance and availability to the birds of aquatic and soil invertebrates. Hence, the suitability of the wider countryside as breeding habitat for these species has been substantially reduced (Sheldon 2002). In lowland England, populations of these species are now largely restricted to nature reserves where wetland habitats are artificially maintained, often by storage of winter rains (Wilson *et al.* 2005). The effects of this change in land use in the wider countryside thus mimic the likely effects upon these species of projected increases in summer droughts.

7.5.3 Protecting areas with high environmental heterogeneity

In this section we consider the benefits of including within protected areas land with high environmental heterogeneity. The rationale for this is that, as just discussed, climate change may result in a species' habitat preferences being altered, or in altitudinal or latitudinal changes in distribution in order that the species remains within its climatic niche. In this case, a protected area which contains a wide range of habitats, particularly variants of a particular habitat and ecotones between habitats, is more likely to accommodate changes in species distribution within its boundaries (Hannah *et al.* 2005). These potential shifts in location and habitat may also require connectivity across a gradient of habitats. This principle suggests that the conservation of mountain areas, with a high altitudinal range and topographical diversity, will be particularly important in a changing climate, as these will naturally encompass a high degree of environmental variability within a relatively small land-surface area. They are likely to protect a wide range of microclimates, which may result in temperature variation occurring over tens or hundreds of metres that is analogous to distances of hundreds of kilometres across a flat landscape (Suggitt *et al.* 2011). Conservation of natural and semi-natural habitats along an elevational gradient and including sites with different aspects would potentially allow a species to track a changing climate by changing its elevational limit upwards or changing from slopes facing away from the pole to those which face towards it. Some taxa may therefore be able to persist in cool or moist microclimate refugia at latitudes that otherwise would be too hot or dry for them.

Although there is increasing evidence for such refugia being important for plants and invertebrates, the degree to which birds are likely to benefit from this principle remains uncertain, because most have home ranges that extend over hundreds of metres, and as already discussed, require the maintenance of a significant population size to be robust to extinction risk. Indeed, the range expansion of the Dartford warbler in the UK, a relatively sedentary species sensitive to winter temperature, and therefore the sort of species for which microclimate might be important, appears to have been only weakly affected by micro-variation in slope and aspect (Bradbury *et al.* 2011). Stronger evidence of the importance of microclimate is highlighted by a study of whinchat *Saxicola rubetra* distribution in Scotland. This previously widespread farmland bird is now largely restricted to upland areas of the UK, where it appears strongly associated with south-facing slopes, which of course have a warmer microclimate. Indeed, above 500 m, the only territories recorded in some locations were on south-facing slopes (Calladine & Bray 2012). Therefore, variation in microclimate may have the potential to influence the fine-scale distribution of some bird species. Thus, in a warming world, north-facing slopes may provide cool refugia for birds against climate warming, although this potential may depend upon the spatial scale at which birds make settlement decisions and the minimum area required to maintain viable populations, and certainly requires testing.

Areas of high environmental heterogeneity, such as mountains, tend to support a high degree of species endemism (Simberlof 1976, Ohlemuller et al. 2008). This is a second strong case for the conservation of such habitats regardless of climate change. Species which occupy mountainous areas, especially at low latitudes, tend to have small geographical ranges and small populations, making them more vulnerable to extinction. Areas of tropical montane forest should therefore be a focus for detailed research on changes in the fine-scale distribution of species as a result of changes in climate, to assess how resilient such small populations are likely to be to future climate change. This will help assess for such species whether topographical heterogeneity may help to buffer them against extinction. Many of these species have only recently diverged from allopatric sibling species as a result of geographical barriers such as mountain ranges and river systems (Section 5.3), and it remains unclear the extent to which they may be vulnerable to climatic shifts in distribution which may lead to the re-mixing of previously allopatric populations.

7.5.4 Prioritising centres of endemism

Concentrating conservation effort on areas where several bird species with small global ranges are found together has been recognised as a good use of conservation resources for many years (Stattersfield et al. 1998). Such areas, termed Endemic Bird Areas by BirdLife International, are concentrated in tropical mountains, tropical forests and on islands. Measures of endemism give an indication of the irreplaceability of the biodiversity of a particular region. If the habitats within that region are damaged, then endemic species affected are at higher risk of global extinction (Brooks et al. 2006). Basing priorities on the distribution of species with restricted ranges tends to give very different results from using measures of the local richness of all species (e.g. Orme et al. 2005; Brooks et al. 2006). Maps of species richness (e.g. Figure 5.2) tend to reflect patterns of the distribution of common and widespread species rather than those of greatest rarity or vulnerability due to their restricted range size. Hence, there are considerable differences in the spatial pattern of conservation priority areas around the globe depending on whether they are defined on the basis of species richness, threatened species richness or endemism. The targeting of highly threatened regions of high biodiversity for conservation would prioritise areas of endemism and threat, leading to greatest conservation effort in tropical mountain and island chains and areas of rapid habitat loss, whilst targeting the most diverse regions would give greater priority to extensive lowland tropical forest areas with lower levels of endemism but high diversity. However, using various approaches that combine information about the distribution of different taxonomic groups and indicators of the degree of threat

(Myers *et al.* 2000; Possingham & Wilson 2005; Lamoreux *et al.* 2006), it is possible to appropriately prioritise the conservation of both highly threatened environments of high conservation importance and highly diverse regions currently subject to reduced threat, particularly at large spatial scales (Reid 1998; Brooks *et al.* 2006).

It has been proposed that areas with high biological diversity, especially of species with small global ranges, and high levels of current threat, should remain as high priorities for conservation when climate change is also taken into account (Hodgson *et al.* 2009). This approach might not only minimise the risk of further species' loss due to existing pressures, but may also maximise the protection of species in the future, because such areas support high environmental heterogeneity, particularly in the tropical mountain areas of the Andes, Africa and Asia. Here, protected areas should be as large as possible to maximise this heterogeneity and the size of protected populations to increase their long-term viability.

What about potential shifts of species' ranges caused by future climate change? As outlined previously, the performance of existing priority areas for birds in Africa under projected climate change has recently been assessed using climate envelope models. Models of 815 priority species distributions indicated that, by 2085 under an intermediate emissions scenario, approximately 88–92% of species would continue to have some potential future range with suitable climate within Important Bird Areas (IBAs) designated for them, whilst a further 8–11% would have suitable climate in other IBAs (Hole *et al.* 2009). Less than 1% of species were modelled to have no suitable climate within the current IBA network. However, rates of species turnover at the individual sites were projected to approach 35–45%, particularly in south-central Africa. Hence, a high capacity for dispersal would be needed for species to maintain their current range extents. Despite the potential impact that climate change may have upon species' distributions, these results suggest that African IBAs, which are identified on the basis of current avian biodiversity, should continue to form a high priority for protection (see Table 7.3). However, it should be noted that almost half of IBAs are completely unprotected, and much of the remainder face severe threats (Butchart *et al.* 2012).

Unfortunately, the level of threat that protected areas will face is likely to continue to increase as a result of continued human pressure upon the environment (McKee *et al.* 2004). For example, in a study of 198 protected forests around the world, 70% have become more isolated over the last 20 years as a result of habitat loss in surrounding areas, whilst 25% have also lost habitat within their boundaries (DeFries *et al.* 2005). Changes have been particularly severe in parts of South America and south-east Asia (Figure 7.7). Not only do these changes reduce the distribution and abundance of the forest species present, increasing their current threat level (Buchanan *et al.* 2008), but they also reduce the capacity of those species to cope with climate change by further fragmenting their habitat, limiting their ability to track their climate niche through time, and reducing their populations, increasing their vulnerability to extinction.

More widely, given that many of the IBAs discussed above are not currently protected, such anthropogenic pressures are of significant concern for their likely long-term viability. For example, in South Africa both avian biodiversity and human populations tend to be concentrated in areas of high rainfall. As demand for water resources is likely to increase, and be potentially exacerbated by future drought (Solomon *et al.* 2009), this is likely to

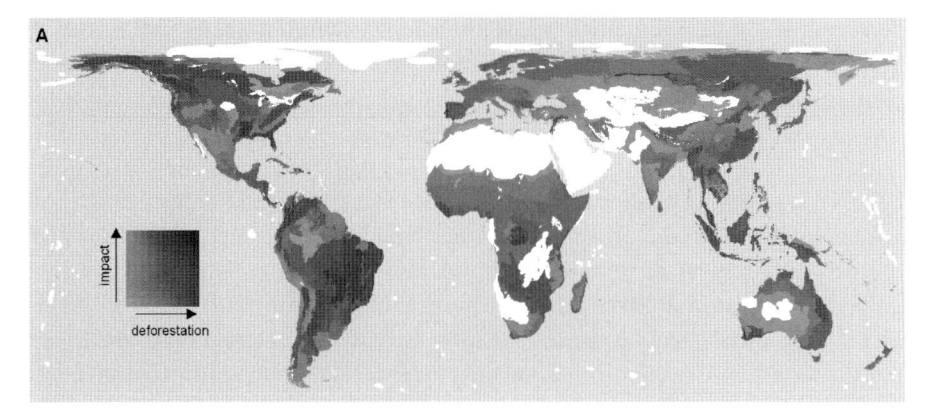

Figure 7.7. Global assessment of deforestation rates during 2000–2005 in relation to their impact on forest-dependent birds (from Buchanan *et al.* 2011, which gives a colour version).

increase pressure on both avian biodiversity and human populations, potentially leading to conflict between the two (van Rensburg *et al.* 2004). Maximising the protection of areas of natural and semi-natural habitats is therefore a robust long-term conservation priority, but it will be a real challenge to implement in many parts of the world. As habitats become increasingly degraded, fragmented and isolated by human pressures, combined with increasing severity of climate change, management to facilitate the movement of species across the wider landscape between protected areas will become increasingly important (Section 7.7). Achieving this will require sustainable development to support increased human populations in the areas between protected areas in a way which minimises the isolation and fragmentation of the protected habitats. Given these difficulties, ensuring appropriate management of protected sites to maximise their resilience to climate change will also be increasingly important as they are likely to support higher and higher fractions of the world's vulnerable bird species.

7.6 Adaptation management of core sites

The management of core sites is a vital tool for existing conservation action in order to prevent or reverse harm to species of conservation interest within protected areas. The same approach may be applied to adaptation to increase the resistance of a particular population or site to the effects of climate change, and may be extended across a protected area network impacted by climate change (Table 7.3). The intention of such adaptation is to reduce the magnitude of, or eliminate, negative effects of climate change at that site on the demographic rates of the species of concern. This principle differs little from the model already well-established and outlined for the implementation of management to address any other conservation problems (Section 7.2.3) and indeed is based upon that same model, of attempting to reduce negative effects of anthropogenic change (Pearce-Higgins 2011b).

Given the timescale over which climate change is occurring and the degree of inter-annual variation in weather conditions, robust long-term monitoring of bird abundance, distribution and demography is needed to identify the impacts of climate change. Most of the examples of species whose populations have been demonstrated to be affected by climate change cited in Chapters 3 and 4 are not necessarily those most sensitive to change, but often simply the species most amenable to study. Thus, great tits and pied flycatchers may not be the species most seriously affected by phenological mismatch, but because they nest in artificial nest boxes, they have been studied in detail, providing the long-term data with the power to examine variation in breeding phenology and breeding success with respect to temperature and mismatch (Both 2010b). Similarly, Eurasian golden plover are not necessarily the most susceptible upland bird to climate change, and indeed, others may be more vulnerable by virtue of their diet (Pearce-Higgins 2010), but the long run of monitoring data collected by Derek Yalden from Snake Summit in the Peak District has made it possible to understand the climatic drivers of population change (Pearce-Higgins *et al.* 2010). The existence of robust long-term data on species populations greatly facilitates the understanding of how bird populations are affected by climate change, albeit from a small and biased set of the world's bird species.

Research on the demographic mechanisms by which climate change is impacting upon a species (Chapter 4) provides insights into potential adaptive management approaches. We suggest that management for climate adaptation can have two different objectives which we call *counteracting* and *compensatory*. Counteracting management acts by reversing the change in external conditions which is having a negative effect on the demographic rates of a species and causing its population to decline. Compensatory management accepts the negative change that is causing the population decline. However, it compensates for it through other management to enhance demographic rates to a degree which cancels out the continuing negative influence of the change. Counteracting management must, by definition, reverse the negative change in the demographic rate which is the demographic mechanism underlying the population decline. However, compensatory management might affect that rate but it could affect any other demographic rate instead.

7.6.1 Examples of counteracting adaptation management

Research into adaptation management is relatively new, and there are few studies so far which have examined this issue in detail. As far as we are aware, none have demonstrated that site-specific adaptation may successfully increase the resistance of a population to climate change. However, research on southerly populations of the Eurasian golden plover, vulnerable to potential effects of warming mediated through reductions in prey abundance, go some way towards this. Here, there are proposals for a potential counteracting adaptation method based upon an understanding of impacts of annual variations in weather on golden plover populations (Section 4.3.3) and a demographic model to predict the consequences of climate change adaptation (Pearce-Higgins 2011a). As outlined in Chapter 4, an important mechanism by which golden plover populations are affected by climate change is through the desiccation and death of early larval instars of their cranefly prey in the soil during hot summers. In springs when the supply of craneflies is low, golden plover chick survival and breeding productivity are reduced.

This understanding suggests a method for counteracting management for golden plover populations affected by a trend towards warmer summers. Much of the UK uplands in

7.6 Adaptation management of core sites · 283

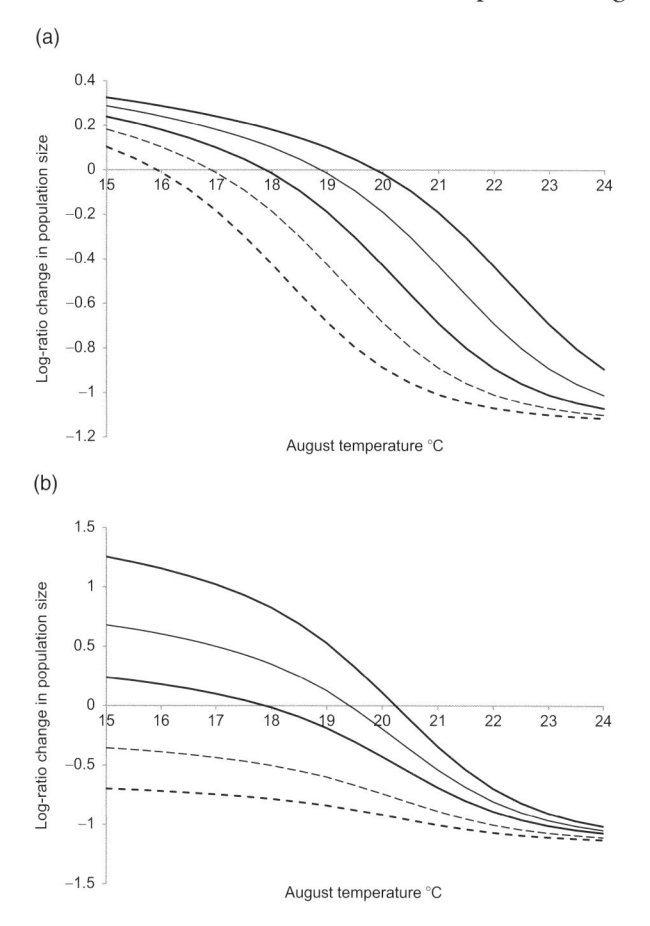

Figure 7.8 Modelled variation in the log-ratio of annual change in a golden plover population as a function of mean daily maximum August temperature with a two-year lag in relation to varying scenarios of cranefly abundance (a), and nest and chick predation (b). The thick central line is based on values for the Snake Summit study area of Pearce-Higgins *et al.* (2010). Thick outlying lines represent fourfold increases (solid – going up) or decreases (dashed – going down) in cranefly abundance (a), or doubling/halving of nest and chick predation rates (b). Intermediate lines represent values half-way between the two. Reproduced with permission from Pearce-Higgins (2011a).

which golden plovers breed has been drained (Holden *et al.* 2007). Reversing this land drainage by a programme of drain blocking might reduce soil desiccation and increase the survival of cranefly larvae and, consequently, golden plover chicks. Modelling suggests that if habitat manipulation were able to double the abundance of emerged craneflies for a given summer temperature, then this would enable golden plovers to resist a 1 °C rise in mean August temperature (Figure 7.8a). A fourfold increase in cranefly abundance for a given temperature would be equivalent to increasing the resistance of golden plovers to a 2 °C temperature rise (Pearce-Higgins 2011a).

Recent experiments where the consequence of drain blocking has been tested suggest that it may increase the abundance of emerged craneflies within at least 10 m of the drains by up to 4.5 times (Carroll *et al.* 2011). How this translates into an improvement in food supply for an average brood of plover chicks will depend upon the distance over which this effect extends beyond the drains, the spacing between them and their distribution within the home range of a typical brood. For example, conservatively, if this effect extends to only 10 m from the drains, at a site where the drains are 100 m apart, this would translate to a 1.7 times improvement in cranefly abundance. This crude assessment is based upon a fixed relationship between drain blocking and cranefly abundance, but drain blocking may change the relationship between August temperature and abundance. Given that the mechanism for this effect is likely to be drought, raising water levels is likely to reduce the slope of the negative relationship between temperature and cranefly abundance, and therefore between August temperature and golden plover population change. This means that the analysis just outlined may underestimate the magnitude of benefit for golden plovers. Further work is required to test this fully, but in the meantime, drain blocking is being conducted widely across the UK uplands as a means of habitat restoration. This management will also deliver effective and evidence-based climate change adaptation. Because this proposal directly reverses the postulated mechanism by which climate change produces an adverse effect on golden plover populations, it is an example of counteracting adaptation management.

Another example of counteracting management concerns the effects of flooding on a population of black-tailed godwits breeding on wet grassland in Cambridgeshire, UK. This species has a small population in the UK, concentrated at the Ouse Washes which was designated as a Special Protection Area for the species, and also at the nearby Nene Washes (Ratcliffe *et al.* 2005). During periods of heavy rain, the Ouse Washes are deliberately flooded by diverting high river flows away from highly productive adjacent farmland. If this occurs during the breeding season, it causes the loss of godwit nests. The birds have a short breeding season, so there is no opportunity for the birds to recover by re-nesting (Section 4.3.3). In a detailed study of this problem, nest and chick survival probabilities were measured in a small number of years of intensive fieldwork, and then used to construct a demographic model to simulate the effects of changing the frequency of summer floods. This showed that recent increases in the frequency of spring flooding, which have been caused by a combination of changes in rainfall patterns and catchment management, were sufficient to account for the observed 90% godwit population decline at the Ouse Washes. By contrast, there was high breeding productivity at the nearby Nene Washes, where flooding rarely occurred because of its different river catchment characteristics. The godwit population was increasing at the Nene Washes at the same time that the Ouse Washes population was declining, with the difference being consistent with expectations from the population model.

Having been validated in this way, the population model was then used to explore the potential consequences of a range of flood avoidance options of varying cost. This identified the most cost-effective option to be creation of a new wet grassland habitat on arable farmland adjacent to the Ouse Washes. This habitat creation scheme is now in progress. Although only six arable fields alongside the Ouse Washes have been converted to wet grassland and a larger programme would be required to restore the godwit population (Hirons 2010); in 2012, the first pair of godwits successfully bred on those fields. This is also an example of counteracting adaptation because provision of alternative habitat free from flooding directly avoids the negative effects of flooding on breeding productivity.

The effect of climate change on passerine birds of temperate woodland that rely on caterpillars taken from the foliage of trees to feed their chicks was discussed in Chapter 3. Here reductions in breeding productivity can occur because climate change causes an increased mismatch in the relative timing of breeding and the peak in caterpillar abundance. The considerable variation in prey abundance and phenology between habitats within the same region (Both 2012) suggests the possibility of a counteracting adaptation management option. The ratio of deciduous to coniferous trees (Tremblay *et al.* 2003, 2005; Pimentel & Nilsson 2007), and tree size (Visser *et al.* 2006) affect the abundance of caterpillars and the timing of the peak. A greater frequency of laying of second clutches occurs in blue tits in higher quality deciduous and mixed woodland than low-quality coniferous woods with fewer, and later emerging, caterpillars (Fargallo 2004). This means that a wood with a mix of tree sizes or species may provide a greater temporal spread of caterpillars than in a wood dominated by a single species, potentially reducing the effects of phenological mismatch. Some evidence for this comes from the fact that pied flycatcher population trends have been more negative in deciduous rather than mixed woodlands (Both 2012). The potential for management of these woodlands to increase the resilience of the flycatcher and other bird populations to climate change has not yet been studied in depth, perhaps because the birds involved are relatively abundant and not the focus of bespoke conservation action. However, were the detrimental effects of phenological mismatch to occur more widely in deciduous woodlands, discussed in Section 3.4.3, then the potential for counteracting habitat management options to reduce such effects should be tested further, particularly as the management decisions to increase the resilience of woodlands to a late twenty-first century climate need to be undertaken now.

Many other widely applied site and habitat management options fall into the category of counteracting adaptation. Their application will depend upon an understanding of ways in which climate change affects a particular system or population of conservation interests, and using that knowledge to identify and trial the most effective intervention measures that may be applied. For example, if climate change is likely to threaten the persistence of a wetland through reduced spring and summer rainfall, management to enhance the flow of water into that wetland, or to construct storage reservoirs to save winter rains to benefit species adversely affected by drying out of wetlands, may be appropriate counteracting adaptation options. Many conservationists are well practised in such hydrological management. Alternatively, if warming is driving the expansion of an invasive non-native species that is having negative impacts on other species of conservation concern, then measures to control and remove that non-native should be favoured. Given that negative effects of climate change on birds may tend to occur through altered species interactions (Cahill *et al.* 2013), an increasing focus of counteracting climate change adaptation is likely to be to manage such species interactions, building on existing conservation practices of habitat and vegetation management, the control of harmful species and the enhancement of prey populations.

7.6.2 Examples of compensatory adaptation management

Counteracting adaptation management options require information about the mechanism through which climate change affects a species. This is not required for compensatory adaptation, which instead relies on an understanding of the likely effects of a management unrelated to climate change upon the population growth rate. We illustrate the principle of compensatory adaptation management with reference again to golden plovers. There is evidence that the population size of these ground-nesting waders may be limited by an abundance of generalist predators, such as red foxes and carrion crows *Corvus corone*, which cause nest and chick predation (Parr 1992; Pearce-Higgins & Yalden 2003a). Perhaps as a result, population densities of golden plover and some other wader species are greater on upland areas in the UK managed for the shooting of red grouse than on areas with similar vegetation without such management (Tharme *et al.* 2001). This difference might be due to predator control, which is widely practiced by grouse moor managers, though other management practices, such as heather burning, also might have contributed to the effect. An experimental study in which predator control was manipulated with other management being held approximately constant indicated that predator control probably accounted for most or all of this difference (Fletcher *et al.* 2010). Golden plover breeding productivity was markedly higher during periods in which predator control was applied and there was also an indication that adult population density also increased during these periods, when compared with trends at unmanaged sites. This management, if applied to a golden plover population being adversely affected by effects of climatic change, could therefore be compensatory, as a simulated reduction in the predation of golden plover nests or chicks to mimic an increase in the intensity of predator control also increased the resistance of a golden plover population to warmer temperatures (Figure 7.8b).

Simulating a combination of both a maximal realistic level of predator control and maximal realistic potential increase in cranefly abundance for Snake Summit (which being relatively undrained is already a good site for golden plovers) might make the population largely resistant to a 2 °C rise in August temperature (Pearce-Higgins 2011a). Although based upon simulation, the results of this modelling exercise are encouraging for the potential of site-based adaptation to successfully enable populations to be resistant to quite significant magnitudes of climate change and, as outlined above, when applied to other, more heavily drained sites, or with a greater abundance of generalist predators, may result in even more positive population outcomes.

The modelling exercise for golden plover lends support to the general principle of continuing and strengthening existing conservation action as a means of successful climate change adaptation. It is interesting to observe from Figure 7.8 that at low summer temperatures, cranefly abundance does not limit golden plover productivity and populations. Here, variation in predation appears the key determinant of population trajectory, perhaps accounting for the current sensitivity of the species to variation in predator control (Tharme *et al.* 2001; Fletcher *et al.* 2010). However, based on the assumptions of this particular simulation, at high temperatures it is cranefly abundance which appears to be limiting. It is therefore important to determine the factor which is population limiting, and understand how that is likely to change with temperature in order to prioritise the most effective adaptation management. At sites where populations appear to be declining as a result of high rates of predation, increases in predator control might confer some resistance to climate change. However, in other cases management may best focus on drain blocking and peatland restoration to raise water levels.

A second example of compensatory adaptation management is that of the interaction between fisheries and climate change on seabirds. Frederiksen *et al.* (2004b) showed that

7.6 Adaptation management of core sites · 287

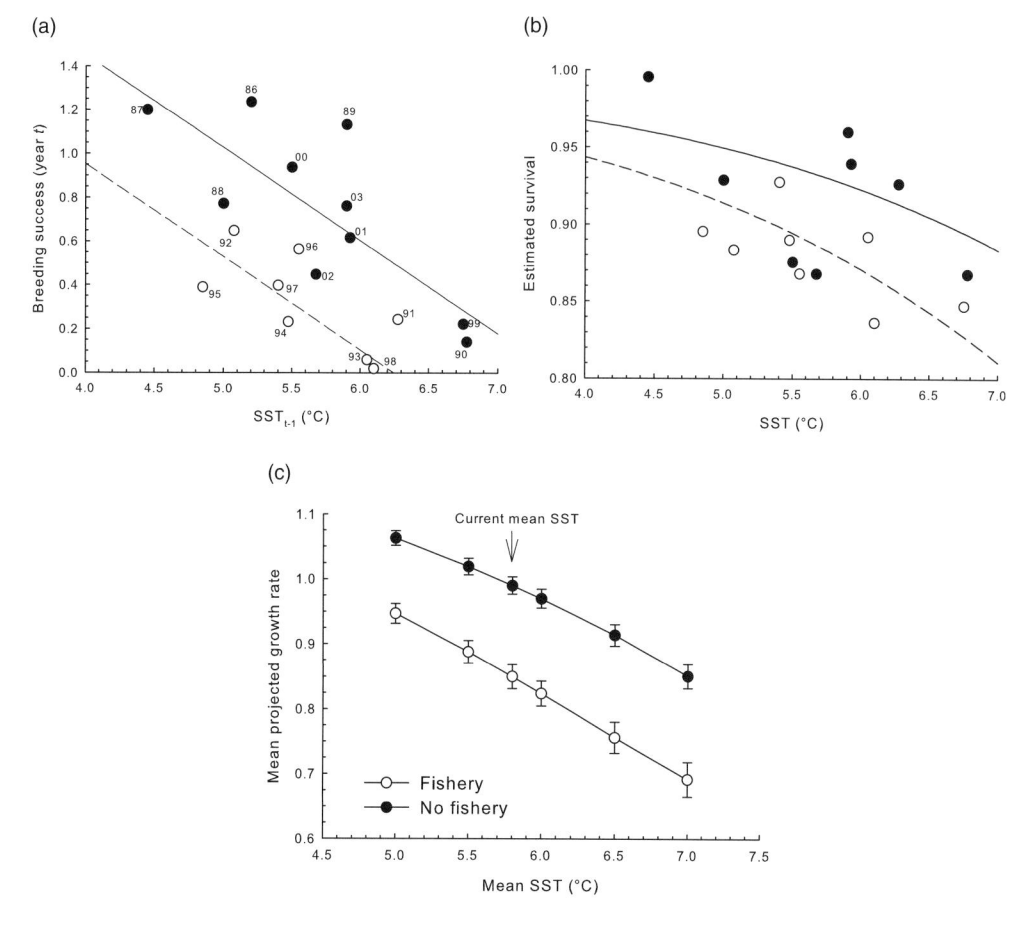

Figure 7.9 Negative effects of sea-surface temperature (SST) upon Kittiwake breeding success (a), Kittiwake survival (b) and projected population growth rate (c) with the sandeel fishery operating (open circles), and without a fishery (filled circles). Reproduced with permission from Frederiksen *et al.* (2004b).

changes in the kittiwake population on the Isle of May, UK, were negatively correlated with sea-surface temperature (SST) in the previous spring, through reductions in both breeding success and adult survival rates mediated by effects of temperature on sandeel prey (Section 4.6). Importantly, for both demographic parameters, there was a significant additive detrimental effect of the existence of a local sandeel fishery (Figure 7.9). A population model was used to indicate that when the sandeel fishery was in operation, the kittiwake population would be expected to be stable only at a February–March SST of 4.5 °C (far below the current mean of 5.7 °C and a temperature reached only once in the 17 years of data presented). However, if the fishery were to be closed, then because of increases in both productivity and survival, the population was expected to remain stable at a temperature of about 5.7 °C, the current mean. Because both temperature and fishing have additive negative impacts upon sandeel abundance and kittiwakes, closing the fishery makes the system more resistant to increases in temperature and shifts the sea-surface temperature at which the population is likely to remain stable by more than 1 °C.

7.6.3 Potential scope of adaptation management

Counteracting adaptation largely follows the existing conservation model for site-based conservation (Norris 2004; Green & Pearce-Higgins 2010; Pearce-Higgins 2011b) whilst compensatory adaptation has strong similarities to compensatory mitigation, a recent proposed solution to reduce the conflict between high-value uses of biological resources and species conservation (Wilcox & Donlan 2007), and that is discussed further in Section 8.8.4 with respect to renewable energy generation. Both approaches build on tried-and-tested conservation actions which means that when considering the adaptive management of core sites, conservationists need not consider radical changes in response to climate change, at least in the short- to medium term. Although some regard these approaches as too expensive to be sustainable in the long term (Lovejoy & Hannah 2005; Mawdsley *et al.* 2009), the same arguments are levelled at much current conservation action (Scott *et al.* 2010). Indeed, given the range of threats and pressures which birds face around the world, building climate change adaptation measures on existing conservation action will also reduce the risk that implementing such adaptation will divert resources away from addressing other conservation threats, which could lead to a net reduction in conservation effectiveness. We suspect that our success in conserving the biodiversity that remains will often depend on bespoke adaptation management underpinned by considerable scientific research, especially in countries where the most widespread ecosystems are strongly modified by humans.

Through time, the magnitude of climate change impacts may well exceed the capacity for site-based management to counteract or compensate for them. There may be a good chance for such management to be successful in a world which is 2 °C warmer than the present, but this will be much reduced in a world that is 4 °C warmer, or more (IPCC 2007c). The associated increases in the magnitude of range shift and extinction risk of birds are clearly shown in Section 6.8.2. At present the limits to adaptation are poorly understood because empirical research on them is in its infancy. Knowing where these limits are will be important in order to prevent the waste of valuable conservation resources. In the absence of further information, we would therefore recommend that much climate change adaptation for protected areas focusses on counteracting and compensatory adaptation management approaches, at least in the short- to medium term. This will often be in accord with existing conservation practice. The monitoring of its effectiveness will provide a valuable resource for the planning of future adaptation. However, in the longer term, more radical solutions may be required, particularly if the severity of realised climate change is high. Even in this case, improving the quality and resilience of protected areas that may ultimately become abandoned in response to further climate change will still have been beneficial to that species by increasing the number of potential colonists from that population to disperse to new or other core sites, as well as protecting an important site for colonisation by other species. Ultimately, however, there may be occasions where management may be required to accommodate and promote change. This may involve changing the focal species for site management and switching objectives to promote shifts in the distribution of species in response to climate change, rather than trying to prevent change. It is this which is examined below.

7.7 Habitat protection and creation to enhance connectivity in the wider landscape

There are two main proposals for ways in which the landscape between core sites for a species may be appropriately managed to promote connectivity between them. The first is the protection or creation of additional areas of similar habitat, to act as stepping stones or corridors between the larger protected areas. The second is the management of the intervening habitat matrix between protected sites and other areas of suitable habitat to make it easier for birds to move successfully between habitat patches. Both approaches have in common that they are intended to increase connectivity between the larger habitat patches, thus reducing the isolation of individual core sites. Increased connectivity is expected, in most circumstances, to increase population size and distribution in a given amount of habitat within the existing range by reducing the risk of local extinction from individual patches and increasing the chance of recolonisation if patch extinction does occur (Section 7.2.4). Thus, action to increase connectivity in part of the current range of a species where climate change is expected to make conditions less favourable may increase resilience against the negative effects of climate change. At the expanding edge of the range, where conditions are becoming more favourable because of climate change, increased connectivity among patches is also expected to facilitate dispersal from the existing range and the colonisation of newly suitable areas. The degree to which it is possible to promote connectivity between core sites through habitat manipulation is an important and active research area of considerable policy interest (e.g. Lawton *et al.* 2010). In situations where enhancing connectivity is impractical or ineffective, there is a third option to facilitate range shifts in response to climate change; that of translocation, which we will also consider as a last resort (Section 7.9).

Following the development of meta-population theory (Hanski & Gilpin 1997; Hanski 1999), and concern over the potential for habitat fragmentation to reduce species diversity and abundance, there has been considerable conservation effort to try and reduce habitat fragmentation and the degree of isolation of habitat patches. However, there is considerable uncertainty about the ability of these interventions to deliver real and tangible conservation benefits (Hobbs 1992; Simberloff *et al.* 1992; Bailey 2007). A range of studies have examined how the abundance of species within habitat patches varies in relation to the availability of suitable habitat in the surrounding landscape outside of the patch. This literature generally shows positive effects of the amount of surrounding habitat on species occurrence or abundance in woodland (van Dorp & Opdam 1987; Baillie *et al.* 2000; Bennett *et al.* 2004; Vergara & Armesto 2009), savanna (Bakker *et al.* 2002), heathland (van den Berg *et al.* 2001) and wetland (Whited *et al.* 2000) habitats. Overall, 143/404 (35%) of species covered by these studies apparently benefited from reduced isolation (as measured either by nearest neighbour distance or the amount of surrounding habitat) through increased abundance or occurrence, suggesting that reducing the degree of habitat fragmentation, for example through the provision of corridors or stepping stones, may be beneficial for them. Whilst there is some evidence that fragmentation and patch isolation have slowed the climate-driven range expansion of some butterfly species (Warren *et al.* 2001; Willis *et al.* 2009), there is as yet little evidence that fragmentation has significantly limited the response of birds to climate change. It is possible, however, that this may be part of the mechanism underlying the lag between avian community or range changes, and the more rapid temperature changes, described in Section 5.4.

This general lack of evidence does not necessarily mean that such management may not have potential benefits for bird conservation by increasing connectivity, but that few studies have so far examined the effectiveness of interventions to increase connectivity between habitat patches through the provision of corridors or stepping stones in increasing species persistence. We are not aware of any that have specifically examined the ability of management to facilitate the colonisation of new habitats as a result of climate change. As a result, we examine the evidence first for the provision of corridors, and secondly, for the provision of stepping stones as being able to improve dispersal, and use this to appraise the likely effectiveness of this management option for climate change adaptation. Before we do so, it is worth emphasising that some authors have suggested that corridors and stepping stones might cause conservation problems, for example through increasing the spread of invasive non-native species (Pienimäki & Leppäkoski 2004). The severity of this potential risk should be considered for a potential species, habitat or network of interest, prior to management to enhance connectivity being implemented. In some cases, such management may be inappropriate.

7.7.1 Providing corridors

The potential role of corridors in reducing the negative effects of habitat fragmentation on birds has been studied across a range of forest habitats from boreal to tropical. Although the results vary, a number of generalisations can be made from these studies. In particular, perhaps unsurprisingly, it is forest species which are most likely to benefit from the provision of corridors. For example, in an experimental test of the role of corridors in reducing rates of community loss in boreal forest fragments, resident forest species were significantly more abundant in the connected fragments and continuous forests than in the isolated fragments, suggesting that increasing connectivity provided benefit for these species. Migratory forest species did not respond to the provision of corridors, but were at highest abundance in continuous forest areas. They therefore were detrimentally affected by fragmentation, but did not appear to benefit from the increase in connectivity associated with corridors. Generalist species, not strongly dependent on forests, were evenly distributed between sites, and least sensitive to the effects of fragmentation (Schmiegelow *et al.* 1997; Hannon & Schmiegelow 2002).

Similar results have been found for temperate deciduous woodland species using non-experimental correlative approaches. In both British and Dutch woodlands, although patch size was the strongest predictor of species occurrence and abundance, the composition of the surrounding landscape was also important (van Dorp & Opdam 1987; Bennett *et al.* 2004). The richness of resident woodland communities was related to the extent of hedgerows (corridors) and woodland cover within a 1 km radius of woodland patches, whilst that of migrant species was not (Bennett *et al.* 2004). However, the number of species shown to benefit specifically from the presence of hedgerows, as a putative corridor between woodlands, was low; being four of eleven species in Holland, and for only one of these, the great-spotted woodpecker, could this effect be disentangled from the fact that hedgerows also provided suitable breeding habitat as well as facilitating dispersal (van Dorp & Opdam 1987). Using an alternative approach of the synchrony of woodland bird fluctuations across areas to infer connections between subpopulations, Bellamy *et al.* (2003) found that synchrony was enhanced between woods connected by hedgerows for three of thirteen species (Eurasian blackbird, hedge accentor and blackcap *Sylvia atricapilla*). The local rate of patch extinction of two (blue tit, Eurasian chaffinch *Fringilla coelebs*) of eight species from woodland patches in the UK was reduced by the presence of hedgerows (Bellamy *et al.* 1996), presumably because of a greater probability of immigration to small patches if they were connected to other woods by hedgerows, for which there was specific evidence for blue tit (Hinsley *et al.* 1995).

Rates of deforestation are currently greatest in the tropics (DeFries *et al.* 2005), and therefore this is where the pressures of habitat fragmentation are most severe now and have the greatest potential to impact upon avian biodiversity. A series of studies on fragmentation and the potential role of corridors in reducing the effects of fragmentation on tropical forest birds in Brazil show similar results to those outlined for temperate woodlands above, that corridors may indeed benefit a number of forest species, but that the proportion of species likely to benefit is relatively small. For example, although five of seven Atlantic forest species studied were sensitive to the effects of fragmentation, only one understory insectivorous species appeared to benefit from the presence of corridors (Uezu *et al.* 2005). In the same habitat, connectivity was a significant correlate of the diversity and density of forest birds in forest fragments (Martensen *et al.* 2008). More detailed work on individual species, using radiotelemetry to track the behaviour of translocated individuals, found that the return rates to their home forest patch of two forest specialists, the Chucao Tapaculo *Scelorchilus rubecula* in temperate rainforest in Chile and the barred antshrike *Thamnophilus doliatus* in tropical dry forest of Costa Rica were enhanced by the existence of wooded corridors between the capture and release locations, whilst that of a third, generalist species, the rufous-naped wren *Camylorhynchus rufinucha*, was unaffected by the presence of corridors (Castellón & Sieving 2006; Gillies & St Clair 2008). These two studies therefore provide important evidence for the role of corridors in facilitating the dispersal of individuals of some species among habitat patches. Overall, of the 76 species examples covered by these studies, for only 21 (28%) was the provision of corridors associated with increased occurrence or abundance within a woodland fragment. Of those species, it was particularly habitat specialists and resident species that move along edge habitats (Levey *et al.* 2005) which appeared most likely to benefit from corridors.

This brief overview ignores considerable detail. A landscape cannot simply be regarded in a binary fashion of good quality habitat patches, corridors and stepping stones, and a hostile matrix. There will be considerable variation in the quality of different patches, and even variation in the matrix, which may provide resources for some species (Dolman 2012). For example, there is increasing evidence that the quality of different corridors can influence their usage by birds. The use of hedgerows, a much discussed corridor habitat between fragmented woodland patches in the heavily modified farmed landscapes of Western Europe, studied by Hinsley and Bellamy (2001), was greatest if those hedges were tall (9/9 woodland species), wide (6/9 woodland species) and contained trees (8/9 woodland species). Hence, hedgerow use increased the more closely the hedgerows resembled the woodland patches they connected (Hinsley & Bellamy 2001). The same principles appear to hold in tropical habitats, where the species richness of birds utilising

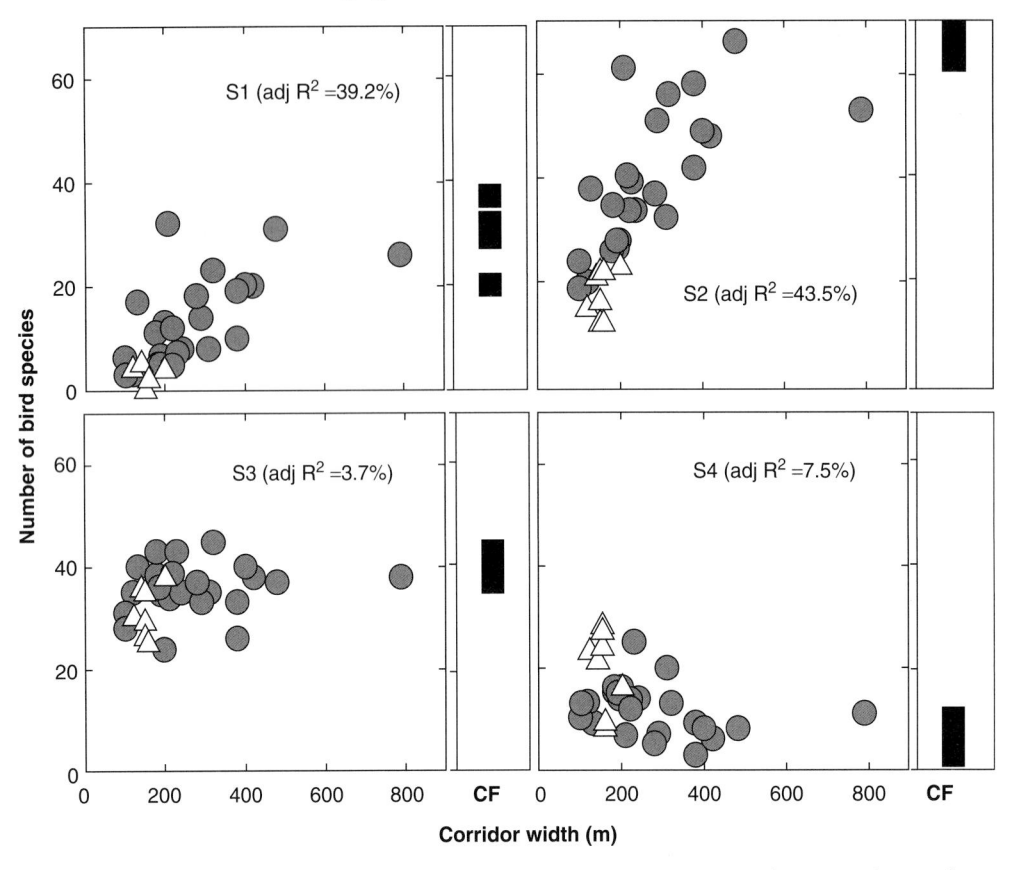

Figure 7.10 Correlation between the number of bird species using forest corridors in the Brazilian Amazon and corridor width, with species separated by varying degrees of habitat sensitivity. S1, all strict forest understory and midstory species; S2, all remaining species dependent on primary forest; S3, forest species able to tolerate secondary or highly degraded forest; S4, primarily non-forest species including scrub and open-habitat countryside species). Open triangles, grey circles, and black squares indicate unconnected corridors, connected corridors, and control riparian sites (CF), respectively. Reproduced with permission from Lees & Peres (2008).

forest corridors in the Brazilian Amazon was positively related to both corridor width and measures of resemblance of the habitat to forest (Lees & Peres 2008), particularly for primary forest species (Figure 7.10).

Thus, it is clear that the use of corridor habitats will be positively correlated with the extent to which they mimic the habitats they are connecting. Forest species will increasingly use wide corridors with characteristics of the forest patches that they connect, such as large trees and closed canopies. As this seems to be a general principle, it explains why corridors are generally only exploited by a relatively small number of species. If, in order to be useful, corridors must closely mimic all the attributes of the forest habitat that a species requires, then they are least likely to benefit the species with the narrowest and most specific requirements. This therefore means that if corridors are created for reasons of

7.7 Habitat protection and creation to enhance connectivity in the wider landscape · 293

climate change adaptation, they are likely to mainly benefit the more widespread species which have less exacting habitat requirements. Creating corridors for rare habitat specialists which, for example, require undisturbed habitats such as old growth forest will be particularly challenging, and yet these are precisely the habitat-limited species which are most likely to need assistance to facilitate range expansion in response to climate change. This conundrum may limit the utility of corridors as a climate change adaptation option for a suite of habitat specialists, and should be examined in greater detail than at present.

As noted earlier, despite this considerable body of evidence on the role of corridors in facilitating species movement between habitat patches, it is noteworthy that none have specifically examined the ability of corridors to facilitate the colonisation of new areas of habitat that exist as a result of climate change. Thus, we do not know what the likely limits to the ability of corridors to facilitate and enhance the potential for species to undertake range expansion are. Martensen *et al.* (2008), working in the Atlantic rainforest of Brazil, suggested that the main benefit of corridors is to enable individuals to utilise multiple fragments and thus to have a larger home range or to utilise it more safely. This would be expected to reduce the negative influence of fragmentation upon species occurrence in patches. This is very different from corridors providing a means for species to advance their range in response to climate change. In order to assess the potential for corridors to facilitate such expansion, some information is needed about the distance over which species will utilise corridors without encountering a larger patch and the effects on their survival of being confined to corridors.

One study which goes partway toward addressing this issue measured how the use of corridors by forest birds declined with increasing distance from source forest patches (Lees & Peres 2008). The diversity of birds utilising patches remained constant to 650 m, but declined significantly by 850 m from the source patches, suggesting most species persisted to at least 650 m along these corridors, but many fewer travelled 850 m. Although measures of bird occurrence on surveys may underestimate the ability of corridors to facilitate long-distance dispersal, these results do suggest that corridors may not facilitate long-distance dispersal anywhere nearly as well as extensive areas of habitat, and therefore cannot be viewed as an equivalent alternative for enhancing dispersal and colonisation.

Were these results to translate to other habitats, this suggests that corridors alone are only likely to play a relatively limited role in facilitating species range spread across the long distances which climate envelope models suggest will be required. In order to maximise their utility, corridors should be as close in character to the habitat characteristics preferred by the species whose movement they are intended to facilitate. However, this requirement may not be possible to achieve for all the species in a diverse assemblage. Hence, the use of corridors for climate change adaptation is most likely to be successful if it involves a sizeable network of large linear habitat features across an otherwise hostile landscape, rather than the provision of narrow strips of poor-quality habitat. In a tropical forest context, corridors of at least 400 m width (Lees & Peres 2008) should connect patches of at least 100 ha or larger (Uezu *et al.* 2005; Stouffer *et al.* 2009) over distances between patches of less than 850 m (Lees & Peres 2008). If these guidelines are applied to a landscape so that a grid of 100 ha patches are connected by 400 m wide corridors of 800 m length, then up to about 50% of the landscape must remain forested in order to maintain

294 · Conservation in a changing climate

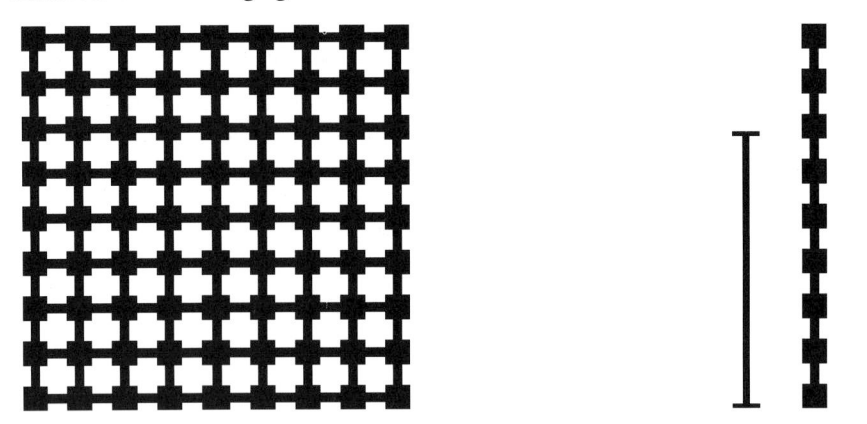

Figure 7.11 Idealised forest habitat (black) matrix to maximise the persistence and movement of forest passerines across a landscape, based on studies of the persistence of tropical passerines in patches (Uezu *et al.* 2005, Stouffer *et al.* 2009) and the movement of birds along forest corridors (Lees & Peres 2008). The vertical black line equals 10 km. What is unclear is the extent to which a matrix of habitats (left) or a single corridor connecting forest patches of 100 ha (right) is sufficient to facilitate the colonisation of species across the landscape from bottom to top.

habitat integrity, depending on how many replicated corridors are required for an effective network (Figure 7.11). This figure is within the range of previous attempts to identify minimum thresholds of suitable habitat within the landscape that a network should contain of 20–60% (Van Teeffelen *et al.* 2012), with the highest thresholds applying to species unable to cross habitat gaps (Wimberly 2006), which certainly applies to many tropical forest bird species. It also matches the estimate of Atlantic forest cover below which rapid losses in response to fragmentation and isolation occur (Martensen *et al.* 2012). This example is not meant to be prescriptive, but simply illustrates the potential scale of corridor or network prevision which may be required in order to be effective at the landscape scale, and as a rough guide, suggests that the long-distance range shift of poor dispersing habitat specialists is unlikely to occur across landscapes with less than 50% coverage of the required habitat. Clearly, maintaining extensive networks of semi-natural and natural habitats will be a much better adaptation option than trying to recreate them using corridors.

7.7.2 Creating stepping stones

In addition to the provision of corridors to link patches of habitat, there has been much discussion about the potential for the creation of stepping stones; small patches of habitat between larger patches that facilitate the movement of species dispersing across unusable areas by reducing the distance between suitable patches. This is perhaps a more realistic option than a continuous corridor because it requires less land. However, the effectiveness of stepping stones depends upon the propensity of species to cross non-utilised habitats and the effect on their survival of doing so. It appears that many tropical forest species are reluctant to cross open areas wider than 100 m (Moore *et al.* 2008) and therefore may also

> **Box 7.3** · *Traits analysis of sensitivity of European woodland birds to fragmentation*
>
> Data on the effects of woodland fragmentation upon European woodland birds were collated from eight references (van Dorp & Opdam 1987; Villiard & Taylor 1994; Enoksson *et al.* 1995; Bellamy *et al.* 1998; Baillie *et al.* 2000; Santos *et al.* 2002; Alderman *et al.* 2005; González-Varo *et al.* 2008), and summarised for each species. The proportion of cases where species occurrence or abundance was found to be significantly correlated with a measure of proximity to woodland in the wider landscape was modelled as a function of the natural log of both body mass (g) and mean dispersal distance (from Paradis *et al.* 1998) using a binomial regression model with a logit link function. Neither term (body mass, $F_{1,\,24} = 0.04$, $P = 0.83$; dispersal distance, $F_{1,\,24} = 0.05$, $P = 0.82$) was significantly correlated with this measure of sensitivity to fragmentation, suggesting that species sensitivity to fragmentation is not a simple function of size or natal dispersal ability.

be unlikely to be able to take advantage of this adaptation measure. Although the role of stepping stones in enabling climate change adaptation by birds has not been specifically examined in the literature, a considerable number of studies have considered the role of landscape context, and particularly the effect of proximity to other habitat patches, as a determinant of species occurrence and abundance. We use these studies to make inferences about the potential for stepping stones to be an effective climate change adaptation option for birds.

Much of this literature has examined birds of temperate European woodland. For example, the occurrence of six of 32 species in Dutch woodland was negatively related to distance to the nearest large woodland patch and positively to the area of surrounding woodland (van Dorp & Opdam 1987). The degree of synchrony in population fluctuations between patches of woodland was negatively related to the distance between woodland patches in England in five of thirteen species, likely to result from limitations in their dispersal ability (Bellamy *et al.* 2003). This suggests that in the heavily fragmented western European landscapes, management to reduce the distance between woodlands, for example through the creation of new woodland stepping stones, may increase the ability of these species to colonise isolated but suitable habitat patches. These effects may not apply to all forest situations, however, as the occurrence of only one of 37 Mediterranean forest species in Spain was negatively correlated with nearest neighbour distance between woodland patches, as a measure of isolation. This was not because the species covered were not dependent upon woodland habitats as there was a widespread relationship between patch size and species occurrence (Santos *et al.* 2002). Overall, there is evidence for some benefit associated with reduced distance between woodland patches for 12% of the 91 species examples covered by the studies reviewed, a lower figure than for corridors, although this was largely due to the lack of effect in the Santos *et al.* study. Clearly there is considerable variation between studies and species, although these do not appear related to either body size or dispersal distance (Box 7.3). The species most likely to benefit from such increasing connectivity may be those towards the generalist end of the habitat-specialisation spectrum (Dolman *et al.* 2007). This is because habitat specialists will be so exacting in their requirements that achieving connectivity for these species across largely hostile landscapes will be very difficult.

296 · Conservation in a changing climate

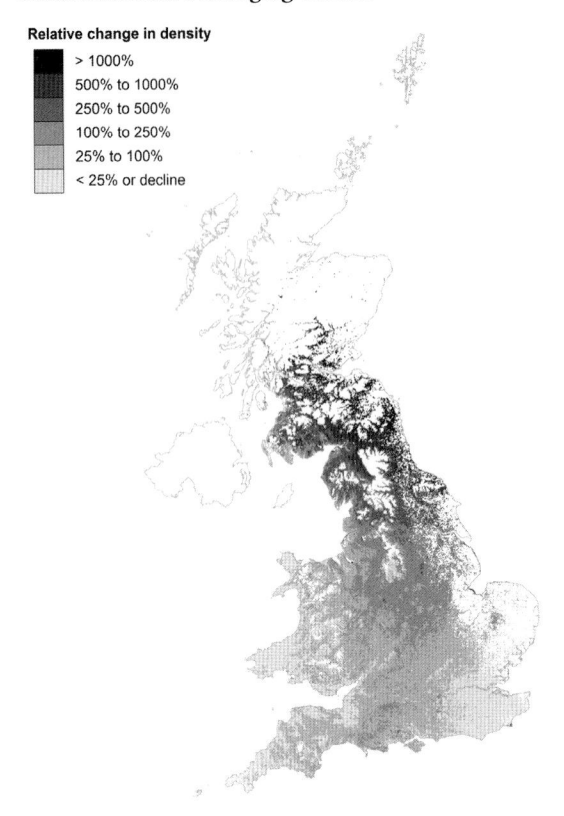

Relative change in density
- > 1000%
- 500% to 1000%
- 250% to 500%
- 100% to 250%
- 25% to 100%
- < 25% or decline

Figure 7.12 The expansion of wood nuthatches into Scotland from 1994/1996 to 2007/2009. Dark areas indicate the greatest proportional increases in nuthatch populations, where colonisations occurred. For more details of the underlying methods, and maps of other species, see British Trust for Ornithology (2013).

One of the best-studied temperate woodland species for which increasing connectivity may be important for climate change adaptation is the wood nuthatch. This is a species whose occurrence within woodland patches has been consistently negatively related to the degree of isolation of those patches from others (e.g. van Dorp & Opdam 1987; Bellamy *et al.* 1998; Villiard & Taylor 1994), and which has been the subject of the development of a number of spatial models to explore the consequences of this (Bellamy *et al.* 1998; van Langevelde 2000; Alderman *et al.* 2005). These models indicate that isolation has restricted the occupancy of otherwise suitable habitat in eastern England, despite these being climatically suitable (Bellamy *et al.* 1998). However, in Scotland much apparently suitable habitat is not occupied because it is climatically unsuitable, or at least has not been occupied until recently. Bellamy's paper is therefore the closest that ornithologists have reached to demonstrating that the colonisation of suitable habitat within areas of suitable climate has been limited by habitat fragmentation, but does not properly examine the effect of fragmentation on the rate of spread of the nuthatch into areas where climatic conditions have recently become suitable (cf. Warren *et al.* 2001). Such a study is now feasible for nuthatch, which has spread northwards in the UK in recent years (Figure 7.12). Nuthatches have a mean natal dispersal distance of 6.5 km (sd ± 9 km) in the UK, similar to that of many other woodland birds (Paradis *et al.* 1998; Dolman *et al.* 2007), but their distributions appear potentially limited by habitat connectivity, perhaps because of high mortality during dispersal across unforested areas (Matthysen & Currie 1996). The implications of a spatially explicit population model (Bellamy *et al.* 1998) for a sparsely wooded landscape in Cambridgeshire, UK, strongly suggested that net immigration from areas with greater woodland cover was key to maintaining the fragmented population. This source–sink situation is potentially analogous to the colonisation of new areas of woodland as they become climatically suitable, and emphasises the importance of large, good quality habitat patches within the existing range, and close to the expanding range margin, to produce large numbers of dispersers to colonise the newly suitable woodland patches. The most effective management option for nuthatches in the Cambridgeshire study area was to increase the size of the largest woodland patches to such a size that they would each be likely to support a secure population (Alderman *et al.* 2005). This is known as the 'key patch' approach to network analysis (Verboom *et al.* 2001) in which the total area of habitat required in a network to sustain a viable population is less if that network includes a key patch. In the case of the nuthatch, a key patch is likely to be an area of woodland which supports more than 10 pairs (Verboom *et al.* 1993).

Similar spatial modelling approaches have been undertaken to assess the conservation of the northern spotted owl in the boreal forests of the USA. Here, it was considered that the most important conservation priority was to develop reserves of sufficient size to support about 20 to 25 territories, beyond which additional resources should be used to increase reserve connectivity, and increase the geographical extent of the reserve network (Lamberson *et al.* 1994). This approach has informed the Northwest Forest Plan which aims to protect old-growth forests to ensure viable spotted owl populations and protect a wide array of other forest biodiversity (Thomas *et al.* 2006b). Although the current network may face increasing stress as a result of projected northward and upward shifts in the distribution of the spotted owl and other species, by maintaining a network approach to reserves which focus on areas of topographical and climatic heterogeneity, it may be possible to design a fixed reserve network that is robust to future climate change (Carroll *et al.* 2010).

Another type of interaction between climatic change and habitat fragmentation is illustrated by a study of the sedge warbler, a wetland bird that breeds in Europe and winters in sub-Saharan Africa. As described in Chapter 4, the overwinter survival of sedge warblers is reduced by drought conditions in their wintering grounds in the Sahel zone. Severe droughts in the Sahel caused a decline in the Dutch sedge warbler population during the late 1970s and early 1980s. Populations in fragmented marshland (surrounded by < 1% similar habitat within a 10 km radius) did not recover from this crash when conditions on the wintering grounds improved, but those in less fragmented marshland (surrounded by 1–30% habitat) recovered. Simulations suggested that this was a result of a combination of a greater probability of local extinction in isolated fragments combined with a reduced probability of colonisation during the recovery phase (Foppen *et al.* 1999). In relation to climate change, not only may increasing the connectivity between habitats potentially facilitate the colonisation of patches of habitat as they become climatically suitable, but it may also increase the resilience of a wider meta-population to negative climate impacts, even when those effects occur in distant wintering or passage areas. Both effects are likely to be important, as the expansion of a species into new habitat is not likely to be a simple smooth transition, but subject to stochastic events such as fluctuations in the weather. Thus, where a resident species distribution is limited by winter weather, a run of mild winters may result in a northward expansion of range, but an occasional cold winter will arrest or even reverse this expansion. Following a cold winter, it is likely that the most connected meta-populations and populations in large habitat fragments will continue to persist, and then recover most rapidly.

As illustrated by the last few examples, much of the research about the potential for increasing connectivity to provide effective climate adaptation for species has resulted from spatial modelling. In particular, as illustrated by the studies on nuthatch, northern spotted owl and sedge warbler, spatially explicit population models based on good demographic and dispersal data have provided a framework for exploring the potential for fragmentation to restrict the future viability of populations. This same approach can specifically address the potential for different landscapes and arrangements of habitat patches to facilitate the expansion of species ranges in response to an increase in climate suitability (as well as potentially increasing the persistence of species in an increasingly unfavourable climate). Vos *et al.* (2008) took this approach for a range of taxa in northwest Europe, including a number of bird species, and modelled both the projected distribution of suitable climate and suitable habitat networks, on the basis of dispersal ability. By simulating the movement of individuals with a number of simple rules, they were able to suggest that habitat fragmentation in the overlap between current and future climatically suitable zones may limit the colonisation of new habitat patches, thus limiting species' responses to climate change. To counter this, Vos *et al.* suggested two types of intervention to facilitate range expansion. They proposed linking otherwise isolated networks to the nearest climate-proof network (increasing connectivity) and increasing colonisation capacity by increasing patch size within the existing range (see Figure 7.3).

There is some empirical evidence in support of both approaches. Firstly, interventions to increase connectivity have been used in the conservation of great bitterns in England, where the distribution of the species was strongly tied to a small number of coastal reedbeds in East Anglia with a high breeding productivity. However, as a result of recent seawater incursions, some of these sites have suffered mortality of fish prey and a consequent reduction in habitat suitability (Section 4.3.3). Future sea-level rise, isostatic sinking of the land and potential increases in storm surges threatened the long-term viability of these sites as bittern habitat (Wotton *et al.* 2009a; Gilbert *et al.* 2010). As a result, the RSPB has created a new wetland area at Lakenheath on former agricultural land, about 80 km inland, but well within the dispersal range of the species. This reserve was colonised by bitterns, and several pairs now breed at this site (Figure 7.5).

Secondly, the number of Dartford warblers undergoing dispersal beyond the boundaries of the breeding range on heathland in southern England was proportionate to the size of the breeding population (Bibby 1979). Indeed, the recent Dartford warbler expansion in the UK was probably driven by milder, warmer temperatures in the core of the range along the south coast, leading to an increase in population density within that range which produced a large enough number of colonists to establish new breeding areas in East Anglia (e.g. shown in the background of Figure 7.5b), Wales and now central England (Bradbury *et al.* 2011). The protection of a network of heathland reserves in southern

England therefore provided the platform for the future expansion of this species' range and the colonisation of these additional areas.

7.7.3 Managing the matrix of unsuitable habitat

An alternative or additional approach for increasing connectivity is to reduce the hazards posed to individuals dispersing through the matrix that surrounds patches of suitable habitat. Such management will be required for species and situations where dispersing individuals are unable to avoid temporarily passing through or over intervening land cover types in which they are unable to find adequate food or cover. It is most likely to apply to species with limited ability to move long distances rapidly in an area with widely spaced suitable habitat patches (Gaston & Blackburn 2002; Hulme 2005; Donald & Evans 2006). The negative consequences of utilising the intervening matrix are likely to increase with the degree of dissimilarity between that matrix and a species' usual habitat. Therefore it is assumed that the character of the intervening matrix will have the greatest effect on the dispersal success of habitat specialists, for which the matrix will be most markedly different (Julliard *et al.* 2003). This might occur because the matrix provides little food or is associated with increased predation risk. A potential example of the latter is the apparent hostility of non-woodland habitats to the nuthatch, which as outlined above is a woodland specialist negatively affected by woodland fragmentation due, in part, to effects on dispersal. Juvenile birds suffer reduced survival when moving through a non-wooded matrix (Matthysen *et al.* 1995; Matthysen & Currie 1996).

Much habitat fragmentation is caused by the conversion of natural and semi-natural habitats to agricultural use (Section 7.2.4). Hence, softening of the matrix for dispersing individuals may be an objective of agri-environment schemes, at least in Western Europe. Donald and Evans (2006) suggest that reptiles, amphibians, mammals and some invertebrates would be more likely beneficiaries of such an approach than birds. There is recent evidence for both invertebrates and mammals that agri-environment schemes in the UK, such as the provision of non-crop vegetation in field margins, or buffer strips along water courses, may increase the quality of farmland habitats for moths and water voles respectively (Macdonald *et al.* 2007; Merckx *et al.* 2009), although we are not aware of any evidence, even for these groups, that specifically links the provision of such suitable habitats in the wider landscape matrix to enhanced dispersal success of individuals. For birds, recent evidence suggests that the amount of un-cropped land on farmland increases the abundance of some key declining farmland bird species (Henderson *et al.* 2012). However, to our knowledge, no studies have specifically tested the extent to which such habitat management may promote the dispersal and movement of individuals across the farmed landscape.

7.8 Management of the wider landscape

Rapid climatic change is unusual as a widespread phenomenon in the past few millennia, but global losses of biodiversity for other reasons began many decades or centuries ago. Hence, it is clear that species are not threatened only by climate change, but also by a wide range of other drivers of long-standing and growing importance, mostly originating from

300 · Conservation in a changing climate

Box 7.4 · *Additive effects of other pressures in addition to climate change*

A simple population model can be used to illustrate how additional pressures on a species may increase the severity of population decline under a changing climate, without any interaction between climate change and other drivers. A randomly generated population trajectory based on a model where $n_t = n_{t-1}(\exp(0.485 - 0.04\ln(n_{-1}) - 0.04T))$ and temperature (T) varied randomly from 5 to 10 produced a fluctuating, but largely stable population (thick line). We simulated the effects of additional hunting pressure as resulting in an additive 2% mortality in each year (thin line), which in this case was reasonably sustainable. We also simulated the effects of chronic loss of suitable habitat through time operating through a linear increase in the magnitude of density dependence by 50% over 100 years (dotted line), which resulted in population decline.

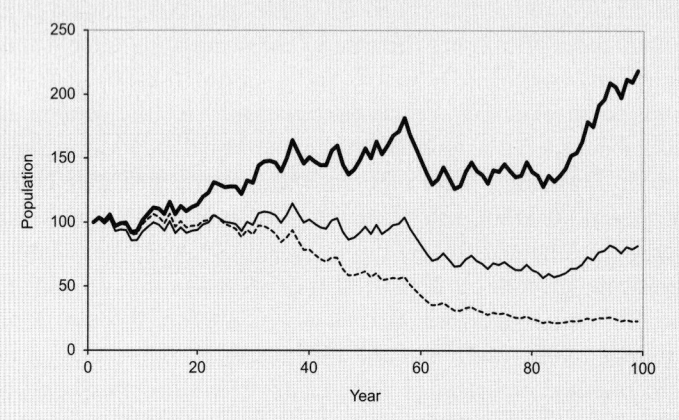

When a 2 °C increase in temperature was superimposed onto the same model and random temperature fluctuations, the population declined under each management scenario. Although the proportional changes were similar with or without climate change, the smaller population size in the former increased the likelihood of extinction as a result of hunting pressure or habitat loss.

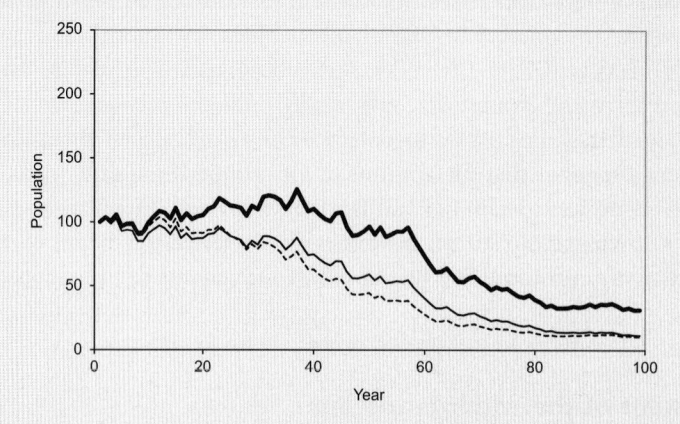

Reducing the rates of hunting and particularly habitat loss will therefore help maintain a stable population now and reduce the future severity of population decline under a changing climate.

the intensity of resource exploitation by increasing and increasingly resource-hungry human populations. These include habitat loss, pollution, hunting, persecution and invasive alien species, and are the current source of the majority of threats facing bird species now (Butchart et al. 2010; Hoffmann et al. 2010). Conservation actions to counter these threats generally must be made within a restricted conservation budget that must also fund climate change adaptation. In some circumstances, there is likely to exist a trade-off between the need to act on conservation pressures now and the need to fund climate change adaptation for the future. If adaptation involves radically different actions to that of existing conservation action, it may exacerbate short- to medium-term conservation problems. Adaptation therefore needs to be fully integrated within a framework of existing conservation action in order to minimise this risk.

Further, there are likely to be combined effects of climate change and these other pressures on species. Where these other drivers and pressures have negative effects on the survival or fecundity of a species, in addition to those that may be caused by climatic change, populations may decline much more rapidly (Box 7.4). A corollary of this is that alleviation of pressures that are not caused by climatic change may allow a species to better tolerate impacts of climate change, as we suggested in our proposals for compensating adaptation management of core sites. For this reason, the third most quoted recommendation for climate change adaptation is that of mitigating other threats (Heller & Zavaleta 2009). Crucially, the benefits of this action are not dependent upon a particular magnitude of climate change occurring, but are tangible now – another no-risk option. Minimising the severity of other pressures is therefore a crucial action, which means that current conservation practice should not be neglected because of the new threat of climate change (Hodgson et al. 2009; Green & Pearce-Higgins 2010).

Ultimately, depending upon the severity of future climate change and the impacts upon a particular species, adaptation management as outlined in this chapter may not be sufficient on its own to prevent long-term population declines and range loss in a changing climate. More radical solutions may be required.

7.9 Captive breeding, re-introduction and assisted colonisation

Many of the climate change adaptation options discussed so far have been focussed on particular sites or landscapes. But if the high end of the climate change projections are realised, which is looking increasingly likely (Section 1.6), then more radical interventions may be needed. Management at individual sites and for particular populations will not be sufficient to increase the resilience of those populations to match the magnitude of climate change For example, drain blocking for Eurasian golden plovers may be effective to about 2 °C warming, but beyond that, it may be necessary to give up on individual sites, or to consider other strategies (Pearce-Higgins 2011a). Closing the sandeel fishery will increase the resilience of black-legged kittiwakes on the Isle of May to warming by 1 °C. Thus, in the face of the likely levels of extinction risk and range shift to be expected above 2 °C of warming (Section 6.8.2), options to accommodate shifts in species' distributions are likely to be required. As just outlined in Section 7.7, management to promote habitat connectivity has been much discussed in this regard. Despite the uncertainties associated with this approach, if it enables climate-driven population declines in one part of the range to be compensated by increases and expansion in another, then the various tools already outlined will have worked effectively. However, given the relatively limited proportion of species that appear to benefit from increased habitat connectivity, there may be many cases where such management proves ineffective, and a species is declining throughout its range as a result of climate change. In this instance, more radical solutions will be required if the extinction of that species is to be avoided.

This may involve direct intervention to alter that species' distribution by taking individuals from climatically unsuitable sink populations to potentially new, suitable areas in order to found new populations. This principle has been demonstrated in butterflies (Willis *et al.* 2009), and could be a management option for birds, building on the considerable expertise that exists in captive breeding and re-introductions of birds to the wild. This is a tried and tested method for existing conservation problems (Section 7.2.6) that has already resulted in the successful re-introduction of many bird species to the wild from captive populations, and facilitated the restoration of historical ranges by translocation of wild birds for many others. The success of many deliberate introductions of alien bird species to countries far beyond their natural ranges also illustrates the potential power of this approach!

However, many baulk at the concept of assisted colonisation beyond the existing historical range of a species, and it is a concept which causes much debate amongst conservationists. In the face of potentially high-magnitude climate change, it is seen by some as a key component of future climate change adaptation, particularly for species with small, isolated populations, low dispersal ability and fragmented populations (Hoegh-Guldberg *et al.* 2008; Loss *et al.* 2011; Thomas 2011), For these species, this may be the only solution to negative climate change impacts short of maintaining them only in captivity. However, this solution is unlikely to be achieved simply. It will require areas of suitable habitat under a favourable climate to which individuals will need to be moved. If a species' range has been limited by direct effects of temperature, as in the butterfly example of Willis *et al.* (2009), then this may be relatively straightforward, as other areas of suitable habitat may exist which the species was previously excluded from by temperature but which it cannot colonise rapidly enough. However, for other species whose range is limited by indirect effects of climate operating through the distribution of other species which provide food and other resources, this will be more difficult to achieve. In particular, ensuring suitable areas of habitat for specialists, which many rare, low dispersal species limited by fragmentation will be, will be non-trivial.

For these reasons, it has been suggested that assisted colonization is not a viable conservation strategy (Ricciardi & Simberloff 2009), particularly given the unpredictable consequences of the arrival of invasive non-native aliens. Invasive non-natives are the third most frequently cited cause of threat to birds around the world, and a major problem for the conservation for all taxa in all biomes. Based on this experience, there are justifiable fears that this adaptation option will have significant unintended and detrimental consequences. For example, the introduction of American red squirrels *Tamiasciurus hudsonicus* to Newfoundland to supplement the diet of declining American martins *Martes americana* significantly increased the predation of spruce cones and caused the probable extinction of the Newfoundland crossbill *Loxia curvirostra percna* (Parchman & Benkman 2002). In addition, assisted colonisation may facilitate the spread of alien diseases. The illegal importation of birds from the Middle East to USA was probably responsible for the transfer of West Nile virus into North America, resulting in significant population declines in a range of bird species and impacts on human health (Lanciotti *et al.* 1999; LaDeau *et al.* 2007). Given the complexities of ecosystems, these risks are very difficult to predict, but the consequences of many previous invasions are not encouraging (Parker *et al.* 1999; Kolar & Lodge 2001).

Assisted colonisation has been considered most often for the conservation of individual species, but there is increasing interest in an ecosystem approach, and potentially the need to consider more wholesale direct interventions or changes to habitats and ecosystems to make them more resilient to climate change. In other words, if climate change is likely to result in significant pressures on particular keystone species within a particular ecosystem, then conservation managers might consider introducing other, equivalent species (which are likely to currently be regarded as non-native species) to perform the same ecosystem function in the future. Further, some species which are traditionally regarded as invasive non-native species may actually form a beneficial ecosystem service and function under climate change and provide an effective functional replacement for other species likely to decline (Pyke *et al.* 2008). Foresters are already thinking long-term and planning for climate change adaptation by using future climate change projections for 60–70 years hence to inform current planting practices (O'Neill *et al.* 2008; Broadmeadow *et al.* 2009; Kirby *et al.* 2009). Should conservationists adopt the same approach?

Proponents of assisted colonisation accept that it should be well-regulated and guided by informed assessment (Hoegh-Guldberg *et al.* 2008). It is envisaged that short-distance assisted colonisations are less likely to result in undesirable consequences than long-distance colonisation (Wilson *et al.* 2009a) and that risk can be further reduced by appropriate decision support frameworks (McDonald-Madden *et al.* 2011). If used, assisted colonisation should not be regarded in isolation, but integrated with other adaptation techniques to facilitate shifts in species ranges such as increasing landscape connectivity (Loss *et al.* 2011) and also adaptive management of core sites to reduce the rate of change, to buy time for risk assessment to reduce the detrimental consequences of colonisation and increase the likelihood of success (McDonald-Madden *et al.* 2011). The current uncertainty and concerns over this tool need to be recognised. Research is required to inform this debate so that, if and when assisted colonisation is required, conservationists are better able to manage the risks and maximise the chances of success, and conversely, to identify the situations where the risks may remain too great. At the same time, potential changes to legislation may be required, since assisted colonisations may involve movements of species across national boundaries and beyond their native range (Shirey & Lamberti 2010).

To our knowledge there are no bird species whose capacity to expand their distribution in response to climate change has been identified empirically as being limited by habitat fragmentation. As and when such species limited by poor dispersal and connectivity are identified, it may be appropriate to conduct similar trials on birds to those which have been conducted on butterflies. There remain significant scientific, technical, policy and legal challenges to doing this, which will need to be overcome if this is to become a viable conservation adaptation tool. In the short term, these constraints should be regarded as

304 · Conservation in a changing climate

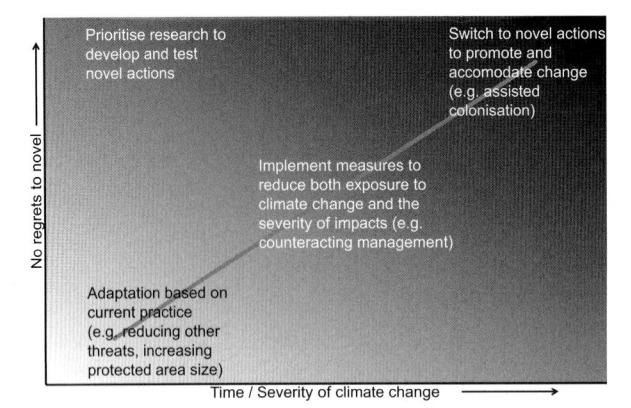

Figure 7.13 With increasing severity of climate change the required shift from climate-smart conservation to build resilience, to novel actions to accommodate change, is indicated by the line. The current uncertainty/risk associated with actions in indicated by the shift from the light (certain/low risk) to dark (uncertain / high risk) background. Priority actions are given in the text.

safeguards, given the large amount of damage which invasive non-natives have done to biodiversity around the world. However, in the longer term, as climate change becomes severe, a more flexible approach to these issues may ultimately be required, particularly as climate change is no respecter of international boundaries.

7.10 Conclusions

We have outlined six tools within the conservationists' toolkit, and how each of those may be adapted to account for climate change. These range from policy and planning instruments to species and habitat management tools. The appropriateness of each of these will depend upon the magnitude of climate change and, indeed, within these six broad categories is variation in the level of intervention. In reality, there is a sliding scale of conservation action required, dependent upon the level of climate change experienced (Dawson *et al.* 2011; Figure 7.13).

As we have emphasised through this chapter, conservation adaptation to climate change should be built on the foundations of existing conservation management now, although requiring modifications to the current toolkit. Much current conservation action is about reducing the impacts of other threats, most of which are, in many places, currently much more important than climate change in driving population declines in birds and putting an increasing range of species at risk of extinction. The impending threat of climate change should not divert conservation efforts so that this action diminishes, otherwise even more biodiversity loss will be experienced in the short term (Butchart *et al.* 2010; Hoffman *et al.* 2010; Rands *et al.* 2010). Further, as we have demonstrated, reducing the magnitude of these other effects will tend to compensate for at least some of the negative impacts of climate change. Species with small populations, fragmented ranges and negative population trajectories are at greatest threat of extinction now. This will continue to be the case, though through time, an increasing magnitude of climate change is likely to exacerbate the severity of these proximate causes of extinction risk as well as put an increasing number of species under threat of extinction directly. The existing conservation tools of species prioritisation and planning, which are particularly important given current restrictions on the size of conservation budgets, are therefore still a crucial first step for conservationists, to help make the most efficient use of those conservation resources. The protection and management of core sites, and the introduction of wider-countryside measures, all heavily employed conservation tools now, will continue to be crucial components of a climate change adaptation strategy.

Conservationists need to recognise that the magnitude of future climate change is likely to cause significant impacts on species distributions and populations and to community structure and function. Through time, and particularly beyond 2050, depending on greenhouse gas emissions in the next 20–30 years (Section 1.6), these impacts may exceed the adaptive capacity associated with many site-based interventions. In order for species to survive, either the potential future range must overlap with areas of the current range, or species must shift their distributions. Habitat protection and creation in the wider landscape will be one mechanism to achieve this, by increasing habitat connectivity to enable species' ranges to track changes in climate, as they have done in response to previous glacial and interglacial periods. However, given the current degree of human impact on populations and habitats, many species may struggle to cope with the projected magnitude of change, and therefore be at considerable risk of extinction. For these species and situations, more urgent interventions will be required, such as assisted colonisation, although this is currently associated with considerable uncertainty and risk.

To summarise, the degree of difference between the climate change adaptation toolkit and the current conservation toolkit will depend upon the magnitude of climate change. In the short- to medium term, or if climate change is kept at manageable levels, much climate change adaptation may be based upon existing conservation practice. As climate change adds to and interacts with other pressures, an increasing level of conservation resource will need to be found. This will be a considerable challenge as current levels of conservation activity are not sufficient to halt current rates of biodiversity loss, and yet, it is becoming increasingly difficult to secure adequate resourcing for these activities due to widespread budgetary restrictions associated with the global economic slowdown of recent years. As the severity of future climate change increases, more radical options may be needed, particularly if the magnitude of climate change exceeds the capacity of systems to adapt (Figure 7.13). Instead of management to prevent or compensate for change, which is the current conservation paradigm, management will need to be implemented to accommodate or facilitate change. This will require a considerable paradigm shift in conservation thinking. In the face of future uncertainty, we should begin to prepare for this eventuality now through appropriate planning, research and development, whilst also doing our best to reduce greenhouse gas emissions to minimise the size of the challenging task ahead. Effective climate change mitigation now is likely to be less costly in the long run than the more difficult task of effective conservation and adaptation in a changed climate (Stern 2007), and should eventually reduce the threat species face from climate change (Warren *et al.* 2013, Section 6.8). However, such mitigation efforts may themselves also affect bird populations. It is these potential effects that we will consider in the next chapter, which will show that addressing the urgent issue of greenhouse gas emissions through mitigation comes with its own significant challenges for bird conservation.

7.11 Summary

- Decades of practical experience and conservation science have increased our understanding of species' requirements and the potential for conservation interventions to reverse population declines and range losses. The tools used for this can be divided into prioritisation and planning, the protection and creation of core sites, management of core sites, habitat protection and creation in the wider landscape, management of the wider landscape and captive breeding, translocation and re-introduction.
- Given that we do not have experience of successfully managing species through previous episodes of climate change, it makes sense to learn from the successful applications of these tools to inform our approach to climate change adaptation. Precisely what these are will vary across a species range, potentially involving interventions at the upper latitudinal/altitudinal range boundary to promote range expansion, and separate interventions at the lower latitudinal/altitudinal limits to slow or prevent loss.
- Methods of conservation prioritisation should be adapted to account for climate change. Models projecting future impacts may be used to identify the species most likely to be vulnerable to climate change, and a number of framework methodologies have been devised to do this in a systematic way, incorporating additional information about other exacerbating factors.
- Key principles for the selection of protected areas in response to climate change include prioritising sites in overlap zones between current distributions and projected future ranges, increasing the size of protected areas, protecting areas of high environmental heterogeneity and prioritising centres of endemism. Although some have suggested that climate change means that a more fluid approach to protected areas is required, there is increasing evidence that existing static protected areas may actually assist species' range expansion in a changing climate by protecting areas of natural and semi-natural habitat for colonisation.
- Appropriate management of core sites may increase their resilience to climate change and that of the species they support. This may be through counteracting adaptation management to directly reverse the impacts of climate change or compensatory adaptation management to offset negative impacts of climate change through an alternative mechanism. Although the magnitude of climate change that such management is likely to be effective against remains uncertain, the application of the existing model for site-based conservation can be used to inform when such management is required or no longer effective.
- Patch isolation detrimentally affects the abundance or occurrence of about 35% of bird species studied, suggesting fragmentation may limit the ability of species to shift their distribution in response to climate change. To counter this, management, such as creating corridors or stepping stones, or reducing the hostility of the matrix between habitat patches, may improve landscape connectivity. There is some limited evidence that increasing connectivity may speed the recovery of populations from

climate-related population declines, which should be tested further. Achieving effective landscape-scale connectivity for the habitat specialists most vulnerable to fragmentation will be difficult.
- The most effective corridors are those which most closely reflect the habitats they are connecting. Given the limited potential for corridors to facilitate long-distance dispersal, we estimate that to facilitate range expansion of highly area-sensitive and non-dispersive individuals, some 50% of the landscape will need to be composed of an interconnected network of the suitable habitat.
- A key adaptation action is to reduce the magnitude of other threats to birds by appropriate management of the wider landscape. Doing so will increase the ability of vulnerable populations to cope with additive effects of climate change, and may also reduce potential interactions between anthropogenic threats and negative climate change impacts on species. Importantly, such action complements and enhances important existing conservation actions required now to prevent population decline and extinction caused by non-climatic threats.
- The greater the magnitude of climate change impacts, the more likely it is that radical intervention options will be required. A much discussed topic is assisted colonisation; introducing species to unoccupied areas as they become climatically suitable. Given the unpredictable consequences of introducing potentially invasive non-native species, this is much more controversial than the well-established conservation intervention of species re-introductions. If used, it must be done in a graduated way, involving well-monitored short-distance colonisations, and fully integrated with other adaptation interventions. It will not be a 'magic' single solution to the problem of climate change.
- Given the uncertain effectiveness of particular methods to successfully conserve particular bird species in a changing climate, the bird conservation responses to climate change in the short- to medium term should be built on the foundation of tried and tested conservation actions. The application of such 'climate-smart' solutions will reduce the likelihood of adaptation taking resources away from urgent conservation interventions now. However, as the severity of climate change increases, more radical options may be required, which will require research and development now in order to be applied successfully and safely. The success of adaptation measures should be monitored, in order to identify the point when a shift from interventions to increase resistance to change, to management to accommodate and promote change, is required.

8 · *Effects of climate change mitigation on birds*

8.1 Introduction

So far in this book we have described the mechanisms by which climate change affects birds, reviewed potential future changes in their distribution and abundance caused by climate change and discussed the implications of these for conservation. It is clear that as the magnitude of warming increases, so will the likely severity of impacts on bird populations. The number of projected bird extinctions is modelled to increase by about 1.6 times from a 2 °C to 4 °C global warming scenario, and differ by approximately 2.5 times between a 2 °C and 6 °C scenario (Box 6.5), when it is estimated one-quarter of global bird species would be at risk of being committed to extinction as a result of climate change (Section 6.8.2). Clearly, addressing the causes of climate change will be an important way of reducing the likely detrimental impacts of climate warming on birds (Warren *et al.* 2013). However, attempts to do this through the reduction of greenhouse gas emissions or the removal of gases from the atmosphere (termed climate change mitigation) may also have a detrimental effect on bird populations.

The principal sources of anthropogenic greenhouse gas emissions are carbon dioxide from the burning of fossil fuels (coal, oil and gas), deforestation and other land use changes leading to the burning or decay of plant material, release of methane from refuse in landfill sites, gut fermentation by ruminant livestock and the farming of rice, and release of nitrous oxide caused by the use of fertilizers in agriculture (Section 1.5). Changes in the ways in which energy is obtained and used, the protection of forests and peatlands and changes in farming practice are therefore the main methods being considered for climate change mitigation. In addition, there might be ways in which the environment could be artificially adapted to remove greenhouse gases from the atmosphere at higher rates. All of these mitigation measures will change the natural environment and could therefore affect bird populations. In this chapter we examine some of these potential effects and assess ways in which potential adverse impacts of mitigation may be reduced, focussing particularly on renewable energy generation.

8.2 The challenge of producing sustainable energy

World energy demand by humans is projected to more than double from 496 EJ per year (exajoules = 10^{18} joules) equivalent in 2008 to 1000 EJ or more by 2050 (Moriarty & Honnery 2012). If realised, there is an urgent and vast challenge to decouple the supply of this energy from greenhouse gas emissions in order to reduce the magnitude of future climate change. According to the Fourth Assessment Report of the IPCC, 85% of global energy production in 2007 was derived from fossil fuels. These were responsible for 57% of

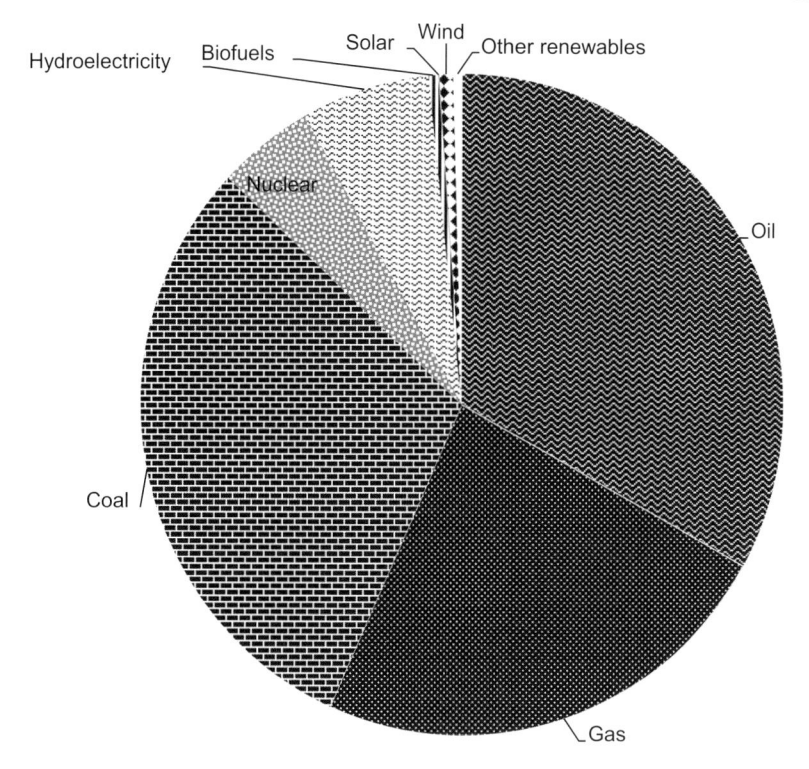

Figure 8.1 Proportion of global energy consumption by source in 2011. Data from BP (2012).

greenhouse gas emissions (IPCC 2007d). At its peak, nuclear power accounted for about 7% of primary energy production, but this share has declined slightly since about 2000. In 2008, the renewable energy sector contributed some 12.9% of global energy supply, of which about 10% was traditional biomass whilst hydropower provided a further 2.5%. Remaining forms of renewable energy, such as wind and solar, contributed only 0.4% of the total. More recent statistics, which exclude traditional biomass usage by individual households, show that the share of global energy production provided by fossil fuels has changed little in recent decades (Figure 8.1). In 2011, 87% of world energy was from fossil fuels, whilst 8% was from renewable sources. Non-biomass and hydropower sources contributed only 1.1% of global energy requirements (BP 2012). If we focus purely on electricity generation, the role of renewable energy is greater, with 16% of global electricity supply produced by hydropower and 3% from other renewable sources in 2008 (IPCC 2011).

Although small in overall magnitude compared to fossil fuels, there have been rapid increases in renewable energy generating capacity in recent years. Between 2008 and 2011 global wind energy production doubled, whilst solar energy production increased by five times (BP 2012). However, there is a vast mismatch between current energy demand and renewable energy production (Figure 8.2). Although the potential for renewable energy generation around the world is large and unlikely to be a limiting factor in reducing greenhouse gas emissions (Table 8.1), our willingness and ability to harness this potential has so far been limited. If the political will to combat climate change gains ground, there is

Table 8.1 *Estimates of the potential energy production from different renewable energy sources (from IPCC 2011). Although these differ widely between studies (hence the wide range for each source), there is a consensus that combined there is sufficient energy production potential to exceed future energy demand (given in Figure 8.2).*

Renewable energy source	Range of estimates of production (EJ/yr)
Geothermal energy	128–1421
Hydropower	50–52
Ocean energy	7–331
Wind energy	85–580
Bioenergy	50–500
Solar energy	1575–49 837

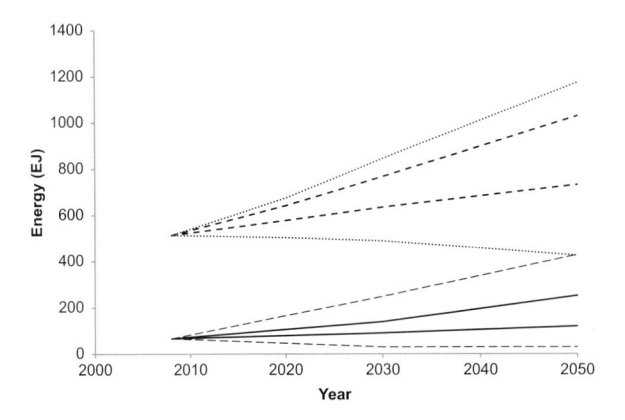

Figure 8.2 Global energy demand projections to 2050 (upper spread of lines). Summaries of ten projections, each of which present a spread of future energy use for 2020, 2030 and 2050. Mean lower and upper values of each range are dashed, whilst the lowest and highest value from across the different projections are indicated by the dotted lines. Data are from Moriarty & Honnery (2012). The lower lines are global projections for renewable energy production for 2030 and 2050 from IPCC (2011). The solid lines are median projections for a baseline scenario (lower) and low emissions scenario for stabilising atmospheric CO_2 concentrations at 440 ppm (upper), which are bounded by the lowest and highest value from the baseline and low emissions scenarios respectively.

likely to be significant expansion of all forms of renewable energy production in the future, far beyond the scale of their current deployment. Even so, models suggest it is unlikely that all energy demands will be met from renewable sources (Figure 8.2). Of the scenarios developed, the maximum contribution of renewable energy by 2050 is 77%; more than half of scenarios give a figure in excess of 27% (IPCC 2011). It is likely that the greatest contributions will come from bioenergy, wind, hydro- and solar power (Figure 8.3). These model predictions do not approach the estimates of global potential (Table 8.1), with a particularly large disparity for solar power. This is probably because of their current substantial costs (Chu & Majumdar 2012), which are likely to decline only after further investment in research and development. Having established the likely future trajectory of renewable energy generation, what are the likely impacts on birds of the widespread promotion of these technologies?

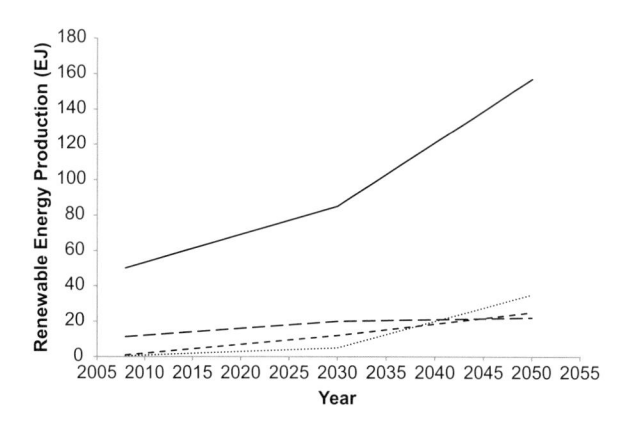

Figure 8.3 Median rates of global energy production from bioenergy (solid line), hydropower (long-dashed line), wind power (short-dashed line) and solar power (dotted line) under a low emissions scenario of stability at atmospheric CO_2 concentrations at 440 ppm (IPCC 2011).

8.3 Wind energy

The wind has long been used as a source of power by humans, whether through sails or windmills, and became an increasingly important source of energy generation during the twentieth century through the development of modern wind turbines. These can generate electricity from blades rotating in a vertical plane on a horizontal axis that can be positioned on land or offshore. Most currently deployed turbines produce some 1–3 MW from 30–80 m high towers, but 120 m tall, 5 MW turbines have been built. Wind energy currently comprises about 0.6% of global energy production or 3% of global electricity generation, having attained some 237 GW capacity by 2011 (World Wind Energy Association 2012; BP 2012). This is anticipated to increase to 9–14% of electricity generation by 2050 (IPCC 2011).

The potential for wind energy production varies around the world, being particularly high in north-west Europe, the coasts of North America, Tierra del Fuego, coastal areas of southern Australia and New Zealand, inland China and the Yellow Sea (Archer & Jacobson 2005; IPCC 2011). As a result, almost 50% of global wind energy potential is found in just two countries (China and USA) and 74% in five (World Wind Energy Association 2012). Onshore wind is currently one of the cheapest and more advanced forms of renewable energy (Chu & Majumdar 2012), leading to recent rapid increases in generating capacity in both the USA and China (IPCC 2011). In Western Europe, because of increasing concerns over visual and environmental impacts of wind farms, there has been a shift towards placing them offshore so that they are not seen by people, although this increases the expense and technical challenge (Bilgili *et al.* 2011). In Denmark, Portugal, Spain and Ireland, more than 10% of electricity generation is now provided by wind energy, showing that it is technically possible for wind farms to play a significant role in climate change mitigation (Wiser & Bolinger 2010). However, this can be associated with detrimental impacts on bird populations, particularly through mortality associated with flying birds colliding with turbine blades or towers, and the displacement of birds away from wind farms (Drewitt & Langston 2006). These impacts are reviewed below.

8.3.1 Collisions of birds with wind turbines

The frequency of recorded collision mortality varies widely between species and between locations. For some species and at some sites, collisions occur very infrequently because birds see and avoid the turbines. Radar tracking of flight routes in the vicinity of wind farms show that birds often divert their course as they approach them (Desholm & Kahlert 2005). However, this is not the case for all species, and long-range avoidance is likely to be affected by visibility, with birds flying at night or in fog being more susceptible to collision (Drewitt & Langston 2008).

There are several well-documented examples of large numbers of birds being killed annually by collisions (Table 8.2). These tend to be where turbines have been placed in sites where birds congregate, such as in migration bottlenecks, or close to breeding sites of colonial nesting species. Raptors are among the list of vulnerable species most likely to occur in high concentrations during migration because they often rely on thermals (upward moving pockets of hot air) for soaring flight. Sufficient thermals are only found over land warmed up by the sun and so migrating raptors concentrate at places where crossings of seas or lakes are at their shortest. They also concentrate in parts of mountain chains where upward deflections of wind facilitate soaring. If wind turbines are placed at these locations, which are also windy, there is the potential for conflict. One of the first cases of large-scale collision mortality to be described was at Altamont Pass in California, a site used by migrating raptors located in the rolling foothills of the Coast Range Mountains which consisted of a maximum of 7300 turbines in 1993, generating 580 MW electricity. A total of 35 000–100 000 birds are estimated to have been killed during the first 20 years of operation at a rate of about 2700 birds per year, of which 1100 were raptors and owls (Thelander & Smallwood 2007; Smallwood & Thelander 2008). Although positioned on a migration route for raptors, additional habitat alteration caused by the construction of the turbines may have increased the abundance of small mammal prey and thereby further attracted raptors to the site, exacerbating collision risk (Thelander *et al.* 2003). Another hazardous wind farm site is at Tarifa, overlooking the straits of Gibraltar in southern Spain. Here, 476 turbines generating 118 MW in 2002 were found to kill 57 griffon vultures and 67 common kestrels per year (Barrios & Rodriguez 2007). A later study of 252 turbines in the same area recorded higher mortality rates of 1.33 birds per turbine per year, of which 36% were raptors (Ferrer *et al.* 2012). It is noteworthy that at both sites, estimates of mortality vary between studies by at least an order of magnitude (Table 8.2), apparently as a result of different turbines being sampled and data being obtained from different years. This variability is a problem as it makes the prediction of the impacts of particular wind farms on birds difficult (De Lucas *et al.* 2008; Ferrer *et al.* 2012).

Concentrations of birds at breeding colonies can also result in a high risk of collision. A line of 25 turbines built at the harbour of Zeebrugge, Belgium killed about 330 terns during 2004 and 2005, 2–4% of the birds breeding on an artificial peninsula built close to the turbines (Everaert & Stienen 2007), leading to a 40% reduction in the size of the breeding colony. Relatively high levels of mortality (birds killed per turbine per year) were also recorded at two further coastal sites at Blyth Harbour and Kreekak Sluices, and three other wind farms in the Netherlands (Table 8.2) where gulls, other seabirds and waterbirds were victims. Large numbers of migrating passerines may also be killed

Table 8.2 *Examples of wind farms where levels of bird collision mortality have been quantified, and average results of review studies.*

Location	Turbine characteristics	Total mortality	Birds/turbine/yr	References
Altamont, California	4000 turbines averaging 0.1 MW output	16 847 birds (1998–2003 and 2005–2007) of which 4112 were raptors	0.19 birds, 0.08 raptors	Smallwood & Thelander (2008)
Altamont, California	52 turbines averaging 0.4 MW output	99 birds and 48 raptors in one year	1.9 birds, 0.9 raptors	Smallwood et al. (2010)
Buffalo Ridge, Minnesota	354 turbines averaging 0.7 MW output	1007 birds (1996–1999)	2.84 birds	Johnson et al. (2002)
Smøla, Norway	68 turbines	28 white-tailed eagles 2005–2009[1]	0.1 eagles	Dahl et al. (2012)
Castellón, Spain	50 turbines	A 30% drop in griffon vulture survival is estimated to represent the loss of 226 adults over 2 years[2]	2.25 adult griffon vultures	Martínez-Abrain et al. (2012)
Navarra, Spain	277 turbines	345 birds (2000–2002) including 227 griffon vultures	0.27 griffon vultures[2]	Lekuona & Ursua (2007)
Tarifa, Spain		5 Egyptian vultures (2004–2008)	> 0.023 Egyptian vultures	Carrete et al. (2009a)
Tarifa, Spain	251 turbines averaging 1.46 MW output	337 birds annually (2005–2008) of which 124 were raptors	1.33 birds, 0.4 griffon vultures	Ferrer et al. (2012)
Tarifa, Spain	256 turbines averaging 0.12 MW output	68 raptors, 30 griffon vultures, 36 common kestrels in 1 year	0.27 raptors, 0.12 griffon vultures, 0.14 kestrels	Barrios & Rodríguez (2004)
Tarifa, Spain	256 turbines averaging 0.12 MW output	151 raptors, 111 griffon vultures, 19 common kestrels	0.06 birds, 0.045 griffon vultures, 0.01 kestrels	De Lucas et al. (2008)
Tarifa, Spain	296 turbines averaging 0.9 MW	135 griffon vultures in 1 year	0.23 griffon vultures	De Lucas et al. (2012)
Blyth Harbour, UK	9, 0.3 MW turbines	148–194 birds killed per year over 11 years	16.5–21.5 birds	Newton & Little (2009)
The Netherlands	25, 1.65 MW turbines at 3 sites	700 birds estimated to be killed per year	28 birds (range 19–68)	Krijgsveld et al. (2009)
Kreekak, The Netherlands	5, 0.25 MW turbines	6 birds killed, a further 3–11 may also have been casualties	3.65 birds	Musters et al. (1996)
Zebruuge Belgium	25 turbines averaging 0.35 MW output	982 birds in 2 years (2004, 2005) of which 329 were breeding terns	18.1 birds, 6.7 terns	Everaert & Stienen (2007)
Tasmania, Australia			1.86 birds	Hötker et al. (2006)

Table 8.2 (*cont.*)

Location	Turbine characteristics	Total mortality	Birds/turbine/yr	References
28 locations across North America (excluding Altamont & Buffalo Ridge)	1–2947 turbines averaging 0.1–1.8 MW output		0.69 (SE ± 0.19) birds or 2.07 (SE ± 0.50) birds when bias corrected[3]	Barclay *et al.* (2007)
9 locations across North America (excluding Altamont & Buffalo Ridge)	3–267 turbines where searches conducted		0.028 raptors (SE ± 0.019)	Sterner *et al.* (2007)
25 locations across Europe (excluding those listed above)			11.89 birds (SE ± 3.99), 1.31 raptors (SE ± 0.86)	Hötker *et al.* (2006)

[1] The number recorded without correction for search effort or carcass removal, so this may be an underestimate of true mortality.

[2] Whilst at the same time the birds also suffered food shortage, this was not regarded as being a major driver of mortality. This estimate does not consider losses of juvenile and sub-adult vultures.

[3] Barclay *et al.* (2007) present two estimates for studies, a raw estimate of mortality and where available, a corrected estimate, accounting for scavenger rates and variation in carcass detection.

(Figure 8.4), particularly when flying during bad weather at night, when they may be attracted to the lights of wind farms, as with other lit installations (Hüppop *et al.* 2006; Newton 2007). The population level consequences of these impacts on such *r*-selected species are likely to be less than for *k*-selected raptors and seabirds.

Although wind turbines seem obvious to us, it is possible that some species of birds collide with them because they see them less well than we do. In many birds, the eyes are oriented so that they do not have much vision, particularly binocular vision, directly in front of the head. In flight, birds often move the head to look downwards with the forward-facing binocular part of the visual field or the sideways-looking monocular part of the visual field. This means that there is a blind area in the visual field immediately ahead of the bird in the direction of flight. Even when the bird is looking forward, frontal vision is likely to be of low resolution compared with that for lateral fields of view. Hence, some birds may not see well enough ahead of them to detect wind turbines (Martin 2011). For vultures in the genus *Gyps* the head usually points downwards at an angle of about 60 degrees below the horizontal when the bird is flying (Figure 8.5). This allows the bird to scan the ground ahead of it with its restricted binocular visual field, but it means that the blind part of the field is oriented in the direction of travel (Martin *et al.* 2012). This may partly explain why griffon vultures *Gyps fulvus* appear particularly susceptible to collisions with wind turbines.

It is clear from this review, and those of others (Hötker *et al.* 2006; Barclay *et al.* 2007; Sterner *et al.* 2007) that mortality rates vary considerably between locations from virtually none, to tens of birds being killed per turbine per year. Across Europe, all sites where collision rates in excess of two birds per turbine per year have been recorded were either

8.3 Wind energy · 315

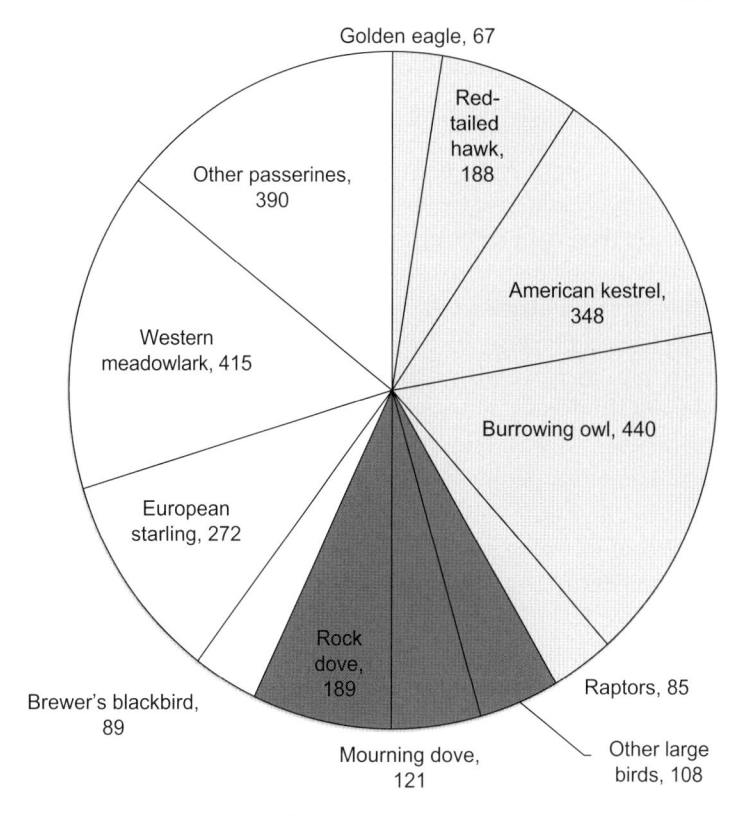

Figure 8.4 Estimated annual bird mortality (numbers per year) at the Altamont Pass Wind Resource Park. Data from Smallwood and Thelander (2008). Raptors and owls are shaded in light grey, other non-passerines in dark grey, and passerines in white.

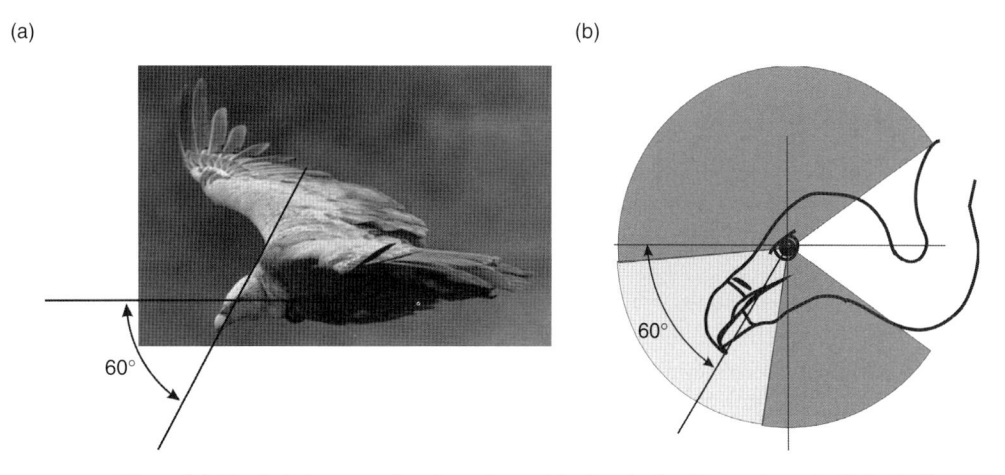

(a) (b)

Figure 8.5 Typical downwards orientation of the head of a *Gyps* vulture in flight (left) and the projection of the blind (dark grey) and binocular (light grey) parts of the birds' visual field in the sagittal plane through the head when it is in this position. Reproduced with permission from Martin *et al.* (2012).

along ridge-tops or close to wetlands (Hötker *et al.* 2006), whilst studies at Zebruuge, the Netherlands and Blyth Harbour suggest that coastal sites may also be associated with a large number of collisions, particularly if located close to breeding colonies of terns and gulls. In addition to these putative habitat differences, there appears to be considerable within-site variation in the mortality rates (Barrios & Rodriguez 2004; Ferrer *et al.* 2012). Often, a small number of turbines are responsible for a high proportion of collisions, presumably because they are associated with a particular micro-topography or wind characteristics that make birds more likely to collide with them. Understanding this further should be the focus of research, in order to understand the factors which influence the ability of birds to avoid particular turbines as a precursor to informing future turbine placement.

In addition, there appears to be significant variation in collision risk associated with different turbine designs. Both Barclay *et al.* (2007) and Hötker *et al.* (2006) suggested that bird collisions may increase with turbine height, although the effect was marginal in the former study. If robust, this relationship may be used to estimate the most efficient way of generating energy for the least number of birds killed. Such an analysis indicates, at least for birds, that overall levels of mortality will be lowest at the most modern and efficient wind farms, where a small number of large turbines will generate the same amount of energy as many small turbines (Box 8.1). This is because despite the fact that larger turbines are associated with a greater collision risk per turbine, this is offset by the reduced number of large turbines required overall to generate the same amount of electricity. Further work is required to test this, and to examine the extent to which such patterns may vary between species' groups; the underpinning data for this analysis was based on all bird collisions. Recent data suggest that most seabirds fly close to the sea surface, indicating that few, large offshore wind farms are also likely to result in fewer bird collisions than more, smaller turbines (Johnston *et al.* 2014), although it is possible that particularly vulnerable groups, such as raptors, may exhibit different relationships. Unfortunately, it appears that such large turbines may cause the greatest mortality of bats (Barclay *et al.* 2007), an additional negative impact of wind farms of significant conservation concern (Voigt *et al.* 2012).

Although these levels of collision mortality sound large, they are in many cases smaller than the numbers of birds killed by other sources. For example, in Canada, it is estimated that the numbers of birds killed by cats or collision with power lines, buildings or road vehicles are each at least three orders of magnitude greater than those killed by collision with wind turbines (Calvert *et al.* 2013). However, collisions with wind turbines may cause a conservation problem when they kill many individuals of species whose life history makes their population trends sensitive to such losses. Bird populations exposed to an additional cause of death, such as hunting, entanglement in fishing gear or collisions, may not decline substantially if the deaths result in a sufficiently large compensatory increase in breeding success or survival. This can happen when demographic rates are density-dependent, leading to higher breeding success or survival when bird population density is low than when it is high. If the death rate is below a certain level which can be compensated for in this way, population size can be maintained albeit at a lower level. Because the survival of birds from fledging to breeding age varies comparatively little among species, the capacity of a bird species to compensate for additional deaths is mostly related to the average longevity of the adults and the average age at first breeding. Species with high adult

Box 8.1 · *Effects of increasing turbine capacity upon bird and bat mortality rates*

There is a strong relationship between hub height (h) and the generating capacity of individual turbines. We estimate the form of this relationship using data on the turbine characteristics of wind farms from Barclay *et al.* (2007) and Pearce-Higgins *et al.* (2012). Across the 49 sites included, this was best described by the following power relationship (Box 8.1a).

We used this relationship to model the predicted number of bird and bat mortalities at a hypothetical 10 MW wind farm comprised of turbine capacities from 0.1–2.5 MW from the following published relationships of annual mortality rates (Box 8.1b):

Bird mortality $= 0.052h - 0.45$, $r = 0.32$ (Barclay *et al.* 2007)
Bird mortality $= 0.30h - 0.45$, $r = 0.28$ (Hötker *et al.* 2006)
Bat mortality rate $= 0.00004e^{0.1757h}$ (Barclay *et al.* 2007)

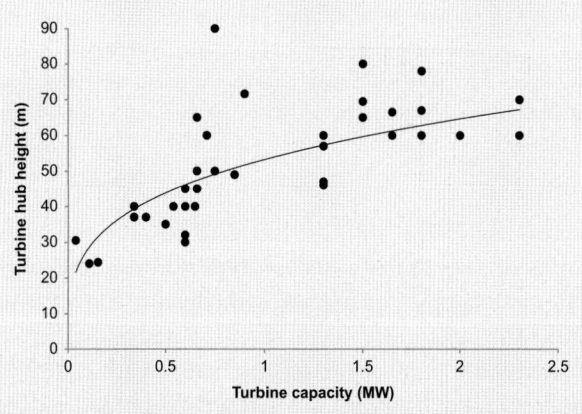

Box 8.1a Relationship between turbine capacity (*c*) and height (*h*) is best described by the following power curve ($h = 53.25c^{0.28}$, $r = 0.76$).

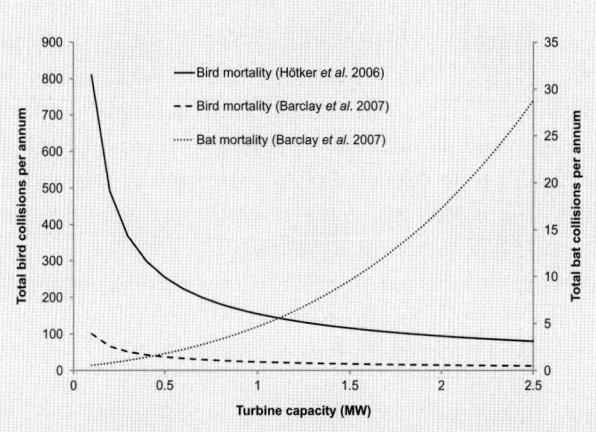

Box 8.1b Modelled variation in annual bird and bat mortality at a hypothetical 10 MW wind farm as a function of the capacity of individual turbines.

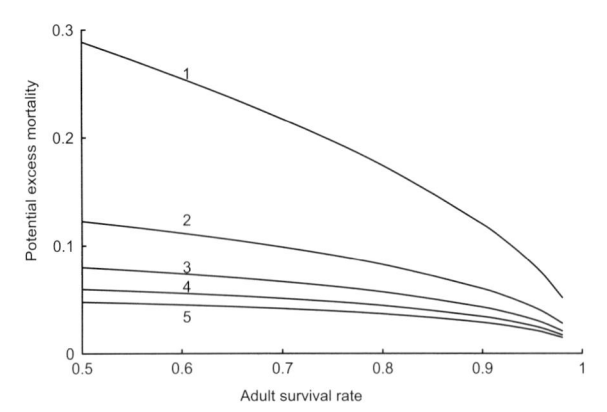

318 · Effects of climate change mitigation on birds

Figure 8.6 The maximum potential excess annual mortality which a population of a bird species might be able to tolerate without declining drastically because it remains within its capacity for density-dependent compensatory improvement of survival or of other demographic rates. The curves show potential excess mortality in relation to the annual survival rate of adults. Each curve is for a different value of the mean age at first reproduction in years, indicated by the numbers. Values were calculated by the method of Niel and Lebreton (2005). Following Dillingham and Fletcher (2008) a value of $\beta = 0.25$ has been used.

survival rate which first breed late in life are least likely to be able to compensate for additional deaths. Large birds of prey, such as eagles and vultures, and large seabirds, such as albatrosses, are extreme examples of species with this life history. An approximate method for calculating the maximum level of additional mortality a species is likely to be able to sustain without a population decline from its adult survival rate and age of first breeding was developed by Niel and Lebreton (2005), and termed the demographic invariant method. This shows how sensitive the level of tolerable additional mortality is to both adult survival and age of first breeding (Figure 8.6). Thus, a species with an adult survival rate of about 0.7 that breeds after one year will decline markedly if excess mortality exceeds 0.2 (or 20% of individuals) or less, depending on the precise details of that population. It should however be stressed that this method is approximate and gives a theoretical *maximum* for the level of additional mortality a species could sustain, rather than an estimate of the *actual* level of additional mortality possible. It should also be noted that the method identifies a level of additional mortality that would not allow stable population to be maintained. However, that level will usually be substantially lower.

The principle is illustrated by the marked population decline of breeding white-tailed eagles *Haliaeetus albicilla* on the island of Smøla, Norway, following the construction of a 68-turbine wind farm within an Important Bird Area. Between 2005 and June 2010, a minimum of 38 individuals were killed as a result of collisions with the turbines, whilst the number of breeding pairs on the island declined from 19 to one (Cole 2011; Ledec *et al.* 2011; Dahl *et al.* 2012). This species is exactly the sort expected to be sensitive by virtue of its high adult survival and late age at first breeding. Poorly sited wind farms can therefore have a significant effect on local populations of vulnerable species. Effects may be more widespread if they kill large numbers of birds from a wide area, as in the case of Egyptian vultures

Box 8.2 · *Effects of wind farms on Egyptian vultures in Spain*

The globally endangered Egyptian vulture has a world population of some 30 000 to 40 000 mature individuals. Of these, 1300 breeding pairs (40% of the European population) breed in Spain, where since 1987 the population has declined by at least 25% (Birdlife International 2012a). Collisions with wind turbines increase the annual mortality rate of territorial birds within 15 km of a wind farm by 0.015 ± 0.03, and of non-territorial birds by 0.008 ± 0.016. About 31% of territories are currently at risk from collision, being within a 15 km radius of at least one wind farm. As a result, the 2005 level of wind farm development (14 145 MW installed wind power capacity) is likely to speed up the current rate of population decline and to advance the time when the population becomes small and subject to chance adverse effects and extinction. By 2010, 20 676 MW had been installed, so the adverse effect of collision is likely to be larger. Expected population trajectories for Egyptian vultures in northern Spain are shown for the following future scenarios: no wind farms, the 2005 level of wind farms, and a fivefold increase in installed wind farm capacity within the same areas as current wind farm development, assuming a linear relationship between the number of wind farms and additional mortality rate.

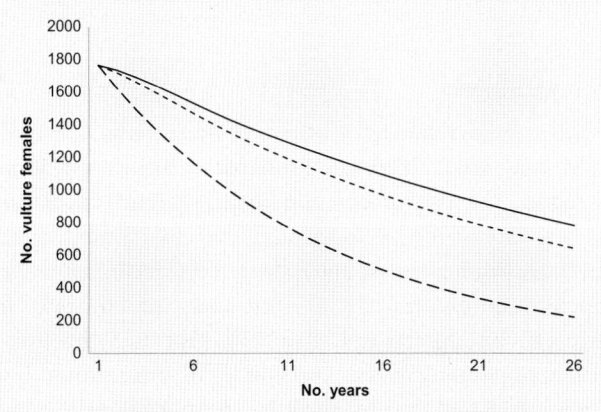

Box 8.2 Modelled changes in the Egyptian vulture population in northern Spain assuming current demographic rates from Grande *et al.* (2008; solid line) and after including additional mortality from Carrete *et al.* (2009a; small dashed line), and with a fivefold increase in wind farm installations beyond the 2005 level (large dashed line).

Neophron percnopterus in Spain, where wind farms have exacerbated the current population decline (Carrete *et al.* 2009a). As a result of collision mortality of this wide-ranging species, any significant future expected increase in wind farm development is likely to exacerbate the decline further and, depending upon its magnitude, may increase the risk of extinction of the Spanish population of this globally endangered species (Box 8.2).

Wind farms in Spain have also affected populations of griffon vultures. Fourteen per cent of Spanish colonies are within 10 km of a wind farm and 33% are within 20 km. As birds range over 50–70 km from their colony, a high proportion of individuals are at increased risk of mortality from collision (Telleria 2009). At one particular colony, sudden changes in food availability caused vultures to switch their main feeding area, which involved them flying near wind turbines. As a result of collision of both adult and immature vultures with the blades, annual survival of individually marked adult vultures was reduced by 30% and the population crashed (Martinez-Abrain et al. 2012).

These studies suggest that where wind farms significantly increase adult mortality, particularly of wide-ranging, long-lived, slow-breeding birds, they are likely to have a negative impact on population trends, not just locally, but across large areas. Many onshore wind farms are in relatively remote and windy areas, such as mountainous areas, which tend to support large numbers of raptors and other similarly long-lived, wide-ranging species vulnerable to human disturbance. There is also increasing development of offshore wind farms, particularly in the seas around Europe, where many seabird breeding colonies support internationally important numbers of a range of species potentially at risk of collision (Langston 2010). As new developments are likely to be sited in areas of relatively shallow water, which also tend to be important spawning grounds for fish, and therefore important foraging grounds for seabirds, there is considerable potential for these to cause problems as well. Careful consideration therefore needs to be given to the potential for onshore and offshore developments to have significant negative impacts on populations of seabird species whose life history characteristics make them sensitive to additional mortality caused by collision.

8.3.2 Disturbance and displacement

In addition to collision, birds may avoid areas of otherwise suitable habitat close to wind turbines. Whilst this might just cause a redistribution of birds without affecting their population size, or even reduce the risk of collision mortality, such displacement may deny the birds access to resources such as food, and therefore could have negative consequences for survival, breeding success or both. If such effects are large enough that a density-dependent compensatory response is insufficient to cancel out their effects, then declines in population size can be expected. It has been proposed that the effect on population size of disturbance preventing access to resources by birds should be estimated by assuming that population size is reduced by the same proportion as the reduction in access to resources (Gill et al. 1996). Compensatory responses might make the true effect smaller than this method would predict, but on the other hand, restriction of access to resources at a critical time of year, when food supplies are scarce or during a migration stopover, might lead to the true effect being larger. Nonetheless, when detailed knowledge of the population ecology of a species is lacking, the approach proposed by Gill et al. (1996) may be a reasonable approximation.

In a review of European studies, Hötker (2006) found that reductions in breeding bird population density at and near to wind farm sites on land following construction, or relative to neighbouring areas without wind farms, occurred in 134 cases (45% of the total reviewed). A greater proportion (57%) of studies of European wintering bird populations indicated negative effects of wind farms on land on the numbers of birds close to the turbines, compared to 126 cases with either no effect or a positive effect. Four species or species' groups of wintering birds (Eurasian wigeon *Anas penelope*, Northern lapwing, Eurasian golden plover and geese *Anser* spp.) appeared to consistently avoid turbines over distances of 200–400 m.

These patterns of greater avoidance during the non-breeding season than the breeding season do not always hold. For example, Deveraux *et al.* (2008) failed to detect any significant

Table 8.3 *Estimated distances from wind turbines over which upland breeding birds in the UK exhibit significantly reduced population density and the size of the estimated reduction in density within a 500 m buffer around the turbines. From Pearce-Higgins* et al. *(2009b).*

Species	Distance	Predicted density reduction
Common buzzard	500 m	41% (16–58%)
Hen harrier	250 m	53% (0–74%)
Eurasian golden plover	200 m	39% (4–59%)
Common snipe	400 m	48% (8–68%)
Eurasian curlew	800 m	42% (3–73%)[a]
Meadow pipit	100 m	15% (3–25%)
Northern wheatear	200 m	44% (5–65%)

[a] Given the apparent avoidance distance to 800 m, this translates to an estimated 30% reduction in density (3–52%) within a 1 km radius of the turbines for curlew.

avoidance of wind turbines by birds during the non-breeding season on UK farmland, whilst a multi-site and multi-species assessment of the distribution and abundance of breeding birds around 12 upland wind farms in the UK showed significant evidence of turbine avoidance after accounting for potentially covarying effects of habitat (Pearce-Higgins *et al.* 2009b). Estimates of the distance over which avoidance occurred ranged from 100 m to 800 m, with the largest effects being for Eurasian curlew *Numenius arquata*, common snipe *Gallinago gallinago* and common buzzard (Table 8.3). Avoidance was not complete, but of sufficient magnitude to result in an estimated 40–50% reduction in breeding densities within 500 m of the turbines. Effects of disturbance from wind farm operation on land birds therefore differ between species and habitats (see also Leddy *et al.* 1999).

Avoidance of wind turbines during the breeding season, when birds tend to be more territorial and widely dispersed, may have greater population-level significance than during the non-breeding season, depending on the concentration of the breeding population and availability of alternative resources in the winter. A meta-analysis of post-construction monitoring data from upland wind farms in the UK as a test of the findings of Pearce-Higgins *et al.* (2009b) found that the species which showed the greatest avoidance of the turbines were those which suffered the greatest population declines at wind farms (Pearce-Higgins *et al.* 2012). Thus, the most notable local declines occurred in Eurasian curlew and common snipe populations. Uniquely, this study indicated that these declines probably occurred during wind farm construction, and therefore appeared likely to result from effects of disturbance during that period of intense construction activity, rather than from the ongoing operation of the wind farm after construction.

Offshore turbines placed in shallow seas near the shore may also displace seaducks, auks and divers. The degree of avoidance also varies substantially among species. Evidence from aerial and boat surveys off the coasts of England and Denmark before and after turbine construction suggests that red-throated *Gavia stellata* and black-throated (Arctic) *G. arctica* divers (loons) may be among the species with the strongest avoidance of wind farms. Not only did they almost completely avoid foraging within the wind farms, they also tended to avoid areas within 2 km or more from the edge of the wind farms (Figure 8.7).

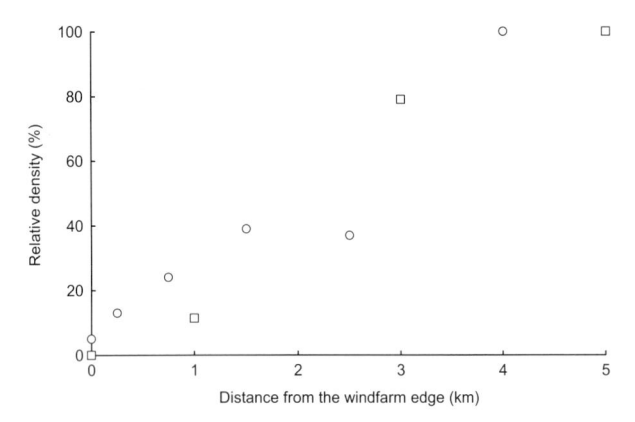

Figure 8.7 Density of wintering red-throated and black-throated divers in relation to the distance from the edge of offshore wind farms. Points represent the mean density of birds for each bin of distance from the wind farm, expressed as a percentage of that expected in the absence of the wind farm, derived from surveys before and after turbine construction. Points are plotted at the midpoint of each distance bin, except that the points at zero distance which represent the relative density of divers within the wind farm and the righthand point for each study is the expected relative density outside the wind farm buffer. Squares represent results from aerial surveys of both species combined in and near the Horns Rev wind farm, Denmark (Petersen *et al.* 2006). Circles represent results for red-throated divers only from boat surveys in the Thames estuary, UK (Percival 2010).

There are few studies of the potential for avoidance of wind farms to affect bird population size or demographic rates over a large geographical area. In one example, the overlap between wind farms and golden plovers, a species whose natural habitat association for flat ridges and plateaus tops matches favoured areas for wind farm development, may lead to conflict. Based on potential avoidance of turbines by breeding golden plovers of 200 m, densities may be reduced on wind farms (Pearce-Higgins *et al.* 2008, 2009b), although such avoidance rates do not seem consistent at all sites (Douglas *et al.* 2011; Pearce-Higgins *et al.* 2012). Overall, the current overlap between wind farms and the Scottish population of this species is low (< 1%), but depending on future wind farm consents, may exceed 5% or more for some regional populations where golden plovers are particularly concentrated on hilltops suitable for wind farm development (Pearce-Higgins *et al.* 2008).

Migrating birds tend to fly around turbine arrays (Desholm & Kahlert 2005). If faced with long strings of turbines, or multiple arrays, individuals may alter their route, forcing them to travel further and increasing energetic costs (Fox *et al.* 2006). However, where studied, the cost associated with flying around wind farm arrays appears minimal compared to the energetic cost of migration (Masden *et al.* 2009). Such barrier effects are therefore unlikely to be a major problem in most circumstances.

8.3.3 Summary of wind farm effects

The effects of wind farms on birds are only likely to be biologically important if developments overlap with large population concentrations, or a high proportion of the population of a dispersed species. In such cases, a reduction in the area of available habitat or an increase in mortality caused by collisions may have a significant negative impact. In the case of rapidly declining species, rare species and those with restricted ranges, inappropriately placed wind farms may pose a serious additional threat to long-term population viability. The impact of overhead power lines on the vulnerable blue crane *Anthropoides paradiseus*, where it is estimated some 12% of birds in the Western Cape population are killed per year through collision with unmarked cables, illustrates how this may occur (Shaw *et al.* 2010).

As a result, care needs to be taken when planning wind farm development, to minimise the potential conflict with bird conservation (see Section 8.8). Potential impacts on bats may also be severe and should also be considered (Barclay *et al.* 2007; Voigt *et al.* 2012), particularly because, although increasing turbine size and efficiency may reduce the risk of mortality to birds, it may increase it for bats (Box 8.1). Although there are relatively few well-documented examples where wind farms have had a significant impact on bird populations to date, as the number of developments increases rapidly in response to the urgent need for climate change mitigation, this may change. There is an increasing risk that new wind farm developments will be located in areas with high concentrations of species susceptible to collision or displacement which may cause or contribute to long-term population declines. Understanding and accounting for these impacts, which are currently relatively poorly understood, should be an increasing priority for bird conservation scientists and decision-makers.

In the case of some legally designated protected areas, any development which reduces the abundance of designated species within that protected area may be deemed unacceptable, even if there is no firm evidence of an impact on the whole population. Outside sites with legal conservation designations, developments may be permitted if they are unlikely to reduce a population below a particular threshold or to increase extinction risk. Individual developments should not be regarded in isolation however, as combined they may have a cumulative impact. Applying some biological common sense leads us to suggest that such cumulative impacts are likely to be greatest where wind farms cause significant mortality of wide-ranging bird species with a high adult survival rate and late age at first breeding (Figure 8.6). This may occur where individual developments in high-risk areas become large-scale population sinks, or where wind farms overlap with a high proportion of a susceptible population. We have already highlighted the particular risk that wind farms may pose to raptor species, but other large species, such as storks, cranes, herons and related species, may also be vulnerable to collision mortality (Ledec *et al.* 2011). Many of these are migratory and concentrate at particular bottlenecks or key sites, such as large wetlands, where wind farm development should be avoided. In addition, the potentially rapid increase in offshore wind development may pose a significant risk to seabird populations which are likely to also be under pressure from other factors, including overfishing and climate change (Chapters 3 and 4). It is worth emphasising that most of the research conducted has been on onshore wind farms, and there is a considerable amount of work to be done to understand the likely impacts of wind farms on seabirds (Langston 2010). The long-term vulnerability of seabirds to increased adult mortality as a result of anthropogenic pressure is well-recognised (Tasker *et al.* 2000), and should therefore be an important consideration when planning new offshore wind power developments.

8.4 Hydroelectricity

There are several different ways in which electricity may be generated from water bodies. In relation to freshwater, two types of scheme may be used – run-of-river schemes take water away from natural water courses, and storage schemes, which use reservoirs to provide a steady flow through the turbines (Copestake 2006). Similar approaches may also generate electricity from tidal currents, which we examine in the next section (8.5).

8.4.1 Run-of-river schemes

Run-of-river schemes divert flows away from the natural river channel through turbines to generate electricity. This is not a problem during periods of high flow volume because an excess of water will maintain river flow, whilst during periods of low flow, abstraction is generally limited or stopped, again to ensure that river flow is sufficient to maintain ecological function. The greatest ecological impacts may therefore occur at intermediate flow levels, when the highest proportion of the total flow of water is diverted. This can lead to long-term impacts on sediment transport, aquatic plants, invertebrate and fish populations (Larinier 2008; McCarthy et al. 2008). Although fish ladders may reduce the obstacle that hydroelectric schemes pose to the movement of fish and other aquatic fauna, they require flows to be maintained over them, which can sometimes be difficult, particularly where water availability is limited (Larinier 2008; Baskaya et al. 2011). This means that run-of-river schemes may lead to the fragmentation of fish populations in river systems. Impacts of these schemes on birds, through reductions in invertebrate and fish prey populations, are possible but poorly documented.

8.4.2 Storage schemes

Water storage schemes are associated with a significant ecological footprint. They often require damming of river valleys, and once the dam is completed and the reservoir created, this causes an immediate loss of terrestrial habitat upstream as a result of flooding (Fearnside 2005). Riparian habitats such as gallery forests and wetlands on river margins are particularly at risk. The watercourse is converted from running water to a large, often deep, still-water system, and species associated with shallow, running water are lost. Particular problems are associated with changes in thermal stratification, sediment loading and eutrophication, as well as the barrier effect of the dam across a once continuous watercourse. It is clear that the environmental impact of such developments may be very significant on both terrestrial and aquatic environments.

The purpose of all storage schemes is to hold back water to release it in a controlled fashion through the turbines, in order to generate electricity. This means that the water level of the storage lake can fluctuate dramatically in response to the amount of water stored. Such short-term instability contrasts strongly with the natural situation of many lakes, where changes in water level are more gradual and caused by precipitation upstream. Rapid fluctuations in water levels may reduce bird breeding success by inundating nests near the water's edge if a sudden increase in water level occurs, or if water level is reduced, by stranding floating nests and putting them at greater risk of predation (Reitan & Thingstad 1999). In Scotland and Scandinavia, the construction of water storage schemes had a significant impact on breeding black-throated divers. The vulnerability of nests to inundation increased because of greater fluctuations in water levels (Mudge & Talbot 1993; Hake et al. 2005). However, the implementation of appropriate mitigation measures has successfully reduced some of these effects. For example, the provision of artificial floating islands on Scottish lochs with hydroelectric schemes has prevented the flooding of nests placed on the shoreline or on islands, and increased breeding productivity at those sites by 2.7 times (Hancock 2000). Similar approaches could be adopted for other vulnerable species. In cases where such intervention is not possible, management to limit the extent of sudden water-level fluctuations during the breeding season, for example by controlling the rate of flow through the turbines, may be possible.

As with run-of-river schemes, negative effects of dams can extend downstream, through high magnitude and rapid changes to water levels in response to changes in flow rate. This may similarly affect the success of birds breeding close to the river, or on sandbanks in the river system, leading to either increased risk of inundation or stranding as water levels rise or fall unpredictably (Hill & Wright 2000; Leslie et al. 2000). Depending on the characteristics of the reservoir, down-stream effects may extend to water quality, which may become de-oxygenated, particularly if the artificial reservoir is deep and still, and contains a high organic content, for example after the inundation of surrounding land (Fearnside 2005). A similar range of downstream effects to those already described for run-of-river schemes can also be expected to be caused by changes in river flow. Where a large number of dams may be built upstream of a large floodplain system, such developments may have significant cumulative impacts on downstream flow.

This is illustrated for the headwaters of the Brahmaputra in India (Box 8.3), a potential problem that extends across the Himalayas (Pandit & Grumbine 2012), where the proposed density of dams exceeds that in other river basins (Figure 8.8). As a result, some 51 km^2 to 115 km^2 of forest could be lost by 2025, depending upon the precise location of the dams. Although a relatively small figure compared to likely background rates of deforestation predicted to occur as a result of other drivers, it is estimated this 1–3% of forest loss could drive the extinction of an additional 2 to 3 bird species beyond the 68 projected to be lost by 2025 as a result of habitat loss (Pandit & Grumbine (2012). Additional negative impacts on riparian and wetland species are also likely (Box 8.3). The same pressures are likely to affect the Andean Amazon, where a large number of dams have also been proposed (Finer & Jenkins 2012). Almost half of these would be likely to have a high ecological impact, resulting in significant fragmentation of Andean headwaters, the expansion of new roads and infrastructure, and significant levels of deforestation in highly biodiverse areas of montane forest.

8.4.3 Summary of hydropower schemes

Hydropower schemes may have a significant impact on wetland and riparian systems and the bird species which rely on them. They may also affect bird populations on marginal terrestrial habitats at increased risk of inundation. Their effects on invertebrate, fish and amphibian populations may be large, but there is relatively little evidence for significant impacts on bird populations, and research is urgently required to address this, particularly given the proposed scale of development in some locations. Storage schemes have a much greater ecological

Box 8.3 · *Potential impacts of hydropower schemes in north-east India*

Plans to construct 135 hydroelectric dams in the Indian region of Arunachal Pradesh to generate 57 000 MW of electricity upstream of the Brahmaputra River are likely to have significant ecological impacts on threatened bird species, their habitats and other biodiversity in the region itself and in the floodplains downstream (Pandit & Grumbine 2012; Vagholikar 2012). Large dams are already under construction in Sikkim, for example on the Teesta River. If the Arunachal Pradesh dams are built, they may lead to large daily fluctuations in downstream water flows which will be low (2% of normal flow levels) for up to 20 hours as water is stored and then increase markedly (600% of normal flow levels) for the remaining 4 hours of electricity generation.

Proposed dams on the Siang, Dibang and Lohit Rivers are likely to result in daily water-level fluctuations of 3–4 m in the Dibru-Saikhowa National Park, some 70 km downstream at confluence of the Brahmaputra River. This park supports a range of globally threatened bird species, including the Bengal florican *Houbaropsis bengalensis*, white-bellied heron *Ardea insignis*, greater adjutant *Leptoptilos dubius*, lesser adjutant *L. javanicus*, white-winged duck *Cairina scutulata*, spotted greenshank *Tringa guttifer* and Baer's pochard *Aythya baeri*, all of which use the riparian grasslands and wetlands potentially affected by the altered water-level regime. Many of these species nest on riverine islands and in reedbed habitats, and so will be extremely vulnerable to the flooding of nesting attempts, aside from any underlying ecological changes to the habitat resulting from the proposed changes. The threatened marsh babbler *Pellorneium palustre* and black-breasted parrotbill *Paradocorbis flavirostris* also occupy grasslands and wetlands in the floodplain.

Away from wetland habitats, the forests and scrub of Arunachal Pradesh contain populations of the globally threatened Blyth's tragopan *Tragopan blythii*, Sclater's monal *Lophophorus sclateri*, rufous-necked hornbill *Aceros nipalensis*, beautiful nuthatch *Sitta formosa*, rusty-throated wren-babbler *Spelaeornis badeigularis* and snowy-throated babbler *Stachyris oglei*. These are species whose habitats might be impacted by habitat loss associated with flooding or by additional developments associated with the roads and other infrastructure resulting from dam construction. Arunachal Pradesh also forms a substantial part of the Eastern Himalayas Endemic Bird Area, which holds many bird species with restricted global ranges and contains populations of an additional ten restricted-range species which are not globally endangered.

Box 8.3 The lesser adjutant has a global population of less than 5000 mature individuals, and may be impacted by the loss of wetlands associated with hydropower schemes.

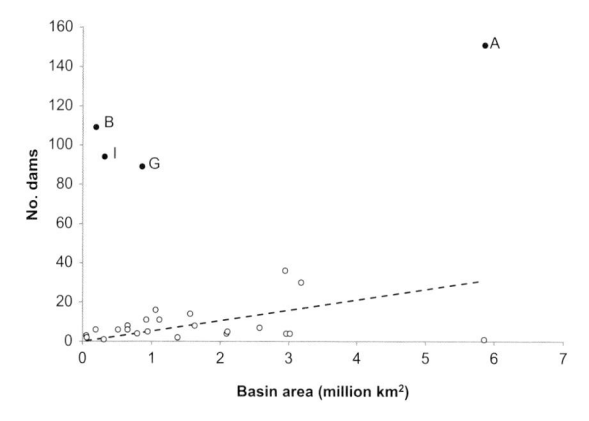

Figure 8.8 The area and number of dams within major river basins of the world, with a fitted line based on mean dam density. The number of proposed dams in the Indus (I), Brahmaputra (B) and Ganga (G) basins are indicated by filled circles (data from Pandit & Grumbine 2012). Also given are the number of proposed dams in the Andean Amazon (A) (Finer & Jenkins 2012).

footprint than run-of-river schemes, potentially destroying or modifying large areas of terrestrial habitats. For example, the area flooded by nine large dams in Amazonia with a generating capacity of 630 MW of electricity totalled 730 km^2 (Fearnside 2005). Across the Indian Himalayas, it is estimated that about 1.5 ha will be lost per MW of the 57 000 MW proposed, with an additional 0.59 ha of habitat lost as a result of associated activities (Pandit & Grumbine 2012). In addition to this loss of terrestrial habitat, they may cause additional impacts on freshwater birds through potential changes in water levels, although it may be possible to reduce some of these effects through appropriate mitigation.

8.5 Tidal and wave power

A number of different methods exist to generate electricity from tidal and wave power. Barrages may be constructed across estuaries with a large tidal range in order to generate electricity from the tidal current. Sluices in the barrage are opened on the rising tide to allow the estuary to fill, but closed when the tide turns. Once there is a sufficient height differential between the water inside and outside the barrage on the falling tide, the turbines are opened and electricity is generated on the ebb flow. It is also possible to generate electricity on both the ebb and flow part of the tide cycle in a dual-mode system. However, this limits the amount of water flowing into the barrage on the rising tide, and so the total net output over both phases of the cycle is reduced (Figure 8.9). A small number of tidal barrage schemes exist, most notably at La Rance, France, which generates 240 MW, and the Bay of Fundy, Canada, which generates 17.8 MW. However, because of the large energy-generating potential, there is currently considerable interest in constructing additional and larger schemes at a number of sites. As an alternative to the barrage system, tidal stream farms involve the placement of turbines in the water column to extract the existing energy from the tide, without the need for a barrage. A variety of other technologies are currently in development to generate electricity from wave energy.

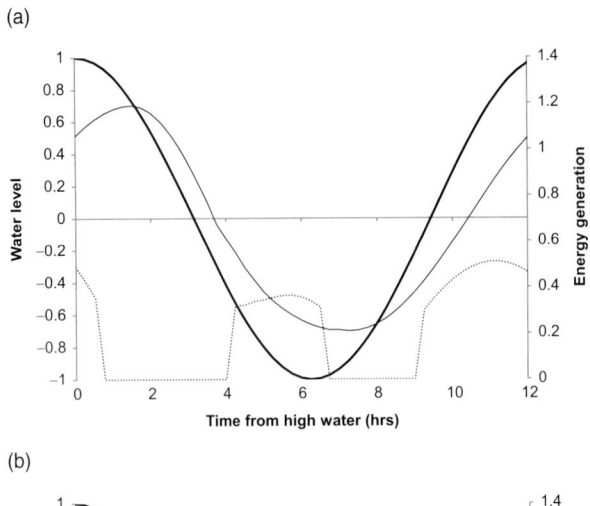

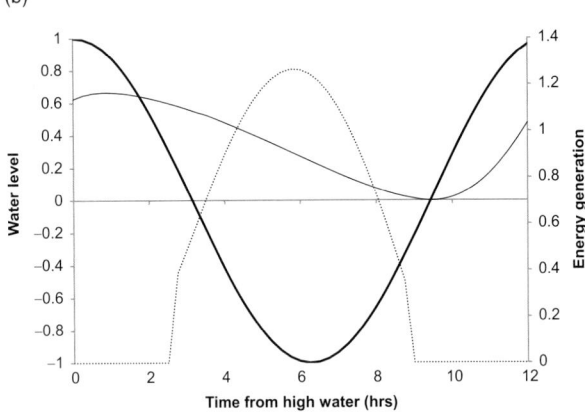

Figure 8.9 Comparison of the effects of a dual-cycle barrage (a) and ebb-only barrage (b) on water level (−1, low water; 1, high water) inside the barrage (thin line) and outside (thick line) in relation to an index of energy generation (dotted line). Adapted from Frid *et al.* (2012).

Both tidal stream and wave energy production remain largely experimental and therefore the ecological impacts of these are relatively unknown and difficult to evaluate, but could involve potential impacts through disturbance, collision, changes in sedimentation, habitat alteration and impacts on aquatic prey species (Grecian *et al.* 2010; McCluskie *et al.* 2012).

8.5.1 Tidal barrages

Estuaries around the world are widely used by both breeding and wintering birds. Being fed by nutrient-rich freshwater from rivers, they are extremely productive habitats supporting high densities of invertebrates which are preyed upon by many millions of wintering waders and waterfowl. Salt marsh and mangrove habitats located on the edge of estuaries also support many wintering and breeding birds. As a result, many such sites are legally protected. The carrying capacity of these sites is extremely sensitive to disruption by human activities; commercial harvesting has frequently led to reductions in waterbird invertebrate prey and the numbers of birds which particular sites support. Examples include the commercial harvesting of cockles *Cerastoderma edule* in the Waddensee, the Netherlands (Kraan *et al.* 2009), cockles and mussels *Mytilus edulis* in the Wash, UK (Atkinson *et al.* 2003), and horseshoe crabs *Limulus polyphemus* in Delaware Bay, USA. At the latter, a reduction in the abundance of horseshoe crab eggs in the spring has adversely affected red knots migrating between the North American Arctic and South America. The birds rely on these eggs to provide a nutritious and easily available food resource in order to gain condition for their onward northward migration to their breeding grounds. As crab abundance declined, adult knot survival dropped significantly, from 85% to 56% (Baker *et al.* 2004). Horseshoe crab harvesting at a single site may have impacted the entire flyway population of a red knot subspecies, causing a 50% population decline in only three years, although there may also be an impact of disrupted lemming cycles in the Arctic that requires further investigation (Fraser *et al.* 2013). Management decisions at Delaware Bay, USA could therefore have ecological consequences for bird communities from the Arctic to Tierra del Fuego. These results suggest that many bird species which use estuaries on migration are likely to be susceptible to reductions in the extent of foraging habitat or densities of prey (Kraan *et al.* 2009). Hence, changes such as those caused by the construction of a barrage are likely to have substantial and far-reaching ecological effects.

Human modification of estuarine habitats, such as through the construction of a barrage, is likely to significantly reduce the carrying capacity of a particular site for migratory waterbirds in a number of ways (Clark 2006; Burton *et al.* 2010; Frid *et al.* 2012). Firstly and most obviously, a barrage scheme will affect water levels. These effects are more pronounced in an ebb-only generation barrage than a dual-cycle barrage (Figure 8.9), which will reduce the tidal range upstream of the barrage by about half, leading to a reduction in the intertidal area of the estuary. The delayed fall in water levels during the ebb–flow before the sluices are opened will reduce the amount of time the mudflats are exposed for the birds to be able to feed, which is likely to have a large and non-linear impact on the carrying capacity of the estuary (West & Caldow 2006). The barrage will also cause significant changes in the flow rates to occur on either side of it. These are likely to be reduced upstream, leading to significant increases in sediment and nutrient deposition within the barrage area. This may increase the productivity of the estuary, boost prey densities and therefore potentially offset some of the reductions in the extent and duration of exposure of the mudflats for foraging birds outlined above. However, it is also likely to increase the proportion of clay and silt in the sediment within the impounded area. Sediment type has an important influence on the composition of estuarine invertebrate species and their functional types. In turn, this is likely to alter the waterbird community composition of the estuary away from species such as sanderling *Calidris alba* and common ringed plover *Charadrius hiaticula*, which associate with sandy estuaries, towards dunlin and bar-tailed godwits *Limosa lapponica* which prefer muddy estuaries (Clark 2006). Downstream of the barrage, increased wave action and reduced rates of sediment deposition may lead to increased erosion of mudflats (Figure 8.10), as observed after the construction of a storm surge barrage on the Dutch Oosterschelde, which reduced the survival and abundance of a local oystercatcher population (Duriez *et al.* 2009).

The negative effects to birds of losses of intertidal habitat have been clearly demonstrated by the consequences of the construction of a freshwater barrage in Cardiff Bay,

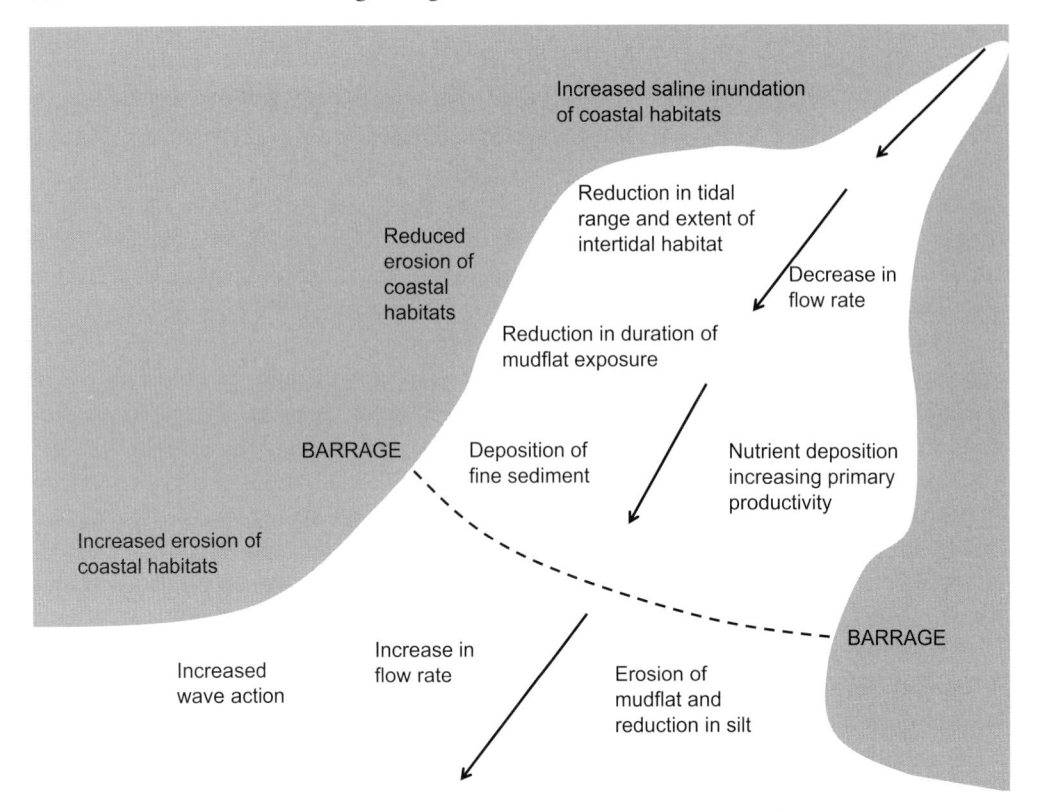

Figure 8.10 Schematic diagram of an estuary to summarise the ecological consequences relevant to bird populations of the construction of a tidal barrage (dashed line) both on land (grey) and in the estuary (white). The downstream direction of water flow is indicated by the arrows.

UK. Common redshank wintering at Cardiff Bay before the construction of the barrage were displaced to nearby intertidal habitat, leading to a reduction in the survival of individually-marked birds relative to both the pre-construction period and to a control group of individuals at nearby unmodified estuarine sites. These effects were probably the results of increased competition among birds at the sites to which the displaced redshank moved and led to an overall population decline (Box 8.4). Barrage schemes on estuaries may therefore reduce the abundance of species relying on intertidal habitats, which may not only reduce the integrity of the particular designated sites that are developed, but could affect the size of flyway or global populations of the species involved. Species for which a relatively small number of sites are of critical importance would be most sensitive to such development, as indicated by the decline in the red knot subspecies *C. c. rufa* using Delaware Bay and declines in the abundance of many east Asian waders due to large-scale development and reclamation of intertidal areas in China and Korea (Amano *et al.* 2010). Any future large-scale tidal power developments would probably be highly detrimental to many migratory waterbird species. As a result, tidal power developments should be subject to thorough environmental impact assessment in order to weigh the potential environmental costs against the anticipated benefits (Section 8.8).

Box 8.4 · *Effects of the Cardiff Bay barrage on redshank populations*

Cardiff Bay is located at the confluence of the Taff and Ely estuaries, at the mouth of the Severn estuary which separates Wales from England. The bay once covered 200 ha, of which 75% was intertidal mudflat. In November 1999, a barrage across the bay was completed to create a freshwater lagoon, as part of development to promote the economic regeneration of the city of Cardiff. Construction work resulted in a significant reduction in waterbird usage of the site (Burton *et al.* 2002). After completion, 300 redshank were displaced to the Severn estuary. These displaced birds suffered a 5% reduction in body condition in the 1999/2000 winter compared to non-displaced individuals wintering in the same area after construction. This resulted in a significant reduction in survival compared to their previous survival rate at Cardiff Bay as well as to the survival of non-displaced birds elsewhere on the Severn (Burton *et al.* 2002, 2006).

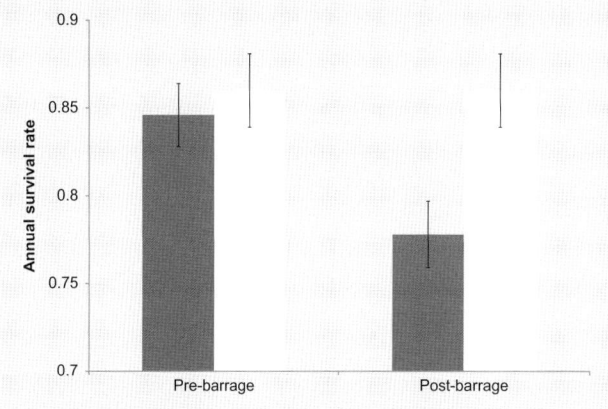

Box 8.4 A comparison of redshank survival rates of birds caught at Cardiff Bay (dark grey) and at a control site on the Severn (white) before the barrage was constructed (pre-barrage) and in the years following barrage construction (post-barrage).

8.5.2 Tidal stream and wave power

Tidal stream and wave power devices are at an earlier stage of research and development than tidal barrages. Because there are few large-scale implementations of these devices, little is known about their ecological effects. Both are likely to be less efficient than barrage schemes, and therefore will require a large footprint in order to generate the same amount of electricity. Given that tidal stream devices involve the deployment of many underwater turbines, there is the potential for these to cause substantial mortality of fish, marine mammals and diving seabirds (Coutant & Whitney 2000; Deng *et al.* 2011). However, it may be possible to reduce these impacts through a range of technical developments, or by limiting turbine velocities (Frid *et al.* 2012). The large-scale deployment of both turbines and wave power devices may have additional localised effects on water flow and sedimentation, although these may be difficult to predict. Such effects of turbines are likely to have the greatest impact on benthic animals, whilst wave power plants are likely to reduce wave energy, with potential impacts on coastal erosion processes and sedimentation patterns. The potential magnitude of these is uncertain. Because they

> **Box 8.5** · *Avian mortality at a solar energy power plant*
>
> Solar One was a pilot concentrating solar power project built in the Mojave Desert in California, USA. Its construction was completed in 1981 and the plant was operational from 1982 to 1986, using reflective mirrors (heliostats) to direct and concentrate the solar energy to a thermal device. At the time it was the largest solar energy power plant in the world. In order to examine bird mortality rates, the plant was searched weekly for carcasses over 40 weeks, whilst bird surveys assessed abundance across the 150 ha site. A total of 70 bird fatalities were documented, involving 26 species. Most of these (57 individuals, including 19 waterbirds) were from collisions with the infrastructure, particularly the mirrors. The other 13 birds (7 of which were aerial insectivores such as swallows) were burnt as they flew through the concentrated beam of solar energy. The plant may have been particularly attractive to birds because it was located near evaporation ponds, likely to concentrate birds in a desert environment (McCrary *et al.* 1986).

float on the sea surface, the shelter provided by wave power plants and their associated anchors is likely to attract fish. The structures may also offer protection from fishing activities which are likely to be restricted in their vicinity. It is therefore possible that they may provide some degree of biodiversity benefit (Inger *et al.* 2009; Grecan *et al.* 2010). Given these uncertainties, large-scale deployment of these technologies should be associated with significant research and monitoring of potential impacts.

8.6 Solar power

Solar energy can be used to heat water through thermal heating systems, or to generate electricity directly through photovoltaic devices. Capture devices may be deployed at a range of scales from supplying electricity and/or warm water to individual buildings, to large-scale facilities devoted to industrial energy generation. Irrespective of the method used, it has been suggested that the potential for negative environmental impacts of solar energy capture devices is relatively small (Tsoutsos *et al.* 2005). There is a risk that birds may collide with solar structures, or in the case of concentrated solar energy plants, be burned when they enter the areas where reflective mirrors are focussing sunlight, but there are few data on the likely severity of such impacts.

At an experimental heliostat solar power site, McCrary *et al.* (1986) crudely estimated, by dividing the mean daily count of individuals by the estimated mortality rate, that 0.6–0.7% of birds died per week (Box 8.5). Given that the majority of birds recorded were migrants, with a high degree of turnover of individuals at the site, this is likely to overestimate the true mortality rate, and the authors regarded these impacts as relatively low. However, for resident birds this would be equivalent to additive annual mortality rates of 27–31%, which seems very high. It may be significant that despite the desert location, among the birds killed were a number of waterbirds, including 11 eared grebes *Podiceps nigricollis*. The reflective nature of the heliostats used might have caused birds flying at night to confuse them with waterbodies, leading to collision. Photovoltaic plants, whose panels are dark and unreflective, are unlikely to be associated with such mortality risk (RSPB 2011), although further research is required to examine in detail the risk associated with different types of devices. Given the current interest in solar power development, the lack of such published research on their impacts on birds should be urgently addressed.

Aside from the risk of collision and heat mortality, large-scale solar power plants are likely to require large areas of land. Based on present technologies, a 5 MW plant is likely to require some 15 ha of land (RSPB 2011). Although this is considerably less than the 80 ha area required for a turbine array to generate the same power (Bright *et al.* 2008), this could represent a significant loss of habitat in otherwise relatively under-developed arid regions, where it has been suggested that large solar power development may be most appropriate (Abbasi & Abbasi 2000). Photovoltaic cells require water or other chemicals for coolant, which may also place significant pressure on scarce water resources in such areas, either through abstraction or pollution risk. Care also needs to be taken that any grid infrastructure associated with solar power plants, such as overhead power transmission lines, does not cause significant bird mortality (Jenkins *et al.* 2010).

If the risk of mortality associated with solar power plants can be minimised, there is potential for the land between the devices to be used for conservation purposes. In relatively poor areas for biodiversity such as farmland, fields converted to solar generation may be sown with wild flowers or sacrificial crops, allowing wildlife-friendly measures to be integrated within the agricultural landscape. Of course, the reduced potential for food production may then lead to expansion or intensification of agricultural production elsewhere, a topic we shall return to later in this chapter.

To conclude, solar power may be a good solution for renewable energy generation that conflicts relatively little with bird conservation, although much more research is required to confirm this. Solar generation is a rapidly expanding energy sector, a trend which is likely to continue (Figure 8.3), and is unlikely to be limited by energy availability (Table 8.1). Such expansion will need to be managed appropriately so that it does not lead to habitat loss or degradation in important areas for bird conservation. More robust information is needed on direct mortality rates requiring monitoring schemes to be implemented at new solar power plants, combined with equivalent monitoring of control sites, in much the same way as are undertaken for wind farms. Following McCrary *et al.* (1986), carcass searches should also be conducted to estimate mortality. Reflecting this uncertainty, the rapid growth of concentrated solar power was included in the top 15 emerging issues of global conservation concern for 2013 (Sutherland *et al.* 2013).

8.7 Bioenergy

Up until the nineteenth century, wood provided most of the energy generated for human use (Chu & Majumdar 2012). Although it is much less important now, biomass still provides the largest renewable contribution to energy production through the use of wood and other vegetable material, charcoal and manure for heating and lighting. There is increasing interest in expanding this contribution further through modern bioenergy approaches to generate heat and light renewably from a wide range of products, most of which are generated from farmed or plantation landscapes (Table 8.4). Sugar, starch and oil crops are grown and converted into liquid biofuels (ethanol or biodiesel), although only a relatively small proportion of the total biomass produced is used for fuel. This

Table 8.4 *Examples of different forms of bioenergy and associated crops and sources*

Crop type	Example sources
Sugar	Sugarcane, beet
Starch	Maize, wheat, cassava
Oil	Soya, rapeseed, oil palm
Biomass	Wood, straw, perennial grass, municipal waste
Gas	Biodegradable waste (sewage, manure, farm and food waste), macroalgae
Micro-organisms	Algae and bacteria

makes them two to five times less efficient than biomass crops, such as woody plants and grasses, in which the entire plant is converted into energy. The main potential impact of bioenergy production on birds is that they require large areas of land in order to be grown. That land must come from somewhere. If grown on farmland, bioenergy crops may replace food crops. Alternatively, they may require the conversion of natural and semi-natural habitats. The ultimate effect of bioenergy crops on birds therefore depends upon the utility of the crop compared to the alternative land cover they replace.

To help understand these impacts, there is much that can be learned from the already extensive literature on the effects of both agricultural and commercial forestry practices on birds. Ecological impacts of bioenergy production are likely to be low if they only involve the conversion of existing agricultural land from food to bioenergy production, but considerably higher if they require the loss of natural or semi-natural habitat. However, given current and increasing demands for global food resources, associated with the increased political importance attached to food security, loss of agricultural land for bioenergy production is likely to increase the conversion of natural vegetation into cropland, or the intensity of use of the remaining land, in order to maintain national, regional or global levels of food production.

8.7.1 The tragedy of biofuel production in the tropics

Unlike most of the other renewable energy sources discussed in this chapter, the expansion of biofuel crops has already been sufficiently large to have had a detectable and significant impact on natural ecosystems and bird populations, particularly in the tropics (Lee *et al.* 2011a). Partly fuelled by Western policies to promote renewable energy sources for reasons of climate change mitigation, biofuels have provided an important export for many countries. For example, deforestation in south-east Asia has been driven by rising global demand for oil palm, which can be used to create diesel as well as a wide range of processed foods and other products (Scharlemann 2008). Global palm oil production increased by 55% from 2001 to 2006 and plantations now cover some 14.5 million hectares globally (Fitzherbert *et al.* 2008; Foster *et al.* 2011). Between 1990 and 2005, at least 55% of oil palm expansion in Malaysia and Indonesia, where some 7% of biodiesel is produced, was in forested habitats (Koh & Wilcove 2007; Bessou *et al.* 2011). Climate change mitigation has therefore contributed to what has perhaps been one of the most rapid and significant large-scale natural habitat conversions in recent decades (exemplified

Box 8.6 · *Effects of oil palm on habitat loss in south-east Asia*

A number of studies have examined the proportional change in both the number of species and the abundance of birds on oil palm plantations compared with native forest habitats (Danielsen & Heegaard 1995; Peh *et al.* 2006; Aratrakorn *et al.* 2006; Edwards *et al.* 2010; Sheldon *et al.* 2010). The results of these studies can be averaged in order to estimate the overall magnitude of impact on native bird populations associated with oil palm plantations.

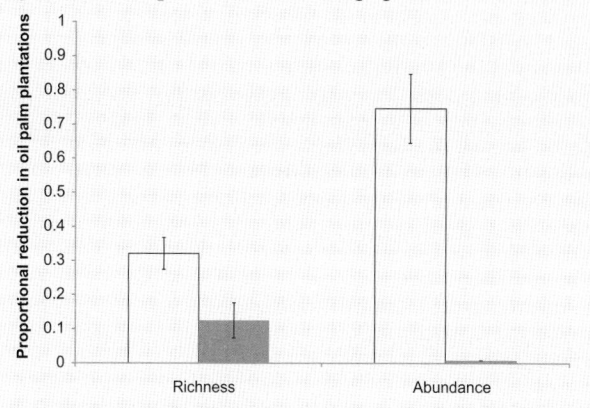

Box 8.6 Average effect sizes of the impact of oil palm plantations ($\pm$ SE) upon the richness and abundance for all bird species (open bars) and forest bird species only (grey bars) relative to natural forests (*y*-axis value of 1).

in Figure 7.2). The net greenhouse gas emissions associated with such forest clearance are large and mean they have delivered no climate change mitigation benefit. Instead, it is estimated that at least 75 years will be required for the emissions saved through biofuel use to exceed those lost by forest clearance, or over 500 years if the forest cleared was on peatland, the case across much of Indonesia (Danielsen *et al.* 2008; Fargione *et al.* 2008). Thus, well-intentioned but poorly thought through 'green' policies have had catastrophic consequences for biodiversity in these regions, as well as having exacerbated, rather than reduced, the likely magnitude of future climate change.

Oil palm plantations support a much lower biodiversity than the primary, secondary and partially logged forests that they replace (Aratrakorn *et al.* 2006; Peh *et al.* 2006). This is because they have a lower structural complexity, lower plant species diversity, and are subject to considerable human disturbance both through their lifespan and when they are cleared and replanted after 25 to 30 years (Fitzherbert *et al.* 2008). They also support far fewer invertebrate species and individuals, and have an altered microclimate compared to primary or secondary forest habitats (Foster *et al.* 2011). This transformation has had a significant negative impact on most bird species, but particularly on forest specialists, many of which have small global ranges and are of high conservation concern. Overall, 90–95% of forest species may be lost as a result of this conversion (Danielsen & Heegaard 1995; Sheldon *et al.* 2010), with oil palm plantations supporting only the most abundant and widespread generalist and open-habitat species (Box 8.6). As a result, plantations contain an order of magnitude fewer bird species and individuals than natural forest, patterns which are reflected in most other taxa (Foster *et al*. 2011). The expansion of these plantations at the expense of tropical forest has therefore resulted in changes to the IUCN Red List status of a number of endemic forest specialists (Buchanan *et al*. 2008).

It has been suggested that plantation management should be modified to maximise structural and habitat diversity and to protect or incorporate fragments of forest habitat within the plantation landscape. However, the most important measure to reduce the impact of such plantations would be to avoid siting them in biodiversity-rich areas (Edwards *et al*. 2010; Nájera & Simonetti 2010; Foster *et al*. 2011). We will return to this topic in Section 8.8. It is not just the growing of oil palm for biofuels which is a threat to natural habitats in Asia. The seeds of the jatropha plant can also be converted into oil. India's national plan for the development of jatropha identifies a total of 3 million hectares of forests available for conversion to plantations (Phalan 2009). It seems likely that this will also detrimentally affect birds and other biodiversity, particularly given projected impacts of forest loss in the Himalayas upon the long-term persistence of many bird species (Pandit & Grumbine 2012).

Across the globe, South America is far from immune to these pressures. A total of 37% of global ethanol production occurs in Brazil, where 21% of domestic fuel consumption is biofuel (Bessou *et al*. 2011). This is produced from the fermentation of sugarcane, whose planting has contributed to continued deforestation and has significantly increased the extinction risk of forest bird species in the Amazon (Bird *et al*. 2011). These impacts also extend far beyond tropical forests to large areas of central South America's savanna and Cerrado systems where many endemic and globally threatened bird species are found (Lopes *et al*. 2009). In addition to sugarcane, soya beans have increasingly been planted to provide oil for biofuel, though it is also used as food for humans and livestock. Soya bean planting has occurred extensively across large areas of the Brazilian Cerrado and also in Argentina, where in 2008 soya was grown on 15.2 million ha – over half of Argentina's agricultural land. Similar trends have occurred in Paraguay and Bolivia (Grau & Aide 2008). Although there appear to be few publications describing the bird communities of sugarcane and soya plantations, they do appear to be associated with reduced raptor diversity (Carrete *et al*. 2009b). The conversion of Amazonian forests to other plantation types has been detrimental to the bird communities present (Barlow *et al*. 2007), as also discussed in Chapter 7. As with palm oil, the expansion of these crops at the expense of natural habitats is therefore likely to have significantly increased the conservation threat faced by many South American birds. The mechanisms are probably similar to those for oil palm: reduced structural complexity and plant species diversity which leads to a reduced avian diversity. These detrimental impacts are also likely to extend to long-distance migrant populations which rely on natural habitats during the high-latitude winter (Yamaura *et al*. 2009; Faaborg *et al*. 2010). Tragically, these habitat losses are again likely to have caused greenhouse gas emissions that will require two to four decades to recoup (Fargione *et al*. 2008). Biodiversity loss will therefore not have been compensated for by climate change mitigation, but both biodiversity and climate change will have lost – a double jeopardy (Danielson *et al*. 2008).

Although Africa has so far been relatively little impacted by large-scale biofuel development, some 2.5 million hectares of land in Mali, Ghana, Sudan, Ethiopia and Madagascar have already been allocated to foreign investors for biofuel production. These are likely to be planted by a variety of crops, ranging from jatropha to produce biodiesel, to sugarcane and cassava for ethanol production. Such wholesale habitat conversion would be likely to threaten both African resident birds and Palaearctic long-distance migrants (Senelwa *et al.* 2012). In the immediate future, however, the main bioenergy issue in Africa will probably relate to continued deforestation for domestic firewood and charcoal production, which together provide an average of 59% of the continent's energy needs, and as much as 80% in some areas.

8.7.2 Biofuel production in North America and Europe

The expansion of biofuel crops in the tropics in the last two decades has been extremely damaging for birds. However, one might expect that increased planting of biofuels across existing agricultural landscapes has been less damaging because it has involved the conversion of already modified habitats. To see whether this is the case, we review evidence from the United States, where some 14% of the country's maize crop is used to produce 51% of global ethanol production, and Europe, where 60% of the world's biodiesel is produced, primarily from rapeseed and sunflower oil (Bessou *et al.* 2011). Large areas of the long-established agricultural landscapes in these areas are now used to produce biofuels, where the impacts of growing these and other crops have been studied in reasonable detail.

This research shows that the intensification of management of agricultural land has generally been associated with significant losses of biodiversity living on that land. One of the best known examples of this has been the decline in grassland and other open-country bird species (farmland birds) as a result of agricultural intensification in both Europe (Krebs *et al.* 1999; Chamberlain *et al.* 2000; Donald *et al.* 2001; Gregory *et al.* 2004; Eglington & Pearce-Higgins 2012) and North America (Brennan & Kuvlesky 2005; Askins *et al.* 2007). Whilst declines of individual species may be attributed to specific changes in farming practice, the main drivers are generally a reduction in structural heterogeneity and a lack of food resources, caused by changes in cropping, time of sowing and the use of herbicides and insecticides (Benton *et al.* 2003; Stephens *et al.* 2003; Newton 2004; Siriwardena *et al.* 2008; Wilson *et al.* 2009b).

Maize, rape and sunflower can each provide seeds for birds in the winter, and therefore may be associated with some benefit for granivorous farmland birds, many of which can otherwise face food shortages at this time (Siriwardena *et al.* 2008). As a result, the spread of oilseed rape in Europe may have benefited a number of otherwise declining bird species. The leaves of this crop, when autumn-sown, also provide food in winter for grazing birds such as the common wood pigeon *Columba palumbis*, a widespread agricultural pest species that has increased in abundance in the UK by 170% since the 1960s (Baillie *et al.* 2013). Rape also provides nesting and foraging habitat during the breeding season for species requiring taller vegetation (Green *et al.* 1994; Newton 2004).

However, where biofuel production is associated with a high intensity of management, its effects on biodiversity tend to be negative. For example, high intensity maize production in the USA is associated with high irrigation and fertiliser inputs, causing eutrophication and loss of wetlands (Fargione *et al.* 2009). As a result, maize and soya crops in the USA support 60% fewer bird species and 25% lower bird abundance when compared to grassland habitats (Fletcher *et al.* 2011). These detrimental effects are particularly severe for bird species of conservation concern, with significant negative effects of the conversion of low input grassland crops to high input biofuel crops on seven characteristic grassland bird species (Bell's vireo *Viero bellii*, boblink *Dolichony orzyivorus*, field sparrow *Spizella pusila*, grasshopper sparrow *Ammodramus savannarum*, Henslow's sparrow *Ammodramus henslowii*, loggerhead shrike *Lanius ludovicianus* and sedge wren *Cistothorus platensis*; Meehan *et al.* 2010). High intensity biofuel production may therefore be more detrimental to grassland birds in the USA than it is to farmland birds in Europe because of the types of crops used and the intensity of their management, although more work is required to quantify this in more detail. Furthermore, the greenhouse gas emissions resulting from crop-based biofuels may be greater than originally thought, particularly once the emissions associated with nitrous oxide (N_2O) release from fertiliser are fully accounted for (Smith & Searchinger 2012). Hence, their value for climate change mitigation may also be limited.

8.7.3 Biomass production in North America and Europe

In addition to the small number of biofuel crop species which are widely planted, there is considerable interest in the planting of biomass crops. These may provide bioenergy either through distillation into biofuels, or to be burnt as dry biomass for energy generation. A wide range of crops, from fast-growing grasses, such as *Miscanthus*, switchgrass, maize and other grass silage, to fast-growing wood crops, such as willow, pine, poplar and eucalyptus, may be grown (Hinchee *et al.* 2009). This potentially allows flexibility for the delivery of conservation benefit alongside bioenergy production, and may also deliver a more efficient energy yield per unit area than biofuel crops (Bessou *et al.* 2011).

As with biofuels, the potential impacts of different biomass crops upon bird populations vary considerably. For example, *Miscanthus* can provide shelter for wintering farmland birds and food resources in the form of the weed species present and the invertebrates they support (Semere & Slater 2007a, 2007b; Bellamy *et al.* 2009). These benefits vary between bird species and in relation to the condition of the crop (Sage *et al.* 2010). Although *Miscanthus* grows tall and dense, farmland birds which prefer open habitats, such as northern lapwing and skylark, may occur where crop establishment and growth are relatively poor (Gove & Bradbury 2010), although if the crop grows well these species should be excluded. There is a significant risk that the widespread and intensive growth of grass biomass crops with a dense litter layer and shade will provide few food resources and be too tall and dense for many farmland birds to nest in (Anderson & Fergusson 2006).

In the USA, switchgrass may fulfil a similar biomass function to other crops, but because it is native, it provides more food resources and shelter for grassland bird species of conservation concern (Robertson *et al.* 2011), as well as a more favourable crop structure than *Miscanthus* (Fargione 2010; Jager *et al.* 2010). Promoting heterogeneity in the structure of such crops across the landscape may be an important mechanism for improving or maintaining grassland bird populations within a biomass production system (Robertson *et al.* 2011). This could be achieved by leaving some areas unharvested each year to provide habitat for species which favour tall vegetation, such as sedge wren and Henslow's sparrow, whilst short, cut swards will be favoured by species such as the upland sandpiper *Bartramia longicauda* and lark sparrow *Chondestes grammacus* (Roth *et al.* 2005; Fuhlendorf *et al.* 2006).

In addition to perennial grasses, a number of short-rotation coppice crops of fast-growing woody plant species have been widely promoted for biomass production, and may also improve the diversity of agricultural landscapes for birds. In the UK, short-rotation willow coppice supports higher diversity and abundance of birds than the equivalent grassland or arable habitats although, depending on where it is planted, it may displace some farmland bird species of conservation concern (Sage *et al.* 2006; Gove & Bradbury 2010). The planting and maintenance of coppice habitats may be a particularly useful way to increase the diversity and range of habitats on farmland as they are a surrogate for natural and semi-natural scrub which is often absent from intensively managed agricultural landscapes (Schulz *et al.* 2009). Short-rotation cropped habitats tend, however, to support a lower diversity and abundance of bird species than woodland habitats (Riffell *et al.* 2011), and are therefore not a good replacement for established woodland. There is potential for traditional coppice woodland practices to be implemented in existing woodlands to provide woodchip for biomass. Such management is widely employed for conservation to promote woodland structural diversity and is favourable for a number of woodland bird species of conservation concern (Fuller & Rothery 2010). Woodfuel may therefore provide an economic return from such conservation management practice, although the expansion of bioenergy power plants relying on wood products may further incentivise the clear-felling of existing forests in boreal and temperate zones of Canada and Russia, rather than supporting more locally grown and small-scale production of conservation-grade bioenergy.

Overall, studies suggest that the introduction of both short-rotation coppice and perennial grass crops for biomass may provide some biodiversity benefits when compared to some other agricultural habitats in the farmed landscape (Figure 8.11). However, the majority of these studies simply compare species diversity, rather than the occurrence and abundance of particular scarce or threatened farmland or grassland bird species. The increase in bird diversity associated with the introduction of biomass crops into the agricultural systems is most likely to result from the increase in vegetation heterogeneity which they bring to the landscape. Previous studies have highlighted the importance of structural and crop heterogeneity as a means to increase bird species diversity on farmland. Particular benefits are likely to accrue if the biomass crop is ecologically similar to unfarmed natural habitats, such as native grasslands, scrub and woodland that already deliver significant biodiversity benefit (Henderson *et al.* 2012). In addition, both coppice and perennial grasses generally have fewer agricultural inputs and require a lower intensity of management than food crops. This often means that they have a greater density and diversity of weeds, particularly in the first year or two after establishment, and a greater abundance of invertebrate food resources than annual food crops. They may also provide important nesting habitat for species requiring tall vegetation, although this may be at the cost of excluding ground-nesting species of open habitats. Thus, small- to moderate-scale implementation of biomass crops within a high-intensity agricultural landscape maximising food production would probably benefit farmland biodiversity at the farm scale. However, based on the negative effect of increasing the scale and intensity of cereal cultivation upon farmland bird populations (Donald *et al.* 2001; Eglington & Pearce-Higgins 2012), similar increases in the scale and intensity of management associated with biomass crops would probably reduce the degree of such biodiversity benefit.

It is suggested that areas of low-intensity perennial grassland with a high plant diversity managed for conservation might be harvested for bioenergy, thus delivering both

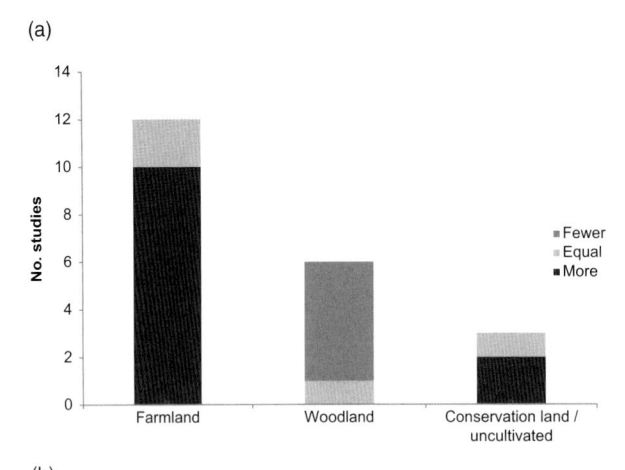

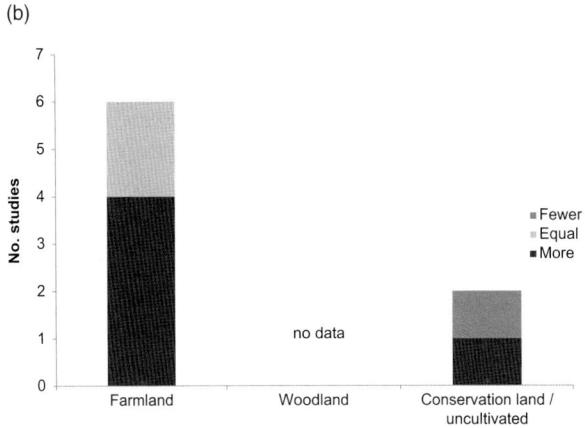

Figure 8.11 Summary of the number of studies in which either short-rotation coppice (a) or perennial grasses (b) grown as biomass supported more, fewer or the same species diversity of birds as farmland, woodland and conservation land (set-aside or conservation reserve programme)/uncultivated land. Updated from Dauber *et al.* (2010).

significant biodiversity benefit and a source of renewable energy (Bakker & Higgins 2009). In order for this to successfully deliver conservation benefit, the biomass crop should be harvested outside of the nesting season, either in early spring or late summer, depending on the species of interest. Crops may also provide important wintering habitats, such as seed-rich stubble (Fargione *et al.* 2009). However, such a low-intensity system is likely to have a lower energy yield than more intensively managed bespoke biomass crops (Adler *et al.* 2009), requiring a greater proportion of land to be employed for biomass production than might otherwise be needed. Furthermore, from a farming perspective, the land most likely to be converted to lower-intensity biomass crops will be the less productive parts of the farm which may already be good for wildlife. This may therefore not be a simple win-win solution that delivers bird conservation and significant climate change mitigation.

A final bioenergy product which may not conflict with bird conservation is the co-products and wastes from food and timber production, such as straw, forestry residues and manure (Anderson & Fergusson 2006; Wiens *et al.* 2011). In the United States it is estimated that these sources could produce some 444 million metric tons of biomass, approximately double that required to produce the 79 billion litres of biofuel target by 2022 (Fargione *et al.* 2009). The use of such co-products and wastes may also make an important contribution to bioenergy requirements in the UK, although as some of these residues are also put to other uses, such as being ploughed into the soil to improve water retention and soil nutrition and to prevent erosion, it is important that these supporting ecosystem services are not lost (Gove & Bradbury 2010). Further research is needed to identify the residues and wastes most likely to deliver the greatest energy at the lowest environmental cost.

8.7.4 Overview of bioenergy impacts

There have been recent large increases in bioenergy production around the world, though in most areas it remains a small part of total energy provision for human use. In tropical areas, bioenergy production has involved the clearance and conversion of extensive areas of forest and savanna, with highly detrimental consequences for tropical biodiversity. The concurrent expansion of bioenergy crops on existing farmland in North America and Europe may have been less damaging ecologically, and by increasing habitat and structural heterogeneity, may have benefited birds if deployed at relatively small scales. However, in order to stabilise greenhouse gas concentrations at an acceptable level, bioenergy crops will need to be grown at a large scale. Globally, it is estimated that some 7.8 million km^2 may be suitable for them, based on the area of grassland and woodland habitats which are currently undesignated as protected areas (IPCC 2011). If entirely converted to biomass production, this land could potentially yield some 171 EJ 1yr, enough to meet 17–23% of predicted mean global energy demand by 2050 (Figure 8.2). One EJ is 10^{18} joules. Based on the above review, this clearly would have significant impacts on bird populations around the world.

Such large-scale bioenergy production will need to involve either the conversion of natural and semi-natural habitats to agriculture and plantation forestry, or the replacement of food production on agricultural land with biofuel and biomass production. This second option may then require compensatory agricultural expansion elsewhere in order to maintain food production. Competition for land between bioenergy and food, and the conservation of ecosystem services and biodiversity, is likely to be a significant feature of future bioenergy expansion around the world. Following recent trends, much of this expansion is most likely to be in the tropics, and therefore likely to overlap with existing biodiversity hotspots (Lee *et al.* 2011a). If not subject to appropriate governance, bioenergy production will continue to be a key driver of large-scale loss of natural habitats in tropical areas and therefore is likely to increase the threat many tropical bird species face. There is an urgent need for policy interventions to reduce this threat.

The expansion of bioenergy generation is largely being driven by the energy policies of western countries, as a result of an increasing need for renewable energy generation. Although policies are being put in place to address this problem, such as the Renewable Energy Directive (RED) in Europe, which sets sustainability targets for biofuel, complex supply and demand interactions across global markets may make solving this issue difficult. For example, the expansion of maize-based ethanol production in the USA has led to a reduction in the soya harvest in that country. The resulting rise in soya prices has increased incentives for the conversion of forest and Cerrado habitats in Brazil to soya production (Scharlemann 2008). In the USA, it is estimated that 141 000–247 000 km^2 of land will be required for biofuel production by 2030 to support domestic requirements. If grown domestically, compensatory agricultural expansion elsewhere would be required in order to produce the same amount of food (McDonald *et al.* 2009). In the UK, 3500 km² of agricultural land is likely to be converted to energy crops (Defra 2007), whilst in Italy, about one-third of agricultural land is needed to meet European targets (Russi 2008). Large-scale land-cover change is already happening in south-east Asia and South America in response to the global biofuel market, which is increasingly also changing agricultural practice in North America and Europe. If bioenergy crops are going to be part of the climate change solution, then the scale at which they will need to be grown will risk their expansion becoming one of the most significant and detrimental consequences of climate change for birds. Choices remain to be made about which bioenergy crops to grow and how intensively to manage them, in order to minimise this risk. We consider the factors which should guide those choices in the next section.

8.7.5 Consequences for bird conservation of growing high- and low-yielding bioenergy crops

Finding policy solutions will require rigorous consideration of the relative merits of land-sparing and land-sharing as a means of obtaining a given amount of agricultural production whilst minimising the harm caused to biodiversity. Should the land required per unit of agricultural (including biofuel) production be minimised by using techniques which maximise the amount of production per unit area? This may result in biodiversity on farmland, including birds, being low. However, minimising the land area required should make the retention, protection and restoration of large areas of natural and semi-natural habitats more practical by reducing the pressure to convert them. For example, it has been estimated that annual bioenergy yield increases of 1.2–1.4% per annum would be sufficient to deliver an extra 100 EJ of energy from bioenergy by 2055, without requiring further expansion of agricultural land (Lotze-Campen *et al.* 2010; Thomson *et al.* 2010). If achievable, this would deliver much of the increase in energy production required from bioenergy under a low-emissions scenario (Figure 8.3). Whether or not this positive effect of high production efficiency on biodiversity away from farmland outweighs the resulting negative impact on farmland biodiversity depends upon the relationship between the population density of individual wild species on farmland and the yield of agricultural products per unit area of land (Green *et al.* 2005; Balmford *et al.* 2012). This is called the density-yield function.

Depending on the proportions of species with different classes of shapes of density-yield functions, it may be better for biodiversity to grow agricultural products using high-yielding methods and allow more natural habitat to remain untouched, or better to use low-yielding methods if that allows higher densities of enough species to persist in the farmed landscape. High-yield farming is called land-sparing because its biodiversity benefits mainly accrue on land with natural vegetation spared from farming by high levels of production. Low-yield farming is called land-sharing because its biodiversity benefits accrue by wild species sharing the landscape with farming. Field studies examining this trade-off in India, Ghana and Uganda show that substantially more species would benefit from high-yield farming than would benefit from low-yield farming (Phalan *et al.* 2011a; Hulme *et al.* 2013). However, the potential biodiversity benefits of high-yield farming indicated by these field studies only materialise if it really does spare land for wild species. If growing staple food crops and bioenergy crops at high yield simply frees up land to be used instead for luxury crops, cities and airports, then land-sparing has not worked. Although there are indications that recent deforestation rates were lower in countries where the yield of staple crops had increased most, and higher in countries where yield had decreased (Ewers *et al.* 2009) the land-sparing effect of high yields was weak. Only if land use and energy policies can be found which link high-yield farming with the effective protection of natural habitats can land sparing work in practice (Phalan *et al.* 2011b).

8.8 Solutions

The generation of renewable energy is likely to expand enormously in the next few decades as we attempt to balance rising energy demands with the need for climate change mitigation. This chapter has demonstrated that this expansion is likely to impact significantly upon bird populations and bird conservation status around the world. Aside from prioritising the least damaging and most efficient sources of energy, it will be important for conservation scientists to be involved in identifying ways to reduce the impact of particular developments to minimise the ecological costs of such expansion. This can be achieved through the following tools.

8.8.1 Strategic Environmental Assessment

The most important step in reducing the impacts on bird populations is to avoid locating renewable energy sources in important areas for birds through full and proper assessments of the risks from any proposed development. Existing legally protected areas and important areas for bird conservation which are not yet protected should be avoided unless developments can be shown not be damaging. Although claims have been made that shifting species' ranges in response to climate change (Chapter 6) reduce the suitability of protected areas through time, in fact, currently important areas are likely to remain important in the future, but potentially for a different suite of species (Section 7.5). The maintenance of protected areas alone will be insufficient, however, given the likely need for such range shifts to occur in response to climate change. Many species are also likely to require areas of intervening habitat to act as stepping stones or corridors between protected areas, or a relatively benign matrix through which to move (Section 7.7). Populations of more dispersed, wider-countryside species, migratory species or species with large home ranges, such as many seabirds or some raptors and vultures, will always require protection in the wider countryside away from protected areas (Section 7.8).

To ensure that vulnerable populations are protected, Strategic Environmental Assessments (SEA) should be conducted. These involve the collation of information about potentially suitable areas for renewable energy development alongside information about the distribution of vulnerable habitats and species, in order to identify potential areas of conflict between energy development and birds (and other biodiversity) within an area. An important aspect of such an assessment is the production of a sensitivity map, which combines an appraisal of species sensitivity to particular types of renewable energy development, with information about their distribution, to highlight hotspots of particular sensitivity. This approach was developed for wind farms (i.e. Bright *et al.* 2008; Eichhorn &

Box 8.7 · *Wind farm sensitivity mapping*

Scotland has one of the best wind resources in Western Europe and has a target for producing 100% of its energy from renewables by 2020. To identify the areas for wind farm development which would do the least harm to bird conservation, Scottish Natural Heritage (SNH) has produced Strategic Location Guidance (Scottish Natural Heritage 2009). One of the layers within this was a bird sensitivity map, produced by RSPB and SNH, based on the distribution and sensitivity of a range of potentially vulnerable bird species to wind farms (Bright *et al.* 2008). This was produced by reviewing the likely sensitivity of species to wind farms, based upon their flight activity, likely collision risk and known vulnerability to disturbance and displacement, and overlaying that information on bird distribution data. Based on this information, locations were classed as being of high, medium or low/unknown vulnerability. The same approach was then extended to England (Bright *et al.* 2009), although with some slight changes based on differing conservation priorities between the two countries.

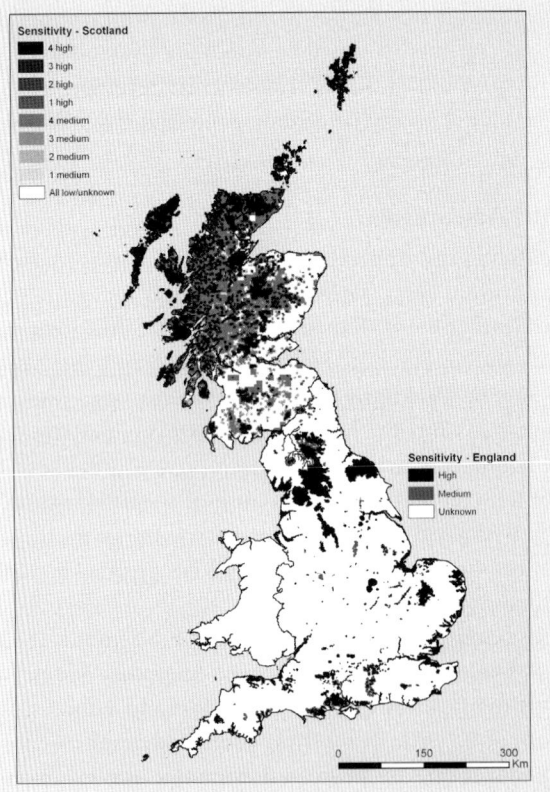

Box 8.7 Combined wind farm sensitivity map for Scotland (Bright *et al.* 2008) and England (Bright *et al.* 2009). Wales is unclassified. Each 2 × 2 km square is shaded by the number of high or medium sensitivity squares it contains.

Drechsler 2010), where information about the likely collision risk of species was combined with information about their distribution and home ranges in order to buffer particularly sensitive areas by appropriate distances (Box 8.7). An SEA therefore provides a strategic overview to assess and minimise the impacts of energy development within a particular region, the size of which should not be based only on political boundaries, but also biological ones, such as those of a flyway for migratory birds or a functioning meta-population.

8.8.2 Environmental Impact Assessment

Suitable areas which apparently do not conflict with other constraints should then be identified within an SEA as preferred locations for potential development. It should be emphasised, however, that due to imperfect data availability, such areas may still contain unknown locations that would be highly damaging to birds if developed. This can be a particular problem across large areas of the globe where detailed information about species' distributions and movements are not available. For this reason, any proposed developments should be subject to detailed Environmental Impact Assessment (EIA) with the aim of assessing, as accurately as possible, the likely impacts of a development upon bird populations of interest (Tucker & Treweek 2008; IEEM 2010). In most cases, targeted fieldwork will be required in order to assess the importance of specific sites to birds. It is important to collect sufficient data at this stage to ensure that a good characterisation of bird activity at the site is achieved (e.g. Douglas *et al.* 2012), and for all the relevant time periods. For example, if a site is thought to be important for migratory birds, then it will be necessary to ensure that there is a sufficient frequency of survey visits during likely passage periods in order to measure what could be high site usage for only a short period. Multiple years of data collection may be required if the importance of a site is thought to vary annually (Scottish Natural Heritage 2010).

Information about bird activity and abundance at a particular location needs to be combined with knowledge about the likely impacts of that development upon the species of interest, based upon the scientific literature, in order to make an appropriate assessment of the potential impacts on their populations. In some cases, simply overlaying the footprint of a particular development with information about the distribution, density and abundance of species likely to overlap with that footprint will provide a reasonable estimate of impact (e.g. Table 8.3). For developments which are likely to cause significant mortality of birds, such as a wind farm or power generating plant requiring overhead transmission lines, then estimates of likely mortality rates should ideally be combined with other demographic information in order to make a proper assessment. Often estimates of background mortality rates will be used within population viability analysis in order to model the population-level consequences of development. This can be a good way of combining multiple negative impacts to assess the overall size of their overall effect (e.g. Carette *et al.* 2009a; Schaub 2012), and may additionally include information about disturbance, displacement and other impacts of development, alongside potential effects of other influences. Where detailed information on population processes is available, it may be possible to assess the potential for density-dependent compensation to reduce or cancel out the negative effects of a development, but this is only likely to be available for a few species. The outputs from such population models will often be associated with considerable error and uncertainty, which should also be presented alongside any underpinning assumptions, as these may have a significant impact on the overall outcome. Quick methods for assessing the potential for density-dependent compensatory responses to additional mortality, such as Potential Biological Removal (Figure 8.6), should be used with caution, as their performance in reliably identifying levels of additional mortality which a population can tolerate without undergoing a substantial decline has not yet been tested empirically with robust validation studies.

The EIA should consider the magnitude, extent, duration and reversibility of impacts, alongside an assessment of their probability of occurrence. Finally, the ecological significance of impacts should be quantified, with reference to legislative or policy guidance. Thus impacts are often not related to the long-term viability or likelihood of extinction risk of species or populations, but to the integrity or condition of a designated site or protected population. Developments which are likely to have a significant negative impact upon the ecological integrity or condition of a legally designated site or protected population will be most serious. If significant ecological impacts are identified, then potential mitigation, compensation and enhancement options should be assessed through the EIA process, again expressing the degree of confidence in, and likely magnitude of potential benefit associated with, these options and how long it will take to implement them effectively. If these measures are likely to be of insufficient magnitude, relative to the size of the potential impact, then a development may not be granted consent, particularly if the environmental cost outweighs the societal benefit.

Where multiple developments affect a bird population within a defined area, cumulative impact assessment (CIA) should be conducted. The methods used for this are less well developed than for SEA and EIAs, but may compare predicted reductions in population against a pre-determined threshold (i.e. 1% of the population considered), or if data permit, use population models to combine multiple impacts when estimating extinction risk.

It is at this planning stage that the most potentially damaging developments should be identified. This framework should be applied as widely as possible to the development of renewable energy in order to minimise the associated damage to bird populations (Figure 8.12). For example, one of the reasons that wind power development in Scotland has had relatively little negative impact on bird populations so far is that the planning process has ensured that developments have been largely kept away from populations of vulnerable species such as raptors (Fielding *et al.* 2006; Bright *et al.* 2008; Warren & Birnie 2009). Although this approach has largely been associated with wind power, spatial modelling of this kind is now being applied to other more widely dispersed forms of renewable energy, such as biofuel production in Indonesia to identify a strategy to facilitate oil palm expansion whilst minimising losses of farmland, biodiversity and carbon stocks (Koh & Ghazoul 2010). Further extending and applying these methodologies in this way will be vital if potentially detrimental impacts of climate change mitigation on bird populations are to be minimised (Northrup & Wittemyer 2013).

8.8.3 Mitigating negative impacts

As part of the consent process, particular mitigation measures may be proposed in order to reduce harmful environmental impacts. If that is not possible, then compensation measures may be applied to another location (see below). Mitigation measures will be specific to each development. For example, there are many potential mitigation measures

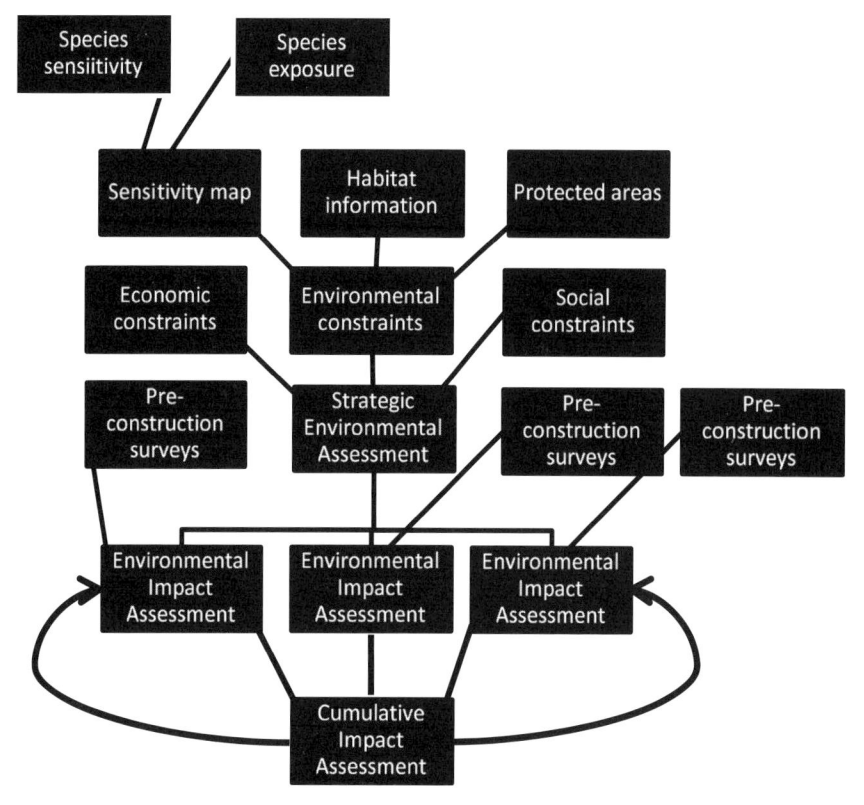

Figure 8.12 Flow diagram to indicate how different information and levels of assessment combine to minimise the impacts of renewable development on birds at the planning stage.

which have been proposed to reduce the impacts of wind farms on birds (Johnson *et al.* 2007; Ledec *et al.* 2011; US Fish and Wildlife Service 2012), though only a few of these are well supported by a good evidence base (Table 8.5). Various mitigation measures are identified in the accounts above, such as managing water levels to minimise the impacts of hydroelectric power on nesting birds, or increasing the heterogeneity associated with bioenergy crops to maximise the abundance and diversity of threatened grassland bird species. There is, however, a lack of studies on the likely effectiveness of mitigating the detrimental effects of renewable energy generation on biodiversity (Northrup & Wittemyer 2013), which makes it difficult to generalise about their likely effectiveness. This knowledge gap should be urgently addressed, as understanding the potential for mitigation will be of critical importance when considering a particular development for consent.

8.8.4 Compensation

In cases where the adverse impacts of a particular development cannot be mitigated against, but the societal benefits of the proposal are seen to outweigh the environmental costs and the project is consented, then compensation may be required. This involves implementing compensatory management or habitat creation to offset any potential

Table 8.5 *Summary of the likely effectiveness of different mitigation options proposed to reduce the magnitude of detrimental impacts of wind farms on birds. H – High priority action with good evidence base, M – Medium priority action with limited effectiveness or evidence base, L – Low priority action because of limited evidence base combined with likely limited effectiveness.*

	Ability to reduce collision	Ability to reduce disturbance
Micro-siting of turbines away from high-use areas	M	M
Selection of appropriate turbine designs to minimise perches	M	
The use of a small number of large turbines to generate the same energy	M	M
Marking of meteorological towers and other structures	M	
Install transmission cables underground to eliminate collision risk	H	
Fit flight diverters to overhead power cables	H	
Install electrocution mitigation measures to overhead power cables	H	
Use good construction practices to reduce detrimental impacts on habitat condition		M
Reduce nocturnal lighting	H	
Use flight diverters to steer birds away from turbines	L	
Paint turbines to increase their visibility	L	
Use behavioural deterrents to scare birds from turbines	L	
Habitat manipulation to reduce attractiveness of wind farm to birds	M	Negative
Increase turbine cut-in speed as collisions tend to happen at low wind speed	H	
Operate short-term shutdown during periods of peak bird activity	H	
Remove problem turbines associated with high collision frequency	M	
Use good maintenance practices	M	M

negative impacts on populations of interest, or to counter any direct habitat loss, as a result of development, and may also be termed biodiversity offsetting (McKenney & Kiesecker 2010). Compensation for habitat loss and disturbance should offer comparable habitat creation or improvement in the relative vicinity of the development. To maximise the likely effectiveness of such management, whenever possible, this should be instigated prior to the negative impact of the development being observed, in order to demonstrate its likely efficacy. Compensation for increased mortality rates or reduced productivity may involve the development of a species' management plan to increase the population elsewhere, which, again, should be implemented in advance of the renewable energy development.

Given the rising interest and use of such compensatory and offsetting schemes as a theoretical means of achieving economic development with net biodiversity gain, it is very important that the uncertainties associated with such compensation should be recognised. Many offsetting schemes have not resulted in a net biodiversity benefit, largely as a result of unrealistic expectations, limited evidence base, poor governance, a lack of appropriate targets and insufficient monitoring of their effectiveness (Quétier & Lavorel 2011; Hill & Arnold 2012; Maron et al. 2012). As a result, there is increasing recognition that the ability of compensatory or offsetting approaches to reduce and prevent biodiversity loss associated with particular developments may be limited (Maron et al. 2012; Brownlie et al. 2013), although this remains a contentious and active area of research.

To conclude, the most important measure to minimise the conflict between renewable energy development and bird conservation is to ensure that such development avoids protected areas, important bird areas and other hotspot locations where vulnerable species are concentrated or occur at high densities. Strategic and planning frameworks are available to minimise these impacts, and are well-used in relation to some energy developments, such as wind farms. The lessons learned from their successful application in some countries, such as Scotland, which has ambitious renewable energy generation targets but has so far achieved this with relatively little impact on birds, should be applied elsewhere.

8.9 Further considerations

As outlined above, some of the renewable energy developments undertaken for reasons of climate change mitigation have been counter-productive. The mitigation benefits have been cancelled out by greenhouse gas emissions to the atmosphere as a result of associated habitat loss and degradation, such as the clearance of tropical forests to plant bioenergy crops (Danielson et al. 2008), or placing wind turbines on carbon-rich peat soils (Lindsay 2010). More widely, about one-third of global greenhouse gas emissions (1.6 GtC/yr) are estimated to originate from land use, land-use change, and forestry (termed LULUCF), although there is considerable uncertainty over this estimate (IPCC 2007d). More than half of this value, 17% of all emissions, is estimated to originate from the clearance of tropical forests, although the precise magnitude of this estimate varies between studies and authors (Gibbs & Herold 2007; van der Werf et al. 2009; Schrope 2009). Additional losses of carbon from agricultural and peatland soils as a result of cultivation and drainage are also important. Because of the size of their contribution to climate change, there has been an increasing policy focus on the need to reduce LULUCF emissions. This is not easy to achieve, because they are a by-product of economically important activities, such as agriculture or forestry, which also provide valuable goods for human use. Whilst these goods can be sold in a market, the greenhouse gas emissions avoided by not producing them are not marketed and are therefore ignored. Up to now, there has been no financial incentive for LULUCF emissions to be reduced.

8.9.1 Reducing emissions

In response to this, the UN Framework Convention on Climate Change (UNFCCC) has proposed a mechanism to pay nations to reduce carbon emissions from deforestation and forest degradation (known as REDD). Many of the nations which still contain sufficient areas of forest to make a significant difference to the global greenhouse gas budget are in developing countries. This mechanism tries to enable developing nations to access revenue to protect their carbon-rich forest habitats where the trees and in some places the underlying peatlands provide a globally significant carbon store. By protecting such habitats, emissions associated with LULUCF may be drastically reduced, thereby contributing significantly to climate change mitigation. Given the large-scale biodiversity loss associated with tropical deforestation (e.g. Box 8.6), conservationists hope that this mechanism may also benefit biodiversity conservation. For example, the carbon market has a global revenue of $125 billion (Point Carbon 2009), of which REDD has already secured $6 billion. This support is sorely needed because existing approaches have largely failed to protect this key habitat for biodiversity (Miles & Kapos 2008), using a global conservation budget of less than $1 billion.

If it works, REDD may slow deforestation, reduce logging and decrease the incidence of forest fires, all of which are associated with greenhouse gas emissions. In addition, a potential expansion of the REDD programme, REDD+, could fund the regeneration and restoration of forest habitats and the large-scale planting of trees to sequester carbon (Stickler et al. 2009). This programme clearly has the potential to provide significant environmental, ecological and biodiversity benefits if it is associated with increased protection for native tropical forests. In particular, the protection of peatland forests in Sumatra, Borneo and Papua New Guinea is likely to both benefit biodiversity and reduce greenhouse gas emissions, as will the protection of parts of southern Amazonia, central America and the Congo (Buchanan et al. 2011). Depending on the magnitude of funding available through REDD+, the programme has the capacity to reduce global extinction rates of nationally endemic forest-dependent species by some two to four times. To realise this potential, efforts should focus on maximising the funding available and ensuring the broadest possible participation (Busch et al. 2011).

However, there are risks associated with these policies which will need to be avoided. Firstly, REDD will preferentially protect carbon-rich habitats over other habitats of high biodiversity value but lower carbon value. Given other pressures and demand on land, this may not lead to a reduction in pressure for habitat conversion, but a shift in that pressure away from carbon-rich tropical forests towards natural habitats such as savanna, scrub and dry forests which contain less carbon (so-called leakage). Where these lower-carbon habitats have a high biodiversity value, this shift may be undesirable. For example, the savannas and scrubland habitats of central South America are among the most threatened habitats in the continent (Stotz et al. 1996), and yet would not be protected through REDD. Secondly, the commercial planting of highly productive non-native tree species may replace slow-growing native trees, as they would be likely to sequester greater rates of carbon from the atmosphere (Stickler et al. 2009). Such non-native plantations would be largely devoid of biodiversity interest. Indeed, these two pressures have already combined to drive the conversion of the highly biodiverse Cerrado habitat of Brazil to *Eucalyptus* plantations (Mansourian et al. 2005). Thirdly, there is concern that rehabilitation of degraded forest habitats through planting seedlings and the cutting of climbers may have negative impacts on some bird species (Putz & Redford 2009), although the overall effect of such management is likely to be largely beneficial, by restoring the bird community towards that of native forests (Ansell et al. 2011). Careful safeguards need to be put in place to ensure that the clearance of native vegetation is not supported through REDD+.

In October 2012, REDD+ was adopted by the CoP 11 of the Convention of Biological Diversity, noting with appreciation a list of biodiversity-related safeguards set out by the UNFCCC. Although viewed as a potential contribution to achieving the objectives of the convention, caution was also expressed about the possible negative impacts on biodiversity. Despite adoption at the CBD CoP 11, there remain significant obstacles to be overcome. If successful, REDD+ could have a positive effect on the prospects of many threatened forest birds, as well as delivering effective climate change mitigation, but it remains to be seen whether this initiative will deliver the large biodiversity and mitigation benefits it has the potential to achieve.

8.9.2 Non-forest habitats

In northern and temperate latitudes, there is concern that carbon and methane emissions from peatlands may also pose a significant source of LULUCF emissions. These organic soils contain high densities of carbon, distributed across lowland raised bogs, fens and blanket peatlands (Montanaralla *et al.* 2006; Lindsey 2010) and locked within the permafrost of the circumpolar region (Schuur *et al.* 2008; Tarnocai *et al.* 2009). Estimates of the amount of carbon stored in the northern circumpolar region (north of 45° N) range from 1400 to 1850 Pg (McGuire *et al.* 2009), some three to five times greater than the carbon stored in all terrestrial vegetation, estimated by Prentice *et al.* (2001) to be 350–540 Pg. These habitats are also important for birds, supporting many ground-nesting shorebirds and waterbirds, as well as grouse, passerines and raptors.

Peatland soils are particularly vulnerable to climate change, as warming increases the rate of decomposition of organic material, leading to emissions of carbon dioxide (CO_2) and methane (CH_4) into the atmosphere. Drought causes the peat to desiccate, leading to the oxidisation of stored carbon (Bridgham *et al.* 2008; Dorrepaal *et al.* 2009; Ise *et al.* 2009). Rising temperatures may further drive the release of stored carbon from permafrost habitats as the stable soil thaws and is exposed to decomposition and carbon release. Carbon-rich wetland habitats created by such thaws may be substantial sources of methane into the atmosphere, whilst increased fire risk may further accelerate CO_2 emissions (Schuur *et al.* 2008; McGuire *et al.* 2009; Turetsky et al. 2010). Present estimates of the current carbon balance of northern circumpolar soils indicate that this region is a sink for CO_2, contributing some 30–60% of the 1 Pg C/yr sequestered by the terrestrial biosphere. However, 3–9% of the 550 Tg CH_4/yr global CH_4 emissions from land also originate from this region (IPCC 2007d; McGuire *et al.* 2009). Given the sensitivity of peatland soils to climate change through impacts of rising temperatures, drought and fire, there is concern that greenhouse gas emissions from these habitats may cause a positive feedback loop to climate change. As outlined in Chapter 4, such warming would also be likely to have significant negative impacts on many of the birds which breed in these habitats (Beale *et al.* 2006b; Pearce-Higgins 2010).

There is considerable interest in what can be done to mitigate these effects. The main management option is to manipulate water levels. Peatlands are wet habitats, and need high water levels in order to sequester carbon from the atmosphere. Although wetland habitats may release methane, it is the relative importance of CO_2 sequestration and CH_4 release which determine the net warming or mitigation effect of a particular site. Many temperate peatlands have been drained and converted for agricultural use, or commercially planted with trees, causing greenhouse gases to be emitted. However, there is potential for rewetting and restoration of such sites back to carbon sinks, although often this is associated with a short-term spike in methane emissions (Bain *et al.* 2011). Many other peatlands remain as natural habitats, but with their carbon balance shifted towards being a carbon source by human interventions. For example, despite being one of the largest areas of blanket peatland in the world, extensive areas of the UK uplands are artificially drained by ditches which were constructed during the twentieth century to lower water levels and enhance livestock grazing. Blocking these drainage ditches raises water levels (Wilson *et al.* 2010; Carroll *et al.* 2011), facilitates peatland restoration and moves the carbon budget back towards being a sink. As outlined in Chapter 7, such management may also increase the resilience of these habitats and associated biodiversity to rising temperatures and drought, including providing benefits to birds (Pearce-Higgins 2010, 2011a, 2011b; Pearce-Higgins *et al.* 2010; Carroll *et al.* 2011). The same management may therefore deliver both climate change mitigation and conservation adaptation, as well as immediate biodiversity benefits.

Many coastal and marine environments are also carbon rich. Mangroves, coastal marshes and sea grasses, so called 'blue carbon', emit large amounts of CO_2 when destroyed (Pendleton *et al.*), for example for shrimp aquaculture, agriculture or urban development (Barbier et al. 2011). These habitats are highly biodiverse, and are not just important for breeding birds, but also for wintering waders and waterbirds. In addition to providing carbon capture and storage potential, they also provide important nursery areas for fish and protect vulnerable coastlines from flooding, which may be increasingly important in the face of climate change. They therefore deliver a wide range of ecosystem services, and should be protected, not just for their biodiversity, but the goods and services they provide to vulnerable societies. As discussed above, this may potentially be achieved through carbon markets related to initiatives such as REDD+ (Murray 2012; Siikamaki *et al.* 2012).

8.10 Conclusions

As we have demonstrated through this book, the impact of climate change on bird populations will increase with increasing magnitude of climate change. The severity of such impacts will affect the likelihood of being able to effectively adapt conservation action in the face of climate change. If the magnitude of climate change can be limited, fewer species will be threatened with extinction, and our ability to increase the resilience of those populations which are threatened will increase. One of the main ways in which climate change may be limited is through mitigation, and particularly by increasingly using low-carbon and renewable sources of energy, as opposed to carbon-rich fossil fuels. Mitigation scenarios where greenhouse gas emissions peak at 2016 or 2030 are likely to reduce the proportion of birds projected to be at risk of losing $\geq 50\%$ of their range from 30% by 2080, to 10–15% respectively (Warren *et al.* 2013). However, as we have shown in this chapter, a number of these mitigation options will also have negative impacts on bird populations, ranging from direct increases in mortality, through reductions in the

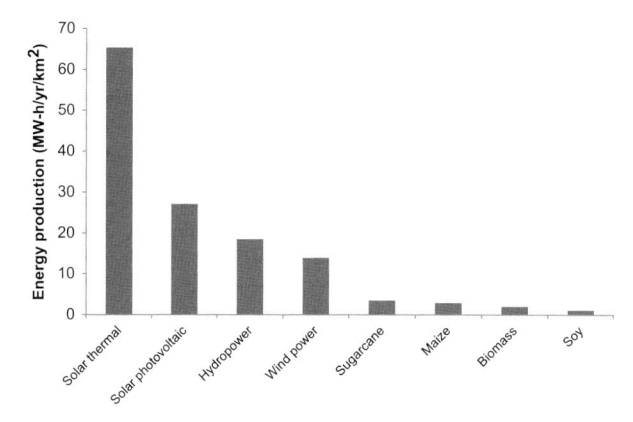

Figure 8.13 Examples of efficiency of different sources of renewable energy as measured by the energy production per unit area of land (IPCC 2011).

suitability of particular habitats, to complete habitat loss. All technologies and options potentially involve some risk, but the magnitude of this risk varies between them.

A key determinant of the effect of a particular energy source upon biodiversity will be the land area it occupies, so a useful way to compare the impacts of different renewable energy options is to examine their efficiency, as measured by the area required per unit energy produced (Figure 8.13). On this basis, solar power, both concentrating thermal and photovoltaic, is the most area-efficient form of renewable energy. Our review also suggests that it is perhaps among the least damaging technologies for birds, albeit based on a limited evidence base. If further research shows that this assessment is robust, then future expansion of solar power may represent the best renewable energy option for birds. Although solar is the energy source with the greatest global potential for production (Table 8.1), because of technological and practical constraints, it is not regarded as likely to overtake many other forms of energy production in terms of net energy production until towards the middle of this century (Figure 8.3). It is also expensive, which is an important obstacle to large-scale implementation, as consumers are likely to be unwilling or unable to pay significantly more to meet their energy needs. Although costs have reduced significantly in recent decades (IPCC 2011), it is likely that other forms of energy will continue to predominate in the short- to medium term.

Of these other renewable energy options, bioenergy crops are likely to be the main source of renewable energy globally (Figure 8.3) because they have the lowest technological requirements, and are the cheapest (IPCC 2011). Unfortunately, they tend to be inefficient in terms of land area required (Figure 8.13), and have even increased greenhouse gas emissions in many areas through the loss of carbon stocks from natural habitats as a result of habitat conversion. Their contribution to climate change mitigation has therefore been questionable. The switch from food to energy production on some farmland may have mixed benefits for farmland birds, but has probably increased the conversion of natural and semi-natural habitats to farmland, again with likely detrimental consequences for bird conservation. Perversely, the most widely used source of renewable energy is therefore probably the most damaging to the conservation of birds and other biodiversity globally, and the least beneficial for climate change mitigation.

Remaining renewable energy options of wind, hydro and marine sources are each associated with some detrimental impacts on birds. Some of these result from habitat loss, for example through the construction of hydroelectric dams which flood large areas of terrestrial habitat and alter riparian systems. Tidal barrage schemes may also significantly reduce the extent and quality of intertidal and coastal habitats. Other effects arise through birds avoiding built structures such as wind turbines, which is really equivalent to habitat loss because habitats and resources which would otherwise be available to the birds are denied them and they are displaced to other areas where they may die or fail to breed because of increased levels of competition with conspecifics. Renewable energy structures may also directly cause mortality, most apparent at wind farms. These effects appear most serious for species which have large home ranges, those whose habitats coincide with landforms and features favourable for energy development, and those which concentrate in particular areas, such as foraging areas for seabirds and raptors, or at bottleneck locations for vulnerable migratory birds. If renewable energy production is concentrated in such places, such as for example a wind farm at a key crossing area for migratory soaring birds susceptible to collision, or in key foraging areas for seabirds, or a tidal barrage across an estuary supporting thousands of waders, there is a significant risk that they will affect a large proportion of regional or national populations. If these places are avoided, then it may be possible for such renewable energy generation to play an important part in the mitigation of climate change, without significantly compromising bird conservation interest.

A final consideration for those involved in planning renewable energy development is that the associated energy transmission infrastructure may also harm birds. Often the cheapest way to transmit electricity is through the use of overhead power lines, but these can pose a significant risk of collision or electrocution to birds. Such risks are most likely to be relevant for renewable technologies which involve energy production in remote areas, such as hydroelectric, wind and large-scale solar power generation, where large populations of sensitive species are also likely to occur. In common with wind farms, there are examples where overhead power lines have been associated with significant mortality of birds through collision. Where those are large, long-lived species with slow reproductive rates, then significant population level impacts have been observed (e.g. Sergio *et al.* 2004; Shaw *et al.* 2010; López-López *et al.* 2011; Angelov *et al.* 2012). Fortunately, a number of mitigation measures exist and can be used to minimise the negative consequences of this type of energy transmission, for example by making power lines more visible to birds, and they should be employed where necessary (AEWA 2008; Prinsen *et al.* 2011), but may not work well for those species which do not see well along the line of travel when flying above a certain height (Martin 2011).

In addition to greenhouse gas emissions from energy generation, the degradation of carbon-rich tropical forests and high-latitude peatlands has also contributed to global climate change. This degradation has also been detrimental to biodiversity, and pushed many bird species closer to extinction. There is increasing recognition that the protection and restoration of forests and peatlands to reduce the magnitude of such LULUCF greenhouse gas emissions may contribute significantly to both climate change mitigation and biodiversity conservation. The potential for significant global benefit to occur as a result of initiatives such as REDD+ and the restoration of degraded peatlands is clear. The challenge for those drafting and implementing these policies is to ensure that they achieve this potential. It is imperative that the funding is made available, potentially through carbon markets, to provide the scale of protection and restoration required, to ensure that the action delivers the intended carbon and biodiversity benefits, and to avoid perverse and unexpected detrimental consequences. This requires rigorous certification and monitoring which can be technically challenging, but potentially achievable through advances in remote sensing. That large-scale policy initiatives can deliver significant action on the ground is clear. From 2000 to 2004, some 40 000 km^2 of Amazonia were converted from forest to farmland, or logged and burnt, and alone contributed 5–6% of global greenhouse gas emissions. Six years later in 2011, rates of destruction had declined by two-thirds as a result of a reduction in market prices for the agricultural goods produced, a moratorium on soya and beef grown on recently cleared lands, increased governmental enforcement and an expanded protected area network (Nepstad 2011). There is hope, if the policy and the funding can be aligned to deliver maximum benefit.

Away from renewable energy generation and REDD, a number of more radical geo-engineering solutions have been proposed to achieve climate change mitigation through the removal of greenhouse gases from the atmosphere. For example, spreading crushed silicate rocks over large areas will absorb CO_2 from the atmosphere. Alternatively, fertilising nutrient-poor ocean areas, using either nitrogren or iron, may increase phytoplankton growth and stimulate the rate of CO_2 absorption by these microscopic plants (Mackay 2008; Boyd 2008a). However, as with biofuel production, both potential interventions, and others that have been suggested, will require large areas of land or sea to be converted for this use, with potentially far-reaching and unintended ecological consequences. Alternatively, injecting sulphur particles into the stratosphere may reverse the impacts of increasing CO_2 concentrations (Crutzen 2006), but again, may be associated with significant risk and uncertainty (Pope *et al.* 2012). Many of these options are also likely to be expensive (Mackay 2008; Boyd 2008b).

There is no single solution to climate change. Mitigation will require the implementation of a range of low-carbon energy generation solutions, most of which have potentially negative impacts on at least some bird species. No single form of renewable energy can be widely, cheaply and rapidly implemented with little impact on biodiversity. Geo-engineering solutions are expensive, uncertain and associated with significant risk. Nuclear power has been suggested by some to be the answer to this problem, but is also associated with significant costs, and considerable public opposition, particularly following the Fukushima disaster of 2011. Nuclear accidents, although very rare, may also bring the risk of environmental damage, as well as public health concerns. The surest way of reducing greenhouse gas emissions without posing a risk to birds is through the implementation of energy efficiency measures that reduce overall energy demand. Although not discussed in detail, reducing global energy consumption through time should be a key policy mechanism for tackling climate change in a biodiversity friendly way.

The benefits of reducing the magnitude of future climate change for humans, and for biodiversity, are clear (Section 6.8). Although developed to reduce the risk of dangerous climate change, mitigation will require very careful implementation to avoid significant biodiversity loss being associated with it. If handled badly, there is the risk we will preside over the large-scale conversion of highly biodiverse natural and semi-natural habitats to intensively managed energy-generation or mitigation landscapes that are of limited bird conservation value. This is what has happened to our agricultural landscapes, and recent experience from the last decade or two has shown how this may happen with respect to energy. Should this happen, the negative impacts of climate change mitigation in terms of driving bird populations into decline and towards extinction, may even exceed those of climate change itself (Powell & Lenton 2013). The challenge for policy-makers is to ensure that many of the negative consequences outlined in this chapter are avoided, so that renewable energy and other appropriate mitigation options play an important part in reducing the magnitude of climate change, without significantly adding to the threat that many bird species face.

8.11 Summary

- About 87% of energy production is currently from fossil fuels, responsible for 57% of anthropogenic greenhouse gas emissions. Global energy demand may double between now and 2050. Rapid increases in renewable energy generation are required to achieve this without significantly exacerbating the magnitude of human-induced climate change.
- Wind energy is one of the most advanced forms of renewable energy, but can be associated with significant collision risk for flying birds. Large, soaring, long-lived and slow-breeding species, such as seabirds and raptors, appear particularly vulnerable to detrimental population-level effects. Wind farms located at migratory bottlenecks, near seabird breeding colonies or feeding areas, and distributed across the home ranges of wide-ranging vulnerable species, have had the greatest negative impacts on bird populations. Individuals may also be displaced from otherwise suitable habitat around turbines, causing population declines, at least locally.
- Hydroelectric power schemes may have significant impacts on freshwater species through rapid alterations in water level which may inundate breeding attempts, or leave them vulnerable to predation. The indirect effects of potential changes in flow regimes, water quality and habitat fragmentation on prey populations and habitat quality are poorly understood. Storage schemes involving the creation of reservoirs may also detrimentally affect terrestrial species through habitat loss.
- Tidal barrages across large estuaries can generate large amounts of electricity from a single scheme, but would be likely to significantly reduce the carrying capacity of these habitats for the large numbers of wintering waders and waterfowl they support. Because populations may be concentrated at a small number of key sites, such schemes have the potential to produce far-reaching consequences along entire migratory flyways. Potential effects of experimental tidal stream and wave power devices are largely unknown.

8.11 Summary

- There has also been relatively little research on the effects of solar power generation on birds. Whilst collisions were recorded at a single heliostat site, which used reflective mirrors to concentrate solar energy, large-scale photovoltaic plants may be more benign for birds, although further research on this is urgently required.
- Bioenergy is the cheapest and least technologically advanced form of renewable energy, and also the most inefficient in terms of yield per unit land area. Driven by international targets, biofuel expansion has contributed to extensive tropical forest and savanna habitat loss in south-east Asia and South America, some of the greatest conservation problems of recent decades.
- Large-scale conversion of North American and European farmland to bioenergy crops has had more equivocal effects on bird populations. Where these have increased habitat heterogeneity or were based on native plant species, they may have benefited farmland birds, but where associated with an increase in agricultural intensification, they probably have not. Bioenergy crop expansion on existing farmland has probably driven losses of natural and semi-natural habitat to food production elsewhere.
- For bioenergy to contribute approximately one-fifth of global energy demand, almost 8 million km^2 of land will need to be converted to their production. Much of this expansion is likely to replace highly biodiverse tropical habitats. The adoption of a land-sparing approach where both food and bioenergy yield is maximised by high-intensity agriculture may reduce such losses of natural and semi-natural habitat.
- To minimise the conflict between renewable energy production and bird conservation, renewable energy sources should be located away from protected areas, Important Bird Areas and other sites of conservation interest. Rigorous Strategic Environmental Assessment and Environmental Impact Assessment are required to avoid the most damaging developments, whilst specific interventions may further reduce the negative impacts of particular schemes. Biodiversity offsetting should only be considered as a last resort as it is associated with much uncertainty over its long-term effectiveness.
- Damage and degradation of carbon-rich habitats, alongside emissions from agriculture and forestry, account for one-third of greenhouse gas emissions. Protecting these habitats, many of which are highly biodiverse, may deliver further climate change mitigation. Programmes such as REDD and REDD+ could protect and restore tropical forest habitats and deliver much benefit for global bird conservation. Policies will need to be implemented carefully if they are not simply going to accelerate rates of loss of other habitats.
- Protection and restoration of northern peatlands may benefit the conservation of many bird species that occupy them, as well as reducing the likelihood of them being a significant source of greenhouse gas emissions. This may be achieved particularly through the appropriate restoration of drained peatlands. For similar reasons, mangrove and salt marsh habitats should also be protected. Crucially, such protection will deliver benefits for climate change mitigation, current conservation needs and future climate change adaptation for the species they support.

- There is no single low-cost renewable energy solution that can be widely and rapidly implemented with little impact on bird populations. Climate change mitigation will therefore need careful implementation around the world in order to minimise the likelihood and magnitude of associated detrimental impacts on bird populations. Energy efficiency measures should be widely implemented to reduce overall energy demand. Reducing greenhouse gas emissions from inappropriate land uses that also threaten biodiversity should be the highest priority from a conservation perspective.

9 · *Overall conclusions*

9.1 Impacts of recent climate change

In the first part of the book, we examined the impacts of climate change on bird populations. We found good evidence that significant changes have occurred in the timing of seasonal events within the annual cycle of birds (Chapter 2). In recent decades, both spring arrival of migratory species and egg-laying dates, as measured for the average individual in a population, have advanced consistently by some 2 days per decade across temperate and boreal latitudes. Phenological changes affecting the timing of the end of the breeding season, and autumn departure dates of migrants have varied much more between species, depending on migration, moult and breeding strategies. A wide range of correlative analyses, supported by a small number of studies of underlying mechanisms, have demonstrated that many of these changes are a consequence of warming. Recent climate change has therefore altered the seasonal pattern of avian life cycles. Although there is currently insufficient monitoring of birds in tropical areas to track their long-term phenological responses to climate change, the studies which have been conducted suggest that here, changes in precipitation, and not temperature, are likely to be the main determinant of the timing of commencement of the breeding season and the movement of individuals. Trends in tropical bird phenology are therefore likely to be related primarily to changes in rainfall patterns.

The effects of climate change on bird species often operate through effects on the availability of resources. As we examined in Chapter 3, changes in the timing of peak food availability relative to the timing of migration or breeding have, in some cases, led to a reduction in the food resources available for either migrating adults or growing chicks. Where this has occurred, survival and/or productivity may be reduced (phenological mismatch). This topic has been the focus of much research, with good evidence for mismatch having affected to some degree about one-third of the species studied. The species most affected tend to be those which occupy highly seasonal habitats and that are dependent upon the availability of a narrow range of food resources, especially if the availability of those peak during a short time window. Another factor in these cases can be that the drivers that determine bird phenology differ from those that determine peak resource availability, potentially leading to divergence in the long-term trends of the two. Of those species which have been studied, the greatest proportion which are potentially sensitive to mismatch occur in the marine environment, although other well-cited examples of mismatch have been documented in deciduous woodland. Despite this body of evidence, a quantitative link between mismatch and population decline has been proposed for only two species, and even here, it has only been a contributory, rather than a primary, factor.

A number of broad-scale correlative studies are suggestive of an association between phenological mismatch and recent population declines in long-distance migrants. This group of species is expected to be particularly vulnerable to mismatch because climatic changes on their wintering and passage areas are often different from those on their breeding grounds, which may constrain their ability to respond to spring warming. However, there remains considerable debate as to the scale of the effects of phenological mismatch on migrants (Knudsen *et al.* 2011). Given this uncertainty, and the lack of strong evidence from a range of species-specific studies that mismatch has caused long-term population declines, it is possible that the lack of phenological advance in declining migrants may be a symptom of some other underlying environmental deterioration on the wintering grounds, which may also be the primary driver of the observed population declines.

Probably of wider significance for bird populations than phenological mismatch is the impact of climate change upon the abundance, rather than the timing, of food supplies (Chapter 4). There are many examples of negative impacts of warming upon the availability of plankton and fish in the marine environment, which have led to reductions in seabird productivity and survival. Seabirds therefore appear to be particularly vulnerable to climate change. Although there are fewer examples from the terrestrial environment that climate change has reduced food availability, evidence is mounting that this process could also be important for landbirds. Food availability is just one of the biotic mechanisms by which climate change is likely to affect species, with a number of studies also providing evidence that variation in levels of predation, disease and competition can be linked to changes in temperature or precipitation (e.g Mustin *et al.* 2007; Geyer *et al.* 2011; Cahill *et al.* 2013). As species ranges shift, we anticipate that such interspecific interactions will become increasingly important mechanisms by which populations are affected by climate change.

Climate change is projected to increase the frequency of extreme weather events which can cause complete breeding failure or high mortality. There are good examples where increasing frequencies of storm and flood events have led to significant population level impacts. There is also evidence that some tropical bird populations may be vulnerable to increased mortality during extreme heat waves (McKechnie *et al.* 2012). The effects on bird populations of catastrophic events caused by climate change are likely to become more widespread over time. Their impacts are likely to be most severe when they affect small populations within a restricted range.

Strong latitudinal gradients in the strength of the relationships between both temperature and precipitation and demographic parameters indicate for the first time how different bird populations around the globe and within a single species' range may be differentially affected by climate change. At high latitudes, populations tend to be cold-limited, and therefore exhibit a strong positive relationship between temperature and productivity or survival. For these species, there are clear negative effects of cold and wet weather, and recent warming is likely to have increased their abundance. However, for some populations, potentially positive effects of warming may be countered by lagged negative effects of warm or dry weather resulting from altered interspecific interactions, as described above (Pearce-Higgins 2011b). At low latitudes, water availability is often limiting, either directly, or indirectly, through its effects on food resources. In the tropics, rainfall tends to have strong effects on plant growth, and therefore is closely linked to subsequent invertebrate, fruit and seed availability. As a result, potential climate change impacts on the frequency, duration and severity of drought may be the main way in which climate change will affect the abundance of tropical bird species.

These latitudinal patterns in the effects of temperature and rainfall on bird population processes are mirrored by the drivers of global patterns of terrestrial bird diversity (Chapter 5). There is a strong latitudinal gradient in species richness, which is highest in the tropics. At high latitudes, variation in richness appears to be associated with temperature, whilst at low latitudes, water availability is more influential (Hawkins *et al.* 2003). These patterns are best explained by the effects of climate upon plant growth and habitat structure, as described by the energy hypothesis.

In response to warming, there is good evidence for poleward expansion in the distribution of species' ranges, driven by generally positive effects of warming on populations at high latitude range margins. Based on the discussion above, we might expect the low latitude range margins of species to decline in response to lagged effects of increases in temperature and drought frequency and severity, probably mediated through altered species interactions. As a result of recent shifts in species' distributions, across temperate and boreal latitudes of Europe where most studies have been conducted, there has been an increase in bird diversity in many areas. Indeed, range shifts and associated changes in bird community composition provide some of the best evidence for recent climate change already having a widespread and detectable impact on bird populations.

There are likely to be many population-level consequences of climate change which remain undetected, even by detailed studies of individual populations. This could happen because the magnitude of effects on individual populations are relatively small compared to stochastic variation or the impacts of other environmental drivers (e.g. Eglington & Pearce-Higgins 2012). However, when combined across many sites and species, they are sufficiently strong for a climate change signal to be detected (e.g. Gregory *et al.* 2009; Devictor *et al.* 2008b, 2012a). It is worth considering whether there are likely to be biases in the sorts of species which have been studied, which may influence our conclusions about the likely impacts of climate change on birds. It is possible that the small proportion of species which have been studied in sufficient detail and for long enough to detect potential impacts of climate change on their populations is a non-random selection. Many of the species studied in most detail for long periods are relatively common and widespread. Species of this kind are likely to be relatively adaptable and tolerant of a range of environmental conditions, and therefore may be amongst the species least susceptible to climate change (Barnagaud *et al.* 2012). At the other extreme are rare or declining species studied in detail to diagnose the causes of decline. By their very nature, populations of these species are strongly limited by effects of land-use change or other anthropogenic drivers. The importance of these non-climatic factors may therefore mask any effect of climate change on their population processes. The species which may have been most vulnerable to climate change to date may be specialised species that have not been strongly affected by other anthropogenic pressures. However, these species may be amongst those least subject to long-term study. If this conjecture is correct, we may be failing to detect detrimental impacts of climate change on specialist species occupying semi-natural or natural habitats. This may account for the fact that seabirds, upland birds and some woodland birds appear to be amongst those for which the evidence of climate change affecting their populations is strongest.

So far, there are only a small number of bird species and populations which can be convincingly demonstrated to be under a current and immediate threat from climate change (e.g. Cahill *et al.* 2013). As well as resulting from the possibility that many vulnerable species have not been the subject of detailed study, bird populations may also show considerable ability to adapt to change, at least to the extent of the climate change they have experienced thus far. Where studied, this adaptive capacity appears largely to have been achieved through phenotypic plasticity (e.g. Nussey *et al.* 2007; Charmantier *et al.* 2008; Husby *et al.* 2011), although there are some examples of selection leading to micro-evolutionary responses to climate change (e.g. Bearhop *et al.* 2005). As many of the phenotypic characteristics influenced by the climate are heritable, we would expect such micro-evolution to become increasingly apparent as the strength of selection increases. However, given our current state of knowledge, it is difficult to assess the extent to which individual bird populations and species may have the capacity to adapt to future climate change (Gienapp *et al.* 2008; Sheldon 2010; Hadfield *et al.* 2010; Martin *et al.* 2011). We might expect the extent and rate of micro-evolutionary change to be constrained by interspecific competition. If a focal species has a potential competitor which currently occupies a geographical range at lower latitude, the competitor's existing adaptations to a warmer climate may allow it to colonise the range of the focal species, take over its ecological niche and displace the focal species. If the competitor had not been present at lower latitudes, the focal species might have shown micro-evolutionary change that would have allowed it to tolerate the warming.

One of the common threads running through our review of impacts in Part I is that, at least on land, temperature appears to be the most important determinant of phenology, demographic and community change at medium and high latitudes, but precipitation is most influential in the tropics. Thus, the same climatic drivers, whether temperature or precipitation, influence the response of individual birds, as they make decisions about where to live and when to breed or migrate. At different scales, these climatic drivers also influence populations, as individuals survive or die in response to fluctuations in temperature and precipitation, and alter communities, as different populations increase or decline in abundance. Each of the processes described in the first chapters of this book are therefore closely interrelated.

At high latitudes, cold weather limits resource availability and increases energetic requirements. When it is cold, birds are less likely to return to their breeding grounds and will persist for longer at warmer locations. They will be less able to obtain sufficient food resources to come into breeding condition, leading to delays in egg-laying. As a result of these stresses, in cold years, productivity and survival may be reduced, leading to a population decline, and if sustained, a contraction in the distribution of the cold-sensitive species. Towards the tropics, where warmth is not limiting, water availability becomes the main driver of resource availability. Thus, it is rainfall which triggers the migration and breeding of many tropical species, either directly or in response to increasing resource availability. It is drought which reduces food availability and causes localised population declines. Given relationships between actual evapotranspiration (AET) and tropical bird communities, it is likely that increasing frequency of drought will tend to reduce community diversity, suggesting that more species and populations are likely to be adversely affected by drier weather. Although there are many exceptions to these broad generalities, the impacts of climate change on the behaviour of individuals, the demography of populations, large-scale patterns in species' distribution and changes in bird community composition are all likely to be mediated through the same ultimate mechanisms.

This review has implications for our understanding of the effects of climate change on birds around the world. Likely positive effects of temperature on survival and productivity towards higher latitude range limits (Chapter 4) are expected to lead to increases in subpopulations located near the high latitude boundary of a species' range. There is increasing evidence that this is occurring. Correspondingly, low latitude range limits are likely to be negatively affected by increasing temperature or drought, leading to declining populations there. Some of the former increases are likely to be caused by abiotic mechanisms associated with the relaxation of thermal limits, whilst negative effects of temperature and drought appear more likely to operate through biotic mechanisms such as disease, predation, competition and declining food resources (Ockendon *et al.* 2014). As a result, these negative impacts of climate change at low-latitude range boundaries may occur at a slower rate and over a longer time frame than the more immediate positive effects associated with warming. This may drive a short-term discrepancy in the magnitude of range shift between leading- and trailing-range edges that we would expect to cause an apparently more positive impact of climate change on bird populations in the short term than in the long term, and could account for the more limited shift in the trailing range margin of species relative to the leading range margin described in Chapter 5.

Although bird distributions can be well described by climate, it is unclear how quickly climate change will drive changes in bird populations and such distributions. In particular, where habitat structure is the proximate factor limiting range, changes in species' distribution may be delayed by decades or centuries relative to what would occur if the species was responding to a direct climatic link. Examples might be the distributions of species specialised in living in woodland being limited by the treeline in montane forests, or the range limits of species specialised in living in savanna being limited by the boundary between this biome and forest in the tropics. Transitions between vegetation communities with different architecture composed of plants of different functional types can be expected to occur in a different way and at a different rate than they did in response to past Quaternary climatic fluctuations, because of the widespread anthropogenic modification of much of the global land cover. Therefore, it is unclear how rapidly or easily shifts in habitat types driven by climate will occur, and hence how long it might take for habitat-specialist bird species to change their distributions.

To conclude, there is evidence that climate change has affected bird populations and bird communities, leading to significant poleward shifts in the distribution of species and changes in community composition. Whilst relatively few species appear to be facing immediate conservation threat as a result of climate change, there is good reason to suspect that, as the magnitude of climate change increases, it is likely to have an increasing impact upon bird populations. The evidence to date suggests that it will be specialist species, such as those with the most restricted habitat requirements or diet, and those already threatened by other factors that may be under the greatest threat. Therefore, there is an urgent need to assess the potential magnitude of negative impacts of climate change on bird populations and consider the implications of this for their conservation status, which was the topic of Part II of the book.

9.2 Conservation responses to the effects of climate change to come

Having examined the evidence concerning the impacts of climate change on bird demography, population size, distribution and community composition, we are left with some uncertainty about the extent to which climate change presents a significant threat to bird populations. There are relatively few good examples of species which have declined as a result of recent climate change and those which do exist are mostly correlative. It is difficult to firmly attribute these recent population changes specifically to anthropogenic climate change. As discussed in the introductory chapter, if we were to base our assessment of climate change purely on recent observed changes, we might conclude that it is not a significant problem. However, this would not be a prudent conclusion, given the short time over which rapid anthropogenic climate change has been occurring, the complexity of the mechanisms by which it influences bird populations and distributions, and the potential time lags over which such impacts may occur.

The likely importance of climate change as a threat to the future of global biodiversity is highlighted when the potential magnitude of future climate change is examined. Based on the current trajectory, by 2100, climate change is likely to result in novel climates not currently present on the planet across some 12–39% of the land surface (Williams *et al.* 2007), with a mean global temperature that has not been experienced by organisms on this planet for at least 2 million years. The distribution of these novel climates will be concentrated in tropical areas, which currently have the greatest concentration of bird species, including those with restricted global geographical ranges. Given the close relationship between climate and species distributions, for all the reasons outlined in the first part of this book, future shifts in climate are likely to result in significant future changes to species populations and ranges, and may particularly threaten birds in the tropics, and especially in Amazonia (Foden *et al.* 2013).

There is a large body of work which has attempted to model likely future changes in species' distributions in response to projected climate change. Reviewing the practice and outputs from such climate envelope modelling was the focus of Chapter 6. Some approaches to climate envelope modelling describe species' distributions in relation to a small number of bioclimatic variables to reduce the risk of uninformative models identified by dredging through a large number of candidate meteorological variables. As might be expected from Section 9.1, these tend to include a measure of winter cold (likely to limit high latitude range margins), mean accumulated temperature as a measure of the potential duration of the plant growing season and moisture availability, such as the ratio of actual to potential evapotranspiration (AET/PET). Projected future shifts in the location of species' ranges are often associated with anticipated reductions in the total extent of the range. The assumptions made about the ability of a species to colonise currently unoccupied parts of the potential future range have a large influence on the projected magnitude of future range change. Despite this, there remains a consistent positive relationship between the magnitude of global warming and the projected magnitude of decline in future potential range extent. If species are regarded as unable to colonise new areas of the potential future range (likely to be an overly pessimistic scenario for all but the most dispersal-limited species and those with long-term ecological lags), then the mean projected range decline, averaged across species, is 41% for a 2 °C warming scenario and 74% for a 6 °C warming scenario. Projected mean range reductions of 11% and 23% for 2 °C and 6 °C warming scenarios respectively are estimated, if colonisations of new areas of suitable climate occur. Barbet-Massin *et al.* (2012) estimated for Europe that the future distribution of some 5–12% of species was likely to be dispersal-limited. This proportion is likely to be much greater for many tropical forest species sensitive to fragmentation, which may be one way in which such tropical species are more vulnerable to future climate change impacts.

Whilst past climatic changes from cold glacial to warm interglacial periods have resulted in significant shifts in the distribution of species over thousands of kilometres (Section 1.9) on many occasions and for many species, these occurred in the absence of significant human impacts on natural landscapes. Given the current extent of human modification to the natural world, there are now likely to be considerable constraints on the ability of species to track shifts in climate, which may mean that they are less able to make the shifts in distribution necessary to occupy their climatic potential future range in full. Hence, changes induced by climatic change in total range extent and population size are likely to be more negative than they would otherwise be. It is not necessarily climate change on its own which is the main threat to species, but the fact that climate change is occurring in a heavily human-modified world that will make it difficult for species to adapt by changing their distribution. Put another way, many species already face significant anthropogenic threats as a result of habitat loss due to land-use change, the spread of invasive non-native species, over-exploitation and a host of other factors. Climate change is likely to interact significantly with and exacerbate these other existing threats, which will magnify the chance of substantial range and population declines and consequently increase the risk of extinction for many species.

As with projected changes in range extent, the likely magnitude of extinction risk for bird species is expected to increase significantly with the magnitude of projected temperature rise. If extinction is only assumed to occur when a species has no area of projected future potential range, then extinction risks are estimated to be 0.6%–1.8% respectively for the 2 °C and 6 °C warming scenarios, a range from 60 to 180 bird species. For comparison, it is estimated that 150 bird species have gone extinct over the last 500 years (BirdLife International 2012a). This is likely to be a conservative assessment of risk, as the species–area relationship suggests that as range extent declines, the probability of species' extinction increases. Hence, extinctions are expected when a species' potential range is reduced by climate change even if some future potential range remains. Studies which estimate extinction risk in this way, or assign species to IUCN threat categories suggest that, on this basis, the proportion of species committed to extinction is 10.2% and 24.5% respectively for the 2 °C and 6 °C warming scenarios. This is much larger than the estimate of the percentage of species with no projected future potential range and is equivalent to approximately 1000–2500 species. Our review has two messages. Firstly, there are considerable differences in projected extinction risk depending upon the assumptions made (e.g. Dormann *et al.* 2008; Diniz-Filho *et al.* 2009), although some of the difference just outlined may represent the contrast between more immediate impacts of climate change versus a longer-term extinction debt involving a greater number of species, which may take decades or centuries to play out (Thomas et al. 2004). This protracted time course would result from lagged effects mediated through biotic interactions and slow habitat changes. In order for conservationists and policy-makers to be more confident about the current outputs of species' risk assessments, much more research is required to reduce this uncertainty about timing. The second message is that, despite this uncertainty, there is a high likelihood that a greater degree of climate change will increase the extinction risk for a wide range of species. We estimate that the difference between the 2 °C and 6 °C global warming scenarios will be a 2.4–2.8-fold increase in extinction risk, depending upon the method used to estimate risk. Therefore, effective climate change mitigation to reduce the likely severity of future climate change will play an important part in reducing the risk that climate change poses to many bird species (Warren et al. 2013).

Extinction risk due to climate change varies among species because of a combination of differences in vulnerability and exposure (Foden et al. 2013). For a given species, exposure to climate change is determined by where it lives and by the magnitude of climate change in that region. One potential way to assess exposure is from the outputs of climate envelope models (Chapter 6), with species for which the greatest discrepancy between current and projected future range exists being the ones likely to be subject to the greatest exposure to potential effects of climate change. The vulnerability of a species to that exposure will ultimately determine the extent to which the potential for damage or enhancement actually occurs. Vulnerability influences whether projected declines in abundance within the current range are realised and whether the species is able to expand into the parts of the potential future range which become newly suitable. It is likely to be strongly influenced by aspects of the species' ecology. A number of frameworks were summarised in Section 7.4.1 that have been used to assess the risk associated with climate change for particular species. These make use of a range of traits such as habitat specialisation, physiological tolerance, migratory status, dispersal ability, population size, range extent, habitat vulnerability, diet and the strength of interspecific interactions likely to be associated with vulnerability (Maclean et al. 2007; Thomas et al. 2010; Gardali et al. 2012). Outputs from Part I of this book may also be used to identify particular features likely to be associated with vulnerability to climate change, thus adding to this list (Table 9.1). For example, many seabirds, which Chapters 3 and 4 suggest may be extremely vulnerable to climate change, would score highly. They are dependent upon seasonal resources with divergent phenological trends, many are long-distance migrants, they have semi-precocial young vulnerable to weather-related reductions in prey availability, many have fragmented populations at only a small number of breeding sites, they are vulnerable to storm events, have a specialised diet, can be vulnerable to predation and are sensitive to heat stress. Such trait-based approaches to assessing vulnerability are relatively new (e.g. Foden et al. 2013), but may provide important new insights. Future research should focus on testing their validity and hence their value in identifying priorities for conservation responses to climate change.

For the species most at risk of potentially significant impacts of climate change, we have examined the potential for human intervention to reduce the severity of those impacts

Table 9.1 *Indicative list of ecological traits likely to be associated with increased vulnerability of species to climate change, based largely on Part I of this book.*

Ecological traits
Dependent upon seasonally available resources with potential for divergent phenological trends between peak resource availability and peak requirements (Chapter 3)
Long-distance migrants (Sections 3.5, 4.6)
Low adaptive capacity. Species with limited phenotypic plasticity, mobility or micro-evolutionary potential in response to climate change (Gienapp *et al.* 2008; Visser 2008)
Precocial, semi-precocial or semi-altricial species vulnerable to weather-related reductions in prey availability (Section 4.3.2)
Small or fragmented populations (Section 4.3.2)
Vulnerable to storm events (Sections 4.3.2, 4.6.2)
Specialised diet with strong variation in food resources linked to climate (Sections 4.3.4, 4.6)
Vulnerable to predation by predators whose distributions/behaviours are likely to be affected by climate change (Section 4.3.4)
Vulnerable to disease whose occurrence varies with climate (Section 4.3.4)
Vulnerable to climate-related expansion of potential competitor (Section 4.4.2)
Sensitive to heat stress (Section 4.5)
Habitat specialist (Section 5.4.1)

(Chapter 7). A wide range of tools currently exist in the conservation toolkit that may be adapted to respond to climate change, and we suggest that they should form the building blocks of a conservation strategy in a changing climate.

Current conservation practice is focussed on attempting to protect species and their habitats from external threats. Implicit in this is often comparison with a historical reference point that is the target for restoration. In the short term, much climate change adaptation can adopt this same approach, using site-based and landscape-scale management to maximise habitat quality, reduce negative impacts of climate change and minimise the severity of other threats, thus increasing the resistance of species and populations to climate change. However, the greater the magnitude of future climate change, the more severe will be the exposure of species to its potentially damaging effects. Higher exposure to risks will reduce the chances of these management approaches working, leading to a growing need to increase the capacity of species to shift their distributions in response to climate change. This is likely to require management to counteract the landscape-scale degradation and fragmentation of natural habitats which characterises many human-dominated landscapes. Doing this will slow climate change-induced population and range declines within the existing range and facilitate expansion into newly suitable parts of the potential range. Such management should focus on maximising the extent and quality of protected areas and increase the connectivity of semi-natural habitats in the wider landscape. However, it should be recognised that there may be cases where this is associated with risk, for example through facilitating the expansion of more competitive generalist species and exotic invasives. Future projections suggest that our ability to increase the dispersal ability of species will be critical in determining the eventual magnitude of climate change impacts on species' distributions and populations. If such management is not feasible or is unsuccessful, more radical solutions will be required to enable species to survive, including assisted colonisation of new sites. With increasing severity of climate change, an increasingly radical set of tools may need to be applied, but their use involves greater risks and uncertainties than those associated with conservation tools that are currently more widely used.

Future climate change is likely to cause significant ecological changes. Whilst it is possible to write a set of potential conservation prescriptions and approaches which may be used to adapt to these changes, there remains considerable uncertainty about their likely effectiveness in the long term. We do not yet know the magnitude of future changes in temperature and precipitation in sufficient detail to make detailed future plans for conservation management. Changes in the severity of climate change are likely to require alterations in the conservation strategies employed, and good ecological monitoring and understanding will be required to identify transition points when a marked shift in strategy is advisable. We also do not fully understand the effects that climate change will have on species' populations and communities, although as we have shown in this book, in many instances, we can make a good guess. Again, continued monitoring and research on species' responses will be essential. In addition, we do not know how effective will be our conservation management responses to a changing climate. Despite these uncertainties, two additional principles should be emphasised. Firstly, the magnitude of non-climatic threats facing species and populations should always be reduced in order to compensate as far as possible for negative effects of climate change. Small and fragmented populations and those suffering from additional anthropogenic causes of mortality and poor breeding will be most vulnerable to the impacts of climate change. Secondly, there is an urgent need to reduce greenhouse gas emissions to minimise the magnitude of future climate change. The greater the amount of climate change, the lower our chances of successful conservation in a changing climate and the greater the probability that the end of this century will be characterised by high levels of species' extinction (Warren *et al.* 2013).

Mitigation to reduce the magnitude of future climate change will, however, require careful management and application if it is not to also cause its own problems and conflicts with bird conservation (Chapter 8). Many of the laudable measures advocated to reduce greenhouse gas emissions are likely to have detrimental effects on some bird populations. Mitigation actions which cause significant and widespread land-use changes, increase the demand for land and conversion of natural habitats, or that result in large increases in bird mortality, are most likely to be detrimental. Unfortunately the cheapest forms of renewable energy, such as bioenergy crops, tend to be the least efficient in terms of energy produced per unit land area, and therefore are likely to be the most damaging, by requiring the greatest conversion of natural habitats to human use. There is good evidence that recent biofuel expansion, particularly across tropical Asia and South America, has had widespread detrimental impacts on the conservation status of many bird species. This has arguably been the most negative impact of climate change so far. Conversely, whilst solar power currently appears to be the most efficient and potentially least damaging form of renewable energy (albeit based on a relatively limited evidence base), it is also the most expensive, creating significant obstacles to its expansion.

In order to minimise the risk of conflict between renewable energy generation and bird conservation, a number of tools should be applied through a rigorous planning process. In particular, Strategic Environmental Assessments should be conducted in order to identify locations where a particular type of development is likely to be least damaging, whilst, once a potential site for a proposed development has been chosen, Environmental Impact Assessments will act as a further check on its effects. This approach should be applied to all types of developments, including extensive conversion of natural or semi-natural habitat to bioenergy crops and construction of wind turbines or tidal barrages. At the strategic level, there should be greater efforts to compare the impact on biodiversity conservation of different types of developments and to use this information to select the least damaging types. In this way, the most damaging effects of developments to reduce greenhouse gas emissions could be avoided. Significant expansion of renewable energy is likely to be necessary to limit greenhouse gas emissions, emphasising the need for these negative impacts to be reduced or compensated for.

These are difficult issues. Climate change itself is likely to detrimentally affect many bird populations, and the greater its magnitude, the larger these impacts are likely to be. Much mitigation action to reduce climate change may also have widespread negative consequences for birds. The most effective way for society to minimise the impacts of climate change on birds and other biodiversity may therefore be through reducing energy consumption, for example through increased efficiency of energy use. Unfortunately, there appears to be little prospect of this occurring, with global greenhouse gas emissions continuing to rise. One potential win-win option for climate change mitigation, which may both reduce the magnitude of climate change and deliver significant biodiversity benefit, is to reduce the level of emissions associated with land use, land-use change and forestry (LULUCF). Considerable effort is currently being invested to develop schemes to protect carbon-rich natural and semi-natural habitats and to restore those which are inappropriately managed in order to maximise their carbon storage potential. Initiatives such as REDD+ are particularly focussed on tropical forest habitats, and if biodiversity-related safeguards are effectively adopted, may deliver large-scale biodiversity and mitigation benefits. There may also be significant potential to increase the protection, and improve the management, of peatland, coastal and marine habitats that also have high carbon stocks, which may further protect the species associated with those habitats.

REDD+ and similar initiatives offer a ray of hope in what is otherwise a bleak assessment of the future. An increasing severity of climate change is likely to threaten more and more bird species with population decline and extinction, whilst many of the measures suggested for climate change mitigation to reduce the magnitude of climate change are also likely to have negative consequences for bird conservation. Whilst there is considerable potential for conservation action to reduce these threats, current limits to the size of the conservation budget which already limit our ability to halt current rates of biodiversity loss (Butchart *et al.* 2010; Hoffmann *et al.* 2010) will continue to be an obstacle to long-term success.

9.3 Impacts of human responses to climate change

Climate change is likely to result in many significant and potentially radical changes to fields of human activity beyond the ways in which energy is generated. Sectors such as agriculture, forestry, water resource management, construction, transport and tourism are going to be affected by climate change, and each will have to adapt as a consequence. These further impacts and adaptive responses are likely to have significant implications for bird populations, particularly given that the greatest threats to birds at present are associated with habitat loss. The main drivers of habitat loss, which contribute to the threatened status of more than 1000 bird species, are timber extraction and agricultural expansion. Overexploitation of birds and impacts of invasive species each affect in excess of 300 species (BirdLife International 2000). We therefore should also consider how these drivers are likely to change in the future as a result of climate change.

Focussing on habitat loss, as the most important driver of extinction risk in birds, global scenarios of land-use change, such as those developed through the Millennium Ecosystem Assessment, project that 25–28% of natural land will be transformed by 2100, although the precise drivers and locations of these impacts varies between scenarios (Jetz et al. 2007). Climate change itself is regarded as the most important driver of future habitat change at temperate and high latitudes, whilst conversion of natural habitats to human use is most likely to drive habitat loss in the tropics, particularly across central Africa. There are a great range of future land-use projections covered by the IPCC's new representative concentration pathways (RCP), which range from large increases in cropland and grassland as a result of increasing global population (RCP8.5) and increases in cropland associated with bioenergy production (RCP2.6), to reductions in cropland and grassland, and increases in natural vegetation cover associated with policies to protect natural carbon stocks (RCP4.5). In the latter, increased agricultural yields and dietary changes are required to ensure that sufficient food is produced (van Vuuren et al. 2011). Even at the regional level, there remains considerable uncertainty about which trajectories are plausible (e.g. Verburg et al. 2010).

The importance of future changes in agricultural yields in determining the likely pace and direction of land-use change is illustrated by detailed modelling for Europe. Here, significant increases in yield associated with CO_2 fertilisation and technological development may drive a reduction in the extent of land required for agriculture. Many areas that are currently farmland may be replaced by abandoned land and forest (Ewart et al. 2005; Rounsevell et al. 2006). The same changes are also anticipated in North America (Radeloff et al. 2012). If true, there may be a future improvement in the conservation status of forest birds across both continents, a process which is already apparent across temperate North America (Foster & Motzkin 2003). These scenarios also suggest that agricultural land will become increasingly polarised. Certain areas are likely to become intensively farmed to deliver high food and probably bioenergy yields (see Section 8.7) and will be unlikely to support many birds of conservation concern (Chamberlain et al. 2000; Donald et al. 2001; Eglington & Pearce-Higgins 2012). Other areas, where farming becomes uneconomic, are likely to become abandoned. Without intervention, this process is likely to have significant negative impacts on some bird species currently associated with relatively low-intensity agriculture. However, species associated with scrub habitats may benefit (Suárez-Seone et al. 2002; Wretenberg et al. 2006; Moreira & Russo 2007; Sirami et al. 2008).

Much will depend upon the likely spatial resolution and arrangement of different habitats within the agricultural landscape (Vickery & Arlettaz 2012). Landscapes could be designed so that areas of forest and low-intensity or abandoned farmland act as stepping stones or corridors for species averse to intensively managed habitats, to enable them to track future changes in the climate (e.g. Vos et al. 2008). These changes may therefore help deliver the habitat protection and creation required to enhance connectivity in the wider landscape (Section 7.7), which will probably benefit species with intermediate levels of specialisation (see Dolman *et al.* 2007). Conversely, if the landscape became polarised at large spatial scales, then large parts of Europe devoted to intensive food production would become relatively hostile to most species, and therefore support smaller populations of fewer bird species. However, if managed appropriately, this loss might be exceeded by benefits to bird populations from the protection and creation of extensive areas of natural and semi-natural habitats that may support large populations of species vulnerable to anthropogenic pressure. This might also deliver a net increase in resilience to climate change, particularly for habitat specialists. This is the land-sparing and land-sharing debate discussed in Section 8.7.5. It is therefore worth re-emphasising that for any long-term biodiversity benefit to accrue from the sacrifice of large areas of countryside to intensive food production, land-sparing must involve more robust protection of extensive existing areas of habitats of high conservation value and, especially in Europe, the re-creation of large tracts of natural habitat (Phalan *et al.* 2011b). Of course, the operation of intensive agriculture must also be sustainable in the long term, to ensure that food yields can be maintained at high levels on the farmland devoted to such production.

In practice, land-use changes in Europe and North America will not simply be determined by national or European Union political processes and policies, but will also be sensitive to changes in food production elsewhere (see Section 8.7.4). In particular, potential reductions in yields from thin tropical soils suffering deterioration in quality, coupled with reductions in agricultural outputs as a result of climate change, may counter some of the benefits associated with increased agricultural yields in parts of the Northern Hemisphere (Eickhout *et al.* 2007; Schlenker & Lobell 2010). Any potentially negative impacts of climate change on the ability of global agriculture to deliver high crop yields will therefore increase the requirement for additional land to be devoted to food production at the expense of natural and semi-natural habitats. There are clear trade-offs between the area of land under agricultural production and the intensity of management of that land required to deliver a particular level of food, or bioenergy, production (Lotze-Campen *et al.* 2010). If it is not possible to continue to increase agricultural yields of food and bioenergy production through the course of this century, for example as a result of potential future climatic limitations to agriculture, then significant expansion of agricultural land at the expense of forest and savanna are projected, particularly across Amazonia, central Africa and south-east Asia (Thomson *et al.* 2010; Beaumont & Duursma 2012).

The impact of climate change on tropical forest habitats is projected to be greatest in South America, where likely increases in drought conditions coupled with significant warming (Section 1.7) are projected to have widespread impacts on the distribution of Amazonian plant species (Feeley *et al.* 2012). As a result, some 81% of Amazonia is projected to be moderately or severely affected by future climate and land use change under a medium to high A2 scenario by 2100 (Asner *et al.* 2010). In Africa, south-east Asia and Oceania, impacts of climate change are projected to be less severe, and therefore the greatest drivers of habitat change are more likely to be directly related to continued increases in demand, rather than impacts of climate change on yield (Asner *et al.* 2010; Thomson *et al.* 2010; Beaumont & Duursma 2012). Although climate change is not projected to be severe enough to drive as much large-scale habitat conversion in these latter regions as in the Neotropics, it may detrimentally affect crop yields in some areas (Schlenker & Lobell 2010). This could still lead to increased rates of habitat loss as a result of the indirect effects of climate change in tropical Africa and Asia.

In this book, our assessment of the impacts of climate change on bird populations has included both direct abiotic effects, and impacts that are mediated through biotic pathways involving effects of climate change on other species. The main exception to this is our discussion of the potential impacts of climate change mitigation upon bird populations in Chapter 8. It is clear, however, that across many parts of the world, the potential indirect impacts of climate change upon human land use and other sectors are also likely to be as, or more, important. The analyses of Jetz *et al.* (2007), although relatively simplistic and based upon gross habitat change (see Section 6.8.2), supports these conclusions and suggest that land-use change will be the predominant threat to bird populations across tropical Africa, much of southern Asia, parts of Central and South America and eastern North America, whilst climate change impacts will be greatest at high latitudes. In response, there is an urgent need to develop models and approaches to improve our ability to understand and project the likely consequences of climate change for human land use, and the potential for, and likely nature of, human adaptive responses. This should be done alongside a compilation of information about the likely impacts of these land-use changes on bird populations. Whilst that may be relatively straightforward for habitat loss and conversion, which has formed the basis of most such assessments to date, potential changes in the management and quality of particular habitats are likely to be much more widespread, and may have equally serious effects. For example, we know how changes in the methods used to grow crops and produce livestock in Europe have had far-reaching and long-lasting impacts on farmland bird populations (e.g. Wilson *et al.* 2009b), even though the gross habitat type has remained farmland throughout the period of change. The impacts of these changes to the farmland system have so far had a much greater impact on the populations of birds using that habitat than climate change (Eglington & Pearce-Higgins 2012; Figure 9.1).

If we are to fully understand and anticipate the potential indirect consequences of climate change upon birds, we need to think carefully about how each sector of human economic activity will respond and adapt to climate change, and what the biodiversity consequences of those responses and adaptations may be. Sadly, given the recent and rapid biodiversity loss associated with the expansion of biofuels, our track record in achieving this is poor. The development of horizon scanning as a starting point for conservation biologists to begin the identification of potential consequences of future changes in human activities (e.g. Sutherland & Woodroof 2009; Sutherland *et al.* 2013) may help to improve our future preparedness in the face of further novel changes.

Species are likely to be affected by the direct impacts of climate change that were discussed in Part I of the book, and modelled in Chapter 6, and the indirect effects of climate change, including mitigation, covered in Chapter 8, as well as the remaining indirect effects just discussed. This combination of pressures can be illustrated with reference to the white stork. This long-distance migrant may be vulnerable to increasing drought frequency in parts of Africa (Solomon *et al.* 2009) which would be likely to reduce its overwinter food resources (Schaub *et al.* 2005; Sæther *et al.* 2006). It may also

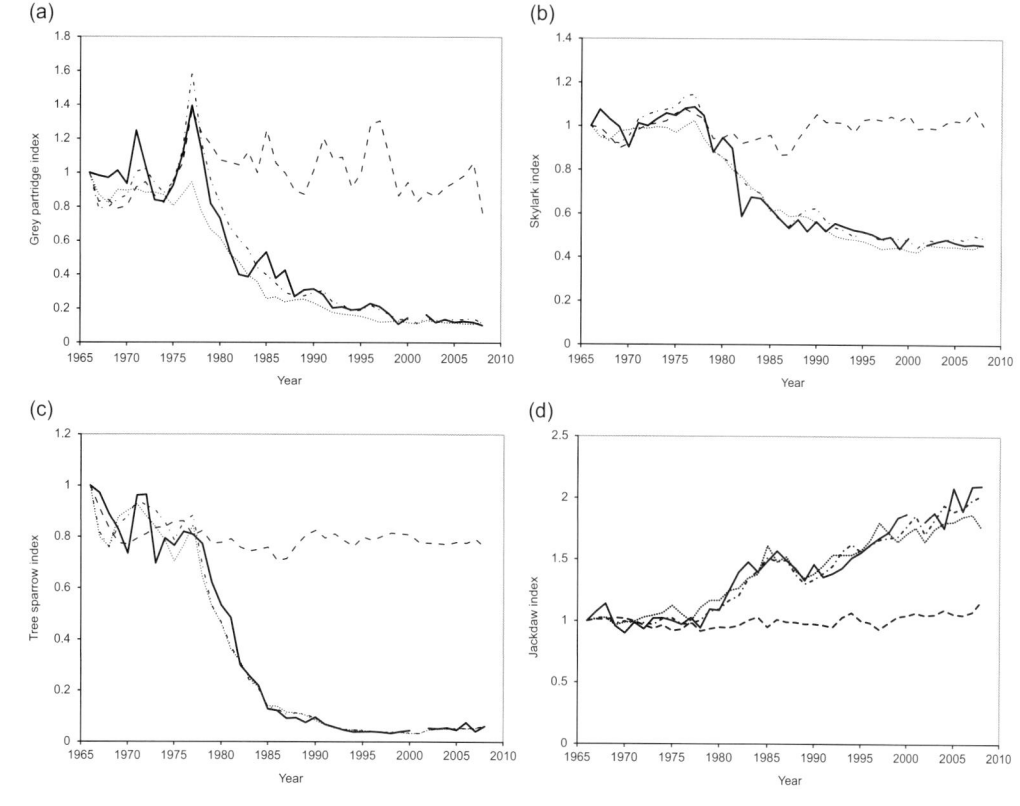

Figure 9.1 Variation in the national abundance (index) of four farmland bird species (a – grey partridge, b – skylark, c – tree sparrow and d – jackdaw) in the UK (solid line) compared to predictions based on models where annual variation in population growth rate was modelled as a function of the weather (dashed line), agricultural intensification (dotted line) or both (dashed and dotted line). In each case, population trends are largely described by changes in agricultural intensification, with changes in the weather (climate change) having only a limited effect. Reproduced from Eglington and Pearce-Higgins (2012).

suffer some contraction of its future potential range in Europe as a result of climate change (Huntley *et al.* 2007). However, the white stork is a generalist species and may have substantial adaptive capacity. It has shown evidence of reduced migratory tendency in recent years in response to warming (Fiedler 2003), which may mean that the potentially negative effects of deteriorating climate in Africa are reduced. Being a migratory soaring bird, it may be vulnerable to collision with wind turbines and associated power lines across its range (Hötker *et al.* 2006), both in Europe and across the Red Sea–Rift Valley migratory flyway, where there is considerable potential for future expansion of renewable energy generation. Conditions on the passage and wintering grounds may deteriorate further through agricultural intensification in Africa which may lead to the drainage and loss of wetland areas. In isolation, each of these impacts may not be severe, but in combination they could pose a long-term threat to the species. For many species, the impact of individual pressures, whether directly or indirectly related to climate change, may be limited when considered in isolation. However, there is a real danger that when combined, these pressures may have either additive or multiplicative negative effects on vulnerable species and cause significant population declines and increased extinction risk. Climate change is not happening in isolation, but alongside many other environmental changes that are also likely to be detrimental to bird conservation. Unfortunately, climate change is likely to interact with these pressures to worsen the conservation status of many species, which makes reducing the severity of these other threats and instigating appropriate management for species across the wider countryside important elements of any adaptive conservation response to climate change (Chapter 7).

9.4 Dealing with uncertainty

There is much uncertainty inherent in assessing impacts of current and future climate change. This is also a highly charged and politically sensitive topic. We have therefore attempted to be as measured and balanced as possible regarding both the evidence for climate change having impacted birds and the potential significance of projected future impacts. However, being cautious is also associated with risk. Recent studies suggest that climate scientists actually have a tendency towards conservatism in their presentation of future projections (Brysse *et al.* 2013). In particular, they have tended to underestimate the magnitude of recent changes (although see Otto *et al.* 2013), and more generally, may consistently underpredict and downplay potential future climate changes for reasons of restraint, objectivity, scepticism, rationality, dispassion, moderation and avoidance of criticism by vested interests. This means some of the material on which our assessments are based may be over-conservative in nature.

Aside from uncertainty over the potential magnitude of climate change, there is significant uncertainty associated with estimating the magnitude of effects of climate change on species and our understanding about the tolerance of species to future climatic conditions. Most of the evidence comes from middle latitudes, whilst the majority of bird species occur at low latitudes (Figure 9.2). In the Northern Hemisphere, the predominant locations of phenological and demographic studies peak at 40–45° N (primarily studies from the USA), and 50–60° N (mainly studies from central and northern Europe). Demographic studies from 40–50° S are largely of seabirds in the Southern Ocean, whilst those further south are from Antarctica, where probably a higher proportion of birds have been subject to study than anywhere else. The paucity of studies from about 40° S to 40° N, where the majority of bird diversity is located, illustrates how little is known about the demography of most bird species and how uncertain our knowledge may be.

There is an urgent need for increased monitoring and research to be conducted in order to help conservationists best adapt their practices to this changing climate (Pearce-Higgins *et al.* 2011a). Throughout the book we have suggested particular knowledge gaps that should be filled in order to improve our understanding, and importantly to reduce the uncertainty for decision-makers and conservationists, which we hope will be useful for the prioritisation of research in this area, both now and into the future. Without doubt, the most important of these must be the improvement of monitoring and ecological research outside of Europe and North America, and particularly in the tropics where the greatest proportion of biodiversity exists. Not only will such knowledge provide ecological understanding about

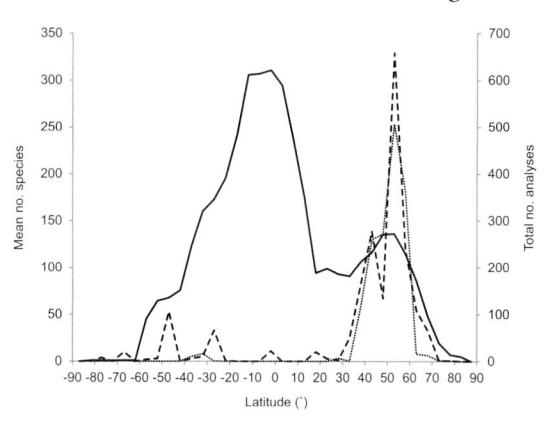

Figure 9.2 Latitudinal gradient of species diversity (thick line) as measured by the mean number of species present per 0.25° grid cell, compared to a measure of the research effort examining phenological change (dotted line) or demographic change (dashed line) within 5° latitudinal bins from the South Pole (−90) to North Pole (90). Research effort is estimated from the total number of published analyses of individual time series collated for this book. Each time series represents a single analysis in relation to year or to a particular climatological variable, and therefore the summed totals given an indication of the total research effort in particular locations (with greater weight to studies covering a large number of species or examining variation with respect to a range of explanatory variables). The number of demographic time series has been multiplied by 10 for ease of plotting on the same axis as the phenological time series, but shows a very similar pattern.

the structure and function of these systems and communities to inform both research and subsequent adaptive responses, but also facilitate future climate change impacts to be documented, as a guide to the implementation of such management.

9.5 Climate change and a real bird species revisited

To conclude the book, let us return to the example of the red grouse, as a subspecies whose populations are highly managed in the UK, yet which still shows considerable climatic influences on its distribution and abundance. We use this species to illustrate how the understanding of climate change impacts, potential future impacts, effects of climate change mitigation and human responses to climate change presented in this book may be used to produce an assessment of the likely impact of climate change on a species. We do so by imagining what the British uplands may be like by the 2080s under two contrasting future scenarios. Although partly based on published projections, these are largely qualitative and descriptive in nature, and should be regarded as illustrative only.

9.5.1 A low emissions scenario

Under a low emissions 1B scenario from UKCP09 (Jenkins *et al.* 2009), by the end of this century, mean UK winter temperature is projected to be about 2.5 °C warmer than the 1961–1990 baseline and mean summer temperature to be about 2.7 °C warmer. Winter precipitation is projected to increase by some 15% whilst summer precipitation may decline by an average of 14%. In response to these changes, climate suitability for blanket peatland in south-west England, south Wales, the South Pennines, North Yorkshire and parts of the Scottish Borders is projected to decline (Clark *et al.* 2010). This is relevant to red grouse, because associated with such peatland areas are craneflies, an important food source for grouse chicks (Park *et al.* 2001), which are likely to decline significantly in abundance in response to warming (Pearce-Higgins *et al.* 2010). Such changes could compromise the long-term persistence of grouse populations in these areas (Fletcher *et al.* 2013), although there may be potential for counteracting management at core sites to increase the resilience of some populations to these pressures (Pearce-Higgins 2011a; Carroll *et al.* 2011).

Although core heather moorland habitats are likely to be fairly resilient to warming, increased frequency of summer drought and heat waves may lead to large-scale accidental fires (McMorrow *et al.* 2009), whilst increases in climatic variability may add to the risk of heather dieback (Hancock 2008). Such events could cause sudden and catastrophic localised deterioration in habitat quality for grouse, to which isolated and fragmented grouse populations may be particularly vulnerable. Depending upon the impacts of climate change upon summer precipitation patterns, rising temperatures may also be associated with increased infection rates of grouse by the nematode parasite *Trichostrongylus tenuis* (Cattadori *et al.* 2005; Hudson *et al.* 2006). Similarly, ticks, which spread louping ill (Gilbert 2010), are also likely to expand their altitudinal range to higher elevations. Both factors may further reduce red grouse abundance in southern Britain and at low altitudes, unless veterinary pharmaceuticals currently deployed by grouse moor managers improve in their effectiveness.

Turning to anthropogenic responses to climate change, it is unclear whether there may be an expansion of more intensive agriculture into some upland areas, to compensate for increases in food demand. Alternatively, general increases in agricultural yield may lead to a reduction in the net extent of farmed land required in the UK (Rounsevell & Reay 2009), which could lead to the abandonment of marginal upland farmland, as has previously occurred in other upland parts of Europe.

In order to achieve a low emissions scenario, there are two potential approaches to mitigation that could be adopted; the first to maximise renewable energy generation, and the second to reduce emissions from LULUCF. For renewable energy generation, significant areas of the uplands may be planted with trees or other bioenergy crops, such as short-rotation willow coppice (Heaton *et al.* 1999; Aylott *et al.* 2008). Such gross changes would result in the exclusion of red grouse from planted areas and nearby areas of open habitat (Hancock *et al.* 2009), but also due to the likely high densities of predators, such as red foxes and carrion crows, harboured within such planted habitats, would significantly increase predation pressure on remaining grouse populations (e.g. Tharme *et al.* 2001; Fletcher *et al.* 2010). Large numbers of wind turbines may also be constructed across the uplands under this low emissions scenario. Whilst such construction may lead to a short-term reduction in grouse abundance, these would be unlikely to have a significant long-term impact on grouse populations, although may affect some other upland species (Pearce-Higgins *et al.* 2009b, 2012; Douglas *et al.* 2011).

Alternatively, or additionally, mitigation may be achieved by altering land management to affect the carbon balance of upland environments. On peatland, the blocking of drainage ditches to raise water levels may reduce net emissions from the soil, although there remains some uncertainty about the precise magnitude of benefit (Lindsay 2010; Bussell *et al.* 2010; Worrall *et al.* 2010). In addition, this would provide a mechanism by which landowners are able to increase the resilience of vulnerable peatland habitats to climate change to benefit red grouse and other upland birds similarly affected (Pearce-Higgins 2010, 2011a, Carroll *et al.* 2011). Pressure to reduce livestock populations in upland areas in order to limit methane emissions (Smith *et al.* 2007) may drive continued long-term reductions in grazing levels on upland hill farms. Depending on the subsequent management of these areas, and the extent to which heather browsing pressure by livestock is offset by expanding deer populations, this could lead to the recovery of heather on previously heavily grazed moorland, which would also benefit red grouse (Pearce-Higgins & Grant 2006). Burning to promote the growth of young heather shoots is an important component of grouse moor management (Hudson 1992), but one that may also be restricted under an approach to reduce greenhouse gas emissions from LULUCF, as burnt peatlands may emit more carbon than pristine ones (Lindsay 2010; Worrall *et al.* 2010). Some controlled burning or cutting may, however, be required to limit the risk of wildfire.

Overall, even under a low emissions scenario, by 2100, climate change is likely to drive significant losses of red grouse populations in southern England, Wales and even in the south Pennines (Pearce-Higgins *et al.* 2010), which is a current stronghold. Populations here may only be maintained through intensive management of water levels to prevent drying out of peatland, prescribed heather management in order to limit the potential for large-scale fires, intensive predator control and dosing with pharmaceuticals to limit disease (McMorrow *et al.* 2009; Pearce-Higgins 2011a; Carroll *et al.* 2011), although rising temperatures and drought may promote heather growth on peatland, potentially offsetting some of these negative effects. Whilst most of these interventions are already undertaken by grouse moor managers (Hudson 1992), they are expensive, and are only likely to be continued if sufficient grouse are produced for sport shooting (Thirgood *et al.* 2000; Baines *et al.* 2008). For this reason, unless there are significant resources devoted to the conservation of the species in these areas, red grouse may become much less abundant, or even vanish from much of southern Britain as a result of the direct impacts of climate change and their indirect effects on upland land uses. Large-scale payments to landowners for the sensitive management of peatlands to reduce greenhouse gas emissions, such as through drain blocking and habitat restoration (Section 8.9.2), may provide a mechanism for funding such management that maximises the resilience of these habitats and the red grouse populations they support to climate change.

Under a low emission scenario, climatic conditions are likely to remain suitable across much of northern Britain, where some grouse moors may remain. Here, it may be the approaches to mitigation that are adopted which have the largest impact on red grouse populations. If extensive upland areas are afforested for reasons of carbon sequestration, and bioenergy crops are widely planted across moorland at lower altitudes, then even in these climatically suitable areas, red grouse densities may decline widely due to habitat loss and increased predation pressure. Alternatively, if mitigation were achieved through payment for carbon-friendly land management, such as peatland restoration and protection, then the suitability of these upland areas for red grouse may be maintained. The future appears uncertain, but it does seem likely from this discussion that the future trajectory of red grouse populations in the UK under a low emissions scenario will depend largely on the mitigation measures adopted. It is worth emphasising that even under this scenario, climate change is projected to make much of southern Britain less climatically suitable for red grouse. As the next section will illustrate, climate change mitigation is therefore required, despite the accompanying challenges.

9.5.2 A high emissions scenario

Under a high emissions A1F1 scenario (Jenkins *et al.* 2009), mean UK winter temperature is projected to be about 3.1 °C warmer by the end of the century than the 1961–1990 baseline and mean summer temperature 4.5 °C warmer. Winter precipitation is projected to increase by some 25% whilst summer precipitation may decline by an equivalent amount. Under this scenario, most areas of blanket peatland are projected to be outside of climate limits currently considered suitable, except in western Scotland, the Western and Northern Isles (Clark *et al.* 2010). As argued above, this suggests that grouse populations across England, Wales and eastern Scotland will struggle due to likely reductions in invertebrate prey, increases in disease risk and potential changes in vegetation condition. In particular, there must be a significant risk of catastrophic and sudden vegetation change across large areas associated with potential wildfires in very hot and dry summers. If sufficiently frequent, these could lead to sudden and large-scale losses of heather moorland and blanket peatland. Under this scenario, we would therefore expect red grouse distribution to be largely limited to western and northern Scotland only, where the species currently only occurs at relatively low densities. It is possible that densities here could increase if heather cover expanded in response to higher temperatures. The drier and more productive moors of eastern Scotland, the Pennines and North Yorkshire may simply become too dry. The future distribution may therefore be similar, or even more limited, than the simulated potential future distributions of Huntley *et al.* (2007) and Huntley and Green (2011), where climate envelope models based upon the willow grouse range project that, under a A1B HadGEM1 scenario, by 2070–2099, red grouse will have only a low to medium probability of occurrence and be restricted to West Scotland only.

Under a high emissions scenario, existing land-use practices may be expected to alter less than the low emissions scenario, because there would be less mitigation. Thus, livestock grazing levels in the uplands may be higher, and would continue to limit heather cover for grouse, whilst fewer areas of peatland may be managed sympathetically in order to maximise the protection of soil carbon stocks. In the longer term, it is possible that greater levels of warming may facilitate the expansion of crops grown more traditionally at lower altitudes into the uplands, although it is unlikely that this would be a significant additional driver of habitat loss for grouse; areas suitable for such crops would probably have lost their grouse many years earlier. Under this scenario of limited mitigation, levels of tree planting across upland areas are likely to be less, which may protect a greater extent of open habitat from afforestation, but there is little doubt that the potential future range of this species within the UK will be much reduced by the magnitude of climate change projected.

9.5.3 Is there a future for red grouse in the UK?

It is clear from both these scenarios that the red grouse is vulnerable to future changes in the UK uplands, depending upon the human responses to climate change. Under a low emissions scenario, where the uplands become important for climate mitigation, there is considerable potential for the red grouse to be detrimentally affected by those mitigation options, particularly large-scale tree planting for carbon sequestration, for which there is currently significant political traction. Such changes would be likely to then have significant consequences for the viability of red grouse management in areas where afforestation is extensive. The alternative mitigation option, of sympathetic peatland management to protect soil carbon stocks, would be more beneficial for grouse, increasing the resilience of the peatlands and their associated biodiversity to climate change. It is unclear the extent to which either mitigation option, or both, may be necessary to limit the magnitude of future climate change, although some mitigation is certainly required to ensure the long-term persistence of red grouse across many upland areas, as under a high emissions scenario, the species' potential future range is likely to be much more restricted to western and northern Scotland.

Based on this discussion, red grouse appears to have a high vulnerability to climate change, but also a high vulnerability to some climate change mitigation solutions. Given sufficient resources, it will probably be possible to maintain populations of red grouse and other upland bird species in the UK within suitably managed protected areas, even in the face of deteriorating climatic conditions, or increasingly hostile landscapes. This could probably be achieved through adaptive management of core sites using techniques such as drain blocking, heather management and predator control, which are already well-understood. Given that many of these processes will also affect many other upland birds (e.g. Pearce-Higgins et al. 2009a; Pearce-Higgins 2010), these conservation interventions would be expected to deliver wider conservation benefits. Potential twin benefits of some management, such as drain blocking to limit greenhouse gas emissions from peatlands, that may also enhance peatland resilience to climate change, mean that they should be appropraitely prioritised and incentivised.

In summary, the long-term future for the red grouse, along with these other upland birds, will depend on the extent to which we are able to reduce greenhouse gas emissions, and therefore to limit the future magnitude of climate change. Their future will also depend upon the mitigation measures adopted to stabilise greenhouse gas concentrations in the atmosphere. If inappropriate mitigation measures are employed, such as large-scale tree planting with non-native species across the uplands for reasons of carbon sequestration, or that mitigation is inadequate, then the long-term future of red grouse in the UK, alongside that of many other upland birds, may appear bleak. Under a scenario of worsening environmental conditions, such vulnerable species will become increasingly reliant upon active conservation measures and protected areas for their long-term persistence. Whilst this may sound pessimistic, the recent past is full of examples of once widespread species which are now conservation-dependent. Ultimately, therefore, the future of such species will depend upon our willingness as a society to make wise decisions and to invest sufficient resources to secure that future.

This example for a single bird species in a small country is likely to apply to many bird species around the world, whether they have highly managed populations, such as the red grouse, or distributions that appear strongly climate-limited, such as the Ethiopian bush-crow (Box 6.2), that we used to illustrate the front of the book. The long-term persistence of many populations will be threatened by anthropogenic climate change, particularly if we fail to limit the magnitude of such change to around 2 °C global warming. Depending on the mitigation approaches used to limit greenhouse gas emissions, many species may also be threatened by industrial scale renewable energy generation. Care will need to be taken when designing the necessary energy production landscapes required for mitigation to ensure that the negative impacts on biodiversity are minimised. Efforts to reduce emissions through biodiversity friendly options such as REDD+ and sympathetic management of other carbon rich habitats, such as peatlands, should be prioritised as most likely to benefit both people and wildlife. Our attitude to climate change, and the decisions we make regarding its mitigation, may therefore ultimately determine the fate of many of the bird species with which we share this planet.

9.6 Summary

- In recent decades, warming has led to significant changes to the seasonality of avian life cycles across medium and high latitudes. In the tropics, it is likely that changes in precipitation will have had the same effect, but fewer empirical studies exist to confirm this.
- Phenological changes have been shown to have the potential to disrupt the timing of migration or breeding relative to the timing of peak resource availability in about one-third of species studied, leading to mismatch of timing. However, for no species has such mismatch been strongly linked to large-scale population decline.
- Changes in temperature or precipitation may also disrupt species interactions by altering predator, competitor or prey populations, rather than just their timing. These effects may be more important than those associated with mismatch. Increases in extreme events such as drought, floods or heat waves may also have catastrophic impacts upon species, particularly affecting small populations occupying a restricted range.
- In response to warming, there is good evidence for poleward expansion in the distribution of species, but weaker evidence for altitudinal shifts upslope. There have already been significant and widespread changes to bird communities that can be related to recent climatic change.
- The same climatic drivers appear to influence phenological, demographic and community changes. Temperature appears to be the main limiter of these processes at medium and high latitudes, but moisture availability is most important in the tropics.
- Only a small proportion of species have been studied in detail and therefore the current assessment of the impacts of climate change as presented in the scientific literature is incomplete and biased towards the most easily studied species. The best available evidence suggests that habitat specialists occupying natural and semi-natural habitats may be most vulnerable to climate change. In particular, there is the greatest evidence for seabirds, upland and some woodland birds being most detrimentally affected, whilst long-distance migrant population declines may also be partly climate-related.

9.6 Summary

- There remains considerable uncertainty about the adaptive capacity of species to climate change. Where studied, most responses appear a function of phenotypic plasticity rather than an evolutionary response.
- Given the close association between climate and species distribution, future warming is likely to result in far more significant future changes to populations and distributions than have already been observed. Published modelling studies consistently show that the extent of a species' potential future range is likely to become smaller with increasing levels of projected warming. The extent of any projected range contraction is also strongly dependent upon the assumptions made about species' ability to colonise new areas which acquire a potentially suitable climate for the species because of climate change. This capacity is limited by dispersal ability, habitat fragmentation and lags caused by delays due to ecological and demographic processes.
- Projections of species extinction risk also increase in severity with warming. The difference between a 2 °C and 6 °C mean global warming scenario equates to a 2.4–2.8 times increase in extinction risk. The precise magnitude of extinction risk also varies widely with the methods used to calculate that risk.
- Many currently adopted conservation tools may be adapted in response to climate change. Site and landscape-scale management interventions should be used to maximise habitat quality and reduce the negative impacts of climate change. With increasing exposure to climate change, measures to facilitate shifts in species' distribution may be required.
- Climate change is likely to interact with and exacerbate other existing threats, and it may be this combination of pressures that poses the greatest danger to species. Reducing the magnitude of non-climatic threats should continue to be prioritised by conservationists in order to compensate for negative climatic impacts.
- Adapting conservation to climate change will be made easier if greenhouse gas emissions can be successfully reduced through appropriate mitigation measures. A lower level of climate change will reduce the risk that species face. However, many mitigation options which involve renewable energy generation which can be associated with significant land-use changes or increased mortality of birds. Inappropriately implemented mitigation options may therefore threaten some bird populations.
- The expansion of bioenergy crops may have been one of the most damaging impacts of climate change on birds so far. Conversely, solar power may be one of the most efficient and least damaging sources of renewable energy. A rigorous planning process should be adopted to minimise the conflict between renewable energy generation and bird populations.
- Policy mechanisms focussed on reducing greenhouse gas emissions from inappropriate land uses may have considerable potential for mitigation and to deliver biodiversity gain. The effective implementation of initiatives such as REDD+ should be prioritised.
- Although not covered in detail, the indirect effects of climate change mediated through adaptive responses of other sectors such as agriculture or forestry are likely to also have wide impacts on bird populations, particularly given the magnitude of the current threat associated with habitat loss.
- Significant future changes to land use are projected as a result of technological advances and climate change impacts. Such changes are perhaps most likely to impact

- upon biodiversity in tropical areas. Much more work is required to identify these potential threats, and to consider their potential impacts on birds, in order to plan and adapt to the future.
- Many of the topics covered in the book are associated with considerable uncertainty. Climate change projections are uncertain, as are the impacts of climate change on biodiversity. There is much uncertainty about the impacts of climate change on tropical species which form the majority of global biodiversity, particularly as the results from well-studied northern temperate and boreal regions may not directly transfer to these other areas. There is an urgent need to improve biodiversity monitoring and ecological research outside of Europe and North America so as to document and understand the impacts of climate change, and to inform any resulting adaptive conservation management.
- The future of many vulnerable bird species will depend upon our ability to limit the severity of future climate change impacts on birds. The means used to reduce greenhouse gas emissions must be adopted carefully in order to ensure that they do not also have widely damaging consequences for biodiversity. Mitigation options which promote the protection and restoration of carbon-rich habitats important for biodiversity should be promoted, whilst the most damaging forms of renewable energy generation should be avoided or located away from the most vulnerable species and populations. It will be our attitude to climate change, and the choices we make regarding its mitigation, which will decide the status of the avifauna that we pass on to future generations.

References

Abbasi, S.A. & Abbasi, N. (2000) The likely adverse environmental impacts of renewable energy sources. *Applied Energy*, **65**, 121–144.

Able, K.P. & Belthoff, J.R. (1998) Rapid 'evolution' of migratory behaviour in the introduced house finch of eastern North America. *Proceedings of the Royal Society of London, Series B*, **265**, 2063–2071.

Adamcik, R.S., Todd, A.W. & Keith, L.B. (1979) Demographic and dietary responses of red-tailed hawks during a snowshoe hare fluctuation. *Canadian Field Naturalist*, **93**, 16–27.

Adamík, P. & Pietrusková, J. (2008) Advances in spring but variable autumnal trends in timing of inland wader migration. *Acta Ornithologica*, **43**, 119–128.

Adler, P.R., Sanderson, M.A., Weimer, P.J. & Vogel, K.P. (2009) Plant species composition and biofuel yields of conservation grasslands. *Ecological Applications*, **19**, 2202–2209.

AEWA (2008) *AEWA Conservation Guidelines No. 11 – Guidelines on how to avoid, minimize or mitigate impact of infrastructural developments and related disturbance affecting waterbirds, 2008.* Agreement on the Conservation of African-Eurasian Migratory Waterbirds. Available from: http://www.unep-aewa.org/publications/conservation_guidelines.htm (last accessed 5 January 2013).

Ahola, M., Laaksonen, T., Eeva, T. & Lehikoinen, E. (2007) Climate change can alter competitive relationships between resident and migratory birds. *Journal of Animal Ecology*, **76**, 1045–1052.

Ahola, M., Laaksonen, T., Sippola, K., Eeva, T., Rainio, K. & Lehikoinen, E. (2004) Variation in climate warming along the migration route uncouples arrival and breeding dates. *Global Change Biology*, **10**, 1610–1617.

Ahola, M., Laaksonen, T., Eeva, T. & Lehikoinen, E. (2012) Selection on laying date is connected to breeding density in the pied flycatcher. *Oecologia*, **168**, 703–710.

Ahumada, J.A. (2001) Comparison of the reproductive biology of two neotropical wrens in an unpredictable environment in northeastern Colombia. *The Auk*, **118**, 191–210

Ainley, D.G. (2002) *The Adélie Penguin: Bellwether of Climate Change*. New York: Columbia University Press.

Ainley, D.G. & Hyenbach, K.D. (2010) Top-down and bottom-up factors affecting seabird population trends in the California current system (1985–2006). *Progress in Oceanography*, **84**, 242–254.

Ainley, D.G., Ribic, C.A., Ballard, G., Heath, S., Gaffney, I., Karl, B.J., Barton, K.J., Wilson, P.R. & Webb, S. (2004) Geographic structure of Adélie penguin populations: overlap in colony-specific foraging areas. *Ecological Monographs*, **74**, 159–178.

Ainley, D.G., Russel, J., Jenouvrier, S., Woehler, E., Lyver, P.O., Fraser, W.R. & Kooyman, G.L. (2010) Antarctic penguin responses to habitat change as Earth's troposphere reaches 2°C above preindustrial levels. *Ecological Monographs*, **80**, 49–66.

Akçakaya, H.R., Butchart, S.H.M., Mace, G.M., Stuart, S.N. & Hilton-Taylor, C. (2006) Use and misuse of the IUCN Red List Criteria in projecting climate change impacts on biodiversity. *Global Change Biology*, **12**, 2037–2043.

Albright, T.P., Pidgeon, A.M., Rittenhouse, C.D., Clayton, M.K., Flather, C.H., Culbert, P.D., Wardlow, B.D. & Radeloff, V.C. (2010a) Effects of drought on avian community structure. *Global Change Biology*, **16**, 2158–2170.

Albright, T.P., Pidgeon, A.M., Rittenhouse, C.D., Clayton, M.K., Wardlow, B.D., Flatcher, C.H., Culbert, P.D. & Radeloff, V.C. (2010b) Combined effects of heat waves and droughts on avian communities across the conterminous United States. *Ecosphere*, **1**, 12.

Alderman, J., McCollin, D., Hinsley, S.A., Bellamy, P.E., Picton, P. & Crockett, R. (2005) Modelling the effects of dispersal and landscape configuration on population distribution and viability in fragmented habitat. *Landscape Ecology*, **20**, 857–870.

Alerstam, T. & Högstedt, G. (1982) Bird migration and reproduction in relation to habitats for survival and breeding. *Ornis Scandinavica*, **13**, 25–37.

Alley, R.B., Andrews, J.T., Brigham-Grette, J., Clarke, G.K.C., Cuffey, K.M., Fitzpatrick, J.J., Funder, S., Marshall, S.J., Miller, G.H., Mitrovica, J.X., Muhs, D.R., Otto-Bliesner, B.L., Polyak, L. & White, J.W.C. (2010) History of the Greenland Ice Sheet: paleoclimatic insights. *Quaternary Science Review*, **29**, 1728–1756.

Alongi, D.M. (2008) Mangrove forests: Resilience, protection from tsunamis, and responses to global climate change. *Estuarine Coastal and Shelf Science*, **76**, 1–13.

Altwegg, R., Broms, K., Erni, B., Barnard, P., Midgley, G.F. & Underhill, L.G. (2012) Novel methods reveal shifts in migration phenology of barn swallows in South Africa. *Proceedings of the Royal Society of London, Series B*, **279**, 1485–1490.

Altwegg, R., Roulin, A., Kestenholz, M. & Jenni, L. (2006) Demographic effects of extreme winter weather in the barn owl. *Oecologia*, **149**, 44–51.

Amano, T. & Sutherland, W.J. (2013) Four barriers to the global understanding of biodiversity conservation: wealth, language, geographical location and security. *Proceedings of the Royal Society of London, Series B*, **280**, 2012–2649.

Amano, T., Szekely, T., Koyama, K.M., Amano, H. & Sutherland, W.J. (2010) A framework for monitoring the status of populations: An example from wader populations in the East Asian-Australasian flyway. *Biological Conservation*, **143**, 2238–2247.

Amar, A., Grant, M., Buchanan, G., Sim, I., Wilson, J., Pearce-Higgins, J.W. & Redpath, S. (2011) Exploring the relationships between wader declines and current land-use in the British uplands. *Bird Study*, **58**, 13–26.

Anders, A.D. & Post, E. (2006) Distribution-wide effects of climate on population densities of a declining migratory landbird. *Journal of Animal Ecology*, **75**, 221–227.

Anderson, B.J., Akçakaya, H.R., Araujo, M.B., Fordham, D.A., Martinez-Meyer, E., Thuiller, W. & Brook, B.W. (2009a) Dynamics of range margins for metapopulations under climate change. *Proceedings of the Royal Society of London, Series B*, **276**, 1415–1420.

Anderson, B.J., Arroyo, B.E., Collingham, Y.C., Etheridge, B., Dernandez-De-Simon, J., Gillings, S., Gregory, R.D., Leckie, F.M., Sim, I.M.W., Travis, J. & Redpath, S.M. (2009b) Using distribution models to test alternative hypotheses about a species' environmental limits and recovery prospects. *Biological Conservation*, **142**, 488–499.

Anderson, G.Q.A. & Fergusson, M.J. (2006) Energy from biomass in the UK: sources, processes and biodiversity implications. *Ibis*, **148** Suppl **1**, 180–183.

Anderson, K. & Bows, A. (2008) Reframing the climate change challenge in light of post-2000 emission trends. *Philosophical Transactions of the Royal Society Series A*, **366**, 3863–3882.

Anderson, K.J. & Jetz, W. (2005) The broad-scale ecology of energy expenditure of endotherms. *Ecology Letters*, **8**, 310–318.

Andersson, M. (1980) Nomadism and site tenacity as alternative reproductive tactics in birds. *Journal of Animal Ecology*, **49**, 175–184.

Ancona, S., Calixto-Albarrán, I. & Drummond, H. (2012) Effect of El Niño on the diet of a specialist seabird, *Sula nebouxii*, in the warm eastern tropical Pacific. *Marine Ecology Progress Series*, **462**, 261–271.

Ancona, S., Sánchez-Colón, S., Rodríguez, C. & Drummond, H. (2011) El Niño in the Warm Tropics: local sea temperature predicts breeding parameters and growth of blue-footed boobies. *Journal of Animal Ecology*, **80**, 799–808.

Angelov, I., Hashim, I. & Oppel, S. (2012) Persistent electrocution mortality of Egyptian Vultures *Neophron percnopterus* over 28 years in East Africa. *Bird Conservation International*, **23**, 1–6.

Ansell, F.A., Edwards, D.P. & Hamer, K.C. (2011) Rehabilitation of logged rain forests: avifaunal composition, habitat structure, and implications for biodiversity-friendly REDD+ *Biotropica*, **43**, 504–511.

Anthes, N. (2004) Long-distance migration of *Tringa* sandpipers adjusted to recent climate change. *Bird Study*, **51**, 203–211.

Aratrakorn, S., Thunhikorn, S. & Donald, P.F. (2006) Changes in bird communities following conversion of lowland forest to oil palm and rubber plantations in southern Thailand. *Bird Conservation International*, **16**, 71–82.

Araújo, M.B., Alagador, D., Cabeza, M., Nogués-Bravo, D. & Thuiller, W. (2011) Climate change threatens European conservation areas. *Ecology Letters*, **14**, 484–492.

Araújo, M.B. & New, M. (2007) Ensemble forecasting of species distributions. *Trends in Ecology and Evolution*, **22**, 42–47.

Araújo, M.B., Pearson, R.G., Thuiller, W. & Erhard, M. (2005a) Validation of species-climate impact models under climate change. *Global Change Biology*, **11**, 1504–1513.

Araújo, M.B., Whittaker, R.J., Ladle, R.J. & Erhard, M. (2005b) Reducing uncertainty in projections of extinction risk from climate change. *Global Ecology and Biogeography*, **14**, 529–538.

Arcese P. & Smith, J.N.M. (1988) Effects of population density and supplemental food on reproduction in Song Sparrows. *Journal of Animal Ecology*, **57**, 119–136.

Archaux, F. (2004) Breeding upwards when climate becomes warmer: no bird response in the French Alps. *Ibis*, **146**, 138–144.

Archaux, F., Balanca, G., Henry, P.Y. & Zapata, G. (2004) Wintering of White Storks in Mediterranean France. *Waterbirds*, **27**, 441–445.

Archer, C.L. & Jacobson, M.Z. (2005) Evaluation of global wind power. *Journal of Geophysical Research*, **110**, D12110.

Arnott, S.A. & Ruxton, G.D. (2002) Sandeel recruitment in the North Sea: demographic, climatic and trophic effects. *Marine Ecology Progress Series*, **238**, 199–210.

Arrigo, K.R., van Dijken, G.L., Ainley, D.G., Fahnestock, M.A. & Markus, T. (2002) Ecological impact of a large Antarctic iceberg. *Geophysical Research Letters*, **29**, 1104.

Artemyev, A.V. (2008) Factors responsible for the long-term population dynamics of the Pied Flycatcher *Ficedula hypoleuca* populations in the taiga of Karelia, Russia. *Acta Ornithologica*, **43**, 10–16.

Asner, G.P., Loarie, S.R. & Heyder, U. (2010) Combined effects of climate and land-use change on the future of humid tropical forests. *Conservation Letters*, **3**, 395–403.

Askins, R.A., Chavez-Famirez, F., Dale, B.C., Haas, C.A., Herkert, J.R., Knopf, F.L. & Vickery, P.D. (2007) Conservation of grassland birds in North America: Understanding of ecological processes in different regions. *Ornithological Monographs*, **64**, 1–46.

Atkinson, C.T. & Utuzzurum, R.B. (2010) *Changes in prevalence of avian malaria on the Alaka'i Plateau, Kaua'i, 1997–2007*. University of Hawai'i at Hilo: Hawai'i Cooperative Studies Unit Technical Report HCSU-017.

Atkinson, P.W., Clark, N.A., Bell, M.C., Dare, P.J., Clark, J.A. & Ireland, P.L. (2003) Changes in commercially fished shellfish stocks and shorebird populations in the Wash, England. *Biological Conservation*, **114**, 127–141.

Auer, S.K. & Martin, T.E. (2013) Climate change has indirect effects on resource use and overlap among coexisting bird species with negative consequences for their reproductive success. *Global Change Biology*, **19**, 411–419.

Austin, G.E. & Rehfisch, M.M. (2003) The likely impact of sea level rise on waders (Charadrii) wintering on estuaries. *Journal for Nature Conservation*, **11**, 43–58.

Austin G.E. & Rehfisch, M.M. (2005) Shifting nonbreeding distributions of migratory fauna in relation to climate change. *Global Change Biology*, **11**, 31–38.

Avery, M.I. & Krebs, J.R. (1984) Temperature and foraging success of great tits *Parus major* hunting for spiders. *Ibis*, **126**, 33–38.

Aylott, M.J., Casella, E., Tubby, I., Street, N.R., Smith, P. & Taylor, G. (2008) Yield and spatial supply of bioenergy poplar and willow short-rotation coppice in the UK. *New Phytologist*, **178**, 358–370.

Bagne, K. E., Friggens, M. M. & Finch, D. M. (2011) *A System for Assessing Vulnerability of Species (SAVS) to Climate Change*. USDA.

Bailey, S. (2007) Increasing connectivity in fragmented landscapes: an investigation of evidence for biodiversity gain in woodlands. *Forest Ecology and Management*, **238**, 7–23.

Baillie, S.M. & Jones, I.L. (2004) Responses of Atlantic puffins to a decline in capelin abundance at the Gannet Islands, Labrador. *Waterbirds*, **27**, 102–111.

Baillie, S.R., Brooks, S.P., King, R. & Thomas, L. (2009) Using a state-space model of the British song thrush Turdus philomelos population to diagnose the cause of a population decline. In *Modelling Demographic Processes in Marked Populations*. Thomson, D.L., Gooch, E.G. & Conroy, M.J.: Springer US, pp. 541–561.

Baillie, S.R., Marchant, J.H., Leech, D.I., Massimino, D., Eglington, S.M., Johnston, A., Noble, D.G., Barimore, C., Kew, A.J., Downie, I.S., Risely, K. & Robinson, R.A. (2013) BirdTrends 2012: trends in numbers, breeding success and survival for UK breeding birds. *Research Report* 644. BTO, Thetford.

Baillie, S.R. & Peach, W.J. (1992) Population limitation in Palaearctic-African migrant passerines. *Ibis*, **134 S1**, 120–132.

Baillie, S.R., Sutherland, W.J., Freeman, S.N., Gregory, R.D. & Paradis, E. (2000) Consequences of large-scale processes for the conservation of bird populations. *Journal of Applied Ecology*, **37 S1**, 88–102.

Bain, C.G., Bonn, A., Stoneman, R., Chapman, S., Coupar, A., Evans, M., Gearey, B., Howat, M., Joosten, H., Keenleyside, C., Labadz, J., Lindsay, R., Littlewood, N., Lunt, P., Miller, C.J., Moxey, A., Orr, H., Reed, M., Smith, P., Swales, V., Thompson, D.B.A., Thompson, P.S., Van de Noort, R., Wilson, J.D. & Worall, F. (2011) *IUCN UK Commission of Inquiry on Peatlands*. Edinburgh, UK: IUCN UK Peatland Programme.

Baines, D., Redpath, S., Richardson, M. & Thirgood, S. (2008) The direct and indirect effects of predation by Hen Harriers *Circus cyaneus* on trends in breeding birds on a Scottish grouse moor. *Ibis*, **150 S1**, 27–36.

Baines, P.G. & Folland, C.K. (2007) Evidence for a rapid global shift across the late 1960s. *Journal of Climate*, **20**, 2721–2744.

Baker, A.J., González, P.M., Piersma, T. Niles, L.J., Serrano do Nscimento, I. de L., Atkinson, P.W., Clark, N.A., Minton, C.D.T., Peck, M.K. & Aarts, G. (2004) Rapid population decline in Red Knots: fitness consequences of decreased refuelling rates and late arrival in Delaware Bay. *Proceedings of the Royal Society of London, Series B*, **271**, 875–882.

Baker, D.J., Freeman, S.N., Grice, P.V. & Siriwardena, G.M. (2012) Landscape-scale responses of birds to agri-environment management: a test of the English Environmental Stewardship scheme. *Journal of Applied Ecology*, **49**, 871–882.

Baker, J.D., Littnan, C.L. & Johnston, D.W. (2006) Potential effects of sea level rise on the terrestrial habitats of endangered and endemic megafauna in the Northwestern Hawaiian Islands. *Endangered Species Research*, **4**, 1–10.

Bakke, J., Lie, Ø., Heergaard, E., Dokken, T., Haug, G.H., Birks, H.H., Dulski, P. & Nilsen, T. (2009) Rapid oceanic and atmospheric changes during the Younger Dryas cold period. *Nature Geoscience*, **2**, 202–205.

Bakker, K.K. & Higgins, K.F. (2009) Planted grasslands and native sod prairie: equivalent habitat for grassland birds? *Western North American Naturalist*, **69**, 235–242.

Bakker, K.K., Naugle, D.E. & Higgins, K.F. (2002) Incorporating landscape attributes into models for migratory grassland bird conservation. *Conservation Biology*, **16**, 1638–1646.

Balazs, G.H. & Chaloupka, M. (2004) Thirty-year recovery trend in the once depleted Hawaiian green sea turtle stock. *Biological Conservation*, **117**, 491–498.

Ballard, G., Geupel, G.R., Nur, N. & Gardali, T. (2003) Long-term declines and decadal patterns in population trends of songbirds in western North America, 1979–1999. *The Condor*, **105**, 737–755.

Ballard, G., Toniolo, V., Ainley, D.G., Parkinson, C.L., Arrigo, K.R. & Trathan, P.N. (2010) Responding to climate change: Adélie Penguins confront astronomical and ocean boundaries. *Ecology*, **91**, 2056–2069.

Ballerini, T., Tavecchia, G., Olmastroni, S., Pezzo, F. & Focardi, S. (2009) Nonlinear effects of winter sea ice on the survival probabilities of Adélie penguins. *Oecologia*, **161**, 253–265.

Balmford, A., Green, R. & Phalan, B. (2012) What conservationists need to know about farming. *Proceedings of the Royal Society of London, Series B*, **279**, 2714–2724.

Banko, P.C., Oboski, P.T., Slotterback, J.W., Dougill, S.J., Goltz, D.M., Johnson, L., Laut, M.E., Murray, T.C. (2002) Availability of food resources, distribution of invasive species, and conservation of a Hawaiian bird along a gradient of elevation. *Journal of Biogeography*, **29**, 789–808.

Barbet-Massin, M., Thuiller, W. & Jiguet, F. (2010) How much do we overestimate future local extinction rates when restricting the range of occurrence data in climate suitability models. *Ecography*, **33**, 878–886.

Barbet-Massin, M., Thuiller, W. & Jiguet, F. (2012) The fate of European breeding birds under climate, land-use and dispersal scenarios. *Global Change Biology*, **18**, 881–890.

Barbet-Massin, M., Walther, B.A., Thuiller, W., Rahbek, C. & Jiguet, F. (2009) Potential impacts of climate change on the winter distribution of Afro-Palaearctic migrant passerines. *Biology Letters*, **5**, 248–251.

Barbier, E.B., Hacker, S.D., Kennedy, C., Koch, E.W., Stier, A.C. & Siliman, B.R. (2011) The value of estuarine and coastal ecosystem services. *Ecological Monographs*, **81**, 169–193.

Barbraud, C., Barbraud, J.C. & Barbraud, M. (1999) Population dynamics of the white stork *Ciconia ciconia* in western France. *Ibis*, **141**, 469–479.

Barbraud, C. & Weimerskirch, H. (2001a) Emperor penguins and climate change. *Nature*, **411**, 183–186.

Barbraud, C. & Weimerskirch, H. (2001b) Contrasting effects of the extent of sea-ice on the breeding performance of an Antarctic top predator, the Snow Petrel *Pagodroma nivea*. *Journal of Avian Biology*, **32**, 297–302.

Barbraud, C. & Weimerskirch, H. (2003) Climate and density shape population dynamics of a marine top predator. *Proceedings of the Royal Society of London, Series B*, **270**, 2111–2116.

Barbraud, D., Rivalan, P., Inchausti, P., Nevoux, M., Rolland, V. & Weimerskirch, H. (2011) Contrasted demographic responses facing future climate change in southern ocean seabirds. *Journal of Animal Ecology*, **80**, 89–100.

Barclay, R.M.R., Baerwald, E.F. & Gruver, J.C. (2007) Variation in bat and bird fatalities at wind energy facilities: assessing the effects of rotor size and tower height. *Canadian Journal of Zoology*, **85**, 381–387.

Barlow, J., Mestre, L.A.M., Gardner, T.A. & Peres, C.A. (2007) The value of primary, secondary and plantation forests for Amazonian birds. *Biological Conservation*, **136**, 212–231.

Barnagaud, J.-Y., Devictor, V., Jiguet, F., Barbet-Massin, M., Le Voil, I. & Archaux, F. (2012) Relating habitat and climatic niches in birds. *PLoS ONE*, **7**, e32819.

Barrett, R.T. (2001) The breeding demography and egg size of North Norwegian Atlantic Puffins *Fractercula arctica* and razorbills *Alca torda* during 20 years of climatic variability. *Atlantic Seabirds*, **3**, 97–140.

Barrios, L. & Rodriguez, A. (2004) Behavioural and environmental correlates of soaring bird mortality at on-shore wind turbines. *Journal of Applied Ecology*, **41**, 72–81.

Barrios, L. & Rodríguez, A. (2007) Spatiotemporal patterns of bird mortality at two wind farms of Southern Spain. In *Birds and Wind Farms*. De Lucas, M., Janss, G.F.E. & Ferrer, M. Madrid, Spain: Quercus, pp. 56–72.

Barrientos, R., Barbosa, A., Valera, F. & Moreno, E. (2007) Temperature but not rainfall influences timing of breeding in a desert bird, the trumpeter finch (*Bucantes githagineus*). *Journal of Ornithology*, **148**, 411–416.

Barshep, Y., Hedenström, A. & Underhill, L.G. (2011) Impact of climate and predation on autumn migration of the Curlew Sandpiper. *Waterbirds*, **34**, 1–9.

Baskaya, S., Baskaya, E. & Sari, A. (2011) The principal negative environmental impacts of small hydro-power plants in Turkey. *African Journal of Agricultural Research*, **6**, 3284–3290.

Battley, P.F. (1997) The northward migration of arctic waders in New Zealand: departure behaviour, timing and possible migration routes of red knots and bar-tailed godwits from Farewell Spit, North-west Nelson. *Emu*, **97**, 108–120.

Battley, P.F. (2006) Consistent annual schedules in a migratory shorebird. *Biology Letters*, **2**, 517–520.

Bauer, S., Gienapp, P. & Madsen, J. (2008a) The relevance of environmental conditions for departure decision changes en route in migrating geese. *Ecology*, **89**, 1953–1960.

Bauer, S., Van Dinthe, M., Hødga, K.-A., Klaassen, M. & Madsen, J. (2008b) The consequences of climate-driven stop-over sites changes on migration schedules and fitness of Arctic geese. *Journal of Animal Ecology*, **77**, 654–660.

Bauer, Z., Trnka, M., Bauerova, J., Mozny, M., Stepanek, P., Bartosova, L. & Zalud, Z. (2010) Changing climate and the phenological response of great tit and collared flycatcher populations in floodplain forest ecosystems in Central Europe. *International Journal of Biometeorology*, **54**, 99–111.

Bayard, T.S. & Elphick, C.S. (2011) Planning for sea-level rise: quantifying patterns of Saltmarsh Sparrow (*Ammodramus caudacutus*) nest flooding under current sea-level conditions. *The Auk*, **128**, 393–403.

Beale, C.M., Baker, N.E., Brewer, M.J. & Lennon, J.J. (2013) Protected area networks and savannah bird biodiversity in the face of climate change and land degradation. *Ecology Letters*, **16**, 1061–1068.

Beale, C.M., Burfield, I.J., Sim, I.M.W., Rebecca, G.W., Pearce-Higgins, J.W. & Grant, M.C. (2006a) Climate change may account for the decline in British ring ouzels *Turdus torquatus*. *Journal of Animal Ecology*, **75**, 826–835.

Beale, C.M., Dodd, S. & Pearce-Higgins, J.W. (2006b) Wader recruitment indices suggest nesting success is temperature dependent in Dunlin *Calidris alpina*. *Ibis*, **148**, 405–410.

Beale, C.M., Lennon, J.J. & Gimona, A. (2008) Opening the climate envelope reveals no macroscale associations with climate in European birds. *Proceedings of the National Academy of Sciences USA*, **105**, 14908–14912.

Beale, C.M., Lennon, J.J., Yearsley, J.M., Brewer, M.J. & Elston, D.A. (2010) Regression analysis of spatial data. *Ecology Letters*, **13**, 246–264.

Bearhop, S., Fieldler, W., Furness, R.W., Votier, S.C., Waldron, S., Newton, J., Bowen, G.J., Berthold, P., Farnsworth, K. (2005) Assortative mating as a mechanism for rapid evolution of a migratory divide. *Science*, **310**, 502–504.

Beaugrand, G., Brander, K.M., Lindley, J.A., Souissi, S. & Reid, P.C. (2003) Plankton effect on cod recruitment in the North Sea. *Nature*, **426**, 661–664.

Beaugrand, G., Reid, P.C., Ibañez, F., Lindley, J.A. and Edwards, M. (2002) Reorganisation of North Atlantic marine copepod biodiversity and climate. *Science*, **296**, 1692–1694.

Beaumont, L.J. & Duursma, D. (2012) Global projections of 21st century land-use changes in regions adjacent to protected areas. *PLoS ONE*, **7**, e43714.

Beaumont, L.J., McAllan, I.A.W. & Hughes, L. (2006) A matter of timing: Changes in the first date of arrival and last date of departure of Australian migratory birds. *Global Change Biology*, **12**, 1339–1354.

Becker, P.H. & Specht, R. (1991) Body mass fluctuations and mortality in common tern *Sterna hirundo* chicks dependent on weather and tide in the Wadden Sea. *Ardea*, **79**, 45–56.

Beerling, D.J., Huntley, B. & Bailey, J.P. (1995) Climate and the distribution of *Fallopia japonica*: use of an introduced species to test the predictive capacity of response surfaces. *Journal of Vegetation Science*, **6**, 269–282.

Beintema, A.J., Thissen, J.B., Tensen, D. & Visser, G.H. (1991) Feeding ecology of charadriiform chicks in agricultural grassland. *Ardea*, **79**, 31–44.

Beintema, A.J. & Visser, G.H. (1989) The effect of weather on time budgets and development of chicks of meadow birds. *Ardea*, **77**, 181–192.

Bellamy, P.E., Brown, N.J., Enoksson, B., Firbank, L.G., Fuller, R.J., Hinsley, S.A. & Schotman, A.G.M. (1998) The influences of habitat, landscape structure and climate on local distribution patterns of the nuthatch (*Sitta europaea* L.). *Oecologia*, **115**, 127–136.

Bellamy, P.E., Croxton, P.J., Heard, M.S., Hinsley, S.A., Hulmes, L., Hulmes, S., Nuttall, P., Pywell, R.F. & Rothery, P. (2009) The impact of growing miscanthus for biomass on farmland bird populations. *Biomass and Bioenergy*, **33**, 191–199.

Bellamy, P.E., Hinsley, S.A. & Newton, I. (1996) Local extinctions and recolonisations of passerine bird populations in small woods. *Oecologia*, **108**, 64–71.

Bellamy, P.E., Rothery, P. & Hinsley, S.A. (2003) Synchrony of woodland bird populations: the effect of landscape structure. *Ecography*, **26**, 338–348.

Belkin, I.M. (2009) Rapid warming of large marine ecosystems. *Progress in Oceanography*, **81**, 207–213.

Bellard, C., Bertelsmeier, C., Leadley, P., Thuiller, W. & Courchamp, F. (2012) Impacts of climate change on the future of biodiversity. *Ecology Letters*, **15**, 365–377.

Bennett, A.F., Hinsley, S.A., Bellamy, P.E., Swetnam, R.D. & MacNally, R. (2004) Do regional gradients in land-use influence richness, composition and turnover of bird assemblages in small woods? *Biological Conservation*, **119**, 191–206.

Benning, T.L., LaPointe, D., Atkinson, C.T. & Vitousek, P.M. (2002) Interactions of climate change with biological invasions and land use in the Hawaiian Islands: Modeling the fate of endemic birds using a geographic information system. *Proceedings of the National Academy of Sciences USA*, **99**, 14246–14249.

Benton, T.G., Vickery, J.A. & Wilson, J.D. (2003) Farmland biodiversity: is habitat heterogeneity the key? *Trends in Ecology and Evolution*, **18**, 182–188.

Berthold, P. (1988) Evolutionary aspects of migratory behavior in European warblers. *Journal of Evolutionary Biology*, **1**, 195–209.

Berthold, P. (1996) *Control of Bird Migration*. London, UK: Chapman & Hall.

Berthold, P., Fliege, G., Querner, U. & Winkler, H. (1986) Die bestandsentwicklung von Kleinvögeln in Mitteleuropa: Analyse von Fangzahlen. *Journal of Ornithology*, **127**, 397–437.

Bertram, D.F., Mackas, D.L. & McKinnell, S.M. (2001) The seasonal cycle revisited: interannual variation and ecosystem consequences. *Progress in Oceanography*, **49**, 283–307.

Bessou, C., Ferchaud, F., Gabrielle, B. & Mary, B. (2011) Biofuels, greenhouse gases and climate change. A review. *Agronomy and Sustainable Development*, **31**, 1–79.

Bibby, C.J. (1979) Mortality and movements of Dartford Warblers in England. *British Birds*, **72**, 10–22.

Bierman, S.M., Fairbairn, J.P., Petty, S.J., Elston, D.A., Tidhar, D. & Lambin, X. (2006) Changes over time in the spatiotemporal dynamics of cyclic populations of field voles (*Microtus agrestis* L.). *American Naturalist*, **167**, 583–590.

Bilgili, M., Yasar, A. & Simsek, E. (2011) Offshore wind power development in Europe and its comparison with onshore counterpart. *Renewable and Sustainable Energy Reviews*, **15**, 905–915.

Bird, J.P., Buchanan, G.M., Lees, A.C., Clay, R.P., Develey, P.F., Ye'pez, I. & Butchart, S.H.M. (2011) Integrating spatially explicit habitat projections into extinction risk assessments: a reassessment of Amazonian avifauna incorporating projected deforestation. *Diversity & Distributions*, **18**, 273–281.

BirdLife International (2000) *Threatened Birds of the World*. Barcelona and Cambridge, UK: Lynx Edicions and BirdLife International.

BirdLife International (2008) *State of the World's Birds: Indicators for our Changing World*. Cambridge, UK: BirdLife International

BirdLife International (2012a) *IUCN Red List for birds*. Downloaded from http://www.birdlife.org on 20/06/2012.

BirdLife International (2012b) The BirdLife checklist of the birds of the world, with conservation status and taxonomic sources. Version 5. Downloaded from http://www.birdlife.info/im/species/checklist.zip.

Blaustein, A.R., Walls, S.C., Bancroft, B.A., Lawler, J.J., Searle, C.L. & Gervasi, S.S. (2010) Direct and indirect effects of climate change on amphibian populations. *Diversity*, **2**, 281–313.

Blomqvist, S., Holmgren, N., Åkesson, S., Hedenström, A. & Pettersson, J. (2002) Indirect effects of lemming cycles on sandpiper population dynamics: 50 years of counts from southern Sweden. *Oecologia*, **133**, 146–158.

Boersma, P.D. (1998) Population trends of the Galápagos penguin: impacts of El Niño and La Niña. *The Condor*, **100**, 245–253.

Bojarinova, J.G., Rymkevich, T.A. & Smirnov, O.P. (2002) Timing of autumn migration of early and late-hatched Great Tits *Parus major* in NW Russia. *Ardea*, **90**, 401–409.

Bond, A.L., Jones, I.L., Sydeman, W.J., Major, H.L., Minobe, S., Williams, J.C. & Byrd, G.V. (2011) Reproductive success of planktivorous seabirds in the North Pacific is related to ocean climate on decadal scales. *Marine Ecology Progress Series*, **424**, 205–218.

Bosque, C., Pacheco, M.A. & García-Amado, M.A. (2004) The annual cycle of *Columbina* ground-doves in seasonal savannas of Venezuela. *Journal of Field Ornithology*, **75**, 1–17.

Both, C. (2010a) Flexibility of timing of avian migration to climate change masked by environmental constraints *en route*. *Current Biology*, **20**, 243–248.

Both, C. (2010b) Food availability, mistiming, and climatic change. In *Effects of Climate Change on Birds*. Møller, A.P., Fiedler, W. & Berthold, P. Oxford, UK: Oxford University Press, pp. 129–147.

Both, C. (2012) Insufficient adaptation to climate change alters avian habitat quality and thereby changes habitat selection. In *Birds and Habitat. Relationships in Changing Landscapes*. Fuller, R.J. Cambridge, UK: Cambridge University Press, pp. 432–452.

Both, C., Artemyev, A.V., Blauuw, B., Cowie, R.J., Dekhuijzen, A.J., Eeva, T., Enemar, A., Gustafsson, L., Ivankina, E.V., Järvinen, A., Metcalfe, N.B., Nyholm, N.E.I., Potti, J., Ravussin, P.-A., Sanz, J.J., Silverin, B., Slater, F.M., Sokolov, L.V., Török, J., Winkel, W., Wright, J., Zang, H. & Visser, M.E. (2004) Large-scale geographical variation confirms that climate change causes birds to lay earlier. *Proceedings of the Royal Society of London, Series B*, **271**, 1657–1662.

Both, C., Biljsma, R.G. & Visser, M.E. (2005) Climate effects on timing of spring migration and breeding in a long-distance migrant, the pied flycatcher *Ficedula hypoleuca*. *Journal of Avian Biology*, **36**, 368–373.

Both, C., Bouwhuis, S., Lessells, C.M. & Visser, M.E. (2006a) Climate change and population declines in a long distance migratory bird. *Nature*, **441**, 81–83.

Both, C., Robinson, R.A., Henk, P. & ven der Jeugd, P. (2012) Long-distance dispersal in migratory pied flycatchers *Ficedula hypoleuca* is relatively common between the UK and the Netherlands. *Journal of Avian Biology*, **43**, 193–197.

Both C., Sanz J.J., Artemyev A.V., Blauuw, B., Cowie, R.J., Dekhuizen, A.J., Enemar, A., Järvinen, A., Nyholm, N.E.I., Potti, J., Ravussin, P.-A., Silverin, B., Slater, F.M., Sokolov, L.V., Visser, M.E., Winkel, W., Wright, J. & Zang, H. (2006b) Pied flycatchers travelling from Africa to breed in Europe: differential effects of winter and migration conditions on breeding date. *Ardea*, **4**, 511–525.

Both, C. & te Marvelde, L. (2007) Climate change and timing of avian breeding and migration throughout Europe. *Climate Research*, **35**, 93–105.

Both, C., van Ash, M., Bijlsma, R.G., van der Burg, A.B. & Visser, M.E. (2009) Climate change and unequal phenological changes across four trophic levels: constraints or adaptations? *Journal of Animal Ecology*, **78**, 73–83.

Both, C., Van Turnhout, C.A.M., Bijlsma, R.G., Siepel, H., Van Strien, A.J. & Foppen, R.P.B. (2010) Avian population consequences of climate change are most severe for long-distance migrants in seasonal habitats. *Proceedings of the Royal Society of London, Series B*, **277**, 1259–1266.

Both, C. & Visser, M.E. (2001) Adjustment to climate change is constrained by arrival date in a long-distance migratory bird. *Nature*, **411**, 296–298.

Both, C. & Visser, M.E. (2005) The effect of climate change on the correlation between avian life-history traits. *Global Change Biology*, **11**, 1606–1613.

Bourgault, P., Thomas, D., Perret, P. & Blondel, J. (2010) Spring vegetation phenology is a robust predictor of breeding date across broad landscapes: a multi-site approach using the Corsican blue tit (*Cyanistes caeruleus*). *Oecologia*, **162**, 885–892.

Boyd, H. & Piersma, T. (2001) Changing balance between survival and recruitment explains population trends in Red Knots *Calidris canutus islandica* wintering in Britain, 1969–1995. *Ardea*, **89**, 301–317.

Boyd, P.W. (2008a) Predicting and verifying the intended and unintended consequences of large-scale ocean iron fertilization. *Marine Ecology Progress Series*, **364**, 295–301.

Boyd, P.W. (2008b) Ranking geo-engineering schemes. *Nature Geoscience*, **1**, 722–724.

BP (2012) *BP Statistical Review of World Energy June 2012*. Available from bp.com/statisticalreview (accessed 25 August 2012).

Brackenridge, G.R. (2012) *Global Active Archive of Large Flood Events*. Dartmouth Flood Observatory, University of Colorado, http://floodobservatory.colorado.edu/Archives/index.html. Accessed February 2012.

Bradbury, R.B., Pearce-Higgins, J.W., Wotton, S.R., Conway, G.J. & Grice, P.V. (2011) The influence of climate and topography in patterns of territory establishment in a range-expanding bird. *Ibis*, **153**, 336–344.

Bradbury, R.B., Wilson, J.D., Moorcroft, D., Morris, A.J. & Perkins, A.J. (2003) Habitat and weather are weak correlates of nestling condition and growth rates of four UK farmland passerines. *Ibis*, **145**, 295–306.

Brashares, J.S., Arcese, P. & Sam, M.K. (2001) Human demography and reserve size predict wildlife extinction in West Africa. *Proceedings of the Royal Society of London, Series B*, **268**, 2473–2478.

Brauer, A., Haug, G.H., Dulski, P., Sigman, D.M. & Negendank, J.F.W. (2008) An abrupt wind shift in western Europe at the onset of the Younger Dryas cold period. *Nature Geoscience*, **1**, 520–523.

Breiman, L. (2001) Random forests. *Machine Learning*, **45**, 5–32.

Brennan, L.A. & Kuvlesky, W.P. Jr (2005) North American grassland birds: an unfolding conservation crisis. *Journal of Wildlife Management*, **69**, 1–13.

Bridgham, S.D., Pastor, J., Dewey, B., Weltzin, J.F. & Updegraff, K. (2008) Rapid carbon response of peatlands to climate change. *Ecology*, **89**, 3041–3048.

Bridle, J.R. & Vines, T.H. (2007) Limit to evolution at range margins: when and why does adaptation fail? *Trends in Ecology and Evolution*, **22**, 140–147.

Bright, J., Langston, R., Bullman, R., Evans, R., Gardner, S. & Pearce-Higgins, J. (2008) Map of bird sensitivities to wind farms in Scotland: a tool to aid planning and conservation. *Biological Conservation*, **141**, 2342–2356.

Bright, J.A., Langston, R.H.W. & Anthony, S. (2009) *Mapped and written guidance in relation to birds and onshore wind energy development in England*. RSPB Research Report No 35. Sandy, UK: Royal Society for the Protection of Birds.

British Trust for Ornithology (2012) *2012 preliminary NRS results.* Downloaded from www.bto.org/volunteer-surveys/nrs/results/2012-preliminary-nrs-results (accessed 29 November 2012).

British Trust for Ornithology (2013) *Maps of population density and trends.* Downloaded from www.bto.org/volunteer-surveys/bbs/latest-results/maps-population-density-and-trends (accessed 4 February 2013).

Broadmeadow, M., Webber, J., Ray, D. & Berry, P. (2009) An assessment of likely future impacts of climate change on UK forests. In *Combating climate change – a role for UK forests. An assessment of the potential of the UK's trees and woodlands to mitigate and adapt to climate change.* Reed, D.J., Morison, J.I.L., Hanley, N., West, C.C. & Snowdon, P. Edinburgh, UK: The Stationary Office, pp. 67–99.

Brohan, P., Kennedy, J.J., Harris, I., Tett, S.F.B. & Jones, P.D. (2006) Uncertainty estimates in regional and global observed temperature changes: a new dataset from 1850. *Journal of Geophysical Research*, **111**, D12106 doi:10.1029/2005JD006548.

Brommer, J.E. (2004) The range margins of northern birds shift polewards. *Annales Zoologici Fennici*, **41**, 391–397.

Brommer, J.E., Merilä, J., Sheldon, B.C. & Gustafsson, L. (2005) Natural selection and genetic variation for reproductive reaction norms in a wild bird population. *Evolution*, **59**, 1362–1371.

Brooke, M. de L. & Davies, N.B. (1987) Recent changes in host usage by cuckoos *Cuculus canorus* in Britain. *Journal of Animal Ecology*, **56**, 873–883.

Brooks, T.M., Mittermeier, R.A., da Fonseca, G.A.B., Gerlach, J., Hoffmann, M., Lamoreux, J.F., Mittermeier, C.G., Pilgrim, J.D. & Rodrigues, A.S.L. (2006) Global biodiversity conservation priorities. *Science*, **313**, 58–61.

Brown, D.R. & Sherry, T.W. (2006) Food supply controls physical condition of a long distance migrant bird wintering in the tropics. *Oecologia*, **149**, 22–32.

Brown, J.H., Allen, A.P. & Gillooly, J.F. (2003) Response to heat and biodiversity (Huston). *Science*, **299**, 512–513.

Brown, J.L., Li, S.H. & Bhagabati, N. (1999) Long-term trend toward earlier breeding in an American bird: a response to global warming? *Proceedings of the Academy Natural Sciences*, **96**, 5565–5569.

Brownlie, S., King, N. & Treweek, J. (2013) Biodiversity tradeoffs and offsets in impact assessment and decision making: can we stop the loss? *Impact Assessment and Project Appriasal*, **31**, 24–33.

Brysse, K., Oreskes, N., O'Reilly, J. & Oppenheimer, M. (2013) Climate change prediction: Erring on the side of least drama? *Global Environmental Change*, **23**, 327–337.

Buchanan, G.M., Butchart, S.H.M., Dutson, G., Pilgrim, J.D., Steininger, M.K., Bishop, K.D. & Mayaux, P. (2008) Using remote sensing to inform conservation status assessment: estimates of recent deforestation rates on New Britain and the impacts upon endemic birds. *Biological Conservation*, **141**, 56–66.

Buchanan, G.M., Donald, P.F. & Butchart, S.H.M. (2011) Identifying priority areas for conservation: a global assessment for forest-dependent birds. *PLoS ONE*, **6**, e29080.

Buchanan, G.M., Pearce-Higgins, J.W., Wotton, S.R., Grant, M.C. & Whitfield, D.P. (2003) Correlates of the change in Ring Ouzel *Turdus torquatus* abundance in Scotland from 1988–91 to 1999. *Bird Study*, **50**, 97–105.

Buchanan, G.M., Pearce-Higgins, J.W., Sanderson, R.A. & Grant, M.C. (2006) The contribution of invertebrate taxa to moorland bird diets and the potential implications of land-use management. *Ibis*, **148**, 615–628.

Buckland, S.T., Anderson, D.R., Burnham, K.P., Laake, J.L., Borchers, D.L. & Thomas, L. (2007) *Advanced Distance Sampling.* New York, USA: Oxford University Press.

Buehler, D.M. & Piersma, T. (2006) Reconstructing palaeoflyways of the late Pleistocene and early Holocene Red Knot (*Calidris canutus*). *Ardea*, **94**, 485–498.

Buisson, L., Thuiller, W., Casajus, N., Lek, S. & Grenouillet, G. (2010) Uncertainty in ensemble forecasting of species distribution. *Global Change Biology*, **16**, 1145–1157.

Bulmer, M.G. & Perrins, C.M. (1973) Mortality in the great tit *Parus major*. *Ibis*, **115**, 277–281.

Burbridge, A.A. & Fuller, P.J. (1982) Banded stilt breeding at Lake Barlee, Western Australia. *Emu*, **82**, 212–216.

Burfield, I.J. (2002) *The Breeding Ecology and Conservation of the Ring Ouzel* Turdus torquatus *in Britain.* Unpublished PhD thesis, University of Cambridge.

Burger, C., Belskii, E., Eeva, T., Laaksonen, T., Mägi, M., Mänd, R., Qvarnström, A., Slagsvold, T., Veen, T., Visser, M.E., Wiebe, K.L., Wiley, C., Wright, J. & Both, C. (2012) Climate change, breeding date and nestling diet: how temperature differentially affects seasonal changes in pied flycatcher diet depending on habitat variation. *Journal of Animal Ecology*, **81**, 926–936.

Burnham, K.R. & Anderson, D.R. (2002) *Model Selection and Multimodel Inference: A Practical Information-Theoretic Approach*. Second Edition. New York: Springer.

Burthe, S., Daunt, F., Butler, A., Elston, D.A., Frederiksen, M., Johns, D., Newell, M., Thackeray, S.J. & Wanless, S. (2012) Phenological trends and trophic mismatch across multiple levels of a North Sea pelagic food web. *Marine Ecology Progress Series*, **454**, 119–133.

Burton, C. & Weathers, W. (2003) Energetics and thermoregulation of the Gouldian Finch (*Erthrura goudiae*). *Emu*, **103**, 1–10.

Burton, N.H.K. (2000) Winter site-fidelity and survival of Redshank *Tringa totanus* at Cardiff, south Wales. *Bird Study*, **47**, 102–112.

Burton, N.H.K., Rehfish, M.M. & Clark, N.A. (2002) Impacts of disturbance from construction work on the densities and feeding behaviour of waterbirds using the intertidal mudflats of Cardiff Bay, UK. *Environmental Management*, **30**, 865–871.

Burton, N.H.K., Rehfish, M.M., Clark, N.A. & Dodd, S.G. (2006) Impacts of sudden winter habitat loss on the body condition and survival of redshank *Tringa totanus*. *Journal of Applied Ecology*, **43**, 464–473.

Burton, N.H.K., Thaxter, C.B., Cook, A.S.C.P., Austin, G.E., Wright, L.J. & Clark, N.A. (2010) Evaluating the potential impacts of tidal power schemes on estuarine waterbirds. *BOU Proceedings – Climate Change and Birds*. http://www.bou.org.uk/bouproc-net/ccb/burton-etal.pdf

Busch, J., Godoy, F., Turner, W.R. & Harvey, C.A. (2011) Biodiversity co-benefits of reducing emissions from deforestation under alternative reference levels and levels of finance. *Conservation Letters*, **4**, 101–115.

Buse, A., Dury, S.J., Woodburn, R.J.W., Perrins, C.M. & Good, J.E.G. (1999) Effects of elevated temperature on multi-species interactions: the case of Pedunculate Oak, Winter Moth and Tits. *Functional Ecology*, **13** (Suppl 1), 74–82.

Bussell, J., Jones, D.L., Healey, J.R. & Pullin, A.S. (2010) How do draining and re-wetting affect carbon stores and greenhouse gas fluxes in peatland soils? *Environmental Evidence*, CEE 08-012. Available at http://www.environmentalevidence.org/SR49.html.

Butchart, S.H.M., Stattersfield, A.J., Baillie, J., Bennun, L.A., Stuart, S.N., Akçakaya, H.R., Hilton-Taylor, C. & Mace, G.M. (2005) Using red list indices to measure progress towards the 2010 target and beyond. *Philosophical Transactions of the Royal Society Series B*, **360**, 255–268.

Butchart, S. H. M., Scharlemann, J. P. W., Evans, M., Quader, S., Aricò, S., Arinaitwe, J., Balman, M., Bennun, L.A., Bertzky, C., Besançon, C., Boucher, T.M., Brooks, T.M., Burfield, I.J., Burgess, N.D., Chan, S., Clay, R.P., Crosby, M.J., Davidson, N.C., De Silva, N., Devenish, C., Dutson, G.C.L., Díaz Fernández, D.F., Fishpool, L.D.C., Fitzgerald, C., Foster, M., Heath, M.F., Hockings, M., Hoffman, M., Knox, D., Larsen, F.W., Lamoreux, J.F., Loucks, C., May, I., Millett, J., Molloy, D., Morling, P., Parr, M., Ricketts, T.H., Seddon, N., Skolnik, B., Stuart, S.N., Upgren, A. & Woodley, S. (2012) Protecting important sites for biodiversity contributes to meeting global conservation targets. *PLoS ONE*, **7**, e32529.

Butchart, S.H.M., Walpole, M., Collen, B., van Strien, A., Scharlemann, J.P.W., Almond, R.E.A., Baillie, J.E.M., Bomhard, B., Brown, C., Bruno, J., Carpenter, K.E., Carr, G.M., Chanson, J., Chenery, A.M., Csirke, J., Davidson, N.C., Dentener, F., Foster, M., Galli, A., Gallloway, J.N., Genovesi, P., Gregory, R.D., Hockings, M., Kapos, V., Lamarque, J.-F., Leverington, F., Loh, J., McGeoch, M.A., McRae, L., Minasyan, A., Hernández Morcillo, M., Oldfield, T.E.E., Pauly, D., Quader, S., Revenga, C., Sauer, J.R., Skolnik, B., Spear, D., Stanwell-Smith, D., Stuart, S.N., Symes, A., Tierney, M., Tyrrell, T.D., Vié, J.-C. & Watson, R. (2010) Global biodiversity: indicators of recent declines. *Science*, **328**, 1164–1168.

Butler, R.W., Williams, T.D., Warnock, N. & Bishop, M.A. (1997) Wind assistance: a requirement for migration of shorebirds? *The Auk*, **114**, 456–466.

Byrkjedal, I. (1980) Nest predation in relation to snow-cover – a possible factor influencing the start of breeding in shorebirds. *Ornis Scandinavica*, **11**, 249–252.

Cahill, A.E., Aiello-Lammens, M.E., Fisher-Reid, M.C., Hua, X., Karanewsky, C.J., Ryu, H.Y., Sbeglia, G.C., Spagnolo, F., Waldron, J.B., Warsi, O., & Weins, J.J. (2013) How does climate change cause extinction? *Proceedings of the Royal Society of London, Series B*, **280**, 21231890.

Calladine, J., Baines, D. & Warren, P. (2002) Effects of reduced grazing on population density and breeding success of black grouse in northern England. *Journal of Applied Ecology*, **39**, 772–780.

Calladine, J. & Bray, J. (2012) The importance of altitude and aspect for breeding whinchats *Saxicola rubetra* in the uplands: limitations of the uplands as a refuge for a declining, formerly widespread species? *Bird Study*, **59**, 43–51.

Calvert, A.M., Bishop, C.A., Elliot, R.D., Krebs, E.A., Kydd, T.M., Machtans, C.S. & Robertson, G.J. (2013) A synthesis of human-related avian mortality in Canada. *Avian Conservation and Ecology*, **8**, 11.

Carlini, A.R., Coria, N.R., Santos, M.M., Negrete, J., Juares, M.A. & Daneri, G.A. (2009) Responses of *Pygoscelis adeliae* and *P. papua* populations to environmental changes at Isla 25 de Mayo (King George Island). *Polar Biology*, **32**, 1427–1433.

Carlisle, J.D., Kaltenecker, G.S. & Swanson, D.L. (2005) Molt strategies and age differences in migration timing among autumn landbird migrants in southwestern Idaho. *The Auk*, **122**, 1070–1085.

Carnicer, J. & Diaz-Delgado, R. (2008) Geographic differences between functional groups in patterns of bird species richness in North America. *Acta Oecologia*, **33**, 253–264.

Carrete, M., Sanches-Zapata, J.A., Benitez, J.R., Lobon, M. & Donazar, J.A. (2009a) Large scale risk-assessment of wind-farms on population viability of a globally endangered raptor. *Biological Conservation*, **142**, 2954–2961.

Carrete, M., Tella, J.L., Blanco, G. & Bertellotti, M. (2009b) Effects of habitat degradation on the abundance, richness and diversity of raptors across neotropical biomes. *Biological Conservation*, **142**, 2002–2011.

Carrete, M., Sanches-Zapata, J.A., Benitez, J.R., Lobon, M., Montoya, F. & Donazar, J.A. (2012) Mortality at wind-farms is positively related to large-scale distribution and aggregation in Griffon Vultures. *Biological Conservation*, **145**, 102–108.

Carroll, C., Dunk, J.R. & Moilanen, A. (2010) Optimising resiliency of reserve networks to climate change: multispecies conservation planning in the Pacific Northwest, USA. *Global Change Biology*, **16**, 891–904.

Carroll, C., Noss, R.F., Paquet, P.C. & Schumaker, N.H. (2003) Use of population viability analysis and reserve selection algorithms in regional conservation plans. *Ecological Applications*, **13**, 1773–1789.

Carroll, M.J., Dennis, P., Pearce-Higgins, J.W. & Thomas, C.D. (2011) Maintaining northern peatland ecosystems in a changing climate: effects of soil moisture, drainage and drain blocking on craneflies. *Global Change Biology*, **17**, 2991–3001.

Carscadden, J.E., Montevecchi, W.A., Davoren, G.K. & Nakashima, B.S. (2002) Trophic relationships among capelin (*Mallotus villosus*) and seabirds in a changing ecosystem. *ICES Journal of Marine Science*, **59**, 1027–1033.

Castellón, T.D. & Sieving, K.E. (2006) An experimental test of matrix permeability and corridor use by an endemic understory bird. *Conservation Biology*, **20**, 135–145.

Castro, G., Myers, J.P., Ricklefs, R.E. (1992) Ecology and energetics of sanderlings migrating to four latitudes. *Ecology*, **73**, 833–844.

Catchpole, E.A., Morgan, B.J.T., Freeman, S.N. & Peach, W.J. (1999) Modelling the survival of British lapwings *Vanellus vanellus* using ring-recovery data and weather covariates. *Bird Study*, **46**, S5–S13.

Cattadori, I.M., Haydon, D.T. & Hudson, P.J. (2005) Parasites and climate synchronize red grouse populations. *Nature*, **433**, 737–741.

Cavé, A.J. (1983) Purple heron survival and drought in tropical West-Africa. *Ardea*, **71**, 217–224.

Cavé, A.J. & Visser, J. (1985) Winter severity and breeding bird numbers in a Coot population. *Ardea*, **73**, 129–138,

Cawthorne, R.A. & Marchant, J.H. (1980) The effects of the 1978/79 winter on British bird populations. *Bird Study*, **27**, 163–172.

Chalfoun, A.D., Thompson, F.R. III & Ratnaswamy, M.J. (2002) Nest predators and fragmentation: a review and meta-analysis. *Conservation Biology*, **16**, 306–318.

Chamberlain, D.E., Arlettaz, R., Caprio, E., Maggini, R., Pedrini, P., Rolando, A. & Zbinden, N. (2012) The altitudinal frontier in avian climate impact research. *Ibis*, **154**, 205–209.

Chamberlain, D.E. & Fuller, R.J. (2001) Contrasting patterns of change in the distribution and abundance of farmland birds in relation to farming system in lowland Britain. *Global Ecology and Biogeography*, **10**, 399–409.

Chamberlain, D.E., Fuller, R.J., Bunce, R.G.H., Duckworth, J.C. & Shrubb, M. (2000) Changes in the abundance of farmland birds in relation to the timing of agricultural intensification in England and Wales. *Journal of Applied Ecology*, **37**, 771–788.

Chamberlain, D.E. & Pearce-Higgins, J.W. (2013) Impacts of climate change on upland birds: complex interactions, compensatory mechanisms and the need for long-term data. *Ibis*, **155**, 451–455.

Chambers, L.E. (2005) Migration dates at Eyre Bird Observatory: links with climate change? *Climate Research*, **29**, 157–165.

Chambers, L.E. (2008) Trends in timing of migration of south-western Australian birds and their relationship to climate. *Emu*, **108**, 1–14.

Chambers, L.E., Quin, B.R., Menkhorst, P., Franklin, D.C. & Smales, I. (2008) The effects of climate on breeding in the Helmeted Honeyeater. *Emu*, **108**, 15–22.

Charmantier, A., McCleery, R.H., Cole, L.R., Perrins, C., Kruuk, L.E.B., & Sheldon, B.C. (2008) Adaptive phenotypic plasticity in response to climate change in a wild bird population. *Science*, **320**, 800–803.

Chase, M.K., Nur, N. & Guepel, G.R. (2005) Effects of weather and population density in reproductive success and population dynamics in a song sparrow (*Melospiza melodia*) population: a long-term study. *The Auk*, **122**, 571–592.

Cheke, R.A., Venn, J.F. & Jones, P.J. (2007) Forecasting suitable breeding conditions for the red-billed quelea *Quelea quelea* in southern Africa. *Journal of Animal Ecology*, **44**, 523–533.

Chen, I.-C., Hill, J.K., Ohlemüller, R., Roy, D.B. & Thomas, C.D. (2011) Rapid range shifts of species associated with high levels of climate warming. *Science*, **333**, 1024–1026.

Cheung, W.W.L., Lam, V.W.Y., Sarmiento, J.L., Kearney, K., Watson, R. & Pauly, D. (2009) Projecting global marine biodiversity impacts under climate change scenarios. *Fish and Fisheries*, **10**, 235–251.

Chevin, L.-M., Lande, R. & Mace, G.M. (2010) Adaptation, plasticity and extinction in a changing environment: towards a predictive theory. *PLoS Biology*, **8**, e1000357.

Cheviron, Z.A., Hackett, S.J. & Capparella, A.P. (2005) Complex evolutionary history of a Neotropical lowland forest bird (*Lepidothrix coronata*) and its implications for historical hypotheses of the origin of Neotropical avian diversity. *Molecular Phylogenetics and Evolution*, **36**, 338–357.

Chu, S. & Majumdar, A. (2012) Opportunities and challenges for a sustainable energy future. *Nature*, **488**, 294–303.

Clark, J.M., Gallego-Sala, A.V., Allott, T.E.H., Chapman, S.J., Farewell, T., Freeman, C., House, J.I., Orr, H.G., Prentice, I.C. & Smith, P. (2010) Assessing the vulnerability of blanket peat to climate change using an ensemble of statistical bioclimatic envelope models. *Climate Research*, **45**, 131–150.

Clark, N.A. (2006) Tidal barrages and birds. *Ibis*, **148** S1, 152–157.

Clarke, A. & Gaston, K.J. (2006) Climate, energy and diversity. *Proceedings of the Royal Society of London, Series B*, **273**, 2257–2266.

Clarke, A. & Johnston, N. M. (1999) Scaling of metabolic rate with body mass and temperature in teleost fish. *Journal of Animal Ecology*, **68**, 893–905.

Clavero, M., Villero, D. & Brotons, L. (2011) Climate change or land use dynamics: do we know what climate change indicators indicate? *PLoS ONE*, **6**, e18581.

Clobert, J., Perrins, C.M., McCleery, R.H. & Gosler, A.G. (1988) Survival rate in the great tit *Parus major* in relation to sex, age, and immigration status. *Journal of Animal Ecology*, **57**, 287–306.

Cohen, J. (1960) A coefficient of agreement for nominal scales. *Educational and Psychological Measurements*, **20**, 37–46.

Cole, S.G. (2011) Wind power compensation is not for the birds: An opinion from an environmental economist. *Restoration Ecology*, **19**, 1–17.

Conde, D.A., Flesness, N., Colchero, F., Jones, O.R. & Scheuerlein, A. (2011) An emerging role of zoos to conserve biodiversity. *Science*, **331**, 1390–1391.

Conlisk, E., Syphard, A.D., Franklin, J., Flint, L., Flint, A. & Regan, H. (2013) Uncertainty in assessing the impacts of global change with coupled dynamic species distribution and population models. *Global Change Biology*, 19, 858–869.

Conrad, K.F., Warren, S.W., Fox, R., Parsons, M.S. & Woiwod, I.P. (2006) Rapid declines of common, widespread British moths provide evidence of an insect biodiversity crisis. *Biological Conservation*, **132**, 279–291.

Conrad, K.F., Woiwod, I.P. & Perrt, J.N. (2003) East Atlantic teleconnection pattern and the decline of a common arctiid moth. *Global Change Biology*, **9**, 125–130.

Conway, G., Wotton, S., Henderson, I., Eaton, M., Drewitt, A., & Spencer, J. (2009) The status of breeding woodlarks *Lullula arborea* in Britain in 2006. *Bird Study*, **56**, 310–315.

Conway, G., Wotton, S., Henderson, I., Langston, R., Drewitt, A. & Curriee, F. (2007) Status and distribution of European nightjars *Caprimulgus europaeus* in the UK in 2004. *Bird Study*, **54**, 98–111.

Cook, A.S.C.P., Parsons, M., Mitchell, I. & Robinson, R.A. (2011) Reconciling policy with ecological requirements in biodiversity monitoring. *Marine Ecology Progress Series*, **434**, 267–277.

Cooke, F., Rockwell, R.F. & Lank, D.B. (1995) *The Snow Geese of La Pérouse Bay: Natural Selection in the Wild*. Oxford, UK: Oxford University Press.

Copestake, P. (2006) Hydropower and environmental regulation – A Scottish perspective. *Ibis*, **148** S1, 169–179.

Coppack, T. & Pulido, F. (2004) Photoperiodic response and the adaptability of avian life cycles to environmental change. *Advances in Ecological Research*, **35**, 131–150.

Coppack, T., Pulido, F. & Berthold, P. (2001) Photoperiodic response to early hatching in a migratory bird species. *Oecologia*, **128**, 181–186.

Coppack, T., Pulido, F., Csich, M., Auer, D.P. & Berthold, P. (2003) Photoperiodic response may facilitate adaptation to climate change in long-distance migratory birds. *Proceedings of the Royal Society of London, Series B*, **270**, S43–S46.

Cormont, A., Vos, C.C., van Turnhout, C.A.M., Foppen, R.P.B. & ter Braak, C.J.F. (2011) Using life-history traits to explain bird population responses to changing weather variability. *Climate Research*, **49**, 59–71.

Cornulier, T., Elston, D.A., Arcese, P., Benton, T.G., Douglas, D.J.T., Lambin, X., Reid, J., Robinson, R.A. & Sutherland, W.J. (2009) Estimating the annual number of breeding attempts from breeding dates using mixture models. *Ecology Letters*, **12**, 1184–1193.

Cotton, P.A. (2003) Avian migration phenology and global climate change. *Proceedings of the Academy Natural Sciences USA*, **100**, 12219–12222.

Coulson, J.C. (1962) The biology of *Tipula subnodicornis* Zetterstedt, with comparative observations on *Tipula paludosa* Meigen. *Journal of Animal Ecology*, **31**, 1–21.

Coutant, C.C. & Whitney, R.R. (2000) Fish behavior in relation to passage through hydropower turbines: a review. *Transactions of the American Fisheries Society*, **129**, 351–380.

Cowley, E. (1979) Sand martin population trends in Britain, 1965–1978. *Bird Study*, **26**, 113–116.

Cox, G.W. (1985) The evolution of avian migration systems between temperate and tropical regions of the New World. *American Naturalist*, **126**, 451–474.

Cox, R.R., Hanson, M.A., Roy, C.C., Euliss, N.H., Johnson, D.H. & Butler, M.G. (1998) Mallard duckling growth and survival in relation to aquatic invertebrates. *Journal of Wildlife Management*, **62**, 124–133.

Cramp, S. & Perrins, C.M. (1994) *The Birds of the Western Palearctic, Volume 9: Buntings and New World Warblers*. Oxford, UK: Oxford University Press.

Crespin, L., Harris, M.P., Lebreton, J.-D., Frederiksen, M. & Wanless, S. (2006) Recruitment to a seabird population depends on environmental factors and on population size. *Journal of Animal Ecology*, **75**, 228–238.

Cresswell, K.A., Wiedenmann, J. & Mangel, M. (2008) Can macaroni penguins keep up with climate- and fishing-induced changes in krill? *Polar Biology*, **31**, 641–649.

Cresswell, W. & McCleery, R. (2003) How great tits maintain synchronization of their hatch date with food supply in response to long-term variability in temperature. *Journal of Animal Ecology*, **72**, 356–366.

Cresswell, W. & Whitfield, D.P. (2008) How starvation risk in Redshanks *Tringa totanus* results in predation mortality from Sparrowhawks *Accipiter nisus*. *Ibis*, **150**, 209–218.

Crick, H.Q.P., Dudley, C., Glue, D.E. & Thomson, D.L. (1997) UK birds are laying eggs earlier. *Nature*, **338**, 526.

Crick, H.Q.P., Gibbons, D.W. & Magrath, R. D. (1993) Seasonal changes in clutch size in British birds. *Journal of Animal Ecology*, **62**, 263–273.

Crick, H.Q.P. & Sparks, T. H. (1999) Climate change related to egg-laying trends. *Nature*, **399**, 423–424.

Croxall, J.P., Trathan, P.N. & Murphy, E.J. (2002) Environmental change and Antarctic seabird populations. *Science*, **297**, 1510–1514.

Crutzen, P.J. (2006) Albedo enhancement by stratospheric sulphur injections: a contribution to resolve a policy dilemma? *Climate Change*, **77**, 211–220.

Currie, D. J. (1991) Energy and large-scale patterns of animal and plant species richness. *American Naturalist*, **137**, 27–49.

Currie, D.J., Mittelbach, G.G., Cornell, H.V., Field, R., Guégan, F., Hawkins, B.A., Kaufman, D.M., Kerr, J.T., Oberdorff, T., O'Brien, E. & Turner, J.R.G. (2004) Predictions and tests of climate-based hypotheses of broad-scale variation in taxonomic richness. *Ecology Letters*, **7**, 1121–1134.

Cushing, D.H. (1982) *Climate and Fisheries*. London, UK: Academic Press.

Cushing, D.H. (1990) Plankton production and year-class strength in fish populations: an update of the match/mismatch hypothesis. *Advances in Marine Biology*, **26**, 249–293.

da Costa, A.C.L., Galbraith, D., Almeida, S., Portela, B.T.T., da Costa, M., de Athaydes Silva Junior, J., Braga, A.P., de Gonçalves, P.H.L., de Oliveria, A.A., Fisher, R., Phillips, O.L., Metcalfe, D.B., Levy, P. & Meir, P. (2010) Effects of 7 years of experimental drought on the aboveground biomass storage of an eastern Amazonian rainforest. *New Phytologist*, **187**, 579–591.

Dahl, E.L., Bevanger, K., Nygard, T., Roskaft, E. & Stokke, B.G. (2012) Reduced breeding success in white-tailed eagles at Smola windfarm, western Norway, is caused by mortality and displacement. *Biological Conservation*, **145**, 79–85.

Dai, A. (2010) Drought under global warming: a review. *WIRES Climate Change*, **2**, 45–65.

Dai, A. (2013) Increasing drought under global warming in observations and models. *Nature Climate Change*, **3**, 52–58.

Daly, K. L. (1990) Overwintering development, growth, and feeding of larval Euphausia superba in the Antarctic marginal ice zone. *Limnology and Oceanography*, **35**, 1564–1576.

Danielsen, F. & Heegaard. M. (1995) Impact of logging and plantation development on species diversity: a case study from Sumatra. In *Management of Tropical Forests: Towards an Integrated Perspective*. Ø. Sandbukt. Oslo, Norway: University of Oslo, pp 73–92.

Danielson, F., Beukema, H., Burgess, N.D., Parish, F., Brühl, C.A., Donald, P.F., Murdiyarso, D., Phalan, B., Reijnders, L., Struebig, M. & Fitzherbert, E.B. (2008) Biofuel plantations on forested lands: double jeopardy for biodiversity and climate. *Conservation Biology*, **23**, 348–358.

Dauber, J., Jones, M.B. & Stout, J.C. (2010) The impact of biomass crop cultivation on temperate biodiversity. *Global Change Biology Bioenergy*, **2**, 289–309.

Davey, C.M., Chamberlain, D.E., Newson, S.E., Noble, D.G. & Johnston, A. (2012) Rise of the generalists: evidence for climate driven homogenization in avian communities. *Global Ecology and Biogeography*, **21**, 568–578.

Davey, C.M., Devictor, V., Jonzén, N., Lindström, Å. & Smith, H.G. (2013) Impact of climate change on communities: revealing species' contribution. *Journal of Animal Ecology*, **82**, 551–561.

Davies, R.G., Orme, D.L., Storch, D., Olson, V.A., Thomas, G.H., Ross, S.G., Ding, T.-S., Rasmussen, P.C., Bennett, P.M., Owens, I.P.F., Blackburn, T.M. & Gaston, K.J. (2007) Topography, energy and the global distribution of bird species richness. *Proceedings of the Royal Society of London, Series B*, **274**, 1189–1197.

Davies, Z.H., Wilson, R.J., Coles, S. & Thomas, C.D. (2006) Changing habitat associations of a thermally constrained species, the silver-spotted skipper butterfly, in response to climate warming. *Journal of Animal Ecology*, **75**, 247–256.

Davis, S.K. (2004) Area sensitivity in grassland passerines: effects of patch size, patch shape and vegetation structure on bird abundance and occurrence in southern Saskatchewan. *The Auk*, **121**, 1130–1145.

Davoren, G.K. & Montevecchi, W.A. (2003) Signals from seabirds indicate changing biology of capelin stocks. *Marine Ecology Progress Series*, **258**, 253–261.

Dawson, A., King, V.M., Bentley, G.E. & Ball, G.F. (2001) Photoperiodic control of seasonality in birds. *Journal of Biological Rhythms*, **16**, 365–380.

Dawson, R.D. & Bortolli, G.R. (2000) Effects of hematozoan parasites on condition and return rates of American Kestrels. *The Auk*, **117**, 373–380.

Dawson, T.P., Jackson, S.T., House, J.I., Prentice, I.C. & Mace, G.M. (2011) Beyond predictions: biodiversity conservation in a changing climate. *Science*, **332**, 53–58.

De'ath, G. & Fabricius, K.E. (2000) Classification and regression trees: a powerful yet simple technique for ecological data analysis. *Ecology*, **81**, 3178–3192.

Dean, W.R.J., Barnard, P. & Anderson, M.D. (2009) When to stay, when to go: trade-offs for southern African arid-zone birds in times of drought. *South African Journal of Science*, **105**, 24–28.

De Lucas, M., Ferrer, M., Bechard, M.J. & Muñoz, A.R. (2012) Griffon vulture mortality at wind farms in southern Spain: Distribution of fatalities and active mitigation measures. *Biological Conservation*, **147**, 184–189.

De Lucas, M., Janss, G.F.E., Whitfield, D.P. & Ferrer, M. (2008) Collision fatality of raptors in wind farms does not depend on raptor abundance. *Journal of Applied Ecology*, **45**, 1695–1703.

Defra (2007) *UK Biomass Strategy*: London, UK: Crown Copyright.

DeFries, R., Hansen, A., Newton, A.C. & Hansen, M.C. (2005) Increasing isolation of protected areas in tropical forests over the past twenty years. *Ecological Applications*, **15**, 19–26.

Dekker, W.R.J. (1989) Predation and the western limits of megapode distribution (Megapodiidae; Aves). *Journal of Biogeography*, **16**, 317–321.

DeLeon, R.L., DeLeon, E.E. & Rising, G.R. (2011) Influence of climate change on avian migrants' first arrival dates. *The Condor*, **113**, 915–923.

Delgado, M.P., Morales, M.B., Traba, J., de la Morena, E.L.G. (2009) Determining the effects of habitat management and climate on the population trends of a declining steppe bird. *Ibis*, **151**, 440–451.

Den Held, J.J. (1981) Population changes in the purple heron in relation to drought in the wintering area. *Ardea*, **69**, 185–191.

Deng, Z., Carlson, T.J., Dauble, D.D. & Ploskey, G.R. (2011) Fish passage assessment of an advanced hydropower turbine and conventional turbine using blade-strike modeling. *Energies*, **4**, 57–67.

Desholm, M. & Kahlert, J. (2005) Avian collision risk at an offshore wind farm. *Biology Letters*, **1**, 296–298.

Devereux, C.L., Denny, M.J.H. & Whittingham, M.J. (2008) Minimal effects of wind turbines on the distribution of wintering farmland birds. *Journal of Applied Ecology*, **45**, 1689–1694.

Devictor, V., Julliard, R., Clavel, J., Jiguet, F., Lee, A. & Couvet, D. (2008a) Functional biotic homogenization of bird communities in disturbed landscapes. *Global Ecology and Biogeography*, **17**, 252–261.

Devictor, V., Julliard, R., Couvet, D. & Jiguet, F. (2008b) Birds are tracking climate warming, but not fast enough. *Proceedings of the Royal Society of London, Series B*, **254**, 2743–2748.

Devictor, V., Julliard, R. & Jiguet, F. (2008c) Distribution of specialist and generalist species along spatial gradients of habitat disturbance and fragmentation. *Oikos*, **117**, 507–514.

Devictor, V., van Swaay, C., Brereteon, T., Brotons, L., Chamberlain, D., Heliölä, J., Herrando, S., Julliard, R., Kuussaari, M., Linström, Å., Reif, J., Roy, D.B., Schweiger, O., Settele, J., Stefanescu, C., Van Strien, A., Van Turnhout, C., Vermouzek, Z., De Vries, M.W., Wynhoff, I. & Jiguet, F. (2012a) Differences in the climate debts of birds and butterflies at a continental scale. *Nature Climate Change*, **2**, 121–124.

Devictor, V., van Swaay, C., Brereteon, T., Brotons, L., Chamberlain, D., Heliölä, J., Herrando, S., Julliard, R., Kuussaari, M., Linström, Å., Reif, J., Roy, D.B., Schweiger, O., Settele, J., Stefanescu, C., Van Strien, A., Van Turnhout, C., Vermouzek, Z., De Vries, M.W., Wynhoff, I. & Jiguet, F. (2012b) Uncertainty in thermal tolerances and climatic debt. Reply. *Nature Climate Change*, **2**, 638–639.

Diamond, A.W. & Devlin, C.M. (2003) Seabirds as indicators of changes in marine ecosystems: ecological monitoring on Machias Seal Island. *Environmental Monitoring and Assessment*, **88**, 153–175.

Dickey, M.-H., Gauthier G. & Cadieux, M.-C. (2008) Climate effects on the breeding phenology and reproductive success of an arctic-nesting goose species, *Global Change Biology*, **14**, 1973–1985.

Dillingham, P.W. & Fletcher, D. (2008) Estimating the ability of birds to sustain additional human-caused mortalities using a simple decision rule and allometric relationships. *Biological Conservation*, **141**, 1783–1792.

Diniz-Filho, J.A.F., Bini, L.M., Rangel, T.F., Loyola, R.D., Hof, C., Nogués-Bravo, D. & Araújo, M.B. (2009) Partitioning and mapping uncertainties in ensembles of forecasts of species turnover under climate change. *Ecography*, **32**, 897–906.

Dodd, A., Hardiman, A., Jennings, K. & Williams, G. (2010) Protected areas and climate change. Reflections from a practitioner's perspective. *Utrecht Law Review*, **6**, 141–150.

Doherty, P.F. & Grubb, T.C. (2002) Survivorship of permanent-resident birds in a fragmented forest landscape. *Ecology*, **83**, 844–857.

Dolman, P.M. (2012) Mechanisms and processes underlying landscape structure effects on bird populations. In *Birds and Habitat. Relationships in Changing Landscapes*. Fuller, R.J. Cambridge, UK: Cambridge University Press, pp. 93–124.

Dolman, P.M., Hinsley, S.A., Bellamy, P.E. & Watts, K. (2007) Woodland birds in patchy landscapes: the evidence base for strategic networks. *Ibis*, **149 Suppl 2**, 146–160.

Donald, P.F. & Evans, A.D. (2006) Habitat connectivity and matrix restoration: the wider implications of agri-environment schemes. *Journal of Applied Ecology*, **43**, 209–218.

Donald, P.F., Gedeon, K., Collar, N.J., Spottiswoode, C.N., Wondafrash, M. & Buchanan, G.M. (2012) The restricted range of the Ethiopian Bush-crow *Zavattariornis stresemanni* is a consequence of high reliance on modified habitats within narrow climatic limits. *Journal of Ornithology*, **153**, 1031–1044.

Donald, P.F., Green, R.E. & Heath, M.F. (2001) Agricultural intensification and the collapse of Europe's farmland bird populations. *Proceedings of the Royal Society of London, Series B*, **268**, 25–29.

Donald, P.F., Sanderson, F.J., Burfield, I.J., Bierman, S.M., Gregory, R.D. & Waliczky, Z. (2007) International conservation policy delivers benefits for birds in Europe. *Science*, **317**, 810–813.

Donnelly, R. & Marzluff, J.M. (2004) Importance of reserve size and landscape context to urban bird conservation. *Conservation Biology*, **18**, 733–745.

Dougall, T.W., Holland, P.K., Mee, A. & Yalden, D.W. (2005) Comparative population dynamics of common sandpipers *Actitis hypoleucos*: living at the edge. *Bird Study*, **52**, 80–87.

Douglas, D.J.T., Bellamy, P.E. & Pearce-Higgins, J.W. (2011) Changes in the abundance and distribution of upland breeding birds at an operational wind farm. *Bird Study*, **58**, 37–43.

Douglas, D.J.T., Follestad, A., Langston, R.H.W. & Pearce-Higgins, J.W. (2012) Modelled sensitivity of avian collision rate at wind turbines varies with number of hours of flight activity input data. *Ibis*, **154**, 858–861.

Douglas, D.J.T., Newson, S.E., Leech, D.I., Noble, D.G. & Robinson, R.A. (2010) How important are climate-induced changes in host availability for population processes in an obligate brood parasite, the European cuckoo? *Oikos*, **119**, 1834–1840.

Dormann, C.F., McPherson, J.M., Araújo, M.B., Bivand, R., Bolliger, J., Carl, G., Davies, R.G., Hirzel, A., Jetz, W., Kissling, W.D., Kühn, I., Ohlemüller, R., Peres-Neto, P.R., Reineking, B., Schröder, B., Schurr, F.M. & Wilson, R. (2007) Methods to account for spatial autocorrelation in the analysis of species distributional data: a review. *Ecography*, **30**, 609–628.

Dormann, C.F., Purschke, P., Marquez, J.R.C., Lautenbach, S. & Schroder, B. (2008) Components of uncertainty in species distribution analysis: a case study of the Great Grey Shrike. *Ecology*, **89**, 3371–3386.

Dorrepaal, E., Toet, S., van Logtestijn, R.S.P., Swart, E., van de Weg, M.J., Callaghan, T.V. & Aerts, R. (2009) Carbon respiration from subsurface peat accelerated by climate warming in the subarctic. *Nature*, **460**, 616–619.

Doswald, N., Willis, S.G., Collingham, Y.C., Pain, D.J., Green, R.E. & Huntley, B. (2009) Potential impacts of climate change in the breeding and non-breeding ranges and migration distances of European *Sylvia* warblers. *Journal of Biogeography*, **36**, 1194–1208.

Doxa, A., Paracchini, M. L., Pointereau, P., Devictor, V. & Jiguet, F. (2012) Preventing biotic homogenization of farmland bird communities: the role of high nature value farmland. *Agriculture, Ecosystems and the Environment*, **148**, 83–88.

Drent, R., Both, C., Green, M., Madsen, J. & Piersma, T. (2003) Pay-offs and penalties of competing migratory schedules. *Oikos*, **103**, 274–292.

Drever, M.C. & Clark, R.G. (2007) Spring temperature, clutch initiation date and duck nest success: a test of the mismatch hypothesis. *Journal of Animal Ecology*, **76**, 139–148.

Drever, M.C., Clark, R.G., Derksen, C., Slattery, S.M., Toose, P. & Nudds, T.D. (2012) Population vulnerability to climate change linked to timing of breeding in boreal ducks. *Global Change Biology*, **18**, 480–492.

Drewitt, A.L. & Langston, R.H.W. (2006) Assessing the impacts of wind farms on birds. *Ibis*, **148 Suppl 1**, 29–42.

Drewitt, A.L. & Langston R.H.W. (2008) Collision effects of wind-power generators and other obstacles on birds. *Annals of the New York Academy of Sciences* **1134**, 233–266.

Ducklow, H.W., Baker, K., Martinson, D.G., Quetin, L.B., Ross, R.M., Smith, R.C., Stammerjohn, S.E., Vernet, M. & Fraser, W. (2007) Marine pelagic ecosystems: the West Antarctic Peninsula. *Philosophical Transactions of the Royal Society B*, **362**, 67–94.

Duckworth, R.A. (2006) Behavioral correlations across reproductive contexts provide a mechanism for a cost of aggression. *Behavioral Ecology*, **17**, 1011–1019.

Duckworth, R.A. (2008) Adaptive dispersal strategies and the dynamics of a range expansion. *American Naturalist*, **172**, S4–S17.

Duckworth, R.A. (2009) Maternal effects and range expansion: A key factor in a dynamic process? *Philosophical Transactions of the Royal Society Series B*, **364**, 1075–1086.

Duckworth, R.A. & Badyaev, A.V. (2007) Coupling of dispersal and aggression facilitates the rapid range expansion of a passerine bird. *Proceedings of the Academy Natural Sciences, USA*, **104**, 15017–15022.

Dugger, K.M., Faaborg, J. & Arendt, W.J. (2000) Rainfall correlates of bird populations and survival rates in a Puerto Rican dry forest. *Bird Populations*, **5**, 11–27.

Dugger, K.M., Faaborg, J., Arendt, W.J. & Hobson, K.A. (2004) Understanding survival and abundance of overwintering warblers: does rainfall matter? *The Condor*, **106**, 744–760.

Duncan, R.P., Cassey, P. & Blackburn, T.M. (2009) Do climate envelope models transfer? A manipulative test using dung beetle introductions. *Proceedings of the Royal Society of London, Series B*, **276**, 1449–1457.

Dunn, P.O. (2004) Breeding dates and reproductive performance. *Advances in Ecological Research*, **55**, 67–85.

Dunn, P.O. & Møller, A.P. (in press) Changes in breeding phenology and population size of birds. *Journal of Animal Ecology*. DOI:10.1111/1365-2656.12162.

Dunn, P.O. & Winkler, D.W. (2010) Effects of climate change on timing of breeding and reproductive success in birds. In *Effects of Climate Change on Birds*. Møller, A.P., Fiedler, W. & Berthold, P. Oxford, UK: Oxford University Press, pp. 113–128.

Dunn, P.O., Winkler, D.W., Whittingham, L.A., Hannon, S.J. & Robertson, R.J. (2011) A test of the mismatch hypothesis: How is timing of reproduction related to food abundance in an aerial insectivore? *Ecology*, **92**, 450–461.

Durant, J.M., Anker-Nilssen, T., Hjermann, D.Ø., & Stenseth, N.C. (2004a) Regime shifts in the breeding of an Atlantic puffin population. *Ecology Letters*, **7**, 388–394.

Durant, J.M., Anker-Nilssen, T., & Stenseth, N.C. (2003) Trophic interactions under climate fluctuations: the Atlantic puffin as an example. *Proceedings of the Royal Society of London, Series B*, **270**, 1461–1466.

Durant, J.M., Anker-Nilssen, T. & Stenseth, N.C. (2006) Ocean climate prior to breeding affects the duration of the nestling period of the Atlantic puffin. *Biology Letters*, **2**, 628–631.

Durant, J.M., Hjermann, D.Ø., Anker-Nilssen, T., Beaugrand, G., Mysterud, A., Pettorelli, N. & Stenseth, N.C. (2005) Timing and abundance as key mechanisms affecting trophic interactions in variable environments. *Ecology Letters*, **8**, 952–958.

Durant, J.M., Hjermann, D.Ø., Ottersen, G. & Stenseth, N.C. (2007) Climate and the match or mismatch between predator requirements and resource availability. *Climate Research*, **33**, 271–283.

Durant, J.M., Stenseth, N.C., Anker-Nilssen, T., Harris, M.P., Thompson, P. & Wanless, S. (2004b) Marine birds and climate fluctuation in North Atlantic. In *Marine Ecosystems and Climate Variation: The North Atlantic*. Stenseth, N.C., Ottersen, G., Hurrell, J.W. & Belgrano, A. Oxford, UK: Oxford University Press, pp. 95–105.

Duriez, O., Sæther, S.A., Ens, B.J., Choquet, R., Pradel, R., Lambeck, R.H.D. & Klaassen, M. (2009) Estimating survival and movements using both live and dead recoveries: a case study of oystercatchers confronted with habitat change. *Journal of Applied Ecology*, **46**, 144–153.

Dutton, D.L., Dutton, P.H., Chaloupka, M. & Boulon, R.H. (2005) Increase of a Caribbean leatherback turtle *Dermochelys coriacea* nesting population linked to long-term nest protection. *Biological Conservation*, **126**, 186–194.

Dynesius, M. & Jansson, R. (2000) Evolutionary consequence of changes in species' geographical distributions driven by Mikalkovitch climate oscillations. *Proceedings of the National Academy of Sciences USA*, **97**, 9115–9120.

Dyrcz, A. & Halupka, L. (2009) The response of the Great Reed Warbler *Acrocephalus arundinaceus* to climate change. *Journal of Ornithology*, **150**, 39–44.

Eaton, M.A., Brown, A.F., Noble, D.G., Musgrove, A.J., Hearn, R.D., Aebischer, N.J., Gibbons, D.W., Evans, A. & Gregory, R.D. (2009) Birds of Conservation Concern 3: the population status of birds in the United Kingdom, Channel Islands and Isle of Man. *British Birds*, **6**, 296–341.

Edwards, D.P., Fisher, B. & Boyd, E. (2010) Protecting degraded rainforests: enhancement of forest carbon stocks under REDD+. *Conservation Letters*, **3**, 313–316.

Edwards, M. & Richardson, A.J. (2004) Impact of climate change on marine pelagic phenology and trophic mismatch. *Nature*, **430**, 881–884.

Eglington, S.M. & Pearce-Higgins, J.W. (2012) Disentangling the relative importance of changes in climate and land-use intensity in driving recent bird population trends. *PLoS ONE*, **7**, e30407.

Eichhorn, M., & Drechsler, M. (2010) Spatial trade-offs between wind power production and bird collision avoidance in agricultural landscapes. *Ecology and Society*, **15**, 10.

Eickhout, B., van Meijl, H., Tabeau, A. & van Rheenen, T. (2007) Economic and ecological consequences of four European land use scenarios. *Land Use Policy*, **24**, 562–575.

Elith, J. & Leathwick, J.R. (2009) Species distribution models: Ecological explanation and prediction across space and time. *Annual Review of Ecology, Evolution, and Systematics*, **40**, 677–97.

Ellegren, H. (1990) Timing of autumn migration in bluethroats *Luscinia svecica svecica* depends on timing of breeding. *Ornis Fennica*, **67**, 13–17.

Elliott, G.P., Merton, D.V. & Jansen, P.W. (2001) Intensive management of a critically endangered species: the kakapo. *Biological Conservation*, **99**, 121–133.

Ellwood, E.R., Primack, R.B. & Talmadge, M.L. (2010) Effects of climate change on spring arrival times of birds in Thoreau's concord from 1851 to 2007. *The Condor*, **112**, 754–762.

Emlen, J.T., DeJong, M.J., Jaeger, M.J., Moermond, T.C., Rusterholz, K.A. & White, R.P. (1986) Density trends and range boundary constraints of forest birds along a latitudinal gradient. *The Auk*, **103**, 791–803.

Enoksson, B., Angelstam, P. & Larsson, K. (1995) Deciduous forest and resident birds: the problem of fragmentation within a coniferous landscape. *Landscape Ecology*, **10**, 267–275.

Enoksson, B. & Nilsson, S.G. (1983) Territory size and population density in relation to food supply in the nuthatch *Sitta europaea* (Aves). *Journal of Animal Ecology*, **52**, 927–935.

Erni, B., Liechti, F., Underhill, L. & Bruderer, B. (2002) Wind and rain govern the intensity of nocturnal bird migration in central Europe – a log-linear regression analysis. *Ardea*, **90**, 155–166.

Etheridge, B., Summers, R.W. & Green, R.E. (1997) The effects of illegal killing and destruction of nests by humans on the population dynamics of the hen harrier *Circus cyaneus* in Scotland. *Journal of Applied Ecology*, **34**, 1081–1105.

Evans, A.D., Smith, K.W., Buckingham, D.L. & Evans, J. (1997) Seasonal variation in breeding performance and nestling diet of Cirl Buntings *Emberiza cirlus* in England. *Bird Study*, **44**, 66–79.

Evans, I.M., Summers, R.W., O'Toole, L., Orr-Ewing, D.C., Evans, R., Snell, N. & Smith, J. (1999) Evaluating the success of translocating Red Kites *Milvus milvus* to the UK. *Bird Study*, **46**, 129–144.

Evans, K.L. & Gaston, K.J. (2005) Can the evolutionary-rates hypothesis explain species–energy relationships? *Functional Ecology*, **19**, 899–915.

Evans, K.L., Greenwood, J.J.D. & Gaston, K.J. (2005a) Dissecting the species-energy relationships. *Proceedings of the Royal Society of London, Series B*, **272**, 2155–2163.

Evans, K.L., Jackson, S.F., Greenwood, J.J.D. & Gaston, K.J. (2006a) Species traits and the form of individual species-energy relationships. *Proceedings of the Royal Society of London, Series B*, **273**, 1779–1787.

Evans, K.L., James, N.A. & Gaston, K.J. (2006b) Abundance, species richness and energy availability in the North American avifauna. *Global Ecology and Biogeography*, **15**, 372–385.

Evans, K.L., Newson, S.E., Storch, D., Greenwood, J.J.D. & Gaston, K.J. (2008) Spatial scale, abundance and the species-energy relationship in British birds. *Journal of Animal Ecology*, **77**, 395–405.

Evans, K.L., Warren, P.H. & Gaston, K.J. (2005b) Species-energy relationships at the macroecological scale: a review of the mechanisms. *Biological Reviews*, **80**, 1–25.

Evans, M.E. (1979) The effects of weather on the wintering of Bewick's Swans *Cygnus columbianus bewickii* at Slimbridge, England. *Ornis Scandinavica*, **10**, 124–162.

Evans, P.R. & Pienkowski, M.W. (1983) Implications for coastal engineering projects of studies at the Tees estuary on the effects of reclamation of intertidal land on shorebird populations. *Water Science and Technology*, **16**, 347–384.

Evans, R.J., O'Toole, L. & Whitfield, D.P. (2012) The history of eagles in Britain and Ireland: an ecological review of placename and documentary evidence from the last 1500 years. *Bird Study*, **59**, 335–349.

Evans, R.J., Wilson, J.D., Amar, A., Douse, A., MacLennan, A., Ratcliffe, N. & Whitfield, D.P. (2009) Growth and demography of a re-introduced population of White-tailed Eagles *Haliaeetus albicalla*. *Ibis*, **151**, 244–254.

Everaert, J. & Stienen, E.W.M. (2007) Impact of wind turbines on birds in Zeebrugge (Belgium). *Biodiversity Conservation*, **16**, 3345–3359.

Ewers, R.M., Scharlemann, J.P.W., Balmford, A.P. & Green R.E. (2009) Do increases in agricultural yield spare land for nature? *Global Change Biology*, **15**, 1716–1726.

Ewert, F., Rounsevell, M.D.A., Reginster, I., Metzger, M.J. & Leemans, R. (2005) Future scenarios of European agricultural land use. I. Estimating changes in crop productivity. *Agriculture, Ecosystems and Environment*, **107**, 101–116.

Faaborg, J. (1982) Avian population fluctuations during drought conditions in Puerto Rico. *Wilson Bulletin*, **94**, 20–30.

Faaborg, J. & Arendt, W.J. (1992) Rainfall correlates of bird population fluctuations in a Puerto Rican dry forest: a 15-year study. *Ornitologia Caribeña*, **3**, 10–19.

Faaborg, J., Arendt, W.J. & Kaiser, M.S. (1984) Rainfall correlates of bird population fluctuations in a Puerto Rican dry forest: a nine year study. *Wilson Bulletin*, **96**, 575–593.

Faaborg, J., Holmes, R.T., Anders, A.D., Bildstein, K.L., Dugger, K.M., Gauthreaux Jr., S.A., Heglund, P., Hobson, K.A., Jahn, A.E., Johnson, D.H., Latta, S.C., Levey, D.J., Marra, P.P., Merkord, C.L., Nol, N., Rothstein, S.I., Sherery, T.W., Sillett, T.S., Thompson III, F.R. & Warnock, N. (2010) Conserving migratory land birds in the New World: Do we know enough? *Ecological Applications*, **20**, 398–418.

Fairhurst, G.D. & Bechard, M.J. (2005) Relationships between winter and spring weather and northern goshawk (*Accipter gentalis*) reproduction in northern Nevada. *Journal of Raptor Research*, **39**, 229–236.

Fargallo, J.A. (2004) Latitudinal trends of reproductive traits in the blue tit *Parus caeruleus*. *Ardeola*, **51**, 177–190.

Fargallo, J.A., Martínez-Padilla, J., Viñuela, J., Blanco, G., Torre, I., Vergara, P. & de Neve, L. (2009) Kestrel-prey dynamic in a Mediterranean Region: the effect of generalist predation and climatic factors. *PLoS ONE*, **4**, e4311.

Fargione, J.E., Cooper, T.R., Flaspohler, D.J., Hill, J., Lehman, C., McCoy, T., McLeod, S., Nelson, E.J., Oberhauser, K.S. & Tilman, D. (2009) Bioenergy and wildlife: threats and opportunities for grassland birds. *Bioscience*, **59**, 767–777.

Fargione, J. (2010) Is bioenergy for the birds? An evaluation of alternative future bioenergy landscapes. *Proceedings of the National Academy of Sciences USA*, **107**, 18745–18746.

Fargione, J., Hill, J., Tilman, D., Polasky, S. & Hawthorne, P. (2008) Land clearing and the biofuel carbon debt. *Science*, **319**, 1235–1238.

Fasola, M., Rubolini, D., Merli, E., Bomcompagni, E. & Bressan, U. (2010) Long-term trends of heron and egret populations in Italy, and the effects of climate, human-induced mortality, and habitat on population dynamics. *Population Ecology*, **52**, 59–72.

Fearnside, P.M. (2005) Brazil's Samuel Dam: Lessons for hydroelectric development policy and the environment in Amazonia. *Environmental Management*, **35**, 1–19.

Feeley, K.J., Malhi, Y., Zelazowski, P. & Silman, M.R. (2012) The relative importance of deforestation, precipitation change and temperature sensitivity in determining the future distributions and diversity of Amazonian plant species. *Global Change Biology*, **18**, 2636–2647.

Ferrer, M., De Lucas, M., Janss, G.F.E., Casado, E., Munoz, A.R., Bechard, M.J. & Calabuig, C.P. (2012) Weak relationship between risk assessment studies and recorded mortality in wind farms. *Journal of Applied Ecology*, **49**, 38–46.

Fiedler, W. (2003) Recent changes in migratory behaviour of birds: a compilation of field observations and ringing data. In *Avian Migration*. Berthold, P., Gwinner, E. & Sonnenschein, E. Berlin, Germany: Springer, pp. 21–38.

Fiedler, W., Bairlien, F. & Köppen, U. (2004) Using large-scale data from ringed birds for the investigation of effects of climate change on migrating birds: pitfalls and prospects. *Advances in Ecological Research*, **35**, 49–67.

Field, R., Hawkins, B.A., Cornell, H.V., Currie, D.J., Diniz-Filho, A.F., Guégan, J.-F., Kaufman, D.M., Kerr, J.T., Mittelbach, G.G., Oberdoff, T., O'Brien, E.M. & Turner, J.R.G. (2009) Spatial species-richness gradients across scales: a meta-analysis. *Journal of Biogeography*, **36**, 132–147.

Fielding, A.H. & Bell, J.F. (1997) A review of methods for the assessment of predictive errors in conservation presence/absence models. *Environmental Conservation*, **24**, 38–49.

Fielding, A.H., Whitfield, D.P. & McLeod, D.R.A. (2006) Spatial association as an indicator of the potential for future interactions between wind energy developments and golden eagles *Aquila chrysaetos* in Scotland. *Biological Conservation*, **131**, 359–369.

Finer, M. & Jenkins, C.N. (2012) Proliferation of hydroelectric dams in the Andeas Amazon and implications for Andes-Amazon connectivity. *PLoS ONE*, **7**, e35126.

Finlayson, H.H. (1932) Heat in the interior of South Australia – holocaust of bird-life. *South Australian Ornithologist*, **11**, 158–160.

Fisher, R., McDowell, N., Purves, D.W., Moorcroft, P.R., Sitch, S., Meir, P., Cox, P., Huntingford, C. & Woodward, F.I. (2010) Assessing uncertainties in a second-generation dynamic vegetation model caused by ecological scale limitations. *New Phytologist*, **187**, 666–681.

Fitzherbert, E.B., Struebig, M.J., Morel, A., Danielsen, F., Bruhl, C.A., Donald, P.F. & Phalan, B. (2008) How will oil palm expansion affect biodiversity? *Trends in Ecology and Evolution*, **23**, 538–545.

Fitzpatrick, M.C. & Hargrove, W.W. (2009) The projection of species distribution models and the problem of non-analog climate. *Biodiversity and Conservation*, **18**, 2255–2261.

Flesch, A.D. (2007) *Population and demographic trends of Ferruginous Pygmy-owls in Northern Sonora Mexico and Implications for Recovery in Arizona*. Unpublished final report.

Fletcher, K., Aebischer, N.J., Baines, D., Foster, R. & Hoodless, A.N. (2010) Changes in breeding success and abundance of ground-nesting moorland birds in relation to the experimental deployment of legal predator control. *Journal of Applied Ecology*, **47**, 263–272.

Fletcher, K., Howarth, D., Kirby, A., Dunn, R. & Smith, A. (2013) Effect of climate change on breeding phenology, clutch size and chick survival of an upland bird. *Ibis* **155**, 456–463.

Fletcher, R.J., Robertson, B.A., Evans, J., Doran, P.J., Alavalapati, J.R.R. & Schemske, D.W. (2011) Biodiversity conservation in the era of biofuels: risks and opportunities. *Frontiers in Ecology and the Environment*, **9**, 161–168.

Foden, W.B., Butchart, S.H.M., Stuart, S.N., Vié, J.-C., Akçakaya, H.R., Angulo, A., DeVantier, L.M., Gutsche, A., Turak, E., Cao, L., Donner, S.D., Katariya, V., Benard, R., Holland, R.A., Hughes, A.F., O'Hanlon, S.E., Garnett, S.T., Şekercioğlu, C.H., Mace, M.C. (2013) Identifying the world's most climate change vulnerable species: a systematic trait-based assessment of all birds, amphibians and corals. *PLoS ONE*, **8**, e65427.

Foppen, R., ter Braak, C.J.F., Verboom, J. & Reijnen, R. (1999) Sedge Warblers *Acrocephalus schoenobaenus* and African rainfall, a low population resilience in fragmented marshlands. *Ardea*, **86**, 113–127.

Forcada, J. & Trathan, P.N. (2009) Penguin responses to climate change in the Southern Ocean. *Global Change Biology*, **15**, 1618–1630.

Fordham, D.A., Akçakaya, H.R., Araújo, M.B., Elith, J., Keith, D.A., Pearson, R., Auld, T.D., Mellin, C., Morgan, J.W., Regan, T.J., Tozer, M., Watts, M.J., White, M., Wintle, B.A., Yates, C. & Brook, B.W. (2012a) Plant extinction risk under climate change: are forecast range shifts alone a good indicator of species vulnerability to global warming? *Global Change Biology*, **18**, 1357–1371.

Fordham, D.A., Wigley, T.M.L., Watts, M.J. & Brook, B.W. (2012b) Strengthening forecasts of climate change impacts with multi-model ensemble averaged projections using MAGICC/SCENGEN 5.3. *Ecography*, **35**, 4–8.

Forero-Medina, G., Terborgh, J., Socolar, S.J. & Pimm, S.L. (2011) Elevational ranges of birds on a tropical montane gradient lag behind warming temperatures. *PLoS ONE*, **6**, e28535.

Foster, D.R. & Motzkin, G. (2003) Interpreting and conserving the openland habitats of coastal New England: insights from landscape history. *Forest Ecology and Management*, **185**, 127–150.

Foster, W.A., Snaddon, J.L., Turner, E.C., Fayle, T.M., Cockerill, T.D., Farnon Ellwood, M.D., Broad, G.R., Chung, A.Y.C., Eggleton, P., Vun Khen, C. & Yusah, K.M. (2011) Establishing the evidence base for maintaining biodiversity and ecosystem function in the oil palm landscapes of South East Asia. *Philosophical Transactions of the Royal Society Series B*, **366**, 3277–3291.

Fox, A.D., Desholm, M., Kahlert, J., Christensen, T.K. & Petersen, I.K. (2006) Information needs to support environmental impact assessment of the effects of European marine offshore wind farms on birds. *Ibis*, **148 S1**, 129–144.

Francis, A.P. & Currie, D.J. (2003) A globally consistent richness–climate relationship for angiosperms. *American Naturalist*, **161**, 523–536.

Francis, C.M. & Saurola, P. (2004) Estimating components of variance in demographic parameters of Tawny Owls, *Strix aluco*. *Animal Biodiversity and Conservation*, **27**, 489–502.

Frank, K. & Wissel, C. (2002) A formula for the mean lifetime of metapopulations in heterogeneous landscapes. *American Naturalist*, **159**, 530–552.

Franklin, A.B., Anderson, D.R., Gutiérrez, R.J. & Burnham, K.P. (2000) Climate, habitat quality, and fitness in northern spotted owl populations in northwestern California. *Ecological Monographs*, **70**, 539–590.

Franklin, J. (2009) *Mapping Species Distributions: Spatial Inference and Prediction*. Cambridge, UK: Cambridge University Press.

Fraser, J.D., Karpanty, S.M., Cohen, J.B. & Truitt, B.R. (2013) The red knot (*Calidris canutus rufa*) decline in the western hemisphere: is there a lemming connection? *Canadian Journal of Zoology*, **91**, 13–16.

Fraser, W.R. & Hofmann, E.E. (2003) A predator's perspective on causal links between climate change, physical forcing and ecosystem response. *Marine Ecology Progress Series*, **265**, 1–15.

Frederiksen, M., Daunt, F., Harris, M.P. & Wanless, S. (2008) The demographic impact of extreme events: stochastic weather drives survival and population dynamics in a long-lived seabird. *Journal of Animal Ecology*, **77**, 1020–1029.

Frederiksen, M., Edwards, M., Richardson, A.J., Halliday, N.C. & Wanless, S. (2006) From plankton to top predators: bottom-up control of a marine food web across four trophic levels. *Journal of Animal Ecology*, **75**, 1259–1268.

Frederiksen, M., Elston, D.A., Edwards, M., Mann, A.D. & Wanless, S. (2011) Mechanisms of long-term decline in size of lesser sandeels in the North Sea explored using a growth and phenology model. *Marine Ecology Progress Series*, **432**, 137–147.

Frederiksen, M., Harris, M.P., Daunt, F. & Wanless, S. (2004a) Scale-dependent climate signals drive breeding phenology of three seabird species. *Global Change Biology*, **10**, 1214–1221.

Frederiksen, M., Wanless, S., Harris, M.P., Rothery, P. & Wilson, L.J. (2004b) The role of industrial fisheries and oceanographic change in the decline of North Sea black-legged kittiwakes. *Journal of Applied Ecology*, **41**, 1129–1139.

Frederiksen, M., Wright, P.J. Harris, M.P., Mavor, R.A., Heubeck, M. & Wanless, S. (2005) Regional patterns of kittiwake *Rissa tridactyla* breeding success are related to variability in sandeel recruitment. *Marine Ecology Progress Series*, **300**, 201–211.

Frid, C., Andonegi, E., Depestele, J., Judd, A., Rihan, D., Rogers, S.I. & Kenchington, E. (2012) The environmental interactions of tidal and wave energy generation devices. *Environmental Impact Assessment Review*, **32**, 133–139.

Friedlingstein, P., Cox, P., Betts, R., Bopp, L., von Bloh, W., Brovkin, V., Cadule, P., Doney, S., Eby, M., Fung, I., Bala, G., John, J., Jones, C., Joos, F., Kato, T., Kawamiya, M., Knorr, W., Lindsay, K., Matthews, H.D., Raddatz, T., Rayner, P., Reick, C., Roeckner, E., Schnitzler, K.-G., Schnur, R., Strassmann, K., Weaver, A.J., Yoshikawa, C. & Zang, N. (2006) Climate-carbon cycle feedback analysis: results from the C^4MIP model intercomparison. *Journal of Climate*, **19**, 3337–3353.

Fuhlendorf, S.D., Harrell, W.C., Engle, D.M., Hamilton, R.G., Davis, C.A. & Leslie, D.M. (2006) Should heterogeneity be the basis for conservation? Grassland bird response to fire and grazing. *Ecological Applications*, **16**, 1706–1716.

Fuller, R.J. & Rothery, P. (2010) Woodfuel management: prospects for reversing declines in woodland birds. *BOU Proceedings – Climate Change and Birds*. http://www.bou.org.uk/bouproc-net/ccb/fuller&rothery.pdf.

Furness, R.W. & Tasker, M.L. (2000) Seabird-fishery interactions: quantifying the sensitivity of seabirds to reductions in sandeel abundance, and identification of key areas for sensitive seabirds in the North Sea. *Marine Ecology Progress Series*, **202**, 253–264.

Galbraith, H., Jones, R., Park, R., Clough, J., Herrod-Julius, S., Harrington, B. & Page, G. (2002) Global climate change and sea level rise: potential losses of intertidal habitat for shorebirds. *Waterbirds*, **25**, 173–183.

García-Navas, V. & Sanz, J.J. (2010) The importance of a main dish: nestling diet and foraging behaviour in Mediterranean blue tits in relation to prey phenology. *Oecologia*, **165**, 639–649.

Gardali, T., Seavy, N.E., DiGaudio, R.T. & Comrack, L.A. (2012) A climate change vulnerability assessment of California's at-risk birds. *PLoS ONE*, **7**, e29507.

Gardarsson, A. & Einarsson, A. (1997) Numbers and production of Eurasian Wigeon in relation to conditions in a breeding area, Lake Myvatn, Iceland. *Journal of Animal Ecology*, **66**, 439–451.

Gaston, A.J., Gilchrist, H.G. & Hipfner, J.M. (2005) Climate change, ice conditions and reproduction in an Arctic nesting marine bird: Brunnich's guillemot (*Uria lomvia* L.). *Journal of Animal Ecology*, **74**, 832–841.

Gaston, A.J., Gilchrist, H.G., Mallory, M.L. & Smith, P.A. (2009) Changes in seasonal events, peak food availability, and consequent breeding adjustment in a marine bird: a case of progressive mismatching. *The Condor* **111**, 111–119.

Gaston, A.J. & Nettleship, D.N. (1981) *The Thick-Billed Murres of Prince Leopold Island*. Ottawa: Environment Canada.

Gaston, A.J. & Woo, K. (2008) Razorbills (*Alca torda*) follow subarctic prey into the Canadian Arctic: colonization results from climate change? *The Auk*, **125**, 939–942.

Gaston, K.J. (2003) *The Structure and Dynamics of Geographic Ranges*. Oxford, UK: Oxford University Press.

Gaston, K.J. & Blackburn, T.M. (2002) Large-scale dynamics in colonization and extinction for breeding birds in Britain. *Journal of Animal Ecology*, **71**, 390–399.

Gaston, K.J. & Chown, S.L. (1999) Why Rapoport's rule does not generalise. *Oikos*, **84**, 309–312.

Gaston, K.J. Jackson, S.F., Cantú-Salazar, L. & Cruz-Piñón, G. (2008) The ecological performance of protected areas. *Annual Reviewsof Ecology, Evolution and Systematics*, **39**, 93–113.

Gaston, K.J., Jackson, S.F., Nagy, A., Cantu-Salazar, L. & Johnson, M. (2008) Protected areas in Europe: principle and practice. *Annals of the New York Academy of Sciences*, **1134**, 97–119.

George, T.L., Fowler, A.C., Knight, R.L. & McEwen, L.C. (1992) Impacts of severe drought on grassland birds in Western North Dakota. *Ecological Applications*, **2**, 275–284.

Gershunov, A., Cayan, D.R. & Iacobellis, S.F. (2009) The great 2006 heat wave over California and Nevada: signal of an increasing trend. *Journal of Climate*, **22**, 6181–6203.

Geyer, J., Kiefer, I., Kreft, S., Chavez, V., Salafsky, N., Jeltsch, F. & Ibisch, P.L. (2011) Classification of climate-change-induced stresses on biological diversity. *Conservation Biology*, **25**, 708–715.

Gibb, J.A. (1960) Populations of tits and goldcrests and their food supply in pine plantations. *Ibis*, **102**, 163–208.

Gibbons, D.W., Amar, A., Anderson, G.Q.A., Bolton, M., Bradbury, R.B., Eaton, M.A., Evans, A.D., Grant, M.C., Gregory, R.D., Hilton, G.M., Hirons, G.J.M., Hughes, J., Johnstone, I., Newbury, P., Peach, W.J., Ratcliffe, N., Smith, J.W., Summers, R.W., Walton, P. & Wilson, J.D. (2007a) *The predation of wild birds in the UK: a review of its conservation impact and management*. RSPB Research Report no 23, RSPB: Sandy, UK.

Gibbons, D.W., Donald, P.F., Bauer, H.-G., Fornasari, L. & Dawson, I.K. (2007b) Mapping avian distributions: the evolution of bird atlases. *Bird Study*, **54**, 324–334.

Gibbons, D.W., Reid, J.B. & Chapman, R.A. (1993) *The New Atlas of Breeding Birds in Britain and Ireland: 1988–1991*. London, UK: Poyser.

Gibbons, D.W., Wilson, J.W. & Green, R.E. (2011) Using conservation science to solve conservation problems. *Journal of Applied Ecology*, **48**, 505–508.

Gibbons, D.W. & Wotton, S. (1996) The Dartford Warbler in the United Kingdom in 1994. *British Birds*, **89**, 203–212.

Gibbs, H. (2007) Climatic variation and breeding in the Australian Magpie (*Gymnorhina tibicen*): a case study using existing data. *Emu*, **107**, 284–293.

Gibbs, H.L. & Grant, P.R. (1987) Oscillating selection in Darwin's finches. *Nature*, **327**, 511–513.

Gibbs, H.L, Grant, P.R. & Weiland, J. (1984) Breeding of Darwin's finches at an unusually early age in an El Niño year. *The Auk*, **101**, 872–874.

Gibbs, H.K. & Herold, M. (2007) Tropical deforestation and greenhouse gas emissions. *Environmental Research Letters*, **2**, 045021.

Gienapp, P., Leimu, R. & Merilä, J. (2007) Responses to climate change in avian migration time – microevolution versus phenotypic plasticity. *Climate Research*, **35**, 25–35.

Gienapp, P., Teplitsky, C., Alho, J.S., Mills, J.A. & Merilä, J. (2008) Climate change and evolution: disentangling environmental and genetic responses. *Molecular Ecology*, **17**, 167–178.

Gilbert, G., Brown, A.F. & Wotton, S.R. (2010) Current dynamics and predicted vulnerability to sea-level rise of a threatened Bittern *Botaurus stellaris* population. *Ibis*, **152**, 580–589.

Gilbert, G., Tyler, G. & Smith, K.W. (2003) Nestling diet and fish preference of Bitterns *Botaurus stellaris* in Britain. *Ardea*, **91**, 35–44.

Gilbert, L. (2010) Altitudinal patterns of tick and host abundance: a potential role for climate change in regulating tick-borne diseases? *Oecologia*, **162**, 217–225.

Gilbert, M., Xiao, X., Pfeiffer, D.U., Epprescht, M., Boles, S. Czarnecki, C., Chaitaweesub, P., Kalpravidh, W., Minh, P.Q., Otte, M.J., Martin, V. & Slingenbergh, J. (2008) Mapping H5N1 highly pathogenic avian influenze risk in Southeast Asia. *Proceedings of the National Academy of Sciences USA*, **105**, 4769–4774.

Gilg, O., Hanski, I. & Sittler, B. (2003) Cyclic dynamics in a simple vertebrate predator-prey community. *Science*, **302**, 866–868,

Gilg, O., Sittler, B. & Hanski, I. (2009) Climate change and cyclic predator-prey population dynamics in the high Arctic. *Global Change Biology*, **15**, 2634–2652.

Gill, J.A., Alves, J.A., Sutherland, W.J., Appleton, G.F., Potts, P.M. & Gunnarsson, T.G. (2014) Why is the timing of bird migration advancing when individuals are not? *Proceedings of the Royal Society of London, Series B*, **281**, 20132161.

Gill, J.A., Norris, K. & Sutherland, W.J. (2001) The effects of disturbance on habitat use by black-tailed godwits *Limosa limosa*. *Journal of Applied Ecology*, **38**, 846–856.

Gill, J.A., Sutherland, W.J. & Watkinson, A.R. (1996) A method to quantify the effects of human disturbance on animal populations. *Journal of Applied Ecology*, **33**, 786–792.

Gillies, C.S. & St. Clair, C.C. (2008) Riparian corridors enhance movement of a forest specialist bird in fragmented forest. *Proceedings of the National Academy of Sciences USA*, **105**, 19774–19779.

Gillings, S. & Sutherland, W.J. (2007) Comparative diurnal and nocturnal diet and foraging in Eurasian Golden Plovers *Pluvialis apricaria* and Northern Lapwings *Vanellus vanellus* wintering on arable farmland. *Ardea*, **95**, 243–257.

Gilman, E., Ellison, J., & Coleman, R. (2007) Assessment of mangrove response to projected relative sea-level rise and recent historical reconstruction of shoreline position. *Environmental Monitoring Assessment*, **124**,105–130.

Ginn, H.B. & Melville, D.S. (1983) *Moult in Birds*. Tring, Hertfordshire, UK: British Trust for Ornithology.

Gjerdrum, C., Vallée, A.M.J., St. Clair, C.C., Bertram, D.F., Ryder, J.L. & Blackburn, G.S. (2003) Tufted puffin reproduction reveals ocean climate variability. *Proceedings of the National Academy of Sciences USA*, **100**, 9377–9382.

Godet, L., Jaffré, M. & Devictor, V. (2011) Waders in winter: long-term changes of migratory bird assemblages facing climate change. *Biology Letters*, **7**, 714–717.

Golawski, A. & Kasprzykowski, Z. (2010) The influence of weather on birds wintering in the farmlands of eastern Poland. *Ornis Fennica*, **87**, 153–159,

González-Varo, J.P., López-Bao, J.V. & Guitián, J. (2008) Presence and abundance of the Eurasian nuthatch *Sitta europaea* in relation to the size, isolation and the intensity of management of chesnut woodlands in the NW Iberian Peninsula. *Landscape Ecology*, **23**, 79–89.

Goodenough, A.E., Elliot, S.L. & Hart, A.G. (2009) The challenges of conservation for declining migrants: are reserve-based initiatives during the breeding season appropriate for the pied flycatcher *Ficedula hypoleuca*? *Ibis*, **151**, 429–439.

Goodenough, A.E., Hart, A.G. & Elliot, S.L. (2011) What prevents phenological adjustment to climate change in migrant bird species? Evidence against the 'arrival constraint' hypothesis. *International Journal of Biometeorology*, **55**, 97–102.

Goodman, R.E., Lebuhn, G., Seavy, N.E., Gardali, T. & Bluso-Demers, J.D. (2012) Avian body size changes and climate change: warming or increasing variability? *Global Climate Change*, **18**, 63–73.

Gordo, O. (2007) Why are bird migration dates shifting? A review of weather and climate effects on avian migratory phenology. *Climate Research*, **35**, 37–58.

Gordo, O., Brotons, L., Ferrer, X. & Comas, P. (2005) Do changes in climate patterns in wintering areas affect the timing of the spring arrival of trans-Saharan migrant birds? *Global Change Biology*, **11**, 12–21.

Gordo, O. & Sanz, J.J. (2006) Climate change and bird phenology: a long-term study in the Iberian Peninsula. *Global Change Biology*, **12**, 1993–2004.

Gosler, A.G., Greenwood, J.J.D. & Perrins, C. (1995) Predation risk and the cost of being fat. *Nature*, **377**, 621–623.

Goss-Custard, J.D. (1970) Dispersion in some overwintering wading birds. In *Social Behaviour in Birds and Mammals*. Crook, J.H. London, UK: Academic Press, pp. 3–35.

Goss-Custard, J.D. (1980) Competition for food and interference among waders. *Ardea*, **68**, 31–52.

Goss-Custard, J.D. & Moser, M.E. (1988) Rates of change in the numbers of dunlin, *Calidris alpina*, wintering in British estuaries in relation to the spread of *Spartina anglica*. *Journal of Applied Ecology*, **25**, 95–109.

Gove, B. & Bradbury, R. (2010) Potential impacts on birds of land-use change to supply growing UK bionmass demand. *Bou Proceedings – Climate Change and Birds*. http://www.bou.org.uk/bouprocnec/ccb/gove&bradbury.pdf

Grande, J.M., Serrano, D., Tavecchia, G., Carrete, M., Ceballos, O., Díaz-Delgado, R., Tella, J.L. & Donázar, J.A. (2008) Survival in a long-lived territorial migrant: effects of life-history traits and ecological conditions in wintering and breeding areas. *Oikos*, **118**, 580–590.

Grant, B.R. & Grant, P.R. (1993) Evolution of Darwin's finches caused by a rare climatic event. *Proceedings of the Royal Society of London, Series B*, **251**, 111–117.

Grant, M.C., Orsman, C., Easton, J., Lodge, C., Smith, M., Thompson, G., Rodwell, S. & Moore, N. (1999) Breeding success and causes of breeding failure of curlew *Numenius arquata* in Northern Ireland. *Journal of Applied Ecology*, **36**, 59–74.

Grant, M.C. & Pearce-Higgins, J.W. (2012) Spatial variation and habitat relationships in moorland bird assemblages: a British perspective. In *Birds and Habitat. Relationships in Changing Landscapes*. Fuller, R.J. Cambridge, UK: Cambridge University Press, pp. 207–236.

Grant, P.R., Grant, B.R., Keller, L.F. & Petren, K. (2000) Effects of El-Niño events on Darwin's finch productivity. *Ecology*, **81**, 2442–2457.

Grau, R.H. & Aide, M. (2008) Globalization and land-use changes in Latin America. *Ecology and Society*, **13**, 16.

Grecian, J.W., Inger, N., Attrill, M.J., Bearhop, S., Godley, B.J., Witt, M.J. & Votier, S.C. (2010) Potential impacts of wave-powered marine renewable energy installations on marine birds. *Ibis*, **152**, 683–697.

Green, R.E. (1995) Diagnosing causes of bird population declines. *Ibis*, **137**, S47–S55.

Green, R.E. (2002) Diagnosing causes of population declines and selecting remedial actions. In *Conserving Bird Biodiversity*. Norris, K. & Pain, D.J. Cambridge, UK: Cambridge University Press, pp. 139–156.

Green, R.E., Collingham, Y.C. Willis, S.G., Gregory, R.D. & Smith, K.W. (2008) Performance of climate envelope models in retrodicting recent changes in bird population size from observed climatic change. *Biology Letters*, **4**, 599–602.

Green, R.E., Cornell, S.J., Scharlemann, J.P.W. & Balmford, A. (2005) Farming and the fate of wild nature. *Science*, **307**, 550–555.

Green, R.E., Osborne, P.E. & Sears, E.J. (1994) The distribution of passerine birds in hedgerows during the breeding season in relation to characteristics of the hedgerow and adjacent farmland. *Journal of Applied Ecology*, **31**, 677–692.

Green, R.E. & Pearce-Higgins, J.W. (2010) Species management in the face of a changing climate. In *Species Management: Challenges and Solutions for the 21st Century*, Baxter, J.M. & Galbraith, C.A. Edinburgh, UK: TSO Scotland, pp. 517–536.

Green, R.E., Tyler, G.A. & Bowden, C.G.R. (2000) Habitat selection, ranging behaviour and diet of the stone curlew (*Burhinus oedicnemus*) in southern England. *Journal of Zoology (London)*, **250**, 161–183.

Greenberg, R. (1986) Competing in migrant birds in the nonbreeding season. *Current Ornithology*, **3**, 281–307.

Greenwood, J.D. & Baillie, S.R. (1991) Effects of density-dependence and weather on population changes of English passerines using a non-experimental paradigm. *Ibis*, **133 S1**, 121–133.

Gregory, R.D., Noble, D.G. & Custance, J. (2004) The state of play of farmland birds; population trends and conservation status of lowland farmland birds in the United Kingdom. *Ibis*, **145 S2**, 1–13.

Gregory, R.D., van Strien, A., Vorisek, P., Meyling, A.W.G., Noble, D.G., Foppen, R.P.B. & Gibbons, D.W. (2005) Developing indicators for European birds. *Philosophical Transactions of the Royal Society Series B*, **360**, 269–288.

Gregory, R.D., Vorisek, P., van Strien, A., Gmelig Meyling, A.W., Jiguet, F., Fornasari, L., Reif, J., Chylarecki, P. & Burfield, I.J. (2007) Population trends of widespread woodland birds in Europe. *Ibis*, **149 Suppl 2**, 78–97.

Gregory, R.D., Willis, S.G., Jiguet, F., Vořišek, P., Klvaňová, A., van Strien, A., Huntley, B., Collingham, Y.C., Couvet, D. & Green, R.E. (2009) An indicator of the impact of climatic change on European bird populations. *PLoS ONE*, **4**, e4678.

Griffin, L., Rees, E. & Hughes, B. (2010) Whooper swan *Cygns cygnus* migration in relation to offshore wind farms. *BOU Proceedings – Climate Change and Birds*. http://www.bou.org.uk/bouprocnec/ccb/Griffin-etal.pdf

Grosbois, V., Harris, M.P., Anker-Nilssen, T., McCleery, R.H., Shaw, D.N., Morgan, B.J.T. & Giminez, O. (2009) Modelling survival at multi-population scales using mark-recapture data. *Ecology*, **90**, 2922–2932.

Grosbois, V., Henry, P.-Y., Blonden, J., Perret, P., Lebreton, J.-D., Thomas, D.W. & Lambrechts, M.M. (2006) Climate impacts on Mediterranean blue tit survival: an investigation across seasons and spatial scales. *Global Change Biology*, **12**, 2235–2249.

Grosbois, V. & Thompson, P.M. (2005) North Atlantic climate variation influences survival in adult fulmars. *Oikos*, **109**, 273–290.

Gross, S.J. & Price, T.D. (2000) Determinants of the northern and southern range limits of a warbler. *Journal of Biogeography*, **27**, 869–878.

Grøtan, V., Sæther, B.-E., Engen, S., van Balen, J.H., Perdeck, A.C. & Visser, M.E. (2009) Spatial and temporal variation in the relative contribution of density dependence, climate variation and migration to fluctuations in the size of great tit populations. *Journal of Animal Ecology*, **78**, 447–459.

Groves, S. (1978) Age-related differences in Ruddy Turnstone foraging and aggressive behaviour. *The Auk*, **95**, 95–103.

Gruar, D., Peach, W. & Taylor, R. (2003) Summer diet and body condition of song thrushes in stable and declining farmland populations. *Ibis*, **145**, 637–649.

Guilhaumon, F., Gimenez, O., Gaston, K.J. & Mouillot, D. (2008) Taxonomic and regional uncertainty in species-area relationships and the identification of richness hotspots. *Proceedings of the National Academy of Sciences USA*, **105**, 15458–15463.

Gunnarsson, T.G., Gill, J.A., Atkinson, P.W., Gélinaud, G., Potts, P.M., Croger, R.E., Gudmundsson, G.A., Appleton, G.F. & Sutherland, W.J. (2006) Population-scale drivers of individual arrival times in migratory birds. *Journal of Animal Ecology*, **75**, 1119–1127.

Gunnarsson, T.G., Waldenström, J. & Fransson, T. (2012) Direct and indirect effects of winter harshness on the survival of Mallards *Anas platyrhynchos* in northwest Europe. *Ibis*, **154**, 307–317.

Gwinner, E. (1996) Circannual clocks in avian reproduction and migration. *Ibis*, **138**, 47–63.

Hadfield, J.D., Wilson, A.J., Garant, D., Sheldon, B.C. & Kruuk, L.E.B. (2010) The misuse of BLUP in ecology and evolution. *American Naturalist*, **175**, 116–125.

Hagemeijer, E.J.M. & Blair, M.J. (1997) *The EBCC Atlas of European Breeding Birds: Their Distribution and Abundance*. London, UK: T & AD Poyser.

Hake, M., Dahlgren, T., Åhlund, M., Lindberg, P. & Eriksson, M.O.G. (2005) The impact of water fluctuation on the breeding success of the black-throated diver *Gavia arctica* in southwest Sweden. *Ornis Fennica*, **82**, 1–12.

Halupka, L., Dyrcz, A. & Borowiec, M. (2008) Climate change affects breeding of reed warblers *Acrocephalus scirpaceus*. *Journal of Avian Biology*, **39**, 95–100.

Hall, K.S.S. & Fransson, T. (2000) Lesser whitethroats under time-constraint moult more rapidly and grow shorter wing feathers. *Journal of Avian Biology*, **31**, 583–587.

Halonen, M., Mapes, T., Meri, T. & Suhonen, J. (2007) Influence of snow cover on food hoarding in Pygmy Owls *Glaucidium passerinum*. *Ornis Fennica*, **84**, 105–111.

Halpin, P.N. (1997) Global climate change and natural-area protection: management responses and research directions. *Ecological Applications*, **7**, 828–843.

Hancock, M. (2000) Artificial floating islands for nesting Black-throated Divers *Gavia arctica*. Scotland: construction, use and effect on breeding success. *Bird Study*, **47**, 165–175.

Hancock, M. (2008) An exceptional *Calluna vulgaris* winter die-back event, Abernethy Forest, Scottish Highlands. *Plant Ecology & Diversity*, **1**, 89–103.

Hancock, M.H., Grant, M.C. & Wilson, J.D. (2009) Associations between distance to forest and spatial and temporal variation in abundance of key peatland breeding bird species. *Bird Study*, **56**, 53–64.

Hannah, L., Midgley, G., Hughes, G. & Bomhard, B. (2005) The view from the cape: Extinction risk, protected areas and climate change. *Bioscience*, **55**, 231–242.

Hannon, S.J. & Schmiegelow, F.K.A. (2002) Corridors may not improve the conservation value of small reserves for most boreal birds. *Ecological Applications*, **12**, 1457–1468.

Hanski, I. (1999) *Metapopulation Ecology*. Oxford, UK: Oxford University Press.

Hanksi, I. & Gilpin, M.E. (1997) *Metapopulation Biology: Ecology, Genetics and Evolution*. San Diego, CA: Academic Press.

Harris, M.P., Anker-Nilssen, T., McCleery, R.H., Erikstad, K.E., Shaw, D.N. & Grosbois, V. (2005a) Effect of wintering area and climate on the survival of adult Atlantic Puffins *Fratercula arctica* in the eastern Atlantic. *Marine Ecology Progress Series*, **297**, 283–296.

Harris, M.P., Buckland, S.T., Russell, S.M. & Wanless, S. (1994) Year- and age-related variation in the survival of adult European shags over a 24-year period. *The Condor*, **96**, 600–605.

Harris, M.P. & Wanless, S. (1985) Fish fed to young guillemots, *Uria aalge*, and used in display on the Isle of May, Scotland. *Journal of Zoology (London)*, **207**, 441–458.

Harris, M.P., Wanless, S., Murray, S. & Mackley, E. (2005b) *Isle of May Seabird Studies in 2004*. JNCC Report no. 375. Peterborough/Banchory, UK: JNCC/CEH.

Hastie, T. & Tibshirani, R. (1990) *Generalized Additive Models*. London, UK: Chapman and Hall.

Hau, M. (2001) Timing of breeding in variable environments: tropical birds as model systems. *Hormones and Behaviour*, **40**, 281–290.

Hau, M., Wikelski, M. & Wingfield, J.C. (1998) A neotropical forest bird can measure the slight changes in tropical photoperiod. *Proceedings of the Royal Society of London, Series B*, **265**, 89–95.

Hawkins, B.A., Diniz-Filho, J.A.F., Jaramillo, C.A. & Soeller S.A. (2007) Climate, niche conservatism, and the global bird diversity gradient. *American Naturalist*, **170**, S16–S27.

Hawkins, B. A., Field, R., Cornell, H. V., Currie, D.J., Guégan, J.-F., Kaufman, D.M., Kerr, J.T., Mittelbach, G.G., Oberdorff, T., O'Brien, E.M., Porter, E.E. & Turner, J.R.G. (2003) Energy, water and broad-scale geographic patterns of species richness. *Ecology*, **84**, 3105–3117.

Hawkins, B.A. & Porter, E.E. (2003) Does herbivore diversity depend on plant diversity? The case of California butterflies. *American Naturalist*, **161**, 40–49.

Heaton, R.J., Randerson, P.F. & Slater, F.M. (1999) The economics of growing short rotation coppice in the uplands of mid-Wales and an economic comparison with sheep production. *Biomass and Bioenergy*, **17**, 59–71.

Hedd, A., Bertram, D.F., Ryder, J.L. & Jones, I.L. (2006) Effects of interdecadal climate variability on marine trophic interactions: rhinoceros auklets and their fish prey. *Marine Ecology Progress Series*, **309**, 263–278.

Heldberg, H. & Fox, A.D. (2008) Long-term population declines in Danish trans-Saharan migrant birds. *Bird Study*, **55**, 267–279.

Heller, N.E. & Zavaleta, E.S. (2009) Biodiversity management in the face of climate change: a review of 22 years of recommendations. *Biological Conservation*, **142**, 14–32.

Helm, B. & Gwinner, E. (2005) Carry-over effects of day length during spring migration. *Journal of Ornithology*, **146**, 348–354.

Hemborg, C., Sanz, J. & Lundberg, A. (2001) Effect of latitude between the trade-off between reproduction and moult: a long-term study with pied flycatcher. *Oecologia*, **129**, 206–212.

Henderson, I.G., Holland, J.M., Storkey, J., Lutman, P., Orson, J. & Simper, J. (2012) Effects of the proportion and spatial arrangement of un-cropped land on breeding bird abundance in arable rotations. *Journal of Applied Ecology*, **49**, 883–891.

Henry, A.C., Hosack, D.A., Johnson, C.W., Rol, D. & Bentrup, G. (1999) Conservation corridors in the United States: benefits and planning guidelines. *Journal of Soil and Water Conservation*, **54**, 645–650.

Herkert, J.R. (1994) The effects of habitat fragmentation on Midwestern grassland bird communities. *Ecological Applications*, **4**, 461–471.

Herkert, J.R., Reinking, D.L., Wiedenfeld, D.A., Winter, M., Zimmerman, J.L., Jensen, W.E., Finck, E.J., Korford, R.R., Wolfe, D.H., Sherrod, S.K., Jenkins, M.A., Faaborg, J. & Robinson, S.K. (2003) Effects of prairie fragmentation on the nest success of breeding birds in the midcontinental United States. *Conservation Biology*, **17**, 587–594.

Herremans, M. (2004) Effects of drought on birds in the Kalahari, Botswana. *Ostrich*, **75**, 217–227.

Hersteinsson, P. & MacDonald, D.W. (1994) Interspecific competition and the geographical distribution of red and arctic foxes *Vulpes vulpes* and *Alopex lagopus*. *Oikos*, **64**, 505–515.

Hewson, C.M. & Noble, D.G. (2009) Population trends of breeding birds in British woodlands over a 32-year period: relationships with food, habitat use and migratory behaviour. *Ibis*, **151**, 464–486.

Hickling, R., Roy, D.B., Hill, J.K., Fox, R. & Thomas, C.D. (2006) The distributions of a wide range of taxonomic groups are expanding polewards. *Global Change Biology*, **12**, 450–455.

Higgins, P.J. (1999) *Handbook of Australian, New Zealand and Antarctic Birds, Vol 4: Parrots to Dollarbird*: Melbourne, Australia: Oxford University Press.

Hiley, J.R., Bradbury, R.B., Holling, M. & Thomas, C.D. (2013) Protected areas act as establishment centres for species colonising the United Kingdom. *Proceedings of the Royal Society of London, Series B*, **280**, 1760 20122310.

Hill, D. & Arnold, R. (2012) Building the evidence base for ecological impact assessment and mitigation. *Journal of Applied Ecology*, **49**, 6–9.

Hill, E.L. & Wright, K.G. (2000) Harlequin duck breeding distribution and hydroelectric operations on the Bridge River, British Columbia. In Darling, L.M. *Proceedings of a Conference on the Biology and Management of Species and Habitats at Risk, Kamloops, B.C., 15 – 19 Feb., 1999. Volume One*. Kamloops, B.C., Canada: Ministry of Environment, Lands and Parks, Victoria, B.C. and University College of the Cariboo, pp. 449–455.

Hill, M.O. (2011) Local frequency as a key to interpreting species occurrence data when recording effort is not known. *Methods in Ecology and Evolution*, **3**, 195–205.

Hinchee, M., Rottmann, W., Mullinax, L., Zhang, C., Chang, S., Cunningham, M., Pearson, L. & Mehra, N. (2009) Short-rotation woody crops for bioenergy and biofuels applications. *In Vitro Cellular and Developmental Biology – Plant*, **45**, 619–629.

Hinke, J.T., Salwicka, K., Trivelpiece, S.G., Watters, G.M. & Trivelpiece, W.Z. (2007) Divergent responses in Pygoscelis penguins reveal a common environmental driver. *Oecologia*, **153**, 845–855.

Hinsley, S.A. & Bellamy, P.E. (2001) The influence of hedge structure, management and landscape context on the value of hedgerows to birds: a review. *Journal of Environmental Management*, **60**, 33–49.

Hinsley, S.A., Bellamy, P.E., Newton, I. & Sparks, T.H. (1995) Habitat and landscape factors influencing presence of individual breeding bird species in woodland fragments. *Journal of Avian Biology*, **26**, 94–104.

Hinsley, S.A., Dogerty Jr, P.F., Bellamy, P.E. & Grubb Jr, T.C. (2006) Consequences of habitat fragmentation for birds: comparison between Europe and North America. *Current Zoology*, **52**, S187–190.

Hinsley, S.A., Rothery, P. & Bellamy, P.E. (1999) Influence of woodland area on breeding success in Great Tits *Parus major* and Blue Tits *Parus caeruleus*. *Journal of Avian Biology*, **30**, 271–281.

Hipfner, J.M. (2008) Matches and mismatches: ocean climate, prey phenology and breeding success in a zooplanktivorous seabird. *Marine Ecology Progress Series*, **368**, 295–304.

Hipfner, J.M., Adams, P.A., & Bryant, R. (2000) Breeding success of black-legged kittiwakes, *Rissa tridactyla*, at a colony in Labrador during a period of low capelin, *Mallotus villosus*, availability. *Canadian Field-Naturalist*, **114**, 413–416.

Hirons, G. (2010) Replacing Ouse Wash habitats. In *RSPB Reserves 2010*. Gilbert, J. & Ausden, M. Sandy, Beds, UK: Royal Society for the Protection of Birds, pp. 26–29.

Hirota, M., Nobre, C., Oyama, M.D. & Bustamante, M.M.C. (2010) The climate sensitivity of the forest, savannah and forest-savanna transition in tropical South America. *New Phytologist*, **187**, 707–719.

Hitch, A.T. & Leberg, P.L. (2007) Breeding distributions of North American bird species moving north as a result of climate change. *Conservation Biology*, **21**, 534–539.

Hobbs, R.J. (1992) The role of corridors in conservation: solution or bandwagon? *Trends in Ecology and Evolution*, **7**, 389–391.

Hochachka, W.M. & Dhondt, A.A. (2000) Density-dependent decline of host abundance resulting from a new infectious disease. *Proceedings of the National Academy of Science USA*, **97**, 5303–5306.

Hockey, P.A.R., Sirami, C., Ridley, A.R., Midgley, G.F. & Babiker, H.A. (2011) Interrogating recent range changes in South African birds: confounding signals from and use and climate change present a challenge for attribution. *Diversity and Distributions*, **17**, 254–261.

Hodgson, J.A., Thomas, C.D., Wintle, B.A. & Moilanen, A. (2009) Climate change, connectivity and conservation decision making: back to basics. *Journal of Applied Ecology*, **46**, 964–969.

Hoegh-Guldberg, O., Hughes, L., McIntyre, S., Lindenmayer, D.B., Parmesan, C., Possingham, H.P. & Thomas, C.D. (2008) Assisted colonization and rapid climate change. *Science*, **321**, 345–346.

Hofmann, R.J., Reichle, R.A., Siniff, D.B. & Muller-Schwarze, D. (1977) The leopard seal (Hydrurga leptonyx) at Palmer Station, Antarctica. In *Adaptations within Antarctic Ecosystems*. Llano, G.A. Washington, DC: Smithsonian Institution, pp. 769–782.

Hoffman, M., Hilton-Taylor, C., Angulo, A. et al. (2010) The impact of conservation on the status of the world's vertebrates. *Science*, **330**, 1503–1509.

Hogstad, O. (2005) Numerical and functional responses of breeding passerine species to mass occurrence of geometrid caterpillars in a subalpine bird forest: a 30-year study. *Ibis*, **147**, 77–91.

Hogstad, O., Selås, V. & Kobro, S. (2003) Explaining annual fluctuations in breeding density of fieldfares *Turdus pilaris* – combined influences of factors operating during breeding, migration and wintering. *Journal of Avian Biology*, **34**, 350–354.

Hogstad, O. & Stenberg, I. (1997) Breeding success, nestling diet and parental care in the White-backed Woodpecker *Dendrocopos leucotos*. *Journal of Ornithology*, **138**, 25–38.

Holden, J., Shotbolt, L., Bonn, A., Burt, T.P., Chapman, P.J., Douill, A.J., Fraser, E.D.G., Hubacek, K., Kirkby, M.J., Reed, M.S., Preli, C., Stagl, S., Stringer, L.C., Turner, A. & Worrall, F. (2007) Environmental change in moorland landscapes. *Earth-Science Reviews*, **82**, 75–100.

Hole, D.G., Willis, S.G., Pain, D.J., Fishpool, L.D., Butchart, S.H.M., Collingham, Y.C., Rahbek, C. & Huntley, B. (2009) Projected impacts of climate change on a continent-wide protected area network. *Ecology Letters*, **12**, 420–431.

Hole, D.G., Huntley, B., Collingham, Y.C., Fishpool, L.D.C., Pain, D.J., Butchart, S.H.M. & Willis, S.G. (2011) Towards a management framework for protected area networks in the face of climate change. *Conservation Biology*, **25**, 305–315.

Holland, P.K. & Yalden, D.W. (1991) Population dynamics of common sandpipers *Actitis hypoleucos* breeding along an upland river system. *Bird Study*, **38**,151–159.

Holland, P.K. & Yalden, D.W. (1995) Who lives and who dies? The impact of severe April weather on breeding common sandpipers *Actitis hypoleucos*. *Ringing and Migration*, **16**, 121–123.

Holmes, R.T. (2007) Understanding population change in migratory songbirds: long-term and experimental studies of Neotropical migrants in breeding and wintering areas. *Ibis*, **149 S2**, 2–13.

Holmes, R.T. & Sherry, T.W. (2001) Thirty-year bird population trends in an unfragmented temperate deciduous forest: Importance of habitat change. *The Auk*, **118**, 589–609.

Holt, S., Whitfield, D.P., Duncan, K., Rae, S. & Smith, R.D. (2002) Mass loss in incubating Eurasian dotterel: adaptation or constraint? *Journal of Avian Biology*, **33**, 219–224.

Hooten, M.B., Wikle, C.K., Dorazio, R.M. & Royale, J.A. (2007) Hierarchical spatiotemporal matrix models for characterizing invasions. *Biometrics*, **63**, 558–567.

Hörnfeld, B. (2004) Long-term decline in numbers of cyclic voles in boreal Sweden: analysis and presentation of hypotheses. *Oikos*, **107**, 376–392.

Hoset, K.S., Espmark, Y., Moksnes, A., Haughan, T., Ingebrigtsen, M. & Lier, M. (2004) Effect of ambient temperature on food provisioning and reproductive success in snow buntings *Plectrophenax nivalis* in the high arctic. *Ardea*, **92**, 239–246.

Hosseini, P.R., Dhondt, A.A. & Dobson, A. (2004) Seasonality and wildlife disease: how seasonal birth, aggregation and variation in immunity affect the dynamics of *Mycoplasma gallisepticum* in house finches. *Proceedings of the Royal Society of London, Series B*, **271**, 2569–2577.

Hötker, H. (2006) *The Impact of Repowering of Wind Farms on Birds and Bats*. Michael-Otto-Institut imNABU, Bergenhusen.

Hötker, H., Thomsen, K.-M., Jeromin, H. (2006) *Impacts on Biodiversity of Exploitation of Renewable Energy Sources: The Example of Birds and Bats*. Michael-Otto-Institut imNABU, Bergenhusen.

Høye, T.T. & Forchhammer, M.C. (2008) Phenology of High-Arctic arthropods: effects of climate on spatial, seasonal and inter-annual variation. *Advances in Ecological Research*, **40**, 299–324.

Høye, T.T., Post, E., Meltofte, H., Schmidt, N.M. & Forchhammer, M.C. (2007) Rapid advancement of spring in the High Arctic. *Current Biology*, **17**, 449–451.

Hubálek, H. (2003) Spring migration of birds in relation to North Atlantic Oscillation. *Folia Zoologica*, **52**, 287–298.

Hudson, P.J. (1992) *Grouse in Space and Time*. Fordingbridge, UK: Game Conservancy Trust.

Hudson, P.J., Cattadori, I.M., Boag, M. & Dobson, A.P. (2006) Climate disruption and parasite-host dynamics: patterns and processes associated with warming and the frequency of extreme climatic events. *Journal of Helminthology*, **80**, 175–182.

Hughes, R.G. (2004) Climate change and loss of saltmarshes: consequences for birds. *Ibis*, **146 S1**, 21–28.

Hulme, M.F., Vickery, J.A., Green, R.A., Phalan, B., Chamberlain, D.E., Pomeroy, D.E., Nalwonga, D., Katebaka, R. & Atkinson, P.W. (2013) Conserving the birds of Uganda's Banana-Coffee Arc: land sparing and land sharing compared. *PLoS ONE*, **8**, e54597.

Hulme, P.E. (2005) Adapting to climate change: is there scope for ecological management in the face of a global threat? *Journal of Applied Ecology*, **42**, 784–794.

Huntley, B., Altwegg, R., Barnard, P., Collingham, Y.C. & Hole, D.C. (2012) Modelling relationships between species spatial abundance patterns and climate. *Global Ecology and Biogeography*, **21**, 668–681.

Huntley, B., Barnard, P., Altwegg, R., Chambers, L., Coetzee, B.W.T., Gibson L., Hockey, P.A.R., Hole, D.G., Midgley, G.F., Underhill, L.G. & Willis, S.G. (2010) Beyond bioclimatic envelopes: dynamic species' range and abundance modelling in the context of climatic change. *Ecography*, **33**, 621–626.

Huntley, B. & Baxter, B. (2003) Insights on synergies: Models and methods. In *Climate Change and Biodiversity: Synergistic Impacts*. Hannah, L. & Lovejoy, T.E. Washington, DC: Conservation International, pp. 15–23.

Huntley, B., Collingham, Y.C., Willis, S.G. & Green, R.E. (2008) Potential impacts of climatic change on European breeding birds. *PLoS ONE*, **3**, e1439.

Huntley, B., & Green, R.E. (2011) Bioclimate models of the distributions of Gyrfalcons and ptarmigan. In *Gyrfalcons and Ptarmigan in a Changing World*. Watson, R.T., Cade, T.J., Fuller, M., Hunt, G. & Potapov, E. Boise, ID, USA: Peregrine Fund.

Huntley, B., Green, R.E., Collingham, Y.C. & Willis, S.G. (2007) *A Climatic Atlas of European Breeding Birds*. Barcelona, Spain: Lynx Edicions.

Huntley, B., Green, R.E., Collingham, Y.C., Hill, J.K., Willis, S.G., Bartlein, P.J., Cramer, W., Hagemeijer, W.J.M. & Thomas, C.J. (2004) The performance of models relating species geographical distributions to climate is independent of trophic level. *Ecology Letters*, **7**, 417–426.

Hüppop, O., Dierschke, J. Exo, K.-M., Frederich, E. & Hill, R. (2006) Bird migration studies and potential collision risk with offshore wind turbines. *Ibis*, **148**, 90–109.

Hüppop, O. & Hüppop, K. (2003) North Atlantic Oscillation and timing of spring migration in birds. *Proceedings of the Royal Society of London, Series B*, **270**, 233–240.

Hüppop, O. & Winkel, W. (2006) Climate change and timing of spring migration in the long-distance migrant *Ficedula hypoleuca* in central Europe: The role of spatially different temperature changes along migration routes. *Journal of Ornithology*, **147**, 344–353.

Hurrell, J.W. (1995) Decadal trends in the North Atlantic Oscillation: regional temperatures and precipitation. *Science*, **269**, 676–679.

Hurrell, J.W., Kushnir, Y., Ottersen, G. & Visbeck, M. (2003) An overview of the North Atlantic Oscillation. *Geophysical Monographs*, **134**, 1–35.

Hurrell, J.W., Kushnir, Y. & Viskeck, M. (2001) The North Atlantic Oscillation. *Science*, **291**, 603–606.

Hurrell, J.W. & Trenberth, K.E. (2010) Climate Change. In *Effects of Climate Change on Birds*. Møller, A.P., Fiedler, W. & Berthold, P. Oxford, UK: Oxford University Press, pp. 9–29.

Husby, A., Kruuk, L.E.B. & Visser, M.E. (2009) Decline in the frequency and benefits of multiple brooding in great tits as a consequence of a changing environment. *Proceedings of the Royal Society of London, Series B*, **276**, 1845–1854.

Husby, A., Visser, M.E. & Kruuk, L.E.B. (2011) Speeding up microevolution: the effects of increasing temperature on selection and genetic variance in a wild bird population. *PLoS Biology*, **9**, e1000585.

Hušek, J. & Adamík, P. (2008) Long-term trends in the timing of breeding and brood size in the Red-backed Shrike *Lanius collurio* in the Czech Republic, 1964–2004. *Journal of Ornithology*, **149**, 97–103.

Hussell, D.J.T. (1972) Factors affecting clutch size in arctic passerines. *Ecological Monographs*, **42**, 317–364.

Hutchinson, G. E. (1959) Homage to Santa Rosalia, or why are there so many kinds of animals? *American Naturalist*, **93**, 145–159.

Hyrenbach, K.D. & Veit, R.R. (2003) Ocean warming and seabird communities of the southern California Current System (1987–1998): response at multiple temporal scales. *Deep Sea Research Part II: Topical Studies in Oceanography*, **50**, 2537–2565.

IEEM (2010) *Guidelines for ecological impact assessment in Britain and Ireland. Marine and Coastal*. IEEM. http://www.ieem.net/docs/Final%20EcIA%20Marine%2001%20Dec%202010.pdf

Impey, A.J., Cote, I.M. & Jones, C.G. (2002) Population recovery of the threatened endemic Rodrigues fody *Foudia flavicans* (Aves, Ploceidae) following reforestation. *Biological Conservation*, **107**, 299–305.

Ims, R.A. & Fuglei, E. (2005) Trophic interaction cycles in tundra ecosystems and the impact of climate change. *Bioscience*, **55**, 311–322.

Ims, R.A., Henden, J.A. & Killengreen, S.T. (2008) Collapsing population cycles. *Trends in Ecology and Evolution*, **23**, 79–86.

Inchausti, P., Guinet, C., Koudil, M., Durbex, J.-P., Barbraud, C., Weimerskirch, H., Cherel, Y. & Jourentin, P. (2003) Inter-annual variability in the breeding performance of seabirds in relation to oceanographic anomalies that affect the Crozet and the Kerguelen sectors of the Southern Ocean. *Journal of Avian Biology*, **34**, 170–176.

Inchausti, P. & Weimerskirch, H. (2001) Risks of decline and extinction of the endangered Amsterdam albatross and the projected impact of long-line fisheries. *Biological Conservation*, **100**, 377–386.

Inger, R., Attrill, M.J., Bearhop, S., Broderick, A.C., Grecian, W.J., Hodgson, D.J., Mills, C., Sheehan, E., Votier, S.C., Witt, M.J. & Godley, B.J. (2009) Marine renewable energy: potential benefits to biodiversity? An urgent call for research. *Journal of Applied Ecology*, **46**, 1145–1153.

Inouye, D.W., Barr, B., Armitage, K.B. & Inouye, B.D. (2000) Climate change is affecting altitudinal migrants and hibernating species. *Proceedings of the Academy Natural Sciences USA*, **97**, 1630–1633.

Insley, H., Peach, W., Swann, B. & Etheridge, B. (1997) Survival rates of redshank *Tringa totanus* wintering on the Moray Firth. *Bird Study*, **44**, 277–289.

IPCC (2000) *Special Report on Emissions Scenarios, Working Group III, Intergovernmental Panel on Climate Change (IPCC)*: Cambridge, UK: Cambridge University Press.

IPCC (2007a) *Climate Change 2007: Synthesis Report*. Contribution of Working Groups I, II and III to the Fourth Assessment Report of the Intergovernmental Panel on Climate Change. Geneva, Switzerland: IPCC.

IPCC (2007b) *Climate Change 2007: Working Group I: The Physical Science Basis*. Contribution of Working Group I to the Fourth Assessment Report of the Intergovernmental Panel on Climate Change. Cambridge, UK and New York: Cambridge University Press.

IPCC (2007c) *Climate Change 2007: Working Group II: Impacts, Adaptation and Vulnerability*. Contribution of Working Group II to the Fourth Assessment Report of the Intergovernmental Panel on Climate Change. Cambridge, UK and New York: Cambridge University Press.

IPCC (2007d) *Climate Change 2007: Working Group III: Mitigation of Climate Change*. Contribution of Working Group III to the Fourth Assessment Report of the Intergovernmental Panel on Climate Change. Cambridge, UK and New York: Cambridge University Press.

IPCC (2011) *IPCC Special Report on Renewable Energy Sources and Climate Change Mitigation*. Cambridge, UK and New York: Cambridge University Press.

Irons, D.B., Anker-Nilssen, T., Gaston, A.J., Byrd, G.V., Gilchrist, G., Hario, M., Hjernquist, M., Krasnov, Y.V., Mosbech, A., Olsen, B., Petersen, A., Reid, J.B., Robertson, G.J., Strøm, H. & Wohl, K.D. (2008) Fluctuations in circumpolar seabird populations linked to climate oscillations. *Global Change Biology*, **14**, 1455–1463.

Ise, T., Dunn, A.L., Wofsy, S.C. & Moorcroft, P.R. (2009) High sensitivity of peat decomposition to climate change through water-table feedback. *Nature Geoscience*, **1**, 763–766.

Jager, H.I., Baskaran, L.M., Brandt, C.C., Davis, E.B., Gunderson, C.A. & Wullschelger, S.D. (2010) Emperical geographical modelling of switchgrass yields in the United States. *Global Change Biology Bioenergy*, **2**, 248–257.

Jagtap, T.G. & Nagle, V.L. (2007) Response and adaptability of mangrove habitats from the Indian Subcontinent to changing climate. *AMBIO*, **36**, 328–334.

Jaksic, F.M., Silva, S.I., Meserve, P.L. & Gutiérrez, J.R. (1997) A long-term study of vertebrate predator responses to an El Niño (ENSO) disturbance in western South America. *Oikos*, **78**, 341–354.

Jansen, R. & Crowe, T.M. (2005) Relationship between breeding activity and rainfall for Swainson's Spurfowl, *Pternistis swainsonii*, within southern Africa, with specific reference to the Springbok Flats, Limpopo Province, South Africa. *Ostrich*, **76**, 190–194.

Jenkins, A.R., Smallie, J.J. & Diamond, M. (2010) Avian collisions with power lines: a global review of causes and mitigation with a South African perspective. *Bird Conservation International*, **20**, 263–278.

Jenkins, G., Murphy, J.M., Sexton, D.H.M., Lowe, J.A., Jones, P. & Kilsby, C.G. (2009) *UK Climate Projections: Briefing Report*. Exeter, UK: Met Office Hadley Centre.

Jenkins, G., Perry, M. & Prior, J. (2008) *The Climate of the UK and Recent Trends*. Exeter, UK: Met Office Hadley Centre.

Jenni, L. & Kéry, M. (2003) Timing of autumn bird migration under climate change: advances in long-distance migrants, delays in short-distance migrants. *Proceedings of the Royal Society of London, Series B*, **270**, 1467–1471.

Jenni, L. & Schaub, M. (2003) Behavioural and physiological reactions to environmental variation in bird migration: a review. In *Avian Migration*. Berthold, P., Gwinner, E. & Sonneschein, E. Berlin Heidelberg, Germany and New York: Springer, pp. 155–171.

Jenouvrier, S., Barbraud, C., Cazelles, B. & Weimerskirch, H. (2005a) Modelling population dynamics of seabirds: importance of the effects of climate fluctuations on breeding proportions. *Oikos*, **108**, 511–522.

Jenouvrier, S., Barbraud, C. & Weimerskirch, H. (2003) Effects of climate variability on the temporal population dynamics of southern fulmars. *Journal of Animal Ecology*, **72**, 576–587.

Jenouvrier, S., Barbraud, C. & Weimerskirch, H. (2005b) Long-term contrasted responses to climate of two Antarctic seabird species. *Ecology*, **86**, 2889–2903.

Jenouvrier, S., Barbraud, C. & Weimerskirch, H. (2006) Sea ice affects the population dynamics of Adélie penguins in Terre Adélie. *Polar Biology*, **29**, 413–423.

Jenouvrier, S., Caswell, H., Barbraud, C., Holland, M., Strœve, J. & Weimerskirch, H. (2009) Demographic models and IPCC climate projections predict the decline of an emperor penguin population. *Proceedings of the National Academy of Sciences USA*, **106**, 1844–1847.

Jenouvrier, S., Holland, M., Strœve, J., Barbraud, C., Wemerskirch, H., Serreze, M. & Caswell, H. (2012) Effects of climate change on an emperor penguin population: analysis of coupled demographic and climate models. *Global Change Biology*, **18**, 2756–2770.

Jetz, W. & Fine, P.V.A. (2012) Global gradients in vertebrate diversity predicted by historical area-productivity dynamics and contemporary environment. *PLoS Biology*, **10**, e1001292.

Jetz, W. & Rahbek, C. (2001) Geometric constraints explain much of the species richness pattern in African birds. *Proceedings of the National Academy of Sciences USA*, **98**, 5661–5666.

Jetz, W., Rahbek, C. & Colwell, R.K. (2004) The coincidence of rarity and richness and the potential signature of history in centres of endemism. *Ecology Letters*, **7**, 1180–1191.

Jetz, W., Thomas, G.H., Job, J.B., Hartmann, K. & Mooers, A.O. (2012) The global diversity of birds in space and time. *Nature*, **491**, 444–448.

Jetz, W., Wilcove, D.S. & Dobson, A.P. (2007) Projected impacts of climate and land-use change on the global diversity of birds. *PLoS Biology*, **5**, e157.

Jiguet, F., Devictor, V., Ottvall, R., Van Turnhout, C., Van der Jeugd, H. & Lindström, Å. (2010) Bird population trends are linearly affected by climate change along species thermal ranges. *Proceedings of the Royal Society of London, Series B*, **277**, 3601–3608.

Jiguet, F., Gadot, A.-S., Julliard, R., Newson, S.E. & Couvet, D. (2007) Climate envelope, life history traits and the resilience of birds facing global change. *Global Change Biology*, **13**, 1672–1684.

Johnson, D. & Igl, L. (2001) Area requirements of grassland birds: a regional perspective. *The Auk*, **118**, 24–34.

Johnson, E.I., Stouffer, P.C. & Bierregaard, R.O. (2012) The phenology of molting, breeding and their overlap in central Amazonian birds. *Journal of Avian Biology*, **43**, 141–154.

Johnson, G.D., Erickson, W.P., Strickland, M.D., Shepherd, M.F., Shepherd, D.A. & Sarappo, S.A. (2002) Collision mortality of local and migrant birds at a large-scale wind-power development on Buffalo Ridge, Minnesota. *Wildlife Society Bulletin*, **30**, 879–887.

Johnson, G.D., Strickland, M.D., Erickson, W.P. & Young, D.P. (2007) Use of data to develop mitigation measures for wind power development impacts on birds. *Birds and Wind Farms*. de Lucas, M., Janss, G.F.E. & Ferrer, M. Madrid, Spain: Quercus, pp. 241–258.

Johnson, M.D., Sherry, T.W., Holmes, R.T. & Marra, P.P. (2006) Assessing habitat quality for a migratory songbird wintering in natural and agricultural habitats. *Conservation Biology*, **20**, 1433–1444.

Johnston, A., Ausden, M., Dodd, A.M., Bradbury, R.B., Chamberlain, D.E., Jiguet, F., Thomas, C.D., Cook, A.S.C.P., Newson, S.N., Ockendon, N., Rehfisch, M.M., Roos, S., Thaxter, C.B., Brown, A., Crick, H.Q.P., Douse, A., McCall, R.A., Pontier, H., Stroud, D.A., Cadiou, B., Crowe, O., Deceuninck, B., Hornmann, M. & Pearce-Higgins, J.W. (2013) Observed and predicted effects of climate change on species abundance in protected areas. *Nature Climate Change*, **3**, 1055–1061.

Johnston, A., Cook, A.S.C.P., Wright, L.J., Humphreys, E.M. & Burton, N.H.K. (2014) Modelling flight heights of marine birds to more accurately assess collision risk with offshore wind turbines. *Journal of Applied Ecology*. **51**, 31–41.

Jones, C. (1998) Saved. *On the Edge*, **81**, 1–2.

Jones, I.L., Hunter, F.M. & Robertson, G.J. (2002) Annual adult survival of Least Auklets (Aves, alcidae) varies with large-scale climatic conditions of the North Pacific Ocean. *Oecologia*, **133**, 38–44.

Jones, J., Doran, P.J. & Holmes, R.T. (2003) Climate and food synchronize regional forest bird abundances. *Ecology*, **84**, 3024–3032.

Jones, T. & Creswell, W. (2010) The phenology mismatch hypothesis: are declines of migrant birds linked to uneven climate change? *Journal of Animal Ecology*, **79**, 98–108.

Jongman, R.H.G., Kulvik, M. & Kristiansen, I. (2004) European ecological networks and greenways. *Landscape and Urban Planning*, **68**, 305–319.

Jonzén, N., Lindén, A., Ergon, T., Knudsen, E., Vik, J.O., Rubolini, D., Piacentinni, D., Brinch, C., Spina, F., Karlsson, L., Stervander, M., Andersson, A., Waldenström, J., Lehikoinen, A., Edvardsen, E., Solvang, R. & Stenseth, N.C. (2006) Rapid advance of spring arrival dates in long-distance migratory birds. *Science*, **312**, 1959–1961.

Julliard, R., Clavel, J., Devictor, V., Jiguet, F. & Couvet, D. (2006) Spatial segregation of specialists and generalists in bird communities. *Ecology Letters*, **9**, 1237–1244.

Julliard, R., Jiguet, F. & Couvet, D. (2003) Common birds facing global changes: what makes a species at risk? *Global Change Biology*, **10**, 148–154.

Kalney, E., Kanamitsu, M., Kistler, R. Collins, W., Deaven, D., Gandin, L., Iredell, M., Saha, S., White, G., Woollen, J., Zhu, Y., Leetmaa, A., Reynolds, R., Chellliah, M., Ebisuzaki, W., Higgins, W., Janowiak, J., Mo, K.C., Ropelewski, C., Want, J., Jenne, R. & Joseph, D. (1996) The NCEP/NCAR 40-year reanalysis project. *Bulletin of the American Meterological Society*, **77**, 437–471.

Kampichler, C., Van Turnhout, C.A.M., Devictor, V. & Van der Jeugd, H.P. (2012) Large-scale changes in community composition: Determining land use and climate change signals. *PLoS ONE*, **7**, e35272.

Kaufmann, R.K., Kauppi, H., Mann, M.L. & Stock, J.H. (2011) Reconciling anthropogenic climate change with observed temperature 1998–2008. *Proceedings of the National Academy of Sciences USA*, **108**, 11790–11793.

Kausrud, K.L., Mysterud, A., Steen, H., Vik, J.O., Østbye, E., Cazelles, B., Framstad, E., Eikeset, A.M., Mysterud, I., Solhøy, T. & Stenseth, N.C. (2008) Linking climate change to lemming cycles. *Nature*, **456**, 93–97.

Kawaguchi, S. & Satake, M. (1994) Relationship between recruitment of the Antarctic krill and the degree of ice cover near the South Shetland Islands. *Fisheries Science*, **60**, 123–124.

Kearney, M., & Porter, W.P. (2009) Mechanistic niche modelling: combining physiological and spatial data to predict species' ranges. *Ecology Letters*, **12**, 334–50.

Keast, A. (1985) Bird community structure in southern forests and northern woodlands: A comparison. In *Birds of Eucalypt Forests and Woodlands: Ecology, Conservation and Management*. Keast, A., Recher, H.F., Ford, H.A. & Saunders, D. Sydney, Australia: Surrey-Beatty, pp. 97–116.

Keith, D.A., Akçakaya, H.R., Thuiller, W., Midgley, G.F., Pearson, R.G., Regan, H.M., Araújo, M.B. & Gebelo, T.G. (2008) Predicting extinction risks under climate change: coupling stochastic population models with dynamic bioclimatic habitat models. *Biology Letters*, **4**, 560–563.

Kelly, J.P., Warnock, N., Page, G.W. & Weathers, W.W. (2002) Effects of weather on daily body mass regulation in wintering dunlin. *Journal of Experimental Biology*, **205**, 109–120.

Kerbiriou, C., Le Viol, I., Jiguet, F. & Devictor, V. (2009) More species, fewer specialists: over a century of biotic homogenization in an island avifauna. *Diversity & Distributions*, **15**, 641–648.

Kéry, M., Masden, J. & Lebreton, J.-D. (2006) Survival of Svalbard pink-footed geese *Anser brachyrhynchus* in relation to winter climate, density and land-use. *Journal of Animal Ecology*, **75**, 1172–1181.

Killengreen, S.T., Ims, R.A., Yoccoz, N.G., Bråthen, K.A., Henden, J.-A. & Schott, T. (2007) Structural characteristics of a low Arctic tundra ecosystem and the retreat of the Arctic fox. *Biological Conservation*, **135**, 459–472,

Kilpatrick, A.M., Chmura, A.A., Gibbons, D.W., Fleischer, R.C., Marra, P.P. & Daszak, P. (2006) Predicting the global spread of H5N1 avian influenza. *Proceedings of the Academy Natural Sciences USA*, **103**, 19368–19373.

Kilpatrick, A.M., LaDeau, S.L. & Marra, P.P. (2007) Ecology of West Nile virus transmission and its impact on birds in the Western Hemisphere. *The Auk*, **124**, 1121–1136.

King, B., Woodcock, M. & Dickinson, E.C. (1975) *A Field Guide to the Birds of South-east Asia*. London, UK: Collins.

Kirby, J.S. & Lack, P.C. (1993) Spatial dynamics of wintering lapwings and golden plovers in Britain and Ireland, 1981/82 to 1983/84. *Bird Study*, **40**, 38–50.

Kirby, K.J., Quine, C.P. & Brown, N.D. (2009) The adaptation of UK forests and woodlands to climate change. In *Combating Climate Change – A Role for UK Forests. An Assessment of the Potential of the UK's Trees and Woodlands to Mitigate and Adapt to Climate Change*. Reed, D.J., Morison, J.I.L., Hanley, N., West, C.C. & Snowdon, P. Edinburgh, UK: The Stationary Office, pp. 164–179.

Kitaysky, A.S. & Golubova, E.G. (2000) Climate change causes contrasting trends in reproductive performance of planktivorous and piscivorous alcids. *Journal of Animal Ecology*, **69**, 248–262.

Klaassen, M. (1995) Moult and basal metabolic costs in two subspecies of stonechats: the European *Saxicola rubicula* and East African *S. t. axillaris*. *Oecologia*, **104**, 424–432.

Klaassen, M., Lindström, Å., Meltofte, H. & Piersma, T. (2001) Arctic waders are not capital breeders. *Nature*, **413**, 794.

Klomp, H. (1970) The determination of clutch size in birds. A review. *Ardea*, **58**, 1–124.

Kluijver, H.N. (1951) The population ecology of the great tit, *Parus m. major* L. *Ardea*, **39**, 1–135.

Kluijver, H.N. & Tinbergen, L. (1953) Territory and the regulation of density in titmice. *Archives Neerlandaises de Zoologie*, **10**, 265–289.

Knudsen, E., Lindén, A., Both, C., Jonzén, N., Pulido, F., Saino, N., Sutherland, W.J., Bach, L.A., Coppack, T., Ergon, T., Gienapp, P., Gill, J.A., Gordo, O., Hedenström, A., Lehikoinen, E., Marra, P.P., Møller, A.P., Nilsson, A.L.K., Péron, G., Ranta, E., Rubolini, D., Sparks, T.H., Spina, F., Studds, C.E., Sæther, S.A., Tryjanowski, P. & Stenseth, N.C. (2011) Challenging claims in the study of migratory birds and climate change. *Biological Reviews*, **86**, 928–946.

Koenig, W.D. & Haydock, J. (1999) Oaks, acorns and the geographical ecology of acorn woodpeckers. *Journal of Biogeography*, **26**, 159–165.

Koenig, W.D., Hochachka, W.M., Zuckerberg, B. & Dickinson, J.L. (2010) Ecological determinants of American crow mortality due to West Nile virus during its North American sweep. *Oecologia*, **163**, 903–909.

Koh, L.P. & Ghazoul, J. (2010) Spatially explicit scenario analysis for reconciling agricultural expansion, forest protection, and carbon conservation in Indonesia. *Proceedings of the National Academy of Sciences USA*, **107**, 11140–11144.

Koh, L.P. & Wilcove, D.S. (2007) Cashing in palm oil for conservation. *Nature*, **448**, 993–994.

Kolar, C.S. & Lodge, D.M. (2001) Process in invasion biology: predicting invaders. *Trends in Ecology and Evolution*, **16**, 199–204.

Koskimies, J. & Lahti, L. (1964) Cold-hardiness of the newly hatched young in relation to ecology and distribution of ten species of European ducks. *Physiological Zoology*, **65**, 803–814.

Kostrzewa, A. & Kostrzewa, R. (1990) The relationship of spring and summer weather with density and breeding performance of the buzzard *Buteo buteo*, goshawk *Accipiter gentilis* and kestrel *Falco tinnunculus*. *Ibis*, **132**, 550–559.

Kostrzewa, R. & Kostrzewa, A. (1991) Winter weather, spring and summer density, and subsequent breeding success of Eurasian kestrels, common buzzards, and northern goshawks. *The Auk*, **108**, 342–347.

Kraan, C., van Gils, J.A., Spaans, B., Dekinga, A., Biljleveld, A.I., Van Roomen, M., Kleefstra, R. & Piersma, T. (2009) Landscape-scale experiment demonstrates that Wadden Sea intertidal flats are used to capacity by molluscivore migrant shorebirds. *Journal of Animal Ecology*, **78**, 1259–1268.

Kraemer, H.C. (1988) Assessment of 2 x 2 associations: generalization of signal-detection methodology. *American Statistical Association*, **42**, 37–49.

Krapu, G.L., Klett, A.T. & Jorde, D.G. (1983) The effect of variable spring water conditions on mallard reproduction. *The Auk*, **100**, 689–698.

Krebs, J.R., Wilson, J.D., Bradbury, R.B. & Siriwardena, G.M. (1999) The second silent spring? *Nature*, **400**, 611–612.

Krijgsveld, K.L., Akershoek, K., Schenk, F., Dijk, F. & Dirksen, S. (2009) Collision risk of birds with modern large wind turbines. *Ardea*, **97**, 3576–366.

Krištín, A. & Patočka, J. (1997) Birds as predators of Lepidoptera: selected examples. *Biologia*, **52**, 319–326.

Krüger, O., Liversidge, R. & Lindström, J. (2002) Statistical modelling of the population dynamics of a raptor community in a semi-desert environment. *Journal of Animal Ecology*, **71**, 603–613.

Kuglitsch, F.G., Toreti, A., Xoplaki, E., Della-Marta, P.M., Zeregos, C.S., Türkes, M. & Luterbacher, J. (2010) Heat wave changes in the eastern Mediterranean since 1960. *Geophysical Research Letters*, **37**, L04802.

Kujala, H., Vepsäläinen, V., Zuckerberg, B. & Brommer, J.E. (2013) Range margin shifts of birds revisited – the role of spatiotemporally varying survey effort. *Global Change Biology*, **19**, 420–430.

Kulka, G.J., Bender, M.L., de Beaulieu, J.-L., Bond, G., Vroecker, W.S., Cleveringa, P., Gavin, J.E., Herbert, T.D., Imbrie, J., Jouzel, J., Keigwin, L.D., Knudsen, K.-L., McManus, J.F., Merkt, J., Muhs, D.R., Müller, H., Poore, R.Z., Porter, S.C., Seret, G., Shackleton, N.J., Turner, C., Tzedakis, P.C. & Winograd, I.J. (2002) Last interglacial climates. *Quaternary Research*, **58**, 2–13.

Kunkel, K.E., Palecki, M.A., Ensor, L. Hubbard, K.G., Robinson, D., Redmond, K. & Easterling, D. (2009) Trends in twentieth century U.S. extreme snowfalls seasons. *Journal of Climate*, **22**, 6204–6216.

Kurki, S., Nikula, A., Helle, P. & Lindén, H. (2000) Landscape fragmentation and forest composition effects on grouse breeding success in boreal forests. *Ecology*, **81**, 1985–1997.

Laaksonen, T., Ahola, M., Eeva, T., Väisänen, Lehikoinen, E. (2006) Climate change, migratory connectivity and changes in laying date and clutch size of the pied flycatcher. *Oikos*, **114**, 277–290.

LaDeau, S.L., Kilpatrick, A.M. & Marra, P.P. (2007) West Nile virus emergence and large-scale declines of North American bird populations. *Nature*, **447**, 710–713.

La Sorte, F.A. & Jetz, W. (2010) Projected range contractions of montane biodiversity under global warming. *Proceedings of the Royal Society of London, Series B*, **277**, 3401–3410.

La Sorte, F.A. & Jetz, W. (2012) Tracking of climatic niche boundaries under recent climate change. *Journal of Animal Ecology*, **81**, 914–925.

La Sorte, F.A., Lee, T.M., Wilman, H. & Jetz, W. (2009) Disparities between observed and predicted impacts of climate change on winter bird assemblages. *Proceedings of the Royal Society of London, Series B*, **276**, 3167–3174.

Lack, D. (1960) Migration across the North Sea studied by radar. Part 2. The spring depature 1956–1959. *Ibis*, **102**, 26–57.

Lack, D. (1966) *Population Studies of Birds*. Oxford, UK: Oxford University Press.

Lack, P. (1986) *The Atlas of Wintering Birds in Britain and Ireland*. London, UK: T. & A.D. Poyser, Calton.

Lahti, K., Orell, M., Rytkönen, S. & Koivula, K. (1998) Time and food dependence in willow tit winter survival. *Ecology*, **79**, 2904–2916.

Lamberson, R.H., Noon, B.R., Voss, C. & McKelvey, K.S. (1994) Reserve design for terrestrial species: the effects of patch size and spacing on the viability of the Northern Spotted Owl. *Conservation Biology*, **8**, 185–195.

Lambert, F., Delmonte, B., Petit, J.R., Bigler, M., Kaufmann, P.R., Hutterli, M.A., Stocker, T.F., Ruth, U., Steffensen, J.P. & Maggi, V. (2008) Dust-climate couplings over the past 800,000 years from the EPICA Dome C ice core. *Nature*, **452**, 616–619.

Lambrechts, M.M., Caro, S., Charmantier, A. Gross, N., Galan, M.-J., Perret, P., Cartan-Son, M., Dias, P.C., Blondel, J. & Thomas, D.W. (2004) Habitat quality as a predictor of spatial variation in blue tit reproductive performance: a multi-plot analysis. *Oecologia*, **141**, 555–561.

Lambrechts, M.M. & Perret, P. (2000) A long photoperiod overrides nonphotoperiodic factors in blue tits' timing of reproduction. *Proceedings of the Royal Society of London, Series B*, **267**, 585–588.

Lamoreux, J.F., Morrison, J.C., Ricketts, T.H., Olson, D.M., Dinerstein, E., McKnight, M.W. & Shugart, H.H. (2006) Global tests of biodiversity concordance and the importance of endemism. *Nature*, **440**, 212–214.

Lampila, P., Mönkkönen, M. & Desrochers, A. (2005) Demographic responses by birds to forest fragmentation. *Conservation Biology*, **19**, 1537–1546.

Lampila, S., Orell, M., Belda, E. & Koivula, K. (2006) Importance of adult survival, local recruitment and immigration in a declining boreal forest passerine, the willow tit *Parus motanus*. *Oecologia*, **148**, 405–413.

Lanciotti, R.S., Roehrig, J.T., Deubel, V., Smith, J., Parker, M., Steele, K., Crise, B., Volpe, K.E., Crabtree, M.B., Scherret, J.H., Hall, R.A., MacKenzie, J.S., Cropp, C.B., Panigrahy, B., Ostlund, E., Schmidt, B., Malkinson, M., Banet, C., Weissman, J., Komar, N., Savage, H.M., Stone, W., McNamara, T. & Gubler, D.J. (1999) Origin of the West Nile virus responsible for an outbreak of Encephalitis in the Northeastern United States. *Science*, **286**, 2333–2337.

Lang, M. (2007) Decline of the Ortolan Bunting *Emberiza hortulana* population in southern Germany – are causes outside the breeding area responsible? *Vogelwelt*, **128**, 179–196.

Langston, R.H.W. (2010) *Offshore wind farms and birds: Round 3 zones, extensions to Round 1 & Round 2 sites & Scottish Territorial Waters*. RSPB Research Report 39. Sandy Beds, UK: The Royal Society for the Protection of Birds.

Larinier, M. (2008) Fish passage experience at small-scale hydroelectric power plants in France. *Hydrobiologia*, **609**, 97–108.

Laura, V., Attrill, M.J. Pinnegar, J.K., Brown, A., Edwards, M. & Votier, S.C. (2012) Influence of climate change and trophic coupling across four trophic levels in the Celtic Sea. *PLoS ONE*, **7**, e47408.

Laurance, W.F., Useche, D.C., Rendeio, J. et al. (2012) Averting biodiversity collapse in tropical forest protected areas. *Nature*, **489**, 290–294.

Lawler, J.J., White, D., Neilson, R.P. & Blaustein, A.R. (2006) Predicting climate-induced range shifts: model differences and model reliability. *Global Change Biology*, **12**, 1568–1584.

Lawson, B., Robinson, R.A., Colvile, K.M., Peck, K.M., Chantrey, J., Pennycott, T.W., Simpson, V.R., Toms, M.P. & Cunningham, A.A. (2012) The emergence and spread of finch trichomonisis in the British Isles. *Philosophical Transactions of the Royal Society Series B*, **367**, 2852–2863.

Lawton, J.H., Brotherton, P.N.M., Brown, V.K., Elphick, C., Fitter, A.H., Forshaw, J., Haddow, R.W., Hilborne, S., Leafe, R.N., Mace, G.M., Southgate, M.P., Sutherland, W.A., Tew, T.E., Varley, J. & Wynne, G.R. (2010) *Making Space for Nature: A Review of England's Wildlife Sites and Ecological Network*. London, UK: Report to Defra.

Le Bohec, C., Durant, J.M., Gauthier-Clerc, M., Stenseth, N.C., Park, Y.-H., Pradel, R., Grémillet, D., Gendner, J.-P. & Le Maho, Y. (2008) King penguin population threatened by Southern Ocean warming. *Proceedings of the National Academy of Sciences USA*, **105**, 2493–2497.

Le Bohec, C., Gauthier-Clerc, M., Grémillet, D., Pradel, R., Bechet, A., Gendner, J. & Le Maho, Y. (2007) Population dynamics in a long-lived seabird: I. Impact of breeding activity on survival and breeding probability in unbanded king penguins. *Journal of Animal Ecology*, **76**, 1149–1160.

Le Voil, I., Jiguet, F., Brotons, L., Herrando, S., Lindström, Å., Pearce-Higgins, J.W., Reif, J., van Turnhout, C. & Devictor, V. (2012) More and more generalists: two decades of changes in the European avifauna. *Biology Letters* **8**, 780–782.

Leathwick, J.R. & Austin, M.P. (2001) Competitive interactions between tree species in New Zealand's old-growth indigenous forests. *Ecology*, **82**, 2560–2573.

Leathwick, J.R. & Whitehead, D. (2001) Soil and atmospheric water deficits and the distribution of New Zealand's indigenous tree species. *Functional Ecology*, **15**, 233–242.

Leberg, P.L., Green, M.C., Adams, B.A., Purcell, K.M. & Luent, M.C. (2007) Response of waterbird colonies in southern Louisiana to recent drought and hurricanes. *Animal Conservation*, **10**, 502–508.

Leddy, K.L., Higgins, K.F. & Naugle, D.E. (1999) Effects of wind turbines on upland nesting birds in conservation reserve program grasslands. *Wilson Bulletin*, **111**, 100–104.

Ledec, G.C., Rapp, K.W. & Aiello, R.G. (2011) *Greening the Wind: Environmental and Social Considerations for Wind Power Development in Latin America and Beyond*. Energy Unit. World Bank – Energy Sector Management Assistance Program. http://www.esmap.org/esmap/sites/esmap.org/files/Greening_The_Wind_LAC_ESMAP_June%202011.pdf

Lee, J.E., Janoin, C., Marais, E., Jansen van Vuuren, B. & Chown, S.L. (2009) Physiological tolerances account for range limits and abundance structure in an invasive slug. *Proceedings of the Royal Society of London, Series B*, **276**, 1459–1468.

Lee, J.S.H., Garcia-Ulloa, J. & Koh, L.P. (2011a) Impacts of biofuel expansion in biodiversity hotspots. *Biodiversity Hotspots*, pp. 277–293.

Lee, P.-Y. & Rotenberry, J. T. (2005) Relationships between bird species and tree species assemblages in forested habitats of eastern North America. *Journal of Biogeography*, **32**, 1139–1150.

Lee, S.-D., Ellwood, E.R., Park, S.-Y. & Primack, R.B. (2011b) Late-arriving barn swallows linked to population declines. *Biological Conservation*, **144**, 2182–2187.

Leech, D.I. & Crick, H.Q.P. (2007) Influence of climate change on the abundance, distribution and phenology of woodland bird species in temperature regions. *Ibis*, **149 Suppl 2**, 128–145.

Lees, A.C. & Peres, C.A. (2008) Conservation value of remnant riparian forest corridors of varying quality for Amazonian birds and mammals. *Conservation Biology*, **22**, 439–449.

Lehikoinen, A., Byholm, P., Ranta, E., Saurola, P., Valkama, J., Korpimäki, E., Pietiäinen, H. & Henttonen, H. (2009) Reproduction of the common buzzard at its northern range margin under climate change. *Oikos*, **118**, 829–836.

Lehikoinen, A. & Jaatinen, K. (2012) Delayed autumn migration in northern European waterfowl. *Journal of Ornithology*, **153**, 563–570.

Lehikoinen, A., Jaatinen, K., Vähätalo, A.V., Clausen, P., Crowe, O., Deceuninck, B., Hearn, R., Holt, C.A., Hornman, M., Keller, V., Nilsson, L., Langendoen, T., Tománková, I., Wahl, J. & Fox, A.D. (2013) Rapid climate driven shifts in wintering distributions of three common waterbird species. *Global Change Biology*, **19**, 2071–2081.

Lehikoinen, E. & Sparks, T.H. (2010) Changes in migration. In *Effects of Climate Change on Birds*. Møller, A.P., Fiedler, W. & Berthold, P. Oxford, UK: Oxford University Press, pp. 89–112.

Lehikoinen, E., Sparks, T.H. & Zalakevicius, M. (2004) Arrival and departure dates. *Advances in Ecological Research*, **55**, 1–31.

Lekuona, J.M. & Ursúa, C. (2007) Avian mortality in wind power plants of Navarra (Northern Spain). *Birds and Wind Farms*. De Lucas, M., Janss, G.F.E. & Ferrer, M. Madrid, Spain: Quercus, pp. 178–192.

Lemoine, N., & Böhning-Gaese, K. (2003) Potential impact of global climate change on species richness of long-distance migrants. *Conservation Biology*, **17**, 577–586.

Lemoine, N., Schaefer, H.-C. & Böhning-Gaese, K. (2007) Species richness of migratory birds is influenced by global climate change. *Global Ecology and Biogeography*, **16**, 55–64.

Lennon, J.J., Greenwood, J.J.D. & Turner, J.R.G. (2000) Bird diversity and environmental gradients in Britain: a test of the species-energy hypothesis. *Journal of Animal Ecology*, **69**, 581–598.

Lesage, L. & Gauthier, G. (1997) Growth and organ development in greater snow goose goslings. *The Auk*, **114**, 229–241.

Lescroël, A., Dugger, K.M., Ballard, G. & Ainley, D.G. (2009) Effects of individual quality, reproductive success and environmental variability on survival of a long-lived seabird. *Journal of Animal Ecology*, **78**, 798–806.

Leslie, D.M., Wood, G.K. & Carter, T.S. (2000) Productivity of endangered Least Terns (*Sterna antillarum athalassos*) below a hydropower and flood-control facility on the Arkansas River. *Southwestern Naturalist*, **45**, 483–489.

Levey, D.J., Bolker, B.M., Tewksbury, J.J., Sargent, S. & Haddad, N.M. (2005) Effects of landscape corridors on seed dispersal by birds. *Science*, **309**, 146–148.

Lewis, S., Wanless, S., Wright, P.J., Harris, M.P., Bull, J. & Elston, D.A. (2001) Diet and breeding performance of black-legged kittiwakes *Rissa tridactyla* at a North Sea cology. *Marine Ecology Progress Series*, **221**, 277–284.

Li, S.-H. & Brown, J. L. (1999) Influence of climate on reproductive success in Mexican Jays. *The Auk*, **116**, 924–936.

Lima, M., Julliard, R., Stenseth, N.C. & Jaksic, F.M. (2001) Demographic dynamics of a neotropical small rodent (*Phyllotis darwini*): feedback structure, predation and climatic factors. *Journal of Animal Ecology*, **70**, 761–775.

Lima, S.L. (1986) Predation risk and unpredictable feeding conditions: determinants of body mass in birds. *Ecology*, **67**, 377–385.

Lindenmayer, D.B., Cunningham, R.B., Donnelly, C.F., Nix, H. & Lindenmayer, B.D. (2002) Effects of forest fragmentation on bird assemblages in a novel landscape context. *Ecological Monographs*, **72**, 1–18.

Lindsay, R. (2010) *Peatbogs and Carbon: A Critical Dynthesis*. Edinburgh, UK: RSPB Scotland. http://www.rspb.org.uk/Images/Peatbogs_and_carbon_tcm9-255200.pdf (accessed 31 August 2012).

Lindström, Å., Green, M., Paulson, G., Smith, H.G. & Devictor, V. (2013) Rapid changes in bird community composition at multiple temporal and spatial scales in response to recent climate change. *Ecography*, **36**, 313–322.

Lindström, E.R., Andrén, H., Angelstam, P., Cederlund, G., Hörnfeldt, B., Jäderberg, L., Lemnell, P., Martinsson, B., Sköld, K. & Swenson, J.E. (1994) Disease reveals the predator: sarcoptic mange, fox predation, and prey populations. *Ecology*, **75**, 1042–1049.

Lips, K.R., Diffendorfer, J., Mendelson III, J.R. & Sears, M.W. (2008) Riding the wave: reconciling the roles of disease and climate change in amphibian declines. *PLoS Biology*, **6**, 441–454.

Liu, J., Curry, J.A., Wang, H., Song, M. & Horton, R.M. (2012) Impact of declining Arctic sea ice on winter snowfall. *Proceedings of the National Academy of Sciences USA*, **109**, E1899–E1900.

Loeb, V., Siegel, V., Holm-Hansen, O., Hewitt, R., Fraser, W., Trivelpiece, W. & Trivelpiece, S. (1997) Effects of sea-ice extent and krill or salp dominance on the Antarctic food web. *Nature*, **387**, 897–900.

Lopes, L.E., Malacco, G.B., Alteff, E.F., de Vasconcelos, M.F., Hoffmann, D. & Silveira, L.F. (2009) Range extensions and conservation of some threatened or little known Brazilian grassland birds. *Bird Conservation International*, **19**, 1–11.

López-López, P., Ferrer, M., Madero, A., Casado E. & McGrady. M. (2011) Solving man-induced large-scale conservation problems: the Spanish imperial eagle and power lines. *PLoS ONE*, **6**, e17196.

Loss, S.R., Terwilliger, L.A. & Peterson, A.C. (2011) Assisted colonization: integrating conservation strategies in the face of climate change. *Biological Conservation*, **144**, 92–100.

Lotze-Campen, H., Popp, A., Beringer, T., Müller, C., Bondeau, A., Rost, S. & Lucht, W. (2010) Scenarios of global bioenergy production: The trade-offs between agricultural expansion, intensification and trade. *Ecological Modelling*, **221**, 2186–2196.

Love, O.P., Gilchrist, H.G., Descamps, S. & Semeniuk, C.A.D. (2010) Pre-laying climatic cues can time reproduction to optimally match offspring hatching and ice conditions in an Arctic marine bird. *Oecologia*, **164**, 277–286.

Lovejoy, T. & Hannah, L. (2005) *Climate Change and Biodiversity*: New Haven, CT: Yale University Press.

Low, T. (2011) *Climate Change and Terrestrial Biodiversity in Queensland*. Brisbane, Australia: Queensland Department of Environment and Resource Management.

Ludwig, G. (2007) Mechanisms of population declines in Boreal Forest Grouse. *Jyväskylä Studies in Biological and Environmental Science*, **176**, 1–48.

Ludwig, G.X., Alatalo, R.V., Helle, P., Lindén, H., Lindström, J. & Siitari, H. (2006) Short- and long-term population dynamical consequences of asymmetric climate change in black grouse. *Proceedings of the Royal Society of London, Series B*, **273**, 2009–2016.

Ludwig, G.X., Alatalo, R.V., Helle, P., Nissinen, K. & Siitari, H. (2008) Large-scale drainage and breeding success in boreal forest grouse. *Journal of Applied Ecology*, **45**, 325–333.

Lundberg, A. & Alatalo, R.V. (1992) *The Pied Flycatcher*. London, UK: Poyser.

Luoto, M., Virkkala, R. & Heikkinen, R.K. (2007) The role of land cover in bioclimatic models depends on spatial resolution. *Global Ecology and Biogeography*, **16**, 34–42.

MacDonald, D.W., Tattersall, F.H., Service, K.M., Firbank, L.G. & Feber, R.E. (2007) Mammals, agri-environment schemes and set-aside – what are the putative benefits? *Mammal Review*, **37**, 259–277.

Mace, G.M., Collar, N.J., Gaston, K.J., Hilton-Taylor, C., Akçakaya, H.R., Leader-Williams, N., Milner-Gulland, E.J. & Stuart, S.N. (2008) Quantification of extinction risk: IUCN's system for classifying threatened species. *Conservation Biology*, **22**, 1424–1442.

Macías-Duarte, A., Montoya, A.B., Hunt, W.G., Lafón-Terrazas, A. & Tafanelli, R. (2004) Reproduction, prey and habitat of the Aplomado Falcon (*Falco femoralis*) in desert grasslands of Chihuahua, Mexico. *The Auk*, **121**, 1081–1093.

MacKay, D.J.C. (2008) *Sustainable Energy – Without the Hot Air*. Cambridge, UK: UIT.

MacKenzie, D.I., Nichols, J.D., Royle, J.A., Pollock, K.H., Bailey, L.L. & Hines, J.E. (2006) *Occupancy Estimation and Modeling*. Burlington, MA: Academic Press.

Maclean, G.L. (1970) The biology of the larks (Alaudidae) of the Kalahari sandveld. *Zoologica africana.* **5**, 7–39.

Maclean, I.M.D., Austin, G.E., Rehfisch, M.M., Blew, J., Crowe, O., Delany, S., Devos, K., Deceuninck, B., Günther, K., Laursen, K., Van Roomen, M. & Wahl, J. (2008) Climate change causes rapid changes in the distribution and site abundance of birds in winter. *Global Change Biology*, **14**, 2489–2500,

Maclean, I.M.D., Rehfisch, M.M., Delany, S. & Robinson, R.A. (2007) *The effects of climate change on migratory waterbirds within the African-Eurasian flyway.* BTO Research Report 486, AEWA/MOP 4.27. Thetford, UK: British Trust for Ornithology.

MacLeod, R., Barnett, P., Clark, J.A. & Creswell, W. (2005) Body mass change strategies in blackbirds *Turdus merula*: the starvation-predation risk trade-off. *Journal of Animal Ecology*, **74**, 292–302.

MacLeod, R., Lind, J., Clark, J. & Cresswell, W. (2007) Mass regulation in response to predation risk can indicate population declines. *Ecology Letters*, **10**, 945–955.

MacMynowski, D.P. & Root, T.L. (2007) Climate and the complexity of migratory phenology: sexes, migratory distance, and arrival distribution. *International Journal of Biometeorology*, **51**, 361–373.

Madsen, J., Bregnballe, T., Frikke, J. & Kristensen, J.B. (1998) Correlates of predator abundance with snow and ice conditions and their role in determining timing of nesting and breeding success in Svalbard light-bellied brent geese (*Branta bernicla hrota*). *Norsk Polarinstitutt Skrifter*, **200**, 221–234.

Maggini, R., Lehmann, A., Kéry, M., Schmid, H., Beniston, M., Jenni, L. & Zbinden, N. (2011) Are Swiss birds tracking climate change? Detecting elevational shifts using response curve shapes. *Ecological Modelling*, **222**, 21–32.

Mallord, J.W., Orsman, C.J., Cristinacce, A., Butcher, N., Stowe, T.J. & Charman, E.C. (2012) Mortality of wood warbler *Phylloscopus sibilatrix* nests in Welsh Oakwoods: predation rates and the identification of nest predators using miniature nest cameras. *Bird Study*, **59**, 286–295.

Mallory, M.L., Gaston, A.J., Forbes, M.R. & Gilchrist, H.G. (2009) Influence of weather on reproductive success of northern fulmars in the Canadian high Arctic. *Polar Biology*, **32**, 529–538.

Manel, S., Williams, H.C & Ormerod, S.J. (2001) Evaluating presence–absence models in ecology: the need to account for prevalence. *Journal of Applied Ecology*, **38**, 921–931.

Mansourian, S. Vallauri, D. & Dudley, N. (2005) *Forest Restoration in Landscapes: Beyond Planting Trees.* New York: Springer.

Manu, S., Peach, W. & Creswell, W. (2007) The effects of edge, fragment size and degree of isolation on avian species richness in highly fragmented forest in West Africa. *Ibis*, **149**, 287–297.

Marchant, J.H. (1992) Recent trends in breeding populations of some common trans-Saharan migrant birds in northern Europe. *Ibis*, **135**, **Suppl 1**, 113–119.

Marchant, S. (1959) The breeding season in S.W. Ecuador. *Ibis*, **101**, 137–152.

Margalida, A., Bertran, J. & Heredia, R. (2009) Diet and food preferences of the endangered Bearded Vulture *Gypaetus barbatus*: a basis for their conservation. *Ibis*, **151**, 235–243.

Marini, M.Â & Durães, R. (2001) Annual patterns of molt and reproductive activity of passerines in south-central Brazil. *The Condor*, **103**, 767–775.

Marion, L., Barbier, L. & Morin, C. (2006) Statut du Blongios nain *Ixobrychus minutus* en France entre 1968 et 2004 et causes probable de l'evolution de ses effectifs. *Alauda*, **74**, 155–170.

Maron, M., Hobbs, R.J., Moilanen, A., Matthews, J.W., Christie, K., Gardner, T.A., Keith, D.A., Lindenmayer, D.B. & McAlpine, C.A. (2012) Faustian bargains? Restoration realities in the context of biodiversity offset policies. *Biological Conservation*, **155**, 141–148.

Marra, P.P., Francis, C.M., Mulvihill, R.S. & Moore, F.R. (2005) The influence of climate on the timing and rate of spring bird migration. *Oecologia*, **141**, 307–315.

Marshall, M.R., Cooper, R.J., DeCecco, J.A., Strazanac, J. & Butler, L. (2002) Effects of experimentally reduced prey abundance on the breeding ecology of the red-eyed vireo. *Ecological Applications*, **12**, 261–280.

Martensen, A.C., Pimtentel, R.G. & Metzger, J.P. (2008) Relative effects of fragment size and connectivity on bird community in the Atlantic Rain Forest: Implications for conservation. *Biological Conservation*, **141**, 2184–2192.

Martensen, A.C., Ribeiro, M.C., Banks-Leite, C., Prado, P.A. & Metzger, J.P. (2012) Associations of forest cover, fragment area, and connectivity with Neotropical understory bird speices richness and abundance. *Conservation Biology*, **26**, 1100–1111.

Martin, G.R. (2011) Understanding bird collisions with man-made objects: a sensory ecology approach. *Ibis*, **153**, 239–254.

Martin, G.R., Portugal, S.J. & Murn, C.P. (2012) Visual fields, foraging and collision vulnerability in Gyps vultures. *Ibis*, **154**, 626–631.

Martin, J.G.A., Nussey, D.H., Wilson, A.J. & Réale, D. (2011) Measuring individual differences in reaction norms in field and experimental studies: a power analysis of random regression models. *Methods in Ecology and Evolution*, **2**, 362–374.

Martin, P.R., Bonier, F., Moore, I.T. & Tewksbury, J.J. (2009) Latitudinal variation in the asynchrony of seasons: implications for higher rates of population differentiation and speciation in the tropics. *Ideas in Ecology and Evolution*, **2**, 9–17.

Martin, T.E. (2001) Abiotic vs. biotic influences on habitat selection of coexisting species, with implications for climate change. *Ecology*, **82**, 175–188.

Martin, T.E. (2007) Climate correlates of 20 years of trophic changes in a high-elevation riparian system. *Ecology*, **88**, 367–380.

Martin, T.E. & Maron, J.L. (2012) Climate impacts on bird and plant communities from altered animal-plant interactions. *Nature Climate Change*, **2**, 195–200.

Martínez-Abrain, A., Tavecchia, G., Regan, H.M., Jiménez, J., Surroca, M. & Oro, D. (2012) Effects of wind farms and food scarcity on a large scavenging bird species following an epidemic of bovine spongiform encephalopathy. *Journal of Applied Ecology*, **49**, 109–117.

Martínez-Meyer, E., Díaz-Porras, D., Peterson, A.T. & Yáñez-Arenas, C. (2013) Ecological niche structure and rangewide abundance patterns of species. *Biology Letters*, **9**, 21210636.

Masden, E.A., Haydon, D.T., Fox, A.D., Furness, R.W., Bullman, R. & Desholm, M. (2009) Barriers to movement: impacts of wind farms on migrating birds. *ICES Journal of Marine Science*, **66**, 746–753.

Matthysen, E. (1989) Nuthatch *Sitta europaea* demography, beech mast and territoriality. *Ornis Scandinavica*, **20**, 278–282.

Matthysen, E., Adraensen, F. & Dhondt, A.A. (1995) Dispersal distances of nuthatches, *Sitta europaea*, in a highly fragmented forest habitat. *Oikos*, **72**, 375–381.

Matthysen, E., Adriaensen, F. & Dhondt, A.A. (2011) Multiple responses to increasing spring temperatures in the breeding cycle of blue and great tits (*Cyanistes caeruleus, Parus major*). *Global Change Biology*, **17**, 1–16.

Matthysen, E. & Currie, D. (1996) Habitat fragmentation reduces disperser success in juvenile nuthatches *Sitta europaea*: evidence from patterns of territory establishment. *Ecography*, **19**, 67–72.

Mawdsley, J.R., O'Malley, R. & Ojima, D. (2009) A review of climate-change adaptation strategies for wildlife management and biodiversity conservation. *Conservation Biology*, **23**, 1080–1089.

Mayr, G. (2005) The Paeogene fossil record of birds in Europe. *Biological Reviews*, **80**, 515–542.

Mazerolle, D.F., Dufour, K.W., Hobson, K.A. & den Haan, H.E. (2005) Effects of large-scale climatic fluctuations on survival and production of young in a Neotropical migrant songbird, the yellow warbler *Dendroica petechia*. *Journal of Avian Biology*, **36**, 155–163.

Mazerolle, D.F., Sealey, S.G. & Hobson, K.A. (2011) Interannual flexibility in the breeding phenology of a Neotropical migrant songbird in response to weather conditions at breeding and wintering areas. *Ecoscience*, **18**, 18–25.

McCain, C.M. (2009) Global analysis of bird elevational diversity. *Global Ecology and Biogeography*, **18**, 346–360.

McCarthy, M.A., Thompson, C.J. & Possingham, H.P. (2005) Theory for designing nature reserves for single species. *American Naturalist*, **165**, 250–257.

McCarthy, M.A., Thompson, C.J. & Williams, N.S.G. (2006) Logic for designing nature reserves for multiple species. *American Naturalist*, **167**, 717–727.

McCarthy, T.K., Frankiewicz, P., Cullen, P., Blaszkowski, M., O'Connor, W. & Doherty, D. (2008) Long-term effects of hydropower installations and associated river regulation on River Shannon eel populations: mitigation and management. *Hydrobiologia*, **609**, 109–124.

McCleery, R.H. & Perrins, C.M. (1998) Temperature and egg-laying trends. *Nature*, **391**, 30–31.

McClintock, J., Ducklow, H. & Fraser, W. (2008) Ecological responses to climate change on the Antarctic Peninsula. *American Scientist*, **96**, 302–310.

McClure, C.J.W., Rolek, B.W., McDonald, K. & Hill, G.E. (2012) Climate change and the decline of a once common bird. *Ecology and Evolution*, **2**, 370–378.

McCluskie, A.E., Langston, R.H.W. & Wilkinson, N.I. (2012) *Birds and wave & tidal stream energy: an ecological review. RSPB Research Report No. 42*, Sandy, UK: RSPB.

McCracken, D.L. & Foster, G.N. (1995) Factors affecting the size of leatherjacket (Diptera: Tipulidae) populations in pastures in the west of Scotland. *Applied Soil Ecology*, **2**, 43–46.

McCrary, M.D., McKernan, R.L., Schreiber, R.W., Wagner, W.D. & Sciarrotta, T.C. (1986) Avian mortality at a solar energy plant. *Journal of Field Ornithology*, **57**, 135–141.

McDonald, P.G., Olsen, P.D. & Cockburn, A. (2004) Weather dictates reproductive success and survival in the Australian brown falcon *Falco berigora*. *Journal of Animal Ecology*, **73**, 683–692.

McDonald, R.I., Fargoine, J., Kiesecker, J., Miller, W.M. & Powell, J. (2009) Energy sprawl or energy efficiency: Climate policy impacts on natural habitat for the United States of America. *PLoS ONE*, **4**, e6802.

McDonald-Madden, E., Runge, M.C., Possingham, H.P. & Martin, T.G. (2011) Optimal timing for managed relocation of species faced with climate change. *Nature Climate Change*, **1**, 261–265.

McGeoch, M.A., Butchart, S.H.M., Spear, D., Marais, E., Kleynhans, E.J., Symes, A., Chanson, J. & Hoffmann, M. (2010) Global indicators of biological invasion: species numbers, biodiversity impact and policy responses. *Diversity and Distributions*, **16**, 95–108.

McGilp, J.N. (1932) Heat in the interior of South Australia and in central Australia. Holocaust of bird-life. *South Australian Ornithologist*, **11**, 160–163.

McGrath, L.J., van Ripper III, C. & Fontaine, J.J. (2009) Flower power: tree flowering phenology as a settlement cue for migrating birds. *Journal of Animal Ecology*, **78**, 22–30.

McGuire, A.D., Anderson, L.G., Christensen, T.R., Dallimore, S., Guo, L., Hayes, D.J., Heimann, M., Lorenson, T.D., Macdonald, R.W. & Roulet, N. (2009) Sensitivity of the carbon cycle in the Arctic to climate change. *Ecological Monographs*, **79**, 523–555.

McKechnie, A. & Erasmus, B. (2006) Climate change and birds in hot deserts: the impacts of increased demand for thermoregulatory water on survival and reproduction. *Journal of Ornithology*, **147 Suppl 1**, 209–210.

McKechnie, A.E., Hockey, P.A.R. & Wolf, B.O. (2012) Feeling the heat: Australian landbirds and climate change. *Emu*, **112**, i–vii.

McKechnie, A.E. & Wolf, B.O. (2010) Climate change increases the likelihood of catastrophic avian mortality events during extreme heat waves. *Biology Letters*, **6**, 253–256.

McKee, J.K., Sciulli, P.W., Fooce, C.D. & Waite, T.A. (2004) Forecasting global biodiversity threats associated with human population growth. *Biological Conservation*, **115**, 161–164.

McKenney, B.A. & Kiesecker, J.M. (2010) Policy development for biodiversity offsets: a review of offset frameworks. *Environmental Management*, **45**, 165–176.

McKinnon, L., Picotin, M., Bolduc, E., Juillet, C. & Béty, J. (2012) Timing of breeding, peak food availability and effects of mismatch on chick growth in birds nesting in the High Arctic. *Canadian Journal of Zoology*, **90**, 961–971.

McMorrow, J., Lindley, S., Aylen, J., Cavan, G., Albertson, K. & Boys, D. (2009) Moorland wildlife risk, visitors and climate change. In *Drivers of Environmental Change in Uplands*. Bonn, A., Allott, T., Hubacek, K. & Stewart, J. Abingdon, UK: Routledge, pp. 404–431.

McNeely, J.A., Miller, K.R., Reid, W.V., Mittermeier, R.A. & Werner, T.B. (1990) *Conserving the World's Biological Diversity*. Gland, Switzerland: IUCN.

Mead, C.J. & Watmough, B.R. (1976) Suspended moult of trans-Saharan migrants in Iberia. *Bird Study*, **23**, 187–196.

Meehan, T.D., Hurlbert, A.H. & Gratton, C. (2010) Bird communities in future bioenergy landscapes of the Upper Midwest. *Proceedings of the National Academy of Sciences USA*, **104**, 18533–18538.

Mehlum, F. & Gabrielsen, G.W. (1993) The diet of high-arctic seabirds in coastal and ice-covered, pelagic areas near the Svalbard archipelago. *Polar Research*, **12**, 1–20.

Meinhausen, M., Smith, S.J., Calvin, K., Daniel, J.S., Kainuma, M.L.T., Lamarque, J.-F., Matsumoto, K., Montzka, S.A., Raper, S.C.B., Riahi, K., Thomson, A., Velders, G.J.M. & van Vuuren, D.P.P. (2011) The RCP greenhouse gas concentrations and their extensions from 1765 to 2300. *Climate Change*, **109**, 213–241.

Meire, P. M. (1991) Effects of a substantial reduction in intertidal area on numbers and densities of waders. In *Proceedings of the XX International Ornithological Congress*. Wellington: New Zealand Ornithological Congress Trust Board, pp. 2219–2227.

Mellin, C., Russell, D.B., Connell, S.D., Brook, B.W. & Fordham, D.A. (2012) Geographic range determinants of two commercially important marine molluscs. *Diversity and Distributions*, **18**, 133–146.

Meltofte, H. & Høye, T.T. (2007) Reproductive response to fluctuating lemming density and climate of the Long-tailed Skua *Stercorarius longicaudus* at Zackenberg, Northeast Greenland, 1996–2006. *Dansk Ornitologisk Forening Tidsskrift*, **101**, 109–119.

Meltofte, H., Høye, T.T., Schmidt, N.M. & Forchhammer, M.C. (2007a) Differences in food abundance cause inter-annual variation in the breeding phenology of High Arctic waders. *Polar Biology*, **30**, 601–606.

Meltofte, H., Piersma, T., Boyd, H., McCaffery, B., Golovnyuk, V.V., Graham, K., Morrison, R.I.G., Nol, E., Schamel, D., Schekkerman, H., Soloviev, M.Y., Tomkovich, P.S., Tracey, D.M., Tulp, I. & Wennerberg, L. (2007b) Effects of climate variation on the breeding ecology of Arctic shorebirds. *Meddelelser om Grønland Bioscience*, **59**, 1–48.

Meltofte, H., Suttler, B. & Hansen, J. (2007c) Breeding performance of tundra birds in High Arctic Northeast Greeland 1988–2007. *Arctic Birds*, **9**, 45–53.

Mendenhall, V.M. & Milne, H. (1985) Factors affecting duckling survival of Eiders *Somateria mollissima* in northeast Scotland. *Ibis*, **127**, 148–158.

Menzel, A., Sparks, T.H., Estrella, N., Koch, E., Aasa, A., Ahas, R., Alm-Kübler, K., Bissolli, P., Braslavská, O., Briede, A., Chmielewski, F.M., Crepinsek, Z., Curnel, Y., Dahl, Å., Defila, C., Donnelly, A., Filella, Y., Jatczak, K., Måge, F., Mestre, A., Nordli, Ø., Peñuelas, J., Pirinen, P., Remišová, V., Scheifinger, H., Striz, M., Susnik, A., van Vliet, A.J.H., Wielgolaski, F.-E., Zach, S. & Zust, A. (2006) European phenological response to climate change matches the warming pattern. *Global Change Biology*, **12**, 1969–1976.

Merckx, T., Feber, R.E, Riordan, P., Townsend, M.C., Bourn, N.A.D., Parsons, M.S. & Macdonald, D.W. (2009) Optimizing the biodiversity gain from agri-environment schemes. *Agriculture, Ecosystems and Environment*, **130**, 177–182.

Metz, C.E. (1978) Basic principles of ROC analysis. *Seminars in Nuclear Medicine*, **4**, 283–298.

Midgley, G.F., Davies, I.D., Albert, C.H., Altwegg, R., Hannah, L., Hughes, G.O., O'Halloran, L.R., Seo, C., Thorne, J.H. & Thuiller, W. (2010) BioMove – an integrated platform simulating the dynamic response of species to environmental change. *Ecography*, **33**, 612–616.

Miles, L. & Kapos, V. (2008) Reducing greenhouse gas emissions from deforestation and forest degradation: global land-use implications. *Science*, **320**, 1454–1455.

Miller, G.B. (2004) *Biological Oceanography*. Oxford, UK: Blackwell Science.

Miller-Rushing, A.J., Lloyd-Evans, T.L., Primack, R.B. & Satzinger, P. (2008) Bird migration times, climate change and changing population sizes. *Global Change Biology*, **14**, 1959–1972.

Miller-Rushing, A.J. & Primack, R.B. (2008) Global warming and flowering times in Thoreau's Concord: a community perspective. *Ecology*, **89**, 332–341.

Mills, K.L., Laidig, T., Ralston, S. & Sydeman, W.J. (2007) Diets of top predators indicate pelagic juvenile rockfish (*Sebastes* spp.) abundance in the California Current System. *Fisheries Oceanography*, **16**, 273–283.

Milsom, T.P., Hart, J.D., Parkin, W.K. & Peel, S. (2002) Management of coastal grazing marshes for breeding waders: the importance of surface topography and wetness. *Biological Conservation*, **103**, 199–207.

Mitchell, T.D., & Jones, P.D. (2005) An improved method of constructing a database of monthly climate observations and associated high-resolution grids. *International Journal of Climatology*, **25**, 693–712,

Møller, A.P. (1989) Population dynamics of a declining swallow *Hirundo rustica* population. *Journal of Animal Ecology*, **58**, 1051–1063.

Møller, A.P. & Fiedler, W. (2010) Long-term time series of ornithological data. In *Effects of Climate Change on Birds*. Møller, A.P., Fiedler, W. & Berthold, P. Oxford, UK: Oxford University Press, pp. 33–38.

Møller, A. P., Flensted-Jensen, E., Klarborg, K., Mardal, W. & Nielsen, J.T. (2010) Climate change affects the duration of the reproductive season in birds. *Journal of Animal Ecology*, **79**, 777–784.

Møller, A.P., Rubolini, D. & Lehikoinen, E. (2008) Populations of migratory bird species that did not show a phenological response to climate change are declining. *Proceedings of the Academy Natural Sciences USA*, **105**, 16195–16200.

Møller, A.P., Saino, N., Adamík, P., Ambrosini, R., Antonov, A., Campobello, D., Sokke, B.G., Fossøy, F., Lehikoinen, E., Martin-Vivaldi, M., Moksnes, A., Moskat, C., Røskaft, E., Rubolini, D., Schulze-Hagen, K., Soler, M. & Shykoff, J.A. (2011) Rapid change in host use of the common cuckoo *Cuculus canorus* linked to climate change. *Proceedings of the Royal Society, Series B*, **278**, 733–738.

Molnár, P.K., Derocher, A.E., Klanjscek, T. & Lewis, M.A. (2011) Predicting climate change impacts on polar bear litter size. *Nature Communications*, **2**, 186.

Molokwu, M.N., Nilsson, J.Å, Ottosson, U. & Olsson, O. (2010) Effects of season, water and predation risk on patch use by birds on the African savannah. *Oecologia*, **164**, 637–645.

Montanarella, L., Jones, R.J.A. & Hiederer, R. (2006) The distribution of peatland in Europe. *Mires and Peat*, **1**, 01.

Montevecchi, W.A., & Myers, R.A. (1997) Centurial and decadal oceanographic influences on changes in northern gannet populations and diets in the north-west Atlantic: implications for climate change. *ICES Journal of Marine Science*, **54**, 608–614.

Monticelli, D., Ramos, J.A. & Quartly, G.D. (2007) Effects of annual changes in primary productivity and ocean indices on the breeding performance of tropical roseate terns in the western Indian Ocean. *Marine Ecology Progress Series*, **351**, 273–286.

Moore, I.T., Bonier, F. & Wingfield, J.C. (2005) Reproductive asynchrony and population divergence between two tropical bird populations. *Behavioural Ecology*, **16**, 755–762.

Moore, R.P., Robinson, W.D., Lovette, I.J. & Robinson, T.R. (2008) Experimental evidence for extreme dispersal limitation in tropical forest birds. *Ecology Letters*, **11**, 960–968.

Moreira, F. & Russo, D. (2007) Modelling the impact of agricultural abandonment and wildfires on vertebrate diversity in Mediterranean Europe. *Landscape Ecology*, **22**, 1461–1476.

Moreno-Rueda, G. & Pizarro, M. (2008) Temperature differentially mediates species richness of birds of different biogeographic types. *Ardea*, **96**, 115–120.

Moriarty, P. & Honnery, D. (2012) What is the global potential for renewable energy. *Renewable and Sustainable Energy Reviews*, **16**, 244–252.

Morris, A.J., Holland, J.M., Smith, B. & Jones, N.E. (2004) Sustainable Arable Farming for an Improved Environment (SAFFIE): managing winter wheat sward structure for Skylarks *Alauda arvensis*. *Ibis*, **146 Suppl 2**, 155–162,

Morrison, C.A., Robinson, R.A., Clark, J.A. & Gill, J.A. (2010) Spatial and temporal variability in population trends in a long-distance migratory bird. *Diversity & Distributions*, **16**, 620–627.

Morrison, C.A., Robinson, R.A., Clark, J.A., Risely, K. & Gill, J.A. (2013) Recent population declines in Afro-Palaearctic migratory birds: the influence of breeding and non-breeding seasons. *Diversity & Distributions*, **19**, 1051–1058.

Morrison, R.I.G., Hobson, K.A. (2004) Use of body stores in shorebirds after arrival on high-Arctic breeding grounds. *The Auk*, **121**, 333–344.

Morrissette, M., Bêty, J., Gauthier, G., Reed, A., & Lefebvre, J. (2010) Climate, trophic interactions, density dependence and carry-over effects on the population productivity of a migratory Arctic herbivorous bird. *Oikos*, **119**, 1181–1191.

Mortensen, H.S., Dupont, Y.L. & Olesen, J.M. (2008) A snake in paradise: disturbance of plant reproduction following extirpation of bird flower-visitors on Guam. *Biological Conservation*, **141**, 2146–2154.

Moser, B.W. & Garton, E.O. (2009) Short-term effects of timber harvest and weather on Northern goshawk reproduction in northern Idaho. *Journal of Raptor Research*, **43**, 1–10.

Moss, R., Oswald, J. & Baines, D. (2001) Climate change and breeding success: decline of the capercaillie in Scotland. *Journal of Animal Ecology*, **70**, 47–61.

Moss, R.H., Edmonds, J.A., Hibbard, K.A., Manniing, M.R., Rose, S.K., van Vuuren, D.P., Carter, T.R., Emori, S., Kainuma, M., Kram, T., Meehl, G.A., Mitchell, J.F.B., Nakicenovic, N., Riahi, K., Smith, S.J., Stouffer, R.J., Thomson, A.M., Weyant, J.P. & Wilbanks, T.J. (2010) The next generation of scenarios for climate change research and assessment. *Nature*, **463**, 747–756.

Moussus, J.-P., Clavel, J., Jiguet, F. & Julliard, R. (2011) Which are the phenologically flexible species? A case study with common passerine birds. *Oikos*, **120**, 991–998.

Moyle, R.G., Filardi, C.E., Smith, C.E. & Diamond, J. (2009) Explosive Pleistocene diversification and hemispheric expansion of a 'great speciator'. *Proceedings of the National Academy of Sciences USA*, **106**, 1863–1868.

Mudge, G.P. & Talbot, T.R. (1993) The breeding biology and causes of failure of Scottish black-throated divers *Gavia arctica*. *Ibis*, **135**, 113–120.

Murray, B.C. (2012) Mangrove's hidden value. *Nature Climate Change*, **2**, 773–774.

Musters, C.J.M., Noordverliet, M.A.W. & Keurs, W.J.T. (1996) Bird casualties caused by a wind energy project in an estuary. *Bird Study*, **43**, 124–127.

Mustin, K., Benton, T.G., Dytham, C. & Travis, J.M.J. (2009) The dynamics of climate-induced range shifting; perspectives from simulation modelling. *Oikos*, **118**, 131–137.

Mustin, K., Sutherland, W.J. & Gill, J.A. (2007) The complexity of predicting climate-induced ecological impacts. *Climate Research*, **35**, 165–175.

Myers, J.H. (1998) Synchrony in outbreaks of forest Lepidoptera: a possible example of the Moran effect. *Ecology*, **79**, 1111–1117.

Myers, N., Mittermeier, R.A., Mittermeier, C.G., da Fonseca, G.A.B. & Kent, J. (2000) Biodiversity hotspots for conservation priorities. *Nature*, **403**, 853–858.

Nagy, L.R. & Holmes, R.T. (2005) Food limits annual fecundity of a migratory songbird: an experimental study. *Ecology*, **86**, 675–681.

Nájera, A. & Simonetti, J.A. (2010) Can oil palm plantations become bird friendly? *Agroforestry Systems*, **80**, 203–209.

Navarro, J.L. & Bucher, E.H. (1992) Annual variation in the timing of breeding of the Monk Parakeet in relation to climatic factors. *Wilson Bulletin*, **104**, 545–549.

Neelin, J.D., Münnich, M., Su, H., Meyerson, J.E. & Holloway, C.E. (2006) Tropical drying trends in global warming models and observations. *Proceedings of the National Academy of Sciences USA*, **103**, 6110–6115.

Nepstad, D.C., McGrath, D.G. & Soares-Filho, B. (2011) Systematic consevation, REDD and the future of the Amazon Basin. *Conservation Biology*, **25**, 1113–1116.

Nevoux, M. & Barbraud, C. (2006) Relationships between sea ice concentration, sea surface temperature and demographic traits of thin-billed prions. *Polar Biology*, **29**, 445–453.

Nevoux, M., Barbraud, J.-C. & Barbraud, C. (2008) Nonlinear impact of climate on survival in a migratory stork population. *Journal of Animal Ecology*, **77**, 1143–1152.

Newson, S.E., Mendes, S., Crick, H.Q.P., Dulvy, N.K., Houghton, J.D.R., Hays, G.C., Hutson, A.M., Macleod, C.D., Pierce, G.J. & Robinson, R.A. (2009) Indicators of the impact of climate change on migratory species. *Endangered Species Research*, **7**, 101–113.

Newton, I. (1979) *Population Ecology of Raptors*: Berkhamsted, UK: T. & A.D. Poyser.

Newton, I. (1986) *The Sparrowhawk*. Berkhamstead, UK: Poyser.

Newton, I. (2004) The recent declines of farmland bird populations in Britain: an appraisal of causal factors and conservation actions. *Ibis*, **146**, 579–600.

Newton, I. (2007) Weather-related mass-mortality events in migrants. *Ibis*, **149**, 453–467.

Newton, I. & Dale, L. (1996) Relationship between migration and latitude among West European birds. *Journal of Animal Ecology*, **65**, 137–146.

Newton, I. & Little, N. (2009) Assessment of wind-farm and other bird casualties from carcasses found on a Northumbrian beach over an 11-year period. *Bird Study*, **56**, 15–167.

Newton, I., Rothery, P. & Dale, L.C. (1998) Density-dependence in the bird populations of an oak wood over 22 years. *Ibis*, **140**, 131–136.

Nicholls, R.J. & Cazenave, A. (2010) Sea-level rise and its impact on coastal zones. *Science*, **328**, 1517–1520.

Nicholson, E. & Possingham, H.P. (2006) Objectives for multiple species conservation planning. *Conservation Biology*, **20**, 871–881.

Nicholson, E. & Possingham, H.P. (2007) Making conservation decisions under uncertainty for the persistence of multiple species. *Ecological Applications*, **17**, 251–265.

Nicholson, E., Westphal, M.I., Frank, K., Rochester, W.A., Pressey, R.L., Lindenmayer, D.B. & Possingham, H.P. (2006) A new method for conservation planning for the persistence of multiple species. *Ecology Letters*, **9**, 1049–1060.

Niehaus, A.C. & Ydenberg, R.C. (2006) Ecological factors associated with the breeding and migratory phenology of high-latitude breeding western sandpipers. *Polar Biology*, **30**, 11–17.

Niel, C. and Lebreton, J.D. (2005) Using demographic invariants to detect overharvested bird populations from incomplete data. *Conservation Biology*, **19**, 826–835.

Nielsen, J.T. (2004) A population study of sparrowhawks *Accipiter nisus* in Vendsyssel, Denmark, 1977–1997. *Dansk Ornitologisk Forening Tidsskrift*, **98**, 147–162.

Nielsen, J.T. & Møller, A.P. (2006) Effects of food abundance, density and climate change on reproduction in the sparrowhawk *Accipiter nisus*. *Oecologia*, **149**, 505–518.

Niemuth, N.D., Solberg, J.W. & Shaffer, T.L. (2008) Influence of moisture on density and distribution of grassland birds in North Dakota. *The Condor*, **110**, 211–222.

Nilsson, J.-Å. & Källander, H. (2006) Leafing phenology and timing of egg laying in great tits *Parus major* and blue tits *P. caeruleus*. *Journal of Avian Biology*, **37**, 357–363.

Nilsson, J.-E. (2008) A 20-year study of a nest-box breeding population with special regard to the pied flycatcher *Ficedula hypoleuca*. *Ornis Svecica*, **18**, 52–64.

Nilsson, S.G. (1987) Limitation and regulation of population density in the nuthatch *Sitta europaea* (aves) breeding in natural cavities. *Journal of Animal Ecology*, **56**, 921–937.

Nilsson, S.G., Olsson, S., Svensson, S. & Wiktander, U. (1992) Population trends and fluctuations in Swedish woodpeckers. *Ornis Svecica*, **2**, 13–21.

Nolet, B.A., Bauer, S., Feige, N., Kokorev, Y.I., Popuv, I.Y. & Ebbinge, B.S. (2013) Faltering lemming cycles reduce productivity and population size of a migratory Arctic goose species. *Journal of Animal Ecology*, **82**, 804–813.

Nores, M. (2009) Are bird populations in tropical and subtropical forests of South America affected by climate change? *Climatic Change*, **97**, 543–551.

Norris, D.R., Marra, P.P., Kyser, T.K., Sherry, T.W. & Ratcliffe, L.M. (2004) Tropical winter habitat limits reproductive success on the temperate breeding grounds in a migratory bird. *Proceedings of the Royal Society of London, Series B*, **271**, 59–64.

Norris, K. (2004) Managing threatened species: the ecological toolbox, evolutionary theory and declining-population paradigm. *Journal of Applied Ecology*, **41**, 413–426.

North, P.W. (1979) Relating grey heron survival rates to winter weather conditions. *Bird Study*, **26**, 23–28.

Northrup, J.M. & Wittemyer, G. (2013) Characterising the impacts of emerging energy development on wildlife, with an eye towards mitigation. *Ecology Letters*, **16**, 112–125.

North American Bird Conservation Initiative, U.S. Committee (2011) *The State of the Birds 2011 Report on Public Land and Waters*. Washington, DC: U.S. Department of the Interior, p. 48.

Novoa, C., Besnard, A., Brenot, J.F. & Ellison, L.N. (2008) Effect of weather on the reproductive rate of Rock Ptarmigan *Lagopus muta* in the eastern Pyrenees. *Ibis*, **150**, 270–278.

Nussey, D.H., Wilson, A.J. & Brommer, J.E. (2007) The evolutionary ecology of individual phenotypic plasticity in wild populations. *Journal of Evolutionary Biology*, **20**, 831–844.

Nyholm, N.E.I. (2011) Dynamics and reproduction of a nest-box breeding population of Pied Flycatcher *Ficedula hypoleuca* in a subalpine birch forest in Swedish Lapland during a period of 46 years. *Ornis Svecica*, **21**, 133–156.

O'Brien, E.M. (1998) Water-energy dynamics, climate, and prediction of woody plant species richness: an interim general model. *Journal of Biogeography*, **25**, 379–398.

Oaks, J.L., Gilbert, M., Virani, M.Z., Watson, R.T., Meteyer, C.U., Rideout, B.A., Shivaprasad, H.L., Ahmed, S., Chaudhrt, M.J.A., Arshad, M., Mahmood, S., Ali, A. & Khan, A.A. (2004) Diclofenac residues as the cause of vulture population decline in Pakistan. *Nature*, **427**, 630–633.

Ockendon, N., Baker, D.J., Carr, J.A., White, E.C., Almond, R.E.A., Amano, T., Bertram, E., Bradbury, R.B., Bradley, C., Butchart, S.H.M., Doswald, N., Foden, W., Gill, D.J.C., Green, R.E., Sutherland, W.J., Tanner, E.U.J. & Pearce-Higgins, J.W. (2014) Mechanisms underpinning climatic impacts on natural populations: altered species interactions are more important than direct effects. *Global Change Biology*. DOI:10.1111/gcb.12559.

Ockendon, N., Hewson, C.H., Johnston, A. & Atkinson, P.W. (2012) Declines in British-breeding populations of Afro-Palaearctic migrant birds and linked to bioclimatic wintering zone in Africa, possibly via constraints on arrival time advancement. *Bird Study*, **59**, 111–125.

Ockendon, N., Leech, D. & Pearce-Higgins, J.W. (2013) Climatic effects on breeding grounds are more important drivers of breeding phenology in migrant birds than carry-over effects from wintering grounds. *Biology Letters*, **9**, 20130669.

O'Donnell, C.F.J. (1996) Predators and the decline of New Zealand forest birds: An introduction to the hole-nesting bird and predator programme. *New Zealand Journal of Zoology*, **23**, 213–219.

O'Donnell, S., Kaspari, M., Kumar, A., Lattke, J. & Powell, S. (2011) Elevation and geographic variation in army ant swarm raids. *Insectes Sociaux*, **58**, 293–298.

O'Grady, J.J., Reed, D.H., Brook, B.W. & Frankham, R. (2004) What are the best correlates of predicted extinction risk? *Biological Conservation*, **118**, 513–520.

Ohlemüller, R., Anderson, B.J., Araújo, M.B., Butchart, S.H.M., Kudrna, O., Ridgely, R.S. & Thomas, C.D. (2008) The coincidence of climate and species rarity: high risk to small-range species from climate change. *Biology Letters*, **4**, 568–572.

Oliver, T.H., Smithers, R.J., Bailey, S., Walsmsley, C.A. & Watts, K. (2012) A decision framework for considering climate change adaptation in biodiversity conservation planning. *Journal of Applied Ecology*, **49**, 1247–1255.

Olivier, F., van Franeker, J.A., Creuwels, J.C.S. & Woehler, E.J. (2005) Variations of snow petrel breeding success in relation to sea-ice extent: detecting local response to large-scale processes? *Polar Biology*, **28**, 687–699.

Oloffson, J., Oksanen, L., Callaghan, T., Hulme, P.E., Oksanen, T. & Suominen, O. (2009) Herbivores inhibit climate-driven shrub expansion on the tundra. *Global Change Biology*, **15**, 2681–2693.

O'Neill, G.A., Hamann, A. & Wang, T. (2008) Accounting for population variation improves estimates of the impact of climate change on species' growth and distribution. *Journal of Applied Ecology*, **45**, 1040–1049.

Opdam, P. & Wascher, D. (2004) Climate change meets habitat fragmentation: linking landscape and biogeographical scale level in research and conservation. *Biological Conservation*, **117**, 285–297.

Orell, M. (1989) Population fluctuations and survival of great tits *Parus major* dependent on food supplied by man in winter. *Ibis*, **131**, 112–127.

Orme, C.D.L., Davies, R.G., Burgess, M., Eigenbrod, F., Pickup, N., Olson, V.A., Webster, A.J., Ding, T.-S., Rasmussen, P.C., Ridgely, R.S., Stattersfield, A.J., Bennett, P.M., Blackburn, T.M., Gaston, K.J. & Owens, I.P.F. (2005) Global hotspots of species richness are not congruent with endemism or threat. *Nature*, **436**, 1016–1019.

Orme, C.D.L., Davies, R.G., Olson, V.A., Thomas, G.H., Ding, T.-S., Rasmussen, P.C., Ridgely, R.S., Stattersfield, A.J., Bennett, P.M., Owens, I.P.F., Blackburn, T.M. & Gaston, K.J. (2006) Global patterns of geographic range size in birds. *PLoS Biology*, **4**, e208.

Oro, D. & Furness, R.W. (2002) Influences of food availability and predation on survival of kittiwakes. *Ecology*, **83**, 2516–2528.

Oro, D., Torres, R., Rodríguez, C. & Drummond, H. (2010) Climate influence on demographic parameters of a tropical seabird varies with age and sex. *Ecology*, **91**, 1205–1214.

Osborne, P.E., al Bowardi, M. & Bailey, T.A. (1997) Migration of the Houbara Bustard *Chlamgdotis undulata* from Abu Dhabi to Turkmenistan; the first results from satellite tracking studies. *Ibis*, **139**, 192–196.

Österblom, H., Casini, M., Olsson, O. & Bignert, A. (2006) Fish, seabirds and trophic cascades in the Baltic Sea. *Marine Ecology Progress Series*, **323**, 233–238.

Oswald, S.A., Bearhop, S., Furness, R.W., Huntley, B. & Hamer, K.C. (2008) Heat stress in a high-latitude seabird: effects of temperature and food supply on bathing and nest attendance of great skuas *Catharacta skua*. *Journal of Avian Biology*, **39**, 163–169.

Otto, A., Otto, F.E.L., Boucher, O., Church, J., Hergel, G., Forster, P.M., Gillett, N.P., Gregory, J., Johnson, G.C., Knutti, R., Lewis, N., Lohmann, U., Marotzke, J., Myhre, G., Shindell, D., Stevens, B. & Allen, M.R. (2013) Energy budget constraints on climate response. *Nature Geoscience*, **6**, 415–416.

Pandit, M.K. & Grumbine, R.E. (2012) Potential effects of ongoing and proposed hydropower development on terrestrial biological diversity in the Indian Himalaya. *Conservation Biology*, **26**, 1061–1071.

Paradis, E., Baillie S.R., Sutherland W.J. & Gregory R.D. (1998) Patterns of natal and breeding dispersal in birds. *Journal of Animal Ecology*, **67**, 518–536.

Parchman, T.L. & Benkman, C.W. (2002) Diversifying coevolution between crossbills and black spruce on Newfoundland. *Evolution*, **56**, 1663–1672.

Park, K.J., Robertson, P.A., Campbell, S.T. Foster, R., Russell, Z.M., Newborn, D. & Hudson, P.J. (2001) The role of invertebrates in the diet, growth and survival of red grouse (*Lagopus lagopus scoticus*) chicks. *Journal of Zoology (London)*, **254**, 137–145.

Parker, D.E., Legg, T.P. & Folland, C.K. (1992) A new daily Central England Temperature Series, 1772–1991. *International Journal of Climatology*, **12**, 317–342.

Parker, I.M., Simberloff, D., Londscale, W.M., Goodell, K., Wonham, P., Kareiva, P.M., Williamson, M.H., Van Holle, B., Moyle, P.B., Byers, J.E. & Goldwasser, L. (1999) Impact: toward a framework for understanding the ecological effects of invaders. *Biological Invasions*, **1**, 13–19.

Parmesan, C. (2007) Influences of species, latitudes and methodologies on estimates of phenological response to global warming. *Global Change Biology*, **13**, 1860–1872.

Parmesan, C. & Yohe, G. (2003) A globally coherent fingerprint of climate change impacts across natural systems. *Nature*, **421**, 37–42.

Parr, R. (1992) The decline to extinction of a population of Golden Plover in north east Scotland. *Ornis Scandinavica*, **23**, 152–158.

Pasinelli, G. (2001) Breeding performance of the Middle Spotted Woodpecker *Dendrocopos medius* in relation to weather and territory quality. *Ardea*, **89**, 353–361.

Pasinelli, G., Schaub, M., Häfliger, G., Frey, M., Jakober, H., Müller, M., Stauber, W., Tryjanowski, P., Zollinger, J.-L. & Jenni, L. (2011) Impact of density and environmental factors on population fluctuations in a migratory passerine. *Journal of Animal Ecology*, **80**, 225–234.

Peach, W., Baillie, S. & Underhill, L. (1991) Survival of British sedge warblers *Acrocephalus schoenobaenus* in relation to west African rainfall. *Ibis*, **133**, 300–305.

Peach, W.J., Denny, M., Cotton, P.A., Hill, I.F., Gruar, D., Barritt, D., Impey, A. & Mallord, J. (2004a) Habitat selection by song thrushes in stable and declining farmland populations. *Journal of Appied Ecology*, **41**, 275–293.

Peach, W.J., du Feu, C. & McMeeking, J. (1995) Site tenacity and survival rates of Wrens *Troglodytes troglodytes* and Treecreepers *Certhia familiaris* in a Nottinghamshire wood. *Ibis*, **137**, 497–507.

Peach, W.J., Robinson, R.A. & Murray, K.A. (2004b) Demographic and environmental causes of the decline of rural Song Thrushes *Turdus philomelos* in lowland Britain. *Ibis*, **146 Suppl 2**, 50–59.

Peach, W.J., Thompson, P.S. & Coulson, J.C. (1994) Annual and long-term variation in the survival rates of British Lapwings *Vanellus vanellus*. *Journal of Animal Ecology*, **63**, 60–70.

Pearce-Higgins, J.W. (2000) The avian community structure of a Bolivian savanna on the edge of the cerrado system. *El Hornero*, **15**, 77–84.

Pearce-Higgins, J.W. (2010) Using diet to assess the sensitivity of northern and upland birds to climate change. *Climate Research*, **45**, 119–130.

Pearce-Higgins, J.W. (2011a) Modelling conservation management options for a southern range-margin population of Golden Plover *Pluvialis apricaria* vulnerable to climate change. *Ibis*, **153**, 345–356.

Pearce-Higgins, J.W. (2011b) How ecological science can help manage the effects of climate change: a case study of upland birds. In *The Changing Nature of Scotland*. Marrs, S.J., Foster, S., Hendrie, C., Mackey, E.C. & Thompson, D.B.A. Edinburgh, UK: TSO Scotland, pp. 397–414.

Pearce-Higgins, J.W., Beale, C.M., Wilson, J. & Bonn, A. (2006) *Analysis of Moorland Breeding Bird Distribution and Change in the Peak District*. Moors for the Future Report 11, Hope, UK: Moors for the Future Partnership.

Pearce-Higgins, J.W., Brace, R.C. & Hornbuckle, J. (2007a) Survival of band-tailed manakins. *The Condor*, **109**, 167–172.

Pearce-Higgins, J.W., Bradbury, R.B., Chamberlain, D.E., Drewitt, A., Langston, R.H.W. & Willis, S.G. (2011a) Targeting research to underpin climate change adaptation for birds. *Ibis*, **153**, 207–211.

Pearce-Higgins, J.W., Dennis, P., Whittingham, M.J. & Yalden, D.W. (2010) Impacts of climate on prey abundance account for fluctuations in a population of a northern wader at the southern edge of its range. *Global Change Biology*, **16**, 12–23.

Pearce-Higgins, J.W. & Gill, J.A. (2010) Unravelling the mechanisms linking climate change, agriculture and avian population declines. *Ibis*, **152**, 439–442.

Pearce-Higgins, J.W. & Grant, M.C. (2006) Relationships between bird abundance and the composition and structure of moorland vegetation. *Bird Study*, **53**, 112–125.

Pearce-Higgins, J.W., Grant, M.C., Robinson, M.C. & Haysom, S.L. (2007b) The role of forest maturation in causing the decline of Black Grouse *Tetrao tetrix*. *Ibis*, **149**, 143–155.

Pearce-Higgins, J.W., Grant, M.C., Beale, C.M., Buchanan, G.M. & Sim, I.M.W. (2009a) International importance and drivers of change in upland bird populations. In *Drivers of Environmental Change in Uplands*. Bonn, A., Allott, T., Hubacek, K. & Stewart, J. Abingdon, UK: Routledge, pp. 209–227.

Pearce-Higgins, J.W., Johnston, A., Ausden, M., Dodd, A., Newson, S.E., Ockendon, N., Thaxter, C.B., Bradbury, R.B., Chamberlain, D.E., Jiguet, F., Rehfisch, M.M. & Thomas, C.D. (2011b) *CHAIN-SPAN Final Report*: Final Report to the Climate Change Impacts on Avian Interests of Protected Area Networks (CHAINSPAN) Steering Group. Defra Ref: WC0750/CR0440. http://randd.defra.gov.

uk/Default.aspx?Menu=Menu&Module=More&Location=None&Completed=2&ProjectID=16731 (last accessed 13 August 2012).

Pearce-Higgins, J.W., Stephen, L., Douse, A. & Langston, R.H.W. (2012) Greater impacts of wind farms on bird populations during construction than subsequent operation: results of a multi-site and multi-species analysis. *Journal of Applied Ecology*, **49**, 386–394.

Pearce-Higgins, J.W., Stephen, L., Langston, R.H.W., Bainbridge, I.P. & Bullman, R. (2009b) The distribution of breeding birds around upland wind farms. *Journal of Applied Ecology*, **46**, 1323–1331.

Pearce-Higgins, J.W., Stephen, L., Langston, R.H.W. & Bright, J.A. (2008) Assessing the cumulative impacts of wind farms on peatland birds: a case study of golden plover *Pluvialis apricaria* in Scotland. *Mires and Peat*, **4**, 1–13.

Pearce-Higgins, J.W. & Yalden, D.W. (2002) Variation in the growth and survival of Golden Plover *Pluvialis apricaria* chicks. *Ibis*, **144**, 200–209.

Pearce-Higgins, J.W. & Yalden, D.W. (2003a) Golden Plover *Pluvialis apricaria* breeding success on a moor managed for shooting Red Grouse *Lagopus lagopus*. *Bird Study*, **50**, 170–177.

Pearce-Higgins, J.W. & Yalden, D.W. (2003b) Variation in the use of pasture by breeding Golden Plovers *Pluvialis apricaria* in relation to prey availability. *Ibis*, **145**, 365–381.

Pearce-Higgins, J.W. & Yalden, D.W. (2004) Habitat selection, diet, arthropod availability and growth of a moorland wader: the ecology of European Golden Plover *Pluvialis apricaria* chicks. *Ibis*, **146**, 335–346.

Pearce-Higgins, J.W., Yalden, D.W., Dougall, T.W. & Beale, C.M. (2009c) Does climate change explain the decline of a trans-Saharan Afro-Palaearctic migrant? *Oecologia*, **159**, 649–659.

Pearce-Higgins, J.W., Yalden, D.W. & Whittingham, M.J. (2005) Warmer springs advance the breeding phenology of golden plovers *Pluvialis apricaria* and their prey (Tipulidae). *Oecologia*, **143**, 470–476.

Pearson, D.J. (1973) Moult of some Palaearctic warblers wintering in Uganda. *Bird Study*, **20**, 24–36.

Pearson, R.G. & Dawson, T.P. (2003) Predicting the impacts of climate change on the distribution of species: are bioclimate envelope models useful? *Global Ecology and Biogeography*, **12**, 361–371.

Pearson, R.G., Dawson, T.P., & Liu, C. (2004) Modelling species distributions in Britain: a hierarchical integration of climate and land-cover data. *Ecography*, **27**, 285–298.

Peery, M.Z., Gutiérrez, R.J., Kirby, R., Ledee, O.E. & Lahaye, W. (2012) Climate change and spotted owls: potentially contrasting responses in the Southwestern United States. *Global Change Biology*, **18**, 865–880.

Peh, K., Sodhi, N.S., de Jong, J., Şekercioğlu, C.H., Yap, C.A.M. & Lim, S.L.H. (2006) Conservation value of degraded habitats for forest birds in southern Peninsular Malaysia. *Diversity and Distributions*, **12**, 572–581.

Peh, K.S.-H. (2007) Potential effects of climate change on elevational distributions of tropical birds in southeast Asia. *The Condor*, **109**, 437–441.

Pendleton, L., Donato, D.C., Murray, M.C., Crooks, S., Jenkins, W.A., Sifleet, S., Craft, C., Fourqurean, J.W., Kauffman, J.B., Marbà, N., Megonigal, P., Pidgeon, E., Herr, D., Gordon, D. & Baldera, A. (2012) Estimating global 'blue carbon' emissions from conversion and degradation of vegetated coastal ecosystems. *PLoS ONE*, **7**, e43542.

Percival, S.M. (2010) *Kentish Flats Offshore Wind Farm: Diver Surveys 2009–10*. Ecology Consulting for Vattenfall Wind Power.

Perdeck, A.C. & Cavé, A.J. (1992) Laying date in the coot: effects of age and mate choice. *Journal of Animal Ecology*, **61**, 13–19.

Perdeck, A.C., Visser, M.E. & van Balen, J.H. (2000) Great tit *Parus major* survival, and the beech-crop cycle. *Ardea*, **88**, 99–108.

Perrins, C.M. (1970) The timing of bird's breeding seasons. *Ibis*, **112**, 242–253.

Perry, M. & Hollis, D. (2005) The generation of monthly gridded datasets for a range of climatic variables over the United Kingdom. *International Journal of Climatology*, **25**, 1041–1054.

Petersen, I.K., Christensen, T.K., Kahlert, J., Desholm, M. & Fox, A.D. (2006) *Final results of bird studies at the offshore wind farms at Nysted and Horns Rev, Denmark*. Natural Environment Research Institute.

Peterson, A.T. (2003) Subtle recent distributional shifts in Great Plains bird species. *Southwestern Naturalist*, **48**, 289–292.

Peterson, A.T., Menon, S. & Li, X. (2010) Recent advances in the climate change biology literature: describing the whole elephant. *WIREs Climate Change*, **1**, 548–555.

Peterson, A.T., Papeş, M. & Soberón, J. (2008) Rethinking receiver operating characteristic analysis applications in ecological niche modeling. *Ecological Modelling*, **213**, 63–72.

Phalan, B. (2009) The social and environmental impacts of biofuels in Asia: a review. *Applied Energy*, **86**, S21–S29.

Phalan, B., Balmford, A., Green, R.E. & Scharlemann, J.P.W. (2011b) Minimising the harm to biodiversity of producing more food globally. *Food Policy*, **36**, S62–S71.

Phalan, B., Onial, M. Balmford, A. & Green, R.E. (2011a) Reconciling food production and biodiversity conservation: land sharing and land sparing compared. *Science*, **333**, 1289–1291.

Phillips, S.J., Anderson, R.P. & Schapire, R.E. (2006) Maximum entropy modeling of species geographic distributions. *Ecological Modelling*, **190**, 231–259.

Picozzi, N., Moss, R. & Kortland, K. (1999) Diet and survival of capercaillie *Tetrao urogallus* chicks in Scotland. *Wildlife Biology*, **5**, 11–23.

Pienimäki, M. & Leppäkoski, E. (2004) Invasion pressure on the Finnish Lake District: invasion corridors and barriers. *Biological Invasions*, **6**, 331–346.

Pienkowski, M.W. (1984) Breeding biology and population dynamics of ringed plovers *Charadrius hiaticula* in Britain and Greenland: nest predation as a possible factor limiting distribution and timing of breeding. *Journal of Zoology (London)*, **202**, 83–114.

Pienkowski, M.W., Lloyd, C.S. & Minton, C.D.T. (1979) Seasonal and migrational weight changes in Dunlins. *Bird Study*, **26**, 134–148.

Piersma, T., Rogers, K.G., Boyd, H., Bunskoeke, E.J. & Jukema, J. (2005) Demography of Eurasian Golden Plovers *Pluvialis apricaria* staging in The Netherlands, 1949–2000. *Ardea*, **93**, 49–64.

Pimtentel, C. & Nilsson, J.Å. (2007) Response of great tits *Parus major* to an irruption of a pine processionary moth *Thaumetopoea pityocampa* population with a shifted phenology. *Ardea*, **95**, 191–199.

Point Carbon. (2009) *Carbon Market Monitor January 2009: a review of 2008*. Oslo, Norway: Point Carbon.

Pomara, L.Y., Ruokalainen, K., Tuomisto, H. & Young, K.R. (2012) Avian composition co-varies with floristic composition and soil nutrient concentration in Amazonian upland forests. *Biotropica*, **44**, 545–553.

Pons, P., Lambert, B., Rigolot, E. & Prodon, R. (2003) The effects of grassland management using fire on habitat occupancy and conservation of birds in a mosaic landscape. *Biodiversity and Conservation*, **12**, 1843–1860.

Pope, F.D., Braesicke, P., Grainger, R.G., Kalberer, M., Watson, I.M., Davidson, P.J. & Cox, R.A. (2012) Stratospheric aerosol particles and solar-radiation management. *Nature Climate Change*, **2**, 713–719.

Popy, S., Bordignon, L. & Prodon, R. (2010) A weak upward elevational shift in the distributions of breeding birds in the Italian Alps. *Journal of Biogeography*, **37**, 57–67.

Porzecanski, A.L. & Cracraft, J. (2005) Cladistic analysis of distributions and endemism (CADE): using raw distributions of birds to unravel the biogeography of the South American aridlands. *Journal of Biogeography*, **32**, 261–275.

Possingham, H.P. & Wilson, K.A. (2005) Turning up the heat on hotspots. *Nature*, **436**, 919–920.

Post, E., Forchhammer, M.C., Bret-Harte, M.S., Callaghan, T.V., Christensen, T.R., Elberling, B., Fox, A.D., Gilg, O., Hik, D.S., Høye, T.T., Ims, R.A., Jeppesen, E., Klein, D.R., Madsen, J., McGuire, D., Rysgaard, S., Schindler, D.E., Stirling, I., Tamstorf, M.P., Tyler, N.J.C., van der Wal, R., Welker, J., Wookey, P.A., Schmidt, N.M. & Aastrup, P. (2009) Ecological dynamics across the Arctic associated with recent climate change. *Science*, **325**, 1355–1358.

Potti, J. (1998) Arrival time from spring migration in male pied flycatchers: individual consistency and familial resemblance. *The Condor*, **100**, 702–708.

Potti, J. (2008) Temperature during egg formation and the effect of climate warming on egg size in a small songbird. *Acta Oecologica*, **33**, 387–393.

Potti, J. (2009) Advanced breeding dates in relation to recent climate warming in a Mediterranean montane population of Blue Tits *Cyanistes caeruleus*. *Journal of Ornithology*, **150**, 893–901.

Poulin, B., Lefebvre, G. & Mauchamp, A. (2002) Habitat requirements of passerines and reedbed management in southern France. *Biological Conservation*, **107**, 315–325.

Poulin, B., Lefebvre, G. & McNeil, R. (1992) Tropical avian phenology in relation to abundance and exploitation of food resources. *Ecology*, **73**, 2295–2309.

Pounds, A., Bustamante, M.R., Coloma, L.A., Consuegra, J.A., Fogden, M.P.L., Foster, P.M., La Marca, E., Masters, K.L., Merino-Viteri, A., Puschendorf, R., Ron, S.R., Sánchez-Azofeifa,

G.A., Still, C.J. & Young, B.E. (2006) Widespread amphibian extinctions from epidemic disease driven by global warming. *Nature*, **439**, 161–167.

Powell, T.W.R. & Lenton, T.M. (2013) Scenarios for future biodiversity loss due to multiple drivers reveal conflict between mitigating climate change and preserving biodiversity. *Environmental Research Letters*, **8**, 025024.

Prakash, V., Green, R.E., Pain, D.J. Ranade, S.P., Saravanan, S., Prakash, N., Venkitachahalam, R., Cuthbert, R., Rahmani, A.R. & Cunningham A.A. (2007) Recent changes in population of resident Gyps vultures in India. *Journal of the Bombay Natural History Society*, **104**, 129–135.

Prakash, V., Pain, D.J., Cunningham, A.A., Donald, P.F., Prakash, N., Verma, A., Gargi, R., Sivakumar, S. & Rahmani, A. R. (2003) Catastrophic collapse of Indian white-backed *Gyps bengalensis* and long-billed *Gyps indicus* vulture populations. *Biological Conservation*, **109**, 381–390.

Pratt, A. & Peach, W. (1991) Site tenacity and annual survival of a willow warbler *Phylloscopus tricholus* population in Southern England. *Ringing & Migration*, **12**, 128–134.

Prentice, I.C., Cramer, W., Harrison, S.P., Leemans, R., Monserud, R.A. & Solomon, A.M. (1992) A global biome model based on plant physiology and dominance, soil properties and climate. *Journal of Biogeography*, **19**, 117–134.

Prentice, I.C., Farquar, G.D., Fasham, M.J.R., Goulden, M.L., Scholes, R.J. & Wallace, D.W.R. (2001) The carbon cycle and atmospheric carbon dioxide. In *Climate Change 2001: The Scientific Basis*. Houghton, J.T., Ding, Y., Griggs, D.J., Noguer, M., van der Linden, P.J., Dai, X., Maskell, K. & Johnson, C.A. Cambridge, UK: Cambridge University Press, pp. 183–237.

Pressey, R.L., Cabeza, M., Watts, M.E., Cowling, R.M. & Wilson, K.A. (2007) Conservation planning in a changing world. *TRENDS in Ecology and Evolution*, **22**, 583–592.

Pressey, R.L., Possingham, H.P. & Margules, C.R. (1996) Optimality in reserve selection algorithms: When does it matter and how much? *Biological Conservation*, **76**, 259–267.

Prinsen, H.A.M., Smallie, J.J., Boere, G.C. & Píres, N. (2011) *Guidelines for mitigating conflict between migratory birds and electricity power grids*. Convention on Migratory Species 2011. Available from: http://www.Convention on Migratory Species2011.int/bodies/COP/cop10/docs_and_inf_docs/doc_30_electrocution_guidlines_e.pdf (accessed 31 August 2012).

Prinzinger, R. (1976) Temperatur- und Stoffwechselregulation der Dohle *Covus monedula* L., Rabenkrähe *Corvus corone corone* L. und Elster *Pica pica* L.: Corvidae. *Anzeiger der Ornithologischen Gesellschaft in Bayern*, **15**, 1–47.

Putz, F.E. & Redford, K.H. (2009) Dangers of carbon-based conservation. *Global Environmental Change*, **19**, 400–401.

Pyke, C.R., Thomas, R., Porter, R.D., Hellmann, J.J., Dukes, J.S., Lodge, D.M. & Chavarria, G. (2008) Current practices and future opportunities for policy on climate change and invasive species. *Conservation Biology*, **22**, 585–592.

Quétier, F. & Lavorel, S. (2011) Assessing ecological equivalence in biodiversity offset schemes: Key issues and solutions. *Biological Conservation*, **144**, 2991–2999.

Qian, F., Wu, H., Gao, L., Zhang, H., Li, F., Zhong, X., Yang, X. & Zheng, G. (2009) Migration routes and stopover sites of Black-necked Cranes determined by satellite tracking. *Journal of Field Ornithology*, **80**, 19–26.

Quintela, M., Berlin, S., Wang, B. & Höglund, J. (2010) Genetic diversity and differentiation among *Lagopus lagopus* populations in Scandinavia and Scotland: evolutionary significant units confirmed by SNP markers. *Molecular Ecology*, **19**, 2380–2393.

Qvarnström, A., Svedin, N., Wiley, C., Veen, T. & Gustafsson, L. (2005) Cross-fostering reveals seasonal changes in the relative fitness of two competing species of flycatchers. *Biology Letters*, **1**, 68–71.

Qvarnström, A., Wiley, C., Svedin, N. & Vallin, N. (2009) Life-history divergence facilitiates regional coexistence of competing *Ficedula* flycatchers. *Ecology*, **90**, 1948–1957.

Radeloff, V.C., Nelson, E., Plantinga, A.J., Lewis, D.J., Hemlers, D., Lawler, J.J., Withey, J.C., Beaudry, F., Martinuzzi, S., Butsic, V., Lonsdorf, E., White, D. & Polasky, S. (2012) Economic-based projections of future land use in the conterminous United States under alternative policy scenarios. *Ecological Applications*, **22**, 1036–1049.

Rahbek, C., Gotelli, N.J., Colwell, R.K., Entsminger, G.L., Fernando, T., Rangel, L.V.B. & Graves, G.R. (2007) Predicting continental-scale patterns of bird species richness with spatially explicit models. *Proceedings of the Royal Society of London, Series B*, **274**, 165–174.

Rahbek, C. & Graves, G.R. (2001) Multiscale assessments of patterns of avian species richness. *Proceedings of the Academy Natural Sciences USA*, **98**, 4534–4539.

Ramos, J.A., Maul, A.M., Bowler, J., Wood, L., Threadgold, R., Johnson, S., Birch, D. & Walker, S. (2006) Annual variation in laying date and breeding success of Brown Noddies on Aride Island, Seychelles. *Emu*, **106**, 81–86.

Randin, C.F., Dirnböck, T., Dullinger, S., Zimmermann, N.E., Zappa, M. & Guisan, A. (2006) Are niche-based species distribution models transferable in space? *Journal of Biogeography*, **33**, 1689–1703.

Rands, M.R.W., Adams, W.M., Bennun, L., Butchart, S.H.M., Clements, A., Coomes, D., Entistle, A., Hodge, I., Kapos, V., Scharlemann, J.P.W., Sutherland, W.J. & Vira, B. (2010) Biodiversity conservation: challenges beyond 2010. *Science*, **329**, 1298–1303.

Rapacciuolo, G., Roy, D.B., Gillings, S., Fox, R., Walker, K. & Purvis, A. (2012) Climatic associations of British species distributions show good transferability in time but low predictive accuracy for range change. *PLoS ONE*, **7**, e40212.

Ratcliffe, N., Catry, P., Hamer, K.C., Klomp, N.I. & Furness, R.W. (2002) The effect of age and year on the survival of breeding adult great skuas *Catharacta skua* in Shetland. *Ibis*, **144**, 384–392.

Ratcliffe, N., Schmitt, S. & Whiffin, M. (2005) Sink or swim? Viability of a black-tailed godwit population in relation to flooding. *Journal of Applied Ecology*, **42**, 834–843.

Rayner, N.A., Brohan, P., Parker, D.E., Folland, C.K., Kennedy, J.J., Vanicek, M., Ansell, T. & Tett, S.F.B. (2006) Improved analyses of changes and uncertainties in sea surface temperature measured in situ since the mid-nineteenth century: the HadSST2 data set. *Journal of Climate*, **19**, 446–469.

Reaser, J.K., Meyerson, L.A., Cronk, Q., De Poorter, M., Elredge, L.G., Green, E., Kairo, M. Latasi, P., Mack, R.N., Mauremootoo, J., O'Dowd, D., Orapa, W., Sastroutomo, S., Saunders, A., Shine, C., Thrainsson, S. & Vaiutu, L. (2007) Ecological and socioeconomic impacts of invasive alien species on island ecosystems. *Environmental Conservation*, **34**, 1–14.

Redpath, S.M., Arroyo, B.E., Etheridge, B., Leckie, F., Bouwman, K. & Thirgood, S.J. (2002) Temperature and hen harrier productivity: from local mechanisms to geographical patterns. *Ecography*, **25**, 533–540.

Reed, T.E., Grøtan, V., Jenouvrier, S., Sæther, B.-E. & Visser, M.E. (2013a) Population growth in a wild bird is buffered against phenological mismatch. *Nature*, **340**, 488–491.

Reed, T.E. Jenouvrier, S. & Visser, M.E. (2013b) Phenological mismatch strongly affects individual fitness but not population demography in a woodland passerine. *Journal of Animal Ecology*, **82**, 131–144.

Reed, T.E., Warzybok, P., Wilson, A.J., Bradley, R.W., Wanless, S. & Sydeman, W.J. (2009) Timing is everything: flexible phenology and shifting selection in a colonial seabird. *Journal of Animal Ecology*, **78**, 376–387.

Regehr, E.V., Lunn, N.J., Amstrup, S.C. & Stirling, I. (2007) Effects of early sea ice breakup on survival and population size of polar bears in Western Hudson Bay. *Journal of Wildlife Management*, **71**, 2673–2683.

Reid, J.M., Bignal, E.M., Bignal, S., McCracken, D.I., Bogdanova, M.I. & Monaghan, P. (2008) Patterns and processes of demographic variation: environmental correlates of pre-breeding survival in red-billed choughs (*Pyrrhocorax pyrrhocorax*). *Journal of Animal Ecology*, **77**, 777–788.

Reid, J.M., Bignal, E.M., Bignal, S., McCracken, D.I. & Monaghan, P. (2004) Identifying the demographic determinants of population growth rate: a case study of red-billed choughs *Pyrrhocorax pyrrhocorax*. *Journal of Animal Ecology*, **73**, 777–788.

Reid, P.C., Edwards, M., Beaugraund, G., Skogen, M. & Stevens, D. (2003) Periodic changes in the zooplankton of the North Sea during the twentieth century linked to oceanic inflow. *Fisheries Oceanography*, **12**, 260–269.

Reid, W.V. (1998) Biodiversity hotspots. *TRENDS in Ecology and Evolution*, **13**, 275–280.

Reid, W.V. & Miller, K.R. (1989) *Keeping Options Alive. The Scientific Basis for Conserving Biodiversity*. Washington, DC: World Resources Institute.

Reif, J. & Flousek, J. (2012) The role of species' ecological traits in climatically driven altitudinal range shifts of central European birds. *Oikos*, **121**, 1053–1060.

Reif, J., Šťastný, K. & Bejček, V. (2010) Contrasting effects of climatic and habitat changes on birds with northern range limits in central Europe as revealed by an analysis of breeding bird distribution in the Czech Republic. *Acta Ornithologica*, **45**, 83–90.

Reif, J., Voříšek, P., Šťastný, K., Koschová, M. & Bejček, V. (2008) The impact of climate change on long-term population trends of birds in a central European country. *Animal Conservation*, **11**, 412–421.

Reitan, O. & Thingstad, P.G. (1999) Responses of birds to damming – a review of the influence of lakes, dams and reservoirs on bird ecology. *Ornis Norvegica*, **22**, 3–37.

Renwick, A.R., Massimino, D., Newson, S.E., Chamberlain, D.E., Pearce-Higgins, J.W. & Johnston, A. (2012) Modelling changes in species' abundance in response to projected climate change. *Diversity & Distributions*, **18**, 121–132.

Repenning, M. & Fontana, C.S. (2011) Seasonality of breeding, moult and fat deposition in subtropical lowlands of southern Brazil. *Emu*, **111**, 268–280.

Reside, A.E., VanDerWal, J.J., Kutt, A.S. & Perkins, G.C. (2010) Weather, not climate, defines distributions of vagile bird species. *PLoS ONE*, **5**, e13569.

Rexstad, E. & Buckland, S. (2012) *Displacement analysis boat surveys Kentish Flats*. Unpublished report to Strategic Ornithological Support Services.

Reynolds, C.M. (1979) The heronries census: 1972–1977 population changes and a review. *Bird Study*, **26**, 7–12.

Ricciardi, A. & Simberloff, D. (2009) Assisted colonization is not a viable conservation strategy. *Trends in Ecology and Evolution*, **24**, 248–253.

Riffell, S., Verschuyl, J., Miller, D. & Wigley, T.B. (2011) A meta-analysis of bird and mammal response to short-rotation woody crops. *Global Change Biology Bioenergy*, **3**, 313–321.

Rindorf, A., Wanless, S. & Harris, M.P. (2000) Effects of changes in sandeel availability on the reproductive output of seabirds. *Marine Ecology Progress Series*, **202**, 241–252.

Ripley, B.D. (1996) *Pattern Recognition and Neural Networks*. Cambridge, UK: Cambridge University Press.

Risely, K., Massimino, D., Johnston, A., Newson, S.E., Eaton, M.A., Musgrove, A.J., Noble, D.G., Proctor, D. & Baillie, S.R. (2012) *The Breeding Bird Survey 2011*. BTO Research Report 624, British Trust for Ornithology, Thetford.

Rivalan, P., Barbraud, C., Inchausti, P. & Weimerskirch, H. (2010) Combined impacts of longline fisheries and climate on the persistence of the Amsterdam Albatross *Diomedea amsterdamensis*. *Ibis*, **152**, 6–18.

Robertson, B.A., Doran, P.J., Loomis, E.R., Robertson, J.R. & Schemske, D.W. (2011) Avian use of perennial biomass feedstocks as post-breeding and migratory stopover habitat. *PLoS ONE*, **6**, e16941.

Robins, M. & Bibby, C.J. (1985) Dartford Warblers in 1984 in Britain. *British Birds*, **78**, 269–280.

Robinson, R.A., Baillie, S.R. & Crick, H.Q.P. (2007a) Weather-dependent survival: implications of climate change for passerine population processes. *Ibis*, **149**, 357–364.

Robinson, R.A., Baillie, S.R. & King, R. (2012) Population processes in European Blackbirds *Turdus merula*: a state-space approach. *Journal of Ornithology*, **152 Suppl 2**, 419–433.

Robinson, R.A., Balmer, D.E. & Marchant, J.H. (2008) Survival rates of hirundines in relation to British and African rainfall. *Ringing & Migration*, **24**, 1–6.

Robinson, R.A., Freeman, S.N., Balmer, D.E. & Grantham, M.J. (2007b) Cetti's Warbler *Cettia cetti*: analysis of an expanding population. *Bird Study*, **54**, 230–235.

Robinson, R.A., Green, R.E., Baillie, S.E., Peach, W.J. & Thomson, D.L. (2004) Demographic mechanisms of the population decline of the song thrush *Turdus philomelos* in Britain. *Journal of Animal Ecology*, **73**, 670–682.

Robinson, R.A, Lawson, B., Toms, M.P., Peck, K.M., Kirkwood, J.K., Chantrey, J., Clatworthy, I.R., Evans, A.D., Highes, L.A., Hutchinson, O.C., John, S.K., Pennycott, T.W., Perkins, M.W., Rowley, P.S., Simpson, V.R., Tyler, K.M. & Cunningham, A.A. (2010) Emerging infection disease leads to rapid population declines of common British birds. *PLoS ONE*, **5**, e12215.

Robinson, T. & Minton, C. (1989) The enigmatic Banded Stilt. *Birds International*, **1**, 72–85.

Robson, C. (2000) *A Guide to the Birds of South-east Asia*. London, UK: New Holland.

Robson, D. & Barriocanal, C. (2011) Ecological conditions of wintering and passage areas as determinants of timing of spring migration in trans-Saharan migratory birds. *Journal of Animal Ecology*, **80**, 320–331.

Rockwell, R.F. & Gormezano, L.J. (2009) The early bear gets the goose: climate change, polar bears and lesser snow geese in western Hudson Bay. *Polar Biology*, **32**, 539–547.

Rockwell, R.F., Gormezano, L.J. & Koons, D.N. (2010) Trophic matches and mismatches: can polar bears reduce the abundance of nesting snow geese in western Hudson Bay? *Oikos*, **120**, 696–709.

Rodenhouse, N.L. & Holmes, R.T. (1992) Results of experimental and natural food reductions for breeding black-throated blue warblers. *Ecology*, **73**, 357–372.

Rodríguez, C. & Bustamante, J. (2003) The effect of weather on lesser kestrel breeding success: can climate change explain historical population declines? *Journal of Animal Ecology*, **72**, 793–810.

Rodríguez, M.Á., Belmontes, J.A. & Hawkins, B.A. (2005) Energy, water and large-scale patterns of reptile and amphibian species richness in Europe. *Acta Oecologia*, **28**, 65–70.

Rodríguez-Sánchez, F., De Frenne, P. & Hampe, A. (2012) Uncertainty in thermal tolerances and climatic debt. *Nature Climate Change*, **2**, 636–637.

Rodríguez-Teijeiro, J.D., Gordo, O., Puigcerver, M., Gallego, S., Vinyoles, D. & Ferrer, X. (2005) African climate warming advances spring arrival of the common quail *Coturnix coturnix*. *Ardeola*, **52**,159–162.

Rogelj, J., Meinhausen, M. & Knutti, R. (2012) Global warming under old and new scenarios using IPCC climate sensitivity range estimates. *Nature Climate Change*, **2**, 248–253.

Rohde, K. (1992) Latitudinal gradients in species-diversity: the search for the primary cause. *Oikos*, **65**, 514–527.

Rolland, V., Nevoux, M., Barbraud, C. & Weimerskirch, H. (2009) Respective impact of climate and fisheries on the growth of an albatross population. *Ecological Applications*, **19**, 1336–1346.

Rompré, G., Robinson, W.D., Desrochers, A. & Angehr, G. (2009) Predicting declines in avian species richness under non-random patterns of habitat loss in a Neotropical landscape. *Ecological Applications*, **19**, 1614–1627.

Rönkä, M.T.H., Saari, L.V., Lehikoinen, E.A., Suolema, J. & Häkkilä, K. (2005) Environmental changes and population trends of breeding waterfowl in northern Baltic Sea. *Annales Zoologici Fennici*, **42**, 587–602.

Root, T.L., Price, J.T., Hall, K.R., Schneider, S.H., Rosenzweig, C. & Pounds, J.A. (2003) Fingerprints of global warming on wild plants and animals. *Nature*, **421**, 57–60.

Rose, R.J., Webb, N.R., Clarke, R.T. & Traynor, C.H. (2000) Changes on the heathlands in Dorset, England, between 1987 and 1996. *Biological Conservation*, **93**, 117–125.

Rosenzweig, M.L. (1968) Net primary productivity of terrestrial communities: prediction from climatological data. *American Naturalist*, **102**, 67–74.

Rotenberry, J.T. & Wiens, J.A. (1991) Weather and reproductive variation in shrubsteppe sparrows: A hierarchical analysis. *Ecology*, **72**, 1325–1335.

Roth, A.M., Sample, D.W., Ribic, C.A., Paine, L., Undersander, D.J. & Bartelt, G.A. (2005) Grassland bird response to harvesting switchgrass as a biomass energy crop. *Biomass and Bioenergy*, **28**, 490–498.

Rounsevell, M.D.A. & Reay, D.S. (2009) Land use and climate change in the UK. *Land Use Policy*, **26S**, S160–S169.

Rounsevell, M.D.A., Reginster, I., Araújo, M.B., Carter, T.R., Dendoncker, N., Ewert, F., House, J.I., Kankaanpää, S., Leemans, R., Metzger, M.J., Schmit, C., Smith, P. & Tuck, G. (2006) A coherent set of future land use change scenarios for Europe. *Agriculture, Ecosystems and Environment*, **114**, 57–68.

Rubolini, D., Massi, A. & Spina, F. (2002) Replacement of body feathers is associated with low premigratory energy stores in a long-distance migratory bird, the barn swallow (*Hirunda rustica*). *Journal of Zoology (London)*, **258**, 441–447.

Rubolini, D., Møller, A.P., Rainio, K. & Lehikoinen, E. (2007) Intraspecific consistency and geographic variability in temporal trends of spring migration phenology among European bird species. *Climate Research*, **35**, 135–146.

Russi, D. (2008) An integrated assessment of a large-scale biodiesel production in Italy. Killing several birds with one stone? *Energy Policy*, **36**, 1169–1180.

Royal Society for Protection of Birds (RSPB). (2011) *Solar Power*. RSPB Briefing. Available from: http://www.rspb.org.uk/Images/Solar_power_briefing_tcm9-273329.pdf (accessed 20 March 2012).

Saari, L. & Mikusiński, G. (1996) Population fluctuations of woodpecker species on the Baltic island of Aasla, SW Finland. *Ornis Fennica*, **73**, 168–178.

Sæther, B.-E. & Bakke, O. (2000) Avian life history variation and contribution of demographic traits to the population growth rate. *Ecology*, **81**, 642–653.

Sæther, B.-E., Engen, S. & Matthysen, E. (2002) Demographic characteristics and population dynamical patterns of solitary birds. *Science*, **295**, 2070–2073.

Sæther, B.-E., Engen, S., Møller, A.P., Matthsen, E., Adriaensen, F., Fiedler, W., Leivits, A., Lambrechts, M.M., Visser, M.E., Anker-Nilssen, T., Both, C., Dhondt, A.A., McCleery, R.H., McMeeking, J., Potti, J., Røstad, O.W. & Thomson, D. (2003) Climate variation and regional gradients in population dynamics of two hole-nesting passerines. *Proceedings of the Royal Society of London, Series B*, **270**, 2397–2404.

Sæther, B.-E., Grøtan, V., Tryjanowski, P., Barbraud, C., Engen, S, & Fulin, M. (2006) Climate and spatio-temporal variation in the population dynamics of a long-distance migrant, the white stork. *Journal of Animal Ecology*, **75**, 80–90.

Sæther, B.-E., Tufto, J., Engen, S., Jerstad, K., Røstad, O.W. & Skåtan, J.E. (2000) Population dynamical consequences of climate change for a small temperate songbird. *Science*, **287**, 854–856.

Sætre, G.P., Post, E. & Král, M. (1999) Can environmental fluctuation prevent competitive exclusion in sympatric flycatchers? *Proceedings of the Royal Society of London, Series B*, **266**, 1247–1251.

Sætre, R., Toresen, R. & Anker-Nilssen, T. (2002) Factors affecting the recruitment variability of the Norwegian spring spawning herring (*Clupea harengus* L.). *ICES Journal of Marine Science*, **59**, 725–736.

Sage, R., Cunningham, M. & Boatman, N. (2006) Birds in willow short-rotation coppice compared to other arable crops in central England and a review of bird census data from energy crops in the UK. *Ibis*, **148 Suppl 1**, 194–197.

Sage, R., Cunningham, M., Haughton, A.J., Mallott, M.D., Bohan, D.A., Riche, A. & Karp, A. (2010) The environmental impacts of biomass crops: use by birds of miscanthus in summer and winter in southwestern England. *Ibis*, **152**, 487–499.

Saino, N., Ambrosini, R., Rubolini, D., von Hardenberg, J., Provenzale, A., Hüppop, K, Hüppop, O., Lehikoinen, A., Lehikoinen, E., Raino, K., Romano, M. & Sokolov, L. (2011) Climate warming, ecological mismatch at arrival and population decline in migratory birds. *Proceedings of the Royal Society of London, Series B*, **278**, 835–842.

Saino, N., Rubolini, D., Lehikoinen, E., Sokolov, L.V., Bonisoli-Alquati, A., Ambrosini, R., Boncoraglio, G. & Møller, A.P. (2009) Climate change effects on migration phenology may mismatch brood parasitic cuckoos and their hosts. *Biology Letters*, **5**, 539–541.

Saino, N., Szep, T., Romano, M., Rubolini, D., Spina, F. & Møller, A.P. (2004) Ecological conditions during winter predict arrival date at the breeding quarters in a trans-Saharan migratory bird. *Ecology Letters*, **7**, 21–25.

Salido, L., Purse, B.V., Marrs, R., Chamberlain, D.E. & Schultz, S. (2011) Flexibility in phenology and habitat use act as buffers to long-term population declines in UK passerines. *Ecography*, **35**, 604–613.

Sanderson, F.J., Donald, P.F., Pain, D.J., Burfield, I.J. & van Bommel, F.P.J. (2006) Long-term population declines in Afro-Palearctic migrant birds. *Biological Conservation*, **131**, 93–105.

Sandvik, H., Coulson, T. & Sæther, B.-E. (2008) A latitudinal gradient in climate effects on seabird demography: results from interspecific analyses. *Global Change Biology*, **14**, 703–713.

Sandvik, H., Erikstad, K.E., Barrett, R.T. & Yoccoz, N.G. (2005) The effect of climate on adult survival in five species of North Atlantic seabirds. *Journal of Animal Ecology*, **74**, 817–831.

Santisteban, L., Benkman, C.W., Fetz, T. & Smith, J.W. (2012) Survival and population size of a resident bird species are declining as temperature increases. *Journal of Animal Ecology*, **81**, 352–363.

Santos, T., Tennen, J.L. & Carbonell, R. (2002) Bird conservation in fragmented Mediterranean forests of Spain: effects of geographical location, habitat and landscape degradation. *Biological Conservation*, **105**, 113–125.

Sanz, J.J. (2003) Large-scale effect of climate change on breeding parameters of pied flycatchers in Western Europe. *Ecography*, **26**, 45–50.

Sanz, J.J., Potti, J., Moreno, J., Merino, S. & Frías, O. (2003) Climate change and fitness components of a migratory bird breeding in the Mediterranean region. *Global Change Biology*, **9**, 461–472.

Saunders, D.A., Mawson, P. & Dawson, R. (2011) The impact of two extreme weather events and other causes of death on Canarby's Black Cockatoo: a promise of things to come for a threatened species? *Pacific Conservation Biology*, **17**, 141–148.

Saunders, S.C., Chen, J., Drummer, T.D., Gustafson, E.J. & Brosofske, K.D. (2005) Identifying scales of pattern in ecological data: a comparison of lacunarity, spectral and wavelet analysis. *Ecological Complexity*, **2**, 87–105.

Schaefer, H.-C., Jetz, W. & Böhning-Gaese (2007) Impact of climate change on migratory birds: community reassembly versus adaptation. *Global Ecology and Biogeography*, **17**, 38–49.

Schaefer, J.A. & Mayor, S.J. (2007) Geostatistics reveal the scale of habitat selection. *Ecological Modelling*, **209**, 401–406.

Schaefer, T., Ledebur, G., Beier, J. & Leisler, B. (2006) Reproductive responses of two related coexisting songbird species to environmental changes: Global warming, competition, and population sizes. *Journal of Ornithology* **147**, 47–56.

Schall, J.J. & Pianka, E.R. (1978) Geographical trends in the numbers of species. *Science*, **201**, 679–686.

Scharlemann, J.P.W. (2008) Can bird research clarify the biodiversity benefits and drawbacks of biofuels. *Ibis*, **150**, 640–642.

Schaub, M. (2012) Spatial distribution of wind turbines is crucial for the survival of red kite populations. *Biological Conservation*, **155**, 111–118.

Schaub, M. & Abadi, F. (2011) Integrated population models: a novel analysis framework for deeper insights into population dynamics. *Journal of Ornithology*, **152 Suppl 1**, 227–237.

Schaub, M., Kania, W. & Köppen, U. (2005) Variation of primary production during winter induces synchrony in survival rates in migratory white storks *Ciconia ciconia*. *Journal of Animal Ecology*, **74**, 656–666.

Schekkerman, H., Tulp, I., Piersma, T. & Visser, G.H. (2003) Mechanisms promoting higher growth rate in arctic than in temperature shorebirds. *Oecologia*, **134**, 332–342.

Schekkerman, H. & Visser, G.H. (2001) Prefledging energy requirements in shorebirds: energetic implications of self-feeding precocial development. *The Auk*, **118**, 944–957.

Schlenker, W. & Lobell, D.B. (2010) Robust negative impacts of climate change on African agriculture. *Environmental Research Letters*, **5**, 014010.

Schmidt, N.M., Ims, R.A., Høye, T.T., Gilg, O., Hansen, L.H., Hansen, J., Lund, M., Fuglei, E., Forchhammer, M.C. & Sittler, B. (2012) Response of an arctic predator guild to collapsing lemming cycles. *Proceedings of the Royal Society of London, Series B*, **279**, 4417–4422.

Schmiegelow, F.K.A., Machtans, C.S. & Hannon, S.J. (1997) Are boreal birds resilient to fragmentation? An experimental study of short-term community responses. *Ecology*, **78**, 1914–1932.

Schoech, S.J. & Hahn, T.P. (2008) Latitude affects degree of advancement in laying by birds in response to food supplementation: a meta-analysis. *Oecologia*, **157**, 369–376.

Schrope, M. (2009) When money grows on trees. *Nature Climate Change*, **3**, 101–103.

Schulz, U., Brauner, O. & Gruss, H. (2009) Animal diversity on short-rotation coppices – a review. *Agriculture and Forestry Research*, **3**, 171–182.

Schuur, E.A.G., Bockheim, J., Canadell, J.G., Euskirchen, E., Field, C.B., Goryachkin, S.V., Hagemann, S., Kuhry, P., Lafleur, P.M., Lee, H., Mazhitova, G., Nelson, F.E., Rinke, A., Romanovsky, V.E., Shiklomanov, N., Tarnocai, C., Venevsky, S., Vogel, J.G. & Zimov, S.A. (2008) Vulnerability of permafrost carbon to climate change: Implications for the global carbon cycle. *BioScience*, **58**, 701–714.

Schwartz, M.D., Ahas, R. & Aasa, A. (2006a) Onset of spring starting earlier across the Northern Hemisphere. *Global Change Biology*, **12**, 343–351.

Schwartz, M.W., Iversson, L.R., Prasad, A.M., Matthews, S.N. & O'Conner, R.J. (2006b) Predicting extinctions as a result of climate change. *Ecology*, **87**, 1611–1615.

Schwertner, T.W., Peterson, M.J. & Silvy, N.J. (2005) Effect of precipitation on Rio Grande wild turkey poult production in Texas. *Proceedings of the National Wild Turkey Symposium*, **9**, 10–15.

Scott, B.E., Sharples, J., Wanless, S. & Ross, O. (2006) The use of biologically meaningful oceanographic indices to separate the effects of climate and fisheries on seabird breeding success. In *Top Predators in Marine Ecosystems: Their Role in Monitoring and Management*. Boyd, I.L., Wanless, S. & Camphuysen, C.J. Zoological Society of London Conservation Biology Series Volume 12. Cambridge, UK: Cambridge University Press, pp. 46–62.

Scott, B., Stead, S.M. & Marrs, S.J. (2011) Changes to Scotland's surrounding seas. In *The Changing Nature of Scotland*. Marrs, S.J., Foster, S., Hendrie, C., Mackie, E.C. & Thompson, D.B.A. Edinburgh, UK: TSO, pp. 153–166.

Scott, J.M., Goble, D.D., Haines, A.M., Wiens, J.A. & Neel, M.C. (2010) Conservation-reliant species and the future of conservation. *Conservation Letters*, **3**, 91–97.

Scottish Natural Heritage (SNH). (2009) *Strategic location guidance for onshore wind farms in respect of the natural heritage* (revised March 2009). Available from: http://www.snh.gov.uk/docs/A328049.pdf (accessed 15 September 2012).

Scottish Natural Heritage (SNH). (2010) *Survey methods for use in assessing the impacts of onshore windfarms on bird communities* (revised December 2010). Available from: http://www.snh.gov.uk/docs/C278917.pdf (accessed 15 September 2012).

Seavy, N.E. (2006) Physiological correlates of habitat association in East African sunbirds (Nectariniidae). *Journal of Zoology (London)*, **270**, 290–297.

Seivwright, L.J., Redpath, S.M., Mougeot, F., Leckie, F. & Hudson, P.J. (2005) Interactions between intrinsic and extrinsic mechanisms in a cyclic species: testosterone increases parasite infection in red grouse. *Proceedings of the Royal Society of London, Series B*, **272**, 2299–2304.

Şekercioğlu, Ç.H., Ehrlich, P.R., Daily, G.C., Aygen, D., Goehring, D. & Sandi, R.F. (2002) Disappearance of insectivorous birds from tropical forest fragments. *Proceedings of the National Academy of Sciences USA*, **99**, 263–267.

Şekercioğlu, Ç.H., Primack, R.B. & Wormworth, J. (2012) The effects of climate change on tropical birds. *Biological Conservation*, **148**, 1–18.

Şekercioğlu, Ç.H., Schneider, S.H., Fay, J.P. & Loarie, S.R. (2008) Climate change, elevational range shifts and bird extinctions. *Conservation Biology*, **22**, 140–150.

Semere, T. & Slater, F.M. (2007a) Ground flora, small mammal and bird species diversity in miscanthus (*Miscanthus x giganteus*) and reed canary-grass (*Phalaris arundinacea*) fields. *Biomass and Bioenergy*, **31**, 20–29.

Semere, T. & Slater, F.M. (2007b) Invertebrate populations in miscanthus (*Miscanthus* x *giganteus*) and reed canary-grass (*Phalaris arundinacea*) fields. *Biomass and Bioenergy*, **31**, 30–39.

Senapathi, D., Nicoll, M.A.C., Teplitsky, C., Jones, C.G. & Norris, K. (2011) Climate change and the risks associated with delayed breeding in a tropical wild bird population. *Proceedings of the Royal Society of London, Series B*, **278**, 3184–3190.

Senelwa, K., Etiégni, L., Osano, O., Balozi, K. & Imo, M. (2012) Environmental impacts of biofuel production in Africa. In *Bioenergy for Sustainable Development in Africa*. Janses, R. & Rutz, D. Netherlands: Springer.

Seone, J. & Carrascal, L.M. (2008) Interspecific differences in population trends of Spanish birds are related to habitat and climatic preferences. *Global Ecology and Biogeography*, **17**, 111–121.

Sergio, F. (2003) From individual behaviour to population pattern: weather-dependent foraging and breeding performance in black kites. *Animal Behaviour*, **66**, 1109–1117.

Sergio, F., Marchesi, L., Pedrini, P., Ferrer, M. & Penteriani, V. (2004) Electrocution alters the distribution and density of a top predator, the eagle owl *Bubo bubo*. *Journal of Applied Ecology*, **41**, 836–845.

Serreze, M.C. (2010) Understanding recent climate change. *Conservation Biology*, **24**, 10–17.

Serreze, M.C. & Francis, J.A. (2006) The Arctic amplification debate. *Climate Change*, **76**, 241–264.

Sharples, J., Ross, O.N., Scott, B.E., Greenstreet, S.P.R. & Fraser, H. (2006) Inter-annual variability in the timing of stratification and the spring bloom in the North-western North Sea. *Continental Shelf Research*, **26**, 733–751.

Sharrock, J.T.R. (1976) *The Atlas of Breeding Birds in Britain and Ireland*. Berkhamstead. UK: T & AD Poyser.

Shaw, J.M., Jenkins, A.R., Smallie, J.J. & Ryan, P.G., (2010) Modelling power-line collision risk for the Blue Crane *Anthropoides paradiseus* in South Africa. *Ibis*, **152**, 590–599.

Shears, N.T., Grace, R.V., Usmar, N.R., Kerr, V. & Babcock, R.C. (2006) Long-term trends in lobster populations in a partially protected vs. no-take Marine Park. *Biological Conservation*, **132**, 222–231.

Sheldon, B.C. (2010) Genetic perspectives on the evolutionary consequences of climate change in birds. In *Effects of Climate Change on Birds*. Møller, A.P., Fiedler, W. & Berthold, P. Oxford, UK: Oxford University Press, pp. 149–168.

Sheldon, B.C., Kruuk, L.E.B. & Merilä, J. (2003) Natural selection and inheritance of breeding time and clutch size in the collared flycatcher. *Evolution*, **57**, 406–420.

Sheldon, F.H., Styring, A. & Hosner, P.A. (2010) Bird species richness in a Bornean exotic tree plantation: a long-term perspective. *Biological Conservation*, **143**, 399–407.

Sheldon, K.S., Yang, S. & Tewksbury, J.J. (2011) Climate change and community disassembly: impacts of warming on tropical and temperate montane community structure. *Ecology Letters*, **14**, 1191–1200.

Sheldon, R.D. (2002) Factors affecting the distribution, abundance and chick survival of the Lapwing (*Vanellus vanellus*). PhD thesis. HarperAdams University College.

Sherry, T.W. & Holmes, R.T. (1996) Winter habitat quality, population limitation, and conservation of Neotropical-Nearctic migrant birds. *Ecology*, **77**, 36–48.

Shirey, P.D. & Lamberti, G.A. (2010) Assisted colonization under the U.S. Endangered Species Act. *Conservation Letters*, **3**, 45–52.

Shoo, L.P., Williams, S.E. & Hero, J.-M. (2005) Climate warming and the rainforest birds of the Australian wet tropics: Using abundance data as a sensitive predictor of change in total population size. *Biological Conservation*, **125**, 335–343.

Short, L.L. (1974) Nesting of southern Sonoran birds during the summer rainy season. *The Condor*, **76**, 21–32.

Shrubb, M. (2003) *Birds, Scythes and Combines. A History of Birds of Agricultural Change.* Cambridge, UK: Cambridge University Press.

Shultz, S., Bradbury, R.B., Evans, K.L., Gregory, R.D. & Blackburn, T.M. (2005) Brain size and resource specialization predict long-term population trends in British birds. *Proceedings of the Royal Society of London, Series B*, **272**, 2305–2311.

Siegel, V. & Loeb, V. (1995) Recruitment of Antarctic Krill *Euphausia superba* and possible causes for its variability. *Marine Ecology Progress Series*, **123**, 45–56.

Siikamaki, J., Sanchirico, J.N. & Jardine, S.L. (2012) Global economic potential for reducing carbon dioxide emissions from mangrove loss. *Proceedings of the National Academy of Sciences USA*, **109**, 14369–14374.

Sillett, T.S., & Holmes, R.T. (2002) Variation in survivorship of a migratory songbird throughout its annual cycle. *Journal of Animal Ecology*, **71**, 296–308.

Sillett, T.S., Holmes, R.T. & Sherry, T.W. (2000) Impacts of a global climate cycle on population dynamics of a migratory songbird. *Science*, **288**, 2040–2042.

Sillett, T.S., Rodenhouse, N.L. & Holmes, R.T. (2004) Experimentally reducing neighbor density affects reproduction and behavior of a migratory songbird. *Ecology*, **85**, 2467–2477.

Silverin, B. (1981) Reproductive effort, as expressed in body and organ weights, in the Pied Flycatcher. *Ornis Scandinavica*, **12**, 133–139.

Silverin, B., Wingfield, J., Stokkan, K., Massa, R., Järvinen, A., Andersson, N.-Å., Lambrechts, M., Sorace, A. & Blomqvist, D. (2008) Ambient temperature effects on photo induced gonadal cycles and hormonal secretion patterns in great tits from three different breeding latitudes. *Hormones and Behaviour*, **54**, 60–68.

Sim, I.M.W., Burfield, I.J., Grant, M.C., Pearce-Higgins, J.W. & Brooke, M. de L. (2007) The role of habitat composition in determining breeding site occupancy in a declining Ring Ouzel *Turdus torquatus* population. *Ibis*, **149**, 374–385.

Sim, I.M.W., Gregory, R.D., Hancock, M.H. & Brown, A.F. (2005) Recent changes in the abundance of British upland breeding birds. *Bird Study*, **52**, 261–275.

Sim, I.M.W., Rebecca, G.W., Ludwig, S.C., Grant, M.C. & Reid, J.M. (2011) Characterising demographic variation and contributions to population growth rate in a declining population. *Journal of Animal Ecology*, **80**, 159–170.

Simberloff, D. (1976) Species turnover and equilibrium island biogeography. *Science*, **194**, 572–578.

Simberloff, D.S., Cox, J. & Mehlman, D.W. (1992) Movement corridors: conservation bargains or poor investments? *Conservation Biology*, **6**, 493–505.

Sinclair, A.R. & Arcese, P. (1995) *Serengeti II: Dynamics, Management, and Conservation of an Ecosystem.* Chicago, IL: University of Chicago Press,.

Sinelschikova, A., Kosarev, V., Panov, I. & Baushev, A.N. (2007) The influence of wind conditions in Europe on the advance in timing of the spring migration of the song thrush (*Turdus philomelos*) in the south-east Baltic region. *International Journal of Biometeorology*, **51**, 431–440.

Singarayer, J.S. & Valdes, P.J. (2010) High-latitude climate sensitivity to ice-sheet forcing over the last 120 kyr. *Quaternary Science Reviews*, **29**, 43–55.

Sirami, C., Brotons, L., Burfield, I., Fonderflick, J. & Martin, J.-L. (2008) Is land abandonment having an impact on biodiversity? A metaanalytical approach to bird distribution changes in the north-western Mediterranean. *Biological Conservation*, **141**, 450–459.

Siriwardena, G.M., Calbrade, N.A. & Vickery, J.A. (2008) Farmland birds and late winter food: does seed supply fail to meet demand? *Ibis*, **150**, 585–595.

Skoglund, P. & Höglund, J. (2010) Sequence polymorphism in candidate genes for differences in winter plumage between Scottish and Scandinavian willow grouse (*Lagopus lagopus*). *PLoS ONE*, **5**, e10334.

Skutch, A.F. (1950) The nesting seasons of central American birds in relation to climate and food supply. *Ibis*, **92**, 185–222.

Slagsvold, T. (1975) Critical period for regulation of great tit (*Parus major* L.) and blue tit (*Parus caeruleus* L.) populations. *Norwegian Journal of Zoology*, **23**, 67–88.

Small-Lorenz, S.L., Culp, L.A., Brandt Ryder, T., Will, T.C. & Marra, P.P. (2013) A blind spot in climate change vulnerability assessments. *Nature Climate Change*, **3**, 91–93.

Smallegange, I.M., Fiedler, W., Köppen, U., Geiter, O. & Bairlein, F. (2010) Tits on the move: exploring the impact of environmental change on blue tit and great tit migration distance. *Journal of Animal Ecology*, **79**, 350–357.

Smallwood, K.S., Bell, D.A., Snyder, S.A. & Didonata, J.E. (2010) Novel scavenger removal trials increase wind turbine – caused avian fatality estimates. *Journal of Wildlife Management*, **74**, 1089–1096.

Smallwood, K.S. & Thelander, C. (2008) Bird mortality in the Altamont Pass Wind Resource Area, California. *Journal of Wildlife Management*, **72**, 215–223.

Smith, K.A. & Searchinger, T.D. (2012) Crop-based biofuels and associated environmental concerns. *Global Change Biology Biofuels*, **4**, 479–484.

Smith, K.W., Smith, L., Charman, E., Briggs, K., Burgess, M., Dennis, C., Harding, M., Isherwood, C., Isherwood, I. & Mallord, J. (2011) Large-scale variation in the temporal patterns of the frass fall of defoliating caterpillars in oak woodlands in Britain: implications for nesting woodland birds. *Bird Study*, **58**, 506–511.

Smith, K.W. & Tyler, G.A. (1993) Trends in numbers of breeding Bitterns in the UK. In *Britain's Birds in 1990–1991: the Conservation and Monitoring Review*. Thetford, UK: British Trust for Ornithology, pp. 139–140.

Smith, P.A., Elliot, K.H., Gaston, A.J. & Gilchrist, H.G. (2010) Has early ice clearance increased predation on breeding birds by polar bears? *Polar Biology*, **33**, 1149–1153.

Smith, P., Martino, D., Cai, Z., Gwary, D., Janzen, H., Kumar, P., McCarl, B., Ogle, S., O'Mara, F., Rice, C., Scholes, B., Sirotekno, O., Howden, M., McAllister, T., Pan, G., Romanenkov, V., Schneider, U., Towprayoon, S., Wattenbach, M. & Smith, J. (2007) Greenhouse gas mitigation in agriculture. *Philosophical Transactions of the Royal Society Series B*, **363**, 789–813.

Smith, T.J. & Hayden, B.P. (1984) Snow goose migration phenology is related to extratropical storm climate. *International Journal of Biometeorology*, **28**, 225–233.

Snow, D.W. (1969) The moult of British thrushes and chats. *Bird Study*, **16**, 115–129.

Sodhi, N.S., Liow, L.H. & Bazzaz, F.A. (2004) Avian extinctions from tropical and subtropical forests. *Annual Review of Ecology and Evolutionary Systematics*, **35**, 323–345.

Sokolov, L.V. (1999) Population dynamics of passerine birds. *Zoologicheskij Zhurnal*, **78**, 311–324.

Sokolov, L.V., Markovets, M.Y. & Morozov, Y.G. (1999) Long-term dynamics of the mean date of autumn migration in passerines on the Courish Spit of the Baltic Sea. *Avian Ecology & Behaviour*, **2**, 1–18.

Sokolov, L.V., Markovets, M.Yu., Shapoval, A.P. & Morozov, Yu.G. (1998) Long-term trends in the timing of spring migration of passerines on the Courish spit of the Baltic Sea. *Avian Ecology & Behaviour*, **1**, 1–21.

Sokolov, L.V. & Payevsky, V.A. (1998) Spring temperatures effects on year-to-year variations in breeding phenology of passerines on the Courish Spit. *Avian Ecology and Behaviour*, **1**, 22–36.

Solomon, S., Plattner, G.-K., Knutti, R. & Friedlingstein, P. (2009) Irreversible climate change due to carbon dioxide emissions. *Proceedings of the National Academy of Sciences USA*, **106**, 1704–1709.

Solonen, T. (2001) Breeding of great tit and blue tit in urban and rural habitats in southern Finland. *Ornis Fennica*, **78**, 131–142.

Sorg, A., Bolch, T., Stoffel, M., Solomina, O. & Benston, M. (2012) Climate change impacts on glaciers and runoff in Tien Shan (Central Asia). *Nature Climate Change*, **2**, 725–731.

Sovon (2012) *Vogels in Nederland*. www.sovon.nl/en/node/1750 (accessed 27 December 2012).

Sparks, T.H. (1999) Phenology and the changing pattern of bird migration in Britain. *International Journal of Biometeorology*, **45**, 212–216.

Sparks, T.H., Bairlein, F., Bojarinova, J.G., Hüppop, O., Lehikoinen, E.A., Rainio, K., Sokolov, L.V. & Walker, D. (2005) Examining the total arrival distribution of migratory birds. *Global Change Biology*, **11**, 22–30.

Sparks, T.H. & Carey, P.D. (1995) The response of species to climate over two centuries: an analysis of the Marsham phenological record, 1936–1947. *Journal of Ecology*, **83**, 321–329.

Sparks, T.H., Collinson, N., Crick, H., Croxton, P., Edwards, M., Huber, K., Jenkins, D., Johns, D., Last, F., Maberly, S., Marquiss, M., Pickup, J., Roy, D., Sims, D., Shaw, D., Turner, A., Watson, A., Woiwod, I. & Woodbridge, K. (2006) *Natural Heritage Trends of Scotland: Phenological Indicators of Climate Change*. Edinburgh, UK: Scottish Natural Heritage Commissioned Report No. 167 (ROAME No. F01NB01).

Sparks, T.H., Huber, K., Bland, R.L., Crick, H.Q.P., Croxton, P.J., Flood, J., Loxton, R.G., Mason, C.F., Newnham, J.A. & Tryanowski, P. (2007) How consistent are trends in arrival (and departure) dates of migrant birds in the UK? *Journal of Ornithology*, **148**, 503–511.

Sparks, T.H., Huber, K. & Tryjanowski, P. (2008) Something for the weekend? Examining the bias in avian phenological recording. *International Journal of Biometeorology*, **52**, 505–510.

Sparks, T.H., & Mason, C.F. (2001) Dates of arrivals and departures of spring migrants taken from the Essex Bird Reports 1950–1998. *Essex Bird Report*, **1999**, 154–164.

Sparks, T.H. & Tryjanowski, P. (2007) Patterns of spring arrival dates differ in two hirundines. *Climate Research*, **35**, 159–164.

Stattersfield, A., Crosby, M.J., Long, A.J. & Wege, D.C. (1998) *Endemic Bird Areas of the World: Priorities for Biodiversity Conservation*. Cambridge, UK: BirdLife International.

Steekhof, K. Kochert, M.N. & McDonald, T.L. (1997) Interactive effects of prey and weather on golden eagle reproduction. *Journal of Animal Ecology*, **66**, 350–362.

Steen, J.B., Grav, H., Borch-Iohnsen, B. & Gabrielsen, G.W. (1989) Strategies of homeothermy in Eider ducklings (Somateria mollissima). In *Physiology of Cold Adaptation in Birds*. Bech, C. & Reinertsen, W. *NATO ASI Series A*, volume 173. New York: Plenum Press, pp 361–370.

Steen, R., Selås, V. & Stenberg, I. (2006) Impact of weather on annual fluctuations in breeding numbers of Lesser Spotted Woodpecker *Dendrocopos minor* in Norway. *Ardea*, **94**, 225–231.

Steffensen, J.P., Andersen, K.K., Bigler, M., Clausen, H.B., Dahl-Jensen, D., Fischer, H., Goto-Azuma, K., Hansson, M., Johnsen, S.J., Jouzel, J., Masson-Delmotte, V., Popp, T., Rasmussen, S.O., Röthlisberger, R., Ruth, U., Stauffer, B., Suggaard-Andersen, M.-L., Sveinbjörnsdóttir, Á.E., Svensson, A. & White, J.W.C. (2008) High-resolution Greenland ice core data show abrupt climate change happens in few years. *Science*, **321**, 680–684.

Stenning, M.J., Harvey, P.H. & Campbell, B. (1988) Searching for density-dependent regulation in a population of pied flycatchers *Ficedula hypoleuca* Pallas. *Journal of Animal Ecology*, **57**, 307–317.

Stephens, P.A., Freckleton, R.P., Watkinson, A.R. & Sutherland, W.J. (2003) Predicting the response of farmland bird populations to changing food supplies. *Journal of Applied Ecology*, **40**, 970–983.

Stern, N. (2007) *The Economics of Climate Change*. Cambridge, UK: Cambridge University Press.

Sterner, D., Orloff, S. & Spiegel, L. (2007) Wind turbine collision research in the United States. In *Birds and Wind Farms*. De Lucas, M., Janss, G.F.E., & Ferrer M. Madrid, Spain: Quercus, pp. 81–100.

Stervander, M., Lindström, Å., Jonzén, N. & Andersson, A. (2005) Timing of spring migration in birds: Long-term trends, North Atlantic Oscillation and the significance of different migration routes. *Journal of Avian Biology*, **36**, 210–221.

Stevens, G.C. (1989) The latitudinal gradient in geographical range: how so many species coexist in the tropics. *American Naturalist*, **133**, 240–256.

Stevenson, I. R. & Bryant, D.M. (2000) Climate change and constraints on breeding. *Nature*, **406**, 366–367.

Stickler, C.M., Nepstad, D.C., Coe, M.T., McGrath, D.G., Rodrigues, H.O., Walker, W.S., Soares-Filho, B.S. & Davidson, E.A. (2009) The potential ecological costs and cobenefits of REDD: a critical review and case study from the Amazon region. *Global Change Biology*, **15**, 2803–2824.

Stirling, C., Esat, T.M., Lambeck, K. & McCulloch, M.T. (1998) Timing and duration of the Last Interglacial: implications for a restricted interval of widespread coral growth. *Earth and Planetary Science Letters*, **160**, 745–762.

Stirling, I., Lunn, N.J. & Iacozza, J. (1999) Long-term trends in the population ecology of polar bears in western Hudson Bay in relation to climatic change. *Arctic*, **52**, 294–306.

Stockwell, D.R.B. & Noble, I.R. (1992) Induction of sets of rules from animal distribution data: a robust and informative method of data analysis. *Mathematics and Computers in Simulation*, **33**, 385–390.

Stokke, B.G., Møller, A.P., Sæther, B.-E., Rheinwald, G. & Gutscher, H. (2005) Weather in the breeding area and during migration affects the demography of a small long-distance passerine migrant. *The Auk*, **122**, 637–647.

Stone, P.H., & Carlson, J.H. (1979) Atmospheric lapse rate regimes and their parameterization. *Journal of the Atmospheric Sciences*, **36**, 415–423.

Storch, D. (2003) Comment on 'global biodiversity, biochemical kinetics, and the energy-equivalence rule'. *Science*, **299**, 346b.

Stotz, D.F., Fitzpatrick, J.W., Parker III, T.A. & Moskovits, D.K. (1996) *Neotropical Birds: Ecology and Conservation*: Chicago, IL: Chicago University Press.

Stouffer, P.C. & Bierregaard, R.O. Jr (1995a) Effects of forest fragmentation on understory hummingbirds in Amazonian Brazil. *Conservation Biology*, **9**, 1085–1094.

Stouffer, P.C., Bierregaard, R.O. Jr (1995b) Use of Amazonian forest fragments by understory insectivorous birds. *Ecology*, **76**, 2429–2445.

Stouffer, P.C., Cockle, K.L., Aleixo, A., Areta, J.I., Barnett, J.M., Bodrati, A., Cadena, C.D., Di Giacomo, A.S., Herzog, S.K., Hosner, P., Johnson, E.I., Naka, L.N. & Sánchez, C. (2011) No evidence for widespread bird declines in protected South American forests. *Climatic Change*, **108**, 383–386.

Stouffer, P.C., Strong, C. & Naka, L.N. (2009) Twenty years of understorey bird extinctions from Amazonian rain forest fragments: consistent trends and landscape-mediated dynamics. *Diversity and Distributions*, **15**, 88–97.

Stralberg, D., Jongsomjit, D., Howell, C.A., Snyder, M.A., Alexander, J.D., Wiens, J.A. & Root, T.L. (2009) Re-shuffling of species with climate disruption: A no-analog future for California birds? *PLoS ONE*, **4**, e6825.

Stratford, J.A. & Stouffer, P.C. (1999) Local extinctions of terrestrial insectivorous birds in a fragmented landscape near Manaus, Brazil. *Conservation Biology*, **13**, 1416–1423.

Strode, P.K. (2003) Implications of climate change for North American wood warblers (Parulidae). *Global Change Biology*, **9**, 1137–1144.

Studds, C.E. & Marra, P.P. (2005) Nonbreeding habitat occupancy and population processes: an upgrade experiment with a migratory bird. *Ecology*, **86**, 2380–2385.

Studds, C.E. & Marra, P.P. (2007) Linking fluctuations in rainfall to nonbreeding season performance in a long-distance migratory bird. *Setophaga ruticulla. Climate Research*, **35**, 115–122.

Studds, C.E. & Marra, P.P. (2011) Rainfall-induced changes in food availability modify the spring departure programme of a migratory bird. *Proceedings of the Royal Society of London, Series B*, **278**, 3437–3443.

Suárez-Seone, S., Osborne, P.E. & Baudry, J. (2002) Responses of birds of different biogeographic origins and habitat requirements to agricultural land abandonment in northern Spain. *Biological Conservation*, **105**, 333–344.

Suggitt, A.J., Gillingham, P.K., Hill, J.K., Huntley, B., Kunin, W.E., Roy, D.B. & Thomas, C.D. (2011) Habtiat microclimates drive fine-scale variation in extreme temperatures. *Oikos*, **120**, 1–8.

Summers, R.W., Green, R.E., Proctor, R., Dugan, D., Lambie, D., Moncrieff, R., Moss, R. & Baines, D. (2004) An experimental study of the effects of predation on the breeding productivity of capercaillie and black grouse. *Journal of Applied Ecology*, **41**, 513–525.

Summers, R.W. & Underhill, L.G. (1987) Factors relating to breeding production of Brent Geese *Branta b. bernicla* and waders (Charadrii) on the Taimyr Peninsula. *Bird Study*, **34**, 161–171.

Summers, R.W., Underhill, L.G., Nicoll, M., Rae, R. & Piersma, T. (1992) Seasonal, size- and age-related patterns in body-mass and composition of Purple Sandpipers *Calidris maritima* in Britain. *Ibis*, **134**, 346–354.

Sun, J., Wang, H., Yuan, W. & Chen, H. (2010) Spatial-temporal features of intense snowfall events in China and their possible change. *Journal of Geophysical Research*, **115**, D16110.

Sunday, J.M., Bates, A.E. & Dulvy, N.K. (2012) Thermal tolerance and the global redistribution of animals. *Nature Climate Change*, **2**, 686–690.

Surman, C.A., Nicholson, L.W. & Santora, J.A. (2012) Effects of climate variability on breeding phenology and performance of tropical seabirds in the eastern Indian Ocean. *Marine Ecology Progress Series*, **454**, 147–157.

Sutherland, W.J. & Woodroof, H.J. (2009) The need for environmental horizon scanning. *Trends in Ecology & Evolution*, **24**, 523–527.

Sutherland, W.J., Bardsley, S., Clout, M., Depledge, M.H., Dicks, L.V., Fellman, L., Fleishman, E., Gibbons, D.W., Keim, B., Lickorish, F., Margerison, C., Monk, K.A., Norris, K., Peck, L.S., Prior, S.V., Scharlemann, J.P.W., Spalding, M.D. & Watkinson, A.R. (2013) A horizon scan of global conservation issues for 2013. *Trends in Ecology & Evolution*, **28**, 16–22.

Svažas, S., Meissner, W., Serebryakov, V., Kozulin, A. & Grishanov, G. (2001) *Changes of wintering sites of waterfowl in Central and Eastern Europe. OMPO Special Publication. Oiseaux Migrateurs du Palearctique Occidental. Vilneus*, Lithuania: OMPO Vilnius and Lithuanian Institude of Ecology.

Svensson, E., & Nilsson, J.-Å. (1995) Food supply, territory quality and reproductive timing in the blue tit (*Parus caeruleus*). *Ecology*, **76**, 1804–1812.

Swann, R.L. & Baillie, S.R. (1979) The suspension of moult by trans-Saharan migrants in Crete. *Bird Study*, **26**, 55–58.

Swann, R.L. & Etheridge, B. (1989) Variations in mid-winter weights of Moray Basin waders in relation to temperature. *Ringing & Migration*, **10**, 1–8.

Swenson, J.E., Alt, K.L. & Eng, R.L. (1986) Ecology of bald eagles in the Greater Yellowstone Ecosystem. *Wildlife Monographs*, **95**, 3–46.

Sydeman, W.J., Hester, M.M., Thayer, J.A., Gress, F., Martin, P. & Buffa, J. (2001) Climate change, reproductive performance and diet composition of marine birds in the southern California Current system, 1969–1997. *Progress in Oceanography*, **49**, 309–329.

Szabo, J.K., Fuller, R.A. & Possingham, H.P. (2012) A comparison of estimates of relative abundance from a weakly structured mass-participation bird atlas survey and a robustly designed monitoring scheme. *Ibis*, **154**, 468–479.

Szabo, J.K., Vesk, P.A., Baxter, P.W.J. & Possingham, H.P. (2010) Regional avian species declines estimated from volunteer-collected long-term data using List Length Analysis. *Ecological Applications*, **20**, 2157–2169.

Szép, T. (1995) Relationship between west African rainfall and the survival of central European Sand Martins *Riparia riparia*. *Ibis*, **137**, 162–168.

Tarnocai, C. (2006) The effect of climate change on carbon in Canadian peatlands. *Global and Planetary Change*, **53**, 222–232.

Tarnocai, C., Canadell, J.G., Schuur, E.A.G., Kuhry, P., Mazhitova, G. & Zimov, S. (2009) Soil organic carbon pools in the northern circumpolar permafrost region. *Global Biogeochemical Cycles*, **23**, GB2023.

Tasker, M.L., Camphuysen, C.J., Cooper, J., Garthe, S., Montevecchi, W.A. & Blaber, S.J.M. (2000) The impacts of fishing on marine birds. *ICES Journal of Marine Science*, **57**, 531–547.

Telleria, J.L. (2009) Overlap between wind power plants and Griffon Vultures *Gyps fulvus* in Spain. *Bird Study*, **56**, 268–271.

te Marvelde, L., Webber, S.L., Meijer, H.A.J. & Visser, M.E. (2011) Mismatched reproduction is energetically costly for chick feeding female great tits. *Functional Ecology*, **25**, 1302–1308.

te Marvelde, L., Webber, S.L., Meijer, H.A.J. & Visser, M.E. (2012) Energy expenditure during egg laying is equal for early and late breeding free-living female great tits. *Oecologia*, **168**, 631–638.

Terborgh, J. (1985) The role of ecotones in the distribution of Andean birds. *Ecology*, **66**, 1237–1246.

Thackeray, S.J., Sparks, T.H., Frederiksen, M., Burthe, S., Bacon, P.J., Bell, J.R., Botham, M.S., Brereton, T.M., Bright, P.W., Carvalho, L.C., Clutton-Brock, T., Dawson, A., Edwards, M., Elliott, M., Harrington, R., Johns, D., Jones, I.D., Jones, J.T., Leech, D.I., Roy, D.B., Scott, W.A., Smith, M., Smithers, R.J., Winfield, I.J. & Wanless, S. (2010) Trophic level asynchrony in rates of phenological change for marine, freshwater and terrestrial environments. *Global Change Biology*, **16**, 3304–3313.

Tharme, A.P., Green, R.E., Baines, D., Bainbridge, I.P. & O'Brien, M. (2001) The effect of management for red grouse shooting on the population density of breeding birds on heather-dominated moorland. *Journal of Applied Ecology*, **38**, 439–457.

Thaxter, C.B., Joys, A.C., Gregory, R.D., Baillie, S.R. & Noble, D.G. (2010) Hypotheses to explain patterns of population change among breeding bird species in England. *Biological Conservation*, **143**, 2006–2019.

Thaxter, C.B., Lascelles, B., Sugar, K., Cook, A.S.C.P., Roos, S., Bolton, M., Langston, R.H.W. & Burton, N.H.K. (2012) Seabird foraging ranges as a preliminary tool for identifying candidate Marine Protected Areas. *Biological Conservation*, **156**, 53–61.

Thayer, J.A. & Sydeman, W.J. (2007) Spatio-temporal variability in prey harvest and reproductive ecology of a piscivorous seabird, *Cerorhinca monocerata*, in an upwelling system. *Marine Ecology Progress Series*, **329**, 253–265.

Thelander, C.G. & Smallwood, K.S. (2007) The Altamont pass wind resource area's effect on birds: a case history. In *Birds and Wind Farms*. De Lucas, M., Janss, G.F.E. & Ferrer, M. Madrid, Spain: Quercus, pp. 25–46.

Thelander, C.G., Smallwood, K.S. & Rugge, L. (2003) *Bird Risk Behaviours and Fatalities at the Altamont Pass Wind Resource Area*. Report to the National Renewable Energy Laboratory, Colorado, USA.

Thingstad, P.G., Nyholm, N.E.I. & Fjedheim, B. (2006) Pied flycatcher *Ficedula hypoleuca* population dynamics in peripheral habitats in Scandinavia. *Ardea*, **94**, 211–223.

Thirgood, S.J., Redpath, S., Rothery, P., Newton, I. & Hudson, P. (2000) Habitat loss and raptor predation: disentangling long and short term causes of red grouse declines. *Proceedings of the Royal Society of London, Series B*, **267**, 651–656.

Thomas, C.D. (2011) Translocation of species, climate change and the end of trying to recreate past ecological communities. *Trends in Ecology and Evolution*, **26**, 216–221.

Thomas, C.D., Cameron, A., Green, R.E., Bakkenes, M., Beaumont, L.J., Collingham, Y.C., Erasmus, B.F.N., de Siquieira, M.F., Grainger, A., Hannah, L., Hughes, L., Huntley, B., van Jaarsveld, A.S., Midgley, G.F., Miles, L., Ortega-Huerta, M.A., Peterson, A.T., Phillips, O.L. & Williams, S.E. (2004) Extinction risk from climate change. *Nature*, **427**, 145–148.

Thomas, C.D., Franco, A.M.A. & Hill, J.K. (2006a) Range retractions and extinction in the face of climate warming. *Trends in Ecology & Evolution*, **21**, 415–416.

Thomas, C.D., Gillingham, P.K., Bradbury, R.B., Roy, D.B., Anderson, B.J., Baxter, J.M., Bourn, N.A.D., Crick, H.Q.P., Findon, R.A., Fox, R., Hodgson, J.A., Holt, A.R., Morecroft, M.D., O'Hanlon, N., Oliver, T.H., Pearce-Higgins, J.W., Procter, D.A., Thomas, J.A., Walker, K.J., Walmsley, C.A., Wilson, R.J. & Hill, J.K. (2012) Protected areas facilitate species' range expansions. *Proceedings of the National Academy of Sciences USA*, **109**, 14063–14068.

Thomas, C.D., Hill, J.K., Anderson, B.J., Bailey, S., Beale, C.M., Bradbury, R.B., Bulman, C.R., Crick, H.Q.P., Eigenbrod, F., Griffiths, H.M., Kunin, W.E., Oliver, T.H., Walsmley, C.A., Watts, K., Worsfold, N.T. & Yardley, T. (2010) A framework for assessing threats and benefits to species responding to climate change. *Methods in Ecology and Evolution*, **2**, 125–142.

Thomas, C.D. & Lennon, J.J. (1999) Birds extend their ranges northwards. *Nature*, **399**, 213.

Thomas, D.W., Blonde, J., Perret, P. Lambrechts, M.M. & Speakman, J.R. (2001) Energetic and fitness costs of mismatching resource supply and demand in seasonally breeding birds. *Science*, **291**, 2598–2600.

Thomas, J.W., Franklin, J.F., Gordon, J. & Johnson, K.N. (2006b) The Northwest Forest Plan: origins, components, implementation experience, and suggestions for change. *Conservation Biology*, **20**, 277–287.

Thompson, D.B.A., MacDonald, A.J., Marsden, H. & Galbraith, C.A. (1995) Upland heather moorland in Great Britain. *Biological Conservation*, **71**, 163–178.

Thompson, P. M. & Ollason, J. C. (2001) Lagged effects of ocean climate change on fulmar population dynamics. *Nature*, **413**, 417–420.

Thomson, A.M., Calvin, K.V., Chini, L.P., Edmonds, J.A., Bond-Lamberty, B., Frolking, S., Wise, M.A. & Janetos, A.C. (2010) Climate mitigation and the future of tropical landscapes. *Proceedings of the National Academy of Sciences USA*, **107**, 19633–19638.

Thomson, D.L. (1994) Growth and development of dotterel chicks *Charadrius morinellus*. *Bird Study*, **41**, 61–67.

Thomson, D. L., van Noordwijk A. & Hagemeijer W. (2003) Estimating avian dispersal distances from data on ringed birds. *Journal of Applied Statistics*, **30**, 1003–1008.

Thuiller, W., Araujo, M.B., & Lavorel, S. (2004) Do we need land-cover data to model species distributions in Europe? *Journal of Biogeography*, **31**, 353–361.

Tingley, M.W., Koo, M.S., Moritz, C., Rush, A.C. & Beissinger, S.R. (2012) The push and pull of climate change causes heterogeneous shifts in avian elevtional ranges. *Global Change Biology*, **18**, 3279–3290.

Tingley, M.W., Monahanc, W.B., Beissinger, S.R. & Moritz, C. (2009) Birds track their Grinnellian niche through a century of climate change. *Proceedings of the National Academy of Sciences USA*, **106**, 19637–19643.

Topp, W. & Kirsten, K. (1991) Synchronisation of pre-imaginal development and reproductive success in the winter moth, *Operophtera brumata* L. *Journal of Applied Entomology*, **111**, 137–146.

Toresen, R., & Østvedt, O.J. (2000) Variations in abundance of Norwegian spring-spawning herring (*Clupea harengus*, Clupeidae L.) throughout the 20th century and the influence of climatic fluctuations. *Fish and Fisheries*, **1**, 231–256.

Tøttrup, A.P., Rainio, K., Coppack, T., Lehikoinen, E., Rahbek, C. & Thorup, K. (2010) Local temperature fine-tunes the timing of spring migration in birds. *Integrative and Comparative Biology*, **50**, 293–304.

Tøttrup, A.P., Thorup, K., Rainio, K., Yosef, R., Lehikoinen, E. & Rahbek, C. (2008) Avian migrants adjust migration in response to environmental conditions en route. *Biology Letters*, **4**, 685–688.

Trathan, P.N., Croxall, J.P. & Murphy, E.J. (1996) Dynamics of Antarctic penguin populations in relation to inter-annual variability in sea-ice distribution. *Polar Biology*, **16**, 321–330.

Tremblay, I., Thomas, D., Blondel, J., Perret, P. & Lambrechts, M.M. (2005) The effect of habitat quality on foraging patterns, provisioning rate and nestling growth in Corsican blue tits *Parus caeruleus*. *Ibis*, **147**, 17–24.

Tremblay, I., Thomas, D.W., Lambrechts, M.M., Blondel, J. & Perret, P. (2003) Variation in blue tit breeding performance across gradients in habitat richness. *Ecology*, **84**, 3033–3043.

Trivelpiece, W.Z., Hinke, J.T., Miller, A.K., Reiss, C.S., Trivelpiece, S.G. & Watters, G.M. (2011) Variability in krill biomass links harvesting and climate warming to penguin population changes in Antarctica. *Proceedings of the National Academy of Sciences USA*, **108**, 7625–7628.

Trouwborst, A. (2010) International nature conservation law and the adaptation of biodiversity to climate change: a mismatch? *Journal of Environmental Law*, **21**, 419–442.

Trouwborst, A. (2011) Conserving European biodiversity in a changing climate: The Bern convention, the European Union Birds and Habita's Directives and the adaptation of nature to climate change. *Review of European Community and International Environmental Law*, **20**, 62–77.

Trouwborst, A. (2012) Transboundary wildlife conservation in a changing climate: adaptation of the Bonn convention on migratory species and its daughter instruments to climate change. *Diversity*, **4**, 258–300.

Tryjanowski, P., Kuźniak, S. & Sparks, T.H. (2002) Earlier arrival of some farmland migrants in western Poland. *Ibis*, **144**, 62–68.

Tryjanowski, P., Kuźniak, S. & Sparks, T.H. (2005) What affects the magnitude of change in first arrival dates of migrant birds? *Journal of Ornithology*, **146**, 200–205.

Tryjanowski, P. & Sparks, T.H. (2001) Is the detection of first arrival of migrating birds influenced by population size? A case study of red-backed shrike. *International Journal of Biometeorology*, **45**, 217–219.

Trzcinski, M.K., Fahrig, L. & Merriam, G. (1999) Independent effects of forest cover and fragmentation on the distribution of forest breeding birds. *Ecological Applications*, **9**, 586–593.

Tsoutsos, T., Frantzeskaki, N. & Gekas, V. (2005) Environmental impacts from the solar energy technologies. *Energy Policy*, **33**, 289–296.

Tucker, G. & Treweek, J. (2008) *Guidance on how to avoid, minimise or mitigate the impact of infrastructure developments and related disturbance affecting waterbirds*. AEWA Conservation Guidelines No. 11, AEWA Technical Series No. 26, Bonn, Germany.

Tulp, I., Schekkerman, H., Klaassen, R.H.G., Ens, B.J. & Visser, G.H. (2009) Body condition of shorebirds upon arrival at their Siberian breeding grounds. *Polar Biology*, **32**, 481–491.

Turetsky, M.R., Kane, E.S., Harden, J.W., Ottmar, R.D., Manies, K.L., Hoy, E. & Kassischke, E.S. (2010) Recent acceleration of biomass burning and carbon losses in Alaskan forests and peatlands. *Nature Geoscience*, **4**, 27–31.

Turner, J.R.G., Gatehouse, C.M. & Corey, C.A. (1987) Does solar energy control organic diversity? Butterflies, moths and the British climate. *Oikos*, **48**, 195–205.

Tyrberg, T. (1995) Palaeobiogeography of the genus *Lagopus* in the Western Palearctic. *Courier Forschunginsitut Senckenberg*, **181**, 275–291.

Tyrberg, T. (1998) *Pleistocene Birds of the Palearctic: A Catalogue*. Cambridge, MA: Nuttall Ornithological Club.

Tyler, G.A. & Green, R.E. (2004) Effects of weather on the survival and growth of Corncrake *Crex crex* chicks. *Ibis*, **146**, 69–76.

Tyler, G.A., Smith, K.W. & Burgess, D.J. (1998) Reedbed management and breeding Bitterns *Botaurus stellaris* in the UK. *Biological Conservation*, **86**, 257–266.

Uezu, A., Metzger, J.P. & Vielliard, J.M.E. (2005) Effects of structural and functional connectivity and patch size on the abundance of seven Atlantic Forest bird species. *Biological Conservation*, **123**, 507–519.

US Fish and Wildlife Service (2012) *Land-based Wind Energy Guidelines*. Available from: http://www.fws.gov/windenergy/docs/WEG_final.pdf (accessed 12 November 2012).

Uttley, J., Monaghan, P. & White, S. (1989) Differential effects of reduced sandeel availability on two sympatrically breeding species of tern. *Ornis Scandinavica*, **20**, 273–277.

Vagholikar, N. (2012) Dams and threatened birds in the Brahmaputra floodplains. In *Threatened Birds of India – Their Conservation Requirements*. Rahmani, A.R. India: Oxford University Press, pp. 92–104.

Vähätalo, A.V., Rainio, K., Lehikoinen, A. & Lehikoinen, E. (2004) Spring arrival of birds depends on the North Atlantic Oscillation. *Journal of Avian Biology*, **35**, 210–216.

Valdez-Hernández, M., Andrade, J.L., Jackson, P.C. & Rebolledo-Vieyra, M. (2010) Phenology of five tree species of a tropical dry forest in Yucatan, Mexico: effects of environmental and physiological factors. *Plant and Soil*, **329**, 155–171.

Vallin, N., Rice, A.M., Arnsten, H., Kulma, K. & Qvarnström, A. (2012) Combined effects of interspecific competition and hybridization impede local coexistence of *Ficedula* flycatchers. *Evolutionary Ecology*, **26**, 927–942.

Van de Pol, M., Ens, B.J., Heg, D., Brouwer, L., Krol, J., Maier, M., Exo, K.-M., Oosterbeek, K., Lok, T., Eising, C.M. & Koffijberg, K. (2010a) Do changes in the frequency, magnitude and timing of extreme climatic events threaten the population viability of coastal birds? *Journal of Applied Ecology*, **47**, 720–730.

Van de Pol, M., Vindenes, Y., Sæther, B.-E., Engen, S., Ens, B.J., Oosterbeek, K. & Tinbergen, J.M. (2010b) Effects of climate change and variability on population dynamics in a long-lived shorebird. *Ecology*, **91**, 1192–1204.

Van den Berg, L.J.L., Bullock, J.M., Clarke, R.T., Langston, R.H.W. & Rose, R.J. (2001) Territory selection by the Dartford warbler (*Sylvia undata*) in Dorset, England: the role of vegetation type, habitat fragmentation and population size. *Biological Conservation*, **101**, 217–228.

VanDerWal, J., Murphy, H.T., Kutt, A.S., Perkins, G.C., Bateman, B.L., Perry, J.J. & Reside, A.E. (2013) Focus on poleward shifts in species' distribution underestimates the fingerprint of climate change. *Nature Climate Change*, **3**, 239–243.

van der Werf, G.R., Morton, D.C., DeFries, R.S., Olivier, J.G.J., Kasibhatla, P.S., Jackson, R.B., Collatz, G.J. & Randerson, J.T. (2009) CO_2 emissions from forest loss. *Nature Geoscience*, **2**, 737–738.

van Dorp, J. & Opdam, P.F.M. (1987) Effects of patch size, isolation and regional abundance on forest bird communities. *Landscape Ecology*, **1**, 59–73.

Van Langevelde, F. (2000) Scale of habitat connectivity and colonization in fragmented nuthatch populations. *Ecography*, **23**, 614–622.

Van Rensburg, B.J., Chown, S.L. & Gaston, K.L. (2002) Species richness, environmental correlates, and spatial scale: a test using South African birds. *American Naturalist*, **159**, 566–577.

Van Rensburg, B.J., Erasmus, B.F.N., van Jaarsveld, A.S., Gaston, K.J. & Chown, S.L. (2004) Conservation during times of change: correlations between birds, climate and people in South Africa. *South African Journal of Science*, **100**, 266–272.

van Riper, C., III, van Riper, S. G., Goff, M. L. & Laird, M. (1986) The epizootiology and ecological significance of Malaria in Hawaiian land birds. *Ecological Monographs*, **56**, 327–344.

van Strien, A.J., Pannekoek, J. & Gibbons, D.W. (2001) Indexing European bird population trends using results of national monitoring schemes: a trial of a new method. *Bird Study*, **48**, 200–213.

Van Teeffelen, A.J.A., Cabeza, M. & Moilanen, A. (2006) Connectivity, probabilities and persistence: comparing reserve selection strategies. *Biodiversity & Conservation*, **15**, 899–919.

Van Teeffelen, A.J.A., Vos, C.C. & Opdam, P. (2012) Species in a dynamic world: consequences of habitat network dynamics on conservation planning. *Biological Conservation*, **153**, 239–253.

van Turnhout, C., Foppen, R., Leuven, R., van Strien, A. & Siepel, H. (2010) Life-history and ecological correlates of population change in Dutch breeding birds. *Biological Conservation*, **143**, 173–181.

van Vliet, A.J.H., de Groot, R.S., Bellens, Y., Braun, P., Bruegger, R., Bruns, E., Clevers, J., Esterguil, C., Flechsig, M., Jeanneret, F., Maggi, M., Martens, P., Menne, B., Menzel, A. & Sparks, T. (2003) The European phenology network. *International Journal of Biometeorology*, **47**, 202–212.

van Vliet, J., Musters, C.J.M. & Ter Keurs, W.J. (2009) Changes in migration behaviour of blackbirds *Turdus merula* from the Netherlands. *Bird Study*, **56**, 276–281.

van Vuuren, D.P., Edmonds, J., Kainuma, M., Riahi, K., Thomson, A., Hibbard, K., Hurtt, G.C., Kram, T., Krey, V., Lamarque, J.-F, Masui, T., Meinshausen, M., Nakicenovic, N., Smith, S.J. & Rose, S.K. (2011) The representative concentration pathways: an overview. *Climate Change*, **109**, 5–31.

Vardanis, Y., Klaassen, R.H.G., Strandberg, R. & Alerstam, T. (2011) Individuality in bird migration: routes and timing. *Biology Letters*, **7**, 502–505.

Vatka, E., Orell, M. & Rytkönen, S. (2011) Warming climate advances breeding and improves synchrony of food demand and food availability in a boreal passerine. *Global Change Biology*, **17**, 3002–3009.

Veen, T., Sheldon, B.C., Weissing, F.J., Visser, M.E., Qvarnström, A. & Sætre, G.-P. (2010) Temporal differences in food abundance promote coexistence between two congeneric paserines. *Oecologica*, **162**, 873–884.

Veit, R., McGowan, J., Ainley, D., Wahl, T. & Pyle, P. (1997) Apex marine predator declines ninety percent in association with changing oceanic climate. *Global Change Biology*, **3**, 23–28.

Végvári, Z., Bókony, V., Barta, Z. & Kovács, G. (2010) Life history predicts advancement of avian spring migration in response to climate change. *Global Change Biology*, **16**, 1–11.

Velásquez-Tibatá, J., Salaman, P., Graham, C.H. (2013) Effects of climate change on species distribution, community structure and conservation of birds in protected areas in Colombia. *Regional Environmental Change*, **13**, 235–248.

Verboom, J., Foppen, R., Chardon, P., Opdam, P. & Luttikhuien, P. (2001) Introducing the key patch approach for habitat networks with persistent populations: an example for marshland birds. *Biological Conservation*, **100**, 89–101.

Verboom, J., Metz, J.A.J. & Meelis, E. (1993) Metapopulation models for impact assessment of fragmentation. In *Landscape Ecology of a Stressed Environment, IALE Studies in Landscape Ecology*. Vos, C.C. & Opdam, P. London, UK: Chapman and Hall, pp. 172–191.

Verboven, N., Tinbergen, J. M. & Verhulst, S. (2001) Food, reproductive success and multiple breeding in the great tit *Parus major*. *Ardea*, **89**, 387–406.

Verburg, P.H., van Berkel, D.B., van Doorn, A.M., van Eupen, M. & van den Heiligenberg, H.A.R.M. (2010) Trajectories of land use change in Europe: a model-based exploration of rural futures. *Landscape Ecology*, **25**, 217–232.

Vergara, P.M. & Armesto, J.J. (2009) Responses of Chilean forest birds to anthropogenic habitat fragmentation across spatial scales. *Landscape Ecology*, **24**, 25–38.

Verner, J. & Purcell, K.L. (1999) Fluctuating populations of house wrens and Bewick's wrens in foothills of the Western Sierra Nevada of California. *The Condor*, **101**, 219–229.

Vernon, C.J. (1978) Breeding seasons of birds in deciduous woodland at Zimbabwe, Rhodesia, from 1970 to 1974. *Ostrich*, **49**, 102–115.

Vernon, C.J. (1984) Population dynamics of birds in Brachystegia woodland. In *Proceedings of the 5th Pan-African Ornithological Congress*, J. Ledger. Johannesburg, South Africa: SOAS, pp. 201–216.

Vickery, J. & Arlettaz, R. (2012) The importance of habitat heterogeneity at multiple scales for birds in European agricultural landscapes. In *Birds and Habitat. Relationships in Changing Landscapes*. Fuller, R.J. Cambridge, UK: Cambridge University Press, pp. 177–204.

Village, A. (1986) Breeding performance of kestrels at Eskdalemuir, south Scotland. *Journal of Zoology (London)*, **208**, 367–378.

Villard, M., Trzcinkski, M.K. & Merriam, G. (1999) Fragmentation effects on forest birds: relative influence of woodland cover and configuration on landscape occupancy. *Conservation Biology*, **13**, 774–783.

Villiard, M.A. & Taylor, R.D. (1994) Tolerance to habitat fragmentation influences colonisation of new habitat by forest birds. *Oecologia*, **98**, 393–401.

Virkkala, R., Heikkinena, R.K., Leikolab, N. & Luotoc, M. (2008) Projected large-scale range reductions of northern-boreal land bird species due to climate change. *Biological Conservation*, **141**, 1343–1353.

Virkkala, R. & Rajasärkkaä, A. (2011) Climate change affects populations of northern birds in boreal protected areas. *Biology Letters*, **7**, 395–398.

Visser, J. (1978) Fat and protein metabolism and mortality in the coot *Fulica atra*. *Ardea*, **66**, 173–183.

Visser, M.E. (2008) Keeping up with a warming world; assessing the rate of adaptation to climate change. *Proceedings of the Royal Society Series B*, **275**, 649–659.

Visser, M.E., Adriaensen, F. & van Balen, J.H., du Feu, C., Ivankina, E.V., Kerimov, A.B., de Laet, J., Matthysen, E., McCleery, R., Orell, M. & Thomson, D.L. (2003) Variable responses to large-scale climate change in European *Parus* populations. *Proceedings of the Royal Society of London, Series B*, **270**, 367–372

Visser, M.E. & Both, C. (2005) Shifts in phenology due to global climate change: the need for a yardstick. *Proceedings of the Royal Society of London, Series B*, **272**, 2561–2569.

Visser, M.E., Both, C. & Lambrechts, M.M. (2004) Global climate change leads to mistimed avian reproduction. *Advances in Ecological Research*, **35**, 89–110.

Visser, M. E., Holleman, L. J.M. & Caro, S. P. (2009a) Temperature has a causal effect on avian timing of reproduction. *Proceedings of the Royal Society of London, Series B*, **276**, 2323–2331.

Visser, M.E., Holleman, L.J.M. & Gienapp, P. (2006) Shifts in caterpillar biomass phenology due to climate change and its impact on the breeding biology of an insectivorous bird. *Oecologia*, **147**, 164–172.

Visser, M.E., te Marvelde, L. & Lof, M.E. (2012) Adaptive phenological mismatches of birds and their food in a warming world. *Journal of Ornithology*, **153 Suppl 1**, 75–84.

Visser, M.E., Van Noordwijk, A.J., Tinbergen, J.M. & Lessells, C. M. (1998) Warmer springs lead to mistimed reproduction in great tits (*Parus major*). *Proceedings of the Royal Society of London, Series B*, **265**, 1867–1870.

Voigt, C.C., Popa-Lisseanu, A.G., Niermann, I. & Kramer-Schadt, S. (2012) The catchment area of wind farms for European bats: a plea for international regulation. *Biological Conservation*, **153**, 80–86.

Vos, C.C., Berry, P., Opdam, P., Baveco, H., Nijhof, B., O'Hanley, J., Bell, C. & Kuipers, H. (2008) Adapting landscapes to climate change: examples of climate-proof ecosystem networks and priority adaptation zones. *Journal of Applied Ecology*, **45**, 1722–1731.

Waite, T.A. & Strickland, D. (2006) Climate change and the demographic demise of a hoarding bird living on the edge. *Proceedings of the Royal Society of London, Series B*, **273**, 2809–2813.

Wang, D., Wang, C., Yang, X. & Lu, J. (2005) Winter Northern Hemisphere surface air temperature variability associated with the Arctic Oscillation and North Atlantic Oscillation. *Geophysical Research Letters*, **32**, L16706.

Wang, H.-J., Sun, J.-Q., Chen, H.-P., Zhu, Y.-L., Zhang, Y., Jiang, D.-B., Land, X.-M., Fen, K., Yu, E.-T., Yang, S. (2012) Extreme climate in China: facts, simulation and projection. *Meteorologische Zeitschrift*, **21**, 279–304.

Wanless, S., Wright, P.J., Harris, M.P. & Elston, D.A. (2004) Evidence for decrease in the size of lesser sandeels *Ammodytes marinus* in a North Sea aggregation over a 30-yr period. *Marine Ecology Progress Series*, **279**, 237–246.

Wanless, S., Harris, M.P., Redman, P. & Speakman, J.R. (2005) Low energy values of fish as a probable cause of a major seabird breeding failure in the North Sea. *Marine Ecology Progress Series*, **294**, 1–8.

Ward, P. (1971) The migration patterns of *Quelea quelea* in Africa. *Ibis*, **113**, 275–297.

Warren, C.R. & Birnie, R.V. (2009) Re-powering Scotland: wind farms and the 'energy or environment?' debate. *Scottish Geographical Journal*, **125**, 97–126.

Warren, M.S., Hill, J.K., Thomas, J.A., Asher, J., Fox, R., Huntley, B., Roy, D.B., Telfer, M.G., Jeffcoate, S., Harding, P., Jeffcoate, G., Willis, S.G., Greatorex-Davies, J.N., Moss, D. & Thomas, C.D. (2001) Rapid responses of British butterflies to opposing forces of climate and habitat change. *Nature*, **414**, 65–69.

Warren, R., Price, J., De La Nava Santos, S., Fischlin, A. & Midgley, G. (2010) Increasing impacts of climate change upon ecosystems with increasing global mean temperature rise. *Climatic Change*, **106**, 141–177.

Warren, R., VanDerWal, J., Price, J., Welbergen, J.A., Atkinson, I., Ramirez-Villegas, J., Osborn, T.J., Jarvis, A., Shoo, L.P., Williams, S.E. & Lowe, J. (2013) Quantifying the benefit of early climate change mitigation in avoiding biodiversity loss. *Nature Climate Change*, **3**, 512–519.

Watanuki, Y. (2010) Climate induced phenological mismatch: An implication from a long-term monitoring study of seabirds. *Japanese Journal of Ecology*, **60**, 1–11.

Watanuki, Y. & Ito, M. (2012) Climatic effects on breeding seabirds of the northern Japan Sea. *Marine Ecology Progress Series*, **454**, 183–196.

Watanuki, Y., Ito, M., Deguchi, T. & Minobe, S. (2009) Climate-forced seasonal mismatch between the hatching of rhinoceros auklets and the availability of anchovy. *Marine Ecology Progress Series*, **393**, 259–271.

Watson, A. & Moss, R. (2008) *Grouse*. London, UK: Collins.

Watson, A., Moss, R. & Rae, S. (1998) Population dynamics of Scottish rock ptarmigan cycles. *Ecology*, **79**, 1174–1192.

Watson, A., Moss, R. & Rothery, P. (2000) Weather and synchrony in 10-year population cycles of rock ptarmigan and red grouse in Scotland. *Ecology*, **81**, 2126–2136.

Watson, A. & O'Hare, P.J. (1979) Red grouse populations on experimentally treated and untreated Irish bog. *Journal of Applied Ecology*, **16**, 433–452.

Watson, J. (1997) *The Golden Eagle*. London, UK: T & AD Poyser.

Weathers, W.W. (1997) Energetics and thermoregulation by small passerines of the humid, lowland tropics. *The Auk*, **114**, 341–353.

Weathers, W.W. & Greene, E. (1998) Thermoregulatory responses of bridled and juniper titmice to high temperature. *The Condor*, **100**, 365–372.

Weathers, W.W., Hodum, P.J. & Blakesley, J.A. (2001) Thermal ecology and ecological energetics of California Spotted Owls. *The Condor*, **103**, 678–690.

Webster, M.S., Marra, P.P., Haig, S., Bensch, S. & Holmes, R.T. (2002) Links between worlds: unraveling migratory connectivity. *Trends in Ecology and Evolution*, **17**, 76–83.

Wegge, P. & Kastdalen, L. (2008) Habitat and diet of young grouse broods: resource partitioning between capercaillie (*Tetrao urogallus*) and black grouse (*Tetrao tetrix*) in boreal forests. *Journal of Ornithology*, **149**, 237–244.

Wegge, P., Vesterås, T. & Rolstad, J. (2010) Does timing of breeding and subsequent brood hatching in boreal forest grouse match the phenology of insect food for the chicks? *Annales Zoologici Fennici*, **47**, 251–260.

Weidinger, K. & Král, M. (2007) Climatic effects on arrival and laying dates in a long-distance migrant, the Collared Flycatcher *Ficedula albicollis*. *Ibis*, **149**, 836–847.

Wesolowski, T. & Maziarz, M. (2009) Changes in breeding phenology and performance of wood warblers *Phylloscopus sibilatrix* in a primeval forest: a thirty-year perspective. *Acta Ornithologica*, **44**, 69–80.

Wesolowski, T. & Stawarcyk, T. (1991) Survival and population dynamics of nuthatches *Sitta europaea* breeding in natural cavities in a primeval temperate forest. *Ornis Scandinavica*, **22**, 143–154.

West, A.D. & Caldow, R.W.G. (2006) The development and use of individual-based models to predict the effects of habitat loss and disturbance on waders and waterfowl. *Ibis*, **148 suppl 1**, 158–168.

Whited, D., Galatowitsch, S., Tester, J.R., Schik, K., Lehtinen, R. & Husveth, J. (2000) The importance of local and regional factors in predicting effective conservation: Planning strategies for wetland bird communities in agricultural and urban landscapes. *Landscape and Urban Planning*, **49**, 49–65.

Whitehead, P.J. & Saalfeld, K. (2000) Nesting phenology of magpie geese (*Anseranas semipalmata*) in monsoonal northern Australia: responses to antecedent rainfall. *Journal of Zoology (London)*, **251**, 495–508.

Wichmann, M.C., Jeltsch, F., Dean, R.J., Moloney, K.A. & Wissel, C. (2003) Implication of climate change for the persistence of raptors in arid savanna. *Oikos*, **102**, 186–202.

Wiens, J., Fargoine, J. & Hill, J. (2011) Biofuels and biodiversity. *Ecological Applications*, **21**, 1085–1095.

Wikelski, M., Hau, M., Robinson, W.D. & Wingfield, J.C. (2003) Reproductive seasonality of seven neotropical passerine species. *The Condor*, **105**, 683–695.

Wikelski, M., Hau, M., & J. C. Wingfield (2000) Seasonality of reproduction in a neotropical rainforest bird. *Ecology*, **81**, 2458–2472.

Wilcox, C. & Donlan, C.J. (2007) Compensatory mitigation as a solution to fisheries by catch-biodiversity conservation conflicts. *Frontiers in Ecology and the Environment*, **5**, 325–331.

Wilkin, T.A., King, L.E. & Sheldon, B.C. (2009) Habitat quality, nestling diet, and provisioning behaviour in great tits *Parus major*. *Journal of Avian Biology*, **40**, 135–145.

Williams, J.W., Jackson, S.T. & Kutzbach, J.E. (2007) Projecting distributions of novel and disappearing climates by 2100 AD. *Proceedings of the National Academy of Sciences USA*, **104**, 5738–5742.

Williams, J.W., Post, D.M., Cwynar, L.C., Lotter, A.F. & Levesque, A.J. (2002) Rapid and widespread vegetation responses to past climate change in the North Atlantic region. *Geology*, **30**, 971–974.

Willis, S.G., Hill, J.K., Thomas, C.D., Roy, D.B., Fox, R., Blakeley, D.S. & Huntley, B. (2009) Assisted colonization in a changing climate: a test-study using two U.K. butterflies. *Conservation Letters*, **2**, 46–52.

Wilson, A.M., Vickery, J.A., Brown, A., Langston, R.H.W., Smallshire, D., Wotton, S. & Vanhinsberg, D. (2005) Changes in the numbers of breeding waders on lowland wet grasslands in England and Wales between 1982 and 2002. *Bird Study*, **52**, 55–69.

Wilson, J.D., Evans, J., Browne, S.J. & King, J.R. (1997) Territory distribution and breeding success of skylarks *Alauda arvensisi* on organic and intensive farmland in southern England. *Journal of Applied Ecology*, **34**, 1462–1478.

Wilson, J.D., Evans, A.D. & Grice, P.V. (2009b) *Bird Conservation and Agriculture*. Cambridge, UK: Cambridge University Press.

Wilson, J.R., Dormontt, E.E., Prentis, P.J., Lowe, A.J. & Richardson, D.M. (2009a) Something in the way you move: dispersal pathways affect invasion success. *Trends in Ecology and Evolution*, **24**, 136–144.

Wilson, L., Wilson, J., Holden, J., Johnstone, I., Armstrong, A. & Morris, M. (2010) Recovery of water tables in Welsh blanket bog after drain blocking: discharge rates, time scales and the influence of local conditions. *Journal of Hydrology*, **391**, 377–386.

Wilson, P.R., Ainley, D.G., Nur, N., Jacobs, S.S., Barton, K.J., Ballard, G. & Comiso, J.C. (2001) Adélie penguin population change in the Pacific sector of Antarctica: relation to sea-ice extent and the Antarctic Circumpolar Current. *Marine Ecology Progress Series*, **213**, 301–309.

Wilson, S., LaDeau, S.L., Tøttrup, A.P. & Marra, P. (2011) Range-wide effects of breeding- and nonbreeding-season climate on the abundance of a Neotropical migrant songbird. *Ecology*, **92**, 1789–1798.

Wimberly, M.C. (2006) Species dynamics in disturbed landscapes: when does a shifting habitat mosaic enhance connectivity? *Landscape Ecology*, **21**, 35–46.

Wingfield J.C. (2005) Flexibility in annual cycles of birds: implication for endocrine control mechanisms. *Journal of Ornithology*, **146**, 291–304.

Winkel, W. & Hudde, H. (1997) Long-term trends in reproductive traits of tits (*Parus major*, *P. caeruleus*) and pied flycatchers *Ficedula hypoleuca*. *Journal of Avian Biology*, **28**, 187–190.

Wiser, R. & Bolinger, M. (2010) *2009 Wind Technologies Market Report*. Washington, DC: US Department of Energy.

Wolf, S.G., Sydeman, W.J., Hipfner, J.M., Abraham, C.L., Tershy, B.R. & Croll, D.A. (2009) Range-wide reproductive consequences of ocean climate variability for the seabird Cassin's Auklet. *Ecology*, **90**, 742–753.

Wood, S.N. & Augustin, N.H. (2002) GAMs with integrated model selection using penalized regression splines and applications to environmental modelling. *Ecological Modelling*, **157**, 157–177.

Woodworth, B.L., Atkinson, C.T., LaPointe, D.A., Hart, P.J., Spiegel, C.S., Tweed, E.J., Henneman, C., LeBrun, J., Denette, T., DeMots, R., Kozar, K.L., Triglia, D., Lease, D., Gregor, A., Smith, T. & Duffy, D. (2005) Host population persistence in the face of introduced vector-borne diseases: *Hawaii amakihi* and avian malaria. *Proceedings of the National Academy of Sciences USA*, **102**, 1531–1536.

World Wind Energy Association (2012) *The World Wind Energy Association 2011 Report*: Bonn, Germany: World Wind Energy Association. Available from www.wwindea.org/webimages/WorldWindEnergyReport2011.pdf (accessed 26 August 2012).

Worrall, F., Bell, M.J. & Bhogal, A. (2010) Assessing the probability of carbon and greenhouse gas benefit from the management of peat soils. *Science of the Total Environment*, **408**, 2657–2666.

Wotton, S., Brown, A., Burn, A., Dodd, A., Droy, N., Gilbert, G., Hardiman, N., Rees, S., White, G. & Gregory, R. (2009a) Boom or bust – a sustainable future for reedbeds and Bitterns? *British Wildlife*, June 2009, 305–315.

Wotton, S., Conway, G., Eaton, M., Henderson, I. & Grice, P. (2009b) The status of the Dartford Warbler in the UK and Channel Islands in 2006. *British Birds*, **102**, 230–246.

Wretenberg, J., Lindström, A., Svensson, S., Thierfelder, T. & Pärtin T. (2006) Population trends of farmland birds in Sweden and England: similar trends but different patterns of agricultural intensification. *Journal of Applied Ecology*, **43**, 1110–1120.

Wright, D.H. (1983) Species–energy theory: an extension of species-area theory. *Oikos*, **41**, 496–506.

Wright, L.J., Hoblyn, R.A., Green, R.E., Bowden, C.G.R., Mallord, J.W., Sutherland, W.J. & Dolman, P.M. (2009) Importance of climate and environmental change in the demography of a multi-brooded passerine, the woodlark *Lullula arborea*. *Journal of Animal Ecology*, **78**, 1191–1202.

Wright, P.J. (1996) Is there a conflict between sandeel fisheries and seabirds? A case study at Shetland. In *Aquatic Predators and Their Prey*. Greenstreet, S.P.R. & Tasker, M.L. Oxford, UK: Fishing News Books, Blackwell Science, pp. 154–165.

Wyndham, E. (1986) Length of birds' breeding seasons. *American Naturalist*, **128**, 155–164.

Yalden, D.W. (1986) Diet, food availability and habitat selection of breeding common sandpipers *Actitis hypoleucos*. *Ibis*, **128**, 23–36.

Yalden, D.W. & Albarella, U. (2009) *The History of British Birds*: Oxford, UK: Oxford University Press.

Yalden, D.W. & Pearce-Higgins, J.W. (1997) Density-dependence and winter weather as factors affecting the size of a population of Golden Plovers *Pluvialis apricaria*. *Bird Study*, **44**, 227–234.

Yamamura, K. & Kiritani, K. (1998) A simple method to estimate the potential increase in the number of generations under global warming in temperate zones. *Applied Entomology and Zoology*, **33**, 289–298.

Yamamura, Y., Amano, T., Koizumi, T., Mitsuda, Y., Taki, H. & Okabe, K. (2009) Does land-use change affect biodiversity dynamics at a macroecological scale? A case study of birds over the past 20 years in Japan. *Animal Conservation*, **12**, 110–119.

Yap, C.A.-M., Sodhi, N.S. & Peh, K.S.-H. (2007) Phenology of tropical birds in peninsular Malaysia: effect of selective logging and food resources. *The Auk*, **124**, 945–961.

Yoccoz, N.G., Stenseth, N.C., Henttonen, H. & Prévot-Julliard, A.-C. (2001) Effects of food addition on the seasonal density-dependent structure of bank vole *Clethrionomys glareolus* populations. *Journal of Animal Ecology*, **70**, 713–720.

Yom-Tov, Y. (1987) The reproductive rate of Australian passerines. *Journal of Australian Wildlife*, **14**, 319–330.

Young, B., Byers, E., Gravuer, K., Hammerson, G. & Redder, A. (2011) *Guidelines for Using the NatureServe Climate Change Vulnerability Index*. NatureServe.

Žalakevičius, M. (2001) Bird migration and the climate: a review of the studies conducted in Lithuania in the context of climate change. *Acta Zoologica Lituanica*, **11**, 200–21.

Žalakevičius, M., Bartkevičienė, G., Ivanauskas, F. & Nedzinskas, V. (2009) The response of spring arrival dates of non-passerine migrants to climate change: a case study from eastern Baltic. *Acta Zooligica Lituanica*, **19**, 155–171.

Žalakevičius, M., Bartkevičienė, G., Raudonikis, L. & Janulaitis, J. (2006) Spring arrival response to climate change in birds: a case study from eastern Europe. *Journal of Ornithology*, **147**, 326–343.

Zang, H. & Kunze, P. (2007) Wie beeinflussen Buchenmast und Strenge des Winters die Populationsdynamik des Kleibers *Sitta europaea* im Harz außerhalb der Brutzeit? *Vogelwelt*, **128**, 1–10.

Zann, R.A., Morton, S.R., Jones, K.R. & Burley, N.T. (1995) The timing of breeding by zebra finches in relation to rainfall in central Australia. *Emu*, **95**, 208–222.

Zbinden, N. & Salvioni, M. (2004) Bedeutung der Temperatur in der frühen Aufzuchtzeit für den Fortpflanzungsefolg des Birkhuhns *Tetrao tetrix* auf verschiedenen Höhestufen im Tessin Südschweiz. *Der Ornithologische Beobachter*, **101**, 307–318.

Zuckerberg, B., Woods, A.M. & Porter, W.F. (2009) Poleward shifts in breeding bird distributions in New York State. *Global Change Biology*, **15**, 1866–1883.

Zwarts, L., Bijlam, R.G., van der Kamp, J. & Wymenga, E. (2009) *Living on the Edge: Wetlands and Birds in a Changing Sahel*. Zeist, the Netherlands: KNNV Publishing.

Index

abiotic mechanisms, 235, 246, 250, 363, 372
Accipiter gentalis. See northern goshawk
Accipitridae. *See* raptors
Accipter nisus. See sparrowhawk
Aceros nipalensis. See rufous-necked hornbill
Acrocephalus arundinaceus. See great reed warbler
Acrocephalus scheonobaenus. See sedge warbler
Acrocephalus scirpaceus. See Eurasian reed warbler
Actia caja. See garden tiger moth
Actitis hypoleuca. See common sandpiper
actual evapotranspiration (AET), 182, 184, 209–210, 362, 364
adaptive capacity, 70, 195, 262, 305, 362, 373
adaptive hypothesis, 72–73
Adelaide's warbler, 141
Adélie penguin, 159–160
aerosols, 11
Aethia cristatella. See crested auklet
Aethia psittacula. See parakeet auklet
Aethia pusilla. See least auklet
Aethia pygmaea. See whiskered auklet
Africa
    climate change adaptation, 266, 268, 280
    climate change mitigation, 336, 373
    climate projections, 15, 371–372
    climate trends, 5–6
    conservation, 280
    effects of climate variables, 37, 39–40, 110, 136–140, 149
    habitat change, 86, 99
    impacts of climate change, 94, 194
    land-use projections, 370–371, 373
    phenology, 26, 40
    phenology trends, 36, 39–40
    projected impacts of climate change, 220, 227, 261, 268, 280, 372
    species richness, 181, 184, 187, 280
African-Eurasian Waterbirds Agreement (AEWA), 266
agri-environment scheme, 257, 299, 333
Alaska
    climate trends, 5
Alauda arvensis. See skylark
albedo, 4
Alca torda. See razorbill
Alectoris barbara. See Barbary partridge
Alliance for Zero Extinction Area, 252
alpine birds. *See* upland birds
Altamont Pass wind farm, 312, 315
altricial chicks, 121

amakihi, 150
Amazon
    climate change adaptation, 292
    climate change mitigation, 325, 327, 336, 350
    climate projections, 15, 364, 371
    climate trends, 6
    habitat loss, 355
    land-use projections, 371
American crow, *134*
American kestrel, 123, 148
American red squirrel, 302
American redstart, 43, 85, 140–141, 145
American robin, 66
American wigeon, 88
Ammodramus henslowii. See Henslow's sparrow
Ammodramus savannarum. See grasshopper sparrow
Ammodytes hexapterus. See sandeel
Ammodytes marinus. See sandeel
amphibians, *166, 325*
Amphispiza belli. See sage sparrow
Amsterdam albatross, 161, 245
Anas acuta. See pintail
Anas americana. See American wigeon
Anas penelope. See Eurasian wigeon
Anas platyrhynchos. See mallard
Anatidae. *See* waterfowl
anchovy, 91, 92
Anser brachyrhynchus. See pink-footed goose
Anser caerulescens. See snow goose
Anseranas semipalmata. See magpie goose
Anseriformes. *See* wildfowl
Antarctica
    climate projections, 15
    climate trends, 4, 159
    effect of climate variables, 158–161
    ice cores, 8, 10
    impacts of climate change, 158–161
    projected impacts of climate change, 245
Anthropoides paradiseus. See blue crane
Anthus berthelotii. See Berthelot's pipit
Anthus pratensis. See meadow pipit
Aphelocoma wollweberi. See Mexican jay
aphid, 65
Aplomado falcon, 146
Aptenodytes forsteri. See emperor penguin
Aptenodytes patagonicus. See king penguin
Apus affinis. See house swift
aquaculture, 352
Aquila rapax. See tawny eagle

Arctic
- climate projections, 15
- climate trends, 4, 6
- effect of climate variables, 66, 87, 89, 123, 126, 129–132, 156–157, 166
- impacts of climate change, 87, 95, 129–132, 156–157
- phenology, 66, 181
- phenology trends, 42, 51, 63, 66
- projected impacts of climate change, 228

Arctic amplification, 4, 15
Arctic cod, 156–157
Arctic fox, 132, 415
Arctic loon. See black-throated diver
Arctic Oscillation, 87
Arctic tern, 153, 156
Ardea cinerea. See grey heron
Ardea insignis. See white-bellied heron
Ardea purpurea. See purple heron
Ardeola ralloides. See Squacco heron
area under a curve (AUC), 231, 234
Arenaria interpres. See ruddy turnstone
Argentina
- breeding phenology, 57
- climate change mitigation, 336

army ant, 196
artificial neural networks, 213
Asia
- climate change adaptation, 280
- climate change mitigation, 334, 342, 368
- climate projections, 15, 364, 371
- climate trends, 6
- conservation, 280, 330
- land-use projections, 371
- projected impacts of climate change, 372
- range shift, 178
- species richness, 187, 280

assisted colonisation, 260, 269, 301–305, 367
asynchrony. See phenology
Athya spp. See scaup
Atlantic forest
- climate change adaptation, 272, 291, 293–294
- climate projections, 15

Atlantic Ocean
- climate projections, 15
- climate trends, 4
- effects of climate variables, 156, 158

Atlantic puffin, 90, 92–93, 95, 153–158
atlas, 183, 191, 204, 213, 236–238
atmosphere
- circulation system, 4, 14

attribution, 9–10, 245
Audouin's gull, 261
Australia
- climate change adaptation, 272
- climate change mitigation, 311, 313
- climate projections, 15
- climate trends, 7
- effect of climate variables, 56–57, 93, 151, 162
- impacts of climate change, 57, 151
- phenology trends, 31, 39, 56
- projected impacts of climate change, 221, 228, 230

Australian magpie, 56
autocovariate regression, 233
autoregressive model, 233
autumnal moth, 81
avian influenza, 134
avian malaria, 150, 166
avian pox, 150
Aythya baeri. See Baer's pochard

Baer's pochard, 326
Baird's sandpiper, 89
bald eagle, 123
Baltic Sea
- effect of climate variables, 153
- projected impacts of climate change, 229

banded stilt, 56
Barbary partridge, 261
barn owl, 118, 146
barn swallow, 26, 39, 60, 139
barred antshrike, 291
barrier effect of renewable energy, 322, 324
bar-tailed godwit, 329
Bartramia longicauda. See upland sandpiper
basal clades, 183
bateleur, 146
bats, 316, 323
bearded parrotbill, 273
bearded tit. See bearded parrotbill
beautiful nuthatch, 326
beech, 113, 115
Belgium
- climate change mitigation, 312–313, 316
- impacts of climate change, 72
- phenology trends, 47
- red grouse introduction, 18

Bell's vireo, 338
Bengal florican, 326
Berthelot's pipit, 261
Betula spp. See birch
bilberry, 17
bioclimate model. See climate envelope model
biodiversity offsetting, 348–349
bioenergy, 333–343, 349, 353, 369
biofuel, 311, 333–338, 340–343, 346–347, 353, 355, 368, 370–372, 376–377
biomass, 309–310, 334, 338–343
biotic mechanisms, 8, 16, 110, 171, 174, 235, 241, 246, 250, 285, 302, 360–361, 363, 366, 372
birch, 17
bird banding. See bird ringing
bird observatory, 27, 36–37
bird ringing, 1, 39, 47, 116, 135, 152, 217, 219, 244
BirdLife International, 1, 179, 230, 251, 253–254, 257, 264, 270, 279, 365, 370
Birds Directive, 265
black-breasted parrotbill, 326
black-browed albatross, 161, 245
blackcap, 150, 291
black-chested buzzard-eagle, 148
black-crowned night heron, 136, 138

black-footed albatross, 229
black grouse, 84–86, 95, 121, 177, 258
black kite, 123
black-legged kittiwake, 93, 95, 153–158, 287, 301
black-tailed godwit, 121, 125, 141, 284
black-tailed gull, 92
black-throated blue warbler, 139–140, 142, 144–145
black-throated diver, 321–322, 325
blue carbon, 352
blue crane, 323
blue-footed booby, 162
blue petrel, 161
blue tit, 47, 52, 67, 69, 74–77, 86, 95, 114–115, 120, 285, 291
blue-throated black warbler, 122
Blyth's tragopan, 326
boblink, 338
body condition, 43, 77, 119, 140, 158, 331, 360
body size
    effect on sensitivity to fragmentation, 271, 295
    effect on survival, 116
Bolivia
    climate change adaptation, 272
    climate change mitigation, 336
Bonferroni correction, 232
Bonin petrel, 229
Boreogadus saida. *See* Arctic cod
Botaurus stellaris. *See* great bittern
Branta bernicla. *See* brent goose
Brazil
    climate change adaptation, 272, 291
    climate change mitigation, 336, 341, 350
    climate projections, 15
    climate trends, 7
    conservation, 293
    effect of climate variables, 57–58
    phenology, 57
breeding
    phenology. *See* phenology: laying date trends
Breeding Bird Survey (BBS), 182, 188–189, 191, 206, 238
breeding season length, 95
breeding success, 16
    carryover effects. *See* carryover effects
    effect of anthropogenic pressure, 301
    effect of competition. *See* competition
    effect of flooding. *See* flooding
    effect of food availability. *See* food availability
    effect of mismatch. *See* phenology: mismatch
    effect of precipitation. *See* precipitation
    effect of temperature. *See* temperature
    effect on migration phenology, *51*
    effects of parasites. *See* parasites
    effects of predation. *See* predation
brent goose, 130
Brewer's sparrow, 146
brood
    number of
        effect of breeding phenology, 50
        effect of food availability, 149
        effect on migration phenology trend, 35, 51, 54

    effect on mismatch, 71–74
brood parasitism, 90, 271
brooding, 121, 126
Brünnich's guillemot, 94–95, 130, 156
Bubo magellanicus. *See* magellanic horned owl
Bubo scandiacus. *See* snowy owl
Bucanetes githagineus. *See* trumpeter finch
budgerigar, 56, 151
buffer effect, 114, 116
Burhinus oedicnemus. *See* Eurasian thick-knee
burning management, 18, 128, 254, 377
Buteo buteo. *See* common buzzard
Buteo jamaicensis. *See* red-tailed hawk
Buteo polyosoma. *See* red-backed hawk
butterfly, 65, 180, 191, 236, 263, 289, 302

cactus finch, 149
caged bird trade, 257
Cairina scutulata. *See* white-winged duck
Calanus finmarchicus, 152, 155
Calanus helgolandicus, 152
Calidris alba. *See* sanderling
Calidris alpina. *See* dunlin
Calidris bairdii. *See* Baird's sandpiper
Calidris canutus. *See* red knot
Calidris ferruginea. *See* curlew sandpiper
Calidris maritima. *See* purple sandpiper
California condor, 257
Calix spp. *See* willow
Calluna vulgaris. *See* heather
Calonectris diomedea. *See* Cory's shearwater
Calyptorhynchus latirostris. *See* Carnaby's black cockatoo
Camylorhynchus rufinucha. *See* rufous-naped wren
Canada
    climate change adaptation, 272
    climate change mitigation, 327, 339
    climate trends, 4–5
    effect of climate variables, 156
    impacts of climate change, 87–88, 92–94, 129, 157
    phenology trends, 43, 87, 92, 94
capelin, 156–157
Caprimulgus europaeus. *See* Eurasian nightjar
captive breeding, 257, 301–304
carbon dioxide (CO$_2$), 10–11, 308, 311, 351–352, 355
carcass searches, 333
Carduelis chloris. *See* European greenfinch
Caribbean
    climate projections, 15, 141
    effects of climate variables, 110, 139–140
Carnaby's black cockatoo, 151
Carpodacus mexicanus. *See* house finch
carrion crow, 128, 286, 377
carryover effects, 140–142
Cassin's auklet, 93, 95, 155, 157
catastrophic event, 124, 166, 360
    climate change adaptation, 252, 276
    effect on breeding success, 125, 160, 167, 244
    effect on extinction, 124, 256, 271
    effect on habitat quality, 376, 378
    effect on survival, 151
    projected impact of climate change, 229

caterpillar, 63, 69–74, 78, 80–81, 83, 85, 120, 122, 142–143, 148–149, 164, 285
Central America
    climate change mitigation, 350
    climate projections, 15
    projected impacts of climate change, 372
Central England Temperature series, 2, 4, 116
Cerastoderma edule. See cockle
Cerorhinca monocerata. See rhinoceros auklet
Certhia familiaris. See Eurasian treecreeper
Cervus elephas. See elk
Cetti's warbler, 275
Cettia cetti. See Cetti's warbler
Charadrii. *See* shorebirds
Charadriiformes. *See* shorebirds
Charadrius hiaticula. See common ringed plover
Chen caerulescens. See snow goose
Chersophilus duponti. See Dupont's lark
chick
    condition, 69, 81, 93, 121–122, 128, 133, 156
    diet, 72, 122
    food availability, 19, 45, 56, 67, 70, 83, 87–89, 120–122, 126, 128, 142, 152–155, 282, 284, 359, 376
    growth rate, 63–64, 93–94, 120, 126, 128, 156
    survival, 64, 70, 85, 87, 93, 120, 123, 125–126, 244, 282, 284
Chile
    climate change adaptation, 272, 291
    climate projections, 15
    effect of climate variables, 146–147
Chimango caracara, 148
China
    climate change mitigation, 311
    climate trends, 5, 7
    conservation, 330
chinstrap penguin, 159, 161
chironomid, 242
Chondestes grammacus. See lark sparrow
Chucao Tapaculo, 291
cicada, 56
Ciconia ciconia. See white stork
Ciconiformes. *See* herons
Circoniidae. *See* herons
Circus aeruginosus. See western marsh harrier
Circus cyaneus. See hen harrier
cirl bunting, 122, 148, 258
Cistothorus platensis. See sedge wren
citizen science, 1, 102–103, 168, 178, 196, 206, 237–238
Cladorhynchus leucocephalus. See banded stilt
classification trees, 212
climate change adaptation, 168, 244–245, 250, 258–306, 364–368
climate change mitigation, 308–358, 366, 368, 372, 379
climate debt, 191, 196
climate envelope model, 20, 201–244, 246–247, 258, 261–262, 268, 270, 273, 280, 293, 363–364, 366, 378
Climate Response Surfaces (CRS), 212–213, 234, 237
climate stability, 187
climate variables, 203–204, 208–210
climate-proofing, 298
climate-space, 207
cloud, 11
Clupea harengus. See herring
clutch
    number of, 29, 50–51, 72–74, 77, 86, 89, 148, 151, 285
    replacement, 29, 50, 59
    size, 50, 70–71, 77, 79–80, 84, 86–87, 89, 113, 148, 151
    weight, 45
coal tit, 115
coastal squeeze, 229
Coccyzus americanus. See yellow-billed cuckoo
cockle, 329
Cohen's kappa, 231
cold-weather movement, 119
collared flycatcher, 67, 81–82, 86, 95, 143
colonisation, 218–220, 223–224, 230, 235, 241, 250, 256, 259–261, 269–271, 275–277, 293, 296, 299, 365
Columba palumbis. See common wood pigeon
Columbina spp. *See* ground dove
Common Bird Census (CBC), **115**
common buzzard, 84, 95, 118, 123, 321
common chiffchaff, 137, 175–176
common coot, 118
common crane, 258
common cuckoo, 90–91
common eider, 121
common guillemot, 90, 93, 95, 153, 156–157
common kestrel, 118, 123, 146, 313
common redshank, 117, 121, 278, 330–331
common redstart, 52, 135, 137
common ringed plover, 329
common sandpiper, 66, 87, 121, 139
common snipe, 278, 321
common starling, 48, 116
common stonechat, 277
common tern, 153, 156
common whitethroat, 135–137
common wood pigeon, 337
community specialisation index (CSI), 188, 192–193
community temperature index (CTI), 189–192, 194, 240
compensatory management, 254, 282–284, 301, 347, 349
compensatory mitigation, 288, 346
competition
    interspecific, 141, 143, 165, 171, 175, 187, 246, 360, 362–363
    intraspecific, 52, 115, 148, 330
conditional generalised least squares, 233
Congo
    climate change mitigation, 350
coniferous woodland, 73, 80–81, 143, 242, 285
connectivity. *See* habitat connectivity
conservation management, 254, 259, 265–266, 269, 281–289, 367
conservation planning, 253, 267–268, 270, 277, 304–306

Index · 455

conservation prioritisation, 247, 251–252, 261–265, 280
conservation resources, 251, 268, 270, 279, 288, 301, 304–305, 369, 377, 380
conservation science, 250, 253, 257
constraint hypothesis, 73, 82
Convention on Biological Diversity (CBD), 265–266, 351
Convention on Migratory Species (CMS), 265–266
core sites, 252–254, 256, 259, 266–289, 301, 303, 305, 376, 379
cormorants, 33
corn bunting, 191
corncrake, 121, 268
corridor, 256, 259, 289–295, 343, 370
Corvidae. See crows
Corvus brachyrhynchos. See American crow
Corvus corone. See carrion crow
Cory's shearwater, 261
counteracting adaptation, 352
counteracting management, 254, 282–285, 367, 376
coupled niche-population model, 246–247
cranefly, 64, 88–89, 117, 126, 128, 244, 282–283, 286, 376
cranes, 33, 323
cream-coloured courser, 219
crested auklet, 155–156
Crex crex. See corncrake
crossbill, 242
cross-validation, 234
crows, 33
Cuculus canorus, 90
cues hypothesis, 82–83
Culex quinquefasciatus, 150
cumulative impact assessment (CIA), 346
curlew sandpiper, 51
Cursorius cursor. See cream-coloured courser
cyclone, 94
Czech Republic
    impacts of climate change, 71, 82, 89, 173, 189, 194
    phenology trends, 36, 82, 89
    range shift, 178

dam, 324, 327, 354
Dartford warbler, 264, 274–275, 277–278, 298
Darwin's finch. See Galapagos finch
day length. See photoperiod
deciduous woodland, 25, 73–74, 77, 79–81, 83, 85, 96, 99, 167, 285, 290, 359
decision support, 303
deforestation, 10, 255, 281, 308, 325, 334, 336–337, 341, 343, 349–350, 370
demographic model. See population model
Dendcoica adelaidae. See Adelaide's warbler
Dendoica petechia. See yellow warbler , 139
Dendrocopos leucotos. See white-backed woodpecker
Dendrocopos medius. See middle-spotted woodpecker
Dendroica petechia. See yellow warbler
Denmark
    climate change mitigation, 311, 321–322
    impacts of climate change, 86
    phenology trends, 47, 86
density-dependence, 16, 77, 87, 89, 103, 114, 116, 146, 148, 150, 244, 250, 257, 300, 316, 320, 345
density-yield function, 342
desert, 15, 166, 187
desert birds, 146, 195, 332
detectability, 205
diatoms, 152
Dicrostonyx spp. See lemming
diet
    effect of mismatch, 77
    effect on migration phenology trend, 35, 54
    effect on mismatch, 72
    effect on sensitivity to climate variables, 107–108, 110–111, 122, 154, 158
    effect on sensitivity to fragmentation, 271
    effect on vulnerability to climate change, 197, 282, 366
Diomedea exulans. See wandering albatross
Diomedia amsterdamensis. See Amsterdam albatross
disease, 134–135, 150, 165, 246, 360, 363, 377
dispersal, 80, 114, 215–216, 223, 226–228, 241–242, 246–247, 250, 252, 256, 259–261, 268–269, 271, 280, 289–291, 293–295, 298–299, 302, 366
Dolichony orzyivorus. See boblink
drainage, 86, 273, 278, 283, 349, 373
drought
    effect on breeding success, 123, 167
    effect on greenhouse gas emissions, 351
    effect on habitats, 371
    effect on migration phenology, 53
    effect on population trends, 110, 137, 163, 247, 278, 361
    effect on prey abundance, 128, 140, 164, 284, 372
    effect on species richness, 188, 195–196, 362
    effect on survival, 115, 120, 139, 209, 297
    limit of range margin, 363
    projections, 15, 280, 376
    trends, 7
dung beetle, 235
dunlin, 66, 121, 126, 329
dunnock, 90–91, 116, 291
Dupont's lark, 261

eared grebe, 332
earthworm, 89, 117, 120, 126, 209
ecological network, 256, 258
ecological niche model. See species distribution model (SDM)
ecosystem approach, 303
ecosystem services, 303, 352
ectotherms, 16, 174, 180, 181, 217
egg size, 79
Egretta garzetta. See little egret
Egyptian vulture, 313, 319
eider duck, 87, 95
El Niño, 7, 14, 57, 91, 139, 142, 146, 148, 162–164
electricity generation, 309, 311–312, 324, 326–327, 331–332

elevation
    as proxy for climate, 202
    projected range shift, 217–228, 238–239
    range shift, 175–179, 238–239, 277–278, 376
elk, 167
Emberiza calandra. See corn bunting
Emberiza cirlus. See cirl bunting
Emberiza hortulana. See Ortolan bunting
Emberiza pallasi. See Pallas' bunting
Emberiza sahari. See house bunting
emigration, 102
emissions scenario, 13, 15, 214–215, 217, 219–220, 227, 280, 310, 342, 352, 375–379
emperor penguin, 160, 245
Endemic Bird Area (EBA), 181, 279, 326
energetics, 73, 77, 122, 126, 153, 180, 362
energy demand, 308–309, 311, 341, 369
energy hypothesis, 361
Engraulis japonicus. See anchovy
Environmental Impact Assessment (EIA), 330, 345–347, 369
Epirrita aitumnata. See autumnal moth
Eremopterix verticalis. See grey-backed sparrow-lark
Erithacus rubecula. See European robin
estuarine birds, 117, 195, 228–229, 327–331
Ethiopia
    climate change mitigation, 336
    effect of climate variables, 218
Ethiopian bush-crow, 217–218, 380
eucalyptus, 56, 272, 350
Eudromias morinellus. See Eurasian dotterel
Eudyptes chrysolophus. See macaroni penguin
Euphagus carolinus. See rusty blackbird
Euphausia superba. See krill
Eurasian blackbird, 52, 120, 291
Eurasian chaffinch, 120, 135, 291
Eurasian curlew, 230, 321
Eurasian dotterel, 121, 128
Eurasian golden plover, 50, 64, 88, 104, 117, 121, 126–128, 167, 244, 282–286, 301, 320–322
Eurasian green woodpecker, 230
Eurasian nightjar, 276
Eurasian oystercatcher, 166, 244, 329
Eurasian pygmy owl, 119
Eurasian reed warbler, 86, 90, 137
Eurasian thick-knee, 276
Eurasian treecreeper, 115
Eurasian wigeon, 121, 320
Europe
    climate change adaptation, 266
    climate change mitigation, 311, 314, 320, 341–342, 373
    climate projections, 15
    climate trends, 5–7, 32, 78
    conservation, 252, 254, 265, 299
    effect of climate variables, 107, 113, 115, 117
    impacts of climate change, 85–91, 96, 119, 188–191, 194, 196, 238, 361
    land use projection, 370–371
    migration phenology, 36–42
    phenology trends, 29, 31–32, 34–38, 47, 53, 64, 67, 85–91

population trends, 256
projected impacts of climate change, 217–221, 233, 261, 275
European greenfinch, 135
European robin, 116
European shag, 93, 95, 153–154, 158
European turtle dove, 52
evergreen woodland, 74, 77
evolution, 17, 183, 186, 362
evolutionary rates hypothesis, 180
expert assessment, 263, 267
extinction, 150
    current threat, 1
    debt, 226–227, 366
    from climate change, 165
    projected rates, 228
    projected risk, 219, 221–222, 225–228, 230, 244–245, 308, 325, 363, 366, 374
    rate, 182, 365
    risk, 124, 161, 251–252, 257, 261, 267, 271, 277, 279–280, 289, 304, 319, 323, 336, 346, 352, 354, 365

Fagus sylvatica. See beech
Falco femoralis. See Aplomado falcon
Falco naumanni. See lesser kestrel
Falco punctatus. See Mauritius kestrel
Falco sparverius. See American kestrel
Falco tinnunculus. See common kestrel
Falconiformes. See raptors
farming
    conversion of habitat to, 171, 273, 299, 352, 370
    co-products and wastes, 340
    effect of climate change, 370–372
    effect on bird populations, 192, 256, 278, 341, 372
    effects on moths, 143
    greenhouse gas emissions, 10, 308, 349, 352
farmland birds, 116, 120, 191–193, 257, 299, 321, 337–339, 342, 353, 370, 372–373
fat reserves, 66, 118–119
ferruginous pygmy owl, 146
Ficedula albicollis. See collared flycatcher
Ficedula hypoleuca. See pied flycatcher
field sparrow, 338
Finland
    effect of climate variables, 113, 118
    impacts of climate change, 84, 143, 173, 193
    laying interval, 48
    phenology trends, 41, 79, 84
    population trends, 84
    projected climate change impacts, 221
fire
    effect on greenhouse gas emissions, 350–351
    effect on habitats, 376, 378
    projected trends, 166
first arrival date (FAD), 27–37, 41, 46, 50, 64–65, 83, 90
first egg date (FED), 29
first laying date (FLD), 50, 72–73, 88
fish, 25, 63, 90–92, 94, 152–153, 155, 159, 162, 164–165, 180, 273, 320, 324–325, 331–332, 352, 360

fish ladder, 324
fishery, 154, 161, 287, 332
flooding
    effect on breeding success, 125, 158, 166–167, 244, 284, 324
    effect on habitats, 326, 352
    effect on population trends, 360
    trends, 7
food availability, 119, 151–152, 285, 298, 320, 338–339, 362–363, 372
    effect of mismatch, 91
    effect on breeding phenology, 45, 56, 78, 93–94
    effect on breeding success, 42, 73, 82, 85, 90–91, 93, 122, 125–126, 128, 132, 142, 157, 244, 282, 376
    effect on climate change vulnerability, 164, 263
    effect on clutch size, 79
    effect on distribution, 171, 209
    effect on double brooding, 73, 142, 148
    effect on migration phenology, 40, 43–44, 54
    effect on population trends, 115, 163, 337, 378
    effect on species richness, 182
    effect on survival, 73, 113, 115, 117–119, 129, 138–140, 159, 329
    phenology, 61, 63, 67, 70, 73–74, 76–77, 91, 94, 359–360
food caching, 85, 119
food peak width, 72, 74–76, 81, 86
food supplementation, 73, 113–115, 142
forestry
    adaptation to climate change, 303
    climate change mitigation, 340–341, 350, 352, 376–377
    effect on bird populations, 19, 86, 128, 256
fossil fuel, 10, 308, 352
France
    climate change mitigation, 327
    effect of climate variables, 138
    impacts of climate change, 74, 136, 173, 188–189, 191
Fratercula arctica. See Atlantic puffin
Fratercula cirrhata. See tufted puffin
Fratercula corniculata. See horned puffin
freezing tolerance hypothesis, *180*
Fringilla coelebs. See Eurasian chaffinch
Fulica atra. See common coot
Fulmarus glacialis. See northern fulmar
Fulmarus glacialoides. See southern fulmar
future potential range, 207–208, 215, 218–219, 224, 365, 373

Galapagos finch, 56–57, 148–149
Galapagos penguin, 162
Gallinago gallinago. See common snipe
garden feeding. See food supplementation
garden tiger moth, 143
Gavia arctica. See black-throated diver
Gavia stellata. See red-throated diver
General Circulation Model (GCM), 9–11, 13, 15, 204, 210, 214–215, 217, 219–220, 225, 228, 245

feedbacks, 12
Generalised Additive Model (GAM), 212–214, 217, 449
Generalised Estimating Equation (GEE), 233
Generalised Linear Model (GLM), 212–214, 217
genetic algorithm (GARP), 213
gentoo penguin, 161
geo-engineering, 355
geographical barrier, 183, 279
geolocators, 39
Geospiza fortis. See medium ground finch
Geospiza scandens. See cactus finch
Geospiza spp. See Galapagos finch
geothermal energy, 310
Geranoaetus melanoleucus. See black-chested buzzard-eagle
Germany
    effect of climate variables, 123
    impacts of climate change, 194
    phenology trends, 36–37, 41, 52, 69
glaciers, 6
Glaucidium brasilianum. See ferruginous pygmy owl
Glaucidium passerinum. See Eurasian pygmy owl
Glossopsitta porphyrocephala. See purple-crowned lorikeet
golden eagle, 258
grasshopper sparrow, 338
grassland birds, 56, 272, 289, 336, 338–339, 341, 363, 371
grazing, 19, 218, 352, 377–378
grazing management, 128, 177, 254
great bittern, 124, 273–275, 298
great bustard, 258
great reed warbler, 86
great spotted woodpecker, 290
great tit, 45, 47, 51, 63, 67, 69–74, 77, 79, 84, 95, 113–115, 120, 122, 143, 150, 282
greater adjutant, 326
grebes, 33
greenhouse gas
    effects, 10–11
    emission scenarios, 11, 13–14, 305, 308
    emissions, 309, 335–336, 338, 349–354, 368
    trends, 10
Greenland
    ice cores, 8–10
    impacts of climate change, 132
    phenology trends, 66
grey heron, 102–103, 105, 117–118
grey jay, 85, 119
grey partridge, 191, 373
grey-backed sparrow-lark, 55
griffon vulture, 312–314, 319
ground dove, 56
grouse, 107, 110–111, 121–122, 351
grouse moor, 18–19, 133, 286, 378
growing season length, 133, 208, 238, 364
Gruidae. See cranes
Grus grus. See common crane
Gymngyps californianus. See California condor
Gymnorhina tibicen. See Australian magpie
Gypes africanus. See white-backed vulture
Gyps fulvus. See griffon vulture

H5N1 virus. *See* avian influenza
habitat change, 191, 194, 366
habitat connectivity, 252, 256, 261, 267, 269, 278, 289–299, 302–303, 305, 367, 371
habitat creation, 259, 261, 265, 273–274, 284, 298, 347, 350, 371
Habitat Directive, 265
habitat fragmentation, 19, 254, 256, 271, 280–281, 289–299, 303
habitat generalist, 188–189, 290, 295, 335, 367, 373
habitat heterogeneity, 270, 278–279, 297, 338–339, 341
habitat heterogeneity hypothesis, 183
habitat loss, 1, 124, 178, 253–254, 259, 280–281, 300–301, 325, 327, 333–334, 336, 341, 348–349, 354, 365, 370–372, 378
habitat management, 254, 285, 299
habitat matrix, 256, 259, 289, 291, 294, 299, 343
habitat patch, 16, 252, 256, 259, 272, 289–291, 293–299
habitat quality, 77, 143, 291, 293, 297, 367, 372, 376
    effect on abundance, 206, 214, 271
    effect on dispersal, 80
    effect on mismatch, 73–75, 80–81
    effect on phenology, 78, 99
    effect on survival, 114, 139–140
    effects on migrants, 43–44
habitat restoration, 253, 259, 265, 350, 352
habitat specialist, 1, 183, 189, 191, 193, 271, 275, 277, 291, 293–295, 299, 302, 335, 361, 366, 371
Haematopus ostralegus. *See* Eurasian oystercatcher
Haliaeetus albicilla. *See* white-tailed eagle
Haliaeetus leucocephalus. *See* bald eagle
Halobaena caerulea. *See* blue petrel
Harris's hawk, 148
Hawaii
    conservation, 150
    projected impacts of climate change, 166, 229
heat stress, 151, 157, 366
heat wave, 150, 166, 360, 376
    trends, 5
heather, 18–19, 376–377
heathland birds, 192, 276–277, 289, 298
hedge accentor. *See* dunnock
hedgerows, 290–291
heliostat, 332
helmeted honeyeater, 57
Hemignathus virens. *See* amakihi
hen harrier, 123, 321
Henslow's sparrow, 338
herons, 33, 110–111, 125, 137, 163, 323
herring, 90, 92, 155–158, 162
Himalayas
    climate change mitigation, 325, 336
    climate projections, 15
    climate trends, 6
    hotspots of species richness, 326
    species richness, 187
Hirundo rustica. *See* barn swallow
history
    effect on species richness, 183–184, 186
Hoge Veluwe, 70–72, 74, 77, 80, 86

horizon scanning, 372
horned puffin, 156
horseshoe crab, 329
Houbaropsis bengalensis. *See* Bengal florican
house bunting, 219
house finch, 134
house sparrow, 150
house swift, 219
house wren, 148
human
    population, ii, 273, 280–281
human impacts, 1, 305, 365, 369–374
    disturbance, 257, 320, 335
    effect on species distribution, 171, 207, 211, 240, 268, 281
    exploitation, 1, 253, 257, 259, 301, 328, 365, 370
    land use, 273
    persecution, 171, 275, 301
    pesticides, 337
    poisoning, 257
    pollution, 11, 207, 240, 250, 257, 301, 333
Hume's leaf warbler, 171
hummingbird, 57, 272
hunting, 89. *See* human exploitation
hurricane
    effect on breeding colonies, 125
    trends, 7
hybridisation, 143, 181
Hydrobatidae. *See* storm petrels
hydrological management, 254
hydropower, 309–311, 324–332, 347, 354
Hydrurga leptonyx. *See* leopard seal
Hylophylax naevioides. *See* spotted antbird

ibis, 33
ice
    effect on prey availability, 163
    effect on survival, 117, 209
ice age, 8, 17, 19, 183, 187
immigration, 102, 297
Important Bird Area (IBA), 252–253, 268, 280, 318, 349
in situ conservation, 257
income breeder, 45, 66, 77
incubation, 70, 77
India
    climate change mitigation, 325–326, 336
    climate projections, 15
    climate trends, 7
    conservation, 342
    effect of climate variables, 171
    population trends, 257
Indian Ocean
    climate projections, 15
    climate trends, 7
    effect of climate variables, 161–162
    projected impacts of climate change, 245
indicator
    of climate change, 115, 136
Indonesia
    climate change mitigation, 334, 350

Index · 459

integrated population model (IPM), 246
interglacial periods, 9
Intergovernmental Panel on Climate Change, 3–7, 9–13, 15, 21, 225, 288, 308, 310–311, 341, 349, 351, 353
invasive species. *See* non-native species
Ireland
    climate change mitigation, 311
island birds
    conservation, 150, 279
    effects of climate variables, 93, 148
    extinction, 150, 172
    hotspots of species richness, 184, 279
    projected impacts of climate change, 229
    speciation, 184
Italy
    climate change mitigation, 342
    effect of climate variables, 136
    impacts of climate change, 173
    phenology trends, 37
IUCN red list, 224, 226, 230, 251, 261, 264, 336, 365, 386
Ixobrychys minutus. *See* little bittern

jackdaw, 373
Jamaica
    climate trends, 141
    effect of climate variables, 139
    phenology trends, 43
Japan
    effect of climate variables, 92
    impacts of climate change, 92
    phenology trends, 92
    population trends, 99
Japanese cormorant, 92, 95
jatropha, 336

kakapo, 258
Kalahari Desert
    climate projections, 15
    effect of climate variables, 146, 195
Key Biodiversity Area, 252
key patch approach, 297
keystone species, 165, 303
king penguin, 160
Korea
    conservation, 330
krill, 152, 158–161
Kurrichane thrush, 55

La Niña, 58
lagged effects of climate variables, 110, 129, 146, 196, 241–243, 360
Lagopus lagopus. *See* willow grouse
Lagopus lagopus scoticus. *See* red grouse
land abandonment, 370, 376
land sharing, 342–343, 371
land sparing, 342–343, 371
land-use, land-use change and forestry (LULUCF), 349, 351, 354, 369
Lanius collurio. *See* red-backed shrike

Lanius ludovicianus. *See* loggerhead shrike
lantern fish, 161
lappet-faced vulture, 146
lapse rate, 202, 227–228
lark sparrow, 338
larks, 33
Larus audouinii. *See* Audouin's gull
Larus crassirostris. *See* black-tailed gull
last departure date (LDD), 52–53, 60
latitude gradient
    in breeding phenology, 78
    in climate stability, 183
    in disease infection, 134
    in effects of climate variables, 105, 109, 115, 123, 159, 162–163, 360, 362
    in effects of mismatch, 81
    in fat reserves, 118
    in migratory propensity, 112
    in phenology trends, 32–33, 46
    in photoperiod importance, 45
    in range size, 181
    in red grouse density, 18
    in seabird diet, 157
    in species richness, 179, 187, 189, 196, 361, 375
    in synchrony of seasonality, 181
Laysan albatross, 229
Laysan finch, 229
leaf-eared mouse, 146
least auklet, 155, 158
leatherjacket. *See* cranefly
legislation, 265, 267, 303
lemming, 128, 130–132, 146
Lemmus spp. *See* lemming
leopard seal, 159
Leptoptilos dubius. *See* greater adjutant
Leptoptilos javanicus. *See* lesser adjutant
lesser adjutant, 326
lesser kestrel, 123
lesser sandeel. *See* sandeel
lesser spotted woodpecker, 115
lesser whitethroat, 137
Lichenostomus melanops cassidix. *See* helmeted honeyeater
light-mantled albatross, 161
Limnosa lapponica. *See* bar-tailed godwit
Limosa limosa. *See* black-tailed godwit
Limulus polyphemus. *See* horseshoe crab
Lithuania
    phenology trends, 36
little bittern, 136, 275
little bustard, 148
little egret, 275
lodgepole pine, 129
loggerhead shrike, 338
long-tailed skua, 132
Lophophorus sclateri. *See* Sclater's monal
louping ill, 133
low-regrets adaptation, 259
Loxia curvirostra. *See* red crossbill
Loxia curvirostra percna. *See* Newfoundland crossbill
Lullula arborea. *See* woodlark
Lumbricidae. *See* earthworm

macaroni penguin, 160
magellanic horned owl, 146
magpie goose, 56
maize, 337–338, 341
Malaysia
    climate change mitigation, 334
mallard, 88, 121
Mallotus villosus, 156
management plan, 348
mangrove, 140, 229, 328, 352
marsh babbler, 326
Martes americana. See pine martin
Mauritius kestrel, 94–95, 257
Maxent, 213, 239
meadow pipit, 90, 230, 321
mean arrival date (MAD), 27–37, 41, 46, 50, 53, 65, 96
mean departure date (MDD), 52–54, 60
mean laying date (MLD), 29–30, 33, 45–50, 65, 78, 80, 82, 86–90, 92–93, 96
Mediterranean
    climate change adaptation, 295
    climate projections, 15
    climate trends, 5–6
    effect of climate variables, 56, 115, 123, 138, 146
    phenology trends, 36–37, 40
    projected impacts of climate change, 229
    species richness, 187
Mediterranean Sea
    as a barrier, 219
medium ground finch, 149
Melanitta spp. *See* scoter
Meleagris gallopayo. See wild turkey
Melopsittacus undulatus. See budgerigar
Melospiza melodia. See song sparrow
metabolic niche hypothesis, 180
metabolic rate, 16
metapopulation, 16, 175, 241, 256, 259–260, 267, 289, 297, 302, 376
methane (CH_4), 10–11, 351
Mexican jay, 56, 146, 149
Mexico
    conservation, 258
    effect of climate variables, 140, 146, 162
microclimate, 179, 278–279, 335
Middle East
    climate projections, 15
    climate trends, 6
middle-spotted woodpecker, 120
migrant
    population declines, 194
migrant birds, 25–26, 28, 36–45, 47–48, 51–54, 59, 65–67, 83, 85–87, 90, 94, 96–99, 110, 119, 135–144, 164–165, 167, 187, 194–195, 220, 290, 322, 332, 336–337, 345, 354, 359–360, 366–367, 372
migration
    autumn phenology, 51–54
    bottleneck, 312
    changes in distance, 52–53, 138, 221, 373
    effect of distance, 35–38, 47–49, 52–54, 83, 86, 96, 108, 110, 195, 290–291, 366
    mismatch, 66–67, 86, 96–99
    phenology, 25–27
    phenology trends. *See* phenology: migration trends
    route, 135
    speed, 37, 40, 43
    stop-over sites, 144
migratory connectivity, 139, 144
Millennium Ecosystem Assessment, 228, 370
Milvago chimango. See Chimango caracara
Milvus milgrans. See black kite
Milvus milvus. See red kite
Miscanthus, 338
mismatch. *See* phenology:mismatch
mismatch criteria, 82–83
mitigation measures, 325, 348, 354
model averaging, 232, 234
model uncertainty, 246
model validation, 234, 247
modelling ensemble
    climate, 10
    climate envelope model, 214–215, 220
Mongolia
    climate trends, 5
monitoring gaps, 54, 56, 58, 61, 99, 102, 141, 165–166, 168, 195–196, 243, 288, 332, 349, 359, 368, 374
monitoring methods, 345
monitoring scheme, 102, 165, 196, 206, 238, 241, 243, 253, 281, 333
monk parakeet, 57
more individuals hypothesis, 182
Morocco
    effect of climate variables, 139
mortality. *See* survival
mosquito, 150
Motacilla alba. See pied wagtail
Motacilla flava. See yellow wagtail
moth, 63, 65, 85, 142, 299
moult
    effect on migration phenology, 35, 51–52, 59, 359
    of red grouse, 17
    phenology, 26, 55
mountain bluebird, 143
mussel, 329
Mustela erminea. See stoat
Mycoplasma gallisepticum, 134
Myiopsitta monachus. See monk parakeet
Mytilus edulis. See mussel

natal dispersal, 16, 80, 217, 219, 295–296
national park. *See* protected area or core site
Natura 2000 site, 265
nature reserve. *See* protected area or core site
Neophron percnopterus. See Egyptian vulture
net primary productivity (NPP), *182*
New World warbler, 44, 85, 110, 139, 163
New Zealand
    climate change mitigation, 311
    conservation, 258
    phenology trends, 38
Newfoundland crossbill, 302

nitrous oxide (N$_2$O), 10–11, 338
non-climate variables, 206, 210–212, 214, 219
non-native species, 129, 134, 150, 172, 235, 258–259, 285, 290, 301–303, 350, 365, 367, 370
no-regrets adaptation, 259, 270, 275, 301
normalised difference vegetation index (NDVI), 182, 184
North America
    climate change mitigation, 311, 314, 341–342
    climate projections, 15
    climate trends, 6, 32
    conservation, 257
    effect of climate variables, 44, 85–87, 92, 94, 142, 146, 195
    impacts of climate change, 85–88, 92–94, 96, 175, 194
    land use projection, 370–371
    phenology trends, 31, 35–36, 38, 47, 53, 64–66, 85–88, 92, 94
    population trends, 134, 256, 303
    projected impacts of climate change, 227–229, 372
North Atlantic Oscillation (NAO), 36
    effect on breeding phenology, 37
    effect on migration phenology, 34, 36–38, 51, 59
    effect on population trends, 142
    effect on survival, 117, 139, 158
North Pacific Index
    effect on survival, 158
North Sea
    as a barrier, 17
    effect of climate variables, 93, 152–155
    impacts of climate change, 93, 152–155
northern fulmar, 158
northern goshawk, 118, 123
northern harrier. *See* hen harrier
northern house martin, 139–140
northern lapwing, 117, 121, 126, 278, 320, 338
northern wheatear, 321
Norway
    climate change mitigation, 313, 318
    effect of climate variables, 90, 92, 155
    impacts of climate change, 93
    phenology trends, 78–79
novel assemblages, 221
novel climate, 364
nuclear power, 309, 355
null model, 232
number of breeding attempts. *See* clutch: number
Nycticorax nycticorax. *See* black-crowned night heron

oak, 63, 69, 71, 73–74, 77, 79, 81–83, 85
occupancy model, 205
ocean energy, 310
Oceania
    climate projections, 371
Oceanodroma tristrami. *See* Tristram's storm petrel
oceans
    circulation system, 4, 7, 9, 156
    climate change mitigation, 310, 355
    currents, 91–92, 154–156, 163–164
        Leeuwin current, 162
        Tsushima current, 92
    effect of climate variables, 164
    heat absorption, 4
Oenanthe moesta. *See* red-rumped wheatear
Oenanthe oenanthe. *See* northern wheatear
oil palm, 99, 334–336, 346
oilseed rape, 337
Old World warbler, 110, 139, 163, 220
Operophtera brumata. *See* winter moth
Opuntia spp, 149
orange-crowned warbler, 143, 167
Orthoptera, 149
Ortolan Bunting, 89
osprey, 258
Otis tarda. *See* great bustard
ovenbird, 140
owls, 118, 145–147, 164, 312
Oxyura leucocephala. *See* white-headed duck

Pachyptila belcheri. *See* thin-billed prion
Pacific Decadal Oscillation, 175
Pacific Ocean
    climate projections, 15
    climate trends, 4, 7
    effect of climate variables, 92, 155–157, 162
Pacific sandlance. *See* sandeel
Pagodroma nivea. *See* snow petrel
palaeoclimate, 8–9, 365
Pallas' bunting, 261
palm oil. *See* oil palm
Pan European Common Bird Monitoring Scheme, 238
Pandion haliaetus. *See* osprey
Panurus biarmicus. *See* bearded parrotbill
Parabuteo unicinctus. *See* Harris's hawk
Paradocorbis flavirostris. *See* black-breasted parrotbill
Paraguay
    climate change mitigation, 336
parakeet auklet, 156
parasite, 18, 133–134, 150, 165, 376
Paridae. *See* tits
Parulidae. *See* New World warbler
Parus ater. *See* coal tit
Parus major. *See* great tit
Parus montanus. *See* willow tit
Passer domesticus. *See* house sparrow
Passeriformes. *See* passerines
passerines, 39, 47, 57, 86, 108, 111, 115–116, 120–121, 123, 150, 220, 264, 312, 351
patch size, 252, 260, 271–272, 290, 295, 298
peatland, 64, 126–127, 166, 286, 308, 335, 349–351, 354, 369, 376–378
Pelecanidae. *See* pelicans
Pelecaniformes. *See* pelicans
pelicans, 33
Pellorneium palustre. *See* marsh babbler
Perdix perdix. *See* grey partridge
Perisoreus canadensis. *See* grey jay
persecution. *See* human impacts persecution
Peru
    range shift, 176

Phalacrocoracidea. *See* cormorants
Phalacrocorax aristotelis. *See* European shag
Phalacrocorax filamentosus. *See* Japanese cormorant
phenology, 25–62, 152, 285, 359
    climatic drivers of migration, 36–44
    effect on competition, 143
    laying date trends, 26–27, 30, 45–51, 59, 69–94, 359–360
    migration trends, 28, 30–36, 51–54, 59, 66–67, 140, 359
    mismatch, 42, 63–99, 141–142, 152, 155, 175, 282, 285, 359
    trends, 25, 63–66
phenotypic plasticity, 362
Phoebastria immutabilis. *See* Laysan albatross
Phoebastria nigripes. *See* black-footed albatross
Phoebetria fusca. *See* sooty albatross
Phoebetria palpebrata. *See* light-mantled albatross
Phoenicurus phoenicurus. *See* common redstart
photoperiod, 26, 39, 42, 45, 51, 56–57, 93
photovoltaic cell, 332–333
Phylloscopus collybita. *See* common chiffchaff
Phylloscopus humei. *See* Hume's leaf warbler
Phylloscopus sibilatrix. *See* wood warbler
Phylloscopus trochilus. *See* willow warbler
Phyllotis darwini. *See* leaf-eared mouse
physiological tolerance hypothesis, 180
phytoplankton, 25, 91, 93, 152, 162, 355
Picus viridis. *See* Eurasian green woodpecker
pied flycatcher, 39–41, 43, 47–49, 60, 67, 77–83, 85–86, 95–96, 142–143, 282, 285
pied wagtail, 90
pine martin, 302
pink-footed goose, 42
pink-footed shearwater, 157
pintail, 88, 95
Pinus contorta. *See* lodgepole pine
plankton, 8, 25, 91, 93–94, 152–155, 157, 162, 164–165, 355, 360
plant
    growth, 25, 59, 85, 87, 132, 146, 182, 195, 209, 361
    phenology, 65
    productivity, 132, 140, 146, 164, 182, 184, 187–188, 209
Plectrophenax nivalis. *See* snow bunting
Pluvialis apricaria. *See* Eurasian golden plover
Podiceps nigricollis. *See* eared grebe
Podicipedidae. *See* grebes
Podicipediformes. *See* grebes
Poland
    impacts of climate change, 84
    phenology trends, 84
polar bear, 129
population cycles, 18–19, 129–132
population model, 103–104, 124, 244–246, 282, 284, 297–298, 300, 345–346
population trend
    effect of breeding success, 80, 82, 114, 128, 144
    effect of mismatch. *See* phenology: mismatch
    effect of precipitation. *See* precipitation
    effect of survival, 77, 87, 89, 116, 119, 129, 135
    effect of temperature. *See* temperature
    effect of wind energy. *See* wind energy
    projections, 229–231
Portugal
    climate change mitigation, 311
potential biological removal, 318, 346
potential evapotranspiration (PET), 182, 184, 209–210, 364
power transmission
    effect on survival, 257, 333, 345, 354, 373
precipitation
    effect on breeding phenology, 55–58, 63, 94, 359
    effect on breeding success, 109–110, 121, 133, 143, 146–150
    effect on community structure, 191
    effect on food availability, 18, 360
    effect on foraging efficiency, 117–118, 122–123, 140, 145, 149
    effect on migration phenology, 40, 43, 55–58, 359
    effect on mismatch, 94
    effect on population trends, 109–110, 137, 284
    effect on prey abundance, 129, 146
    effect on species richness, 182, 184–185
    effect on survival, 109–110, 135–141, 145, 163, 209
    limit of range margin, 178, 209, 228, 239, 361
    projections, 15, 164
    trends, 6–8
precocial chicks, 121–122, 126, 163
predation, 19, 84, 86–87, 89, 118, 122, 125, 129–133, 143, 146, 149, 159, 165, 167, 171, 177, 246, 258–259, 271, 286, 299, 324, 360, 363, 377
predator control, 18, 254, 286, 377, 379
presence-only data, 204
prey availability, 55, 72, 89, 92, 94, 122–123, 128, 140, 142, 158–161, 163–164, 171, 245, 360. *See also* food availability
Prionops plumatus. *See* white helmet shrike
Procellariiformes. *See* shearwaters
Procellariidae. *See* shearwaters
productive energy, 182, 184–186
projections. *See also* population model, *See also* climate envelope model
    climate change, 11–16, 141, 159, 164, 211, 228, 245, 280, 301, 303, 364, 371–372, 375, 378
    land cover, 211, 219, 221, 370–371, 373, 376, 378
    population trend, 130, 161, 164, 167, 175, 244–246
protected area, 125, 252–253, 265–289, 323, 343, 349, 367, 379
protected area network, 125, 252–254, 258–260, 265, 267–281, 298, 355
Prunella modularis. *See* dunnock
Pterodroma hypoleuca. *See* Bonin petrel
Ptychoramphus aleuticus. *See* Cassin's auklet
Puerto Rico
    effect of climate variables, 195
Puffinus creatopus. *See* pink-footed shearwater
Puffinus griseus. *See* sooty shearwater
Puffinus yelkouan. *See* Yelkouan shearwater
purple heron, 136, 138, 275

purple sandpiper, 63
purple-crowned lorikeet, 56
Pusa hispida. See ringed seal
Pygoscelis adeliae. See Adelie penguin
Pygoscelis antarcticus. See chinstrap penguin
Pygoscelis papua. See gentoo penguin
Pyrrhocorax pyrrhocorax. See red-billed chough

Quelea quelea. See red-billed quelea
Quercus. See oak

radiative forcing, 11, 13
ragworm, 167
rainfall. *See* precipitation
Ramsar Convention, 265–266
Ramsar site, 228
Random Forest, 212
range contraction, 175, 218–221, 223, 226–227, 241, 261, 264, 352, 363, 373
range expansion, 143, 174–175, 188, 217, 259, 262, 265, 267, 278, 293, 296, 298, 363, 367
range margin, 16–17, 165, 228
    leading, 143, 156, 164, 172–175, 178, 180, 189, 208, 241, 259–260, 275, 277, 289, 296–297, 361, 363–364
    trailing, 18, 89, 129, 159, 161, 164–165, 174–178, 189, 209, 241, 250, 259, 361, 363, 377
range shift, 117, 135, 143, 172–179, 189, 194, 197, 220, 239, 242, 250, 266, 273, 277–278, 289, 294, 343, 361, 363, 376
    projected, 81, 217–228, 256, 258, 267, 280, 288, 297, 301, 364
raptors, 107, 110–111, 118, 123, 126, 133, 145–148, 164, 166, 171, 312, 316, 318, 320, 336, 343, 346, 351, 354
razorbill, 93, 95, 153, 156–157
realized future range, 216
red crossbill, 129
red fox, 128, 132, 171, 286, 377
red grouse, 17–20, 128, 133–134, 166, 171, 286, 375–379
red kite, 258
red knot, 121, 329–330
red-backed hawk, 148
red-backed shrike, 89
red-billed chough, 128
red-billed quelea, 149
red-rumped wheatear, 219
red-tailed hawk, 123
red-throated diver, 321–322
reduced emissions from deforestation and forest degradation (REDD), 349–350, 352, 355, 369
refugia, 19, 183, 187, 269, 278–279
regression trees, 212
reintroduction, 257–258, 301–304
renewable energy, 308–349, 352
Renewable Energy Directive (RED), 341
representative concentration pathways (RCP), 13, 370
reproductive rates. *See* breeding success
reptiles, 180

reservoir, 285, 324–325
resilience
    to climate change, 266, 269, 281, 285, 288–289, 297, 301, 304, 352, 371, 376
resistance
    to climate change, 281–283, 286, 301, 367
rhinoceros auklet, 91–92, 95, 155, 157
rhinoceros auklet, 157
ring ouzel, 89, 120, 139, 177
ringed seal, 129
Riparia riparia. See sand martin
Rissa tridactyla. See black-legged kittiwake
rock ptarmigan, 121
rockfish, 90, 92
roseate tern, 93, 95
ruddy turnstone, 66, 121
rufous-collared sparrow, 181
rufous-naped wren, 291
rufous-necked hornbill, 326
run-of-river scheme, 324–325, 327
Russia
    climate change mitigation, 339
rusty blackbird, 175
rusty-throated wren-babbler, 326

sage sparrow, 146
Sahara Desert
    climate projections, 15
Sahel
    carrying capacity, 136
    climate projections, 141
    effect of climate variables, 40, 53, 110, 135–138, 194, 297
salt marsh, 166, 229
sampling hypothesis, 182
sand martin, 135, 139
sandeel, 90, 92–93, 152–158, 287, 301, 445
sanderling, 66, 329
sardine, 92
Sardinops melanostictus. See sardine
satellite tags, 39
savanna, 56, 187, 336, 341, 350, 363, 371
Saxicola rubetra. See whinchat
Saxicola torquata. See common stonechat
Scandinavia
    climate change mitigation, 324
    climate trends, 4
    effect of climate variables, 115
    impacts of climate change, 81, 96
    phenology trends, 36, 40–41, 48, 78–79, 96
    population trends, 81, 96
scaup, 88, 95
Scelorchilus rubecula. See Chucao tapaculo
Sclater's monal, 326
scoter, 88, 95
sea ice
    effect on breeding success, 129, 156, 159–161, 245
    effect on breeding success, 158–161
    effect on mismatch, 94, 156
    effect on prey abundance, 156, 158
    effect on prey availability, 159, 161, 245

sea ice (cont.)
    effect on survival, 159, 161, 245
    projection, 245
    projections, 15, 159
    trends, 4, 7, 129, 159
sea-level rise, 166
    effect on habitat quality, 298
    effect on population trends, 125, 166, 244, 298
    projected impacts of climate change, 228–229
    trends, 6
seabirds, 63, 90–95, 107, 151–164, 229, 245, 286–287, 312, 318, 320–321, 323, 331, 343, 354, 359–361, 366
Sebastes spp. *See* rockfish
sedge warbler, 135, 137, 297–298
sedge wren, 338
Seiurus aurocapilla. *See* ovenbird
semi-altricial chicks, 123, 163
semi-precocial chicks, 121
sensitivity map, 343–344
Setophaga ruticilla. *See* American redstart
severe weather, 66, 166, 360
    effect on breeding success, 151
    effect on extinction, 256
    effect on survival, 67, 116, 118
Seychelles
    effect of climate variables, 93, 162
shearwaters, 33
shorebirds, 1, 39, 51, 63, 66, 107, 117, 121–122, 130–132, 165, 167, 177, 194, 228–229, 264, 278, 286, 328, 330, 351–352, 354
short-rotation coppice, 338–340, 376
Siberia
    climate trends, 5
Simpson's diversity index, 188
simultaneous generalised least squares, 233
sink population, 257, 271, 302, 323
Sitta europaea. *See* wood nuthatch
Sitta formosa. *See* beautiful nuthatch
skylark, 191, 338, 373
small mammal, 118–119, 130–133, 146–148, 163, 165, 312
snow
    effect on breeding phenology, 45, 51, 63, 67, 87
    effect on breeding success, 159, 167
    effect on habitat quality, 167
    effect on migration phenology, 52, 66
    effect on population trends, 104, 116
    effect on prey abundance, 129–132
    effect on prey availability, 118–119, 126, 131, 163
    effect on survival, 63, 66–67, 113, 118
    evolutionary response, 17
    limit of range margin, 117
    projections, 15
    trends, 6–7, 66
snow bunting, 122, 128
snow goose, 38, 87, 95, 130, 132
snow petrel, 161, 245
snowy owl, 130–132
snowy-throated babbler, 326
soil moisture, 120, 127, 129, 182, 209

solar energy. *See* solar power or solar radiation
solar insolation, 4
solar power, 309–311, 332–333, 353, 368
solar radiation, 182, 208
solution-testing, 254
Somateria mollissima, 87
song sparrow, 146, 149
song thrush, 116, 120, 209–210
sooty albatross, 162
sooty shearwater, 157
source–sink dynamics, 297
South Africa
    phenology, 26
    phenology trends, 60
    projected impacts of climate change, 230, 280
    range shift, 172
South America
    climate change mitigation, 311, 336, 342, 368
    climate projections, 15
    conservation, 280, 350
    effects of climate variables, 110, 139
    hotspots of species richness, 183, 187
    impacts of climate change, 196
    phenology, 44, 57
    projected impacts of climate change, 371–372
South Hills crossbill, 129, 134
southern fulmar, 161
Southern Ocean
    effect of climate variables, 158–162
    impacts of climate change, 158–162
    monitoring, 374
Southern Oscillation Index (SOI), 4
    effect on breeding success, 142
    effect on migration phenology, 56
    effect on Nearctic migrants, 145
    effect on population trends, 142
    effect on survival, 139
soya bean, 336–337, 341, 355
Spain
    breeding phenology, 57
    climate change adaptation, 272, 295
    climate change mitigation, 311–312, 319–320
    effect of climate variables, 77, 148
    impacts of climate change, 79, 189, 194
    phenology trends, 78–79
    population trends, 265
sparrowhawk, 63, 85
spatial autocorrelation, 207, 232–234, 240
spatial eigenvector mapping, 233
Special Areas of Conservation (SAC), 265
Special Protection Area (SPA), 252, 254, 265, 284
species discovery curve, 205, 227
species distribution. *See* range margin
species distribution model (SDM), 201, 208, 210
species prioritisation, 251, 261, 263, 267, 305, 366
species richness, 179–189, 279, 335, 339, 361, 363, 375
species risk assessment. *See* species prioritisation
species specialisation index (SSI), 191
species temperature index (STI), 189, 191–192
species-area relationship, 219, 226, 365
species-energy hypothesis, 182–185

Spelaeornis badeigularis. See rusty-throated wren-babbler
Spheniscus mendiculus. See Galapagos penguin
spiders, 122
Spizella breweri. See Brewer's sparrow
Spizella pusila. See field sparrow
spotless starling, 261
spotted antbird, 57
spotted greenshank, 326
spotted owl, 118, 247, 297
Squacco heron, 136, 138
Stachyris oglei. See snowy-throated babbler
stepping stone, 256, 289–291, 294–299, 343, 370
Stercorarius londicaudus. See long-tailed skua
Sterna dougallii. See roseate tern
Sterna hirundo. See common tern
Sterna paradisaea. See Arctic tern
Sternus unicolor. See spotless starling
Sternus vulgaris. See common starling
stoat, *130*
stone curlew. *See* Eurasian thick-knee
storm
    effect on breeding success, 124–125, 159
    effect on migration phenology, 38–40
    effect on population trends, 125, 298, 360
    effect on survival, 66–67, 158
    projected impacts of climate change, 166, 229
    trends, 7–8
storm petrels, 33
Strategic Environmental Assessment (SEA), 343–344, 368
Streptopelia turtur. See European turtle dove
Strigiformes. *See* owls
Strigops habroptila. See kakapo
Strix occidentalis. See spotted owl
sugarcane, 336, 337
Sula nebouxii. See blue-footed booby
sulphur dioxide (SO$_2$), 4, 11
sunflower, 337
survival, 16
    effect of anthropogenic pressure, 301
    effect of density-dependence, 77
    effect of dispersal, 256, 297, 299
    effect of food availability. *See* food availability
    effect of mismatch. *See* phenology
    effect of precipitation. *See* precipitation
    effect of prey availability. *See* prey availability
    effect of snow. *See* snow
    effect of solar power. *See* solar power
    effect of temperature. *See* temperature
    effect of wind energy. *See* wind energy
    habitat quality. *See* habitat quality
Sweden
    impacts of climate change, 82, 143, 188–189, 191
    phenology trends, 41, 47, 78–79, 81
switchgrass, 338
Switzerland
    effect of climate variables, 118
    impacts of climate change, 194
    range shift, 176
Sylvia atricapilla. See blackcap
Sylvia communis. See common whitethroat

Sylvia curruca. See lesser whitethroat
Sylvia warblers. *See* Old World warbler
Sylviidae. *See* Old World warbler

Tachycineta bicolor. See tree swallow
Taeniopygia guttata. See zebra finch
Tamiasciurus hudsonicus. See American red squirrel
Tarifa wind farm, 312–313
tawny eagle, 146
Telespiza cantans. See Laysan finch
temperature
    effect on breeding phenology, 45, 48–51, 56–57, 70–71, 88–89, 92, 359
    effect on breeding success, 77, 86–87, 92–93, 106–109, 120–121, 126–128, 133, 157–162, 167, 244, 287
    effect on brood parasitism, 90
    effect on community structure, 188–195
    effect on disease risk, 150
    effect on extinction risk, 225–227, 365
    effect on foraging efficiency, 122–123, 133
    effect on generation time, 181
    effect on greenhouse gas emissions, 351
    effect on migration phenology, 37–38, 40, 42–43, 67, 359
    effect on mismatch, 70–71, 77, 83, 87, 89, 91
    effect on mutation rate, 181
    effect on parasite abundance, 133
    effect on population trends, 102, 104, 106–109, 128, 142, 160, 163, 245, 247
    effect on prey abundance, 92, 94, 122, 126–127, 152, 155, 157, 171
    effect on prey phenology, 69, 73, 78, 89, 91, 93–94
    effect on prey quality, 152
    effect on productivity, 19
    effect on projected range loss, 223
    effect on species richness, 179–184
    effect on survival, 102, 104, 106–109, 113–118, 129, 151, 158–162, 167, 209, 244, 278
    limit of range margin, 174, 178, 180, 208–209, 218, 239, 275, 277, 298, 302, 361, 363
    projections, 13–15
    trends, 2–7, 32
temperature variability hypothesis, 181
temporal autocorrelation, 235
Terathopius ecaudatus. See bateleur
territoriality, 113, 143, 148
Tetrao tetrix. See black grouse
Tetrao urogallus. See western capercaillie
Tetraonidae. *See* grouse
Tetrax tetrax. See little bustard
Thalassarche melanophrys. See black-browed albatross
Thamnophilus doliatus. See barred antshrike
The Netherlands
    climate change adaptation, 272, 290, 295
    climate change mitigation, 312, 316
    effect of climate variables, 113, 118, 136
    impacts of climate change, 70, 74, 77, 79–81, 83, 115, 189, 192, 297
    phenology trends, 41, 47–48, 69–74, 78–80, 86

The Netherlands (cont.)
  population trends, 77, 80, 142
  projected impacts of climate change, 244
thermal heating system, 332
thermoregulation, 45, 52, 67, 113, 116, 119, 121, 123, 125, 133, 158, 163–164, 179, 209
thick-billed murre. *See* Brunnich's guillemot
thin-billed prion, 161
Threskionithidae. *See* ibis
thrushes, 107, 110–111, 120
tick, 133, 166, 376
tidal barrage, 327–331, 354, 369
tidal stream, 331–332
Tipulidae. *See* cranefly
tits, 63, 69–77, 80, 83, 85, 107, 113–115, 119
Torgos tracheliotos. *See* lappet-faced vulture
tortrix, 63, 77
Tragopan blythii. *See* Blyth's tragopan
translocation, 257–258, 260, 289, 302
tree line, 128
tree sparrow, 373
tree swallow, 86
trichomoniasis, 134, 165
Trichostrongylus tenuis, 18, 133–134, 166, 376
Tringa guttifer. *See* spotted greenshank
Tringa totanus. *See* common redshank
Tristram's storm petrel, 229
Troglodytes aedon. *See* house wren
Troglodytes troglodytes. *See* winter wren
Troglodytidae. *See* wrens
trophic cascade, 85, 155, 161, 164
tropical birds, 54–59, 63, 94, 109, 144–151, 162–163, 183, 187, 196, 226, 230, 253, 259, 271–272, 279–280, 291–294, 325, 333–337, 341, 350–351, 359–362, 364, 374
tropical forest, 15, 40, 57, 61, 183, 196, 272, 279, 291, 293–294, 336, 349–350, 354, 369, 371
tropics
  climate change mitigation, 334–336
  climate projections, 15
  climate trends, 5
  conservation, 291
  effect of climate variables, 55, 109, 140, 144–151, 162–163, 361
  impacts of climate change, 94
  land use projections, 370
  monitoring gaps, 374
  phenology, 25
  photoperiod response, 26
  projected impacts of climate change, 172
  species richness, 181, 183–184, 188, 361
trumpeter finch, 57, 261
tufted puffin, 155, 157
Turdidae. *See* thrushes
Turdus libonyanus. *See* Kurrichane thrush
Turdus merula. *See* Eurasian blackbird
Turdus migratorius. *See* American robin
Turdus philomelos. *See* song thrush
Turdus torquata. *See* ring ouzel
turnover, 214, 269, 280, 332
Tyto alba. *See* barn owl

UK
  climate change adaptation, 275–277, 282–286, 291, 295–296, 298–299, 352
  climate change mitigation, 316, 321–322, 324, 337, 339, 341–342, 344, 346
  climate projection, 375, 378
  climate trends, 2, 238, 282
  conservation, 128, 171, 258, 264, 268, 273, 278, 284
  effect of climate variables, 50, 85, 89, 103, 113, 115–116, 118, 120, 126, 128, 135, 152–155, 209–210, 287
  impacts of climate change, 70, 81, 84, 87–91, 93, 124–125, 128, 133–134, 152–155, 173, 188–189, 192, 194–195, 236, 238–239, 264, 275, 373
  land use projection, 376, 378
  laying interval, 48
  phenology, 81
  phenology trends, 45, 65, 69–70, 79, 88–91
  population trends, 81, 83, 128, 134–136, 176, 264, 373
  projected impacts of climate change, 166, 230, 236–238, 244, 268, 275, 375–380
  range shift, 175, 177, 276, 296, 298
  species distribution, 81
  species richness, 183
UN Framework Convention on Climate Change (UNFCCC), 349, 351
upland birds, 66, 88–89, 126, 128, 133, 150, 176, 178, 183–184, 192, 227–228, 263, 278, 316, 321, 352, 361, 375–380
upland sandpiper, 338
Uria aalge. *See* common guillemot
Uria lomvia. *See* Brunnich's guillemot
Ursus maritimus. *See* polar bear
USA
  climate change adaptation, 272, 297
  climate change mitigation, 311–312, 332, 337–338, 340–341
  climate projections, 15
  climate trends, 5, 7, 239
  conservation, 257, 270, 329
  impacts of climate change, 92, 125, 129, 173, 238–239
  phenology trends, 66, 92
  projected climate change impacts, 247
  range shift, 178

Vaccinium myrtilus. *See* bilberry
Vanellus vanellus. *See* northern lapwing
vegetation structure, 166, 184, 277, 335–339, 341
Venezuela
  breeding phenology, 55–56
Vermivora celata. *See* orange-crowned warbler
Vermivora virginiae. *See* Virginia's warbler
Vireo bellii. *See* Bell's vireo
Virginia's warbler, 143, 167
vision, 314
volcanic eruption, 11

vole, 133, 146
vulnerability framework, 261, 366
Vulpes lagopus. See Arctic fox
Vulpes vulpes. See red fox
vultures, 257, 314–315, 318, 343

wader. *See* shorebird
wandering albatross, 162
water quality, 325
water storage schemes, 324–325
water vole, 299
waterbirds, 56, 87–88, 130–132, 136–139, 171, 228, 266, 312, 329, 332, 352
waterfowl, 33, 38, 42, 52, 63, 66, 87–88, 107, 118, 130–132, 134, 165, 195, 320, 328
wave power, 331–332
West Nile virus, 134, 165, 303
western marsh harrier, 273
western bluebird, 143
western capercaillie, 85–86, 95, 121, 268
wetland birds, 83, 86–88, 110, 124, 136, 163, 171, 195, 228–229, 264–265, 273, 276, 285, 289, 297–298, 316, 323, 325, 337, 373
whale, 157
whinchat, 278
whiskered auklet, 155
white eyes, 184
white helmet shrike, 55
white stork, 138, 140, 144, 372
white-backed vulture, 146
white-backed woodpecker, 121
white-bellied heron, 326
white-headed duck, 261
white-tailed eagle, 258, 313, 318
white-winged duck, 326
wider countryside, 252, 256–257, 273, 275, 278, 305, 343, 374
wild turkey, 146

wildfowl. *See* waterfowl
willow, 17
willow grouse, 17, 19–20
willow ptarmigan. *See* willow grouse
willow tit, 84, 95, 115
willow warbler, 175–176
wind
    effect on foraging efficiency, 158
    effect on migration phenology, 37–39
    effect on ocean current, 92, 155
    impact on heather, 18
    limit of range margin, 228
wind energy, 257, 309–324, 344, 347–349, 354, 369, 373, 376
winter moth, 63
winter wren, 115–116
wood nuthatch, 115, 122, 230, 296, 299
wood warbler, 83
woodfuel, 333, 337, 339
woodland birds, 47, 69–86, 96, 99, 113–116, 191–192, 272, 285, 289–291, 295–297, 339, 359, 362
woodlark, 89, 275–276
World Heritage Convention, 265–266
wrens, 107
Wytham Wood, 45, 70–71

Yelkouan shearwater, 261
Yellow Sea
    climate change mitigation, 311
    conservation, 330
yellow wagtail, 137
yellow warbler, 43–44, 139
yellow-billed cuckoo, 142

Zavattariornis stresemanni. See Ethiopian bush-crow
zebra finch, 56, 151
zooplankton, 25, 91, 93, 152–153, 155, 157–158
Zosteropidae, 184

Alpena Co. Library
211 N. First Ave.
Alpena, MI 49707